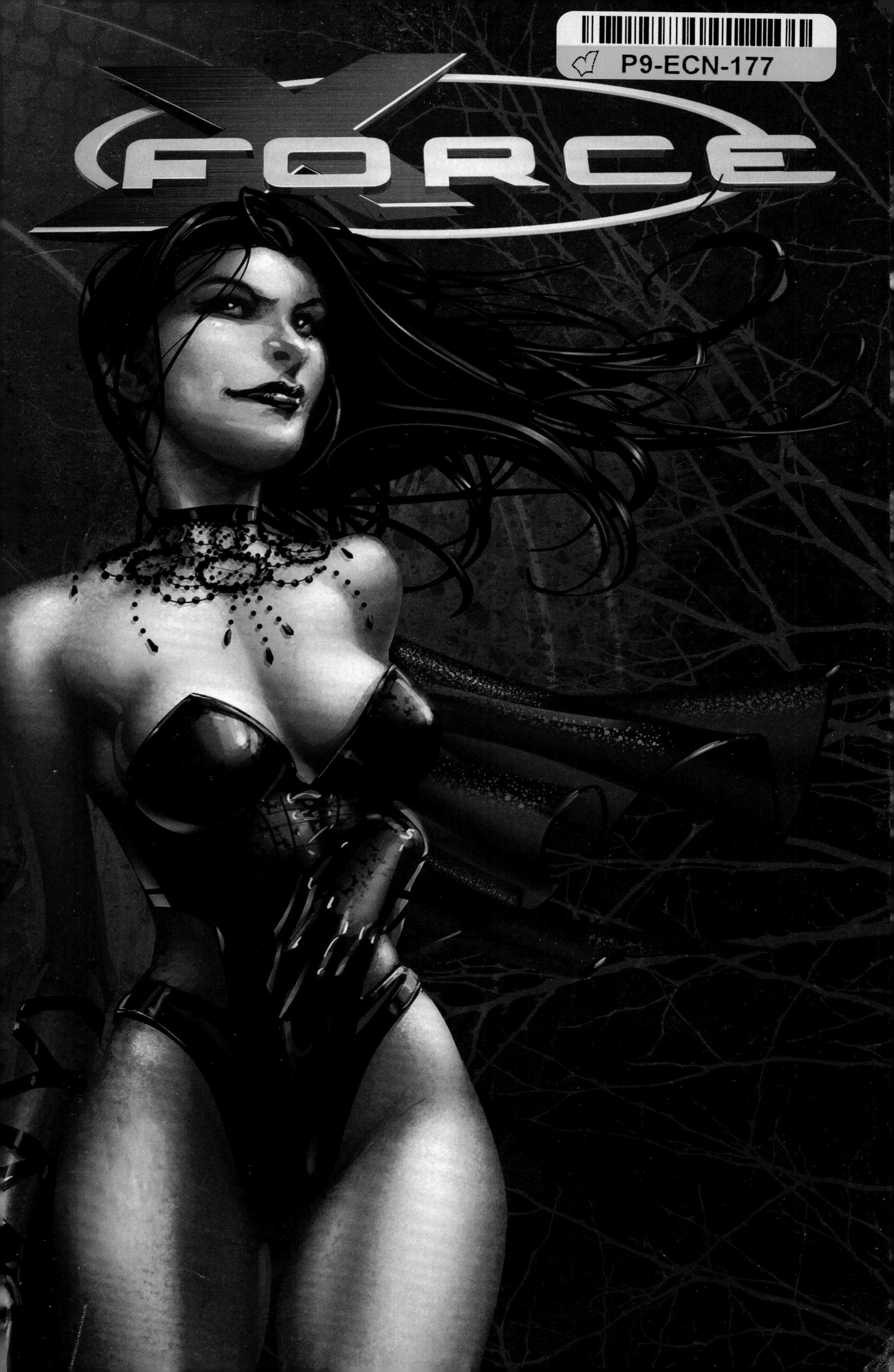
X FORCE

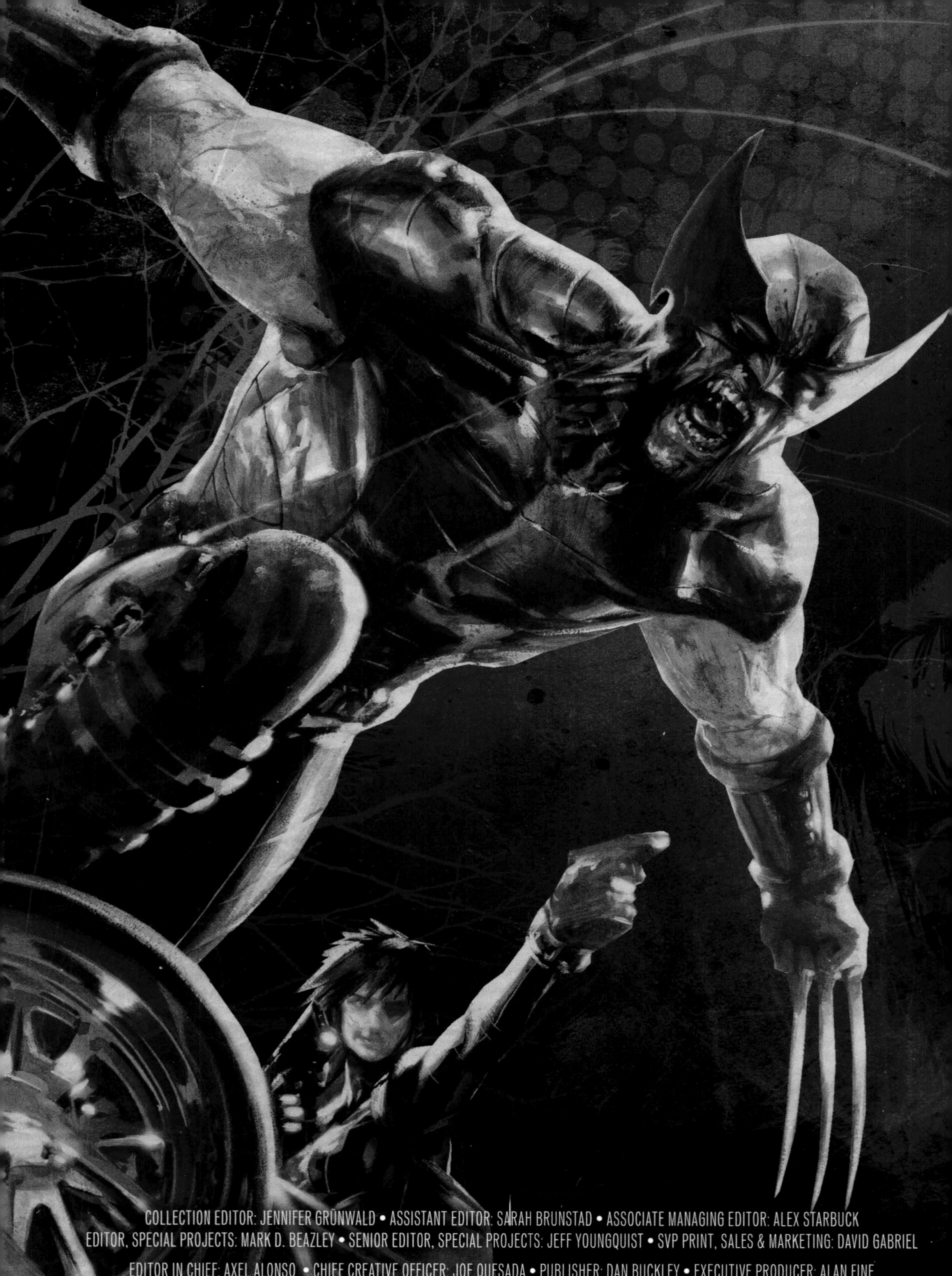

COLLECTION EDITOR: JENNIFER GRÜNWALD • ASSISTANT EDITOR: SARAH BRUNSTAD • ASSOCIATE MANAGING EDITOR: ALEX STARBUCK
EDITOR, SPECIAL PROJECTS: MARK D. BEAZLEY • SENIOR EDITOR, SPECIAL PROJECTS: JEFF YOUNGQUIST • SVP PRINT, SALES & MARKETING: DAVID GABRIEL

EDITOR IN CHIEF: AXEL ALONSO • CHIEF CREATIVE OFFICER: JOE QUESADA • PUBLISHER: DAN BUCKLEY • EXECUTIVE PRODUCER: ALAN FINE

X-FORCE BY CRAIG KYLE & CHRIS YOST: THE COMPLETE COLLECTION VOL. 2. Contains material originally published in magazine form as X-FORCE #17-25 and ANNUAL #1, X NECROSHA, X-NECROSHA: T GATHERING, and X-FORCE: SEX AND VIOLENCE #1-3. First printing 2014. ISBN# 978-0-7851-9000-4. Published by MARVEL WORLDWIDE, INC., a subsidiary of MARVEL ENTERTAINMENT, LLC. OFFICE OF PUBLICATIC 135 West 50th Street, New York, NY 10020. **Printed in Canada.** ALAN FINE, EVP - Office of the President, Marvel Worldwide, Inc. and EVP & CMO Marvel Characters B.V.; DAN BUCKLEY, Publishe President - Print, Animation & Digital Divisions; JOE QUESADA, Chief Creative Officer; TOM BREVOORT, SVP of Publishing; DAVID BOGART, SVP of Operations & Procurement, Publishing; C.B. CEBULSKI, SVP of Creato Content Development; DAVID GABRIEL, SVP Print, Sales & Marketing; JIM O'KEEFE, VP of Operations & Logistics; DAN CARR, Executive Director of Publishing Technology; SUSAN CRESPI, Editorial Operations Manag ALEX MORALES, Publishing Operations Manager; STAN LEE, Chairman Emeritus. For information regarding advertising in Marvel Comics or on Marvel.com, please contact Niza Disla, Director of Marvel Partnerships, ndisla@marvel.com. For Marvel subscription inquiries, please call 800-217-9158. **Manufactured between 7/4/2014 and 8/11/2014 by SOLISCO PRINTERS, SCOTT, QC, CANADA.**

10 9 8 7 6 5 4 3 2 1

X-FORCE

BY

CRAIG KYLE & CHRIS YOST

X-FORCE #17-20
ARTIST: MIKE CHOI
COLOR ARTIST: SONIA OBACK
LETTERER: VC'S CORY PETIT
COVER ART: MIKE CHOI
& SONIA OBACK

X-FORCE: NECROSHA
& X-FORCE #21-25
ARTIST: CLAYTON CRAIN
LETTERER: VC'S CLAYTON COWLES
COVER ART: CLAYTON CRAIN

X-FORCE ANNUAL #1
"UNDEADPOOL"
PENCILER: CARLO BARBERI
INKER: SANDU FLOREA
COLORIST: EDGAR DELGADO
LETTERER: JEFF ECKLEBERRY
COVER ART: JASON PEARSON
& DAVE STEWART

X-NECROSHA: THE GATHERING

"WITHER"
ARTIST: IBRAIM ROBERSON
COLORIST: SOTOCOLOR'S L. MOLINAR
"BLINK"
ARTIST: GABRIEL HERNANDEZ WALTA
"SENYAKA"
ARTIST: LEONARDO MANCO
COLORIST: SOTOCOLOR'S C. FIDLER

"MORTIS"
PENCILER: KALMAN ANDRASOFSZKY
INKER: CAM SMITH
COLORIST: SOTOCOLOR'S J. ROBERTS
"ELIPHAS"
ARTIST: MATEUS SANTOLOUCO

COVER ART: CLAYTON CRAIN

X-FORCE: SEX AND VIOLENCE #1-3
ARTIST: GABRIELE DELL'OTTO
LETTERER: VC'S CORY PETIT
COVER ART: GABRIELE DELL'OTTO

ASSISTANT EDITORS: JODY LEHEUP & SEBASTIAN GIRNER • ASSOCIATE EDITOR: DANIEL KETCHUM
EDITORS: JEANINE SCHAEFER & JOHN BARBER • EXECUTIVE EDITOR: AXEL ALONSO

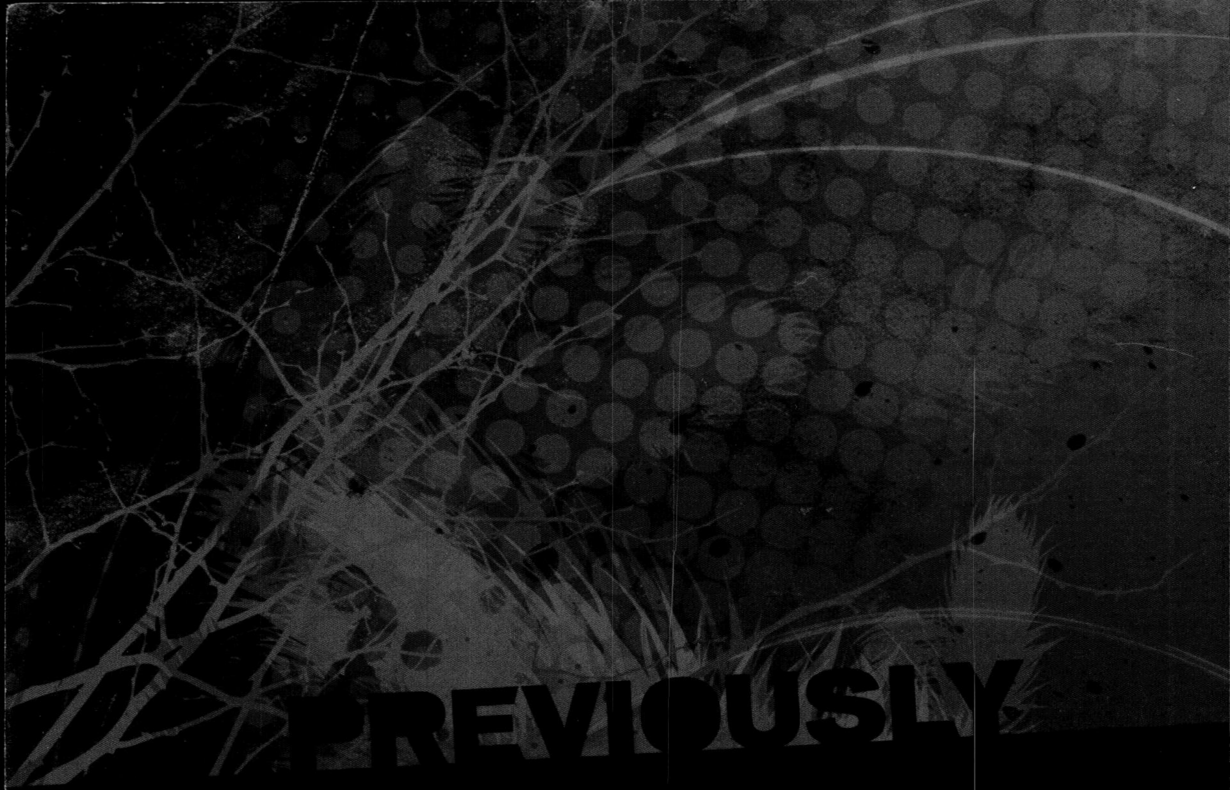

PREVIOUSLY

The mutant-hating cyborg, Bastion, has revived many of the X-Men's enemies, including the villainous pairing of Stephen Lang and Bolivar Trask, as well as the murderer of mutants, the Leper Queen. Their first order of business was to publicly call for an armed response to the mutant threat and to privately steal a mutated strain of the Legacy virus, the contagion that once threatened to annihilate all mutantkind.

This new strain amplifies the powers of those afflicted, and with the right mutant those strengthened abilities can be lethal to anyone nearby. Now — with anti-mutant sentiment on the rise — the Leper Queen has begun abducting and injecting mutants with the virus and releasing them into human populations. So far, hundreds have been killed…and now the young mutants Hellion, Surge, and Boom-Boom have been taken.

X-Force tracks the Leper Queen to her lair, but as they're seconds away from rescuing Boom-Boom, Cyclops — leader of the X-Men — teleports the team to the future to track down his missing son and a young girl who might be the mutant messiah. After a deadly battle, X-Force attempts to return to the exact moment they left. While Vanisher escapes to upstate New York and Wolfsbane is still missing with her lover, Hrimhari, the Wolf Prince of Asgard, the majority of the team heads toward the U.N. to stop Surge and Hellion from detonating, and X-23 alone strives to protect Boom-Boom.

But the Leper Queen isn't finished yet…

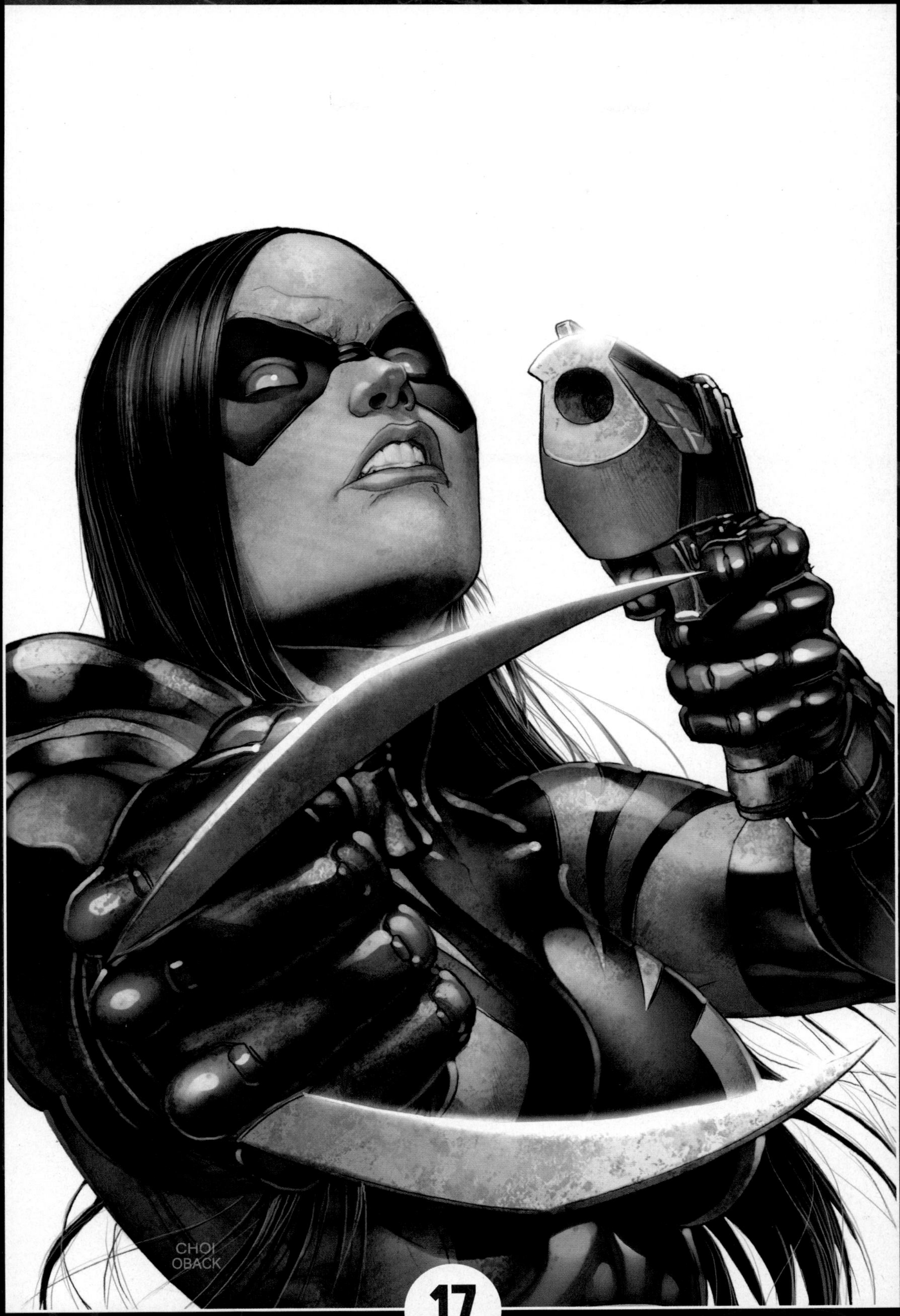
CHOI
OBACK

17

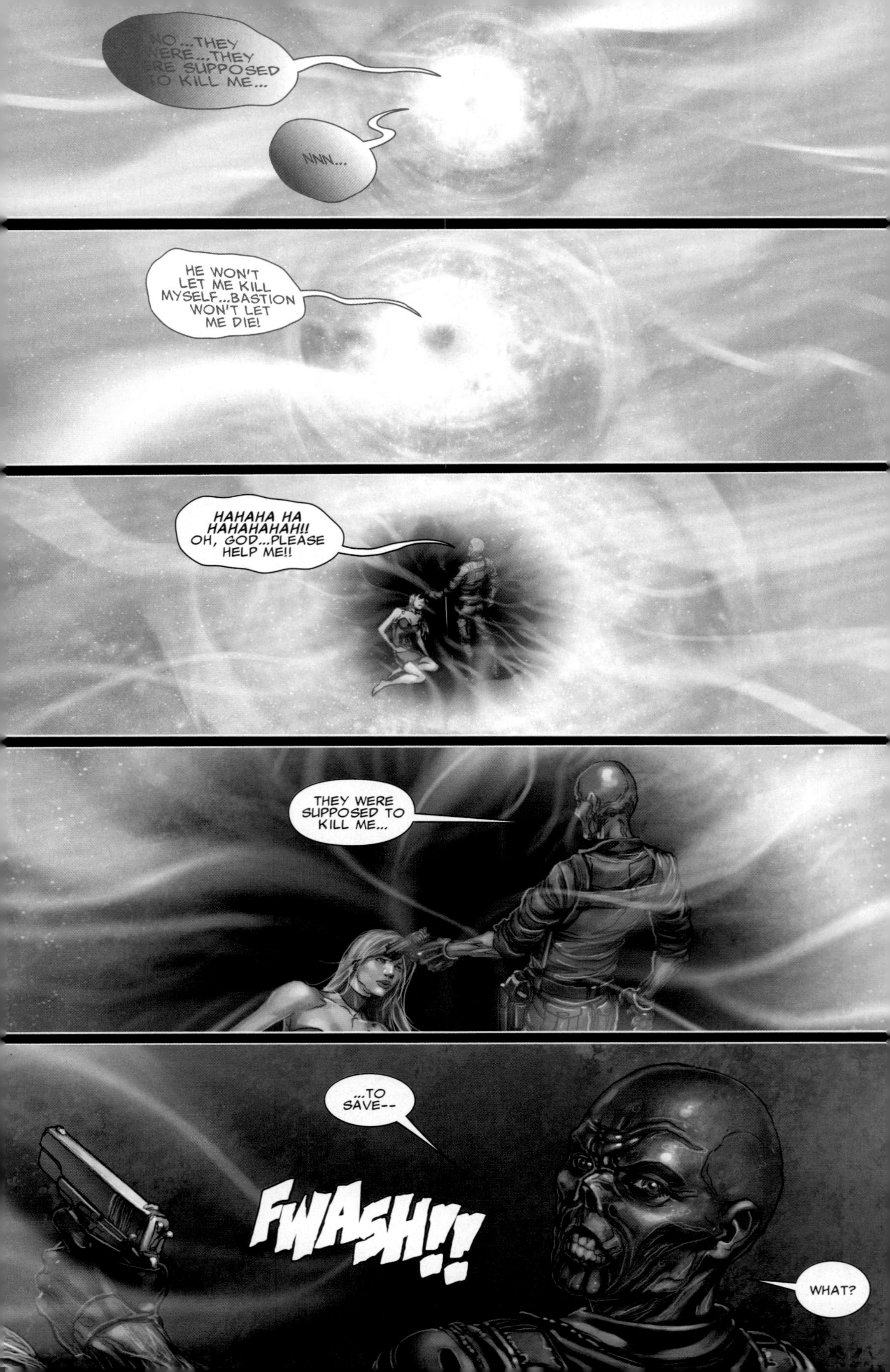
NO...THEY WERE...THEY WERE SUPPOSED TO KILL ME...
NNN...
HE WON'T LET ME KILL MYSELF...BASTION WON'T LET ME DIE!
HAHAHA HA HAHAHAHAH!! OH, GOD...PLEASE HELP ME!!
THEY WERE SUPPOSED TO KILL ME...
...TO SAVE--
FWASH!!
WHAT?

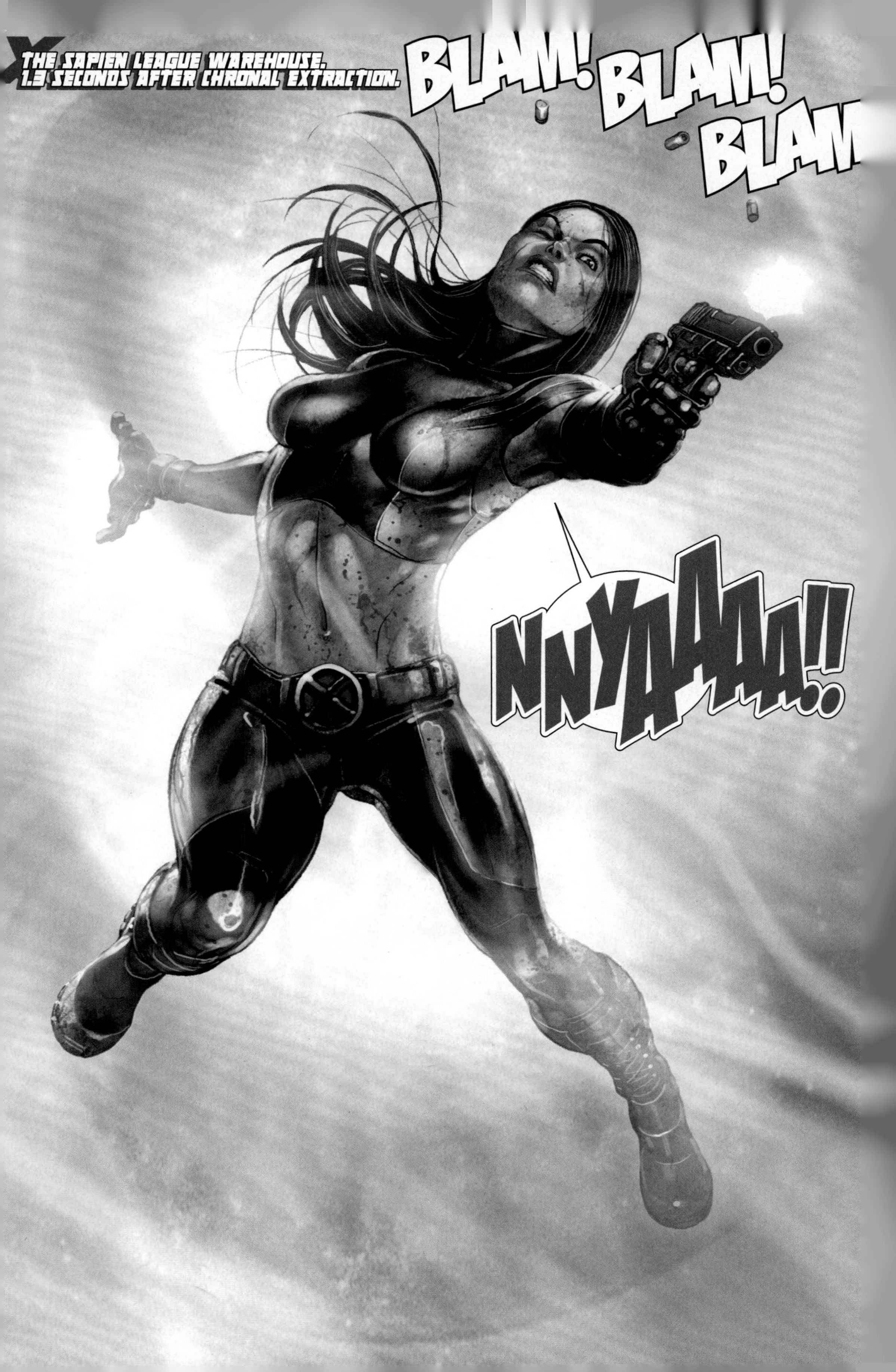
THE SAPIEN LEAGUE WAREHOUSE.
1.3 SECONDS AFTER CHRONAL EXTRACTION.
BLAM! BLAM!
BLAM
NNYAAAA!!

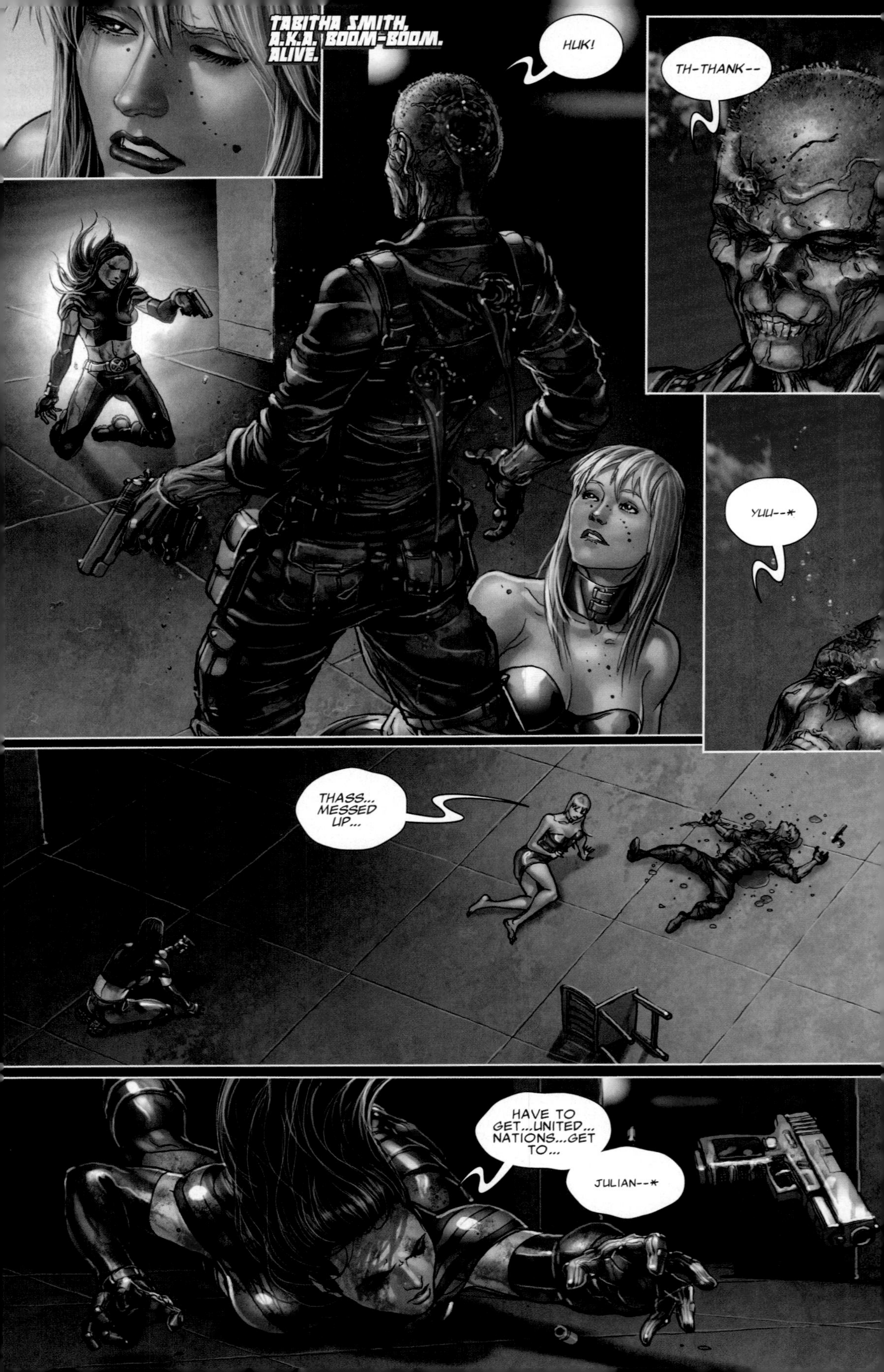
TABITHA SMITH,
A.K.A. BOOM-BOOM.
ALIVE.
HUK!
TH-THANK--
YUU--*
THASS... MESSED UP...
HAVE TO GET...UNITED... NATIONS...GET TO...
JULIAN--*

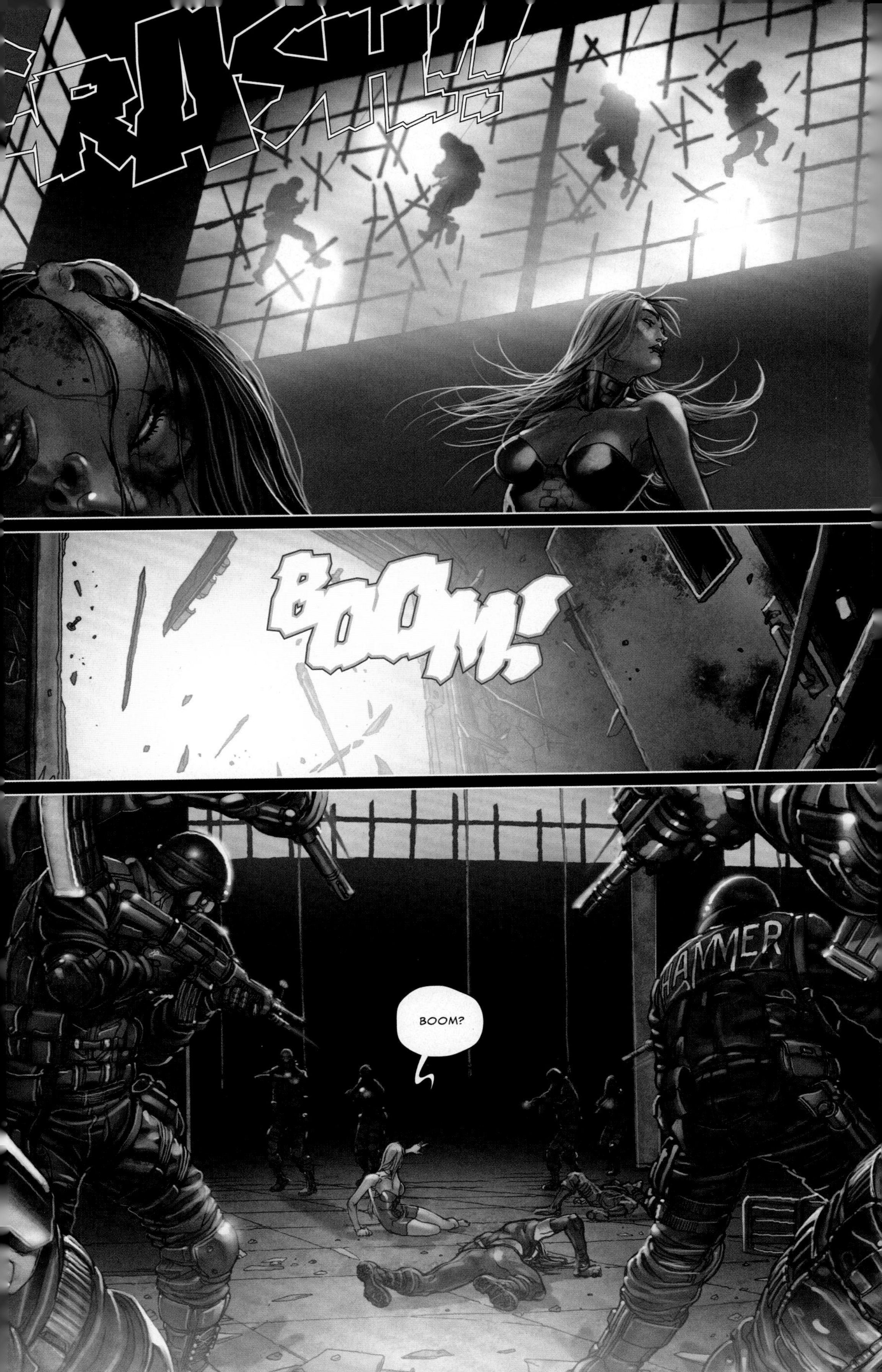
BOOM!
HAMMER
BOOM?

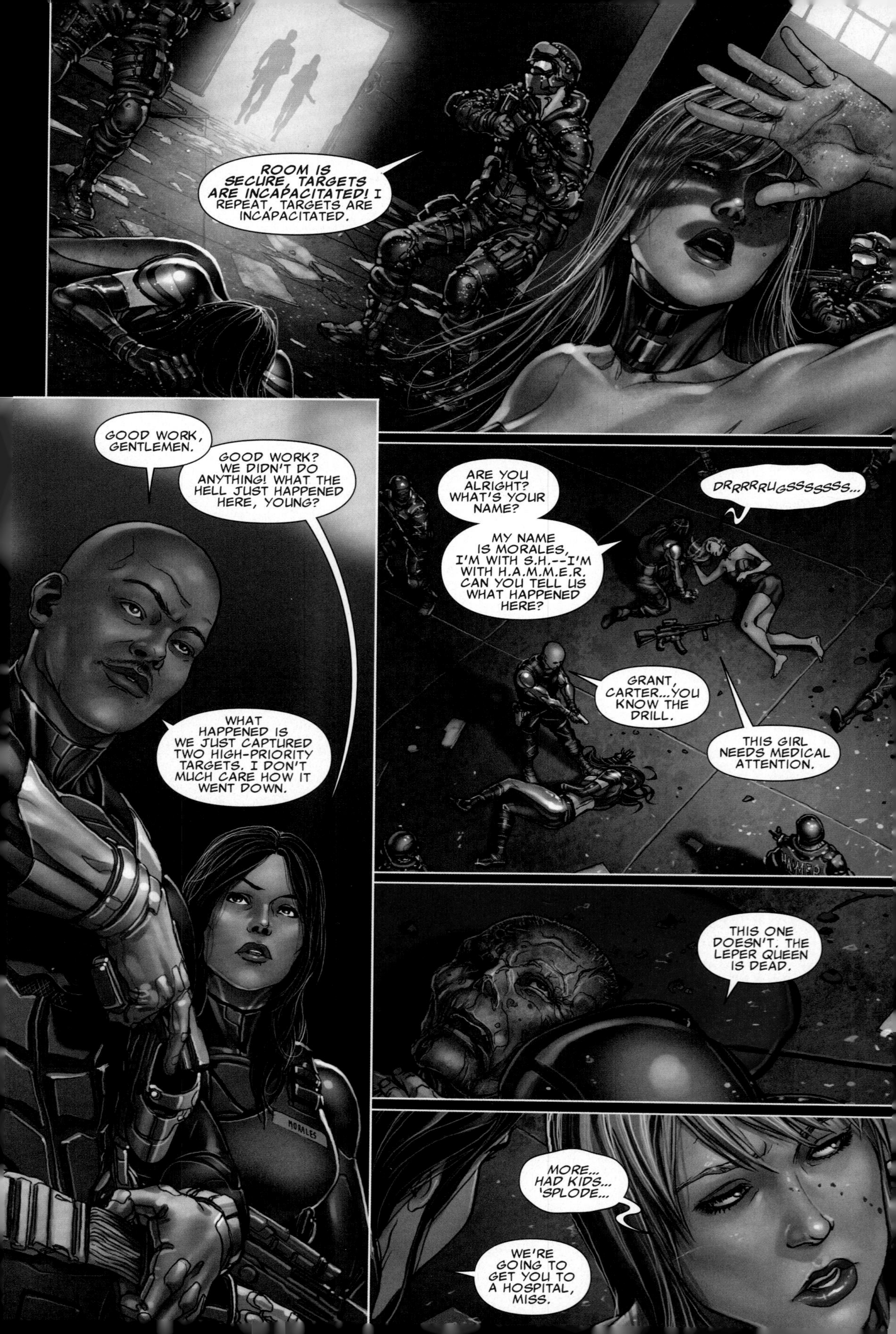
ROOM IS SECURE, TARGETS ARE INCAPACITATED! I REPEAT, TARGETS ARE INCAPACITATED.
GOOD WORK, GENTLEMEN.
GOOD WORK? WE DIDN'T DO ANYTHING! WHAT THE HELL JUST HAPPENED HERE, YOUNG?
WHAT HAPPENED IS WE JUST CAPTURED TWO HIGH-PRIORITY TARGETS. I DON'T MUCH CARE HOW IT WENT DOWN.
MORALES
ARE YOU ALRIGHT? WHAT'S YOUR NAME?
DRRRRRUGSSSSSSS...
MY NAME IS MORALES, I'M WITH S.H.--I'M WITH H.A.M.M.E.R. CAN YOU TELL US WHAT HAPPENED HERE?
GRANT, CARTER...YOU KNOW THE DRILL.
THIS GIRL NEEDS MEDICAL ATTENTION.
THIS ONE DOESN'T. THE LEPER QUEEN IS DEAD.
MORE... HAD KIDS... 'SPLODE...
WE'RE GOING TO GET YOU TO A HOSPITAL, MISS.

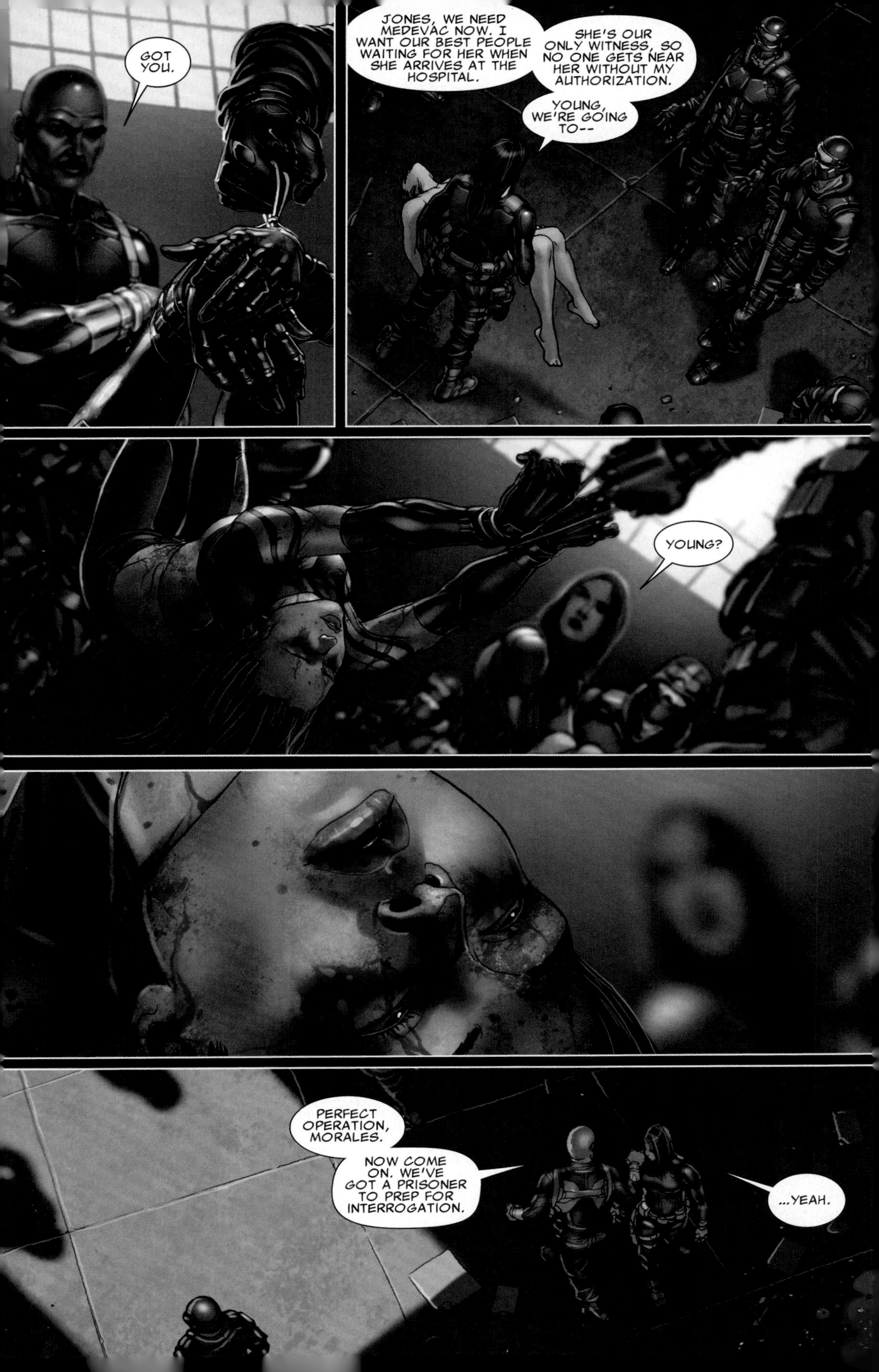
GOT YOU.
JONES, WE NEED MEDEVAC NOW. I WANT OUR BEST PEOPLE WAITING FOR HER WHEN SHE ARRIVES AT THE HOSPITAL.
SHE'S OUR ONLY WITNESS, SO NO ONE GETS NEAR HER WITHOUT MY AUTHORIZATION.
YOUNG, WE'RE GOING TO--
YOUNG?
PERFECT OPERATION, MORALES.
NOW COME ON. WE'VE GOT A PRISONER TO PREP FOR INTERROGATION.
...YEAH.

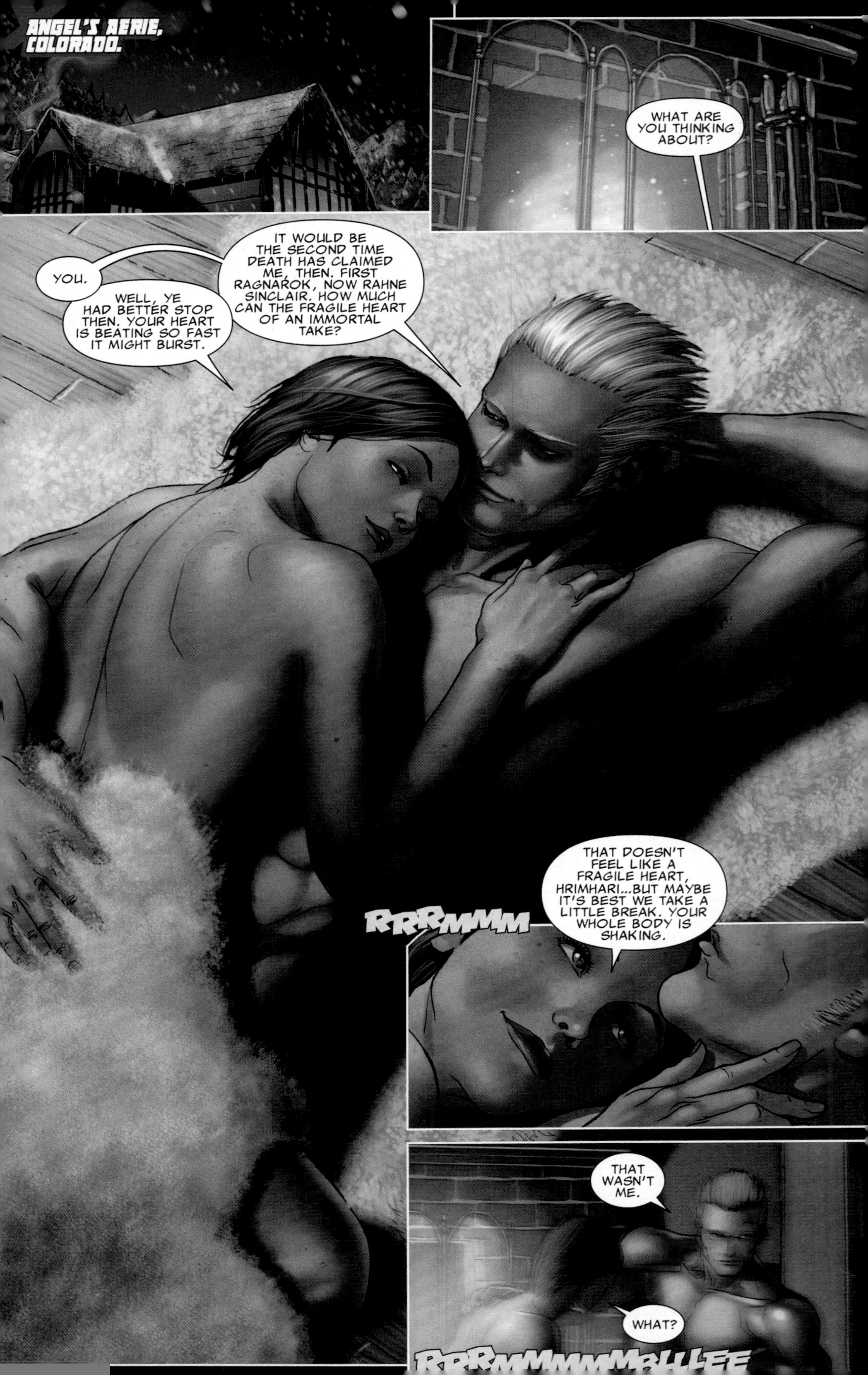
ANGEL'S AERIE, COLORADO.
WHAT ARE YOU THINKING ABOUT?
YOU.
IT WOULD BE THE SECOND TIME DEATH HAS CLAIMED ME, THEN. FIRST RAGNAROK, NOW RAHNE SINCLAIR. HOW MUCH CAN THE FRAGILE HEART OF AN IMMORTAL TAKE?
WELL, YE HAD BETTER STOP THEN. YOUR HEART IS BEATING SO FAST IT MIGHT BURST.
RRRMMMM
THAT DOESN'T FEEL LIKE A FRAGILE HEART, HRIMHARI...BUT MAYBE IT'S BEST WE TAKE A LITTLE BREAK. YOUR WHOLE BODY IS SHAKING.
THAT WASN'T ME.
WHAT?
RRRMMMMMMBLLEE

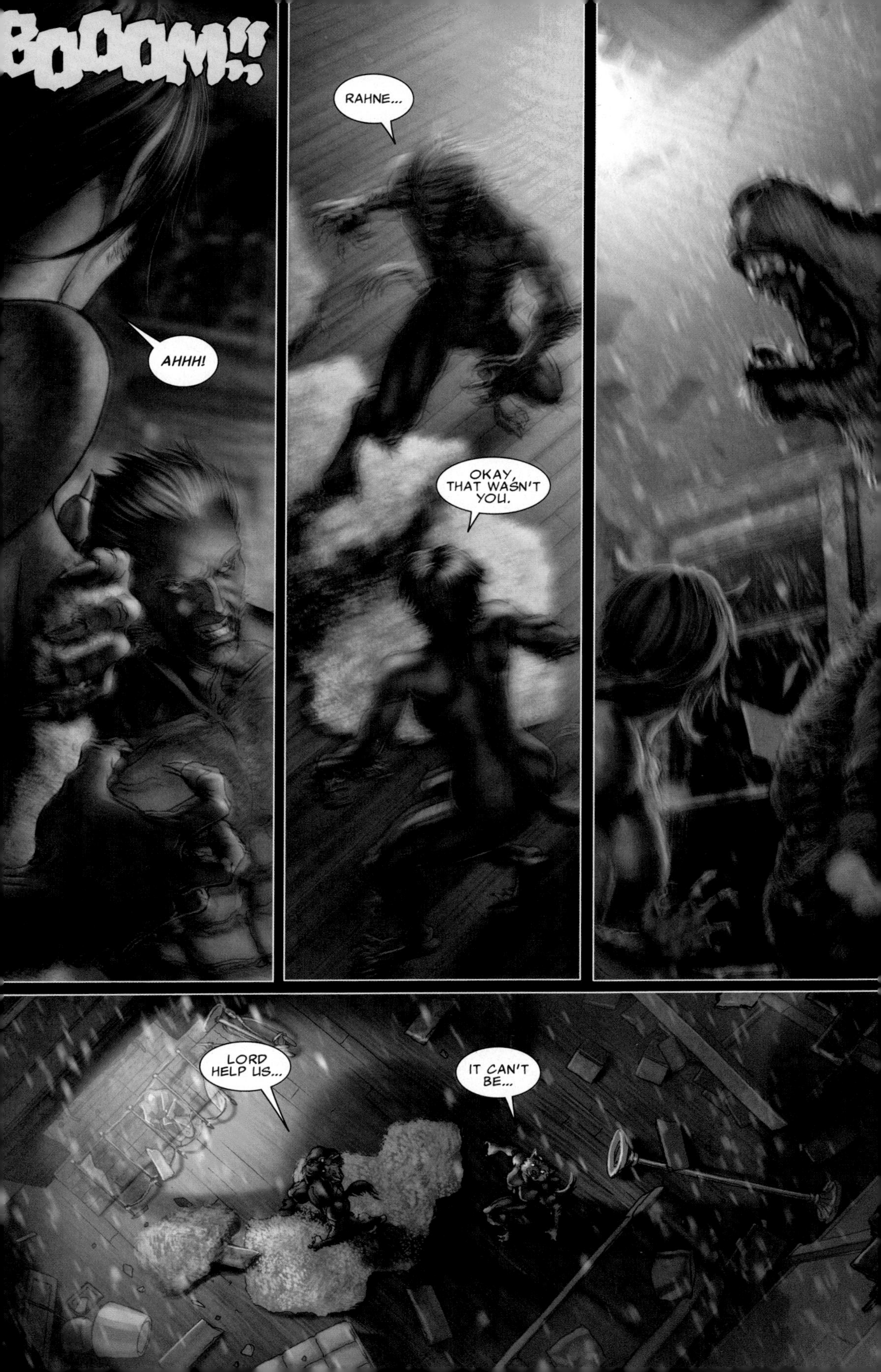
BOOOM!!
AHHH!
RAHNE...
OKAY, THAT WASN'T YOU.
LORD HELP US...
IT CAN'T BE...

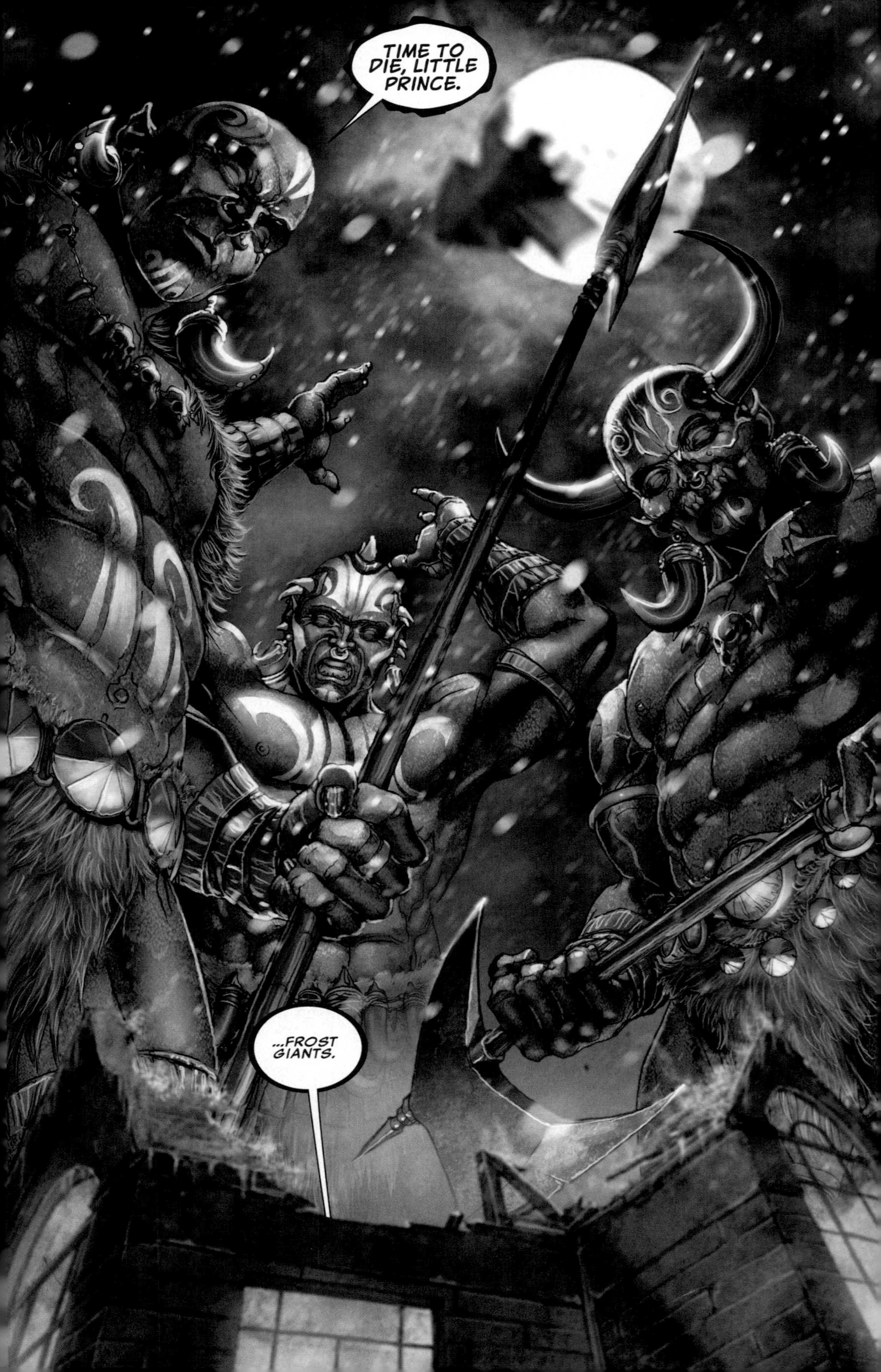
TIME TO DIE, LITTLE PRINCE.
...FROST GIANTS.

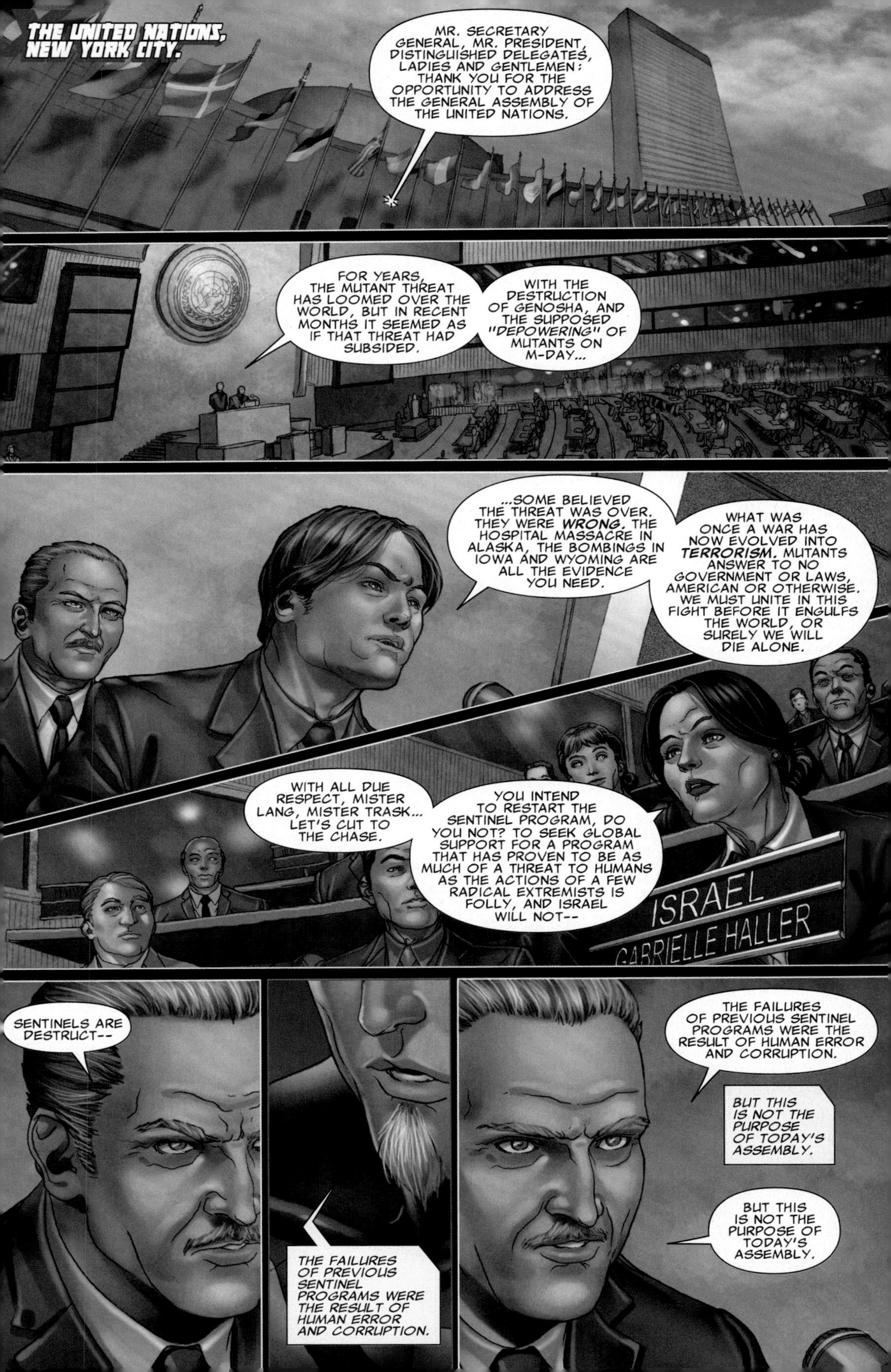
THE UNITED NATIONS, NEW YORK CITY.
MR. SECRETARY GENERAL, MR. PRESIDENT, DISTINGUISHED DELEGATES, LADIES AND GENTLEMEN: THANK YOU FOR THE OPPORTUNITY TO ADDRESS THE GENERAL ASSEMBLY OF THE UNITED NATIONS.
FOR YEARS, THE MUTANT THREAT HAS LOOMED OVER THE WORLD, BUT IN RECENT MONTHS IT SEEMED AS IF THAT THREAT HAD SUBSIDED.
WITH THE DESTRUCTION OF GENOSHA, AND THE SUPPOSED "DEPOWERING" OF MUTANTS ON M-DAY...
...SOME BELIEVED THE THREAT WAS OVER. THEY WERE WRONG. THE HOSPITAL MASSACRE IN ALASKA, THE BOMBINGS IN IOWA AND WYOMING ARE ALL THE EVIDENCE YOU NEED.
WHAT WAS ONCE A WAR HAS NOW EVOLVED INTO TERRORISM. MUTANTS ANSWER TO NO GOVERNMENT OR LAWS, AMERICAN OR OTHERWISE. WE MUST UNITE IN THIS FIGHT BEFORE IT ENGULFS THE WORLD, OR SURELY WE WILL DIE ALONE.
WITH ALL DUE RESPECT, MISTER LANG, MISTER TRASK... LET'S CUT TO THE CHASE.
YOU INTEND TO RESTART THE SENTINEL PROGRAM, DO YOU NOT? TO SEEK GLOBAL SUPPORT FOR A PROGRAM THAT HAS PROVEN TO BE AS MUCH OF A THREAT TO HUMANS AS THE ACTIONS OF A FEW RADICAL EXTREMISTS IS FOLLY, AND ISRAEL WILL NOT--
ISRAEL
GABRIELLE HALLER
SENTINELS ARE DESTRUCT--
THE FAILURES OF PREVIOUS SENTINEL PROGRAMS WERE THE RESULT OF HUMAN ERROR AND CORRUPTION.
THE FAILURES OF PREVIOUS SENTINEL PROGRAMS WERE THE RESULT OF HUMAN ERROR AND CORRUPTION.
BUT THIS IS NOT THE PURPOSE OF TODAY'S ASSEMBLY.
BUT THIS IS NOT THE PURPOSE OF TODAY'S ASSEMBLY.

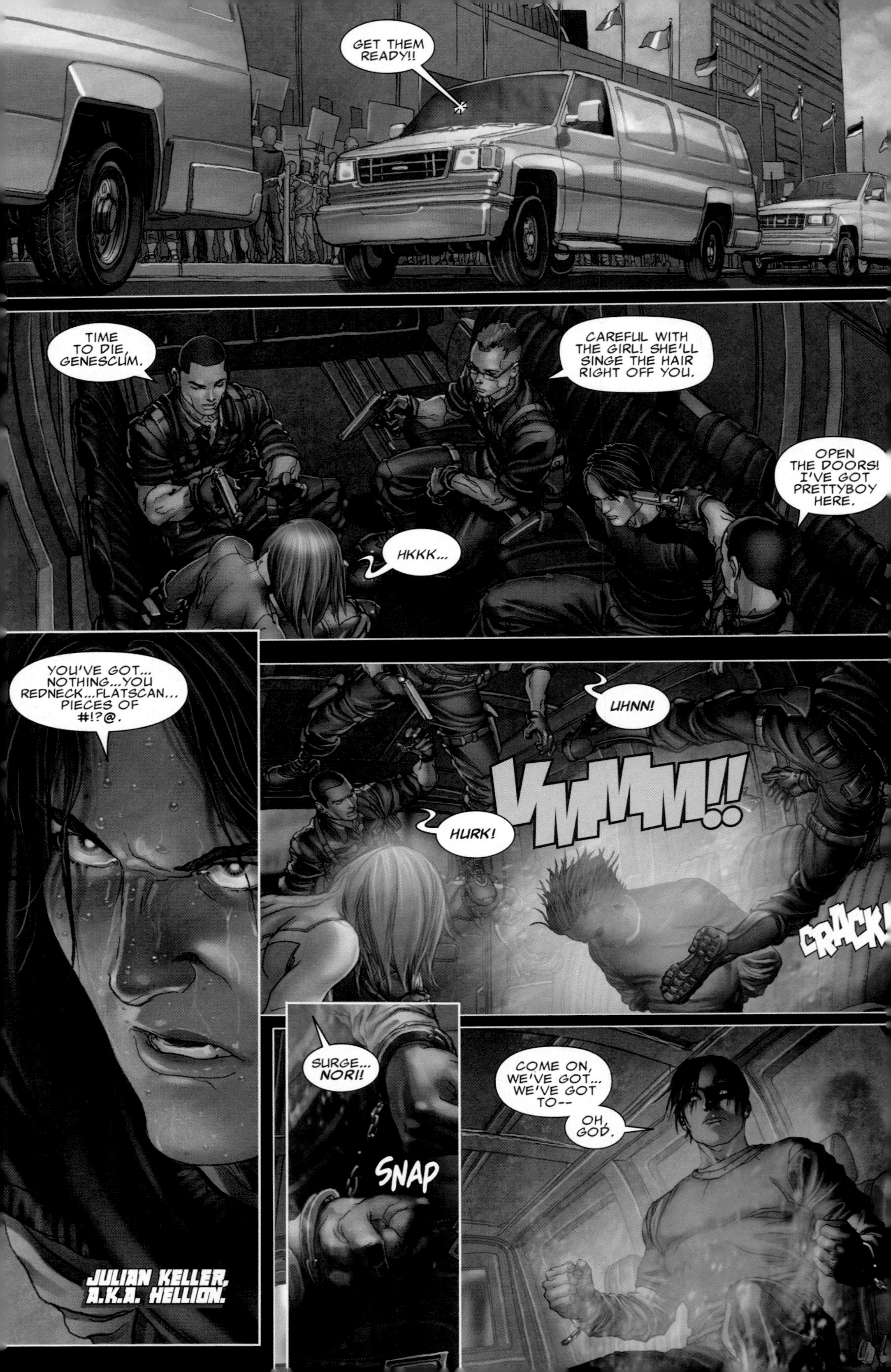
GET THEM READY!!
TIME TO DIE, GENESCUM.
CAREFUL WITH THE GIRL! SHE'LL SINGE THE HAIR RIGHT OFF YOU.
OPEN THE DOORS! I'VE GOT PRETTYBOY HERE.
HKKK...
YOU'VE GOT... NOTHING...YOU REDNECK...FLATSCAN... PIECES OF #!?@.
JULIAN KELLER, A.K.A. HELLION.
UHNN!
VMMMM!!
HURK!
CRACK!
SURGE... NORI!!
SNAP
COME ON, WE'VE GOT... WE'VE GOT TO--
OH, GOD.

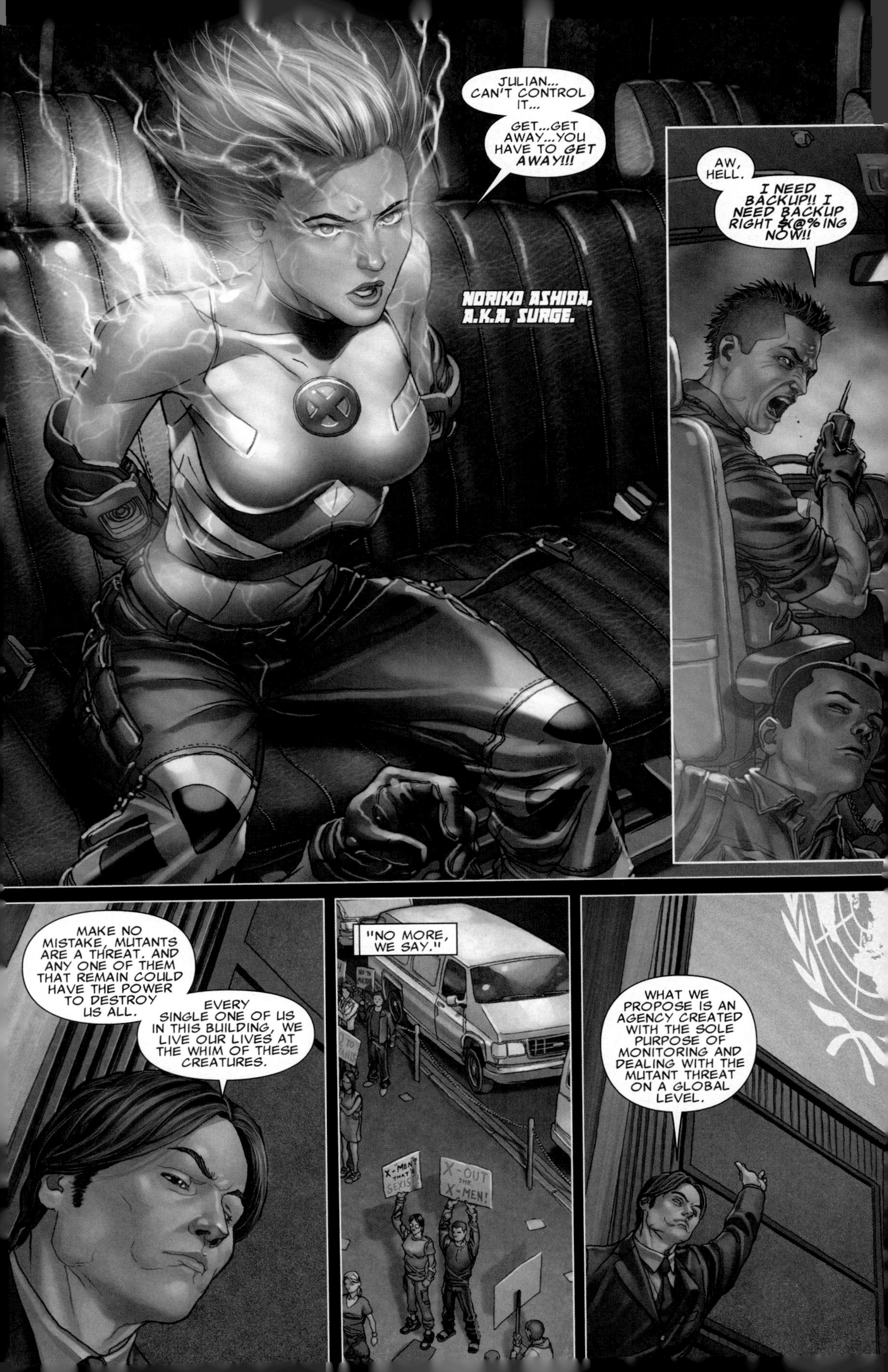
JULIAN... CAN'T CONTROL IT...
GET...GET AWAY...YOU HAVE TO GET AWAY!!!
NORIKO ASHIDA, A.K.A. SURGE.
AW, HELL.
I NEED BACKUP!! I NEED BACKUP RIGHT $(@% ING NOW!!
MAKE NO MISTAKE, MUTANTS ARE A THREAT. AND ANY ONE OF THEM THAT REMAIN COULD HAVE THE POWER TO DESTROY US ALL.
EVERY SINGLE ONE OF US IN THIS BUILDING, WE LIVE OUR LIVES AT THE WHIM OF THESE CREATURES.
"NO MORE, WE SAY."
X-MEN? THAT'S SEXIST!
X-OUT THE X-MEN!
WHAT WE PROPOSE IS AN AGENCY CREATED WITH THE SOLE PURPOSE OF MONITORING AND DEALING WITH THE MUTANT THREAT ON A GLOBAL LEVEL.

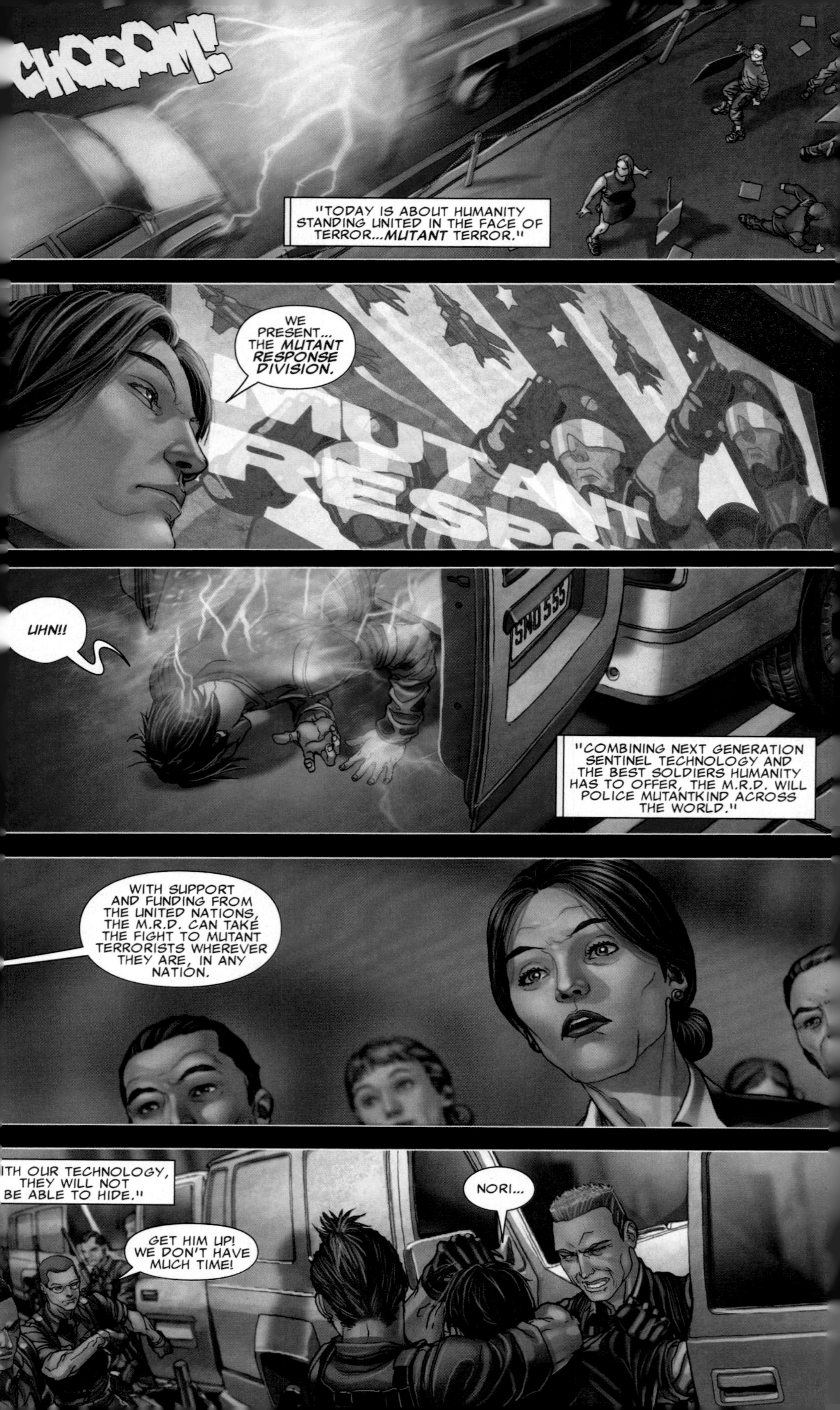
CHOOOM!
"TODAY IS ABOUT HUMANITY STANDING UNITED IN THE FACE OF TERROR...MUTANT TERROR."
WE PRESENT... THE MUTANT RESPONSE DIVISION.
UHN!!
SMD 555
"COMBINING NEXT GENERATION SENTINEL TECHNOLOGY AND THE BEST SOLDIERS HUMANITY HAS TO OFFER, THE M.R.D. WILL POLICE MUTANTKIND ACROSS THE WORLD."
WITH SUPPORT AND FUNDING FROM THE UNITED NATIONS, THE M.R.D. CAN TAKE THE FIGHT TO MUTANT TERRORISTS WHEREVER THEY ARE, IN ANY NATION.
ITH OUR TECHNOLOGY, THEY WILL NOT BE ABLE TO HIDE."
GET HIM UP! WE DON'T HAVE MUCH TIME!
NORI...

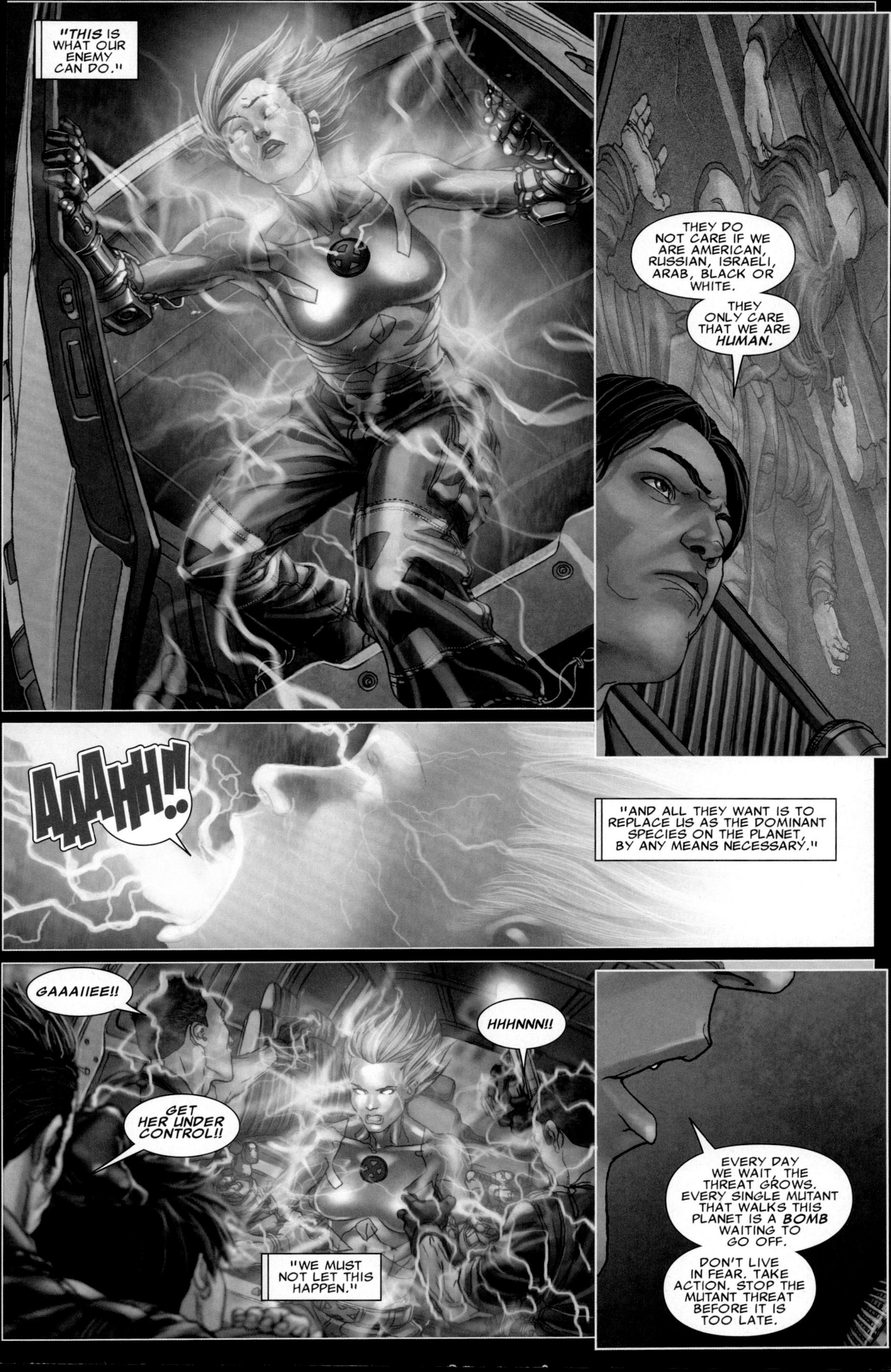
"THIS IS WHAT OUR ENEMY CAN DO."
THEY DO NOT CARE IF WE ARE AMERICAN, RUSSIAN, ISRAELI, ARAB, BLACK OR WHITE.
THEY ONLY CARE THAT WE ARE HUMAN.
AAAHHH!!..
"AND ALL THEY WANT IS TO REPLACE US AS THE DOMINANT SPECIES ON THE PLANET, BY ANY MEANS NECESSARY."
GAAAIIEE!!
HHHNNN!!
GET HER UNDER CONTROL!!
"WE MUST NOT LET THIS HAPPEN."
EVERY DAY WE WAIT, THE THREAT GROWS. EVERY SINGLE MUTANT THAT WALKS THIS PLANET IS A BOMB WAITING TO GO OFF.
DON'T LIVE IN FEAR. TAKE ACTION. STOP THE MUTANT THREAT BEFORE IT IS TOO LATE.

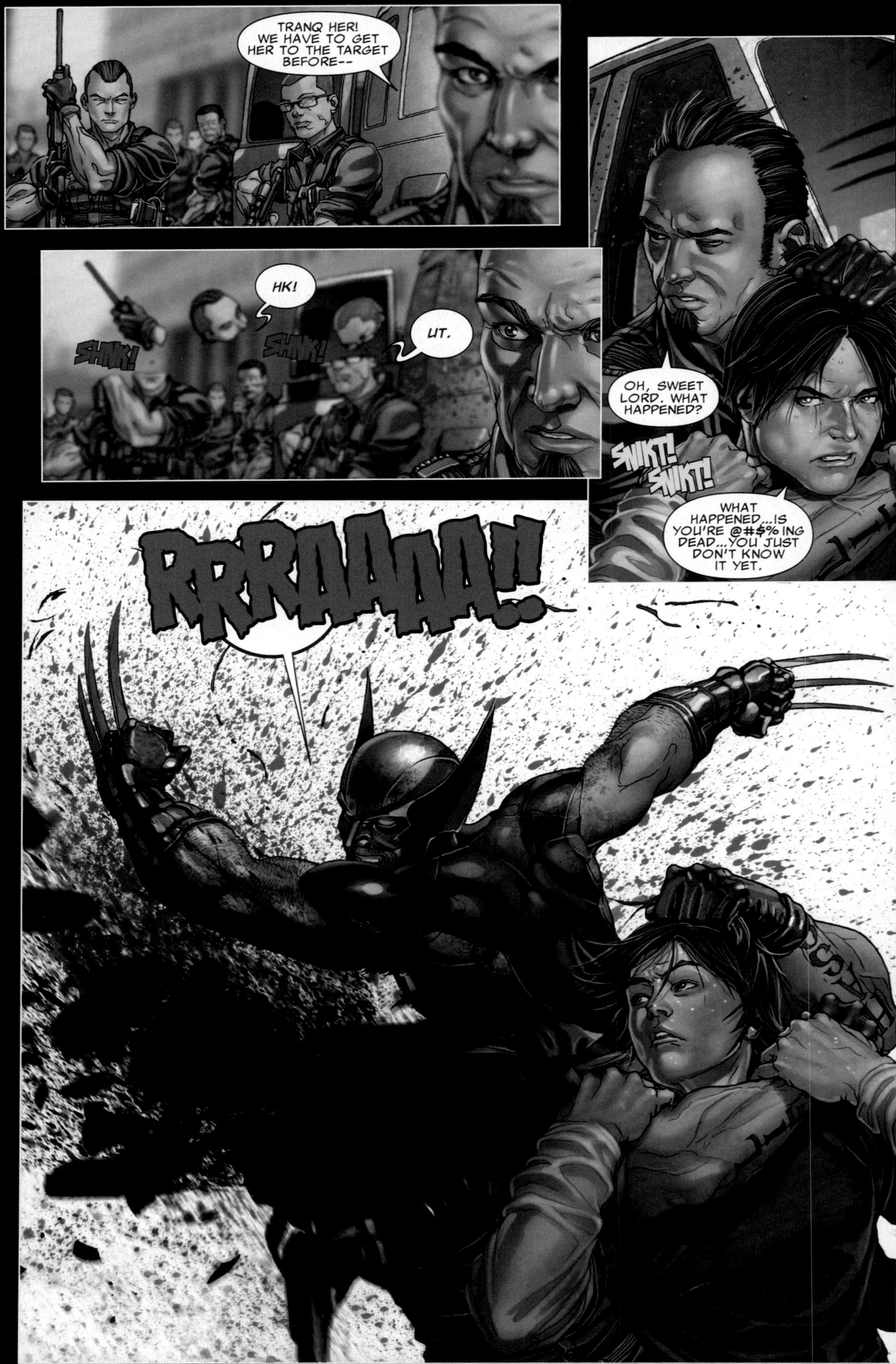
TRANQ HER! WE HAVE TO GET HER TO THE TARGET BEFORE--
HK!
SHNK!
SHNK!
UT.
OH, SWEET LORD. WHAT HAPPENED?
SNIKT! SNIKT!
WHAT HAPPENED...IS YOU'RE @#$% ING DEAD...YOU JUST DON'T KNOW IT YET.
RRRAAAA!!

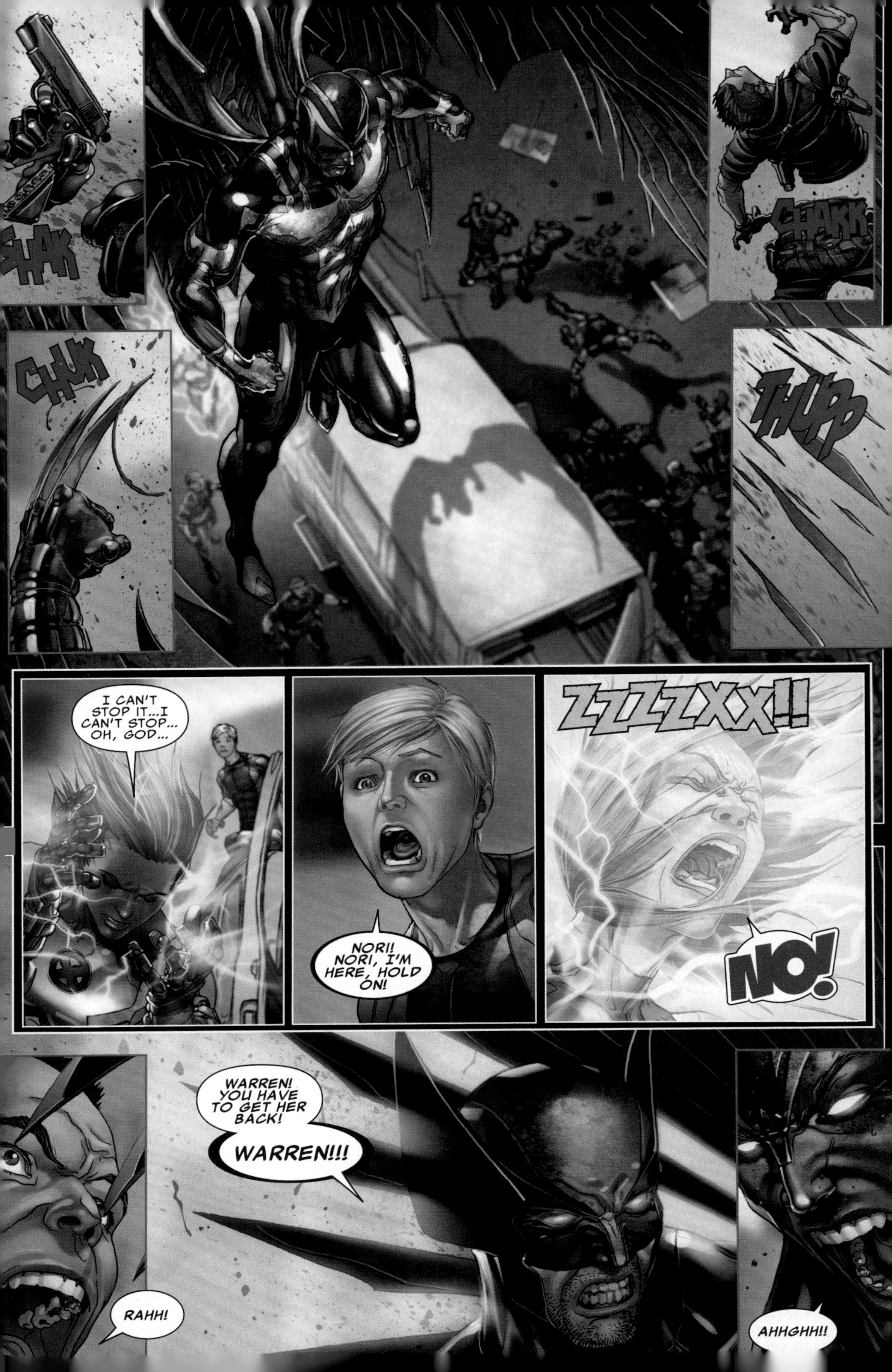
SHAK
CHAKK
CHUK
THUPP
I CAN'T STOP IT...I CAN'T STOP... OH, GOD...
NORI! NORI, I'M HERE, HOLD ON!
ZZZZXX!!
NO!
WARREN! YOU HAVE TO GET HER BACK!
WARREN!!!
RAHH!
AHHGHH!!

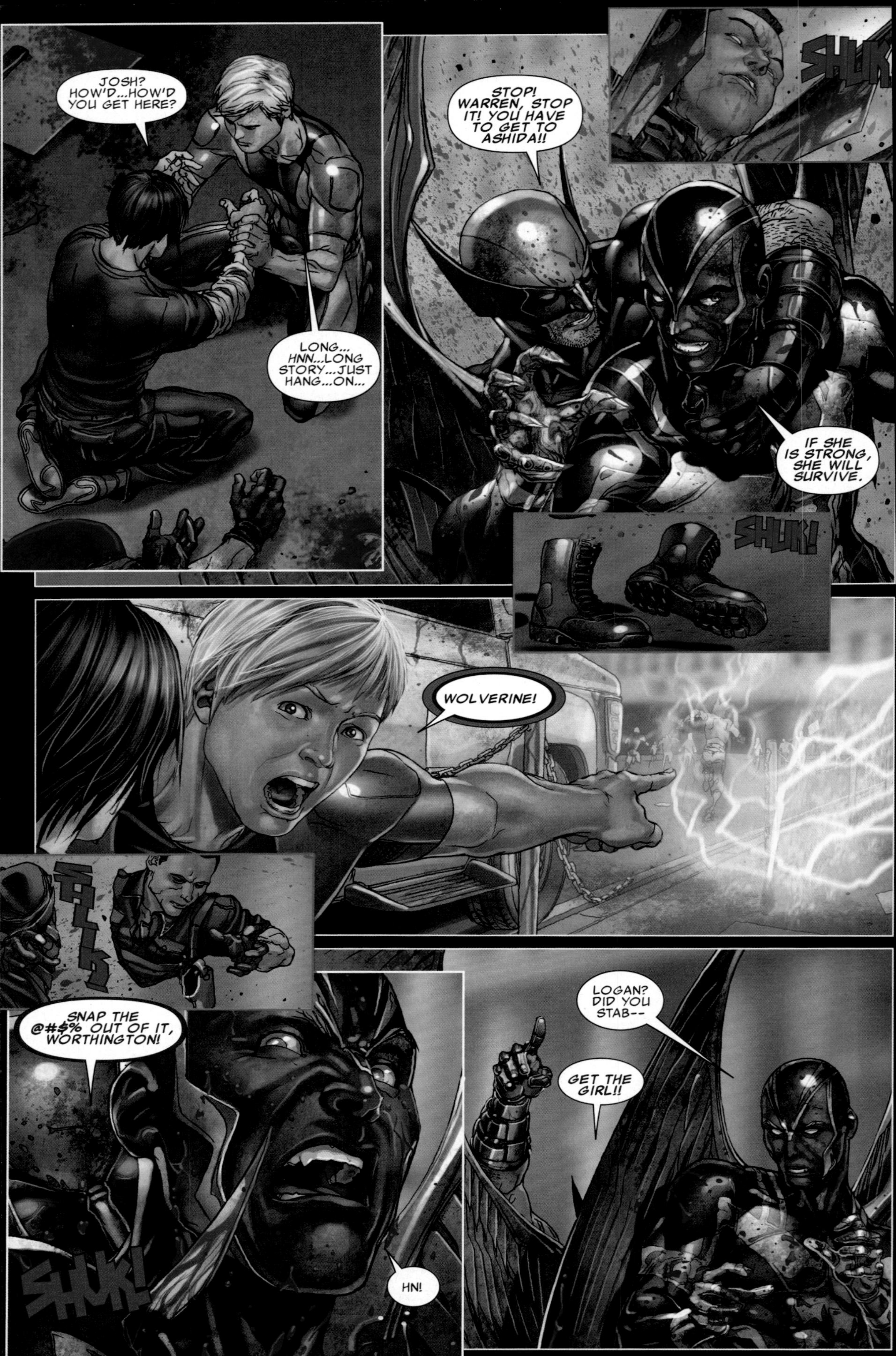
JOSH? HOW'D...HOW'D YOU GET HERE?
LONG... HNN...LONG STORY...JUST HANG...ON...
STOP! WARREN, STOP IT! YOU HAVE TO GET TO ASHIDA!!
SHUK
IF SHE IS STRONG, SHE WILL SURVIVE.
SHUK!
WOLVERINE!
SNAP THE @#$% OUT OF IT, WORTHINGTON!
SHUK!
HN!
LOGAN? DID YOU STAB--
GET THE GIRL!!

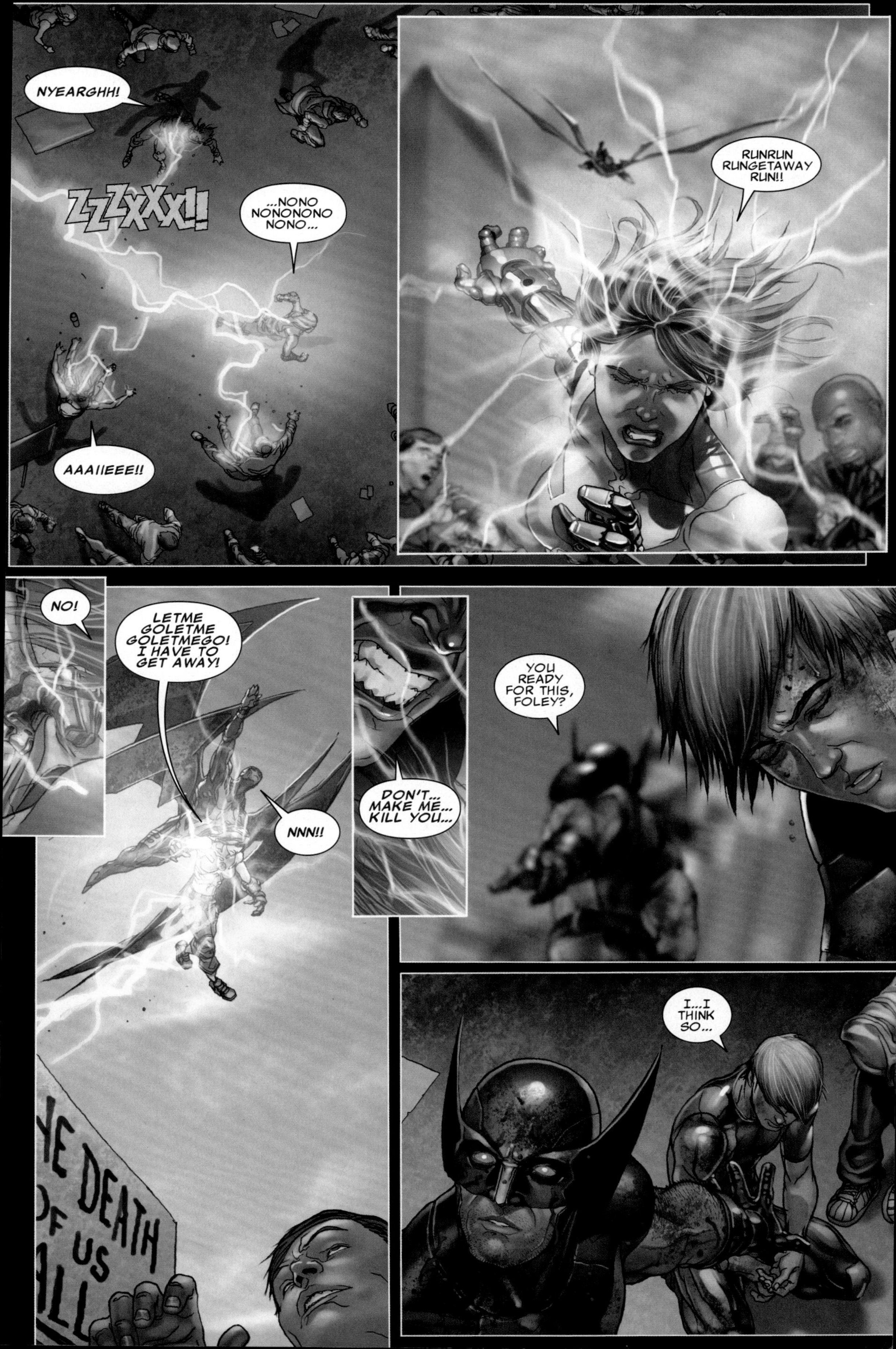
NYEARGHH!
ZZZXXX!!
...NONO NONONONO NONO...
AAAIIEEE!!
RUNRUN RUNGETAWAY RUN!!
NO!
LETME GOLETME GOLETMEGO! I HAVE TO GET AWAY!
NNN!!
DON'T... MAKE ME... KILL YOU...
YOU READY FOR THIS, FOLEY?
I...I THINK SO...
YE DEATH OF US ALL

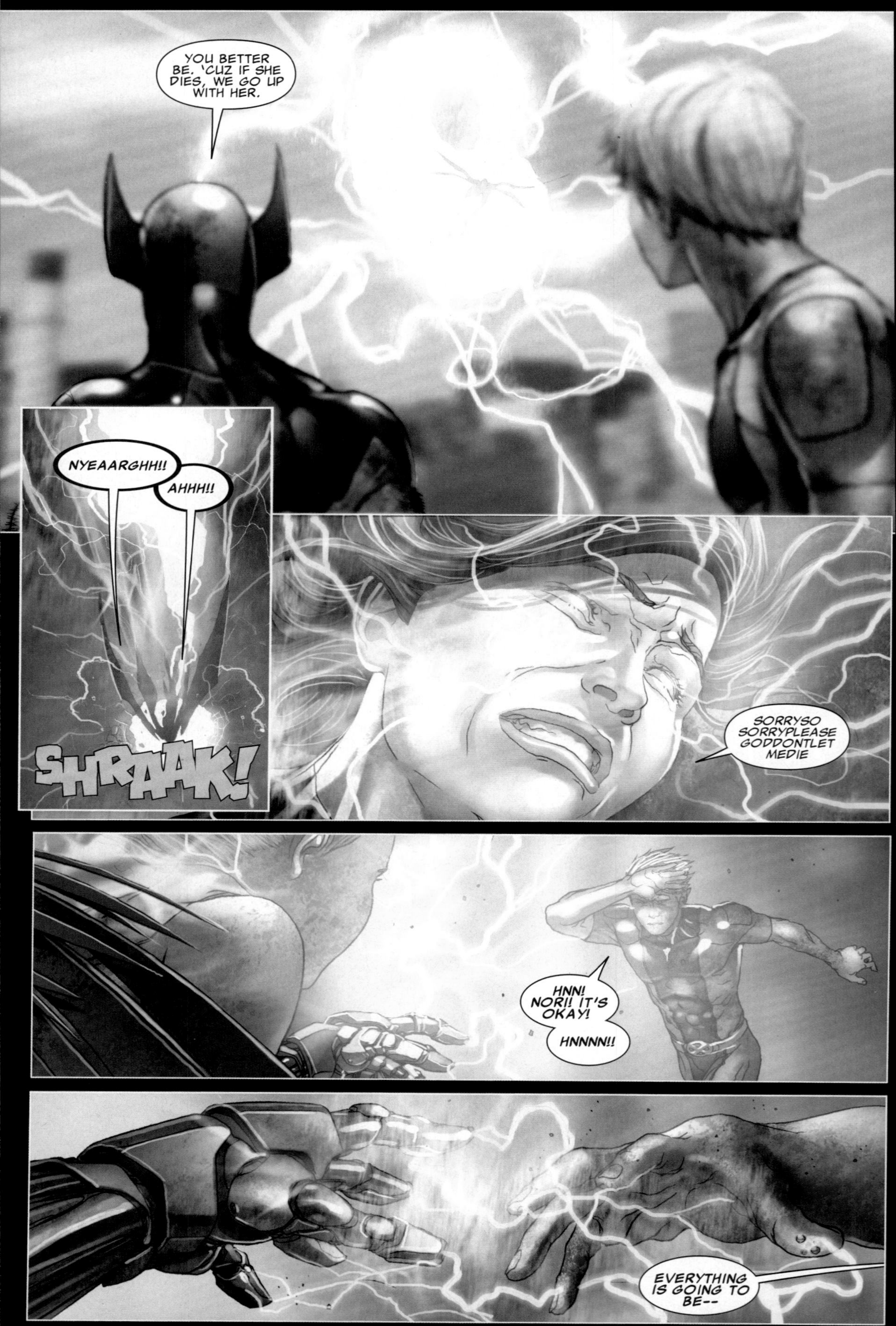

YOU BETTER BE. 'CUZ IF SHE DIES, WE GO UP WITH HER.
NYEAARGHH!!
AHHH!!
SHRAAK!
SORRYSO SORRYPLEASE GODDONTLET MEDIE
HNN! NORI! IT'S OKAY!
HNNNN!!
EVERYTHING IS GOING TO BE--

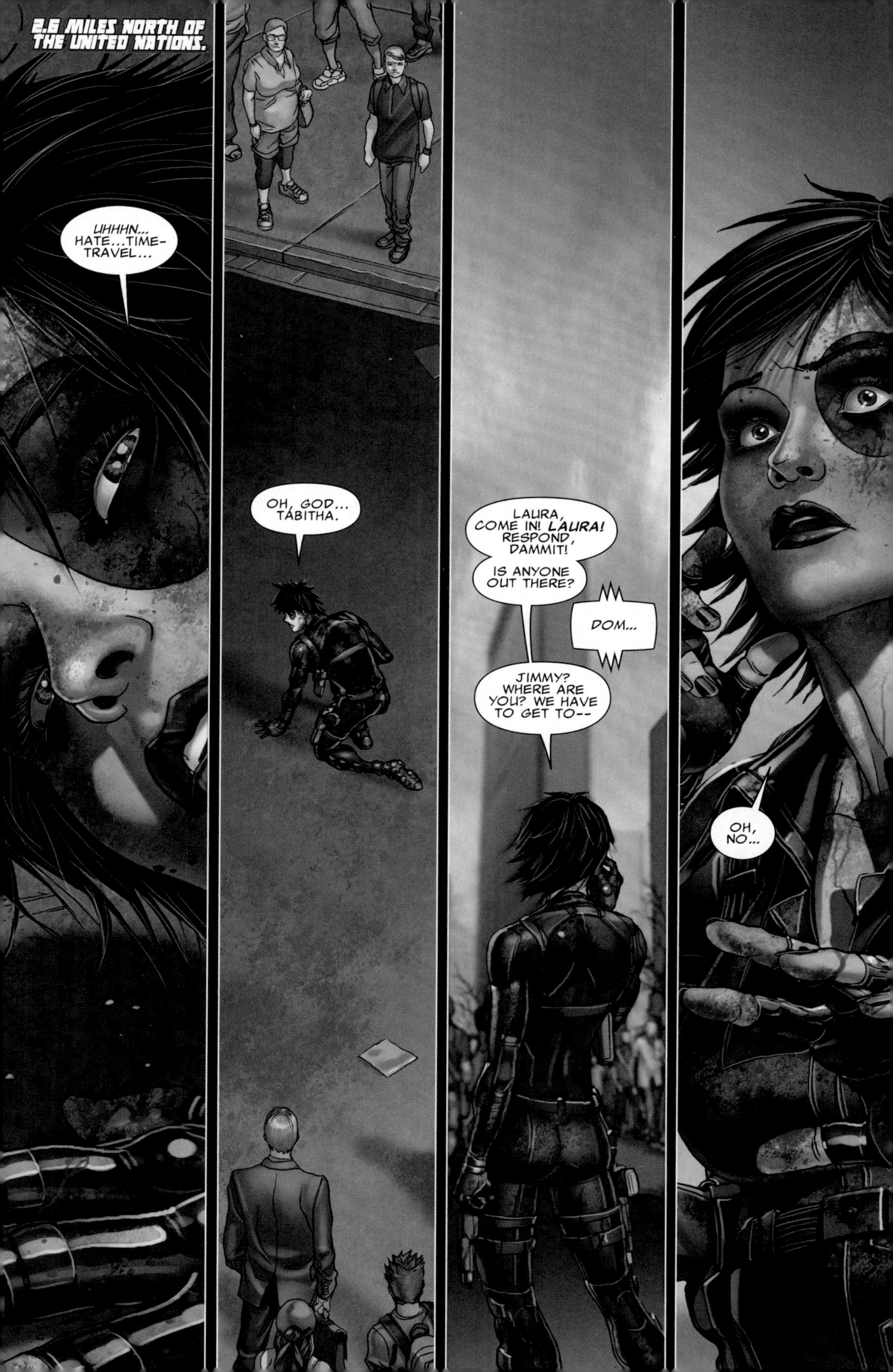
2.6 MILES NORTH OF THE UNITED NATIONS.
UHHHN... HATE...TIME-TRAVEL...
OH, GOD... TABITHA.
LAURA, COME IN! LAURA! RESPOND, DAMMIT!
IS ANYONE OUT THERE?
DOM...
JIMMY? WHERE ARE YOU? WE HAVE TO GET TO--
OH, NO...

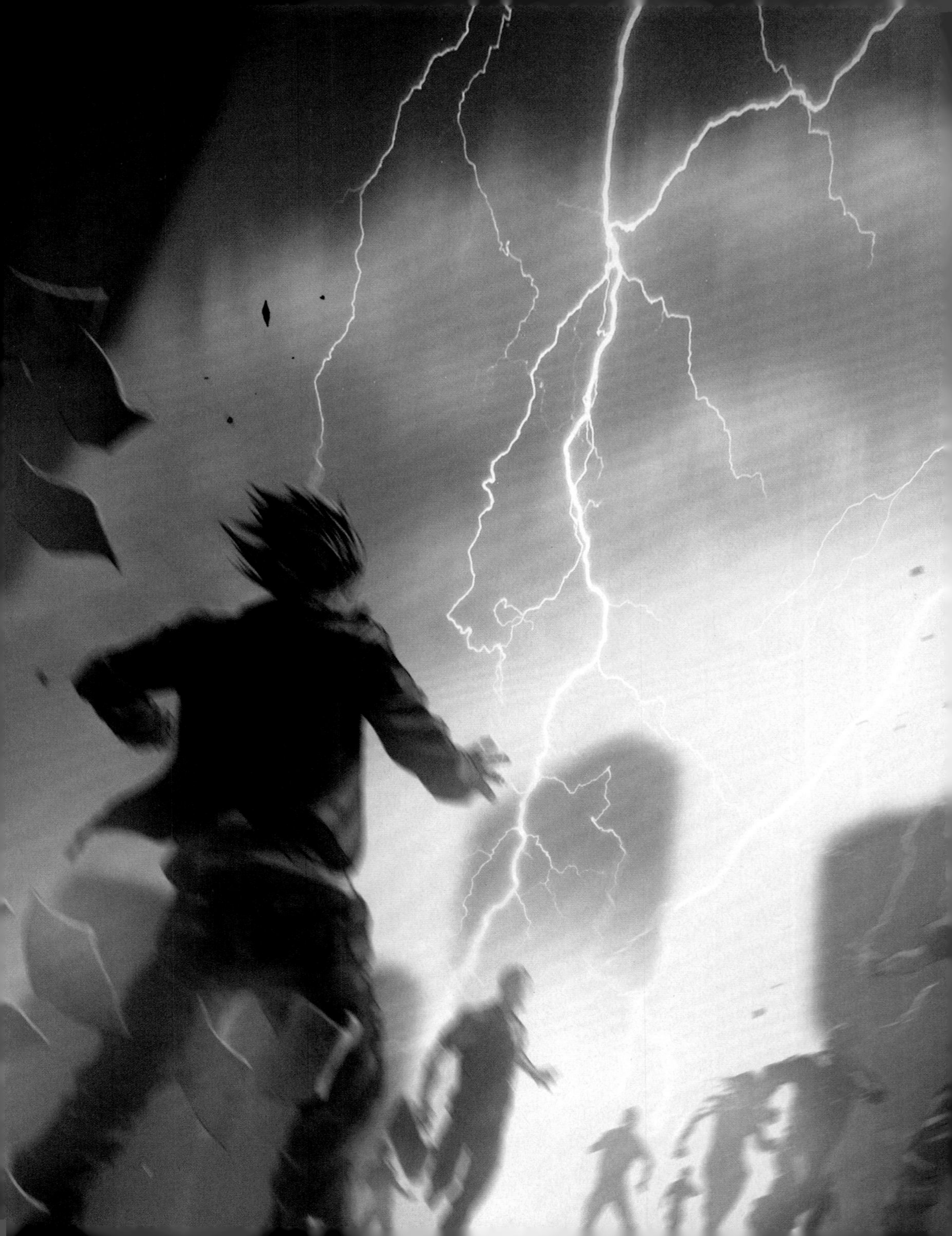

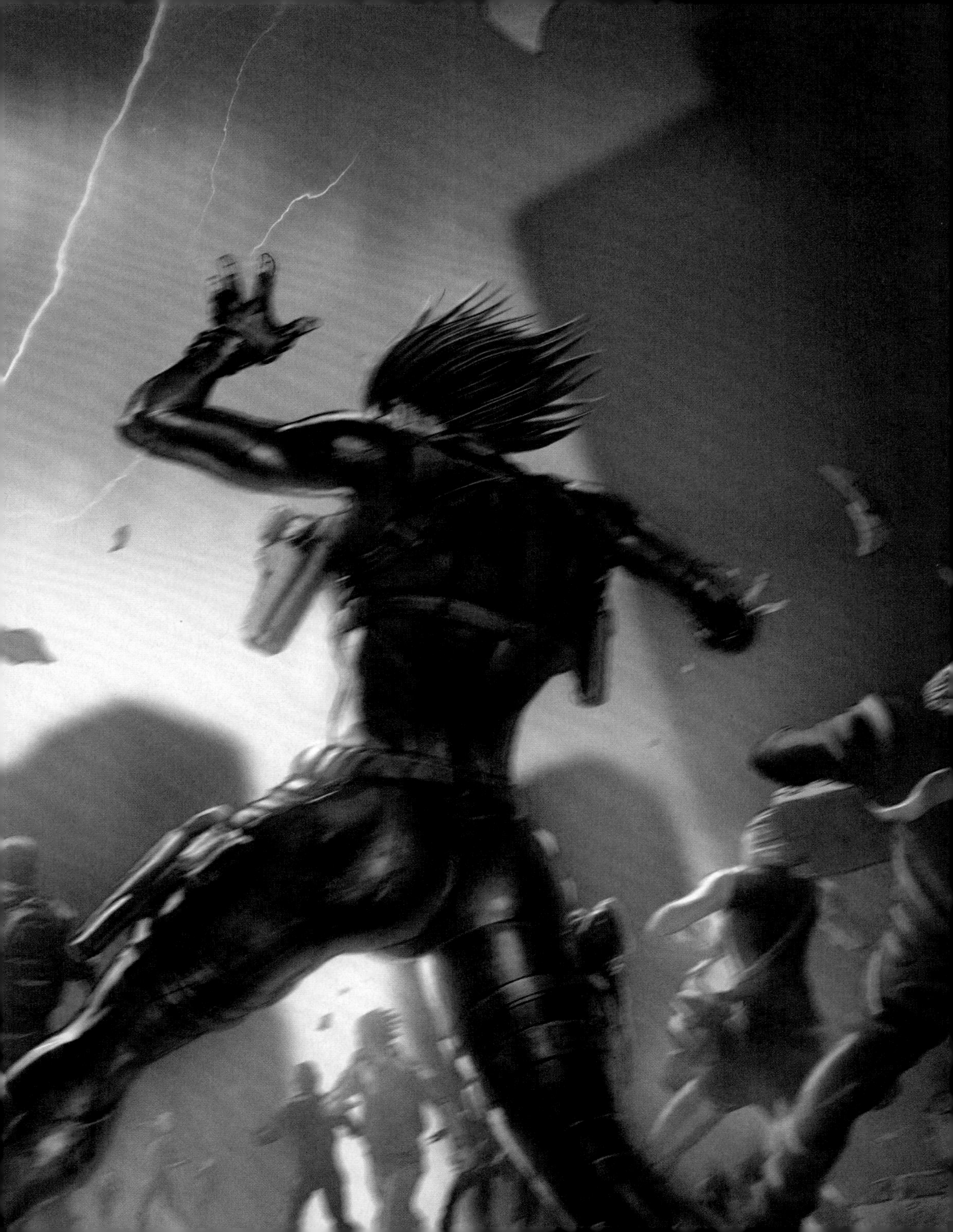

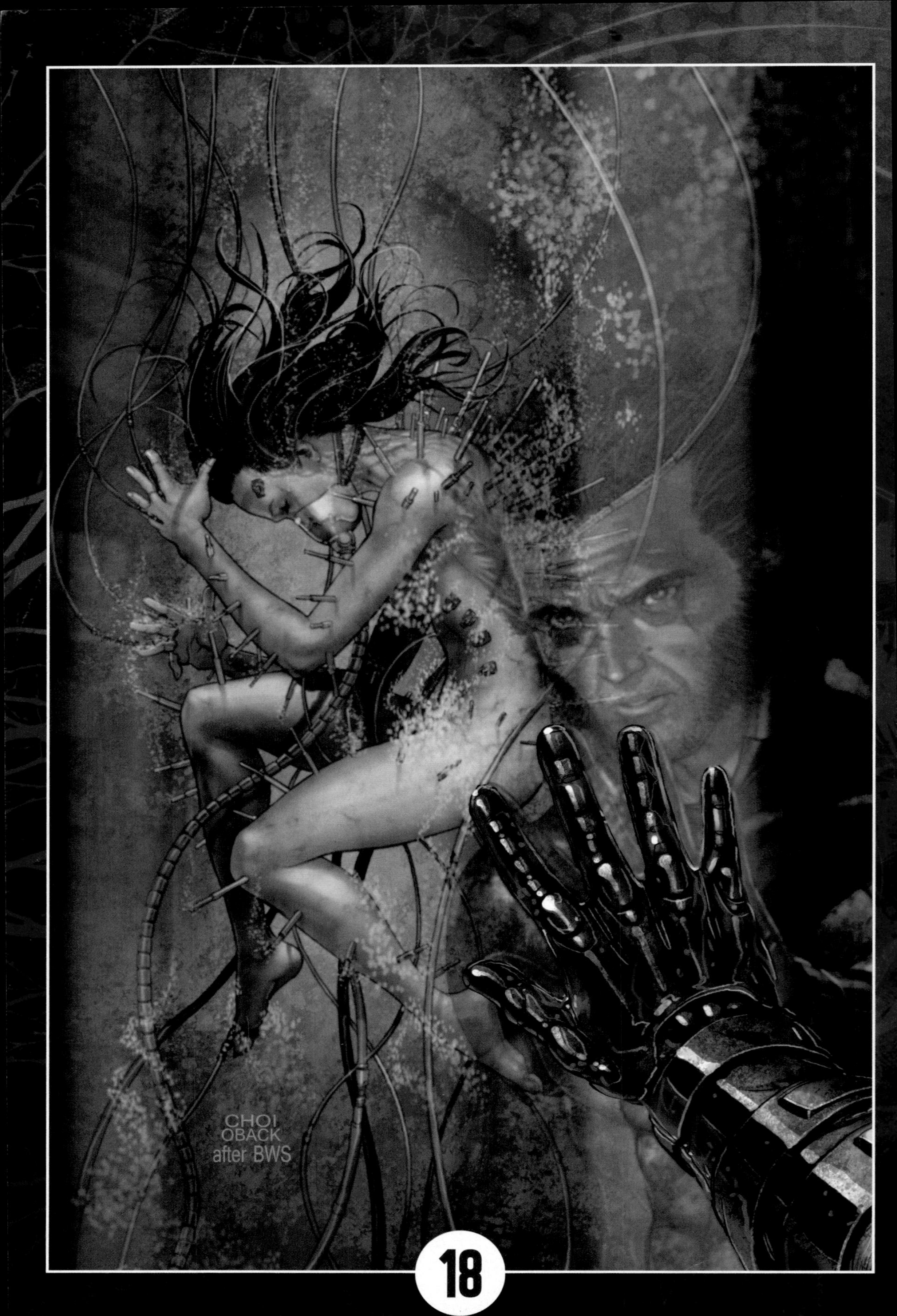
CHOI
OBACK
after BWS
18

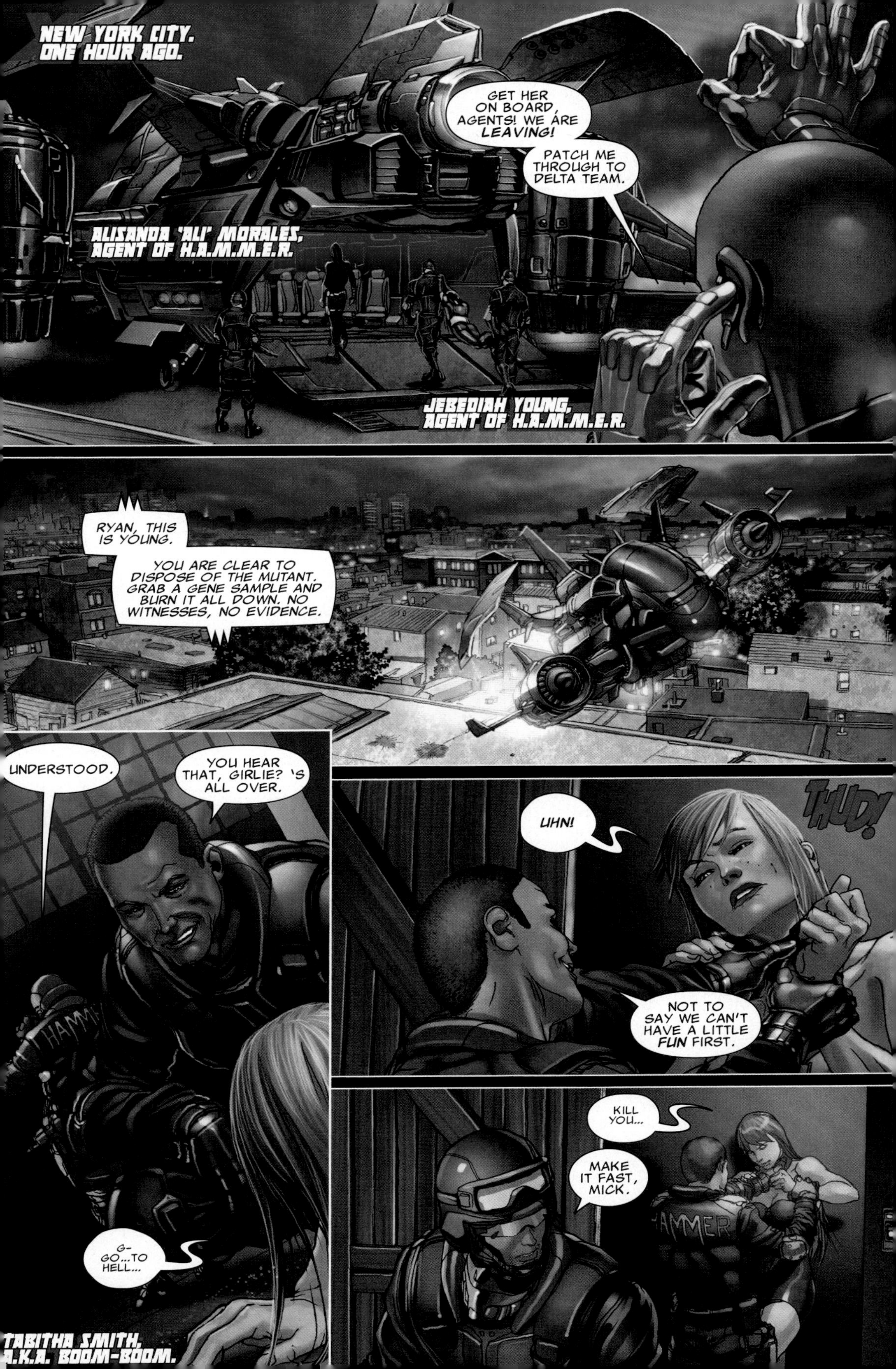
NEW YORK CITY. ONE HOUR AGO.
GET HER ON BOARD, AGENTS! WE ARE LEAVING!
PATCH ME THROUGH TO DELTA TEAM.
ALISANDA 'ALI' MORALES, AGENT OF H.A.M.M.E.R.
JEBEDIAH YOUNG, AGENT OF H.A.M.M.E.R.
RYAN, THIS IS YOUNG.
YOU ARE CLEAR TO DISPOSE OF THE MUTANT. GRAB A GENE SAMPLE AND BURN IT ALL DOWN. NO WITNESSES, NO EVIDENCE.
UNDERSTOOD.
YOU HEAR THAT, GIRLIE? 'S ALL OVER.
G-GO...TO HELL...
TABITHA SMITH, A.K.A. BOOM-BOOM.
THUD!
UHN!
NOT TO SAY WE CAN'T HAVE A LITTLE FUN FIRST.
KILL YOU...
MAKE IT FAST, MICK.
HAMMER

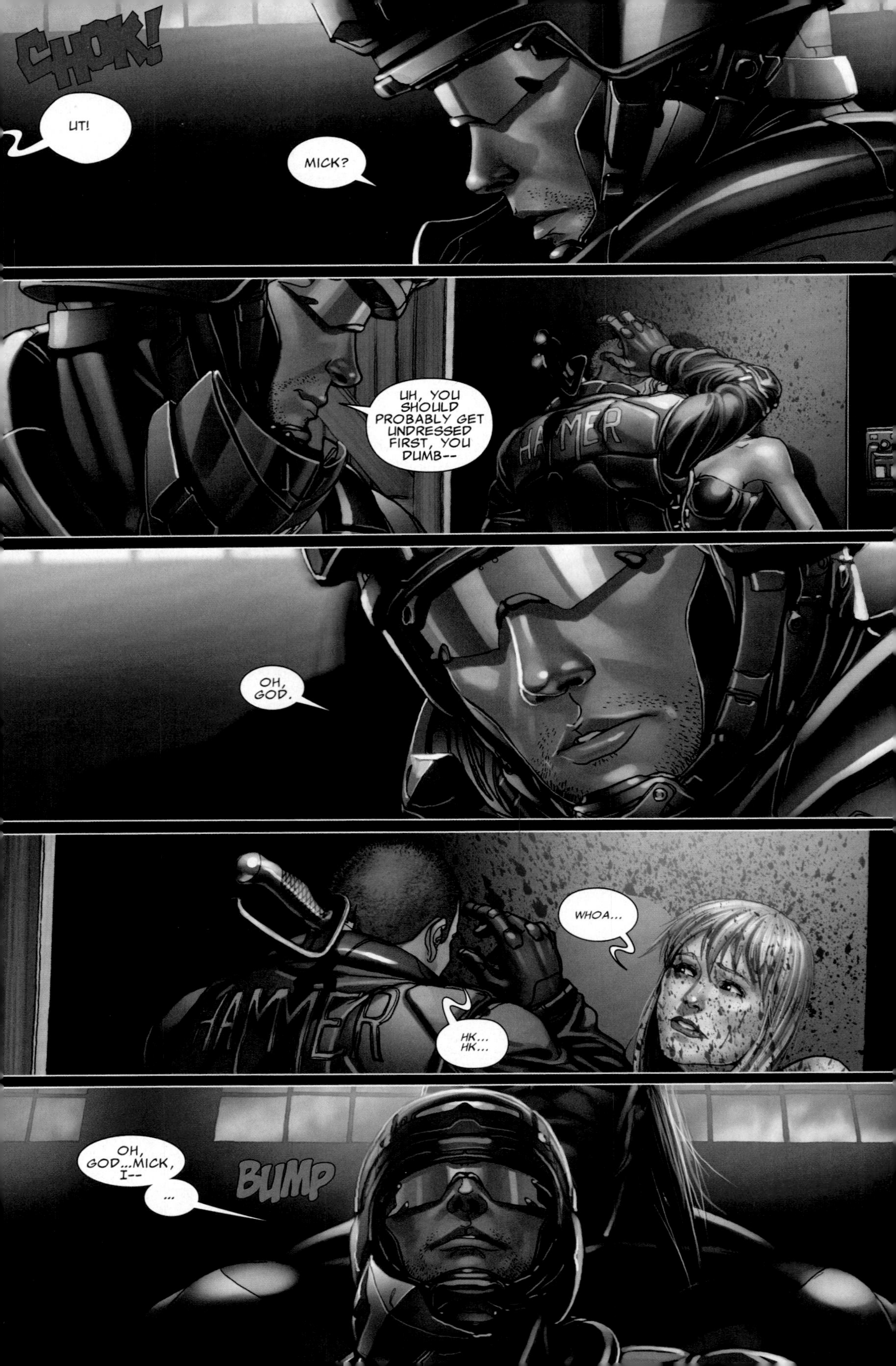
CHOK!
UT!
MICK?
UH, YOU SHOULD PROBABLY GET UNDRESSED FIRST, YOU DUMB--
OH, GOD.
WHOA...
HK... HK...
OH, GOD...MICK, I--
BUMP
...

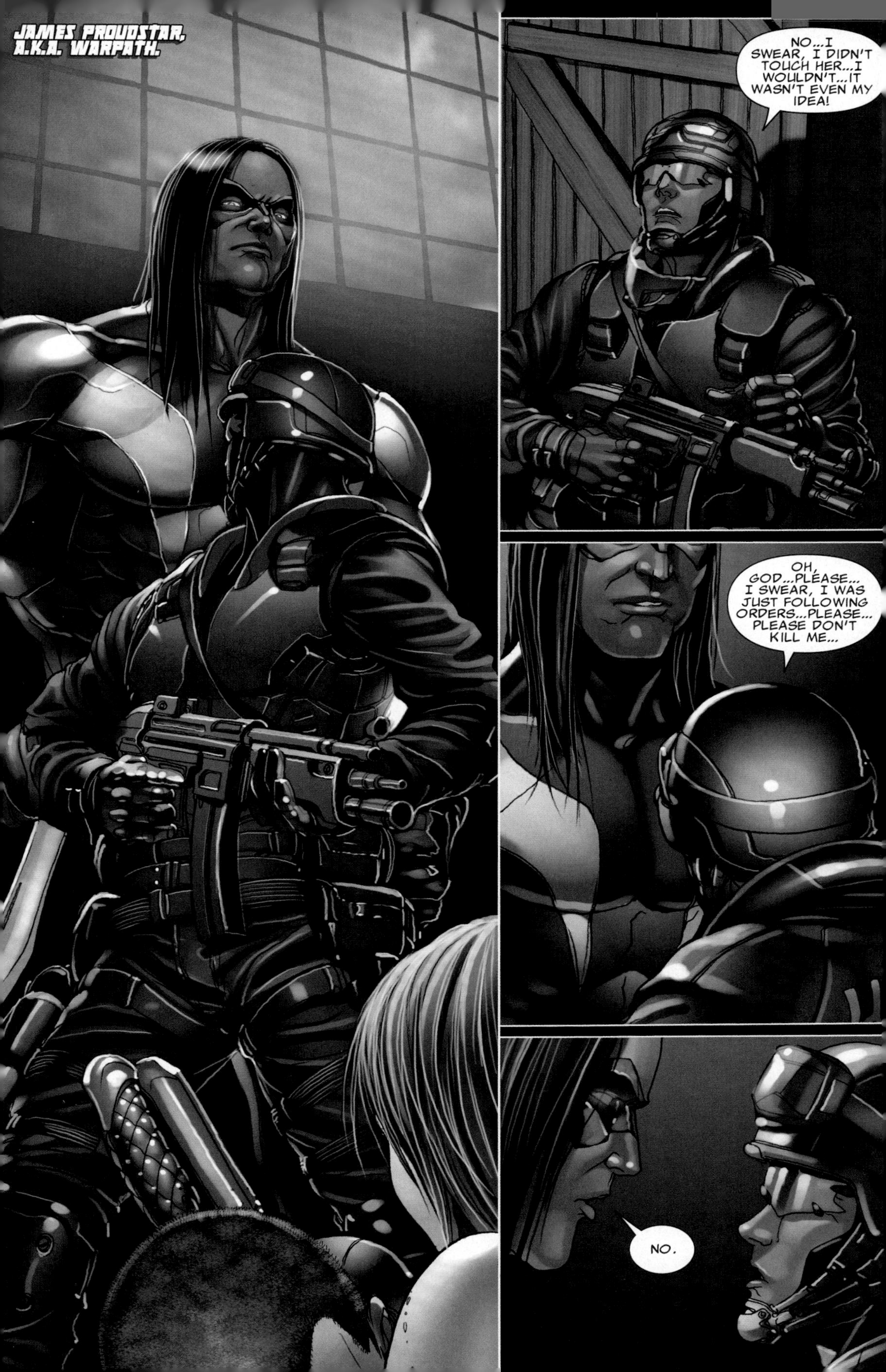
JAMES PROUDSTAR, A.K.A. WARPATH.
NO...I SWEAR, I DIDN'T TOUCH HER...I WOULDN'T...IT WASN'T EVEN MY IDEA!
OH, GOD...PLEASE... I SWEAR, I WAS JUST FOLLOWING ORDERS...PLEASE... PLEASE DON'T KILL ME...
NO.

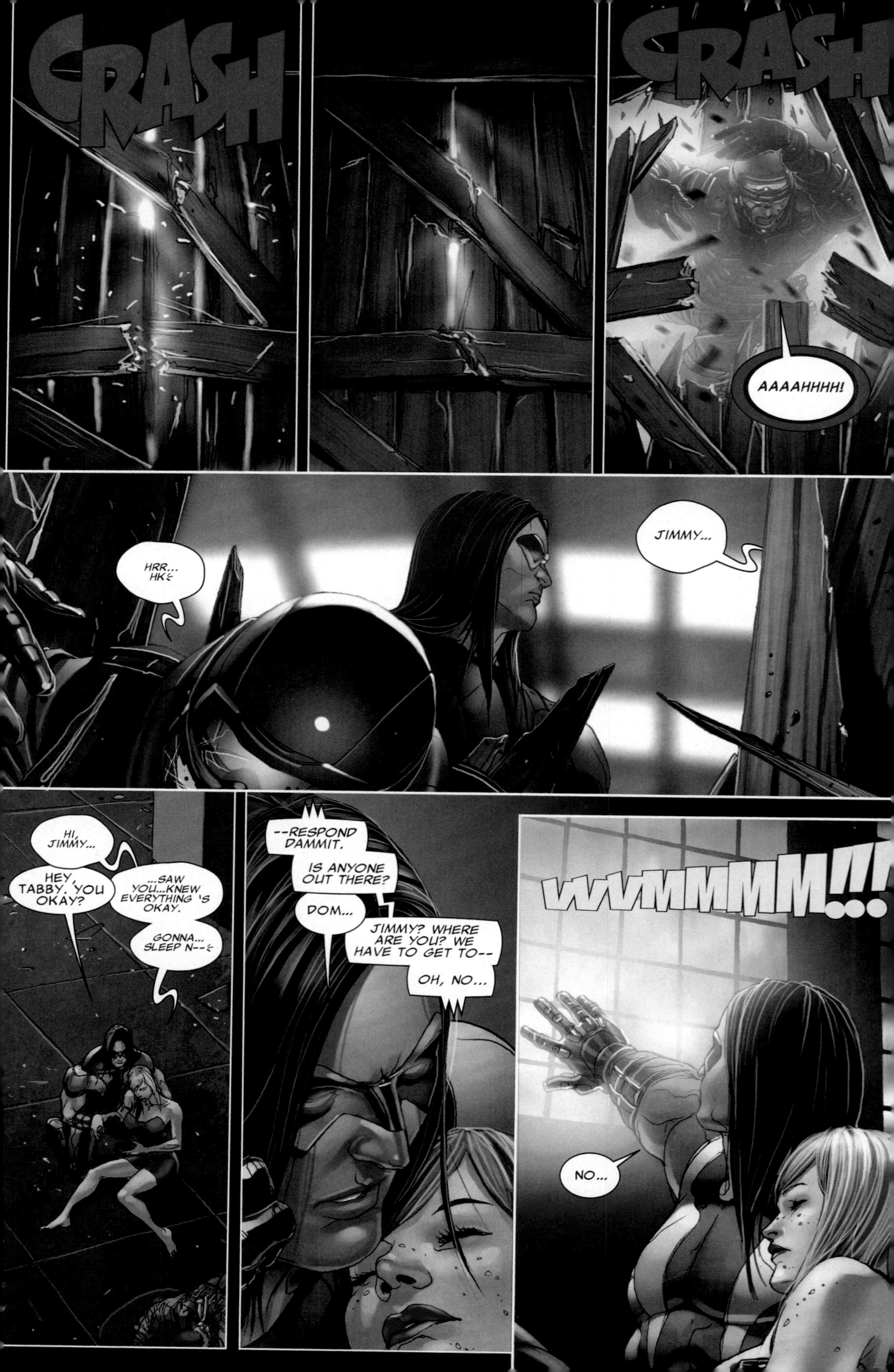

CRASH
CRASH
AAAAHHHH!
HRR... HK≤
JIMMY...
HI, JIMMY...
HEY, TABBY. YOU OKAY?
...SAW YOU...KNEW EVERYTHING 'S OKAY.
GONNA... SLEEP N--≤
--RESPOND DAMMIT.
IS ANYONE OUT THERE?
DOM...
JIMMY? WHERE ARE YOU? WE HAVE TO GET TO--
OH, NO...
WVMMMMM!!!
NO...

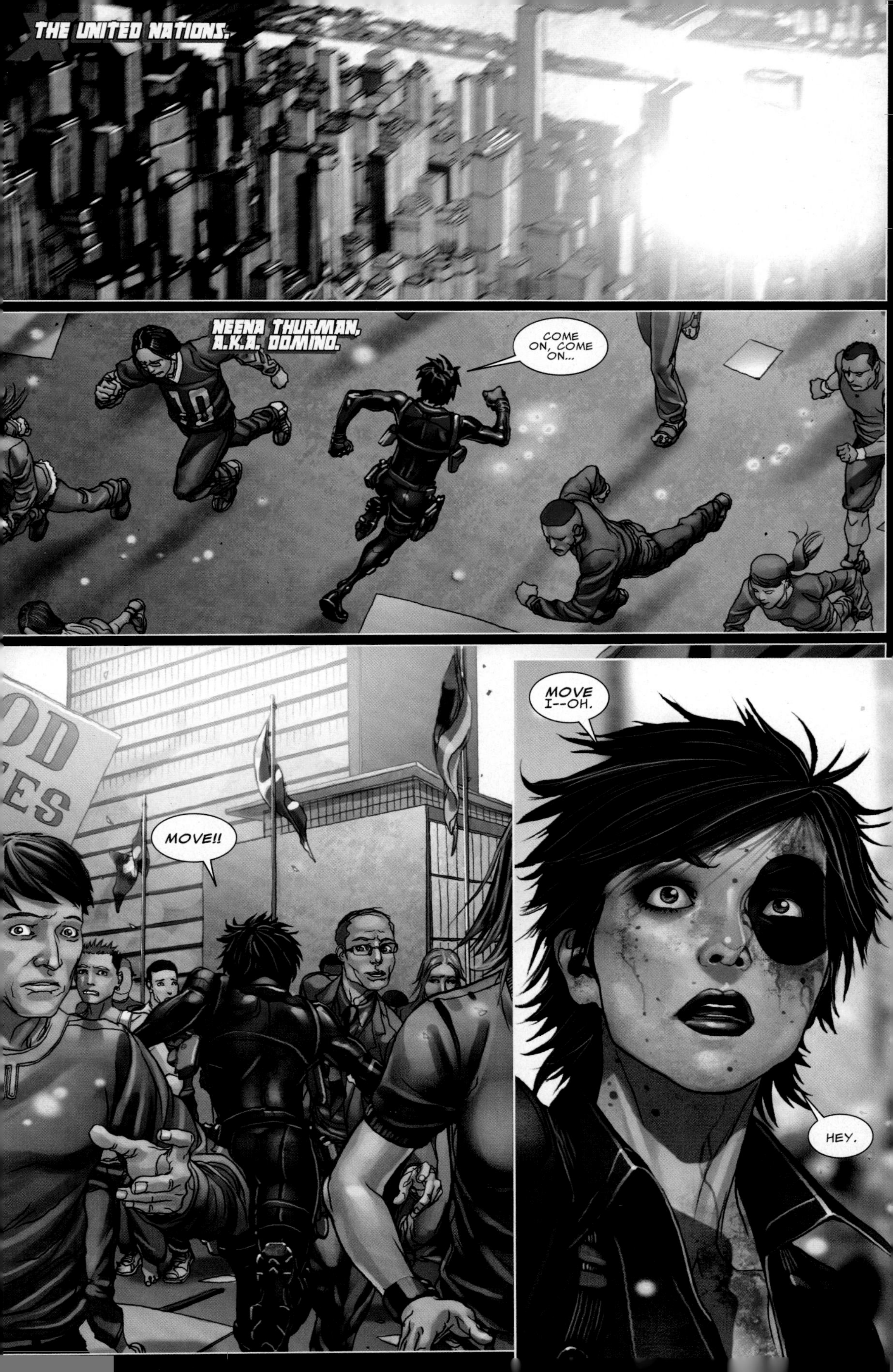
THE UNITED NATIONS.
NEENA THURMAN, A.K.A. DOMINO.
COME ON, COME ON...
OD
ES
MOVE!!
MOVE I--OH.
HEY.

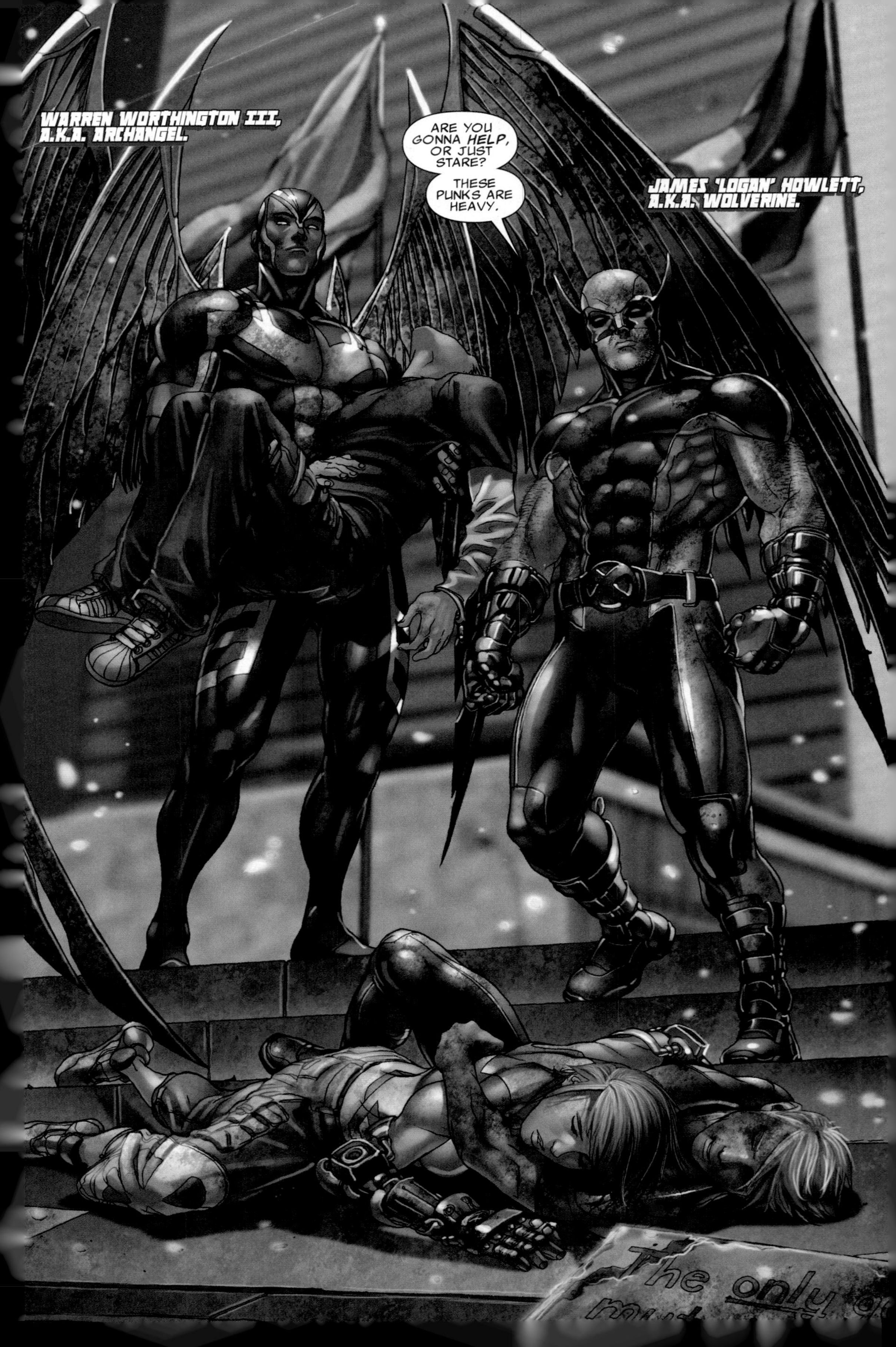
WARREN WORTHINGTON III, A.K.A. ARCHANGEL.
ARE YOU GONNA HELP, OR JUST STARE?
THESE PUNKS ARE HEAVY.
JAMES 'LOGAN' HOWLETT, A.K.A. WOLVERINE.
The only

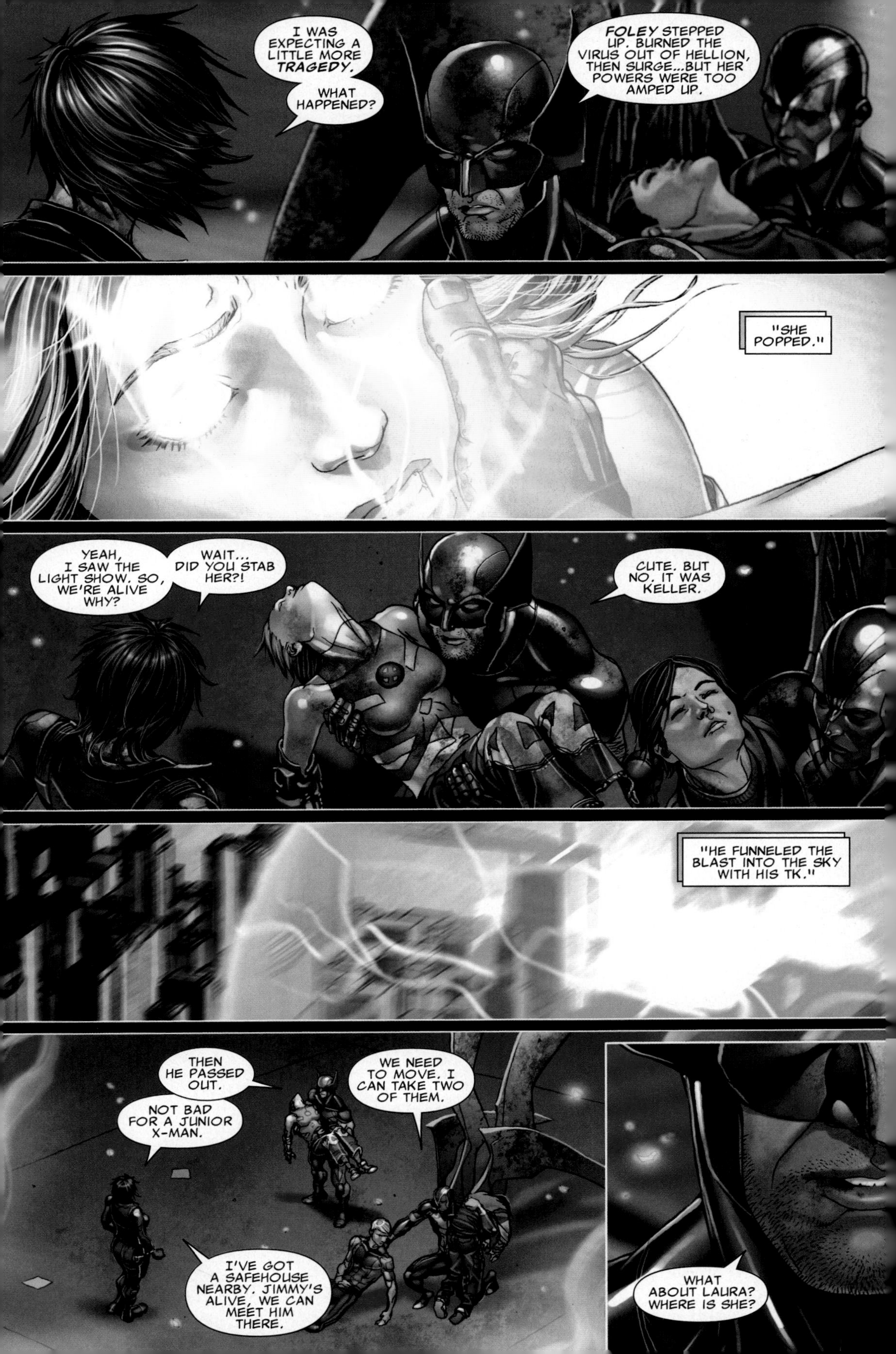

I WAS EXPECTING A LITTLE MORE TRAGEDY.
WHAT HAPPENED?
FOLEY STEPPED UP. BURNED THE VIRUS OUT OF HELLION, THEN SURGE...BUT HER POWERS WERE TOO AMPED UP.
"SHE POPPED."
YEAH, I SAW THE LIGHT SHOW. SO, WE'RE ALIVE WHY?
WAIT... DID YOU STAB HER?!
CUTE. BUT NO. IT WAS KELLER.
"HE FUNNELED THE BLAST INTO THE SKY WITH HIS TK."
THEN HE PASSED OUT.
NOT BAD FOR A JUNIOR X-MAN.
WE NEED TO MOVE. I CAN TAKE TWO OF THEM.
I'VE GOT A SAFEHOUSE NEARBY. JIMMY'S ALIVE, WE CAN MEET HIM THERE.
WHAT ABOUT LAURA? WHERE IS SHE?

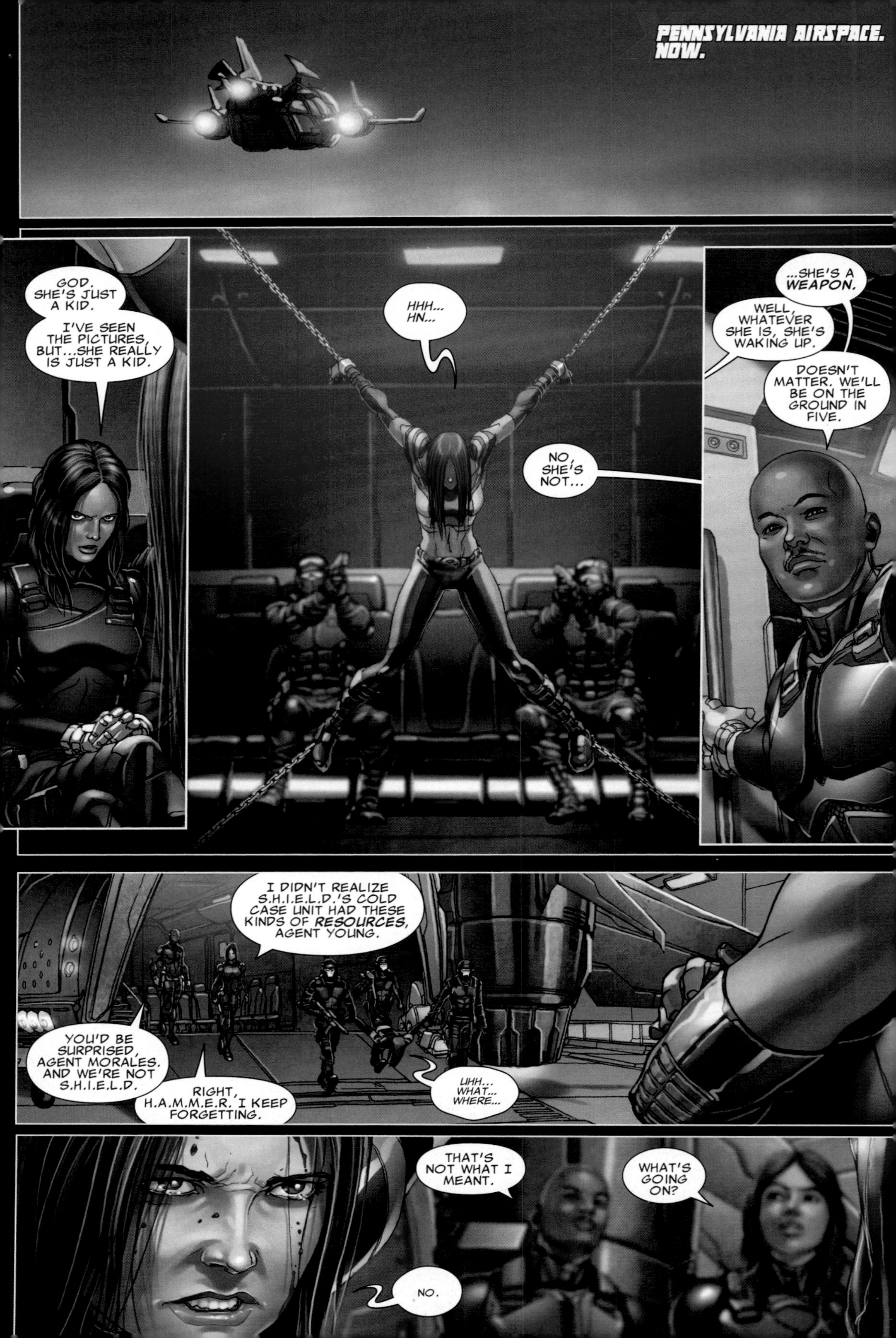
PENNSYLVANIA AIRSPACE. NOW.
GOD. SHE'S JUST A KID.
I'VE SEEN THE PICTURES, BUT...SHE REALLY IS JUST A KID.
HHH... HN...
...SHE'S A WEAPON.
WELL, WHATEVER SHE IS, SHE'S WAKING UP.
DOESN'T MATTER. WE'LL BE ON THE GROUND IN FIVE.
NO, SHE'S NOT...
I DIDN'T REALIZE S.H.I.E.L.D.'S COLD CASE UNIT HAD THESE KINDS OF RESOURCES, AGENT YOUNG.
YOU'D BE SURPRISED, AGENT MORALES. AND WE'RE NOT S.H.I.E.L.D.
RIGHT, H.A.M.M.E.R. I KEEP FORGETTING.
UHH... WHAT... WHERE...
THAT'S NOT WHAT I MEANT.
WHAT'S GOING ON?
NO.

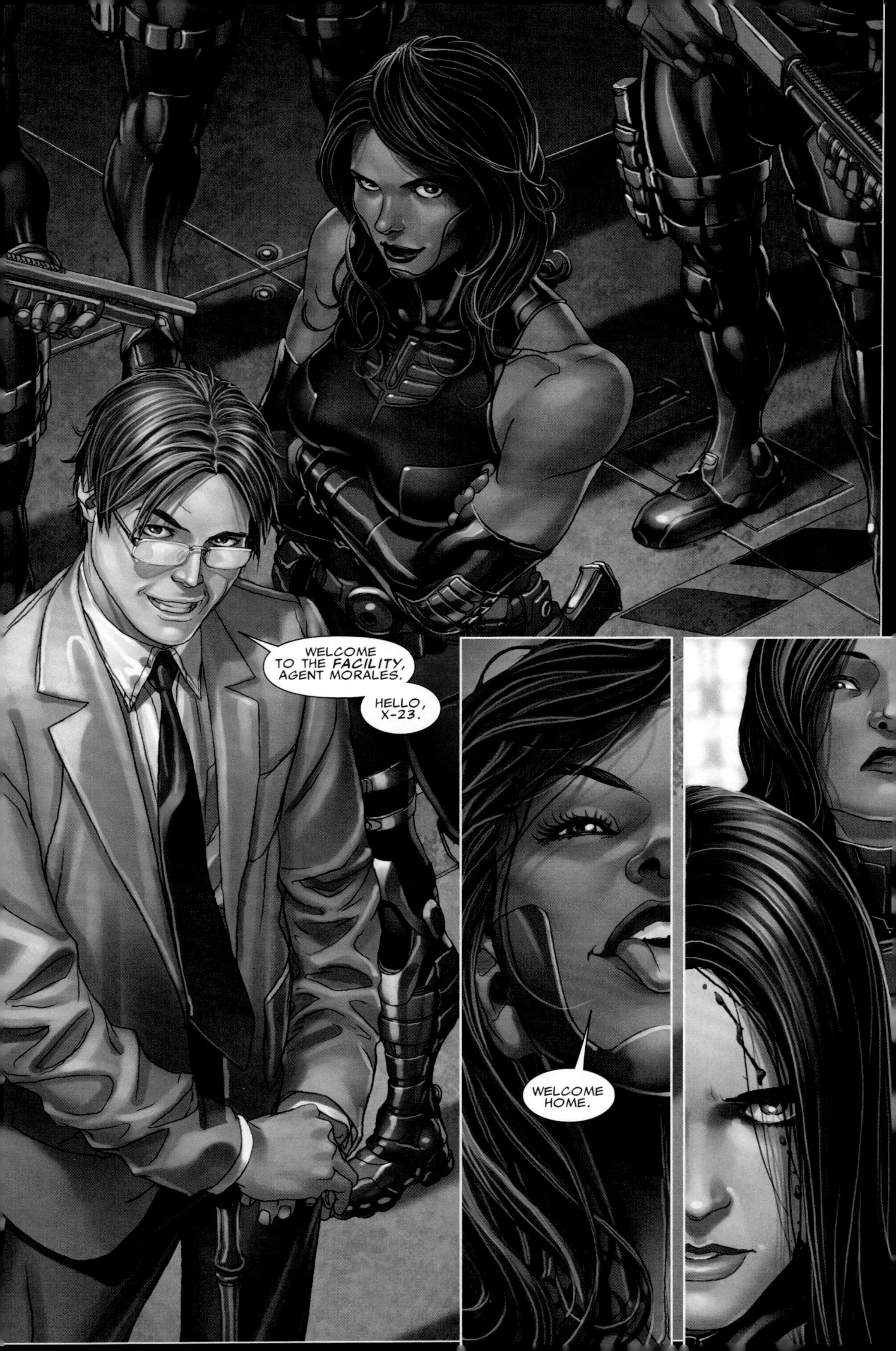
WELCOME TO THE FACILITY, AGENT MORALES.
HELLO, X-23.
WELCOME HOME.

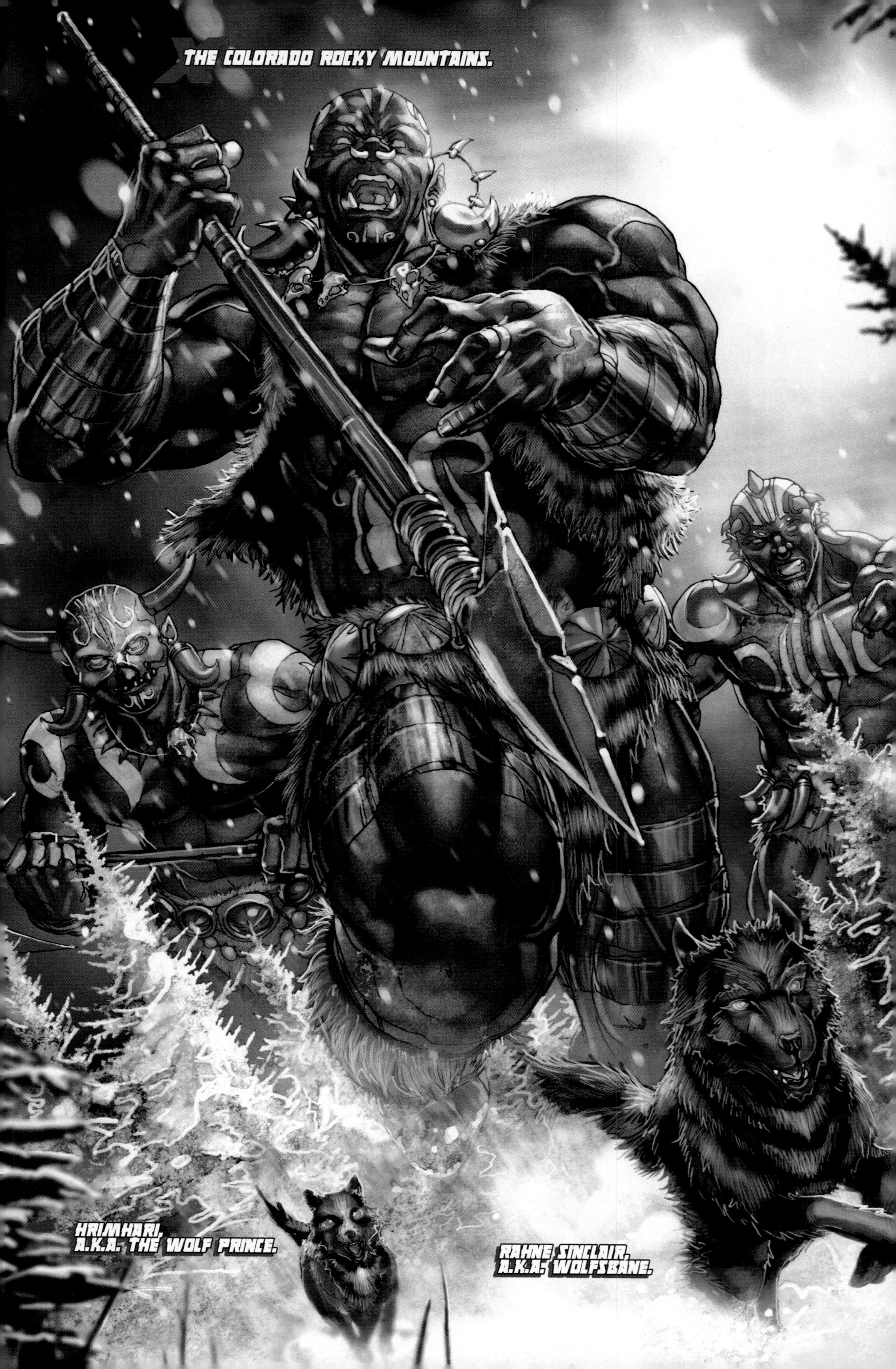
THE COLORADO ROCKY MOUNTAINS.
HRIMHARI,
A.K.A. THE WOLF PRINCE.
RAHNE SINCLAIR,
A.K.A. WOLFSBANE.

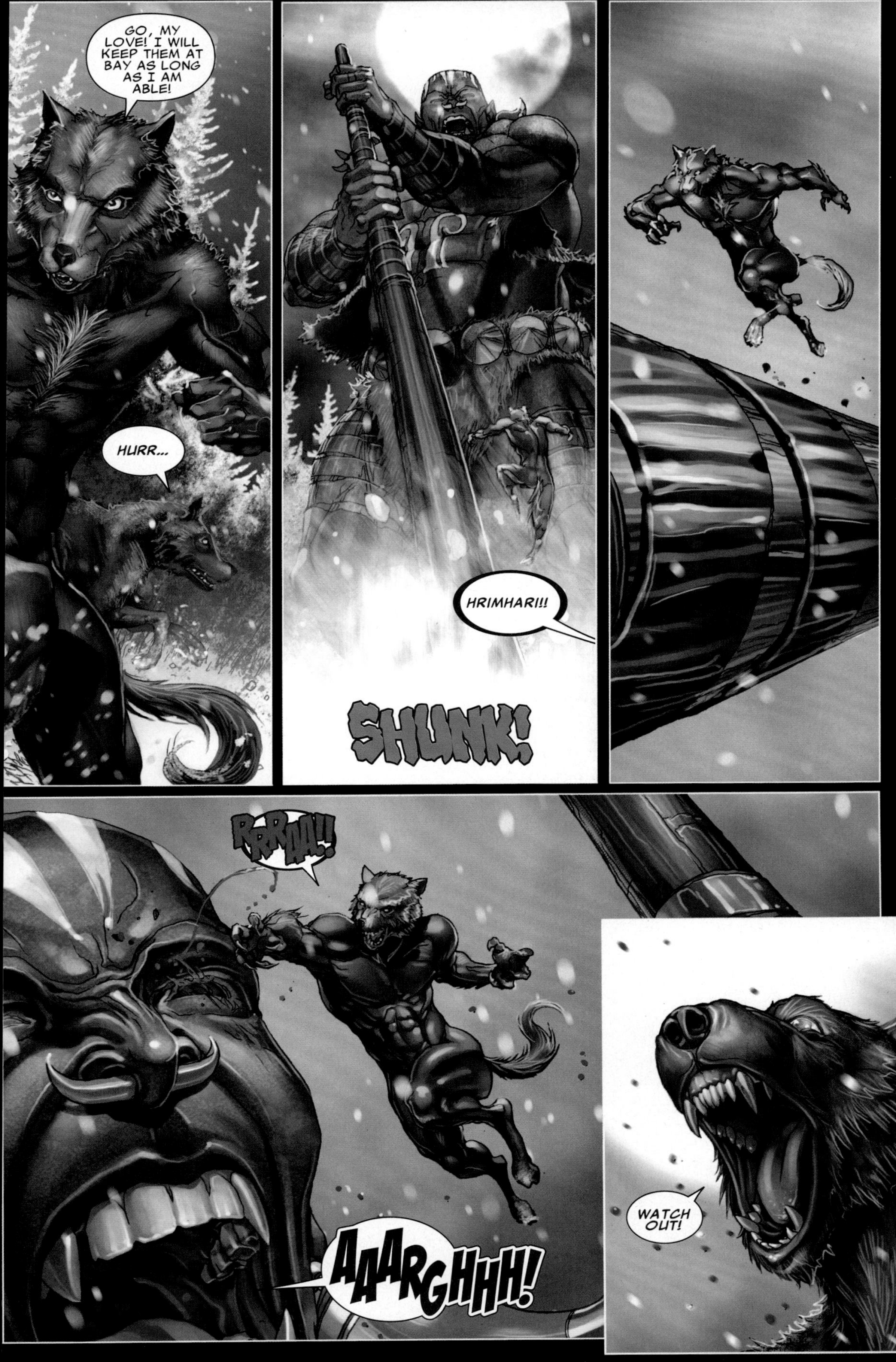
GO, MY LOVE! I WILL KEEP THEM AT BAY AS LONG AS I AM ABLE!
HURR...
HRIMHARI!!
SHUNK!
RRRAA!!
AAARGHHH!
WATCH OUT!

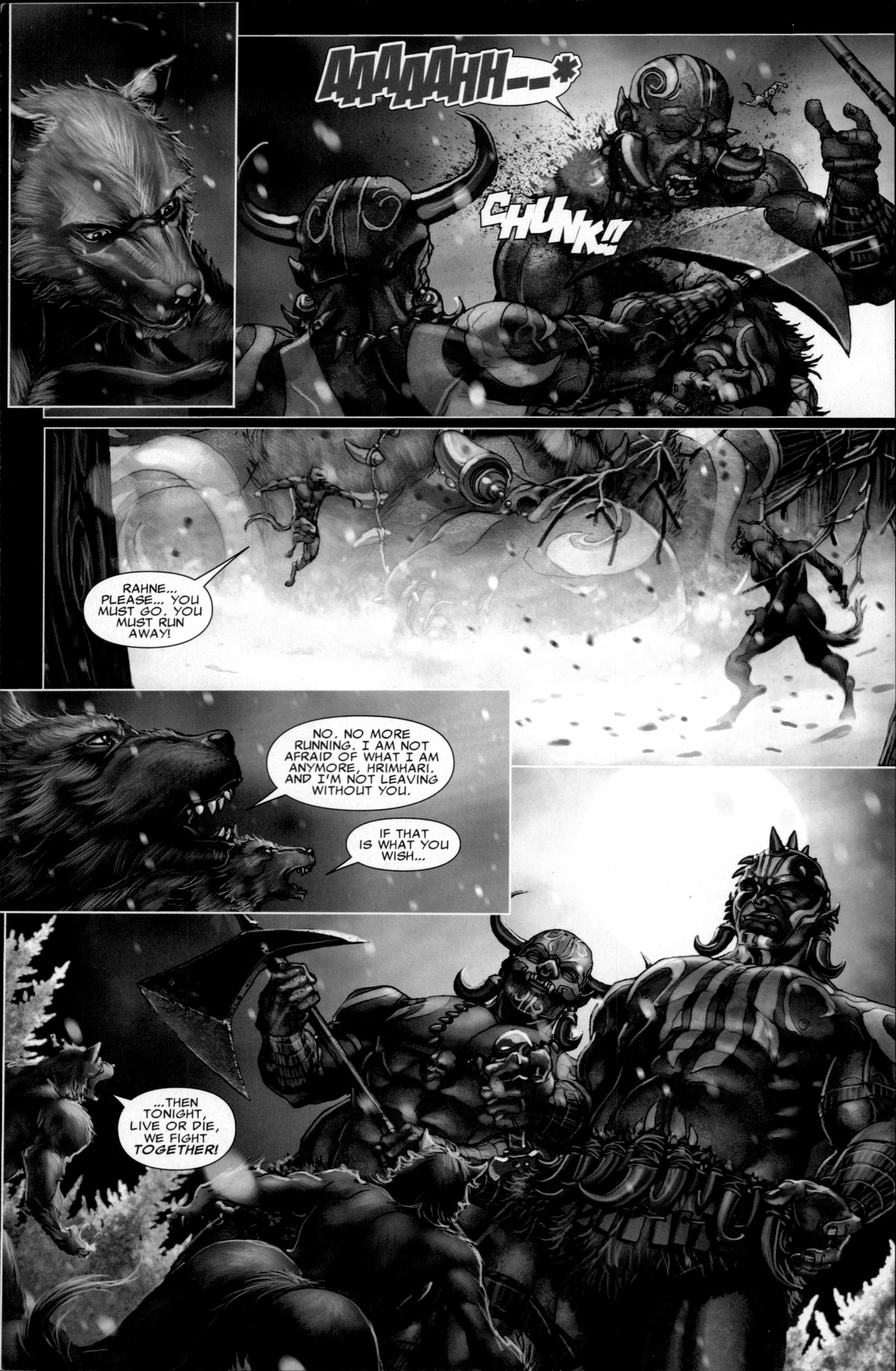
AAAAAHH--*
CHUNK!!
RAHNE... PLEASE... YOU MUST GO. YOU MUST RUN AWAY!
NO. NO MORE RUNNING. I AM NOT AFRAID OF WHAT I AM ANYMORE, HRIMHARI. AND I'M NOT LEAVING WITHOUT YOU.
IF THAT IS WHAT YOU WISH...
...THEN TONIGHT, LIVE OR DIE, WE FIGHT TOGETHER!

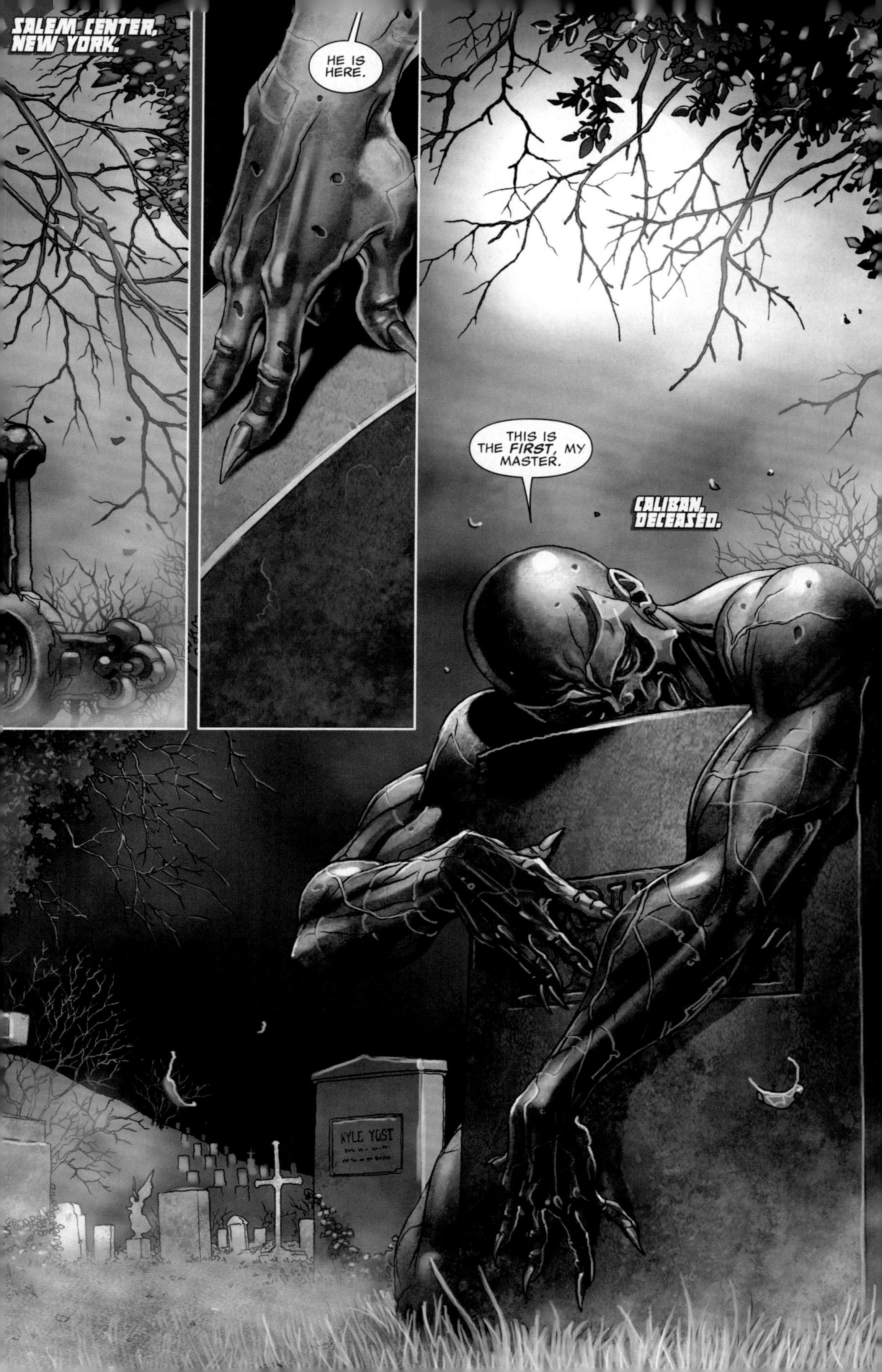
SALEM CENTER, NEW YORK.
HE IS HERE.
THIS IS THE FIRST, MY MASTER.
CALIBAN, DECEASED.
KYLE YOST

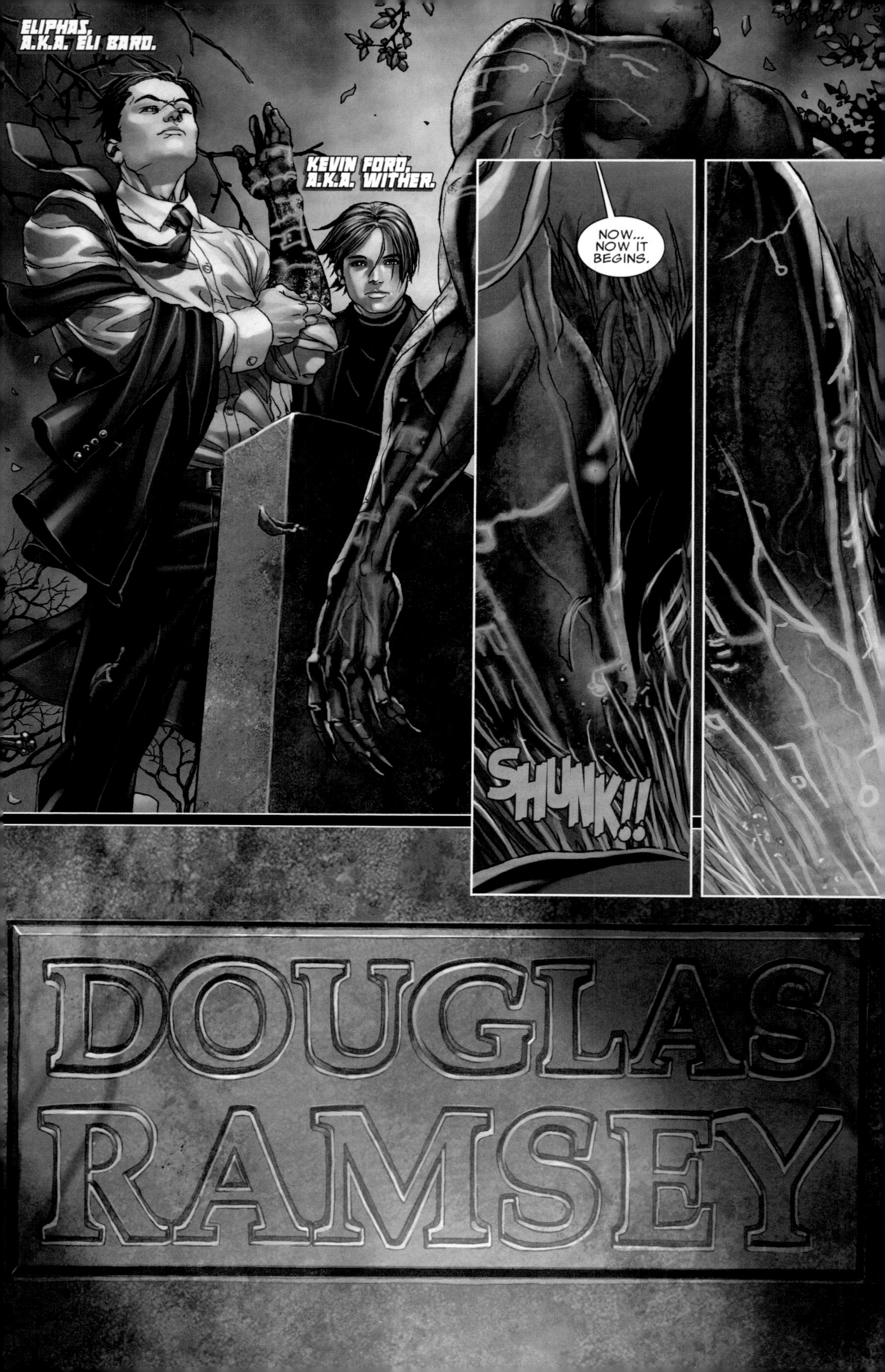
ELIPHAS, A.K.A. ELI BARD.
KEVIN FORD, A.K.A. WITHER.
NOW... NOW IT BEGINS.
SHUNK!!
DOUGLAS RAMSEY

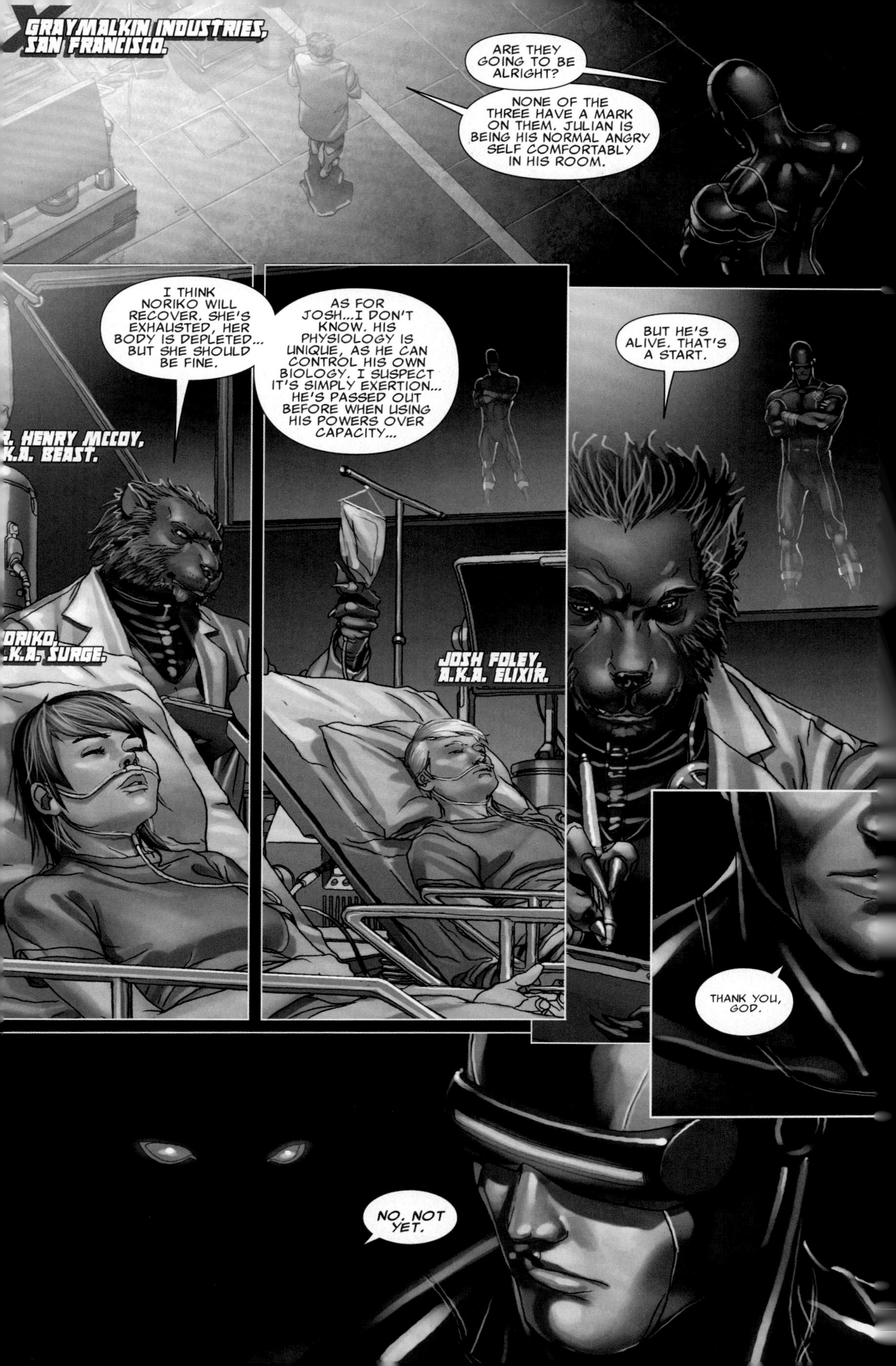
GRAYMALKIN INDUSTRIES, SAN FRANCISCO.
ARE THEY GOING TO BE ALRIGHT?
NONE OF THE THREE HAVE A MARK ON THEM. JULIAN IS BEING HIS NORMAL ANGRY SELF COMFORTABLY IN HIS ROOM.
I THINK NORIKO WILL RECOVER. SHE'S EXHAUSTED, HER BODY IS DEPLETED... BUT SHE SHOULD BE FINE.
R. HENRY MCCOY, .K.A. BEAST.
ORIKO, .K.A. SURGE.
AS FOR JOSH...I DON'T KNOW. HIS PHYSIOLOGY IS UNIQUE, AS HE CAN CONTROL HIS OWN BIOLOGY. I SUSPECT IT'S SIMPLY EXERTION... HE'S PASSED OUT BEFORE WHEN USING HIS POWERS OVER CAPACITY...
JOSH FOLEY, A.K.A. ELIXIR.
BUT HE'S ALIVE. THAT'S A START.
THANK YOU, GOD.
NO. NOT YET.

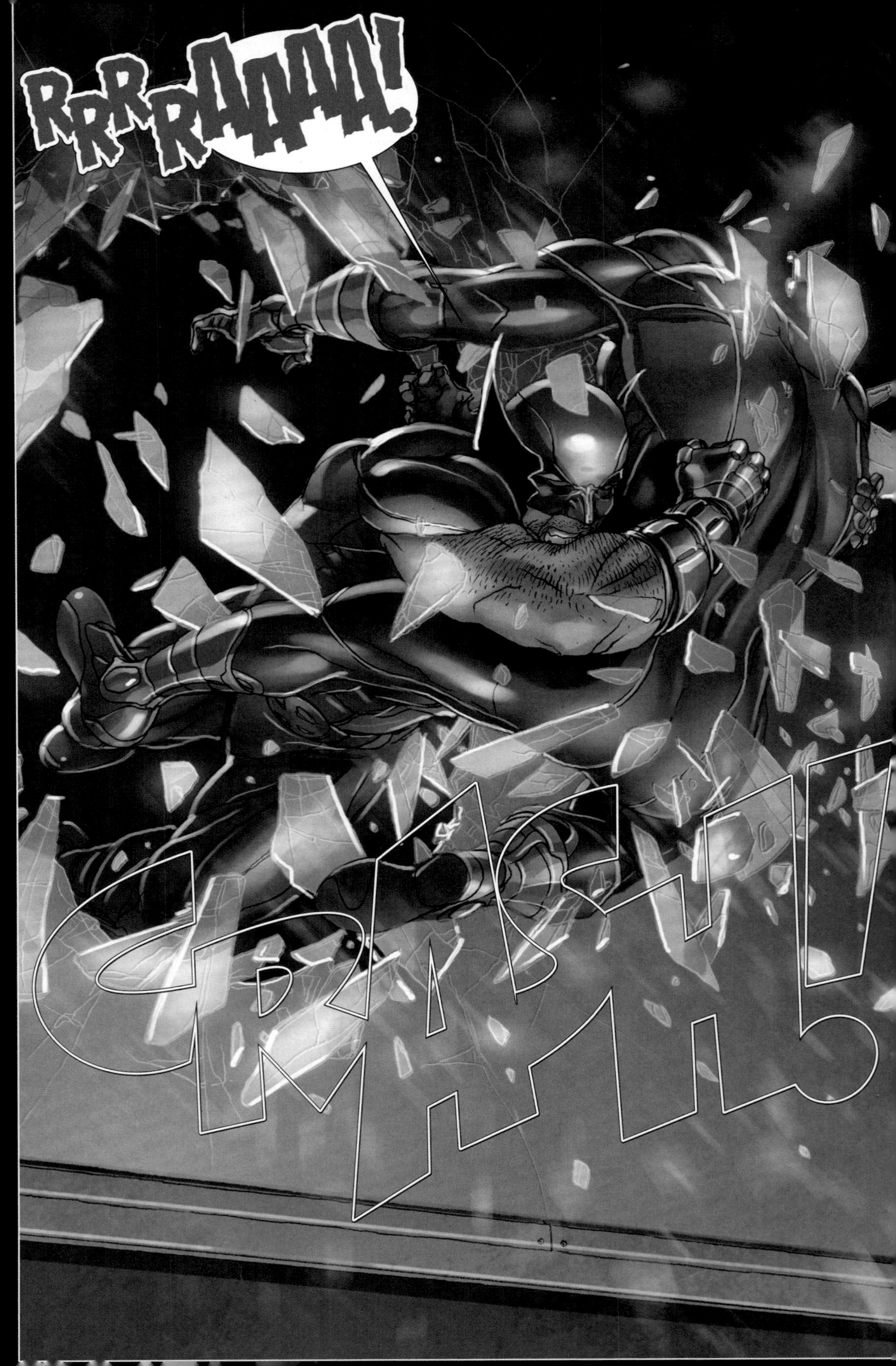
RRRRAAAA!
CRASH!

UHN!!

SCOTT!!

IT'S OKAY, HANK. IT'S--

HUK!!

CHOK!

I KNOW.

HOPE AND CABLE ARE ALIVE.

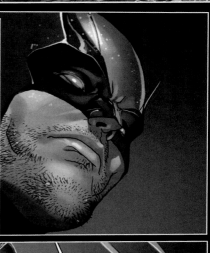

IT'S ABOUT AS FAR FROM "OKAY" AS YOU CAN GET, BOSS MAN.

I TOLD YOU TO WAIT!! YOU SIGNED THEIR DEATH WARRANTS WITHOUT BATTING AN EYE!

IF EITHER ONE OF THOSE KIDS DIES, IT'S ON YOU.

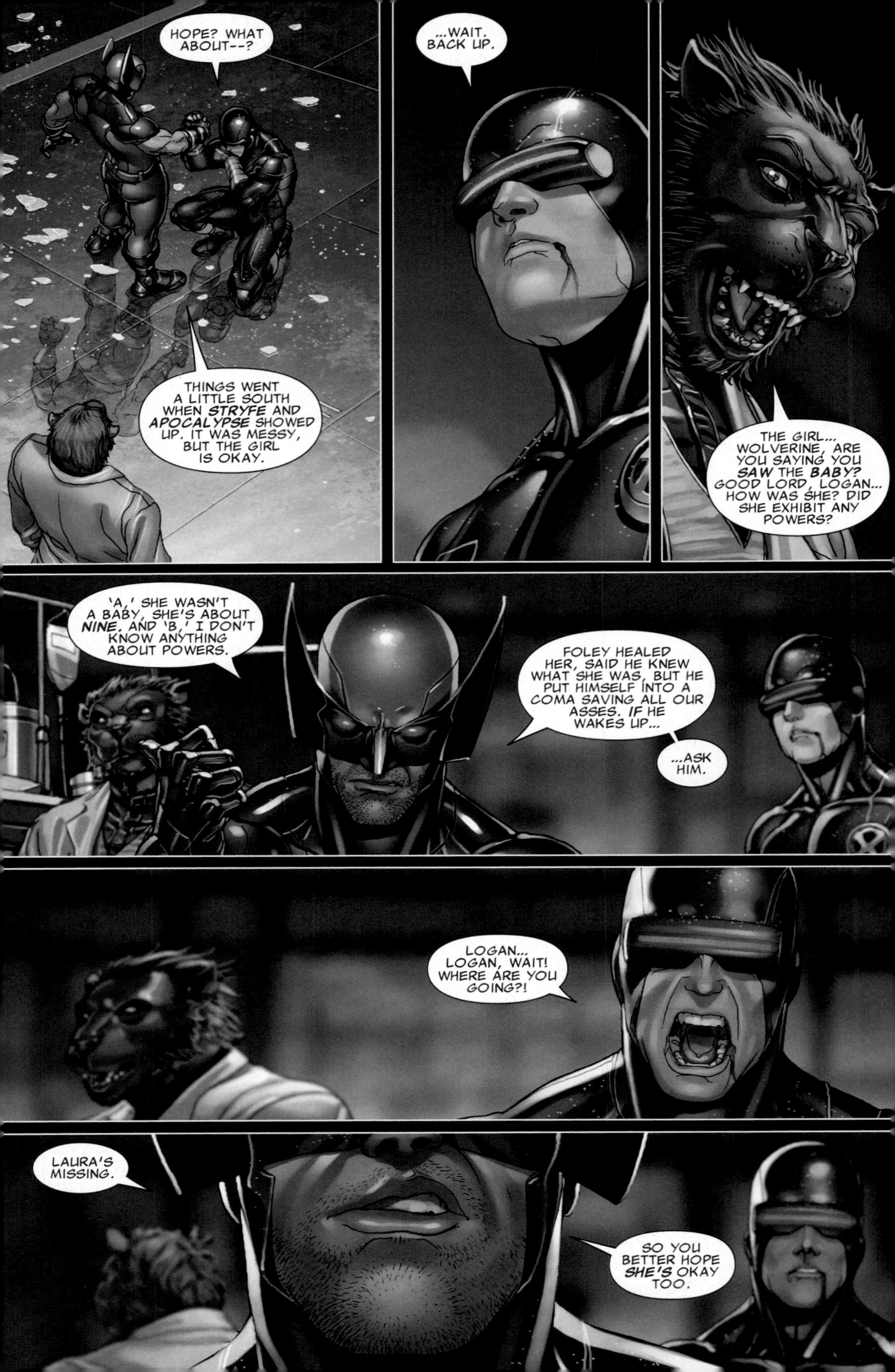
HOPE? WHAT ABOUT--?
THINGS WENT A LITTLE SOUTH WHEN STRYFE AND APOCALYPSE SHOWED UP. IT WAS MESSY, BUT THE GIRL IS OKAY.
...WAIT. BACK UP.
THE GIRL... WOLVERINE, ARE YOU SAYING YOU SAW THE BABY? GOOD LORD, LOGAN... HOW WAS SHE? DID SHE EXHIBIT ANY POWERS?
'A,' SHE WASN'T A BABY, SHE'S ABOUT NINE. AND 'B,' I DON'T KNOW ANYTHING ABOUT POWERS.
FOLEY HEALED HER, SAID HE KNEW WHAT SHE WAS, BUT HE PUT HIMSELF INTO A COMA SAVING ALL OUR ASSES. IF HE WAKES UP...
...ASK HIM.
LOGAN... LOGAN, WAIT! WHERE ARE YOU GOING?!
LAURA'S MISSING.
SO YOU BETTER HOPE SHE'S OKAY TOO.

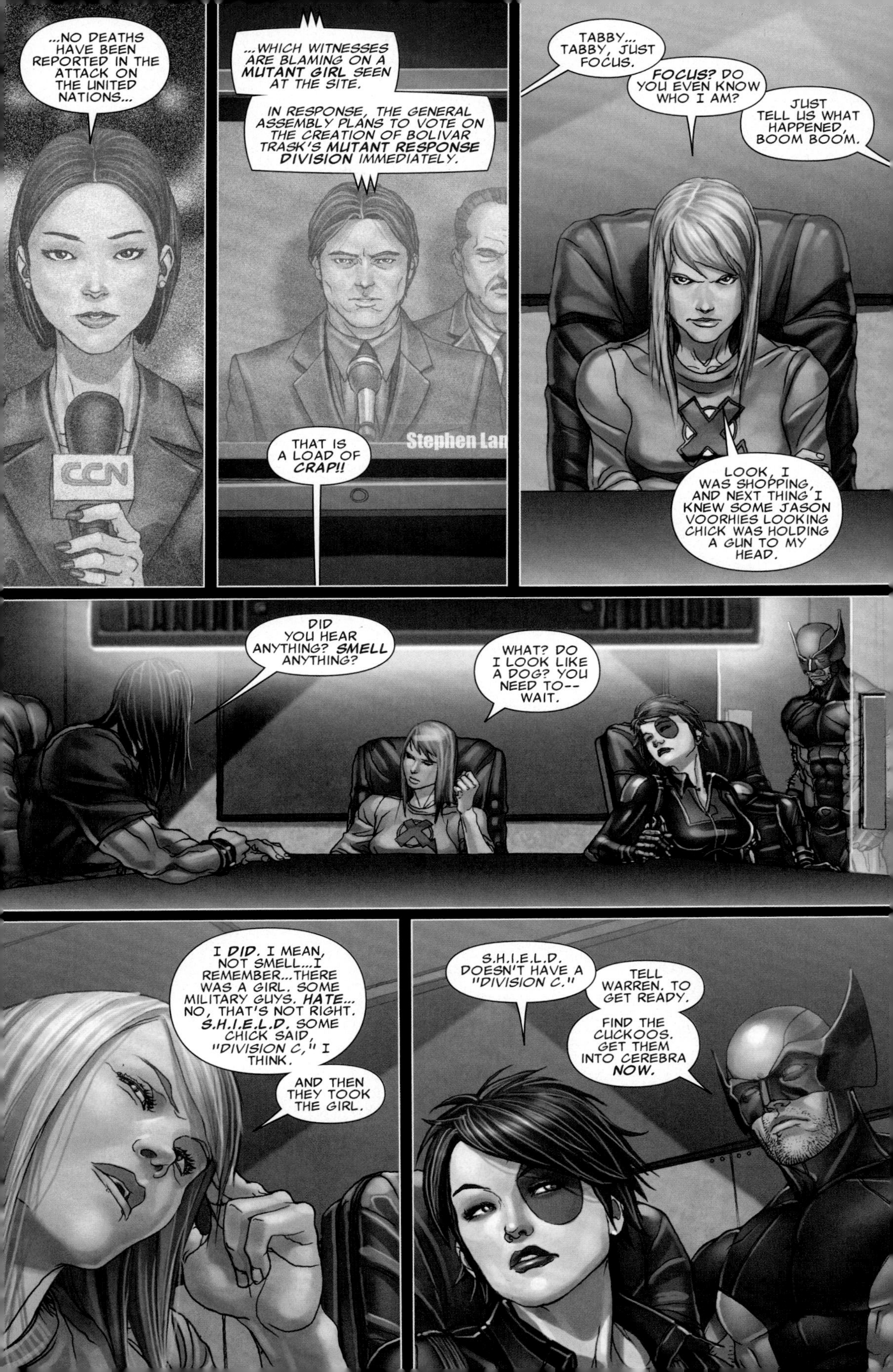
...NO DEATHS HAVE BEEN REPORTED IN THE ATTACK ON THE UNITED NATIONS...
...WHICH WITNESSES ARE BLAMING ON A MUTANT GIRL SEEN AT THE SITE.
IN RESPONSE, THE GENERAL ASSEMBLY PLANS TO VOTE ON THE CREATION OF BOLIVAR TRASK'S MUTANT RESPONSE DIVISION IMMEDIATELY.
CCN
Stephen Lan
THAT IS A LOAD OF CRAP!!
TABBY... TABBY, JUST FOCUS.
FOCUS? DO YOU EVEN KNOW WHO I AM?
JUST TELL US WHAT HAPPENED, BOOM BOOM.
LOOK, I WAS SHOPPING, AND NEXT THING I KNEW SOME JASON VOORHIES LOOKING CHICK WAS HOLDING A GUN TO MY HEAD.
DID YOU HEAR ANYTHING? SMELL ANYTHING?
WHAT? DO I LOOK LIKE A DOG? YOU NEED TO-- WAIT.
I DID. I MEAN, NOT SMELL...I REMEMBER...THERE WAS A GIRL. SOME MILITARY GUYS. HATE... NO, THAT'S NOT RIGHT. S.H.I.E.L.D. SOME CHICK SAID, "DIVISION C," I THINK.
AND THEN THEY TOOK THE GIRL.
S.H.I.E.L.D. DOESN'T HAVE A "DIVISION C."
TELL WARREN. TO GET READY.
FIND THE CUCKOOS. GET THEM INTO CEREBRA NOW.

RRKRRRRRRRREEEEEEEEEEEEEE!!
THERE'S MY GIRL.
HNN... NNN...
HNN...NO... KIMURA...
I MISSED YOU, TOO.
I...I DON'T...

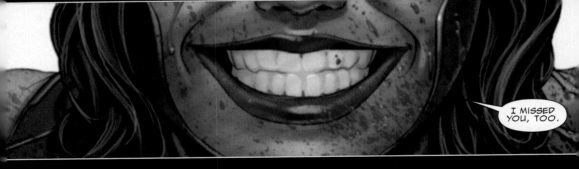

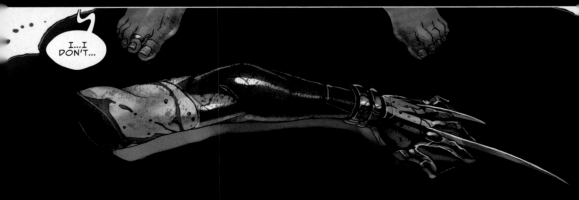

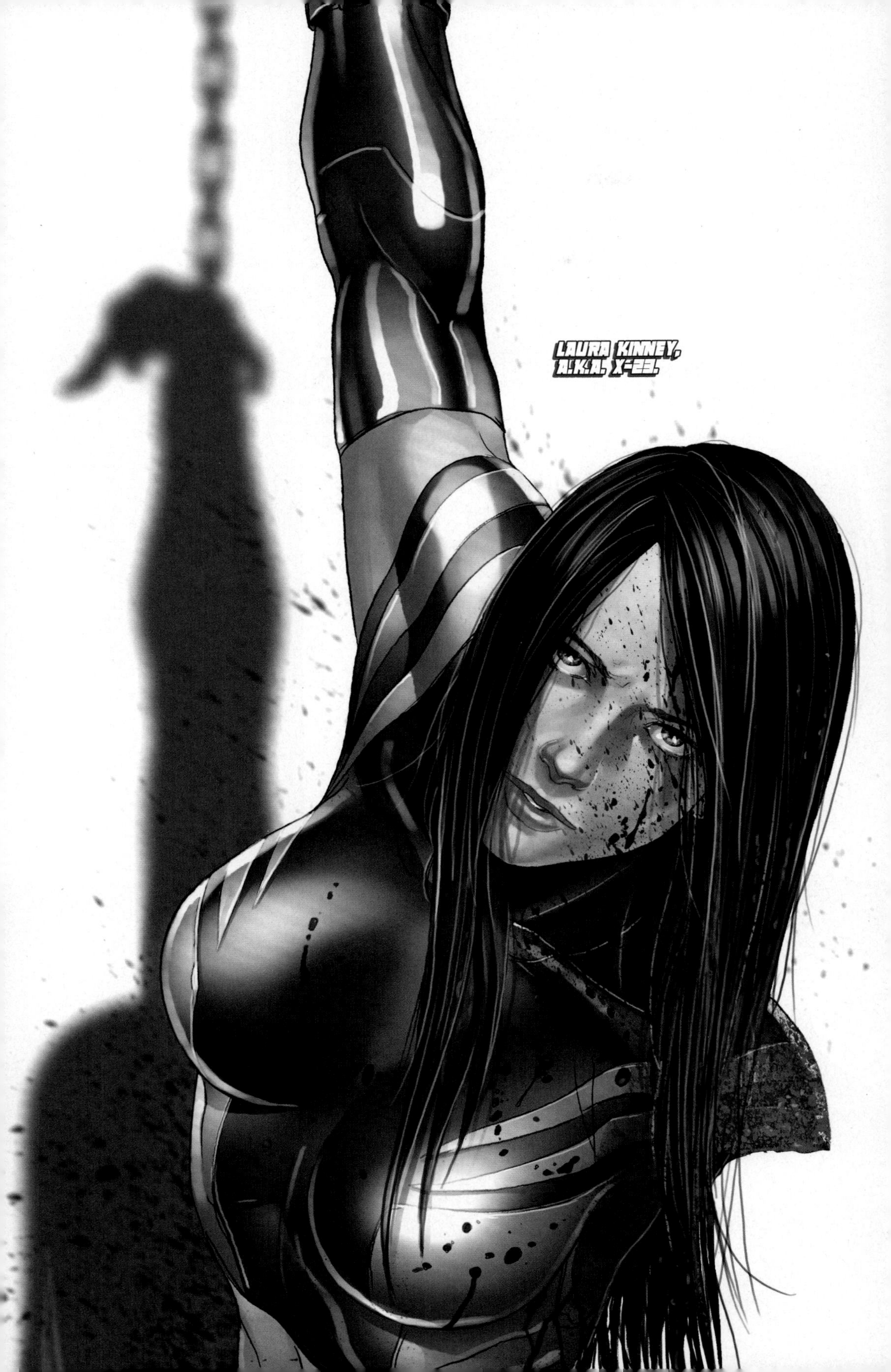
LAURA KINNEY, A.K.A. X-23.

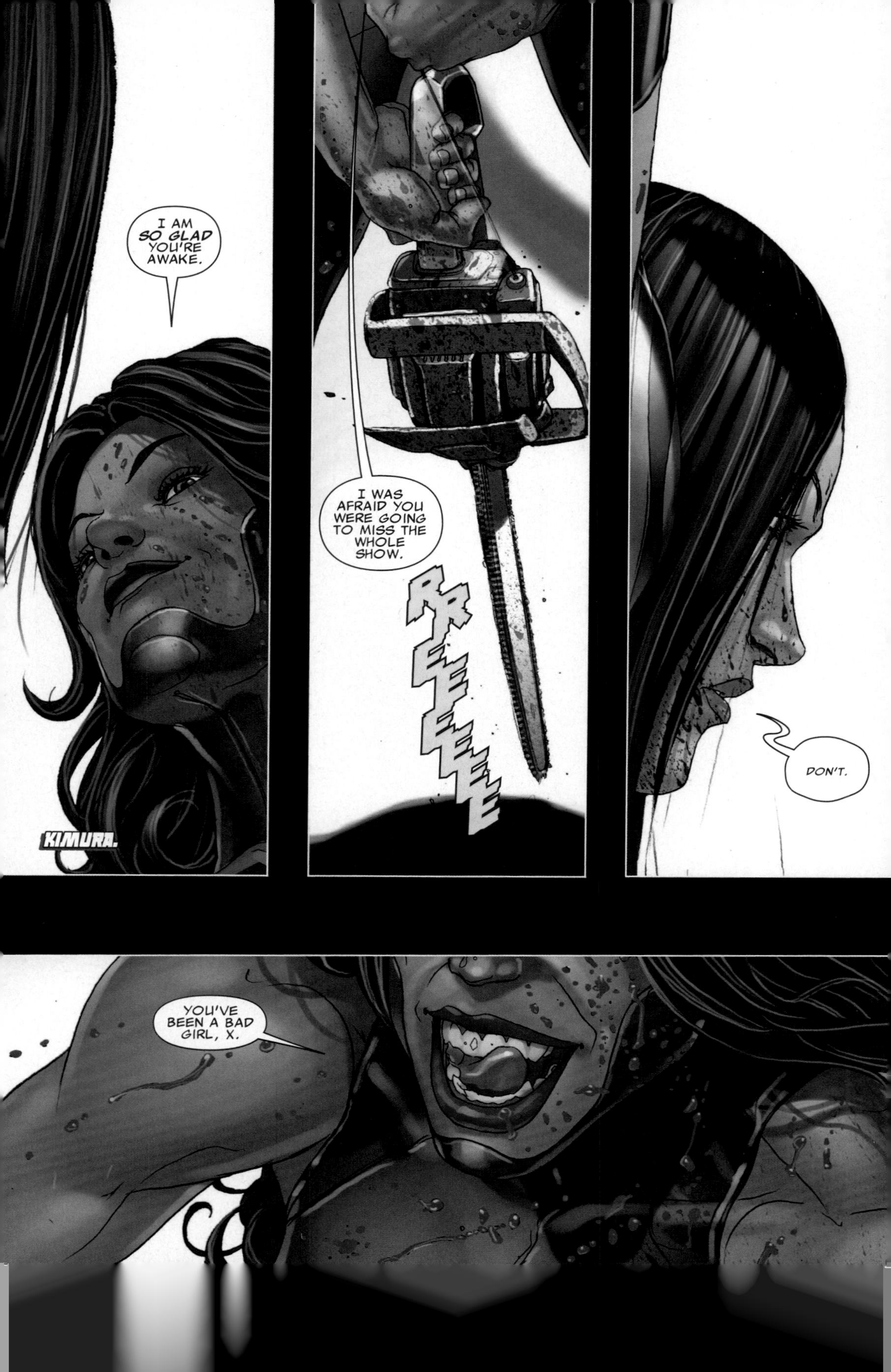
I AM SO GLAD YOU'RE AWAKE.
I WAS AFRAID YOU WERE GOING TO MISS THE WHOLE SHOW.
RRREEEEEE
DON'T.
YOU'VE BEEN A BAD GIRL, X.
KIMURA.

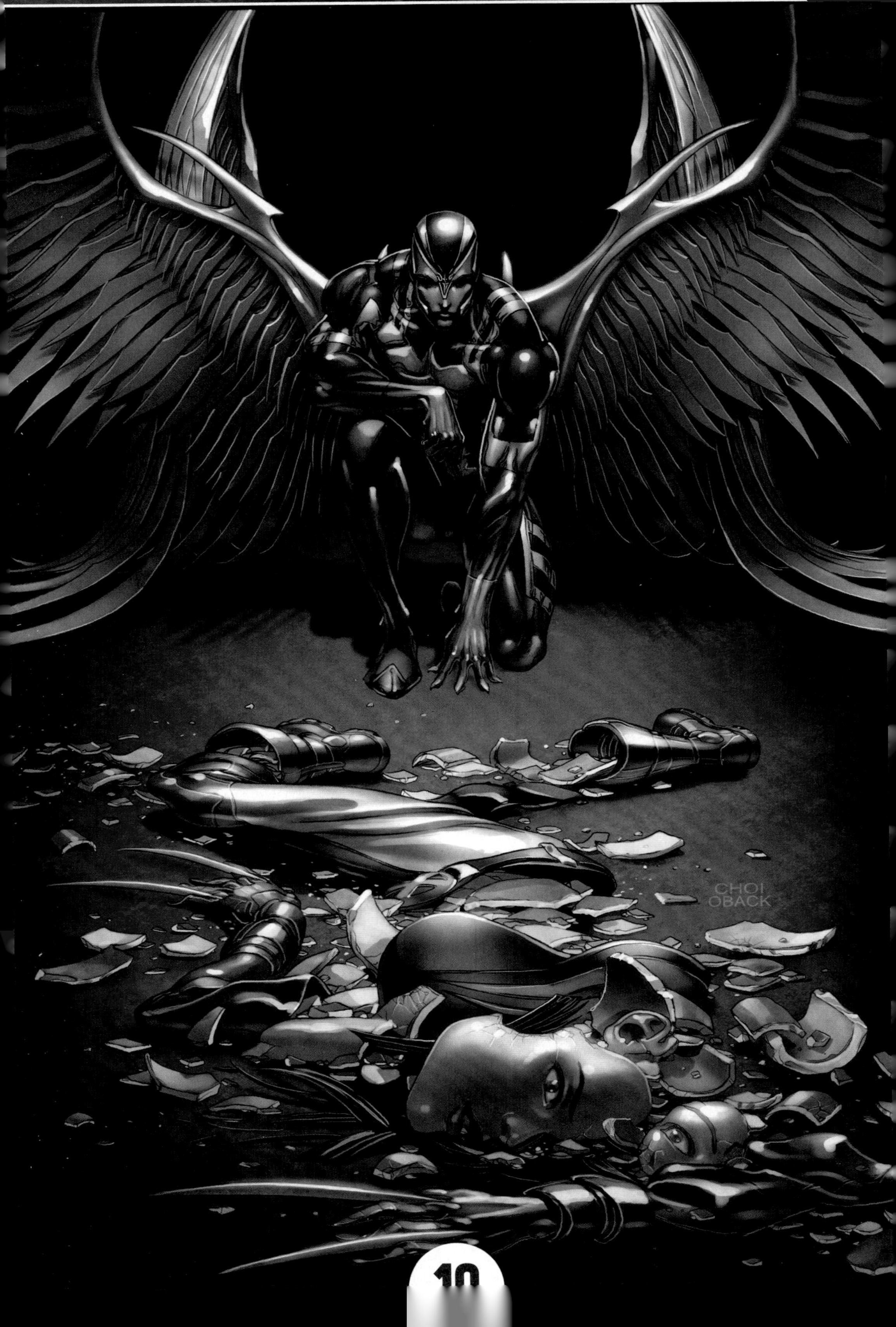
CHOI
OBACK
10

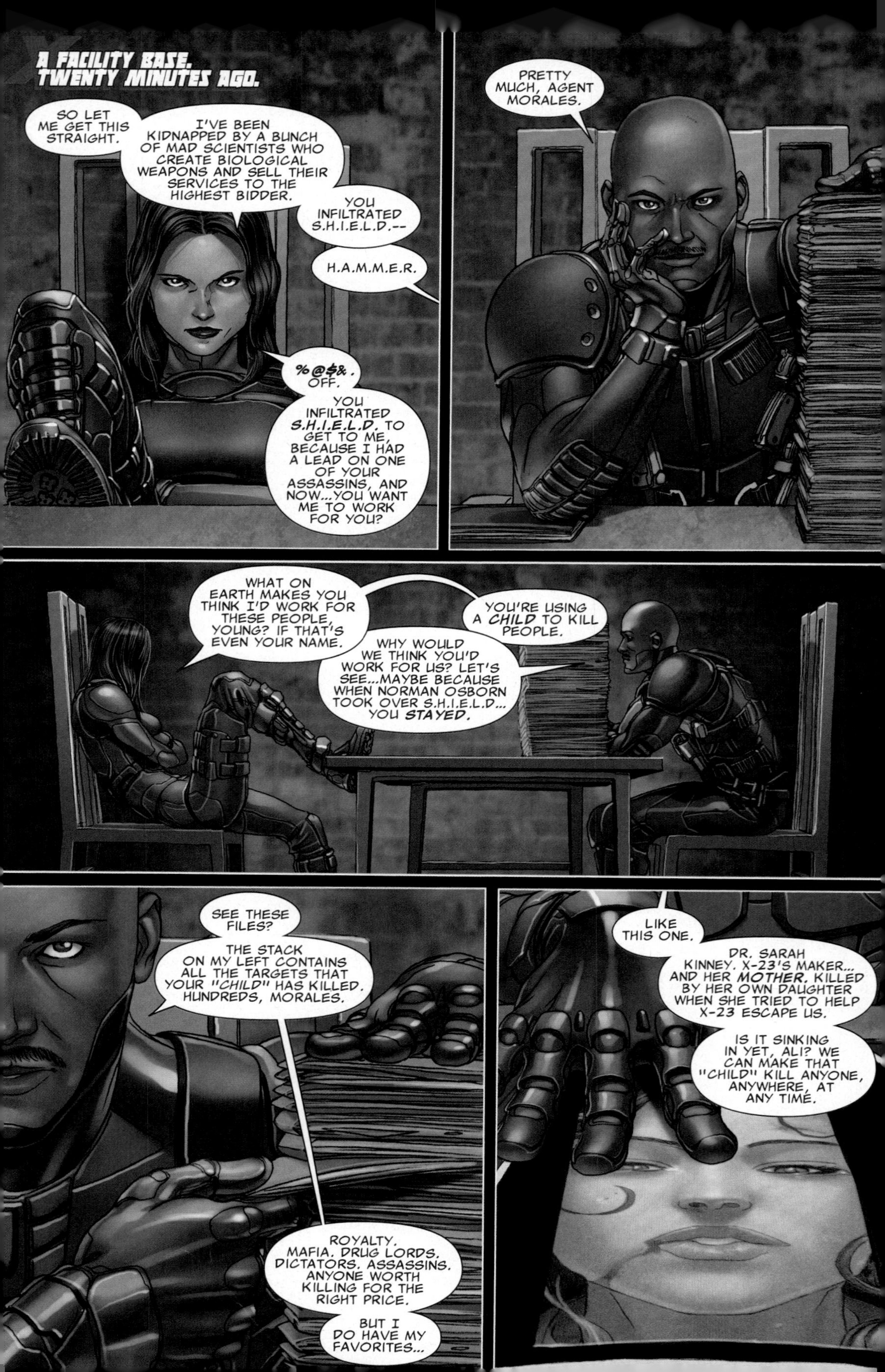
A FACILITY BASE. TWENTY MINUTES AGO.
SO LET ME GET THIS STRAIGHT.
I'VE BEEN KIDNAPPED BY A BUNCH OF MAD SCIENTISTS WHO CREATE BIOLOGICAL WEAPONS AND SELL THEIR SERVICES TO THE HIGHEST BIDDER.
YOU INFILTRATED S.H.I.E.L.D.--
H.A.M.M.E.R.
%@$&. OFF.
YOU INFILTRATED S.H.I.E.L.D. TO GET TO ME, BECAUSE I HAD A LEAD ON ONE OF YOUR ASSASSINS, AND NOW...YOU WANT ME TO WORK FOR YOU?
PRETTY MUCH, AGENT MORALES.
WHAT ON EARTH MAKES YOU THINK I'D WORK FOR THESE PEOPLE, YOUNG? IF THAT'S EVEN YOUR NAME.
YOU'RE USING A CHILD TO KILL PEOPLE.
WHY WOULD WE THINK YOU'D WORK FOR US? LET'S SEE...MAYBE BECAUSE WHEN NORMAN OSBORN TOOK OVER S.H.I.E.L.D... YOU STAYED.
SEE THESE FILES?
THE STACK ON MY LEFT CONTAINS ALL THE TARGETS THAT YOUR "CHILD" HAS KILLED. HUNDREDS, MORALES.
ROYALTY. MAFIA. DRUG LORDS. DICTATORS. ASSASSINS. ANYONE WORTH KILLING FOR THE RIGHT PRICE.
BUT I DO HAVE MY FAVORITES...
LIKE THIS ONE.
DR. SARAH KINNEY. X-23'S MAKER... AND HER MOTHER. KILLED BY HER OWN DAUGHTER WHEN SHE TRIED TO HELP X-23 ESCAPE US.
IS IT SINKING IN YET, ALI? WE CAN MAKE THAT "CHILD" KILL ANYONE, ANYWHERE, AT ANY TIME.

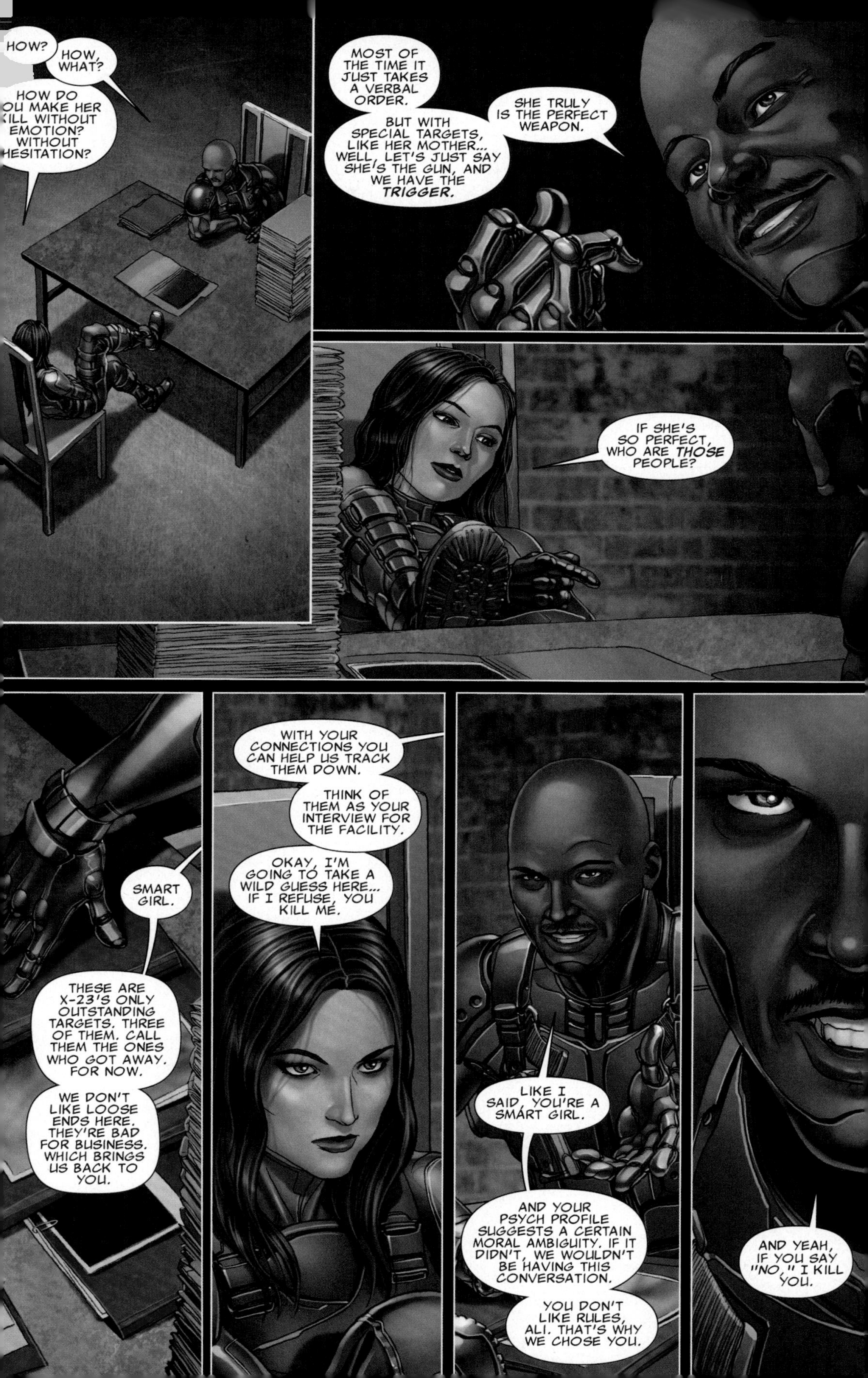
HOW?
HOW, WHAT?
HOW DO YOU MAKE HER KILL WITHOUT EMOTION? WITHOUT HESITATION?
MOST OF THE TIME IT JUST TAKES A VERBAL ORDER.
BUT WITH SPECIAL TARGETS, LIKE HER MOTHER... WELL, LET'S JUST SAY SHE'S THE GUN, AND WE HAVE THE TRIGGER.
SHE TRULY IS THE PERFECT WEAPON.
IF SHE'S SO PERFECT, WHO ARE THOSE PEOPLE?
SMART GIRL.
THESE ARE X-23'S ONLY OUTSTANDING TARGETS. THREE OF THEM. CALL THEM THE ONES WHO GOT AWAY. FOR NOW.
WE DON'T LIKE LOOSE ENDS HERE. THEY'RE BAD FOR BUSINESS. WHICH BRINGS US BACK TO YOU.
WITH YOUR CONNECTIONS YOU CAN HELP US TRACK THEM DOWN.
THINK OF THEM AS YOUR INTERVIEW FOR THE FACILITY.
OKAY, I'M GOING TO TAKE A WILD GUESS HERE... IF I REFUSE, YOU KILL ME.
LIKE I SAID, YOU'RE A SMART GIRL.
AND YOUR PSYCH PROFILE SUGGESTS A CERTAIN MORAL AMBIGUITY. IF IT DIDN'T, WE WOULDN'T BE HAVING THIS CONVERSATION.
YOU DON'T LIKE RULES, ALI. THAT'S WHY WE CHOSE YOU.
AND YEAH, IF YOU SAY "NO," I KILL YOU.

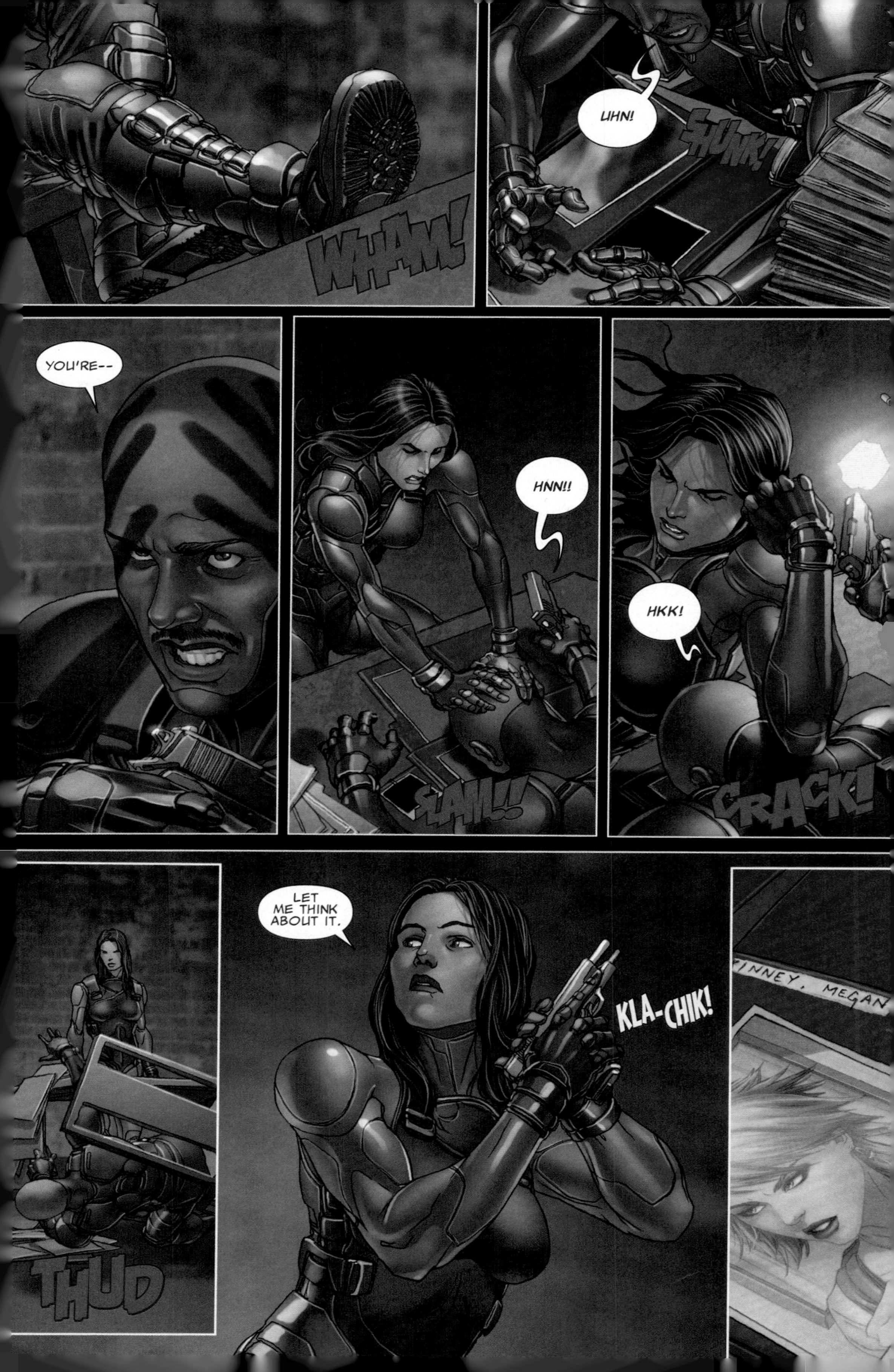
WHAM!
UHN!
SHUNK!
YOU'RE--
HNN!!
SLAM!!
HKK!
CRACK!
THUD
LET ME THINK ABOUT IT.
KLA-CHIK!
INNEY, MEGAN

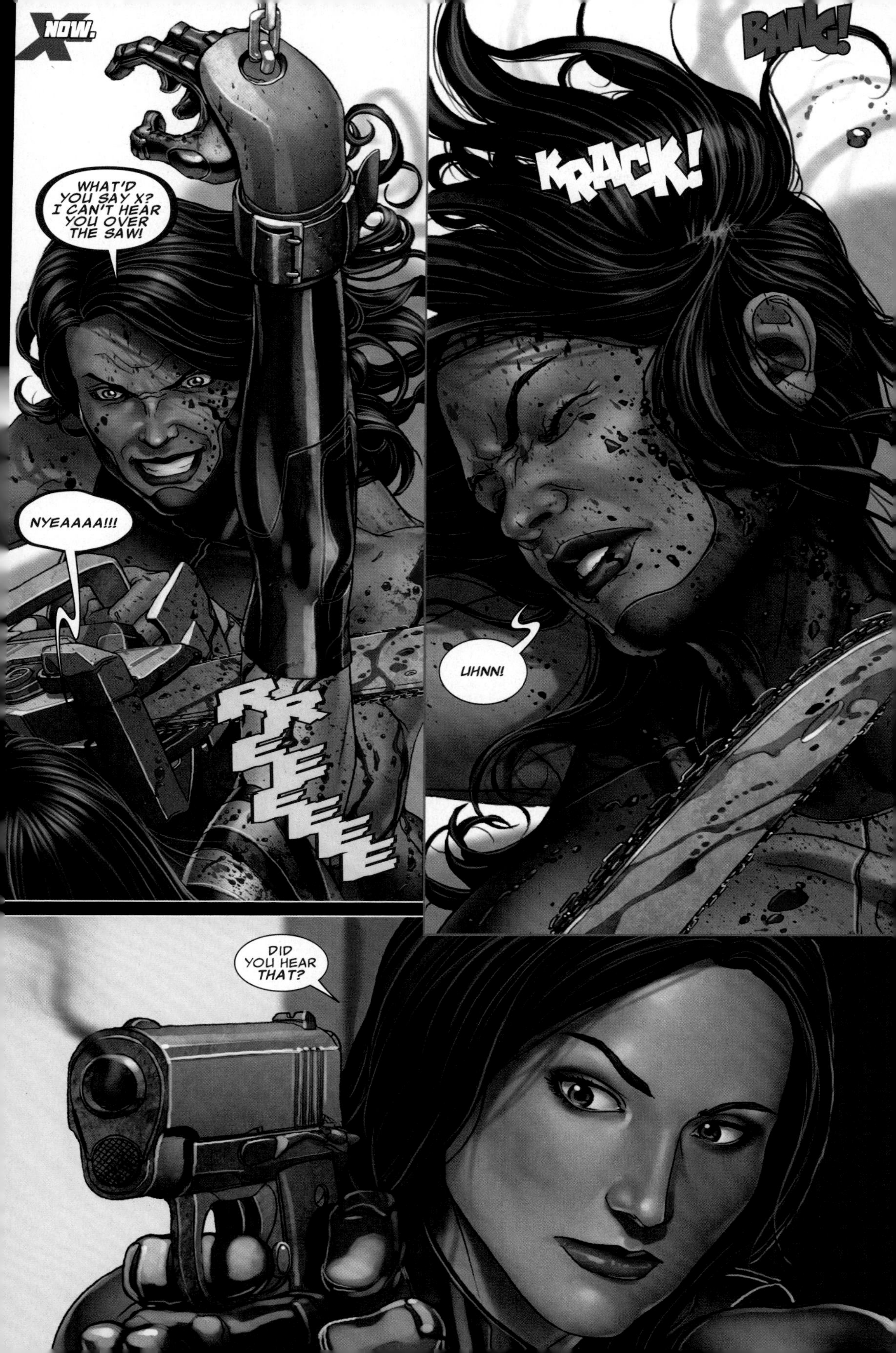
NOW.
WHAT'D YOU SAY X? I CAN'T HEAR YOU OVER THE SAW!
NYEAAAA!!!
RREEEEEEE
BANG!
KRACK!
UHNN!
DID YOU HEAR THAT?

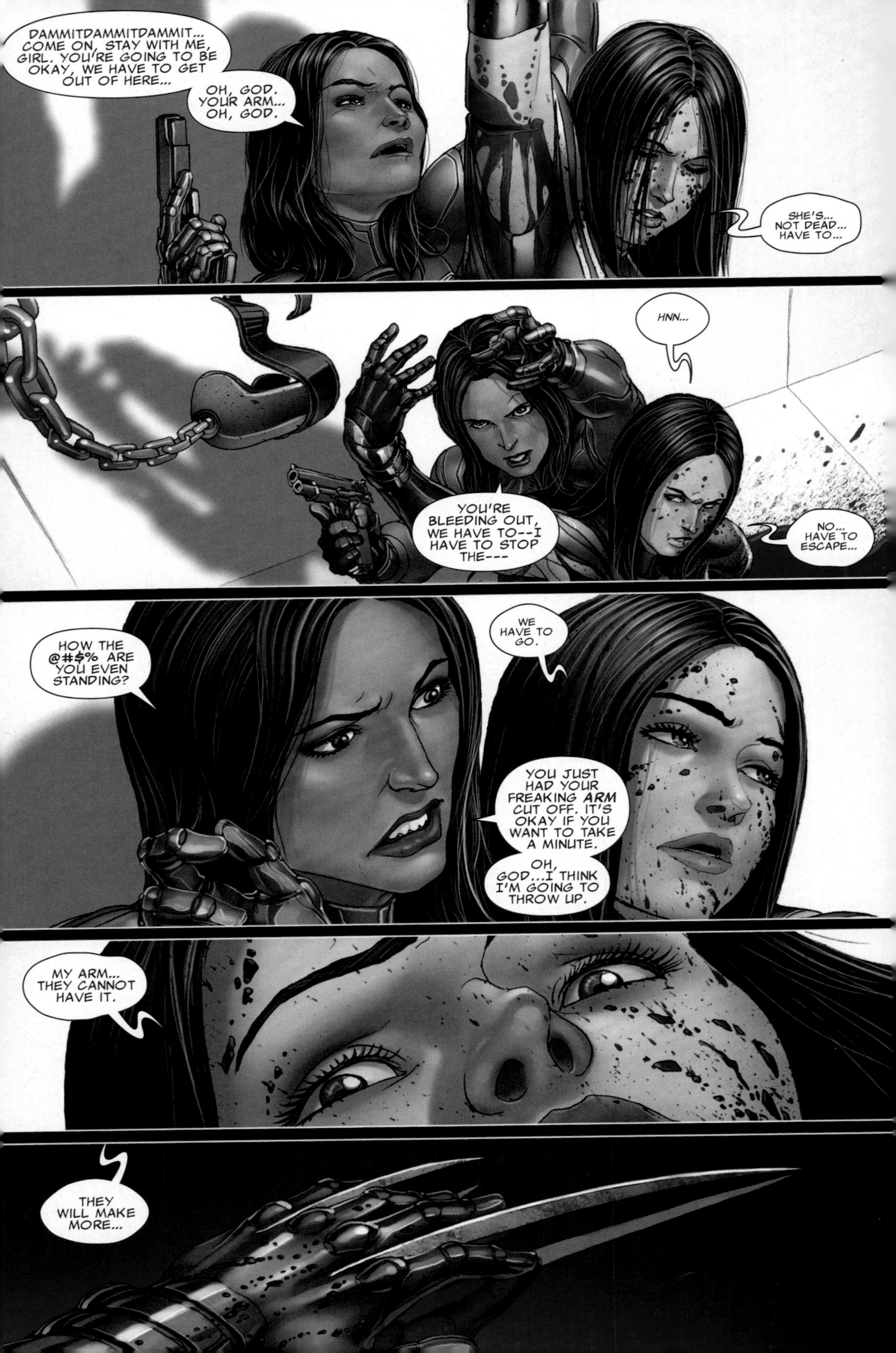
DAMMITDAMMITDAMMIT... COME ON, STAY WITH ME, GIRL. YOU'RE GOING TO BE OKAY, WE HAVE TO GET OUT OF HERE...
OH, GOD. YOUR ARM... OH, GOD.
SHE'S... NOT DEAD... HAVE TO...
HNN...
YOU'RE BLEEDING OUT, WE HAVE TO--I HAVE TO STOP THE---
NO... HAVE TO ESCAPE...
HOW THE @#$% ARE YOU EVEN STANDING?
WE HAVE TO GO.
YOU JUST HAD YOUR FREAKING ARM CUT OFF. IT'S OKAY IF YOU WANT TO TAKE A MINUTE.
OH, GOD...I THINK I'M GOING TO THROW UP.
MY ARM... THEY CANNOT HAVE IT.
THEY WILL MAKE MORE...

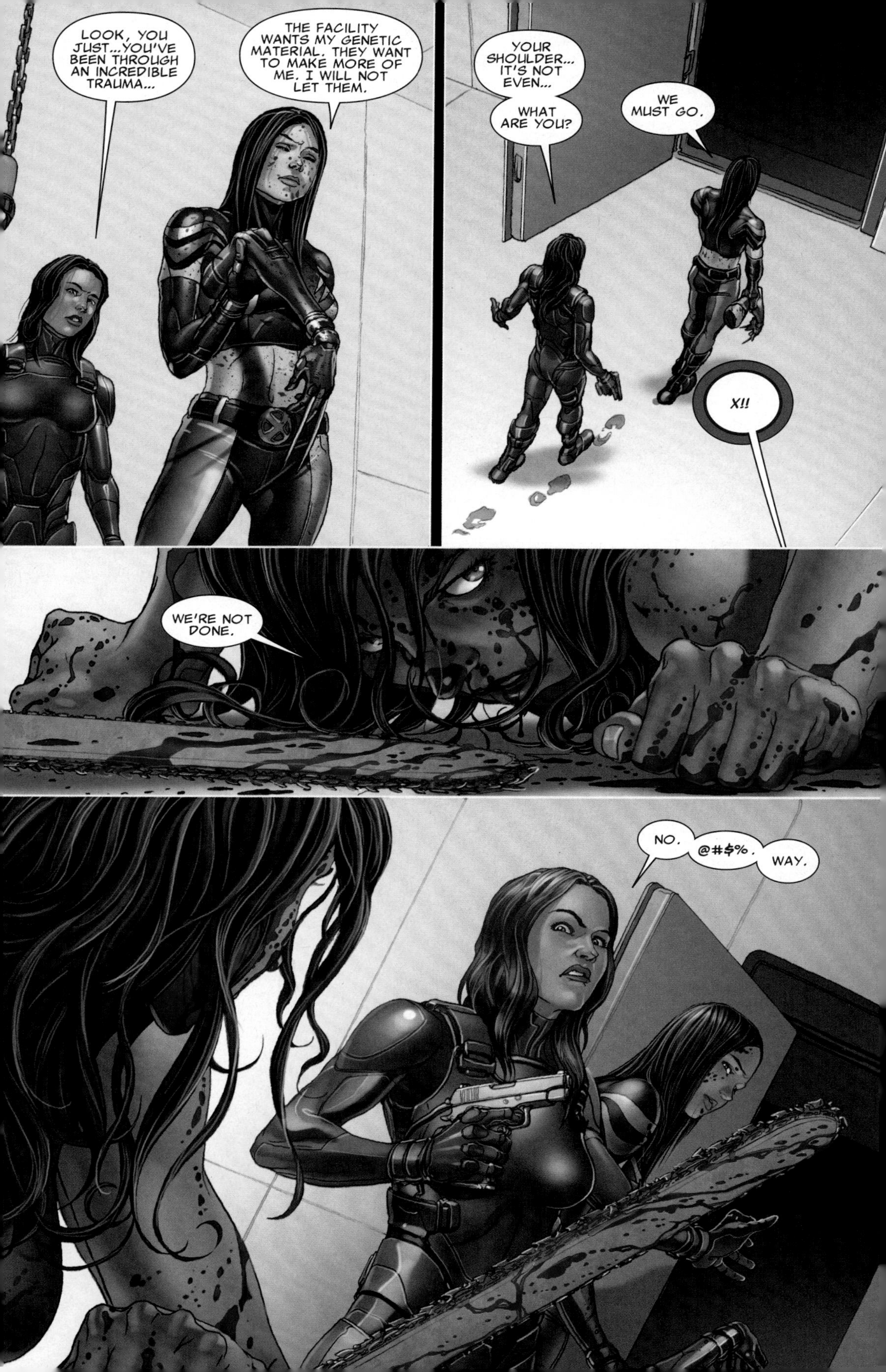
LOOK, YOU JUST...YOU'VE BEEN THROUGH AN INCREDIBLE TRAUMA...
THE FACILITY WANTS MY GENETIC MATERIAL. THEY WANT TO MAKE MORE OF ME. I WILL NOT LET THEM.
YOUR SHOULDER... IT'S NOT EVEN...
WHAT ARE YOU?
WE MUST GO.
X!!
WE'RE NOT DONE.
NO.
@#$%.
WAY.

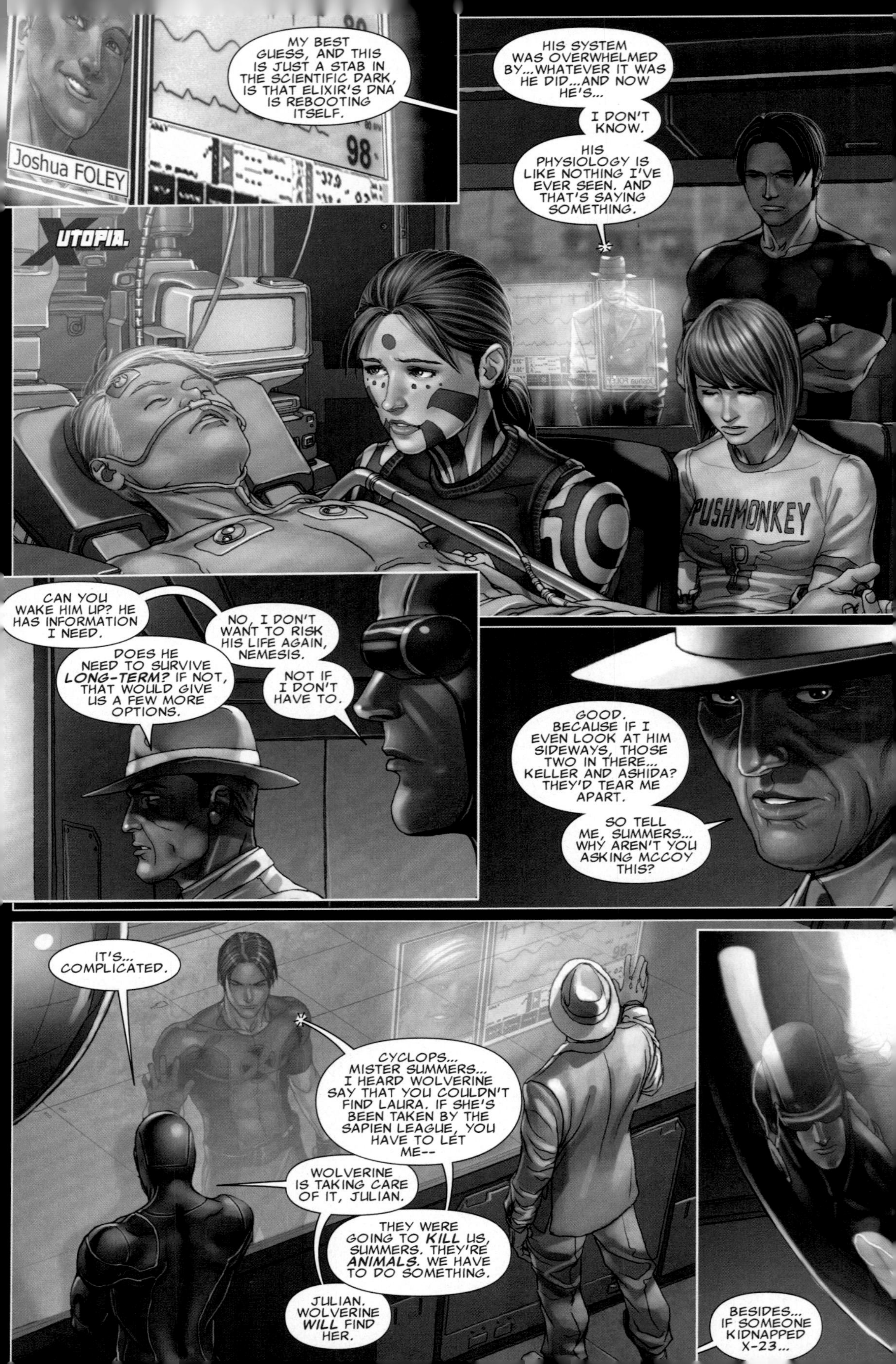

Joshua FOLEY
MY BEST GUESS, AND THIS IS JUST A STAB IN THE SCIENTIFIC DARK, IS THAT ELIXIR'S DNA IS REBOOTING ITSELF.
HIS SYSTEM WAS OVERWHELMED BY...WHATEVER IT WAS HE DID...AND NOW HE'S...
I DON'T KNOW.
HIS PHYSIOLOGY IS LIKE NOTHING I'VE EVER SEEN. AND THAT'S SAYING SOMETHING.
UTOPIA.
PUSHMONKEY
CAN YOU WAKE HIM UP? HE HAS INFORMATION I NEED.
NO, I DON'T WANT TO RISK HIS LIFE AGAIN, NEMESIS.
DOES HE NEED TO SURVIVE LONG-TERM? IF NOT, THAT WOULD GIVE US A FEW MORE OPTIONS.
NOT IF I DON'T HAVE TO.
GOOD. BECAUSE IF I EVEN LOOK AT HIM SIDEWAYS, THOSE TWO IN THERE... KELLER AND ASHIDA? THEY'D TEAR ME APART.
SO TELL ME, SUMMERS... WHY AREN'T YOU ASKING MCCOY THIS?
IT'S... COMPLICATED.
CYCLOPS... MISTER SUMMERS... I HEARD WOLVERINE SAY THAT YOU COULDN'T FIND LAURA. IF SHE'S BEEN TAKEN BY THE SAPIEN LEAGUE, YOU HAVE TO LET ME--
WOLVERINE IS TAKING CARE OF IT, JULIAN.
THEY WERE GOING TO KILL US, SUMMERS. THEY'RE ANIMALS. WE HAVE TO DO SOMETHING.
JULIAN. WOLVERINE WILL FIND HER.
BESIDES... IF SOMEONE KIDNAPPED X-23...

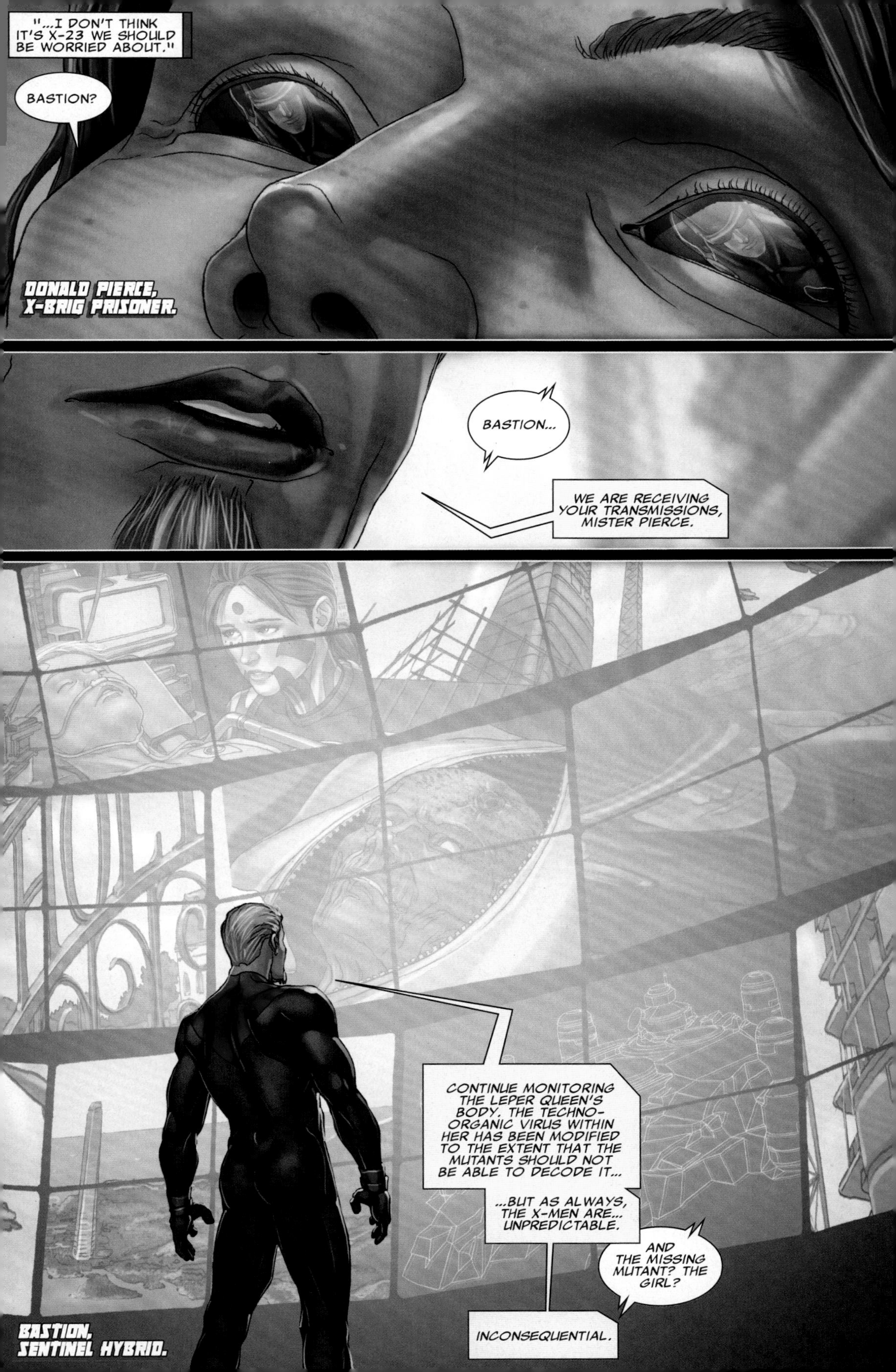
"...I DON'T THINK IT'S X-23 WE SHOULD BE WORRIED ABOUT."
BASTION?
DONALD PIERCE, X-BRIG PRISONER.
BASTION...
WE ARE RECEIVING YOUR TRANSMISSIONS, MISTER PIERCE.
CONTINUE MONITORING THE LEPER QUEEN'S BODY. THE TECHNO-ORGANIC VIRUS WITHIN HER HAS BEEN MODIFIED TO THE EXTENT THAT THE MUTANTS SHOULD NOT BE ABLE TO DECODE IT...
...BUT AS ALWAYS, THE X-MEN ARE... UNPREDICTABLE.
AND THE MISSING MUTANT? THE GIRL?
INCONSEQUENTIAL.
BASTION, SENTINEL HYBRID.

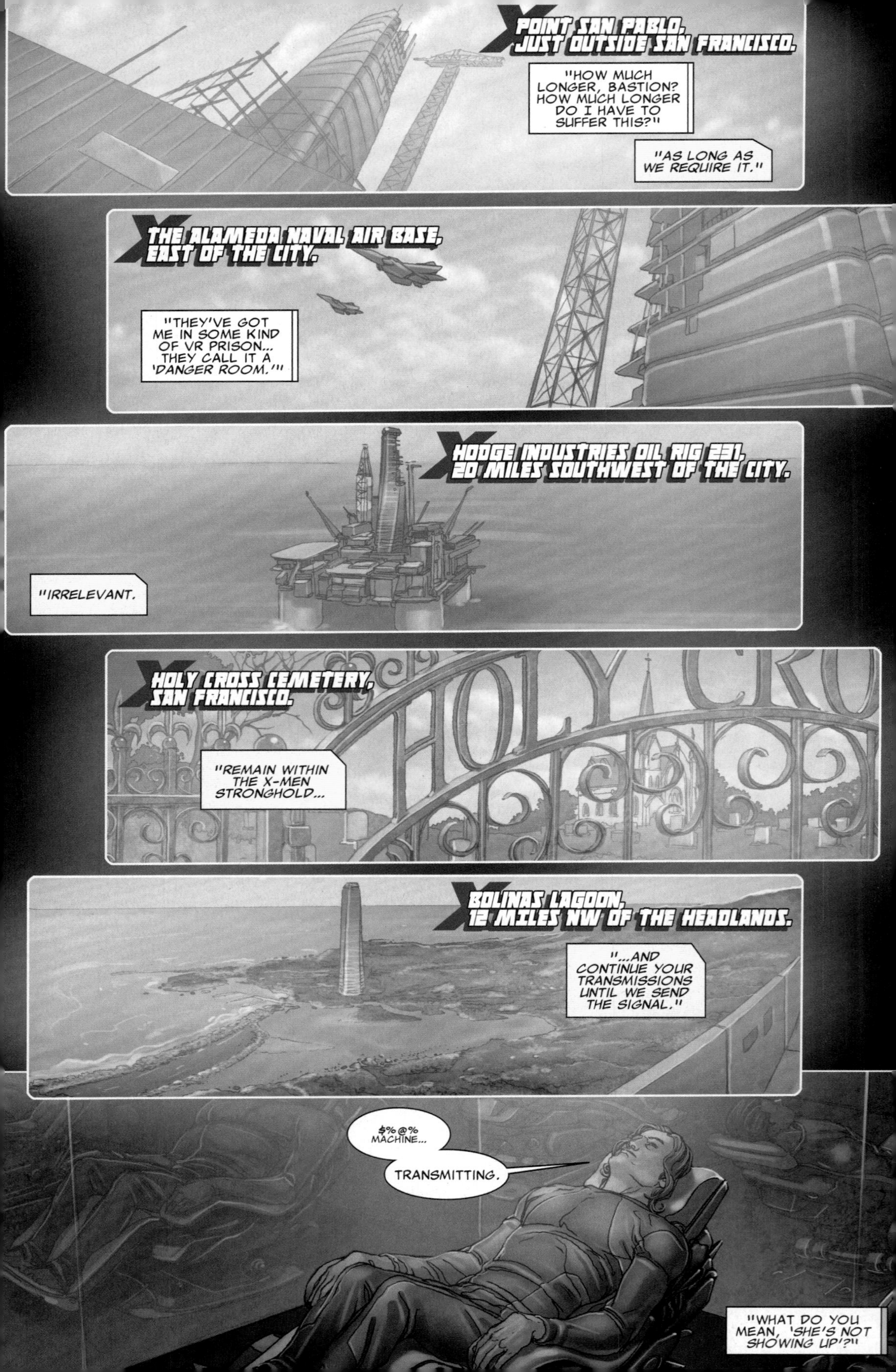
POINT SAN PABLO, JUST OUTSIDE SAN FRANCISCO.
"HOW MUCH LONGER, BASTION? HOW MUCH LONGER DO I HAVE TO SUFFER THIS?"
"AS LONG AS WE REQUIRE IT."
THE ALAMEDA NAVAL AIR BASE, EAST OF THE CITY.
"THEY'VE GOT ME IN SOME KIND OF VR PRISON... THEY CALL IT A 'DANGER ROOM.'"
HODGE INDUSTRIES OIL RIG 231, 20 MILES SOUTHWEST OF THE CITY.
"IRRELEVANT.
HOLY CROSS CEMETERY, SAN FRANCISCO.
"REMAIN WITHIN THE X-MEN STRONGHOLD...
BOLINAS LAGOON, 12 MILES NW OF THE HEADLANDS.
"...AND CONTINUE YOUR TRANSMISSIONS UNTIL WE SEND THE SIGNAL."
$%@% MACHINE...
TRANSMITTING.
"WHAT DO YOU MEAN, 'SHE'S NOT SHOWING UP'?"

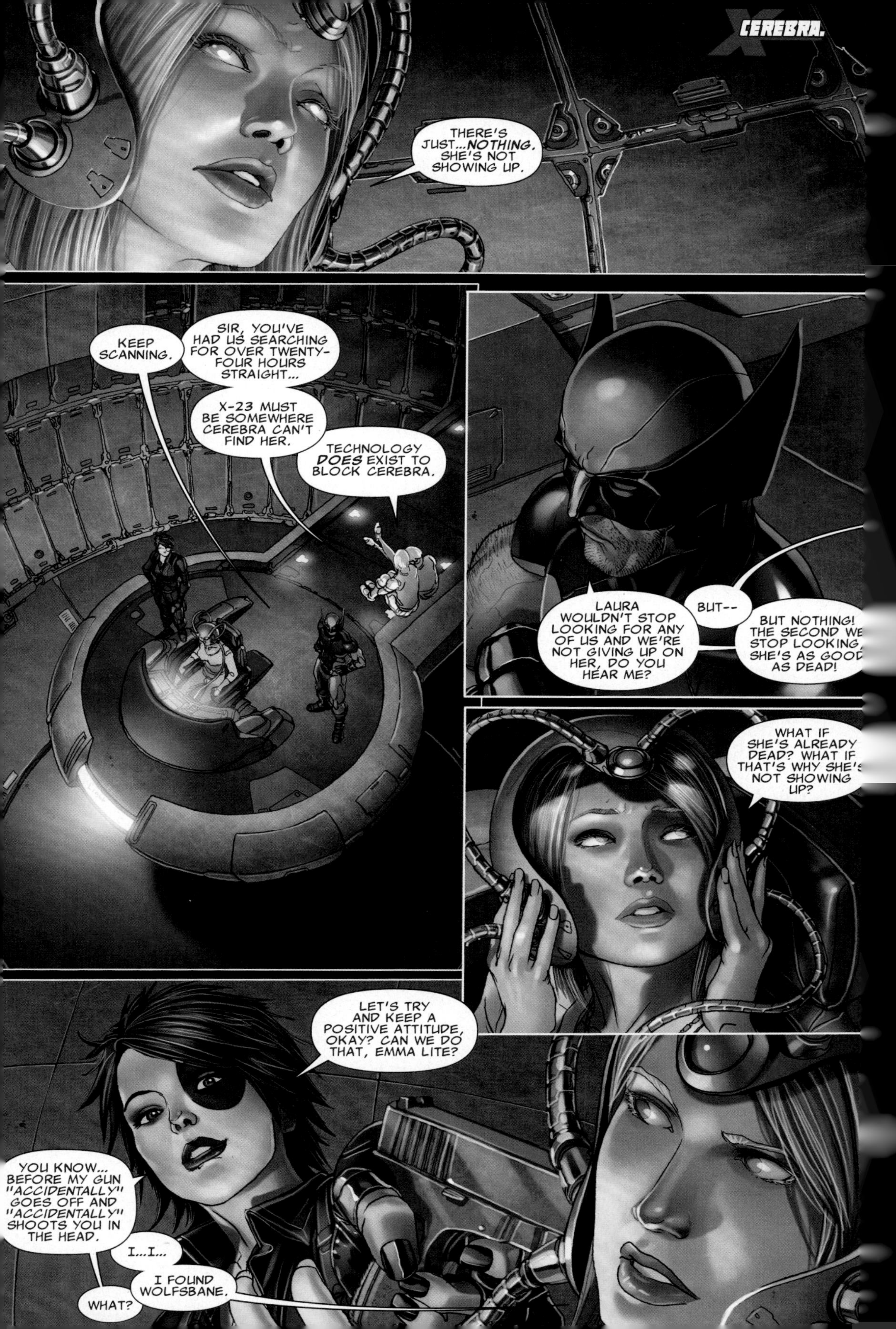
CEREBRA.
THERE'S JUST...NOTHING. SHE'S NOT SHOWING UP.
KEEP SCANNING.
SIR, YOU'VE HAD US SEARCHING FOR OVER TWENTY-FOUR HOURS STRAIGHT...
X-23 MUST BE SOMEWHERE CEREBRA CAN'T FIND HER.
TECHNOLOGY DOES EXIST TO BLOCK CEREBRA.
LAURA WOULDN'T STOP LOOKING FOR ANY OF US AND WE'RE NOT GIVING UP ON HER, DO YOU HEAR ME?
BUT--
BUT NOTHING! THE SECOND WE STOP LOOKING, SHE'S AS GOOD AS DEAD!
WHAT IF SHE'S ALREADY DEAD? WHAT IF THAT'S WHY SHE'S NOT SHOWING UP?
LET'S TRY AND KEEP A POSITIVE ATTITUDE, OKAY? CAN WE DO THAT, EMMA LITE?
YOU KNOW... BEFORE MY GUN "ACCIDENTALLY" GOES OFF AND "ACCIDENTALLY" SHOOTS YOU IN THE HEAD.
I...I...
I FOUND WOLFSBANE.
WHAT?

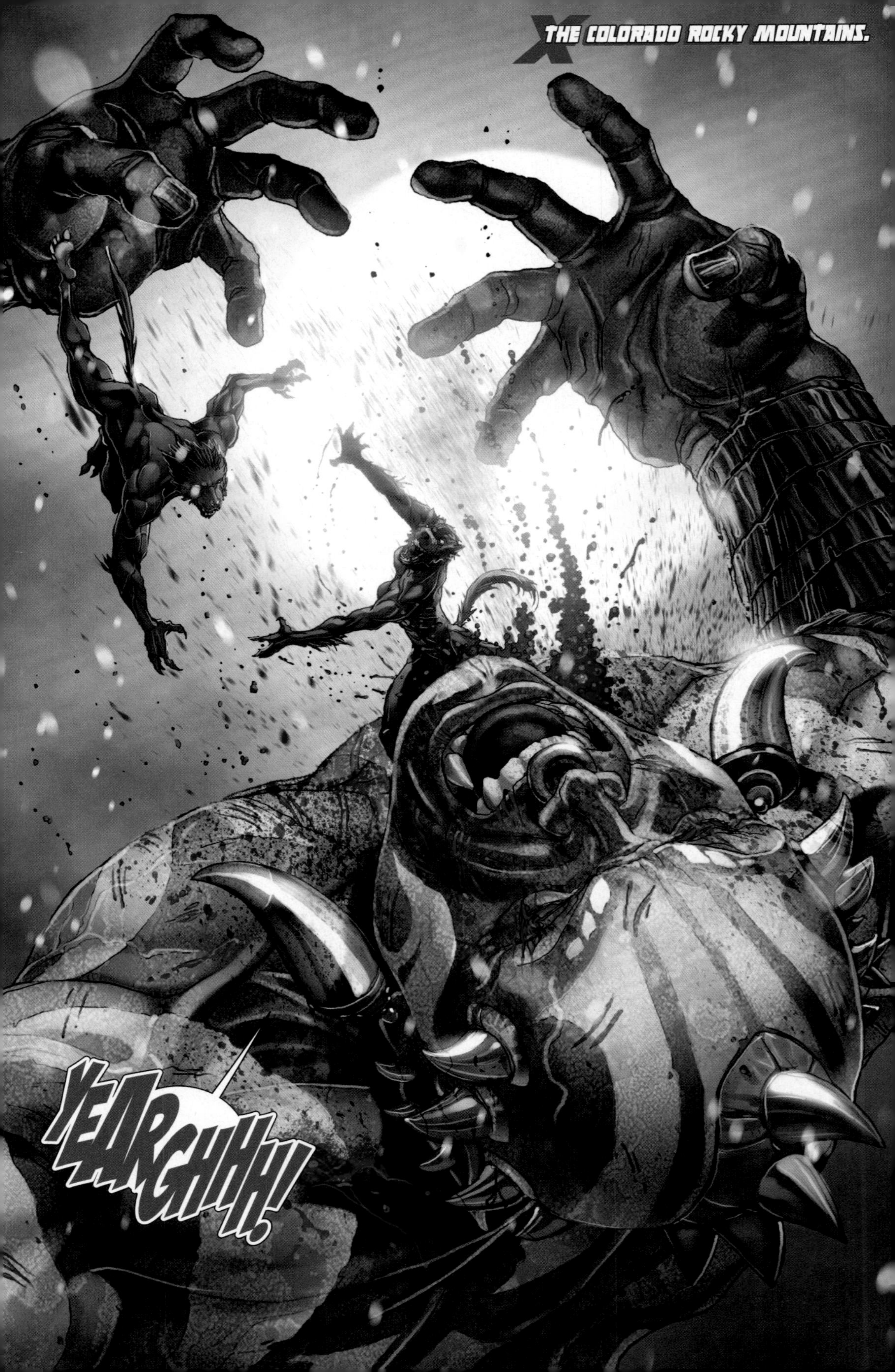
THE COLORADO ROCKY MOUNTAINS.
YEARGHHH!

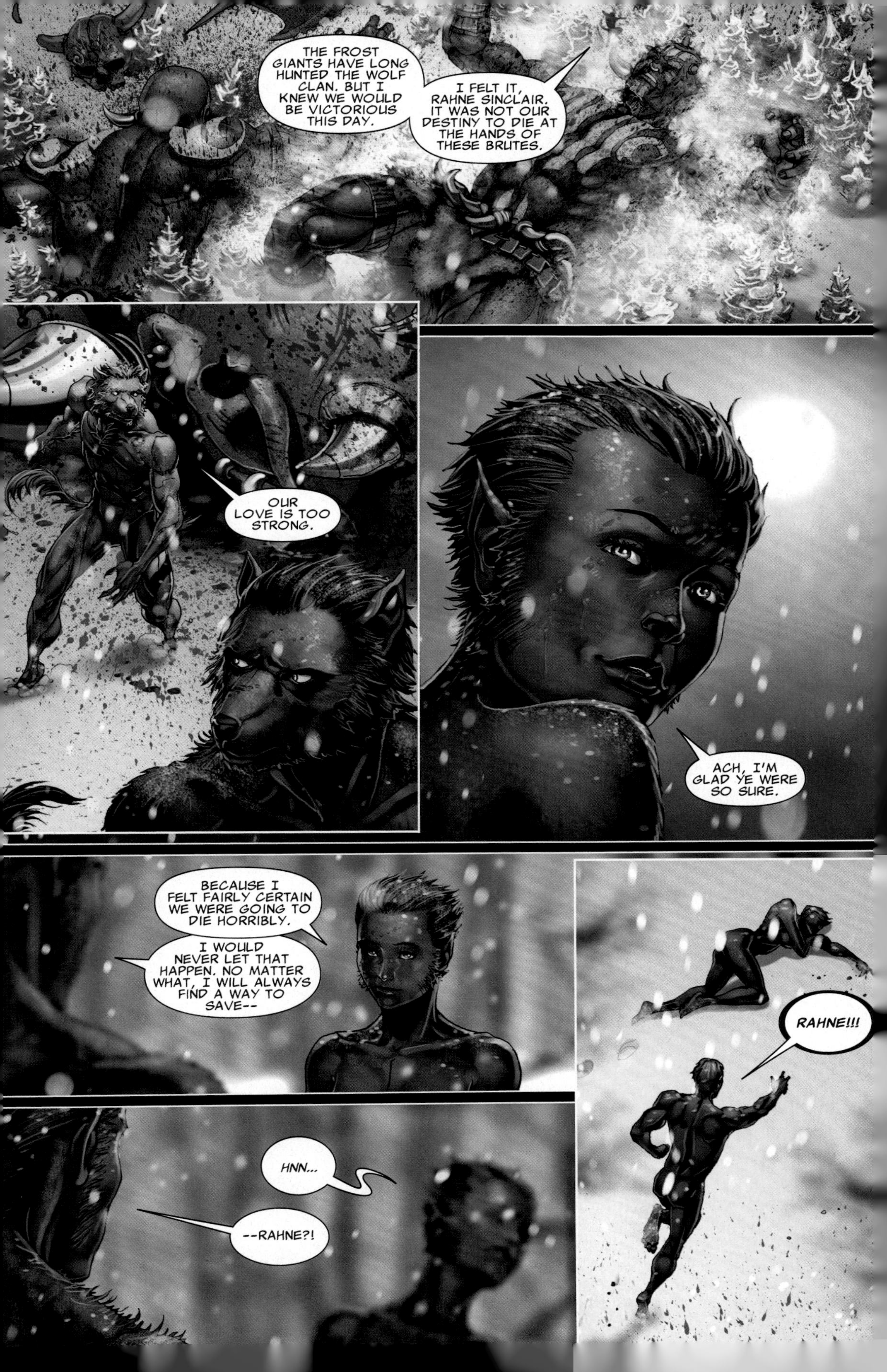
THE FROST GIANTS HAVE LONG HUNTED THE WOLF CLAN. BUT I KNEW WE WOULD BE VICTORIOUS THIS DAY.
I FELT IT, RAHNE SINCLAIR. IT WAS NOT OUR DESTINY TO DIE AT THE HANDS OF THESE BRUTES.
OUR LOVE IS TOO STRONG.
ACH, I'M GLAD YE WERE SO SURE.
BECAUSE I FELT FAIRLY CERTAIN WE WERE GOING TO DIE HORRIBLY.
I WOULD NEVER LET THAT HAPPEN. NO MATTER WHAT, I WILL ALWAYS FIND A WAY TO SAVE--
HNN...
--RAHNE?!
RAHNE!!!

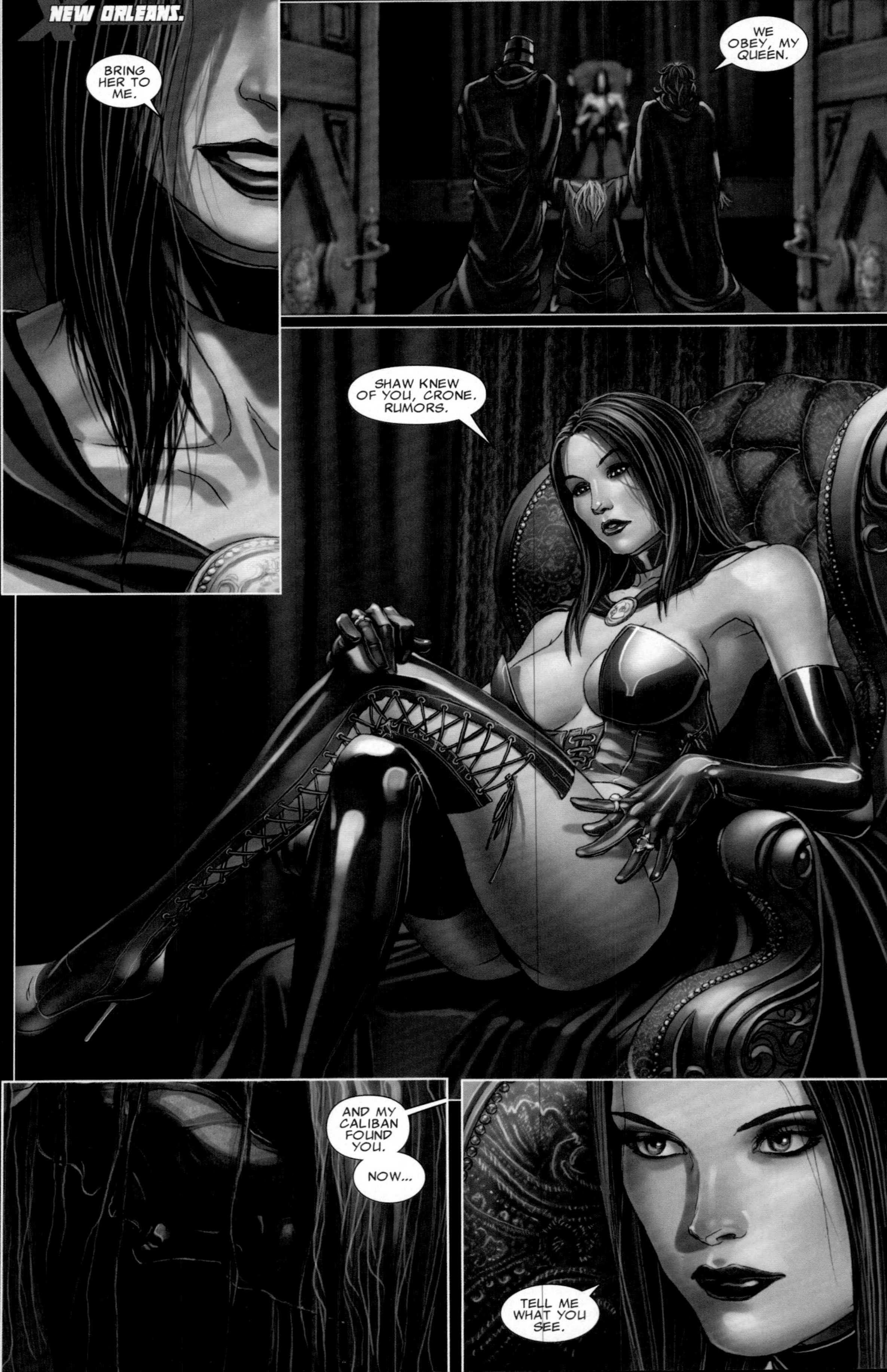
NEW ORLEANS.
BRING HER TO ME.
WE OBEY, MY QUEEN.
SHAW KNEW OF YOU, CRONE. RUMORS.
AND MY CALIBAN FOUND YOU.
NOW...
TELL ME WHAT YOU SEE.

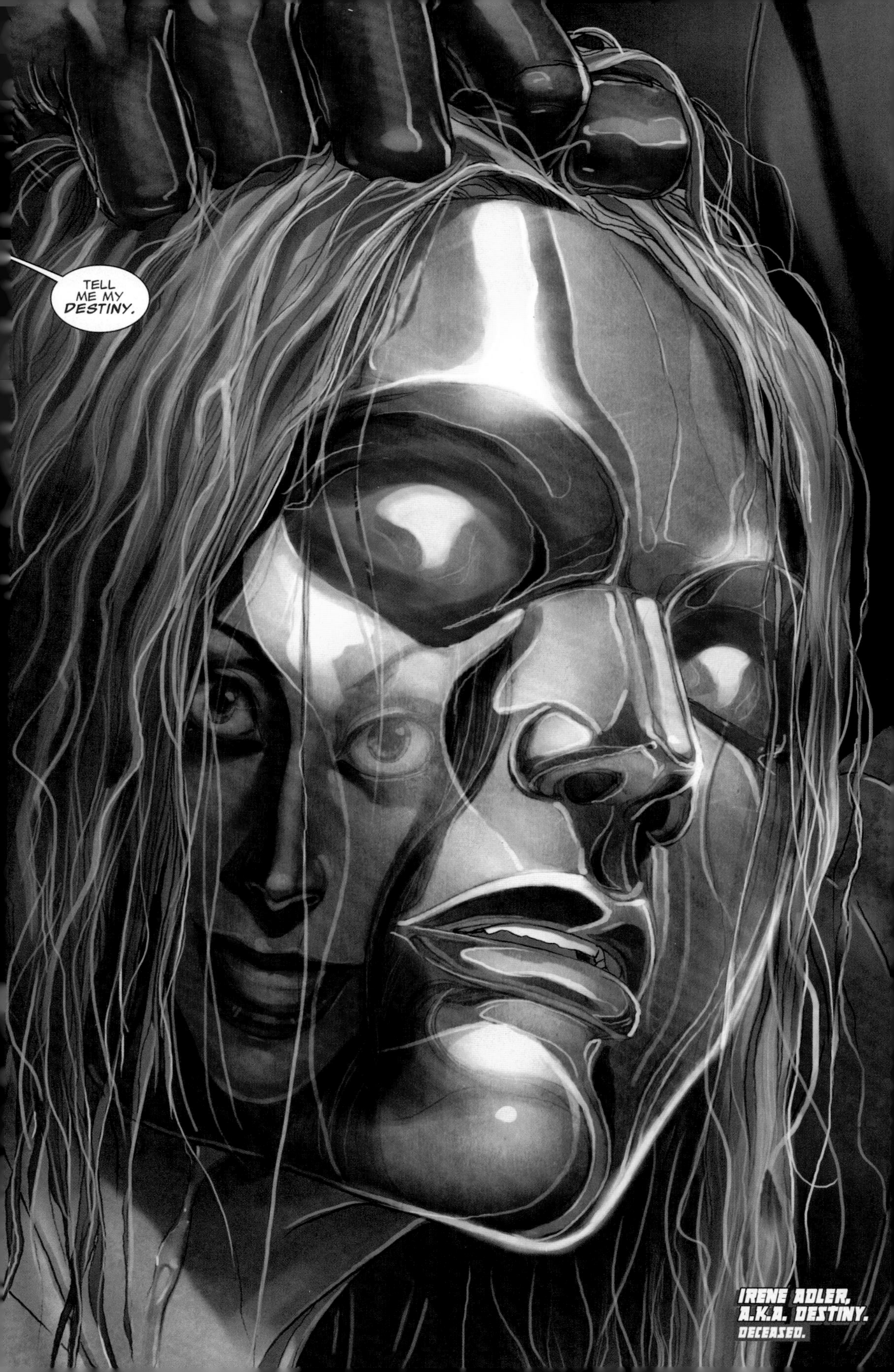
TELL ME MY DESTINY.
IRENE ADLER, A.K.A. DESTINY.
DECEASED.

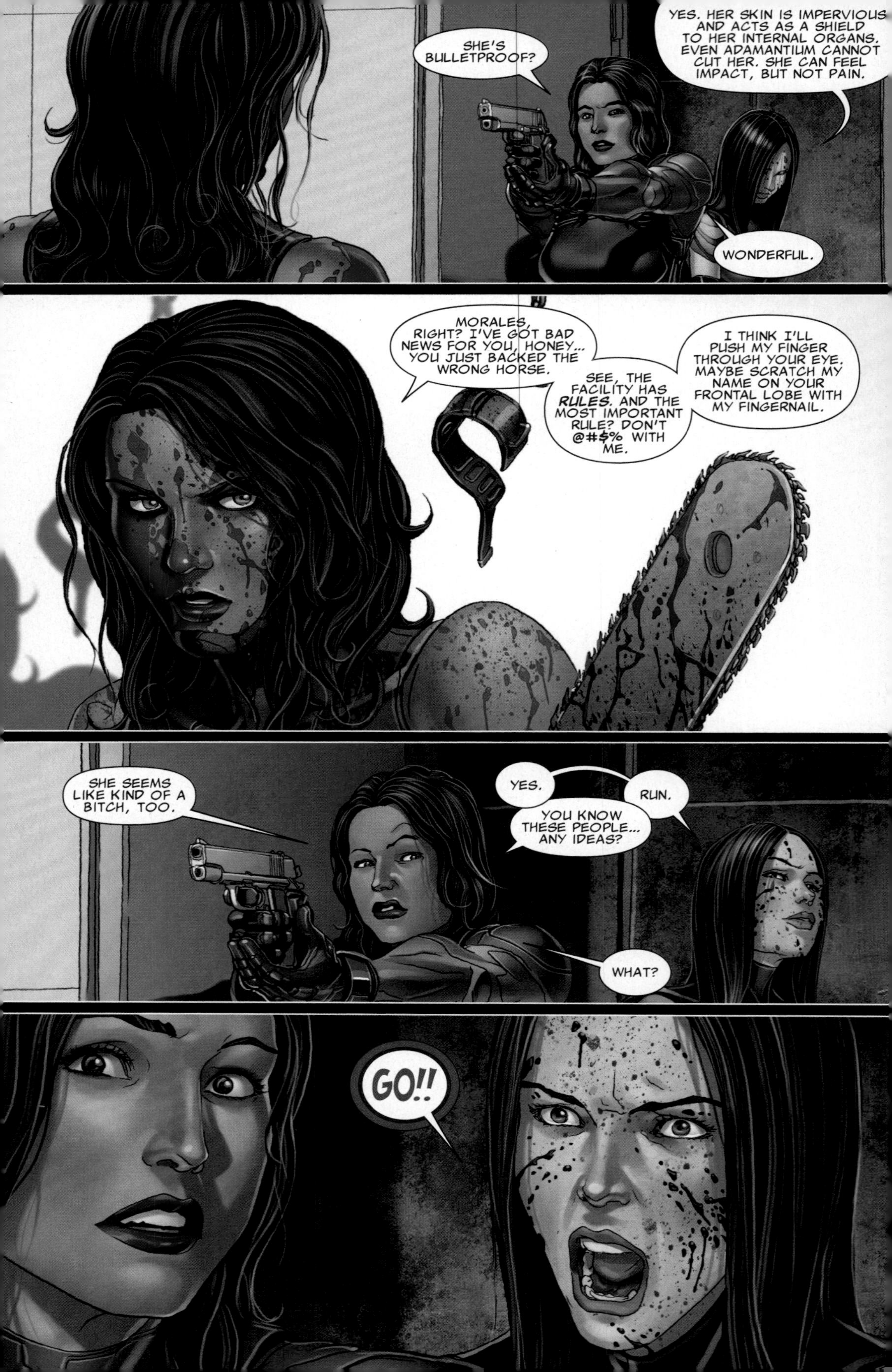
SHE'S BULLETPROOF?
YES. HER SKIN IS IMPERVIOUS AND ACTS AS A SHIELD TO HER INTERNAL ORGANS. EVEN ADAMANTIUM CANNOT CUT HER. SHE CAN FEEL IMPACT, BUT NOT PAIN.
WONDERFUL.
MORALES, RIGHT? I'VE GOT BAD NEWS FOR YOU, HONEY... YOU JUST BACKED THE WRONG HORSE.
SEE, THE FACILITY HAS RULES. AND THE MOST IMPORTANT RULE? DON'T @#$% WITH ME.
I THINK I'LL PUSH MY FINGER THROUGH YOUR EYE. MAYBE SCRATCH MY NAME ON YOUR FRONTAL LOBE WITH MY FINGERNAIL.
SHE SEEMS LIKE KIND OF A BITCH, TOO.
YOU KNOW THESE PEOPLE... ANY IDEAS?
YES.
RUN.
WHAT?
GO!!

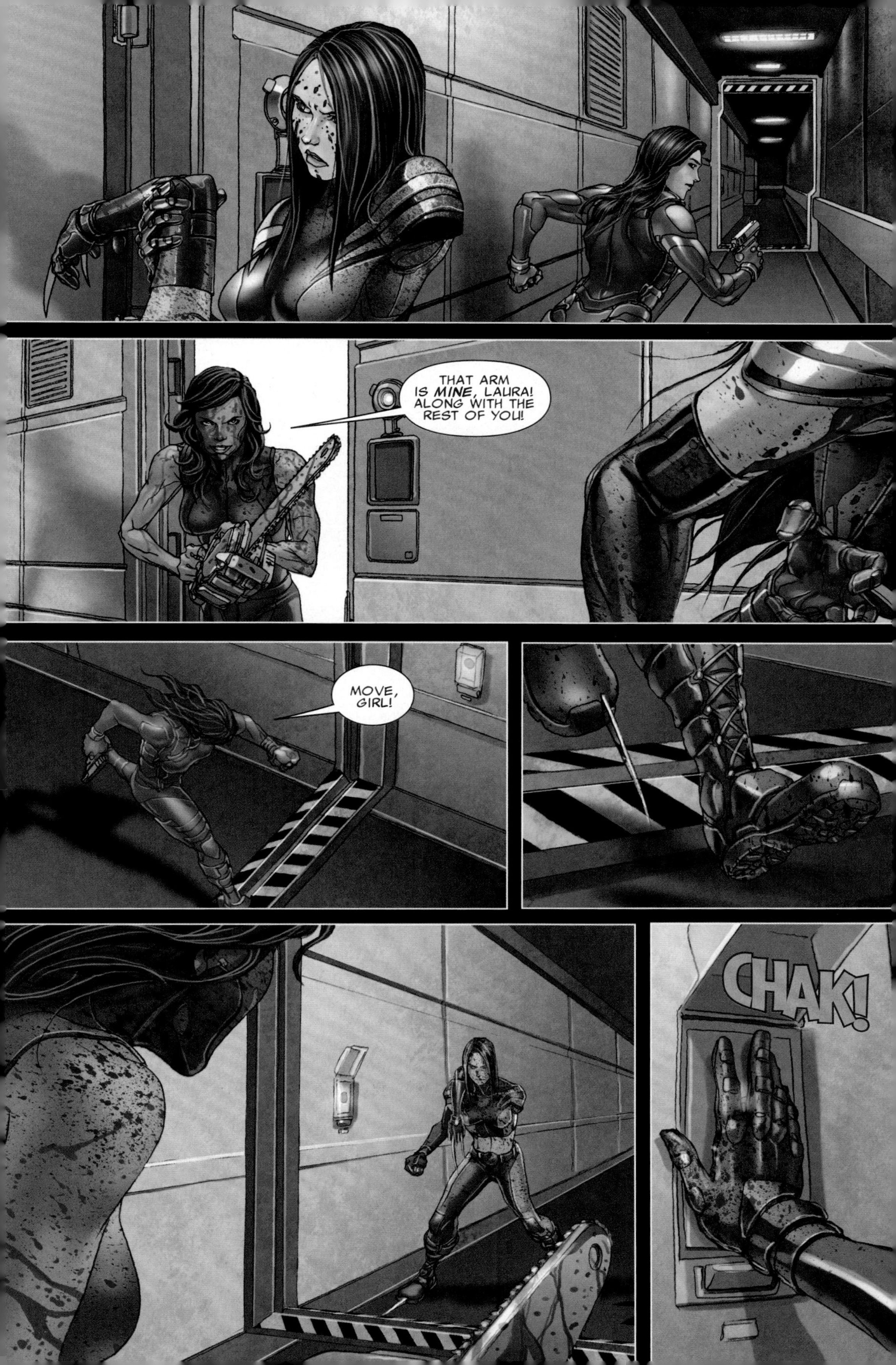
THAT ARM IS MINE, LAURA! ALONG WITH THE REST OF YOU!
MOVE, GIRL!
CHAK!

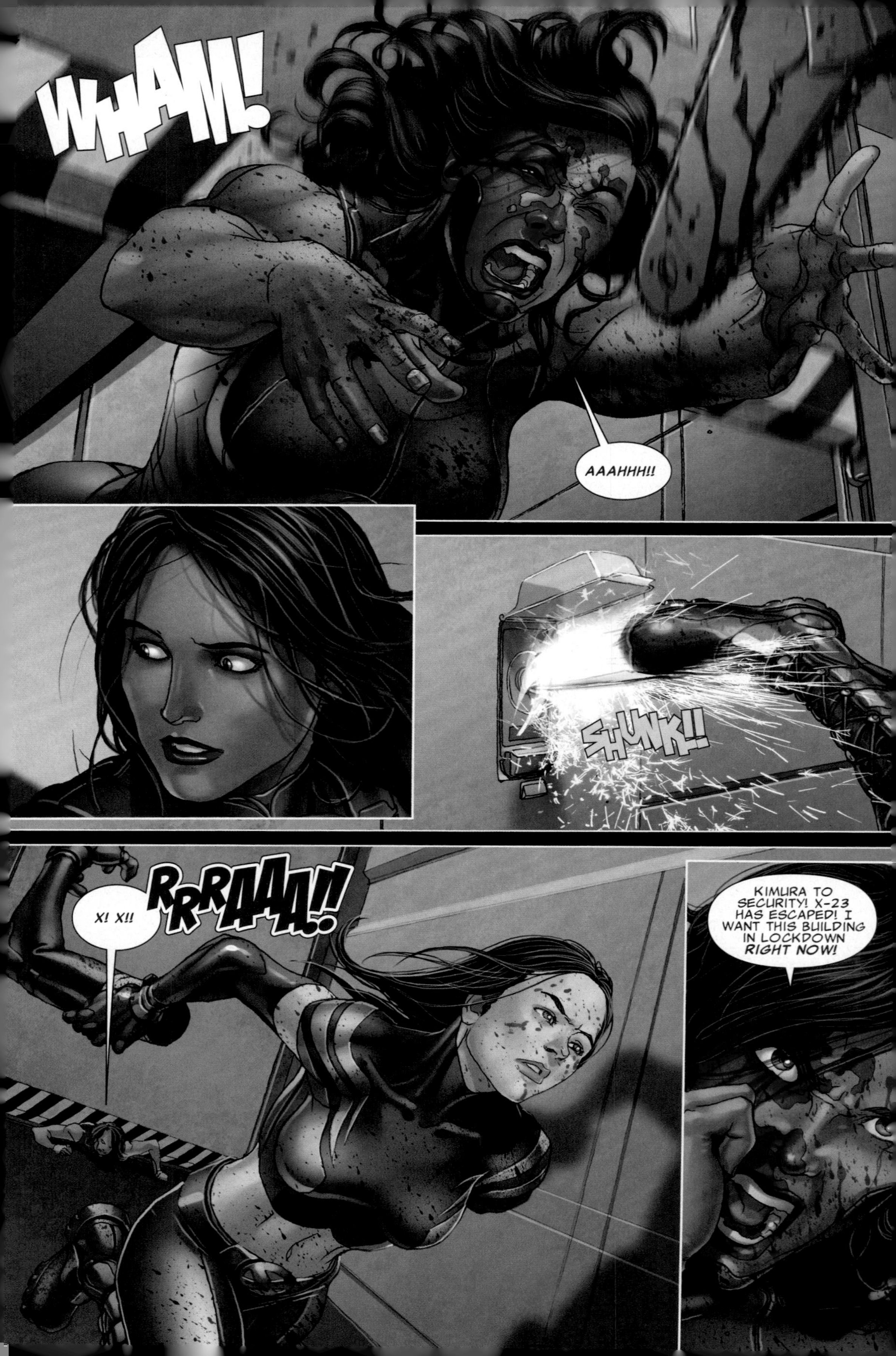
WHAM!
AAAHHH!!
SHUNK!!
RRRAAAA!!
X! X!!
KIMURA TO SECURITY! X-23 HAS ESCAPED! I WANT THIS BUILDING IN LOCKDOWN RIGHT NOW!

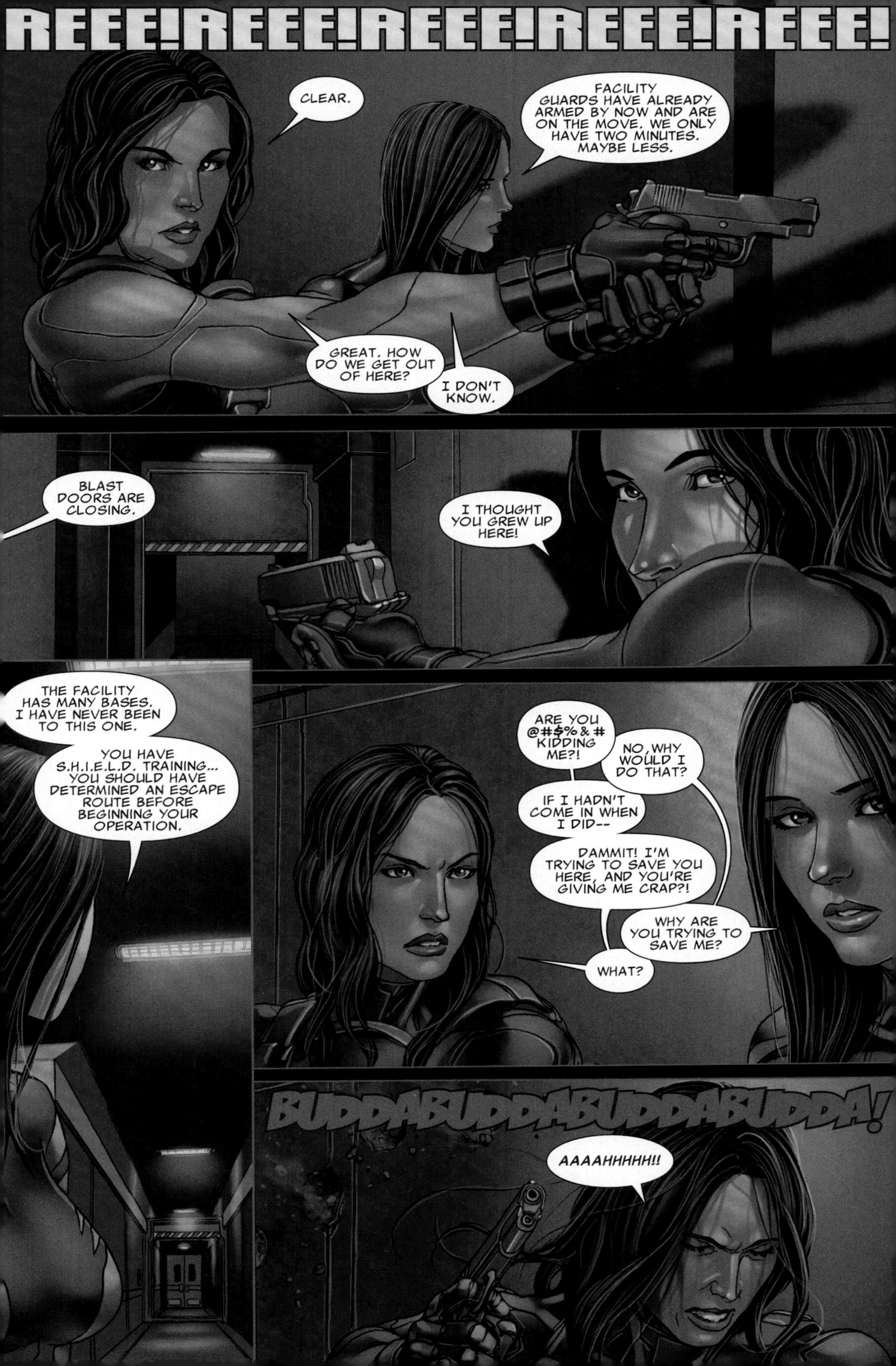
REEE!REEE!REEE!REEE!REEE!
CLEAR.
FACILITY GUARDS HAVE ALREADY ARMED BY NOW AND ARE ON THE MOVE. WE ONLY HAVE TWO MINUTES. MAYBE LESS.
GREAT. HOW DO WE GET OUT OF HERE?
I DON'T KNOW.
BLAST DOORS ARE CLOSING.
I THOUGHT YOU GREW UP HERE!
THE FACILITY HAS MANY BASES. I HAVE NEVER BEEN TO THIS ONE.
YOU HAVE S.H.I.E.L.D. TRAINING... YOU SHOULD HAVE DETERMINED AN ESCAPE ROUTE BEFORE BEGINNING YOUR OPERATION.
ARE YOU @#$%&# KIDDING ME?!
NO, WHY WOULD I DO THAT?
IF I HADN'T COME IN WHEN I DID--
DAMMIT! I'M TRYING TO SAVE YOU HERE, AND YOU'RE GIVING ME CRAP?!
WHY ARE YOU TRYING TO SAVE ME?
WHAT?
BUDDABUDDABUDDABUDDA!
AAAAHHHHH!!

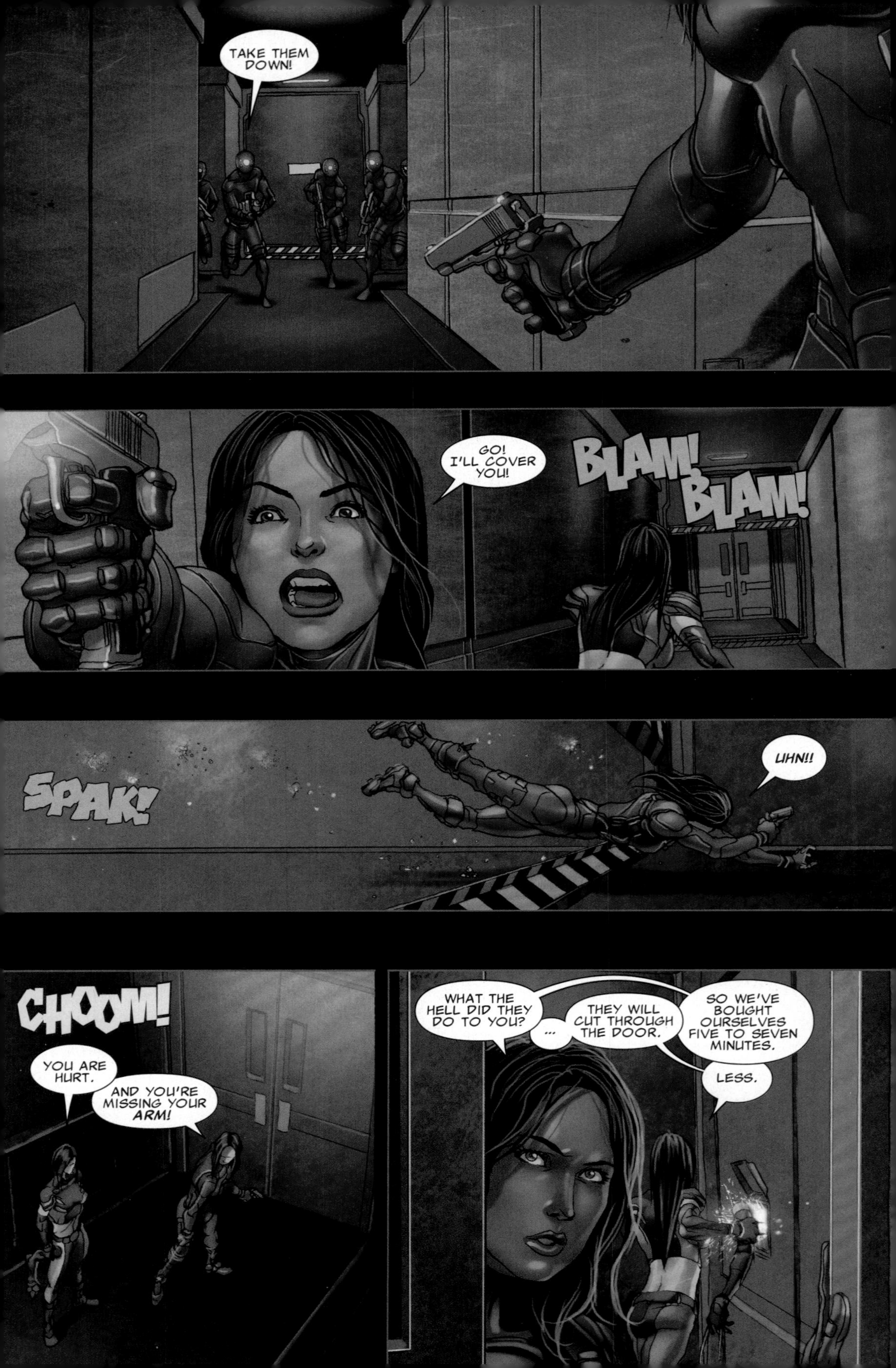
TAKE THEM DOWN!
GO! I'LL COVER YOU!
BLAM! BLAM!
SPAK!
UHN!!
CHOOM!
YOU ARE HURT.
AND YOU'RE MISSING YOUR ARM!
WHAT THE HELL DID THEY DO TO YOU?
...
THEY WILL CUT THROUGH THE DOOR.
SO WE'VE BOUGHT OURSELVES FIVE TO SEVEN MINUTES.
LESS.

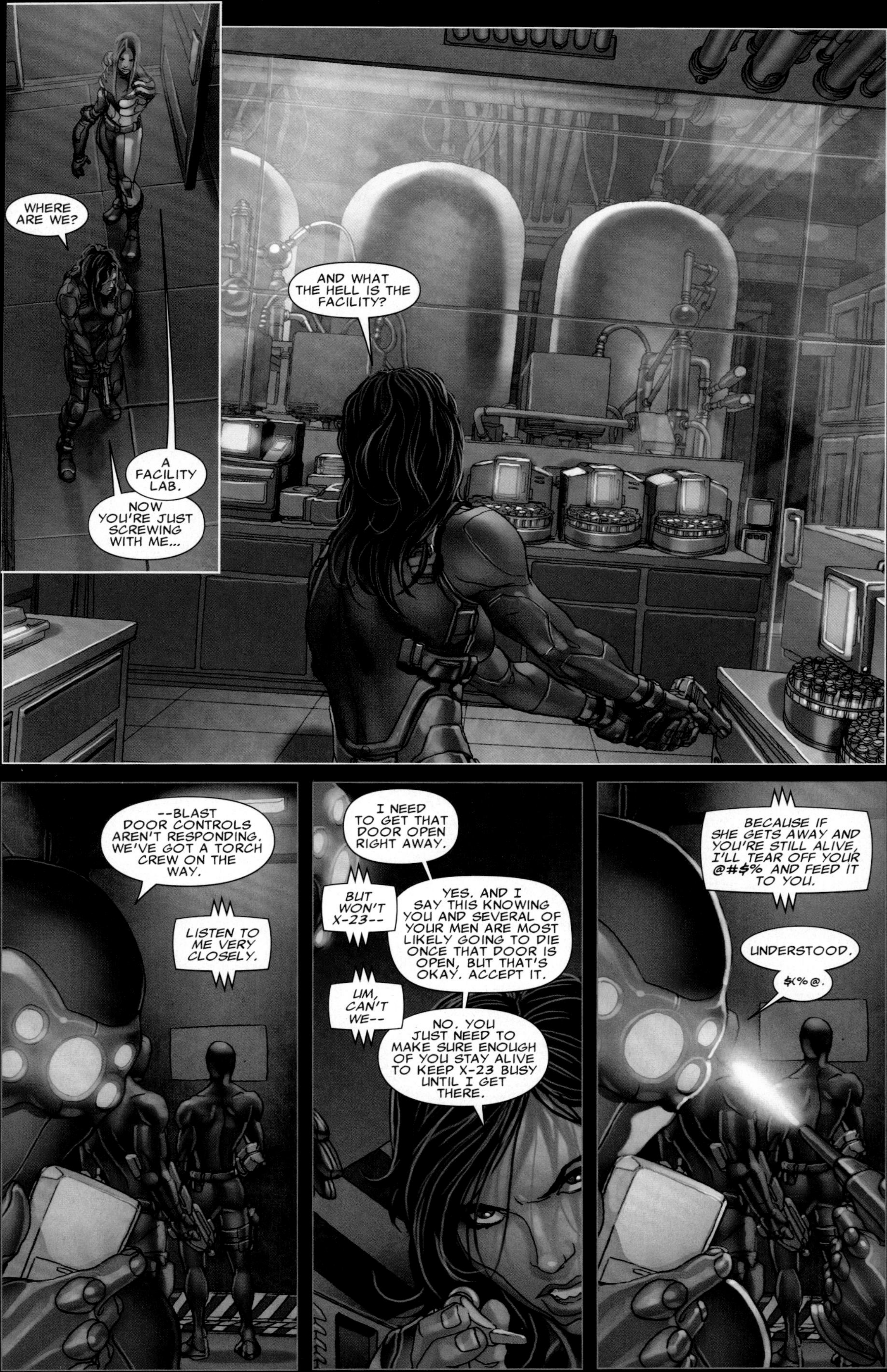
WHERE ARE WE?
AND WHAT THE HELL IS THE FACILITY?
A FACILITY LAB.
NOW YOU'RE JUST SCREWING WITH ME...
--BLAST DOOR CONTROLS AREN'T RESPONDING. WE'VE GOT A TORCH CREW ON THE WAY.
LISTEN TO ME VERY CLOSELY.
I NEED TO GET THAT DOOR OPEN RIGHT AWAY.
BUT WON'T X-23--
YES. AND I SAY THIS KNOWING YOU AND SEVERAL OF YOUR MEN ARE MOST LIKELY GOING TO DIE ONCE THAT DOOR IS OPEN, BUT THAT'S OKAY. ACCEPT IT.
UM, CAN'T WE--
NO. YOU JUST NEED TO MAKE SURE ENOUGH OF YOU STAY ALIVE TO KEEP X-23 BUSY UNTIL I GET THERE.
BECAUSE IF SHE GETS AWAY AND YOU'RE STILL ALIVE, I'LL TEAR OFF YOUR @#$% AND FEED IT TO YOU.
UNDERSTOOD.
$(%@.

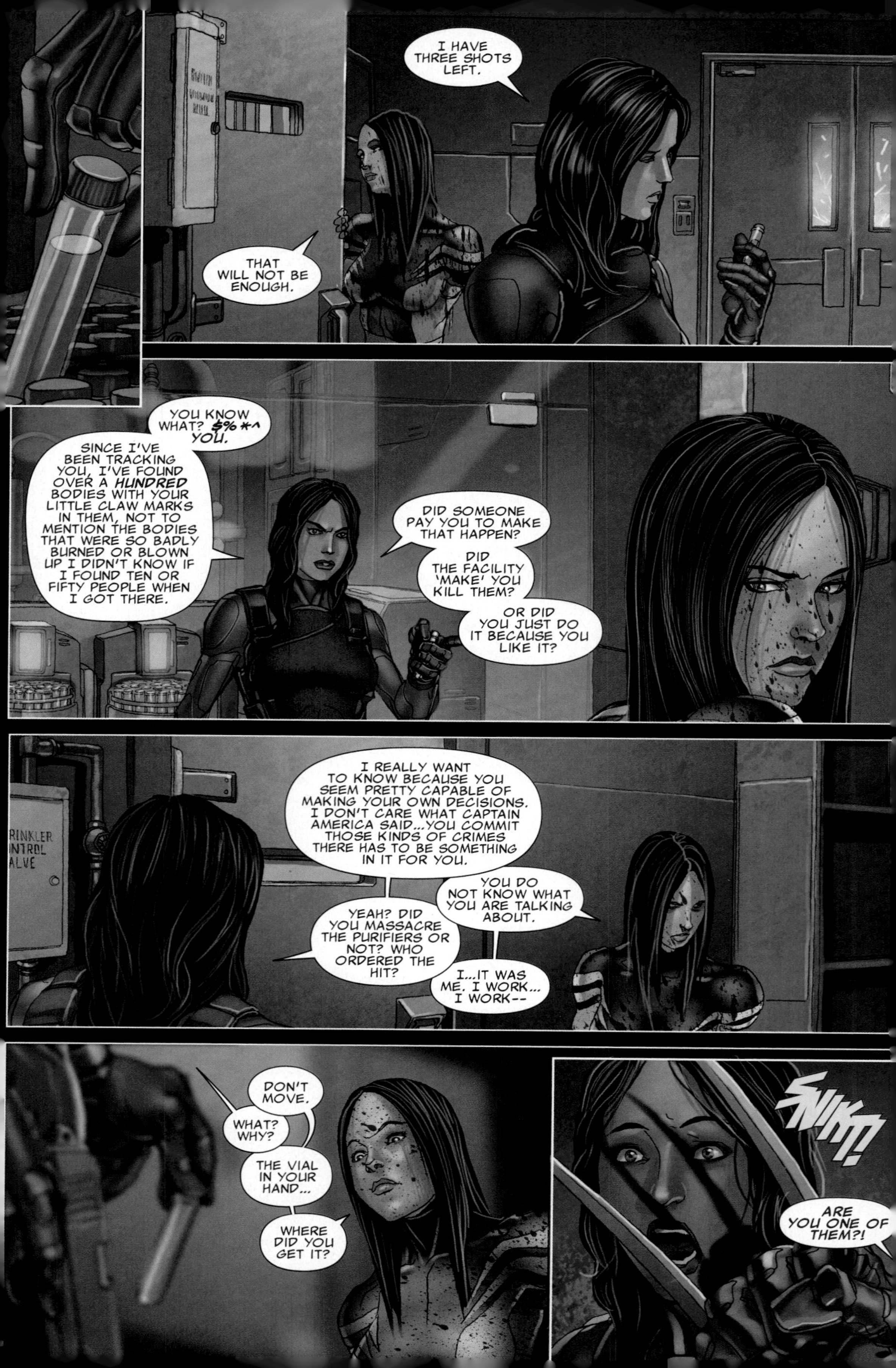
I HAVE THREE SHOTS LEFT.
THAT WILL NOT BE ENOUGH.
YOU KNOW WHAT? $%*^ YOU.
SINCE I'VE BEEN TRACKING YOU, I'VE FOUND OVER A HUNDRED BODIES WITH YOUR LITTLE CLAW MARKS IN THEM, NOT TO MENTION THE BODIES THAT WERE SO BADLY BURNED OR BLOWN UP I DIDN'T KNOW IF I FOUND TEN OR FIFTY PEOPLE WHEN I GOT THERE.
DID SOMEONE PAY YOU TO MAKE THAT HAPPEN?
DID THE FACILITY 'MAKE' YOU KILL THEM?
OR DID YOU JUST DO IT BECAUSE YOU LIKE IT?
RINKLER NTROL ALVE
I REALLY WANT TO KNOW BECAUSE YOU SEEM PRETTY CAPABLE OF MAKING YOUR OWN DECISIONS. I DON'T CARE WHAT CAPTAIN AMERICA SAID...YOU COMMIT THOSE KINDS OF CRIMES THERE HAS TO BE SOMETHING IN IT FOR YOU.
YOU DO NOT KNOW WHAT YOU ARE TALKING ABOUT.
YEAH? DID YOU MASSACRE THE PURIFIERS OR NOT? WHO ORDERED THE HIT?
I...IT WAS ME. I WORK... I WORK--
DON'T MOVE.
WHAT? WHY?
THE VIAL IN YOUR HAND...
WHERE DID YOU GET IT?
SNIKT!
ARE YOU ONE OF THEM?!

BACK THE *@%$ AWAY, RIGHT NOW!

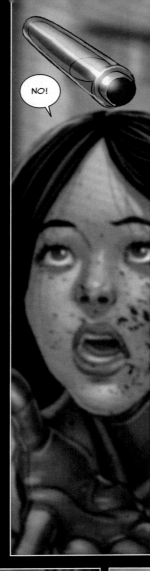

NO!

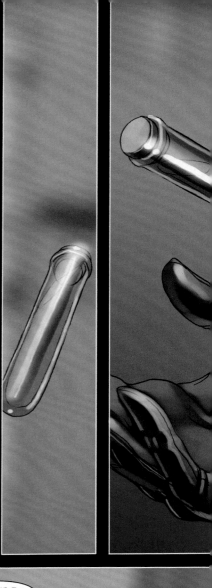

WILL YOU JUST TALK TO ME?! WHAT THE @#$% ARE YOU DOING?

THE FACILITY CREATED ME TO BE A WEAPON. KILLING WAS ALL I KNEW. I DIDN'T KNOW HOW TO SAY "NO."

BUT IF I EVER DID SAY NO, THEY HAD A WAY TO MAKE ME KILL.

A CHEMICAL TRIGGER.

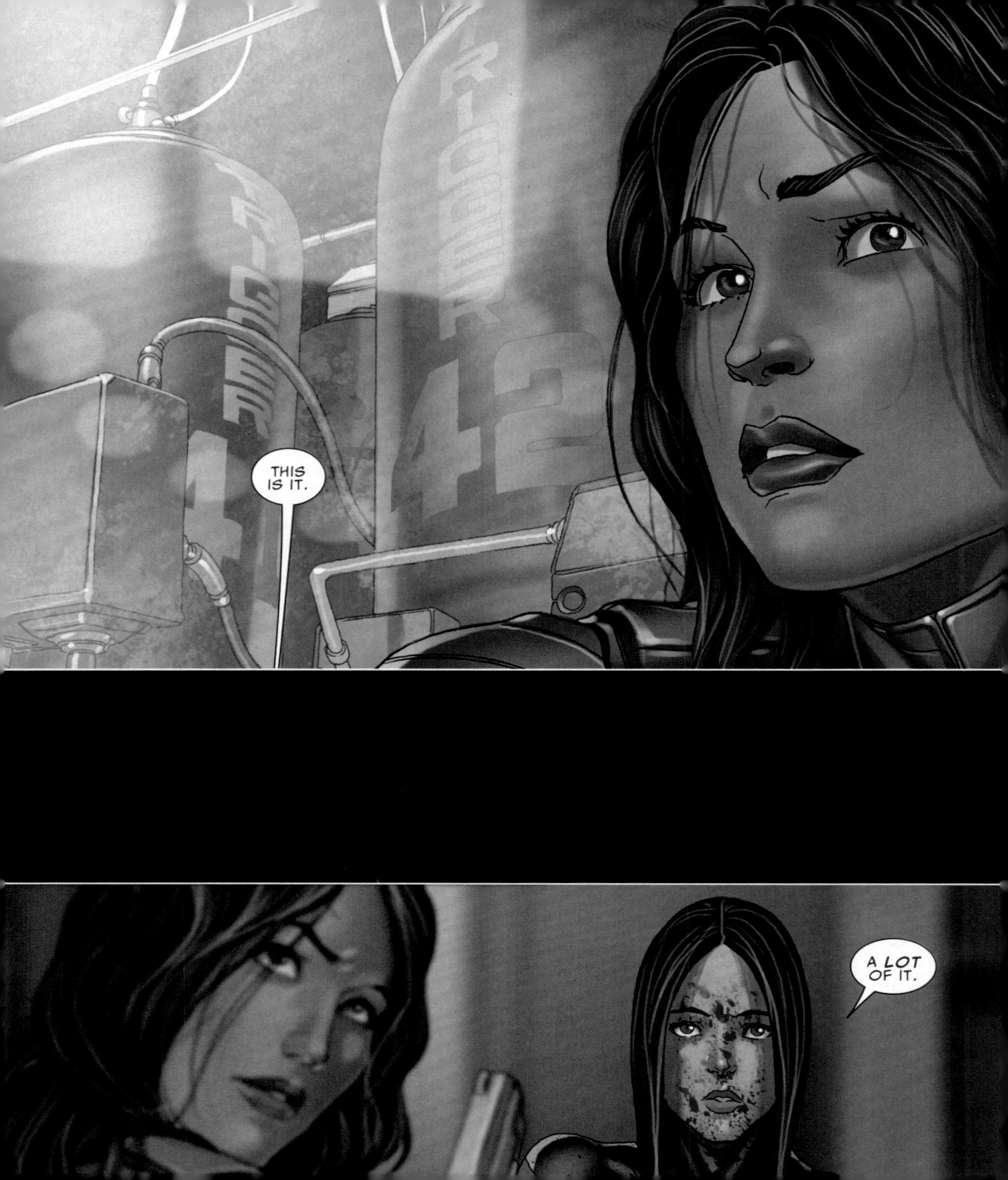
THIS IS IT.
A LOT OF IT.

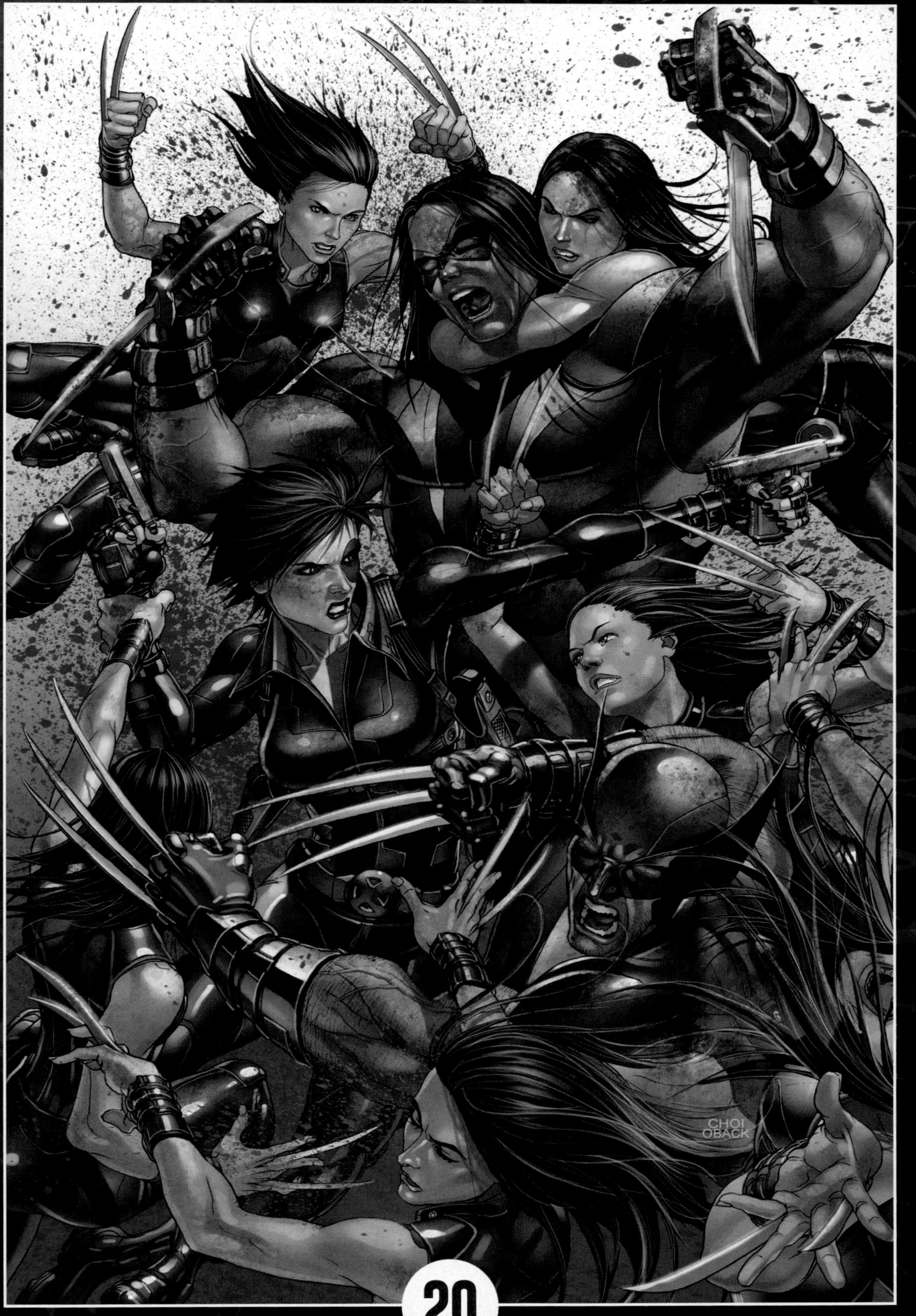
CHOI
OBACK

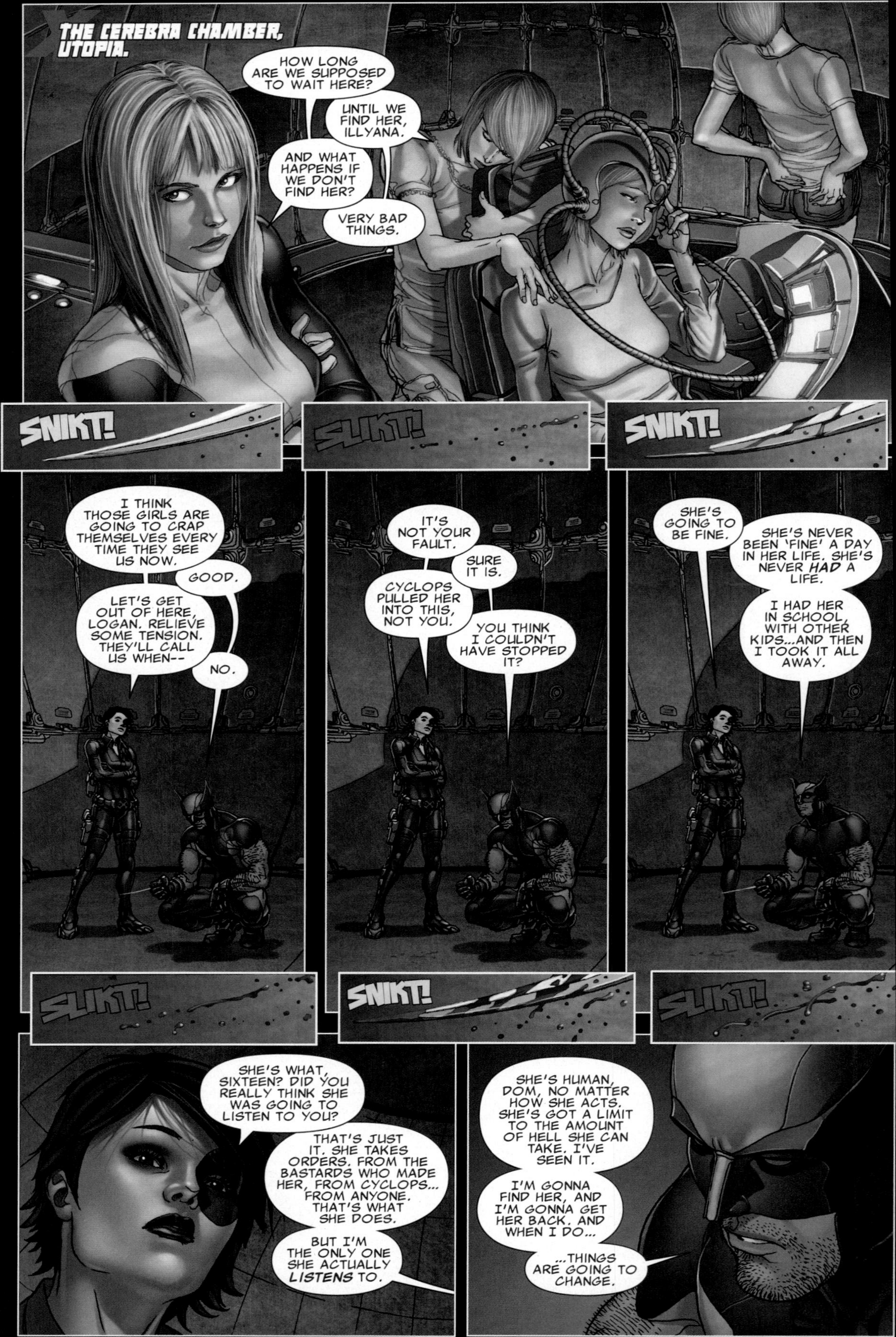
THE CEREBRA CHAMBER, UTOPIA.
HOW LONG ARE WE SUPPOSED TO WAIT HERE?
UNTIL WE FIND HER, ILLYANA.
AND WHAT HAPPENS IF WE DON'T FIND HER?
VERY BAD THINGS.
SNIKT!
SLIKT!
SNIKT!
I THINK THOSE GIRLS ARE GOING TO CRAP THEMSELVES EVERY TIME THEY SEE US NOW.
GOOD.
LET'S GET OUT OF HERE, LOGAN. RELIEVE SOME TENSION. THEY'LL CALL US WHEN--
NO.
IT'S NOT YOUR FAULT.
SURE IT IS.
CYCLOPS PULLED HER INTO THIS, NOT YOU.
YOU THINK I COULDN'T HAVE STOPPED IT?
SHE'S GOING TO BE FINE.
SHE'S NEVER BEEN 'FINE' A DAY IN HER LIFE. SHE'S NEVER HAD A LIFE.
I HAD HER IN SCHOOL, WITH OTHER KIDS...AND THEN I TOOK IT ALL AWAY.
SLIKT!
SNIKT!
SLIKT!
SHE'S WHAT, SIXTEEN? DID YOU REALLY THINK SHE WAS GOING TO LISTEN TO YOU?
THAT'S JUST IT. SHE TAKES ORDERS. FROM THE BASTARDS WHO MADE HER, FROM CYCLOPS... FROM ANYONE. THAT'S WHAT SHE DOES.
BUT I'M THE ONLY ONE SHE ACTUALLY LISTENS TO.
SHE'S HUMAN, DOM, NO MATTER HOW SHE ACTS. SHE'S GOT A LIMIT TO THE AMOUNT OF HELL SHE CAN TAKE. I'VE SEEN IT.
I'M GONNA FIND HER, AND I'M GONNA GET HER BACK. AND WHEN I DO...
...THINGS ARE GOING TO CHANGE.

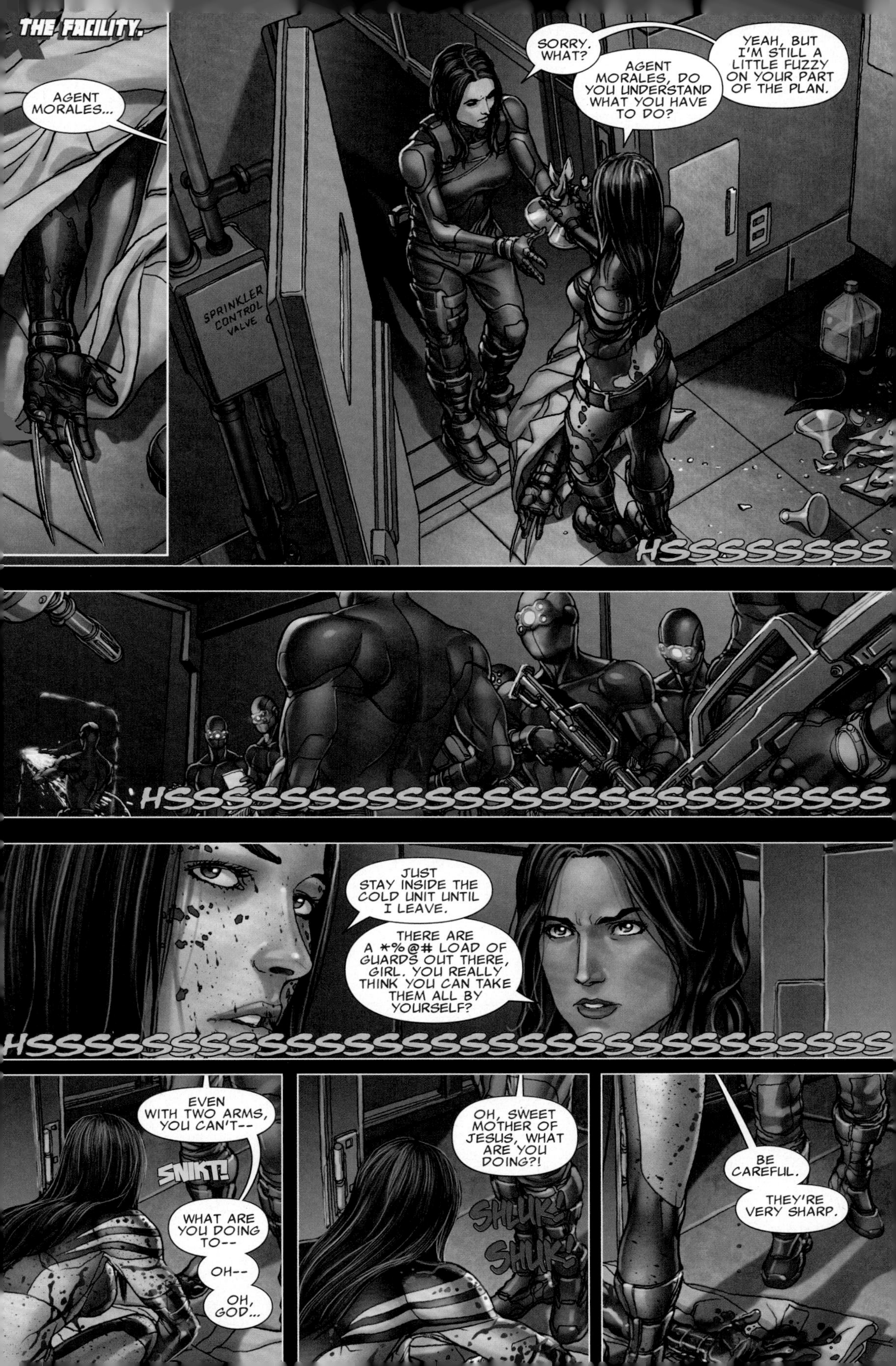
THE FACILITY.
AGENT MORALES...
SORRY. WHAT?
AGENT MORALES, DO YOU UNDERSTAND WHAT YOU HAVE TO DO?
YEAH, BUT I'M STILL A LITTLE FUZZY ON YOUR PART OF THE PLAN.
SPRINKLER CONTROL VALVE
HSSSSSSSSSS
HSSSSSSSSSSSSSSSSSSSSSSSSSSS
JUST STAY INSIDE THE COLD UNIT UNTIL I LEAVE.
THERE ARE A *%@# LOAD OF GUARDS OUT THERE, GIRL. YOU REALLY THINK YOU CAN TAKE THEM ALL BY YOURSELF?
HSSSSSSSSSSSSSSSSSSSSSSSSSSSSSSSSSS
EVEN WITH TWO ARMS, YOU CAN'T--
SNIKT!
WHAT ARE YOU DOING TO--
OH--
OH, GOD...
OH, SWEET MOTHER OF JESUS, WHAT ARE YOU DOING?!
SHUK!
SHUK!
BE CAREFUL.
THEY'RE VERY SHARP.

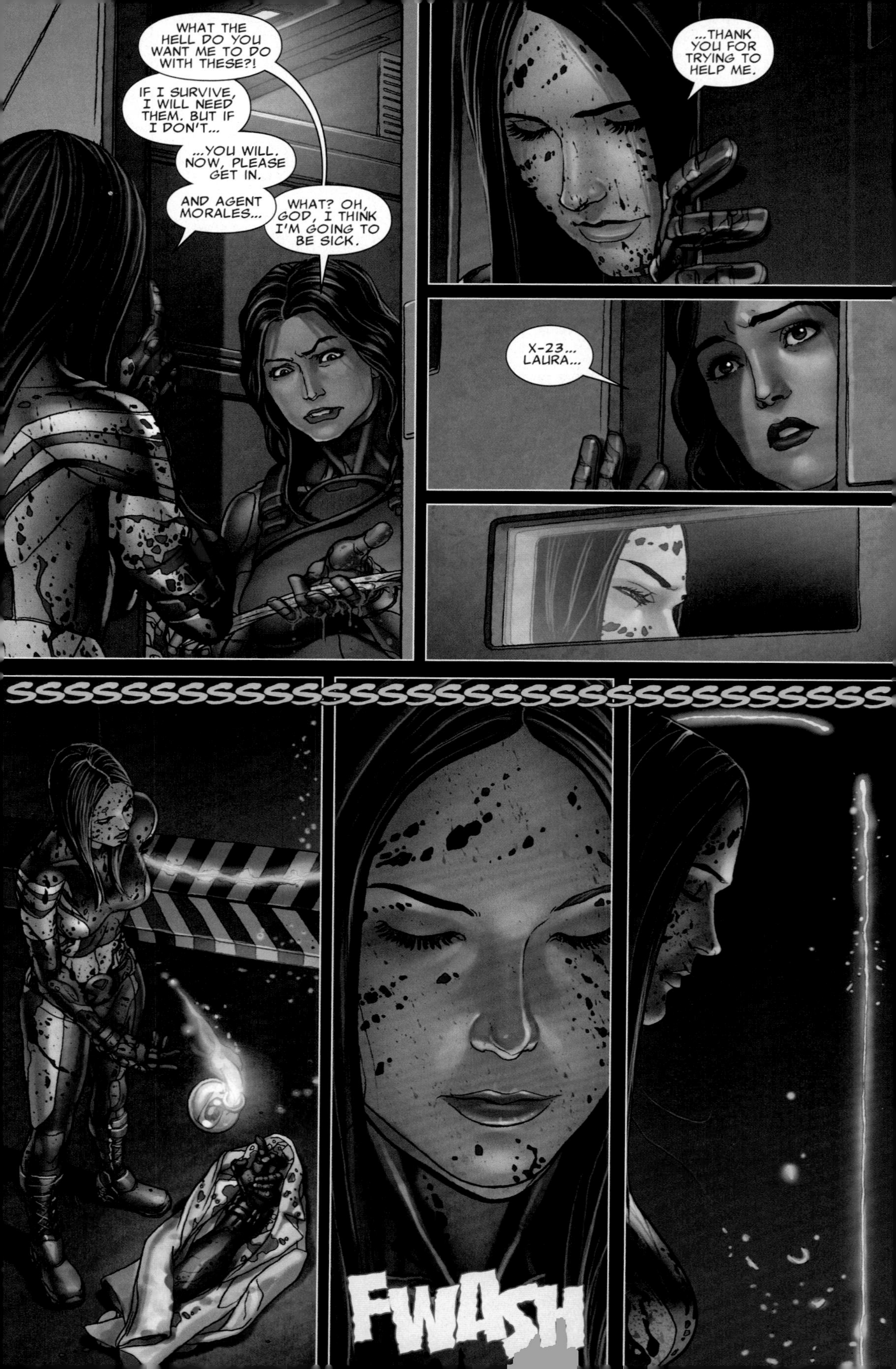

WHAT THE HELL DO YOU WANT ME TO DO WITH THESE?!
IF I SURVIVE, I WILL NEED THEM. BUT IF I DON'T...
...YOU WILL. NOW, PLEASE GET IN.
AND AGENT MORALES...
WHAT? OH, GOD, I THINK I'M GOING TO BE SICK.
...THANK YOU FOR TRYING TO HELP ME.
X-23... LAURA...
SSSSSSSSSSSSSSSSSSSSSSSSSSSSSSSSSSSSSSSSSS
FWASH

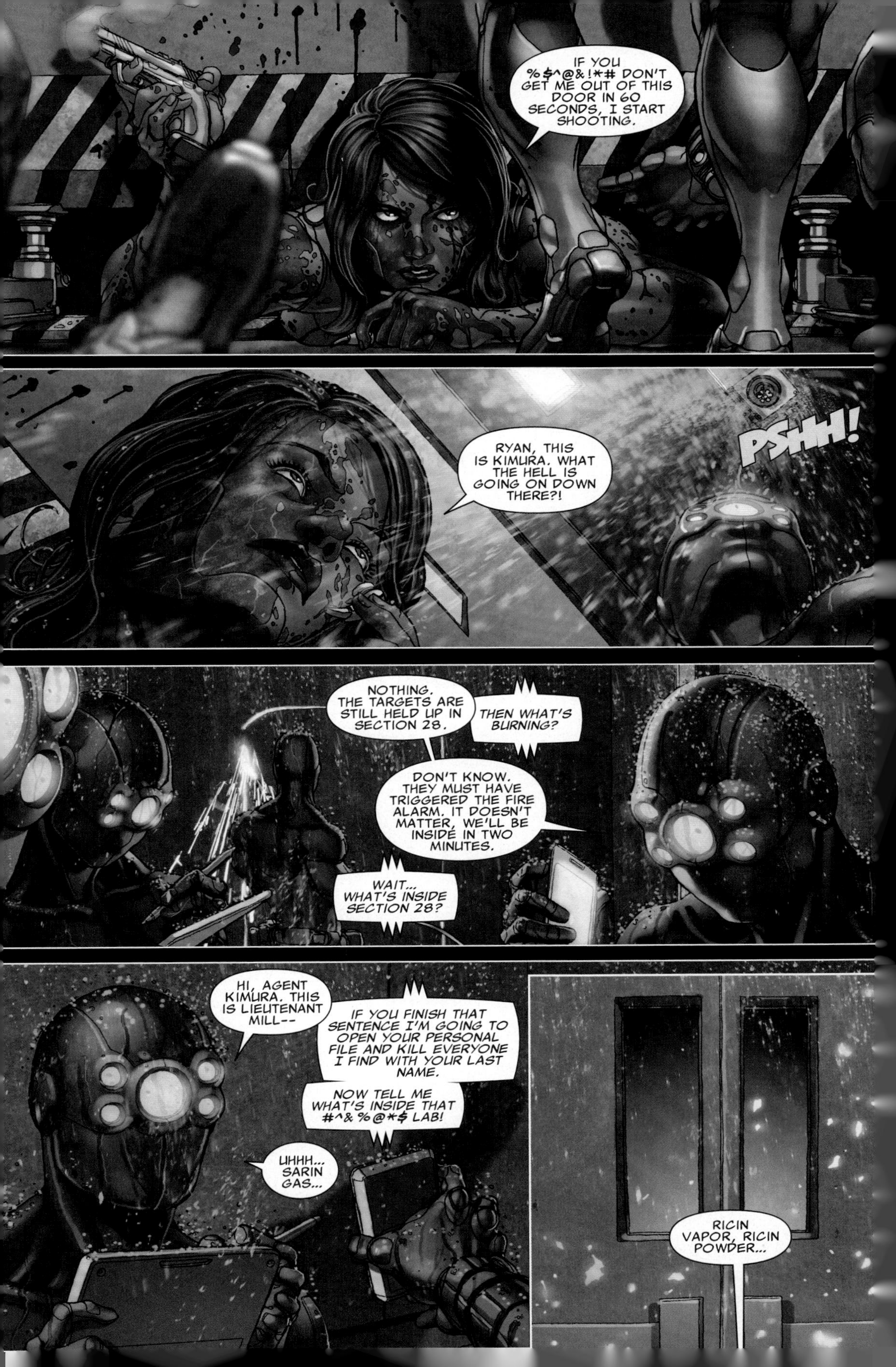
IF YOU %$^@&!*# DON'T GET ME OUT OF THIS DOOR IN 60 SECONDS, I START SHOOTING.
RYAN, THIS IS KIMURA. WHAT THE HELL IS GOING ON DOWN THERE?!
PSHH!
NOTHING. THE TARGETS ARE STILL HELD UP IN SECTION 28.
THEN WHAT'S BURNING?
DON'T KNOW. THEY MUST HAVE TRIGGERED THE FIRE ALARM. IT DOESN'T MATTER, WE'LL BE INSIDE IN TWO MINUTES.
WAIT... WHAT'S INSIDE SECTION 28?
HI, AGENT KIMURA. THIS IS LIEUTENANT MILL--
IF YOU FINISH THAT SENTENCE I'M GOING TO OPEN YOUR PERSONAL FILE AND KILL EVERYONE I FIND WITH YOUR LAST NAME.
NOW TELL ME WHAT'S INSIDE THAT #^&%@*$ LAB!
UHHH... SARIN GAS...
RICIN VAPOR, RICIN POWDER...

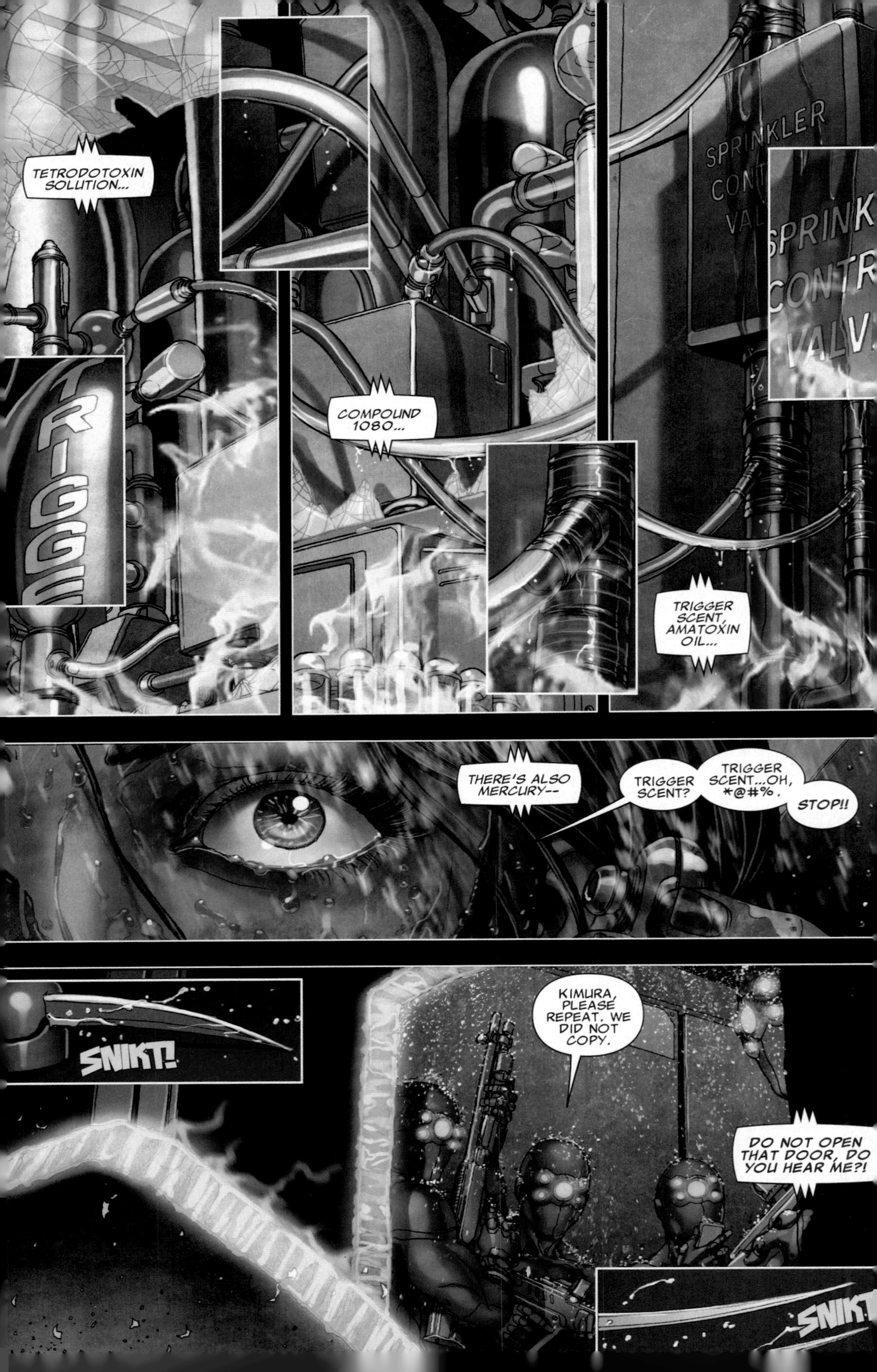

TETRODOTOXIN SOLUTION...
TRIGGER
COMPOUND 1080...
SPRINKLER CONTROL VALVE
SPRINK CONTR VALV
TRIGGER SCENT, AMATOXIN OIL...
THERE'S ALSO MERCURY--
TRIGGER SCENT?
TRIGGER SCENT...OH, *@#%.
STOP!!
SNIKT!
KIMURA, PLEASE REPEAT. WE DID NOT COPY.
DO NOT OPEN THAT DOOR, DO YOU HEAR ME?!
SNIKT

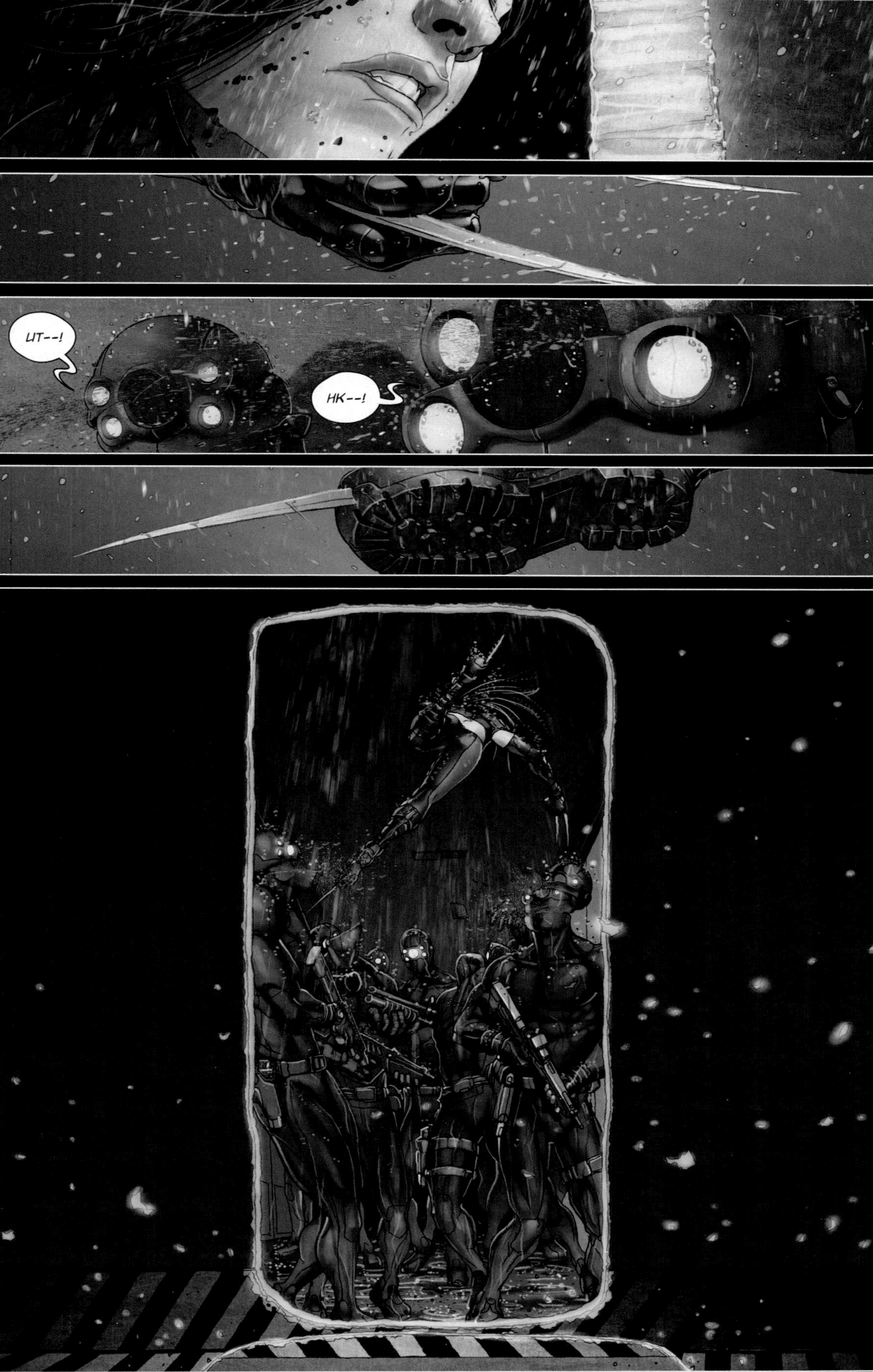

UT--!
HK--!

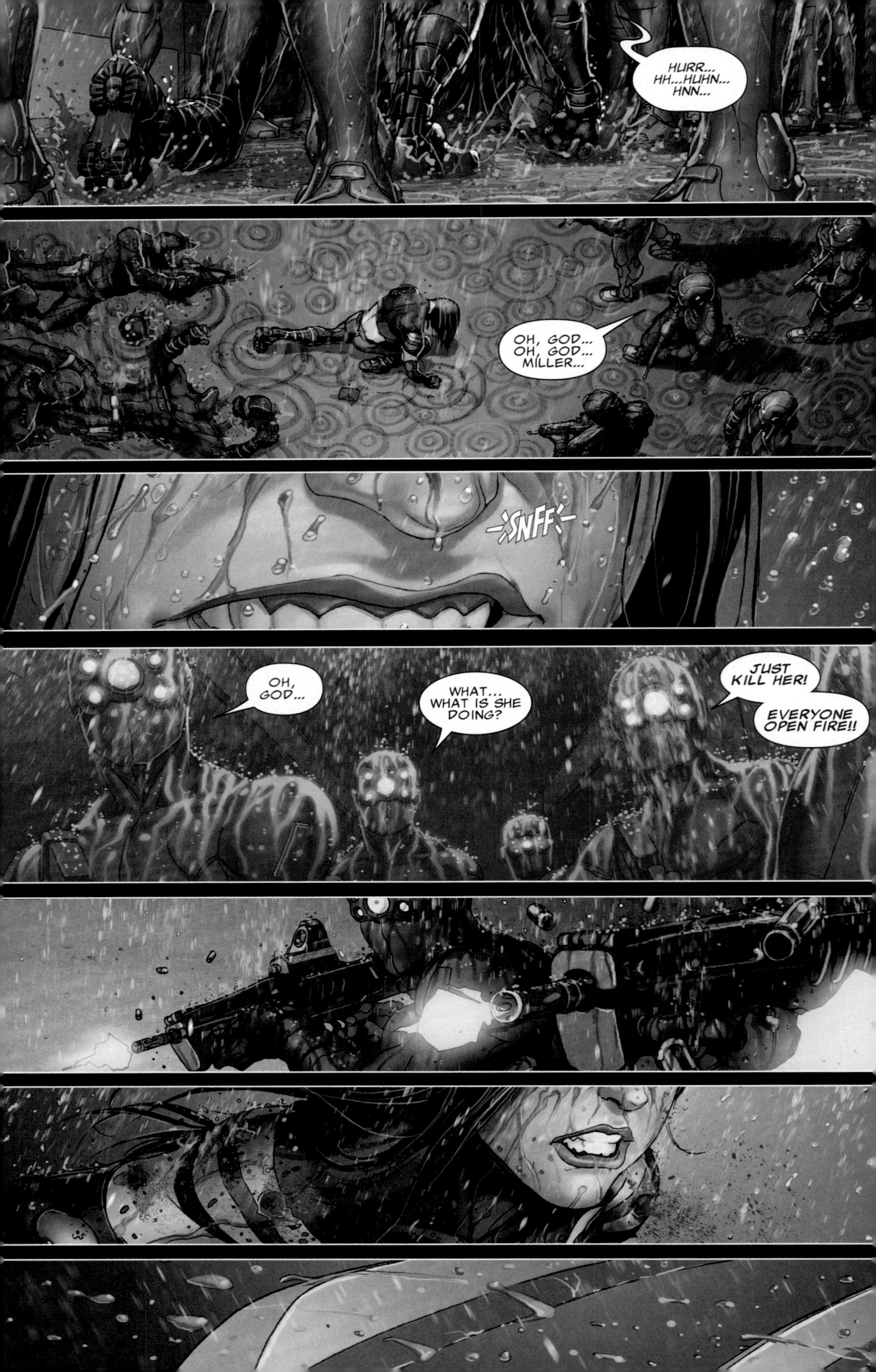
HURR... HH...HUHN... HNN...
OH, GOD... OH, GOD... MILLER...
SNFF
OH, GOD...
WHAT... WHAT IS SHE DOING?
JUST KILL HER!
EVERYONE OPEN FIRE!!

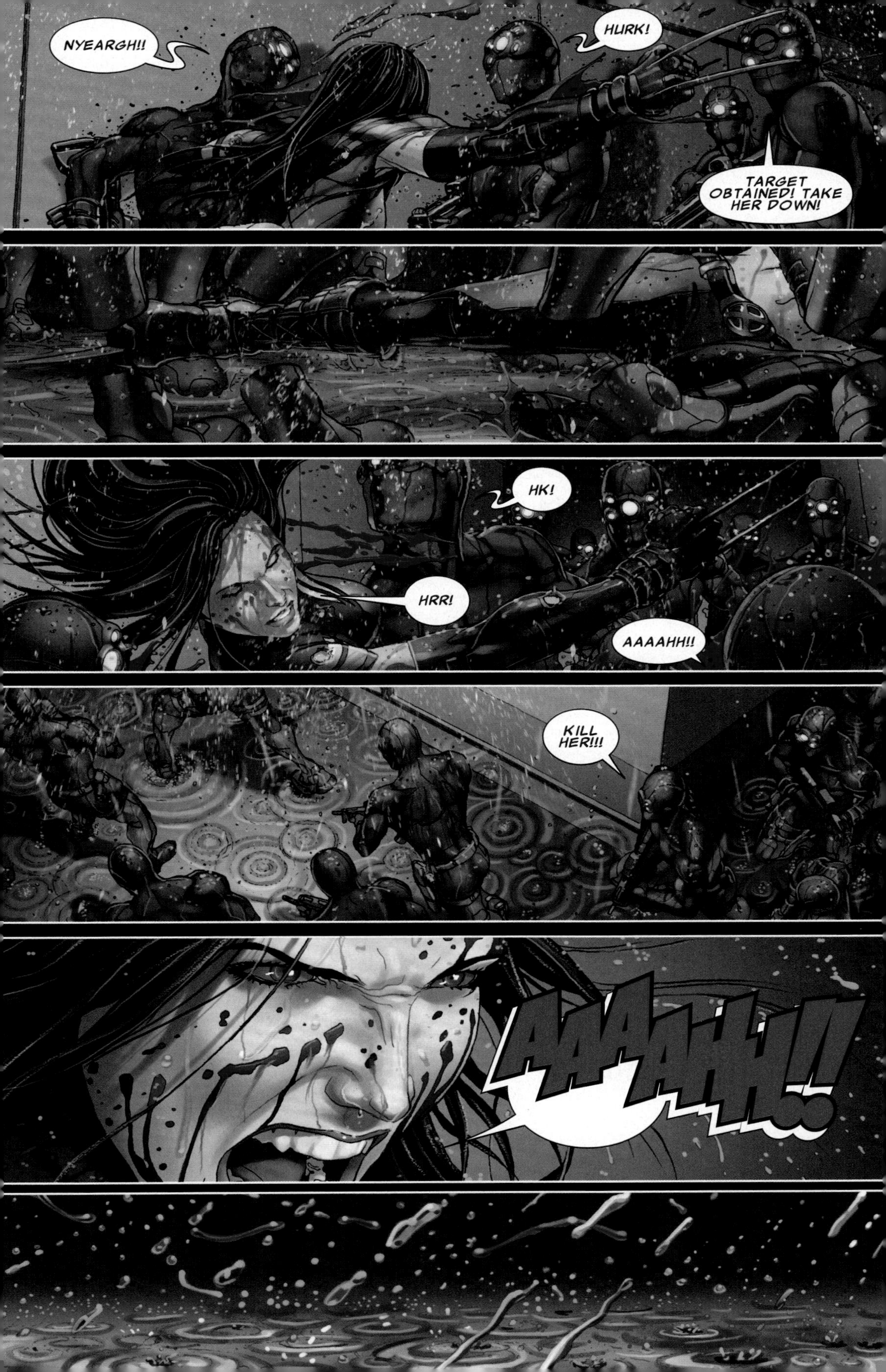
NYEARGH!!
HURK!
TARGET OBTAINED! TAKE HER DOWN!
HK!
HRR!
AAAAHH!!
KILL HER!!!
AAAAHH!!

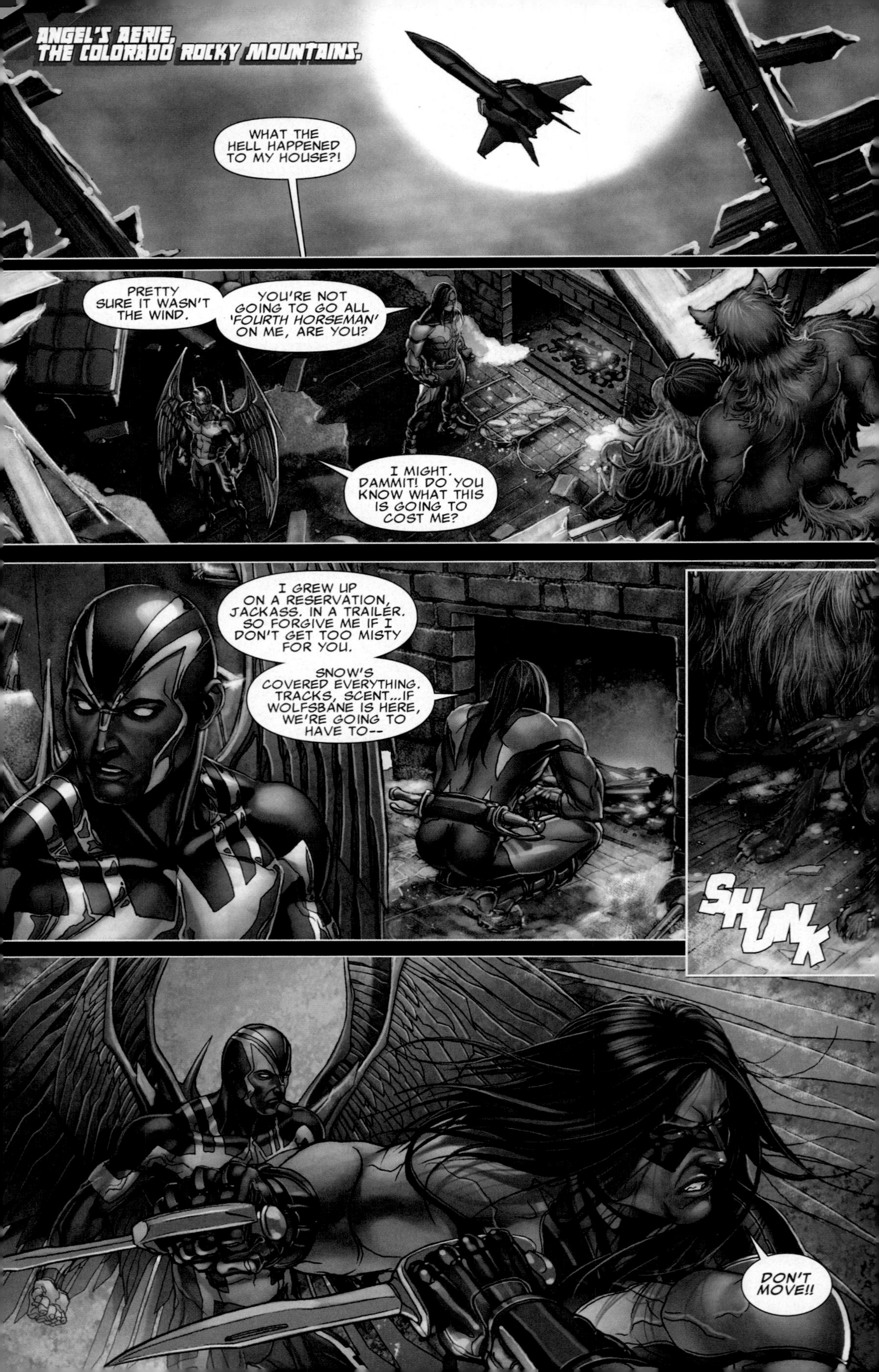
ANGEL'S AERIE, THE COLORADO ROCKY MOUNTAINS.
WHAT THE HELL HAPPENED TO MY HOUSE?!
PRETTY SURE IT WASN'T THE WIND.
YOU'RE NOT GOING TO GO ALL 'FOURTH HORSEMAN' ON ME, ARE YOU?
I MIGHT. DAMMIT! DO YOU KNOW WHAT THIS IS GOING TO COST ME?
I GREW UP ON A RESERVATION, JACKASS. IN A TRAILER. SO FORGIVE ME IF I DON'T GET TOO MISTY FOR YOU.
SNOW'S COVERED EVERYTHING. TRACKS, SCENT...IF WOLFSBANE IS HERE, WE'RE GOING TO HAVE TO--
SHUNK
DON'T MOVE!!

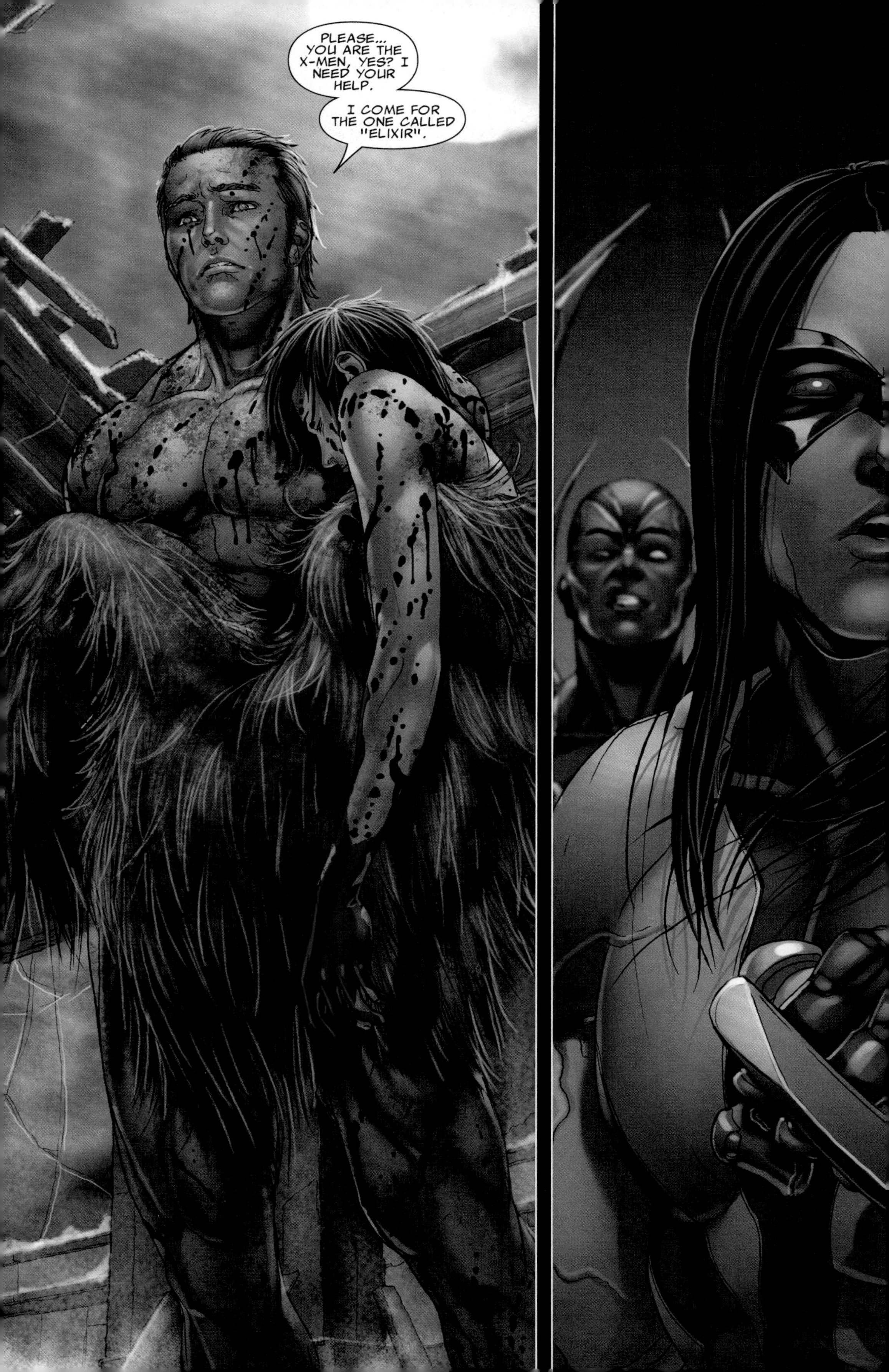
PLEASE... YOU ARE THE X-MEN, YES? I NEED YOUR HELP.
I COME FOR THE ONE CALLED "ELIXIR".

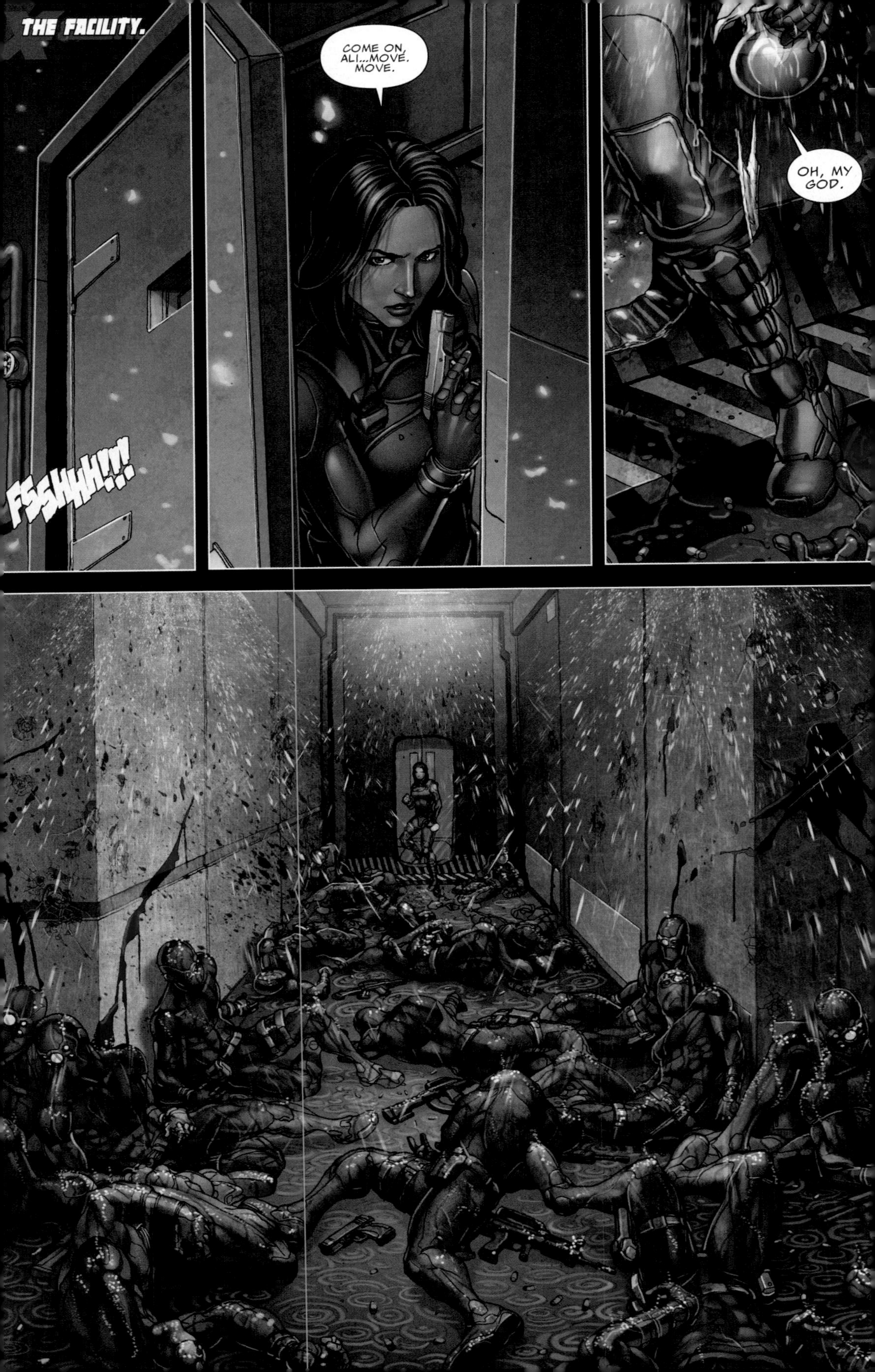
THE FACILITY.
COME ON, ALI...MOVE. MOVE.
FSSHHH!!!
OH, MY GOD.

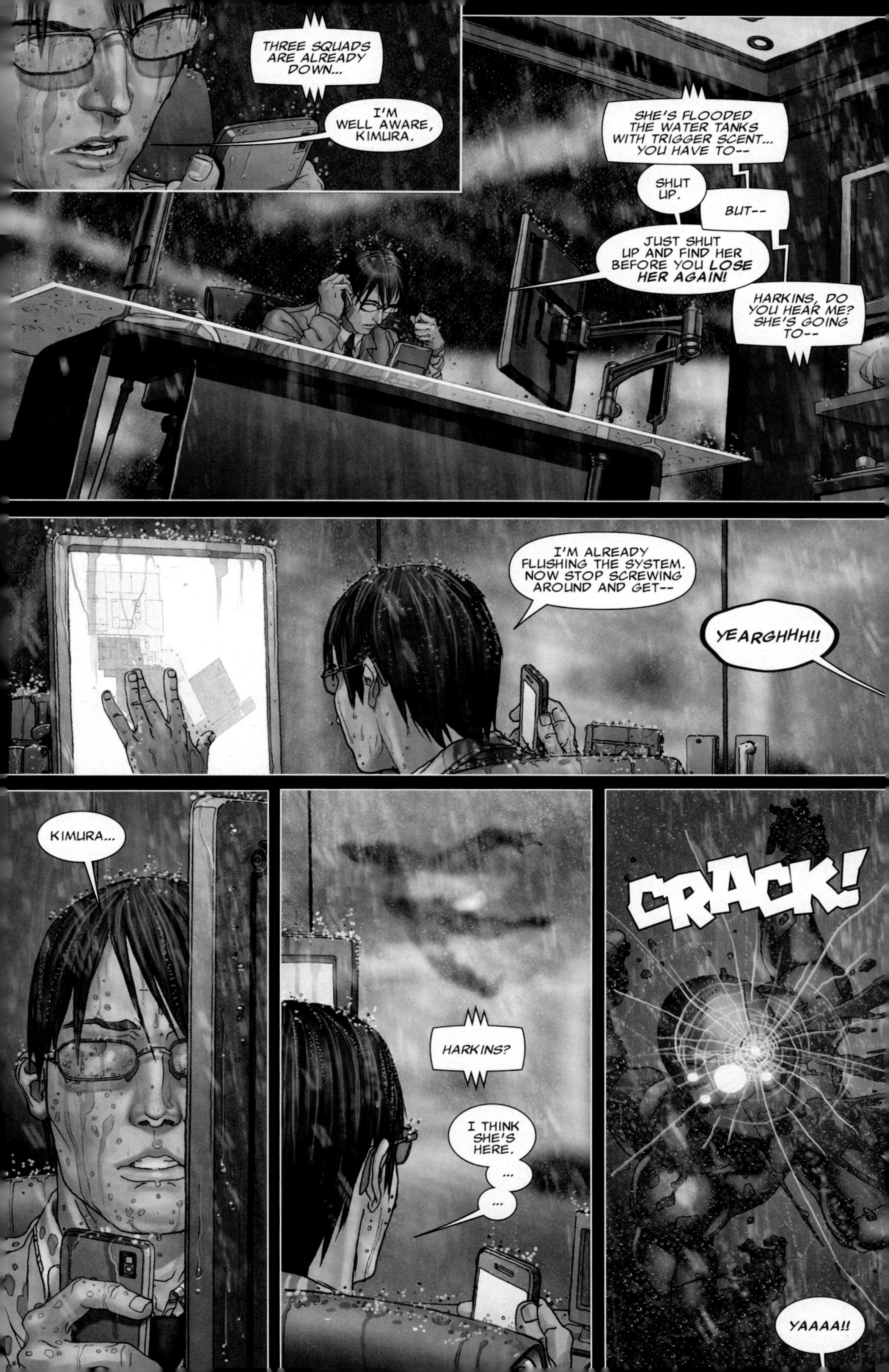
THREE SQUADS ARE ALREADY DOWN...
I'M WELL AWARE, KIMURA.
SHE'S FLOODED THE WATER TANKS WITH TRIGGER SCENT... YOU HAVE TO--
SHUT UP.
BUT--
JUST SHUT UP AND FIND HER BEFORE YOU LOSE HER AGAIN!
HARKINS, DO YOU HEAR ME? SHE'S GOING TO--
I'M ALREADY FLUSHING THE SYSTEM. NOW STOP SCREWING AROUND AND GET--
YEARGHHH!!
KIMURA...
HARKINS?
I THINK SHE'S HERE.
...
...
CRACK!
YAAAA!!

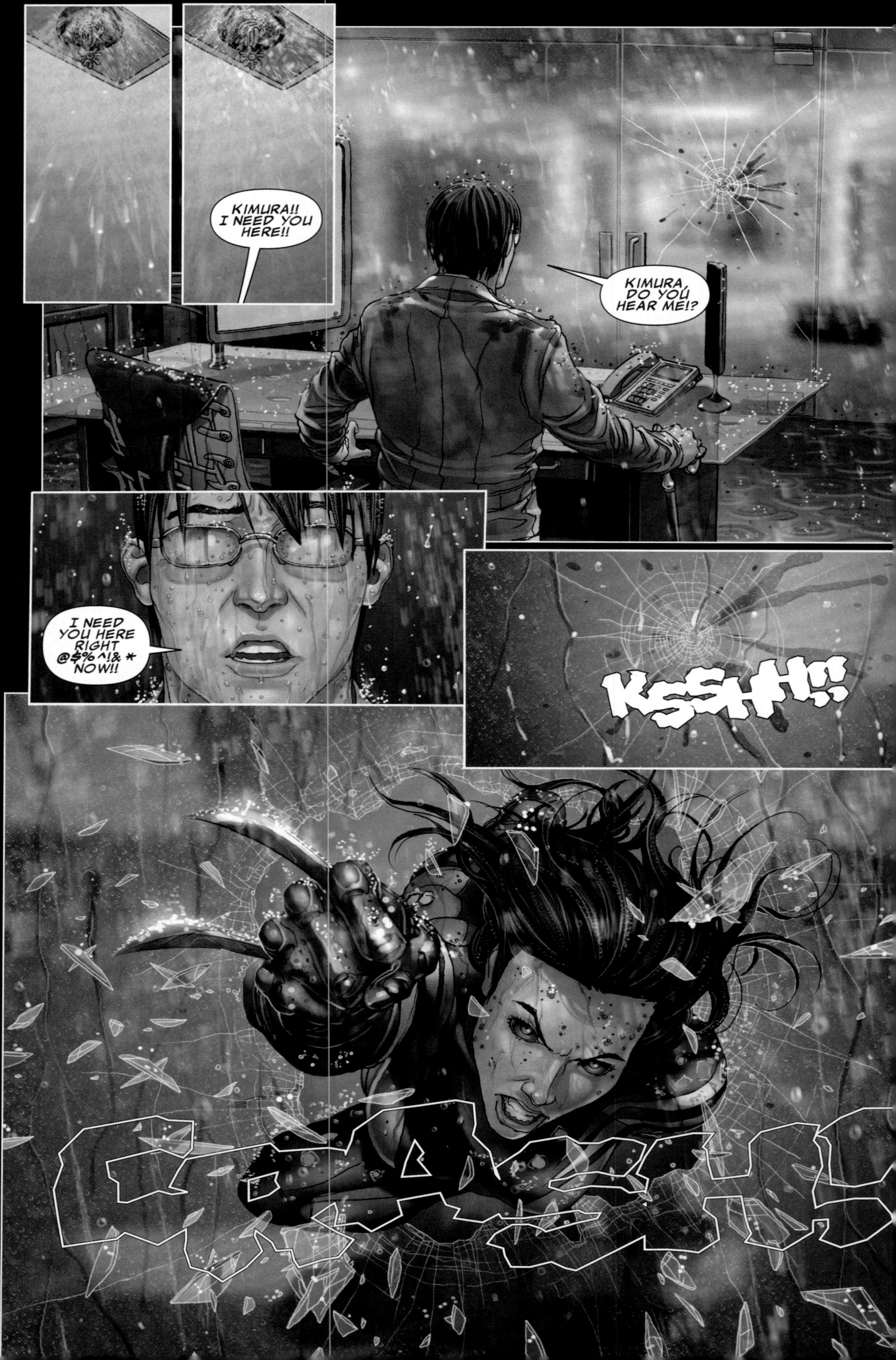
KIMURA!! I NEED YOU HERE!!
KIMURA, DO YOU HEAR ME!?
I NEED YOU HERE RIGHT @$%^!&* NOW!!
KSSH!!

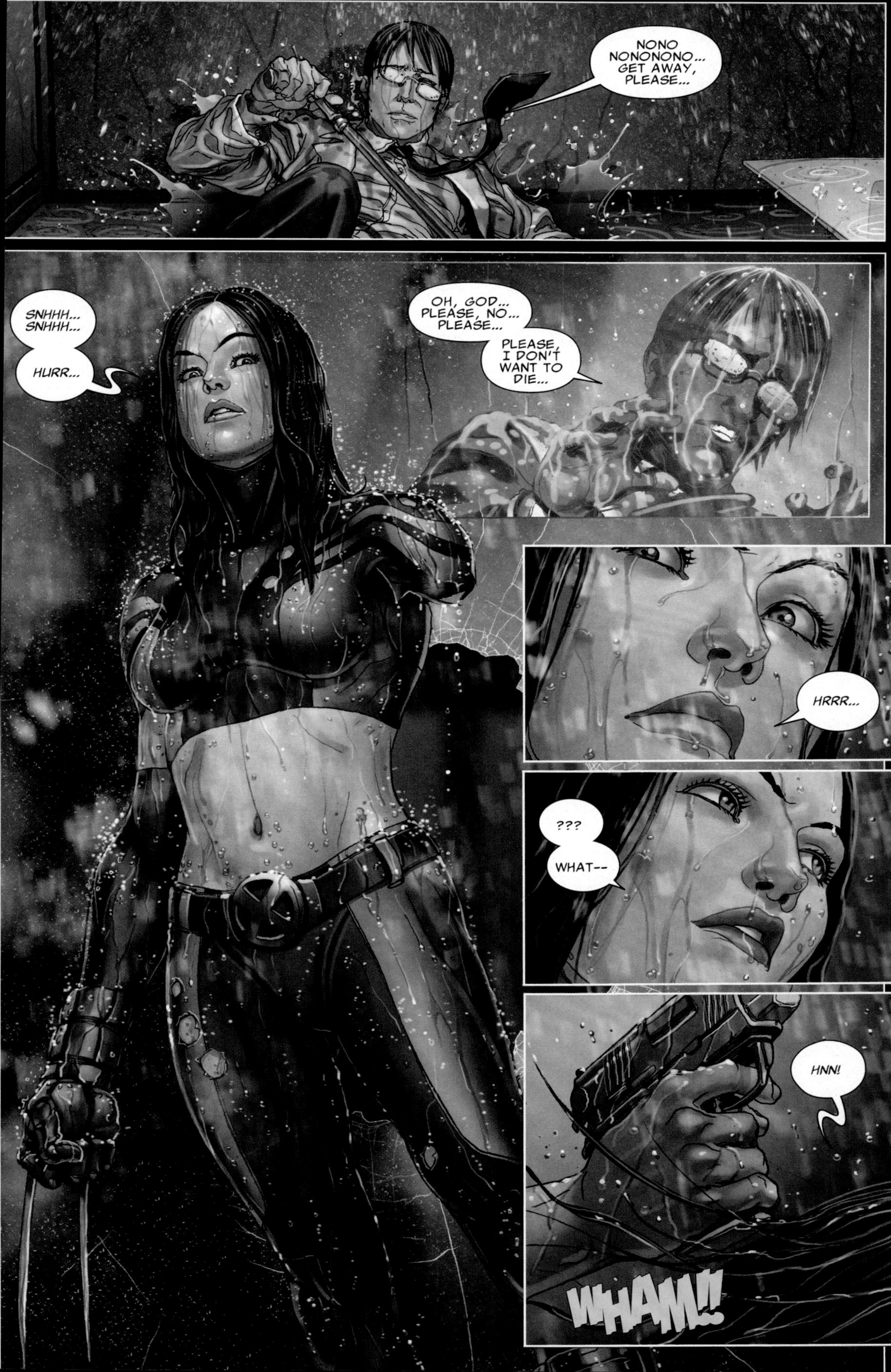

NONO NONONONO... GET AWAY, PLEASE...
SNHHH... SNHHH...
HURR...
OH, GOD... PLEASE, NO... PLEASE...
PLEASE, I DON'T WANT TO DIE...
HRRR...
???
WHAT--
HNN!
WHAM!!

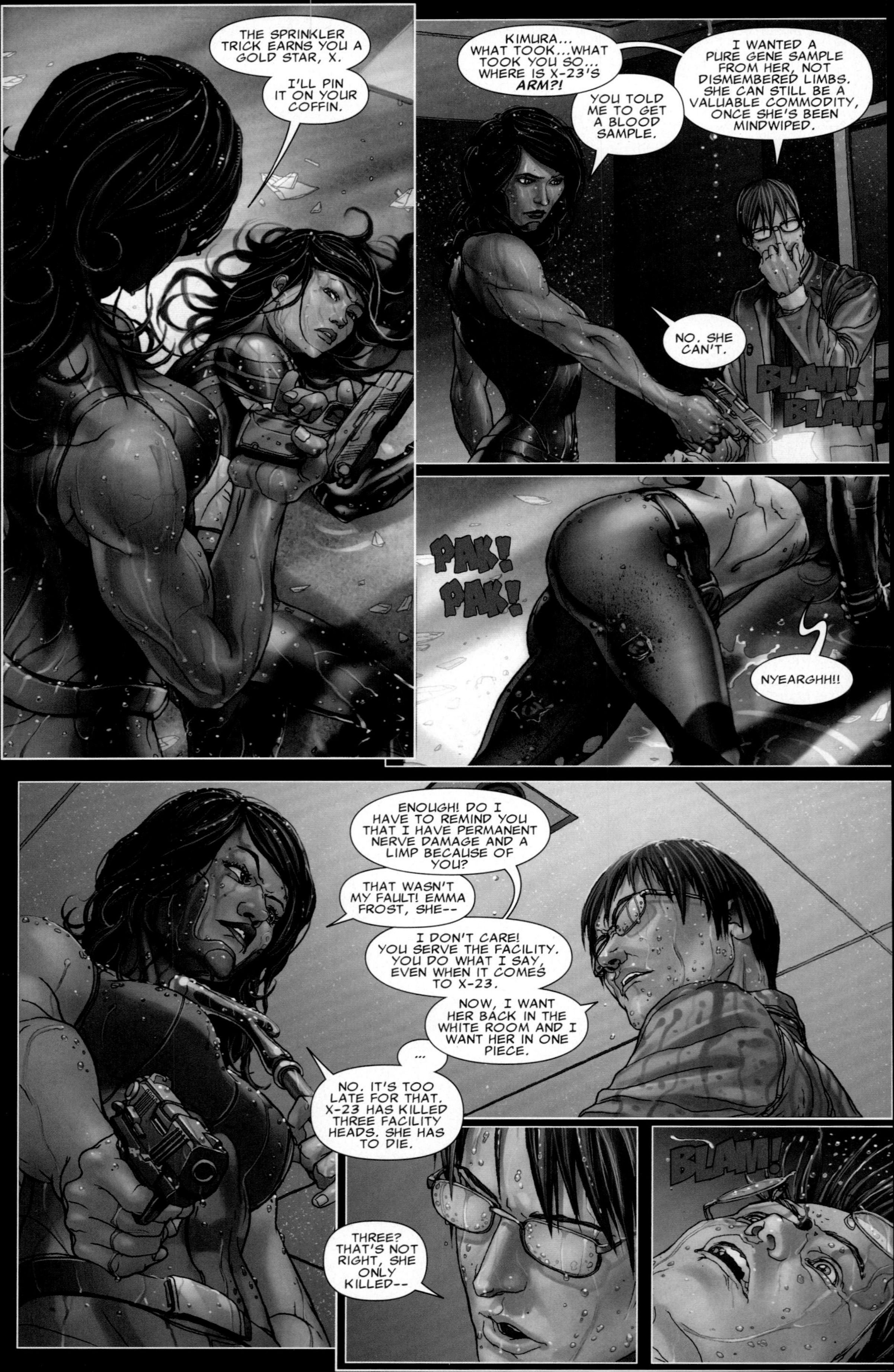
THE SPRINKLER TRICK EARNS YOU A GOLD STAR, X.
I'LL PIN IT ON YOUR COFFIN.
KIMURA... WHAT TOOK... WHAT TOOK YOU SO... WHERE IS X-23'S ARM?!
YOU TOLD ME TO GET A BLOOD SAMPLE.
I WANTED A PURE GENE SAMPLE FROM HER, NOT DISMEMBERED LIMBS. SHE CAN STILL BE A VALUABLE COMMODITY, ONCE SHE'S BEEN MINDWIPED.
NO. SHE CAN'T.
BLAM! BLAM!
PAK! PAK!
NYEARGHH!!
ENOUGH! DO I HAVE TO REMIND YOU THAT I HAVE PERMANENT NERVE DAMAGE AND A LIMP BECAUSE OF YOU?
THAT WASN'T MY FAULT! EMMA FROST, SHE--
I DON'T CARE! YOU SERVE THE FACILITY. YOU DO WHAT I SAY, EVEN WHEN IT COMES TO X-23.
NOW, I WANT HER BACK IN THE WHITE ROOM AND I WANT HER IN ONE PIECE.
...
NO. IT'S TOO LATE FOR THAT. X-23 HAS KILLED THREE FACILITY HEADS. SHE HAS TO DIE.
THREE? THAT'S NOT RIGHT, SHE ONLY KILLED--
BLAM!

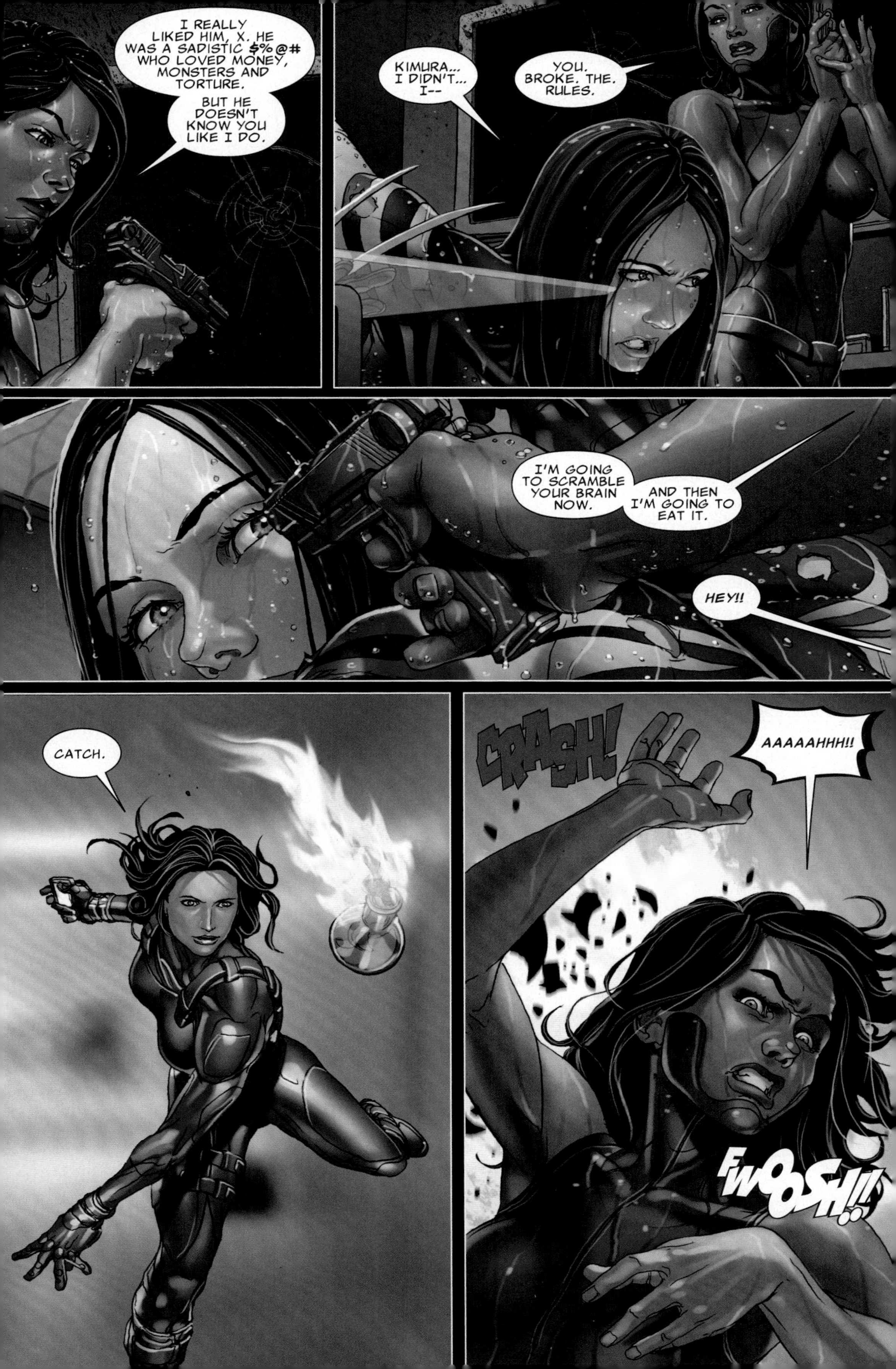

I REALLY LIKED HIM, X. HE WAS A SADISTIC $%@# WHO LOVED MONEY, MONSTERS AND TORTURE.
BUT HE DOESN'T KNOW YOU LIKE I DO.
KIMURA... I DIDN'T... I--
YOU. BROKE. THE. RULES.
I'M GOING TO SCRAMBLE YOUR BRAIN NOW.
AND THEN I'M GOING TO EAT IT.
HEY!!
CATCH.
CRASH!
AAAAAHHH!!
FWOOSH!!

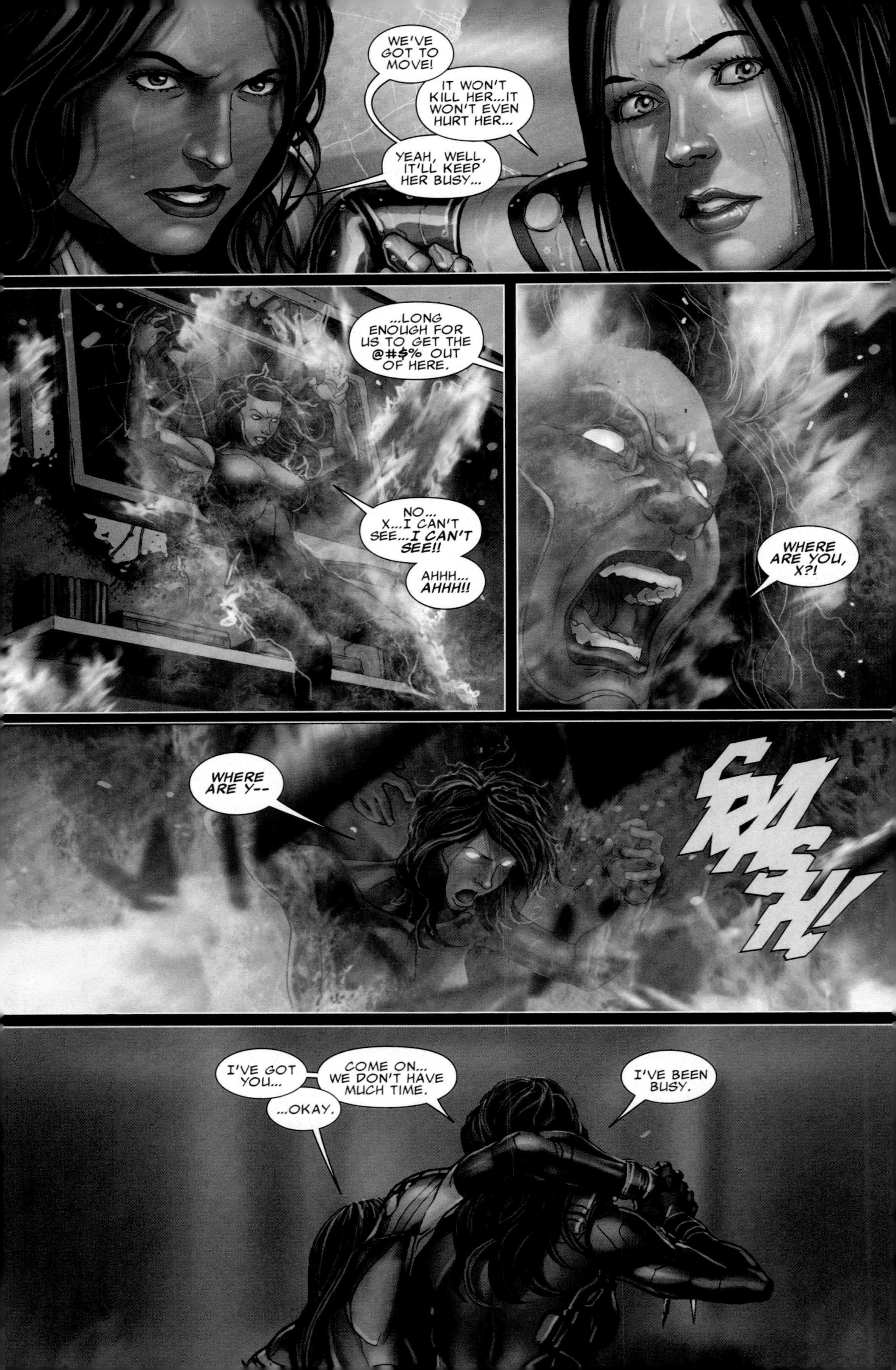
WE'VE GOT TO MOVE!
IT WON'T KILL HER...IT WON'T EVEN HURT HER...
YEAH, WELL, IT'LL KEEP HER BUSY...
...LONG ENOUGH FOR US TO GET THE @#$% OUT OF HERE.
NO... X...I CAN'T SEE...I CAN'T SEE!!
AHHH... AHHH!!
WHERE ARE YOU, X?!
WHERE ARE Y--
CRASH!
I'VE GOT YOU...
...OKAY.
COME ON... WE DON'T HAVE MUCH TIME.
I'VE BEEN BUSY.

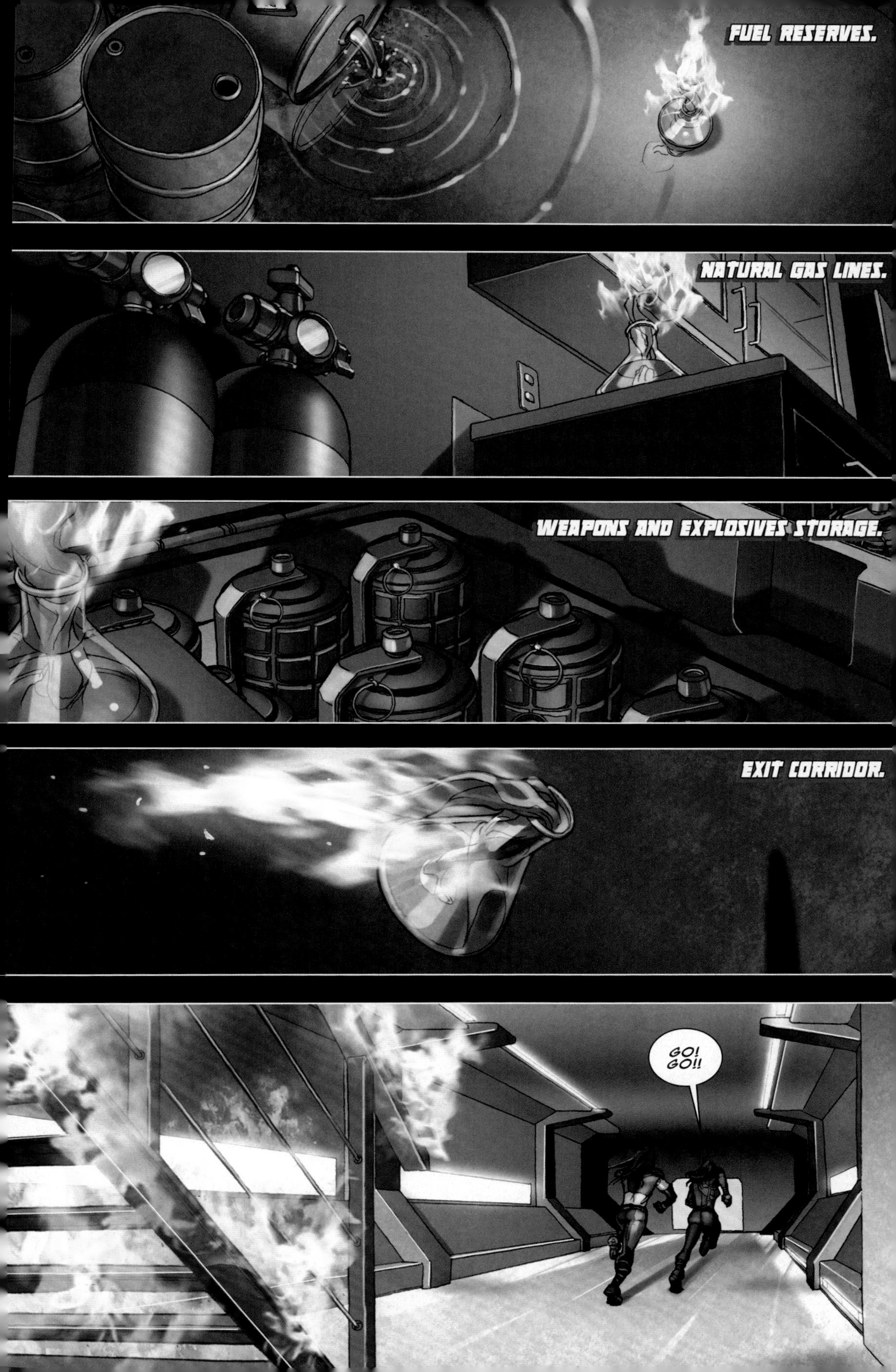
FUEL RESERVES.
NATURAL GAS LINES.
WEAPONS AND EXPLOSIVES STORAGE.
EXIT CORRIDOR.
GO! GO!!

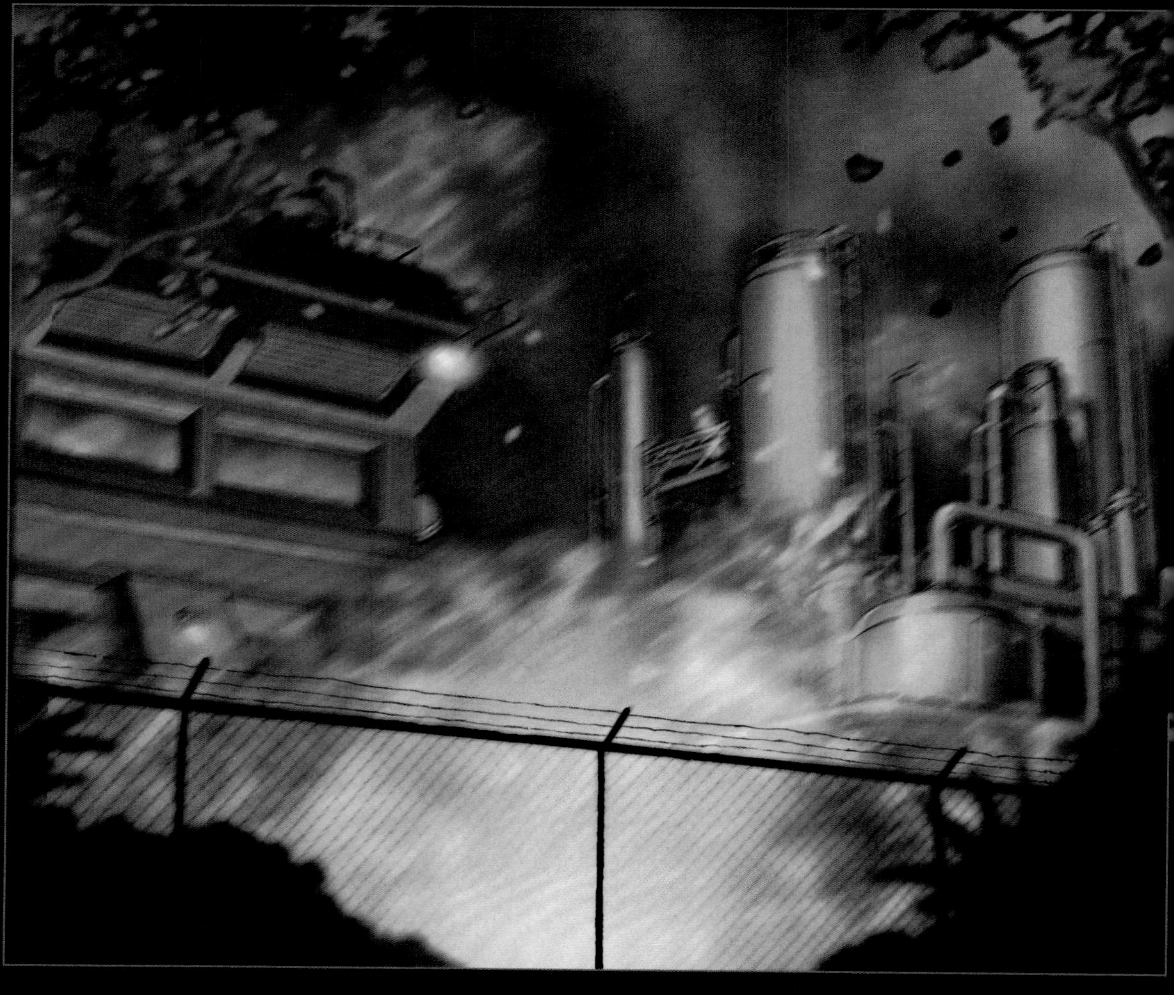

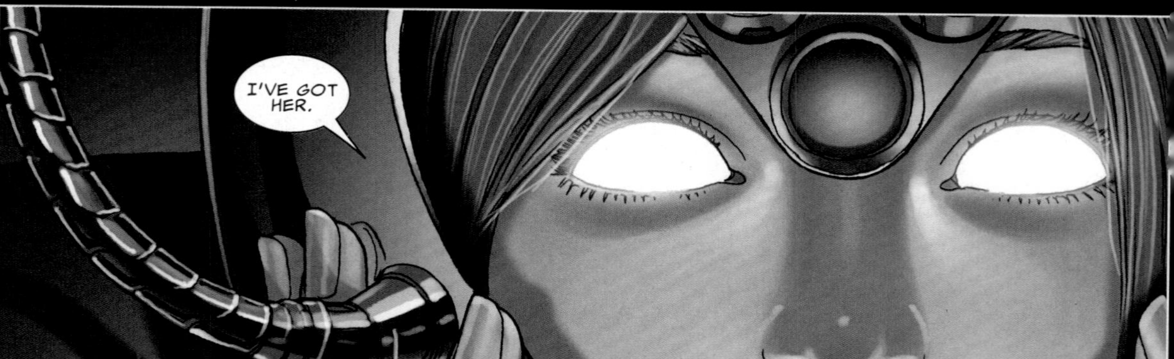
I'VE GOT HER.

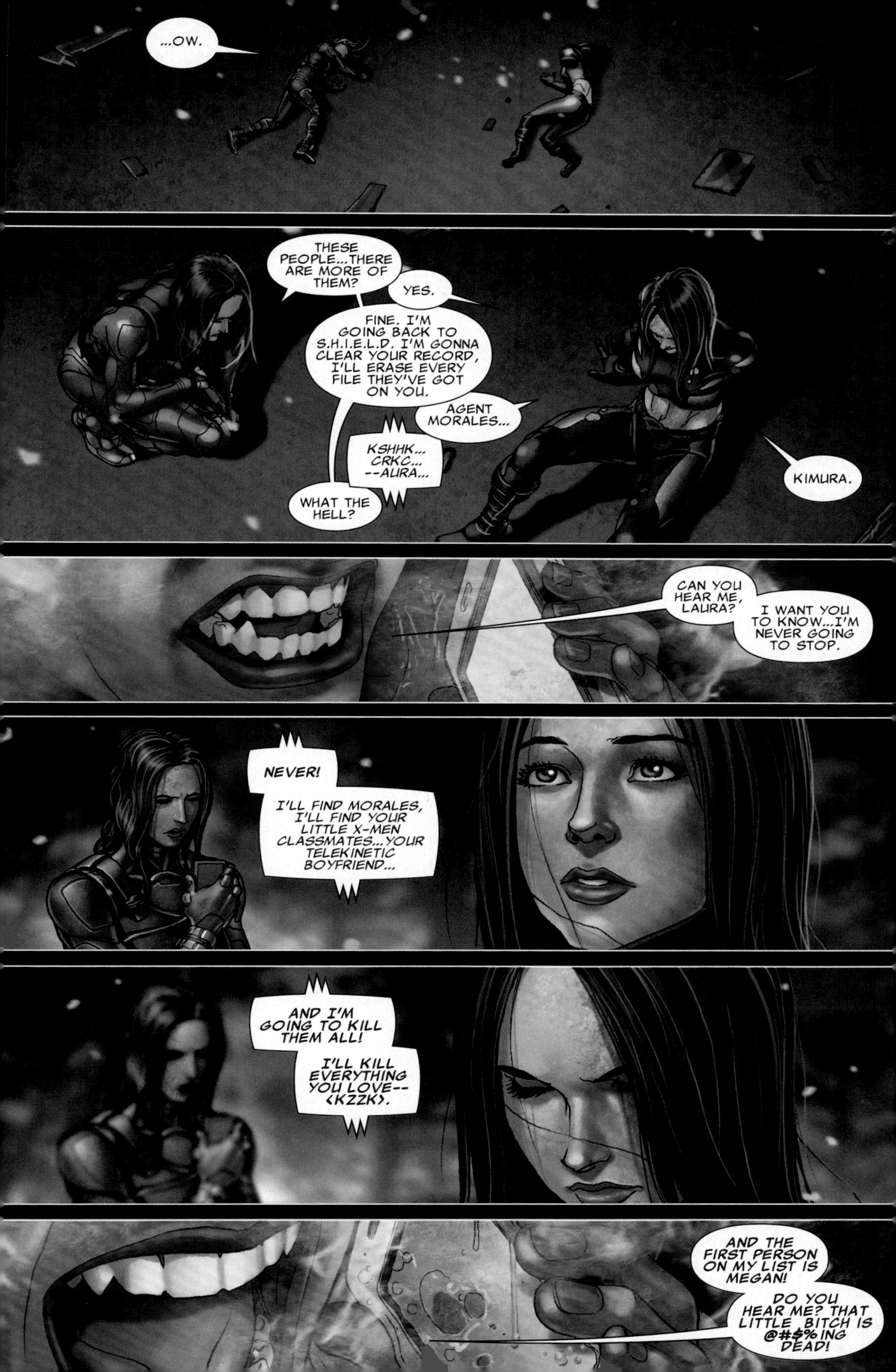
...OW.
THESE PEOPLE...THERE ARE MORE OF THEM?
YES.
FINE. I'M GOING BACK TO S.H.I.E.L.D. I'M GONNA CLEAR YOUR RECORD, I'LL ERASE EVERY FILE THEY'VE GOT ON YOU.
AGENT MORALES...
KSHHK... CRKC... --AURA...
WHAT THE HELL?
KIMURA.
CAN YOU HEAR ME, LAURA?
I WANT YOU TO KNOW...I'M NEVER GOING TO STOP.
NEVER!
I'LL FIND MORALES, I'LL FIND YOUR LITTLE X-MEN CLASSMATES...YOUR TELEKINETIC BOYFRIEND...
AND I'M GOING TO KILL THEM ALL!
I'LL KILL EVERYTHING YOU LOVE-- <KZZK>.
AND THE FIRST PERSON ON MY LIST IS MEGAN!
DO YOU HEAR ME? THAT LITTLE BITCH IS @#$%ING DEAD!

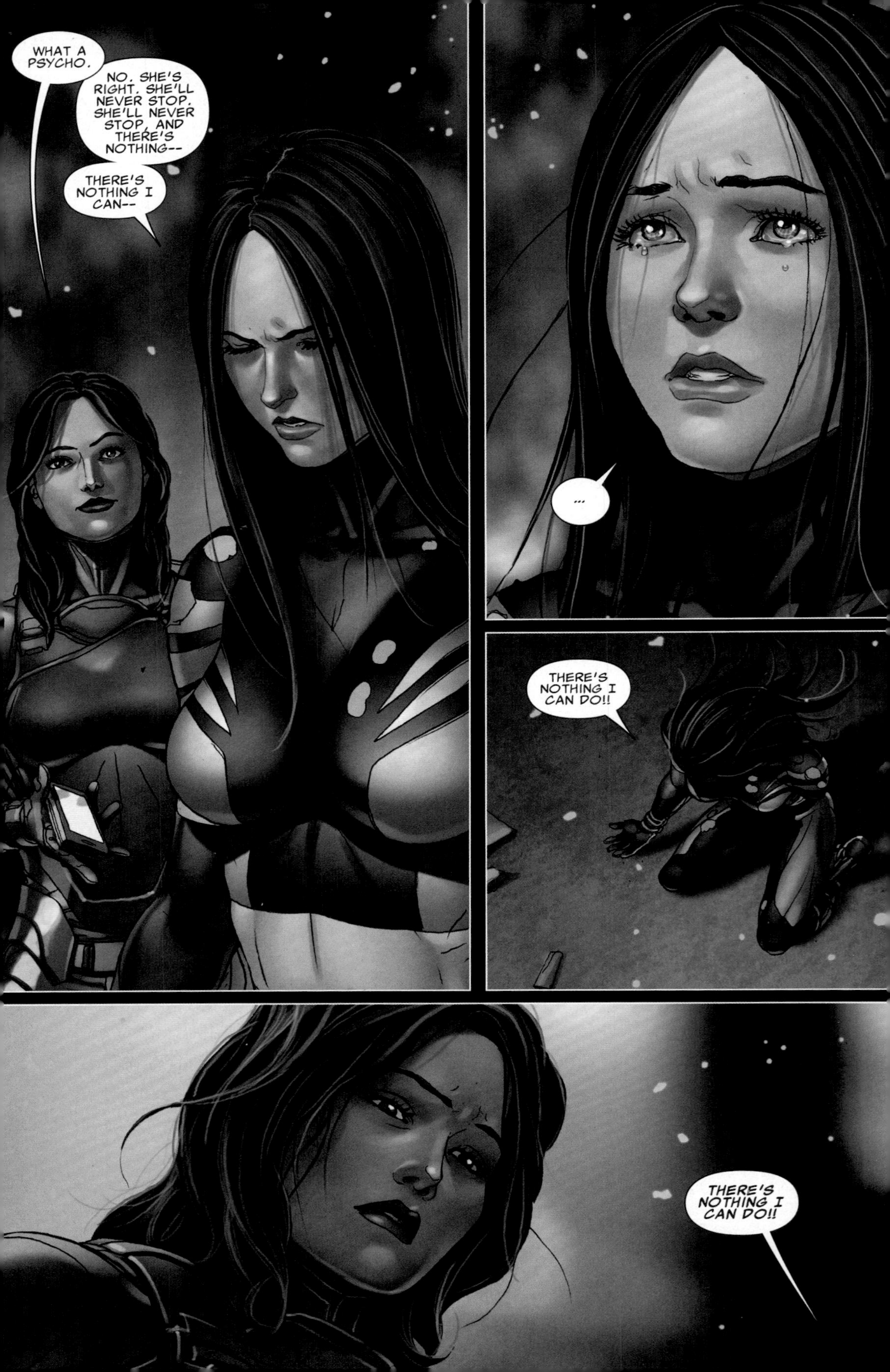
WHAT A PSYCHO.
NO. SHE'S RIGHT. SHE'LL NEVER STOP. SHE'LL NEVER STOP, AND THERE'S NOTHING--
THERE'S NOTHING I CAN--
...
THERE'S NOTHING I CAN DO!!
THERE'S NOTHING I CAN DO!!

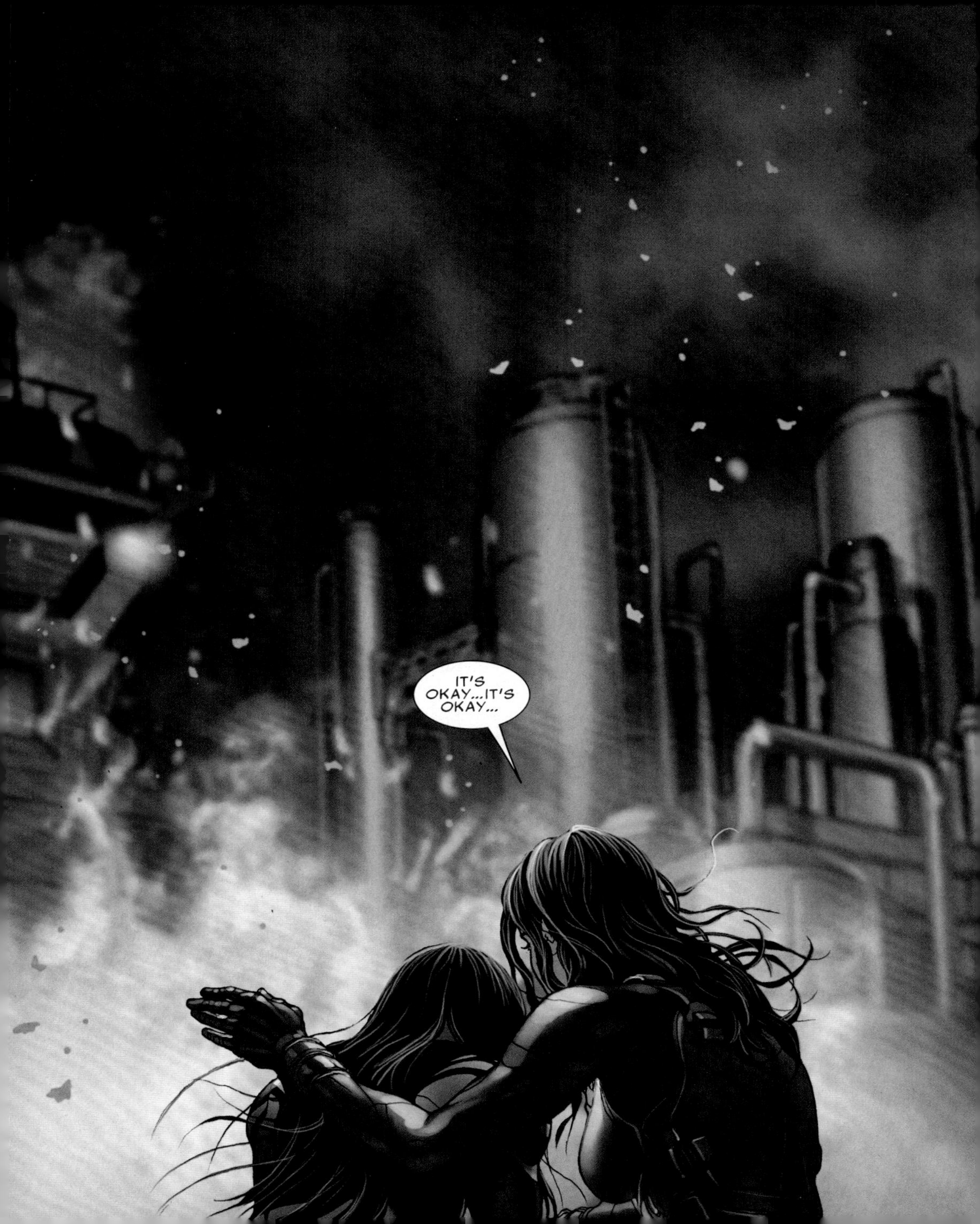
IT'S OKAY...IT'S OKAY...

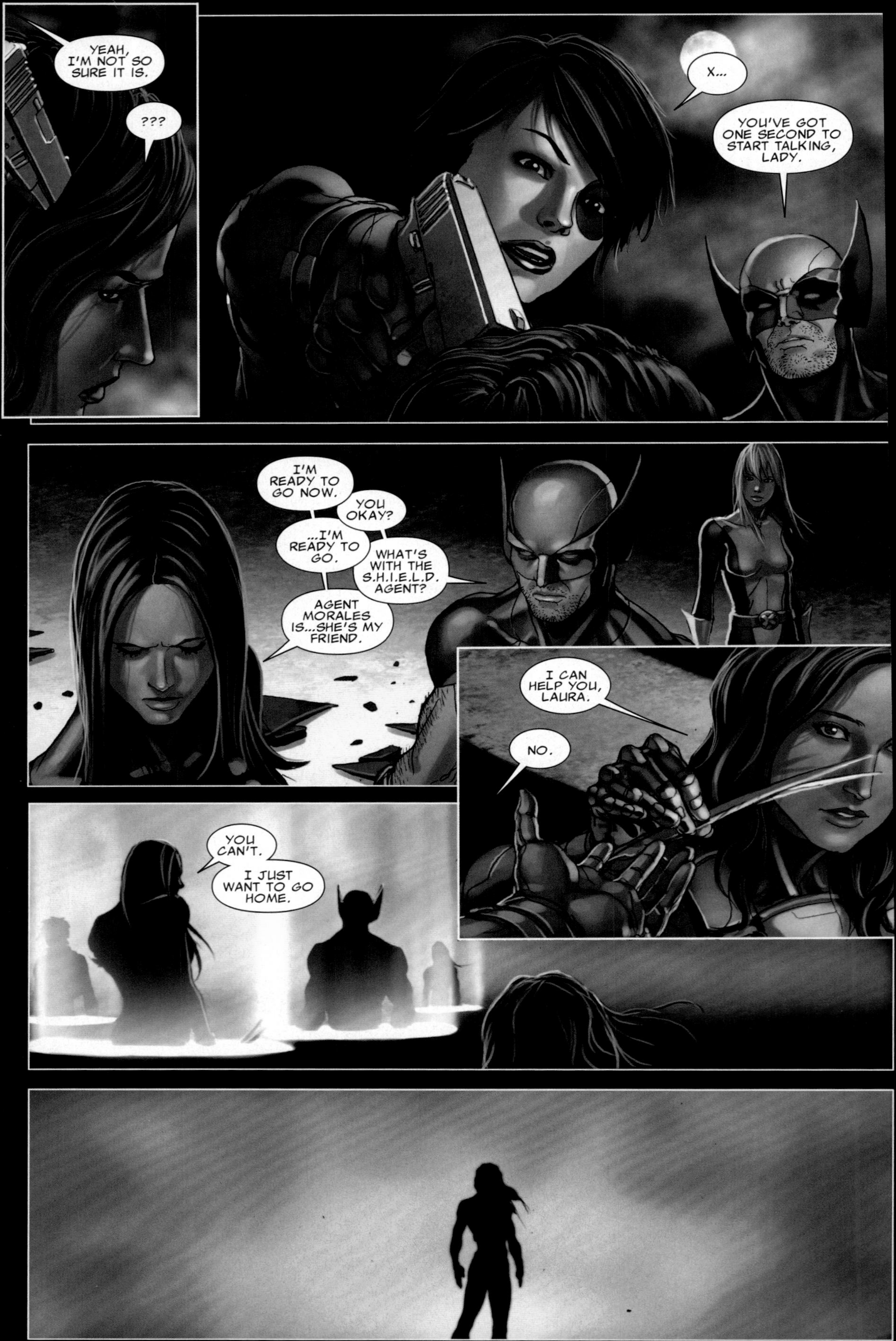
YEAH, I'M NOT SO SURE IT IS.
???
X...
YOU'VE GOT ONE SECOND TO START TALKING, LADY.
I'M READY TO GO NOW.
YOU OKAY?
...I'M READY TO GO.
WHAT'S WITH THE S.H.I.E.L.D. AGENT?
AGENT MORALES IS...SHE'S MY FRIEND.
I CAN HELP YOU, LAURA.
NO.
YOU CAN'T.
I JUST WANT TO GO HOME.

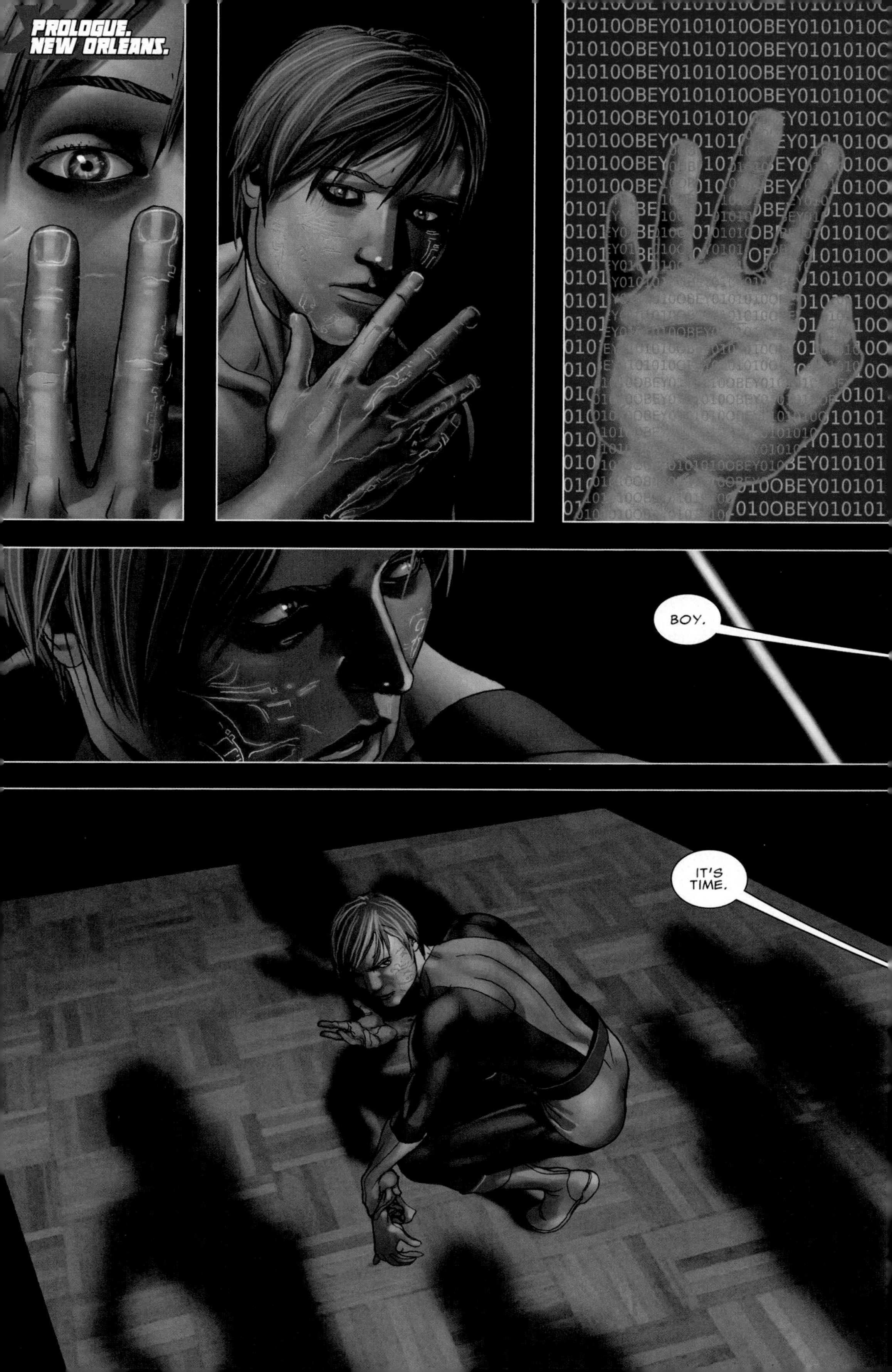
PROLOGUE. NEW ORLEANS.
01010OBEY0101010OBEY0101010C
01010OBEY0101010OBEY0101010C
01010OBEY0101010OBEY0101010C
01010OBEY0101010OBEY0101010C
BOY.
IT'S TIME.

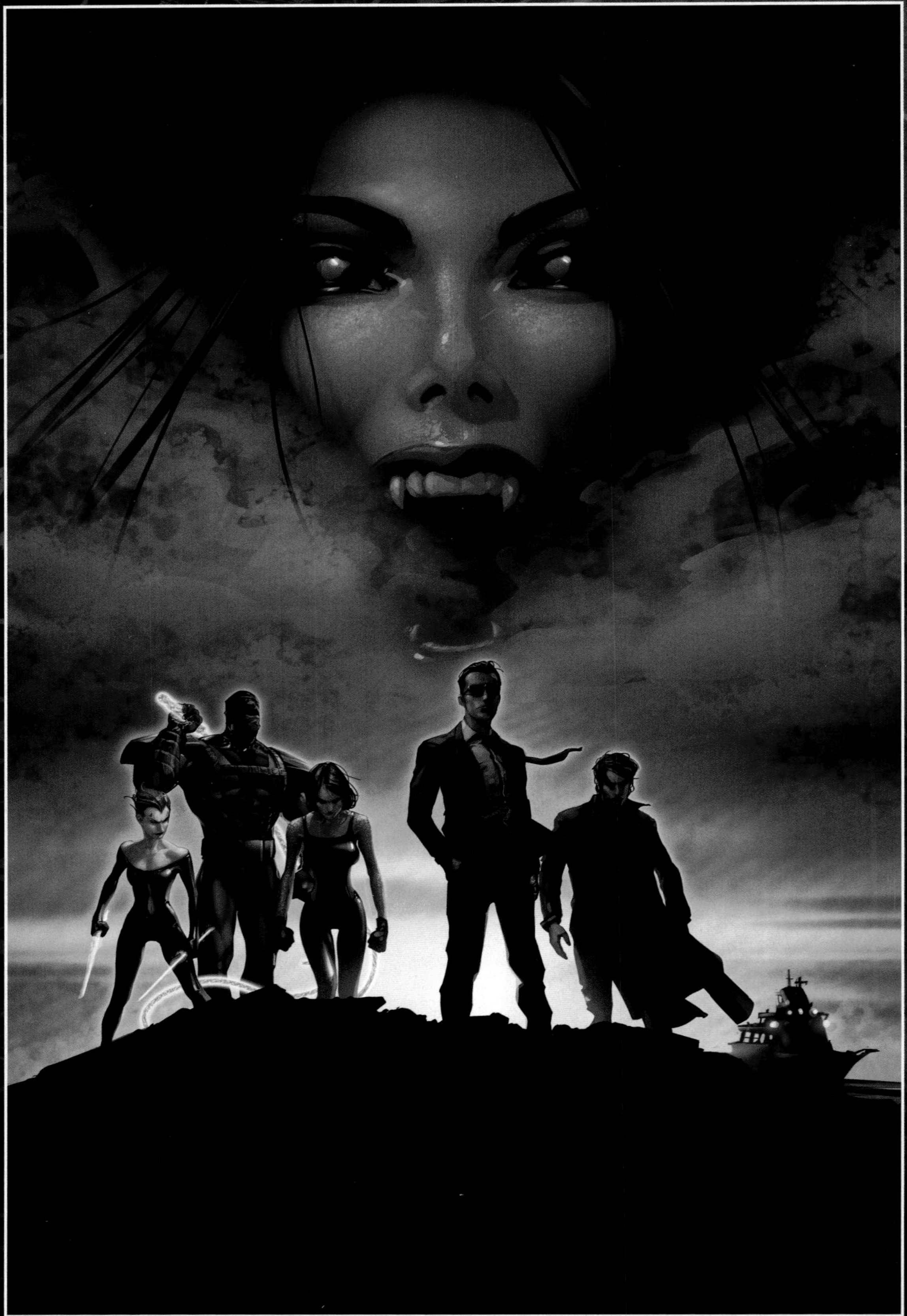

X-NECROSHA: THE GATHERING

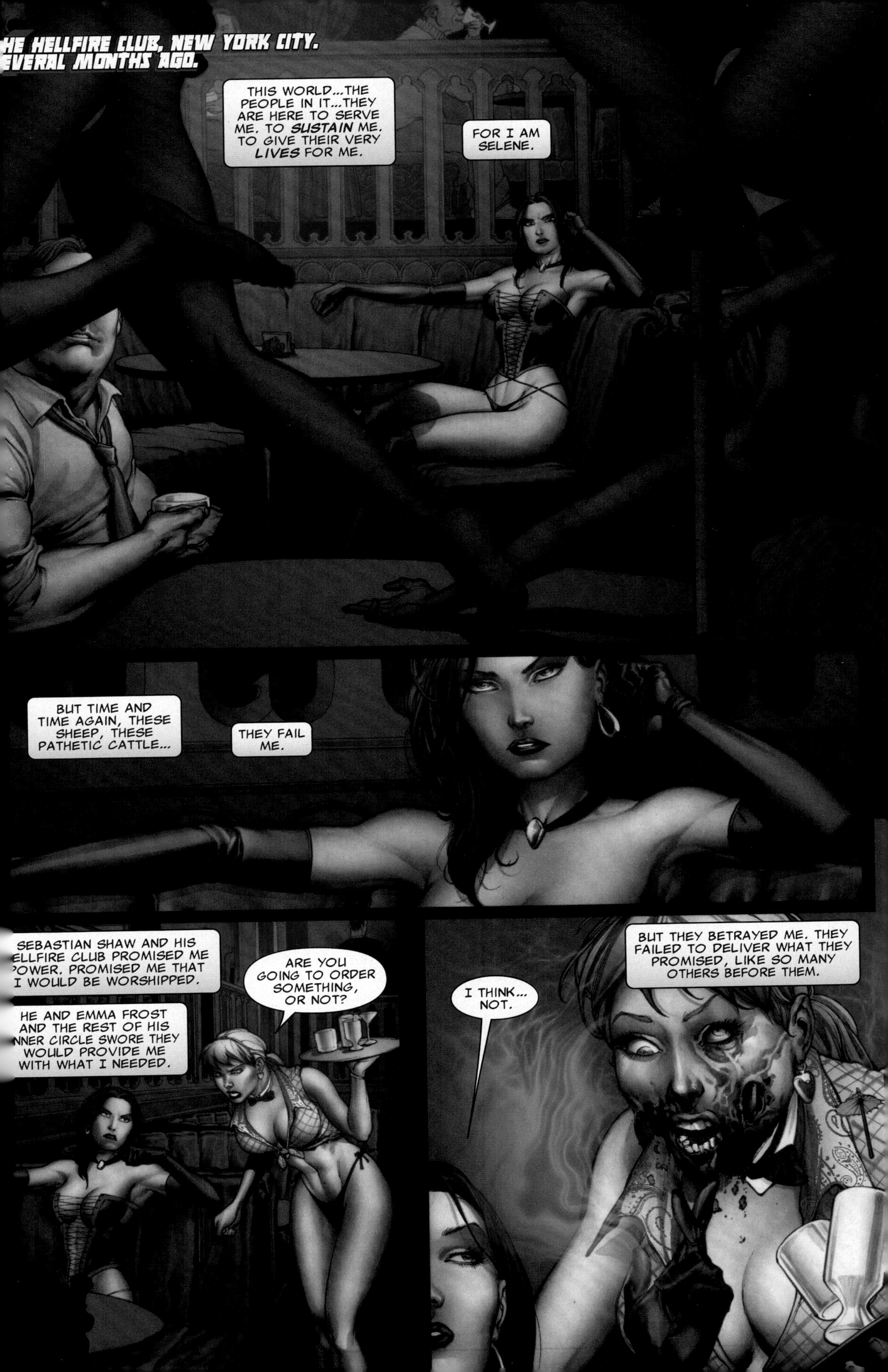
HE HELLFIRE CLUB, NEW YORK CITY.
EVERAL MONTHS AGO.
THIS WORLD...THE PEOPLE IN IT...THEY ARE HERE TO SERVE ME. TO SUSTAIN ME. TO GIVE THEIR VERY LIVES FOR ME.
FOR I AM SELENE.
BUT TIME AND TIME AGAIN, THESE SHEEP, THESE PATHETIC CATTLE...
THEY FAIL ME.
SEBASTIAN SHAW AND HIS ELLFIRE CLUB PROMISED ME POWER. PROMISED ME THAT I WOULD BE WORSHIPPED.
HE AND EMMA FROST AND THE REST OF HIS NNER CIRCLE SWORE THEY WOULD PROVIDE ME WITH WHAT I NEEDED.
ARE YOU GOING TO ORDER SOMETHING, OR NOT?
I THINK... NOT.
BUT THEY BETRAYED ME. THEY FAILED TO DELIVER WHAT THEY PROMISED, LIKE SO MANY OTHERS BEFORE THEM.

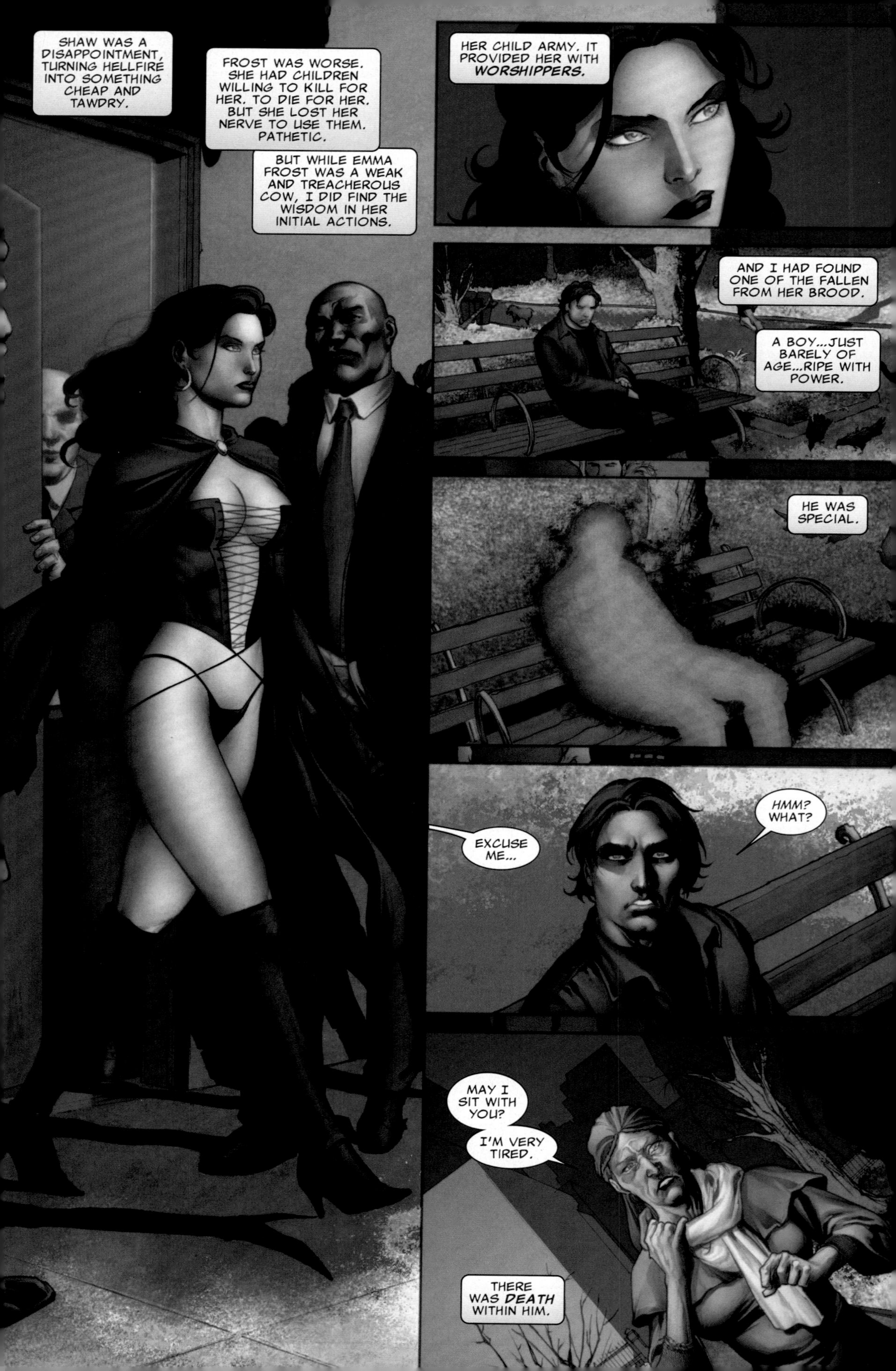
SHAW WAS A DISAPPOINTMENT, TURNING HELLFIRE INTO SOMETHING CHEAP AND TAWDRY.
FROST WAS WORSE. SHE HAD CHILDREN WILLING TO KILL FOR HER. TO DIE FOR HER. BUT SHE LOST HER NERVE TO USE THEM. PATHETIC.
BUT WHILE EMMA FROST WAS A WEAK AND TREACHEROUS COW, I DID FIND THE WISDOM IN HER INITIAL ACTIONS.
HER CHILD ARMY. IT PROVIDED HER WITH *WORSHIPPERS.*
AND I HAD FOUND ONE OF THE FALLEN FROM HER BROOD.
A BOY...JUST BARELY OF AGE...RIPE WITH POWER.
HE WAS SPECIAL.
EXCUSE ME...
HMM? WHAT?
MAY I SIT WITH YOU?
I'M VERY TIRED.
THERE WAS *DEATH* WITHIN HIM.

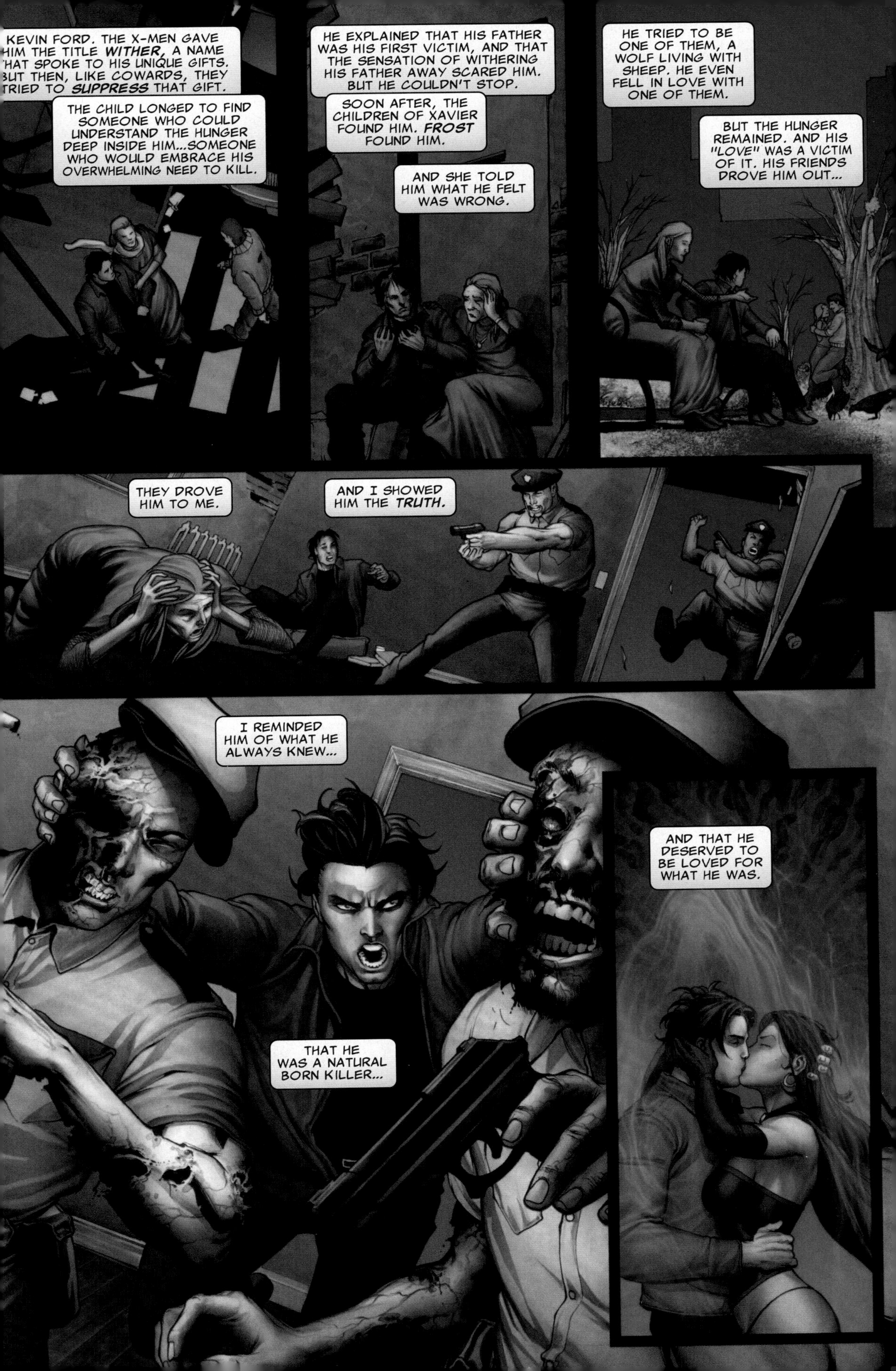
KEVIN FORD. THE X-MEN GAVE HIM THE TITLE WITHER, A NAME THAT SPOKE TO HIS UNIQUE GIFTS. BUT THEN, LIKE COWARDS, THEY TRIED TO SUPPRESS THAT GIFT.
THE CHILD LONGED TO FIND SOMEONE WHO COULD UNDERSTAND THE HUNGER DEEP INSIDE HIM...SOMEONE WHO WOULD EMBRACE HIS OVERWHELMING NEED TO KILL.
HE EXPLAINED THAT HIS FATHER WAS HIS FIRST VICTIM, AND THAT THE SENSATION OF WITHERING HIS FATHER AWAY SCARED HIM. BUT HE COULDN'T STOP.
SOON AFTER, THE CHILDREN OF XAVIER FOUND HIM. FROST FOUND HIM.
AND SHE TOLD HIM WHAT HE FELT WAS WRONG.
HE TRIED TO BE ONE OF THEM, A WOLF LIVING WITH SHEEP. HE EVEN FELL IN LOVE WITH ONE OF THEM.
BUT THE HUNGER REMAINED. AND HIS "LOVE" WAS A VICTIM OF IT. HIS FRIENDS DROVE HIM OUT...
THEY DROVE HIM TO ME.
AND I SHOWED HIM THE TRUTH.
I REMINDED HIM OF WHAT HE ALWAYS KNEW...
THAT HE WAS A NATURAL BORN KILLER...
AND THAT HE DESERVED TO BE LOVED FOR WHAT HE WAS.

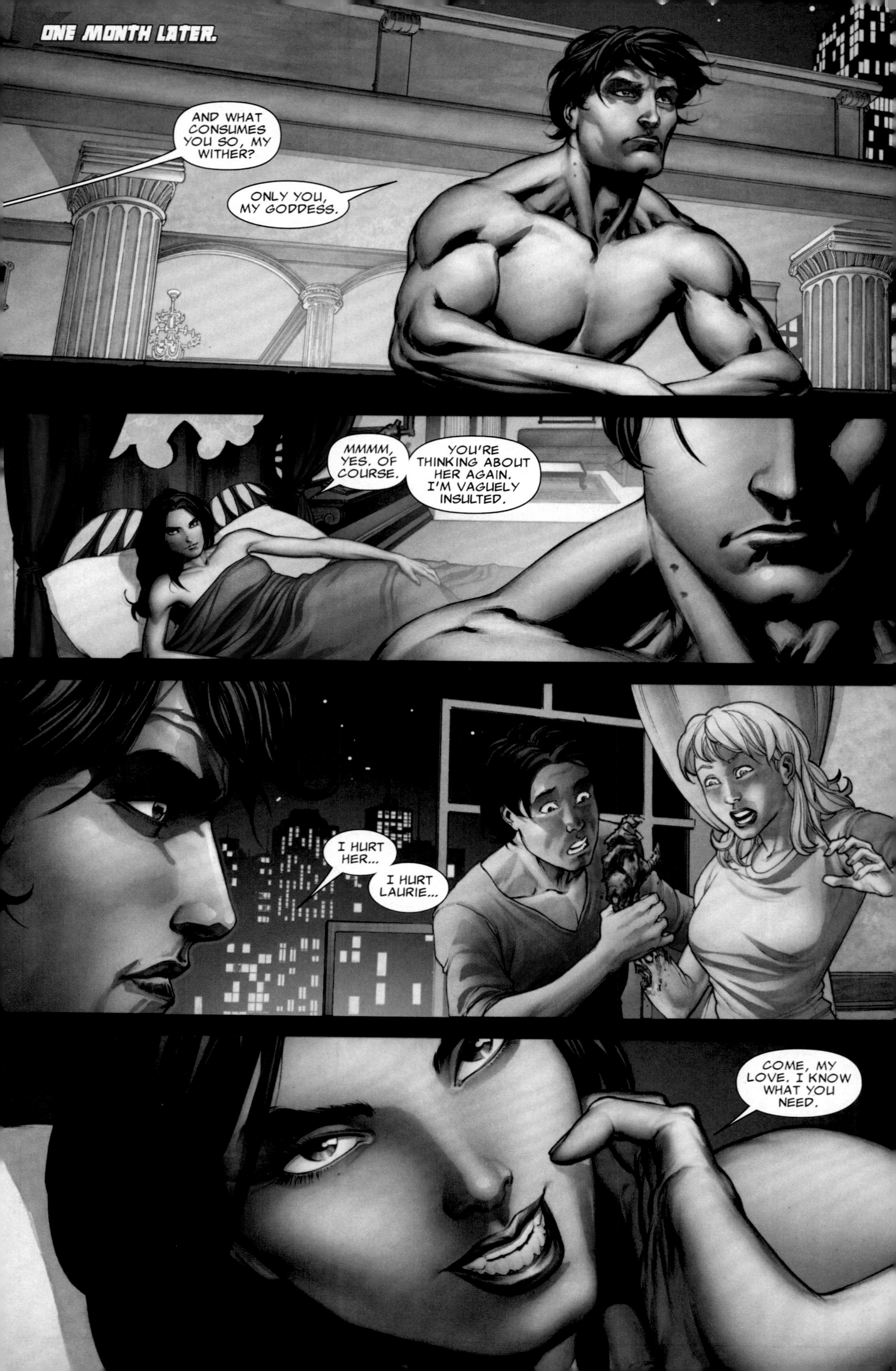
ONE MONTH LATER.
AND WHAT CONSUMES YOU SO, MY WITHER?
ONLY YOU, MY GODDESS.
MMMM, YES. OF COURSE.
YOU'RE THINKING ABOUT HER AGAIN. I'M VAGUELY INSULTED.
I HURT HER...
I HURT LAURIE...
COME, MY LOVE. I KNOW WHAT YOU NEED.

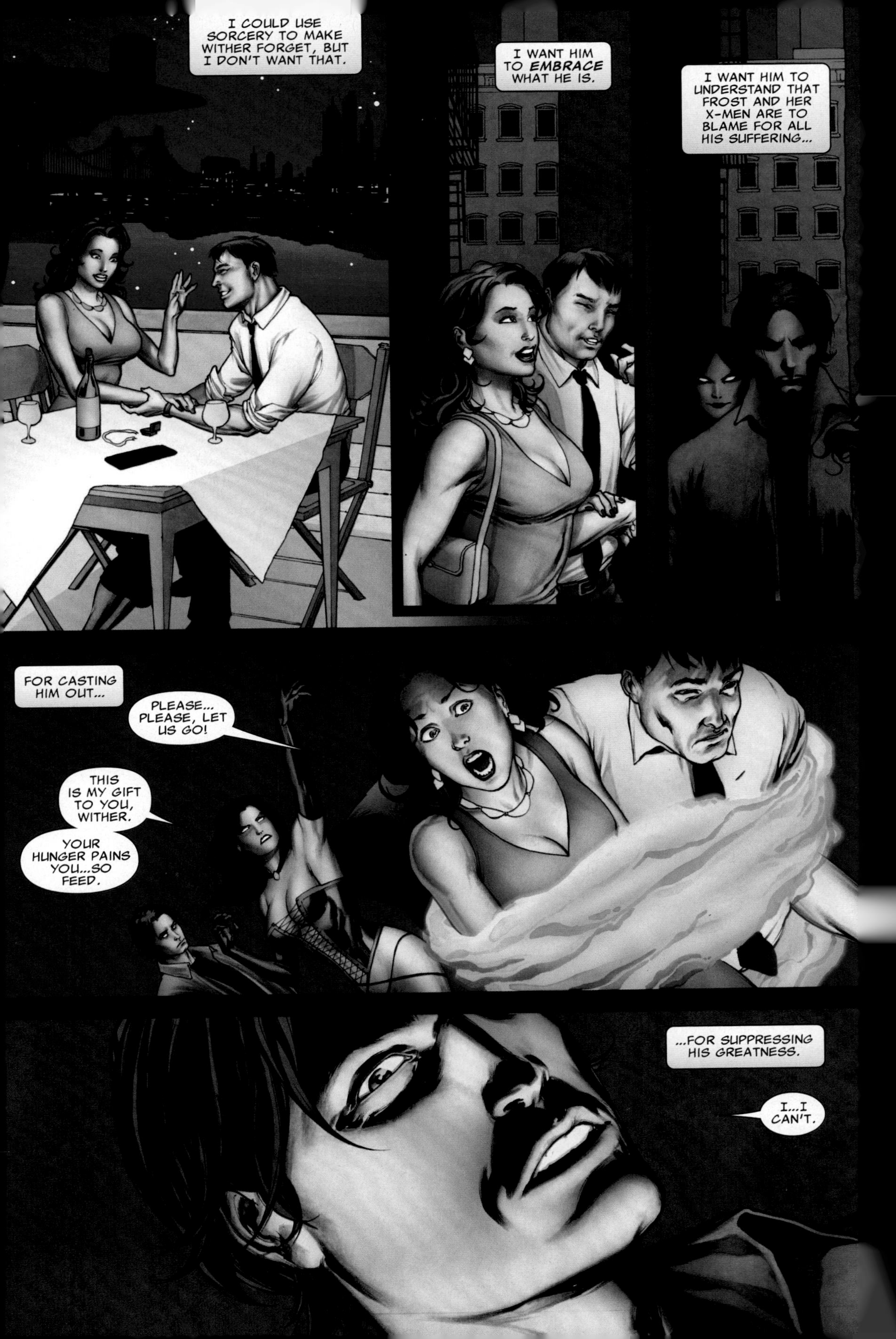
I COULD USE SORCERY TO MAKE WITHER FORGET, BUT I DON'T WANT THAT.
I WANT HIM TO EMBRACE WHAT HE IS.
I WANT HIM TO UNDERSTAND THAT FROST AND HER X-MEN ARE TO BLAME FOR ALL HIS SUFFERING...
FOR CASTING HIM OUT...
PLEASE... PLEASE, LET US GO!
THIS IS MY GIFT TO YOU, WITHER.
YOUR HUNGER PAINS YOU...SO FEED.
...FOR SUPPRESSING HIS GREATNESS.
I...I CAN'T.

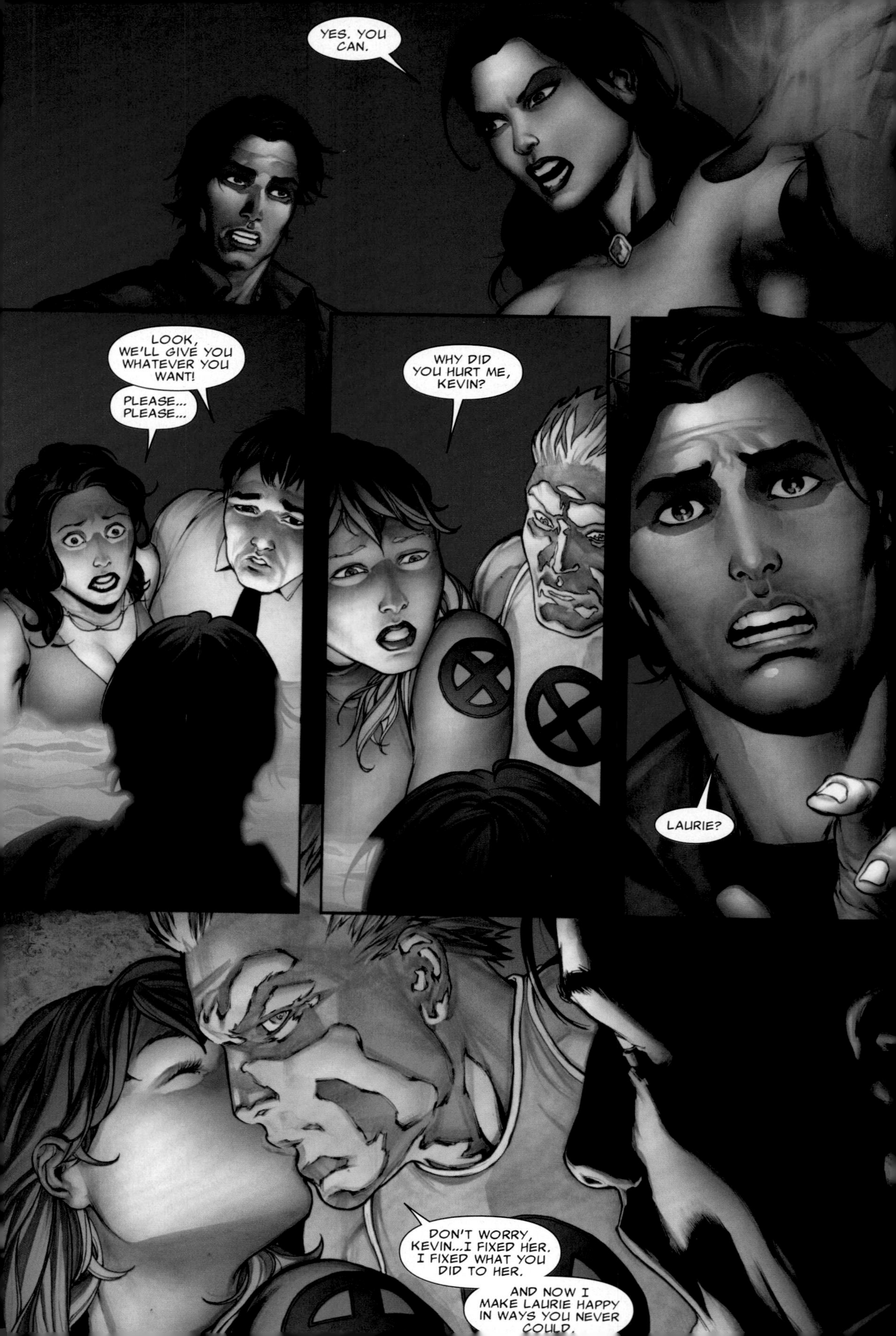
YES. YOU CAN.
LOOK, WE'LL GIVE YOU WHATEVER YOU WANT!
PLEASE... PLEASE...
WHY DID YOU HURT ME, KEVIN?
LAURIE?
DON'T WORRY, KEVIN...I FIXED HER. I FIXED WHAT YOU DID TO HER.
AND NOW I MAKE LAURIE HAPPY IN WAYS YOU NEVER COULD.

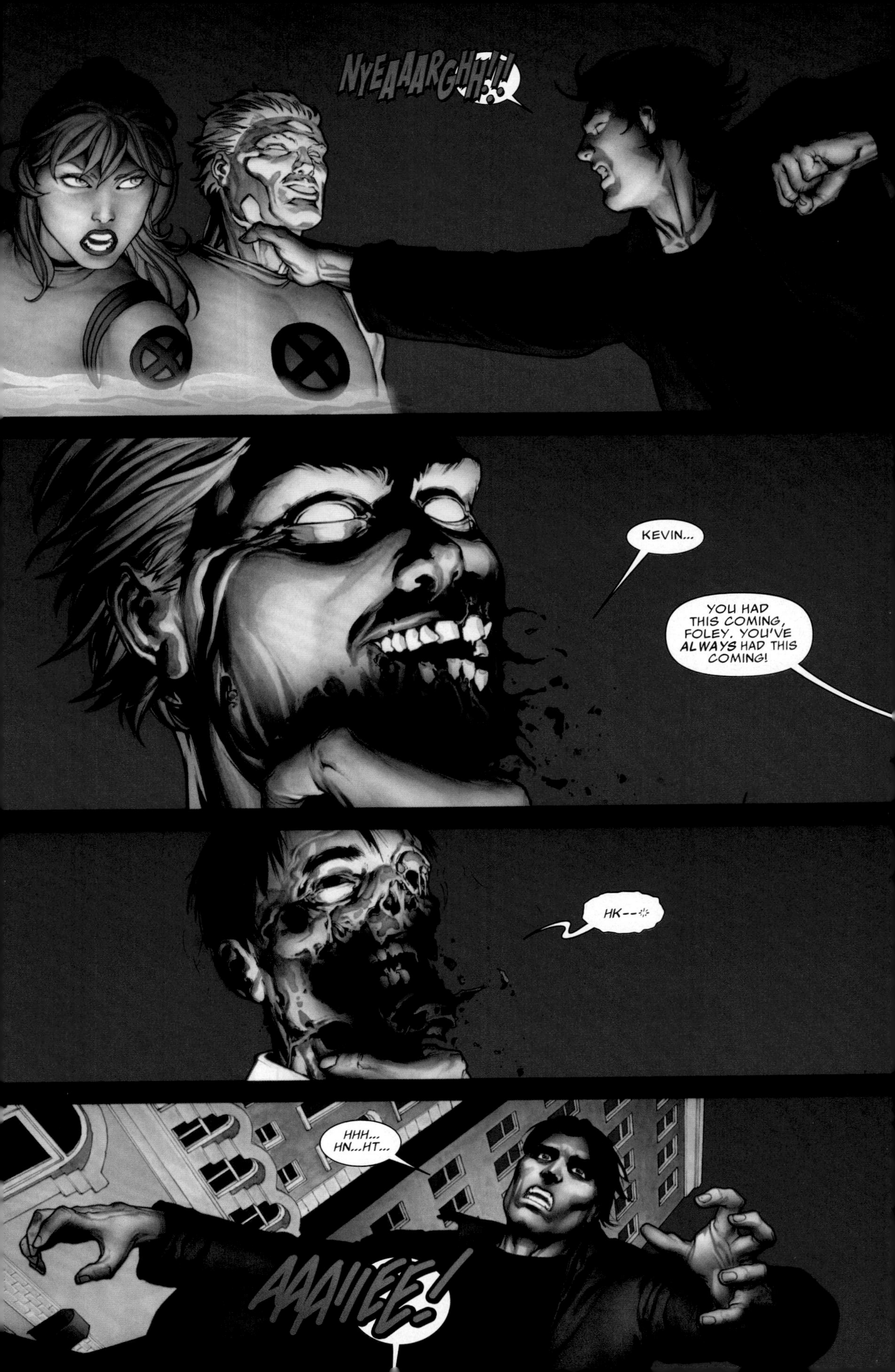
NYEAAARGHH!!!
KEVIN...
YOU HAD THIS COMING, FOLEY. YOU'VE ALWAYS HAD THIS COMING!
HK--
HHH... HN...HT...
AAAIIEEE!

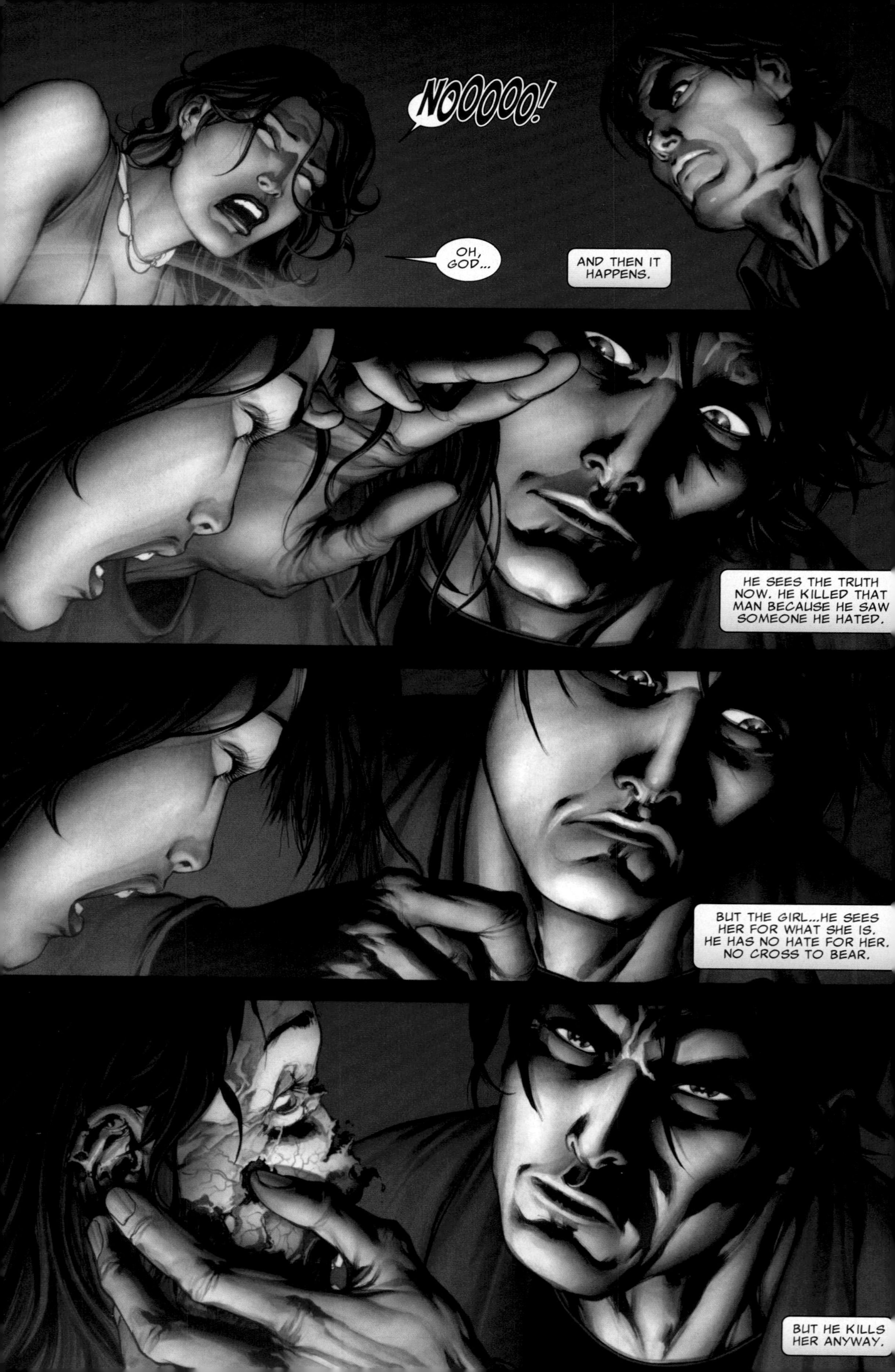
NOOOOO!
OH, GOD...
AND THEN IT HAPPENS.
HE SEES THE TRUTH NOW. HE KILLED THAT MAN BECAUSE HE SAW SOMEONE HE HATED.
BUT THE GIRL...HE SEES HER FOR WHAT SHE IS. HE HAS NO HATE FOR HER. NO CROSS TO BEAR.
BUT HE KILLS HER ANYWAY.

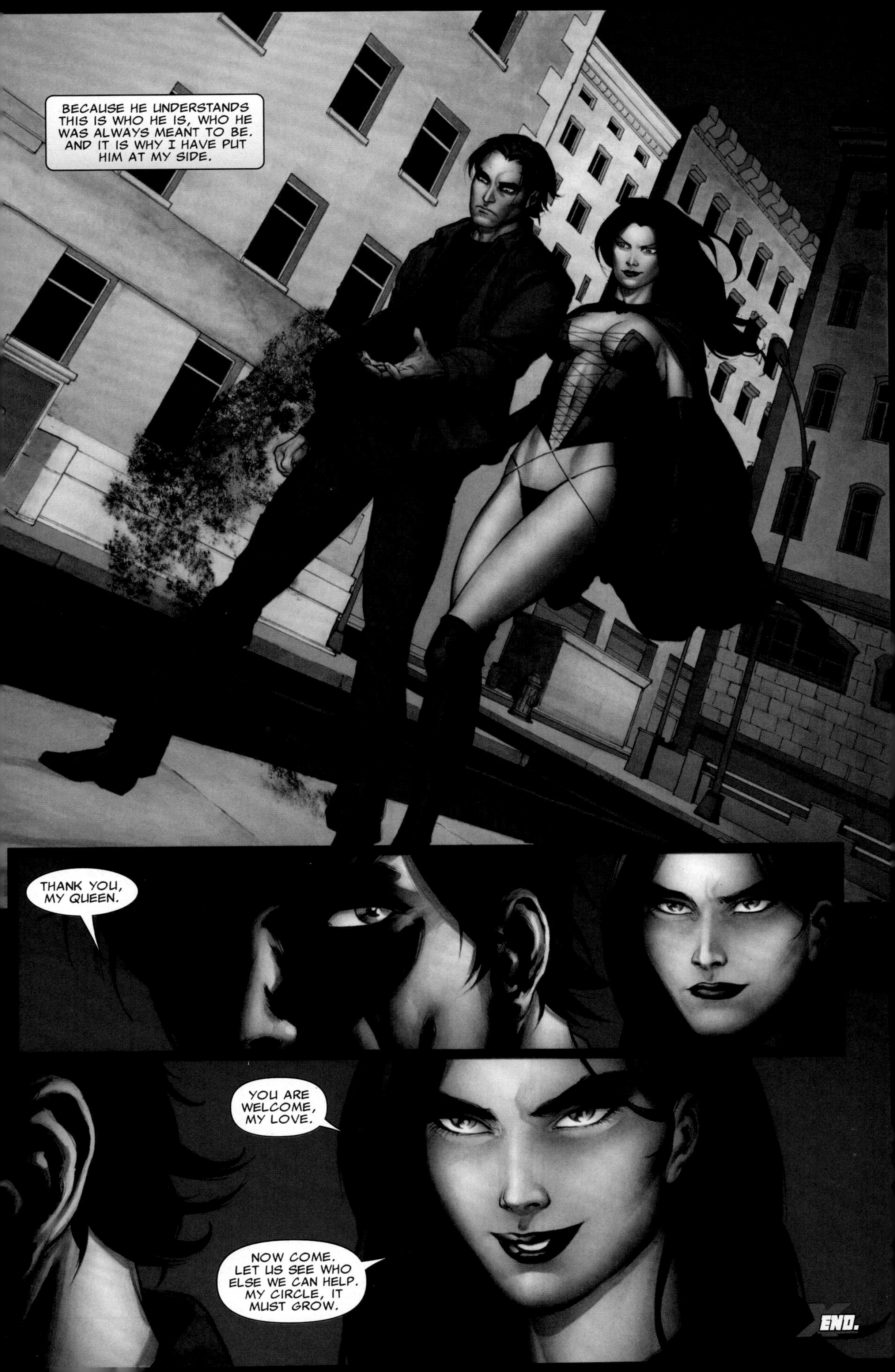
BECAUSE HE UNDERSTANDS THIS IS WHO HE IS, WHO HE WAS ALWAYS MEANT TO BE. AND IT IS WHY I HAVE PUT HIM AT MY SIDE.
THANK YOU, MY QUEEN.
YOU ARE WELCOME, MY LOVE.
NOW COME. LET US SEE WHO ELSE WE CAN HELP. MY CIRCLE, IT MUST GROW.
END.

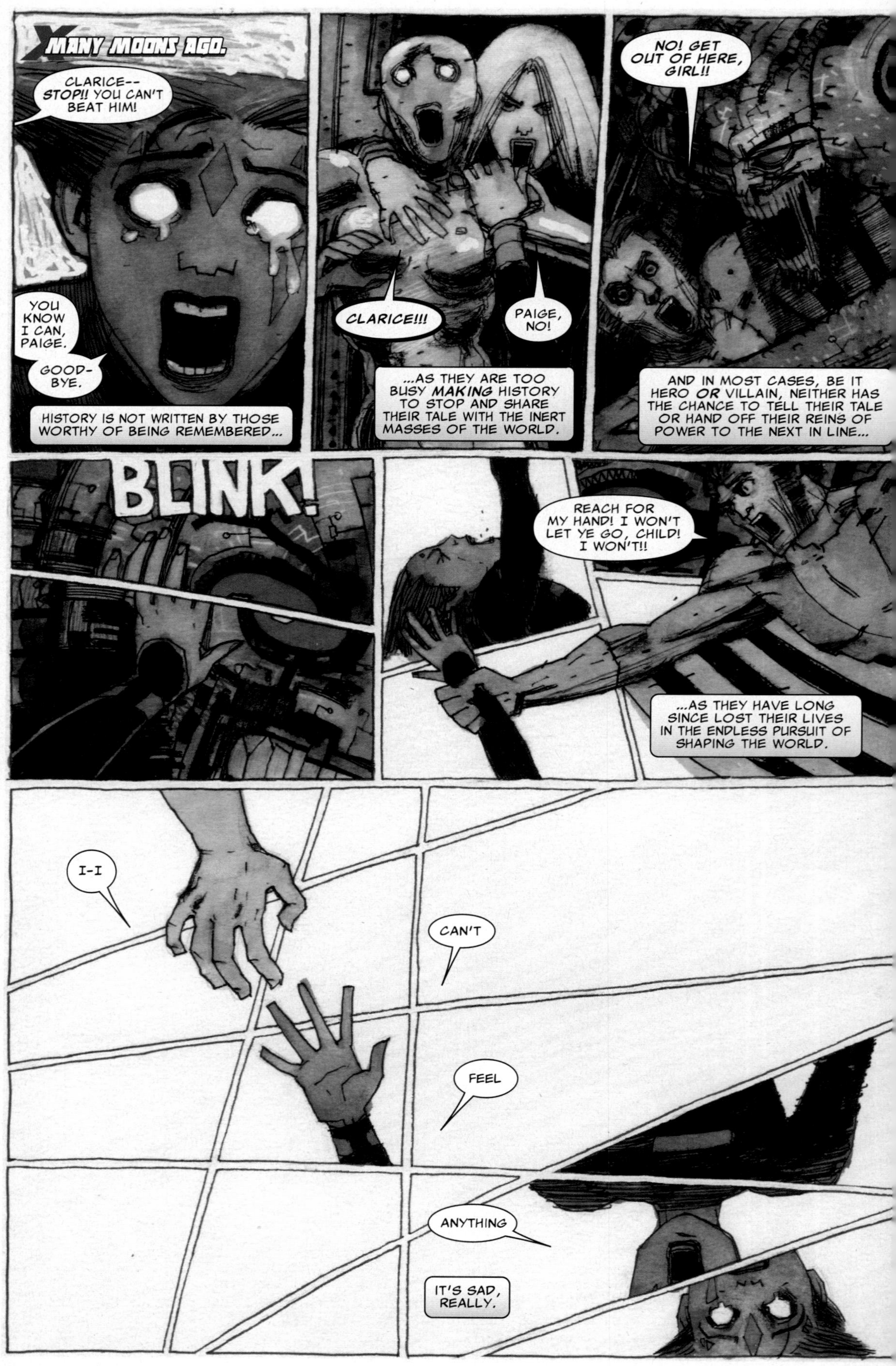
MANY MOONS AGO.
CLARICE-- STOP!! YOU CAN'T BEAT HIM!
YOU KNOW I CAN, PAIGE.
GOOD-BYE.
HISTORY IS NOT WRITTEN BY THOSE WORTHY OF BEING REMEMBERED...
CLARICE!!!
PAIGE, NO!
...AS THEY ARE TOO BUSY MAKING HISTORY TO STOP AND SHARE THEIR TALE WITH THE INERT MASSES OF THE WORLD.
NO! GET OUT OF HERE, GIRL!!
AND IN MOST CASES, BE IT HERO OR VILLAIN, NEITHER HAS THE CHANCE TO TELL THEIR TALE OR HAND OFF THEIR REINS OF POWER TO THE NEXT IN LINE...
BLINK!
REACH FOR MY HAND! I WON'T LET YE GO, CHILD! I WON'T!!
...AS THEY HAVE LONG SINCE LOST THEIR LIVES IN THE ENDLESS PURSUIT OF SHAPING THE WORLD.
I-I
CAN'T
FEEL
ANYTHING
IT'S SAD, REALLY.

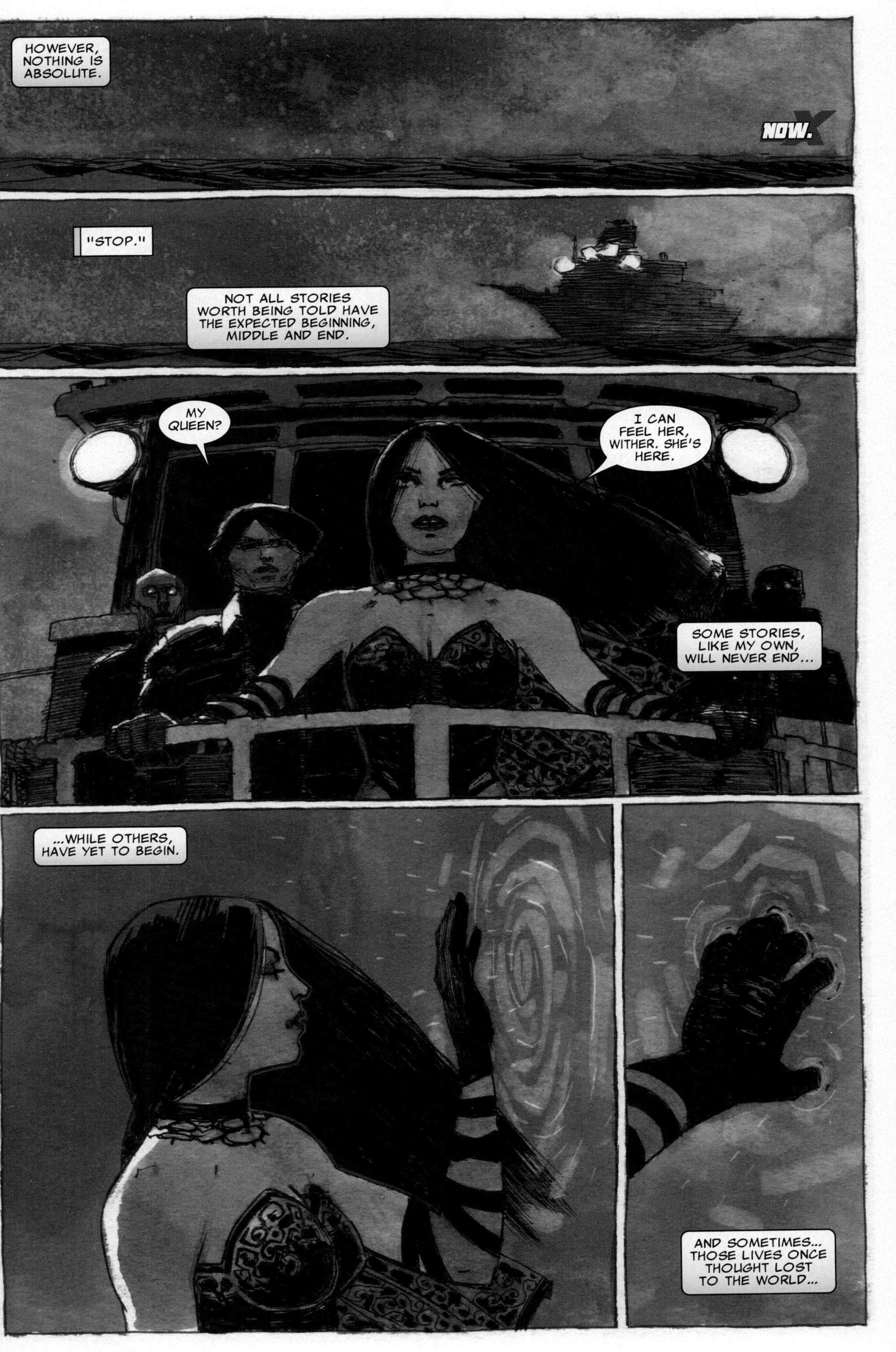

HOWEVER, NOTHING IS ABSOLUTE.
NOW.X
"STOP."
NOT ALL STORIES WORTH BEING TOLD HAVE THE EXPECTED BEGINNING, MIDDLE AND END.
MY QUEEN?
I CAN FEEL HER, WITHER. SHE'S HERE.
SOME STORIES, LIKE MY OWN, WILL NEVER END...
...WHILE OTHERS, HAVE YET TO BEGIN.
AND SOMETIMES... THOSE LIVES ONCE THOUGHT LOST TO THE WORLD...

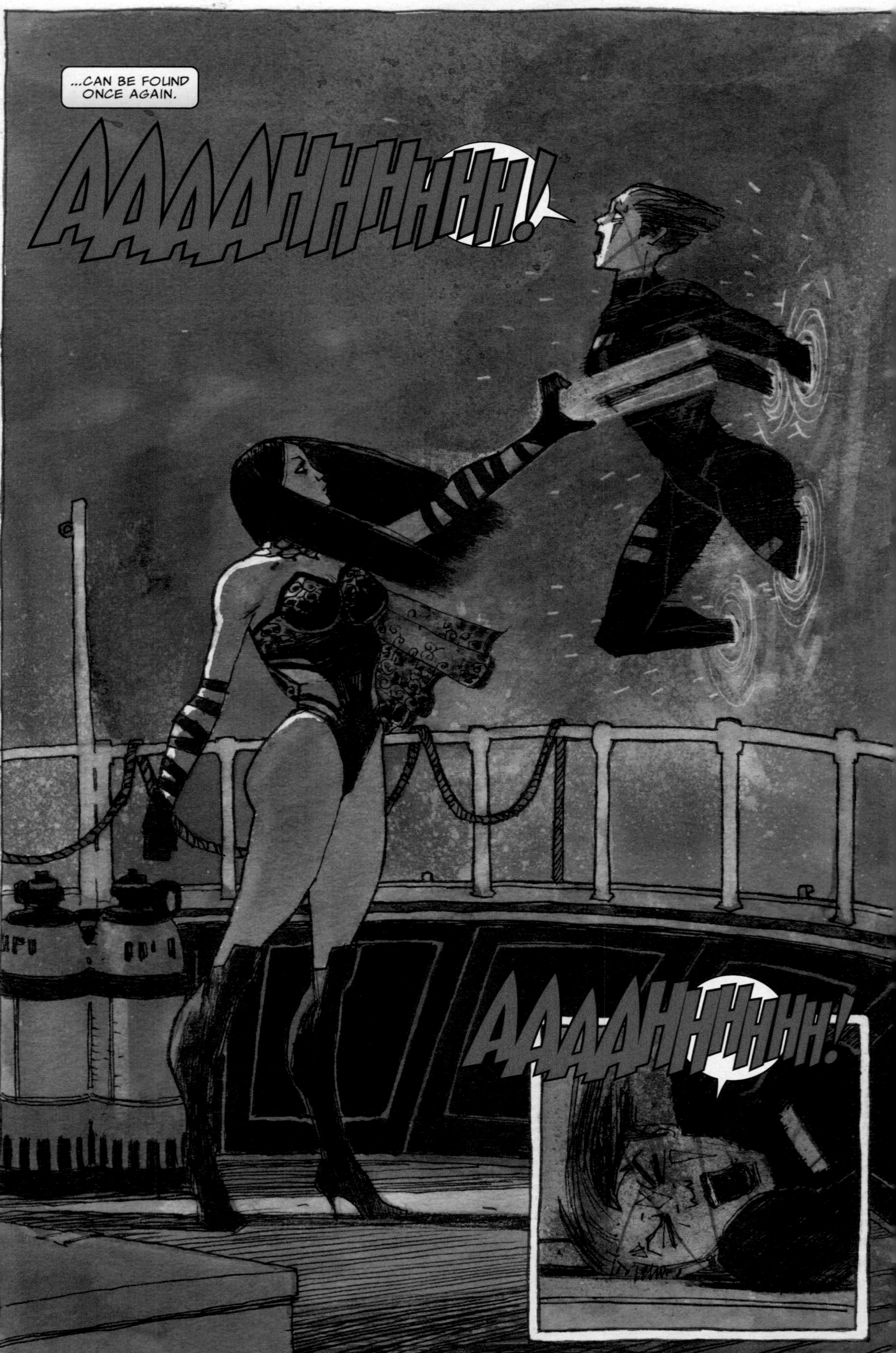
...CAN BE FOUND ONCE AGAIN.
AAAAHHHHHH!
AAAAHHHHHH!

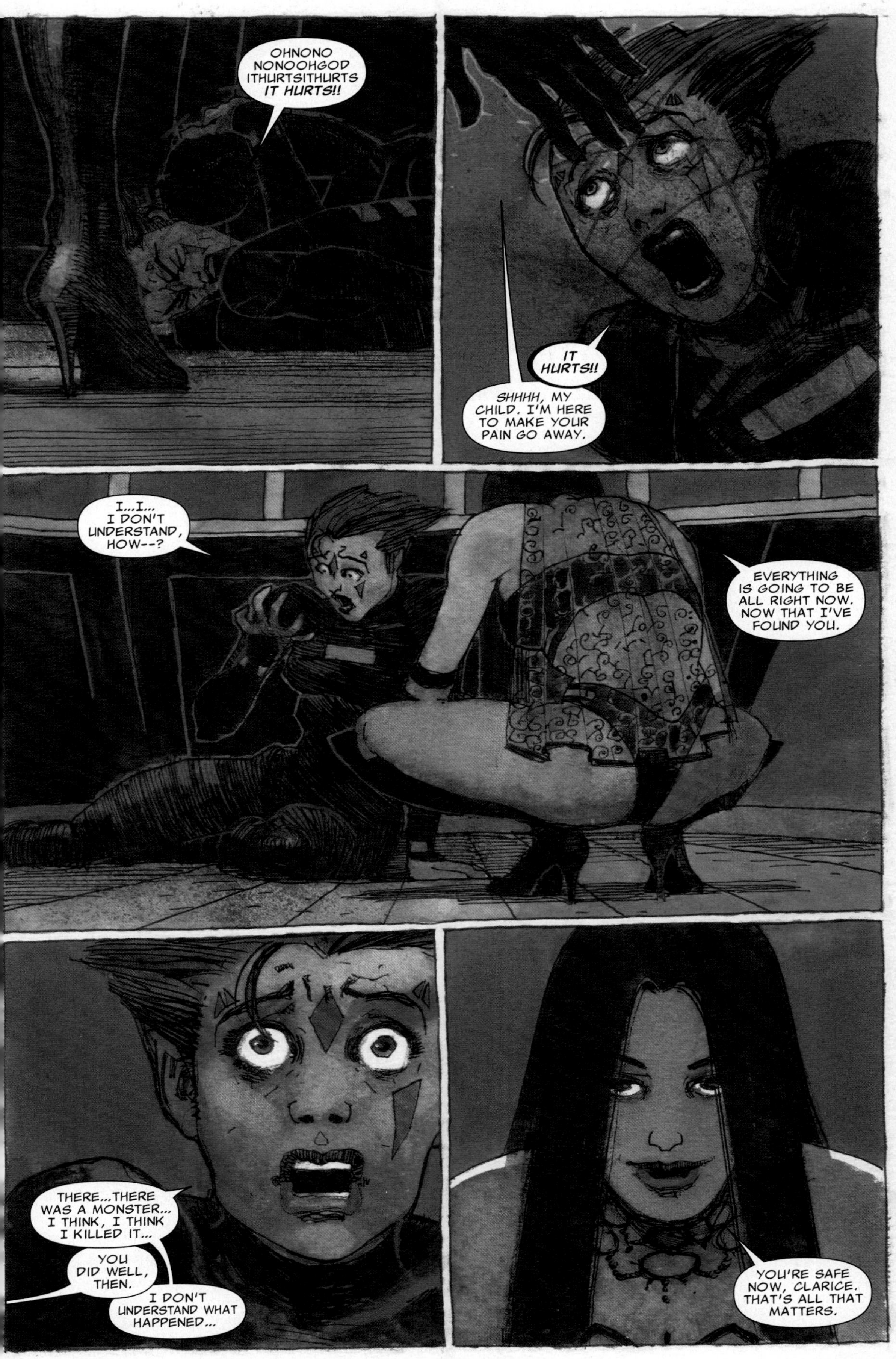
OHNONO NONOOHGOD ITHURTSITHURTS *IT HURTS!!*
IT HURTS!!
SHHHH, MY CHILD. I'M HERE TO MAKE YOUR PAIN GO AWAY.
I...I... I DON'T UNDERSTAND, HOW--?
EVERYTHING IS GOING TO BE ALL RIGHT NOW. NOW THAT I'VE FOUND YOU.
THERE...THERE WAS A MONSTER... I THINK, I THINK I KILLED IT...
YOU DID WELL, THEN.
I DON'T UNDERSTAND WHAT HAPPENED...
YOU'RE SAFE NOW, CLARICE. THAT'S ALL THAT MATTERS.

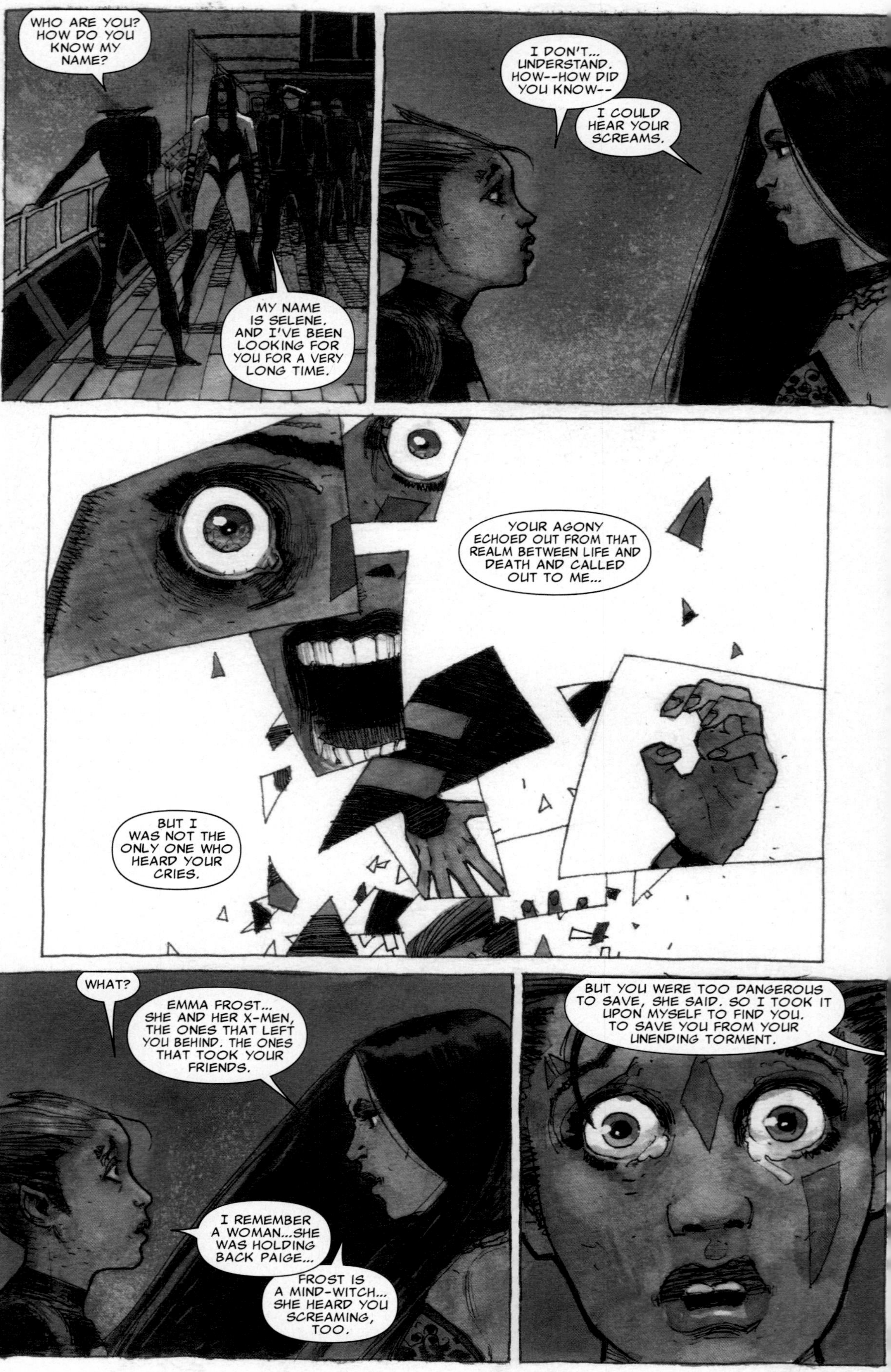
WHO ARE YOU? HOW DO YOU KNOW MY NAME?
MY NAME IS SELENE. AND I'VE BEEN LOOKING FOR YOU FOR A VERY LONG TIME.
I DON'T... UNDERSTAND. HOW--HOW DID YOU KNOW--
I COULD HEAR YOUR SCREAMS.
YOUR AGONY ECHOED OUT FROM THAT REALM BETWEEN LIFE AND DEATH AND CALLED OUT TO ME...
BUT I WAS NOT THE ONLY ONE WHO HEARD YOUR CRIES.
WHAT?
EMMA FROST... SHE AND HER X-MEN, THE ONES THAT LEFT YOU BEHIND. THE ONES THAT TOOK YOUR FRIENDS.
I REMEMBER A WOMAN...SHE WAS HOLDING BACK PAIGE...
FROST IS A MIND-WITCH... SHE HEARD YOU SCREAMING, TOO.
BUT YOU WERE TOO DANGEROUS TO SAVE, SHE SAID. SO I TOOK IT UPON MYSELF TO FIND YOU. TO SAVE YOU FROM YOUR UNENDING TORMENT.

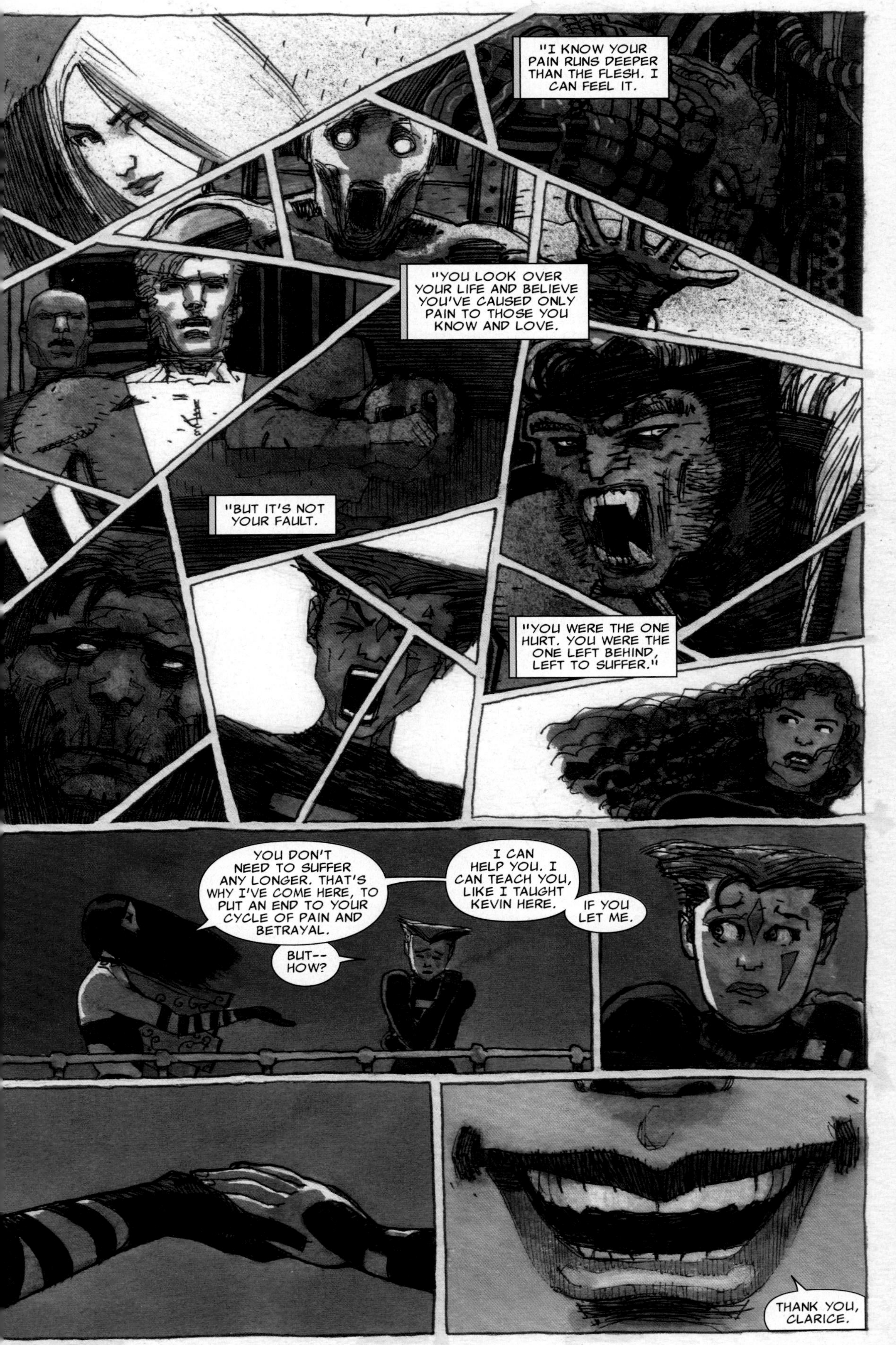
"I KNOW YOUR PAIN RUNS DEEPER THAN THE FLESH. I CAN FEEL IT.
"YOU LOOK OVER YOUR LIFE AND BELIEVE YOU'VE CAUSED ONLY PAIN TO THOSE YOU KNOW AND LOVE.
"BUT IT'S NOT YOUR FAULT.
"YOU WERE THE ONE HURT. YOU WERE THE ONE LEFT BEHIND, LEFT TO SUFFER."
YOU DON'T NEED TO SUFFER ANY LONGER. THAT'S WHY I'VE COME HERE, TO PUT AN END TO YOUR CYCLE OF PAIN AND BETRAYAL.
I CAN HELP YOU. I CAN TEACH YOU, LIKE I TAUGHT KEVIN HERE.
IF YOU LET ME.
BUT-- HOW?
THANK YOU, CLARICE.

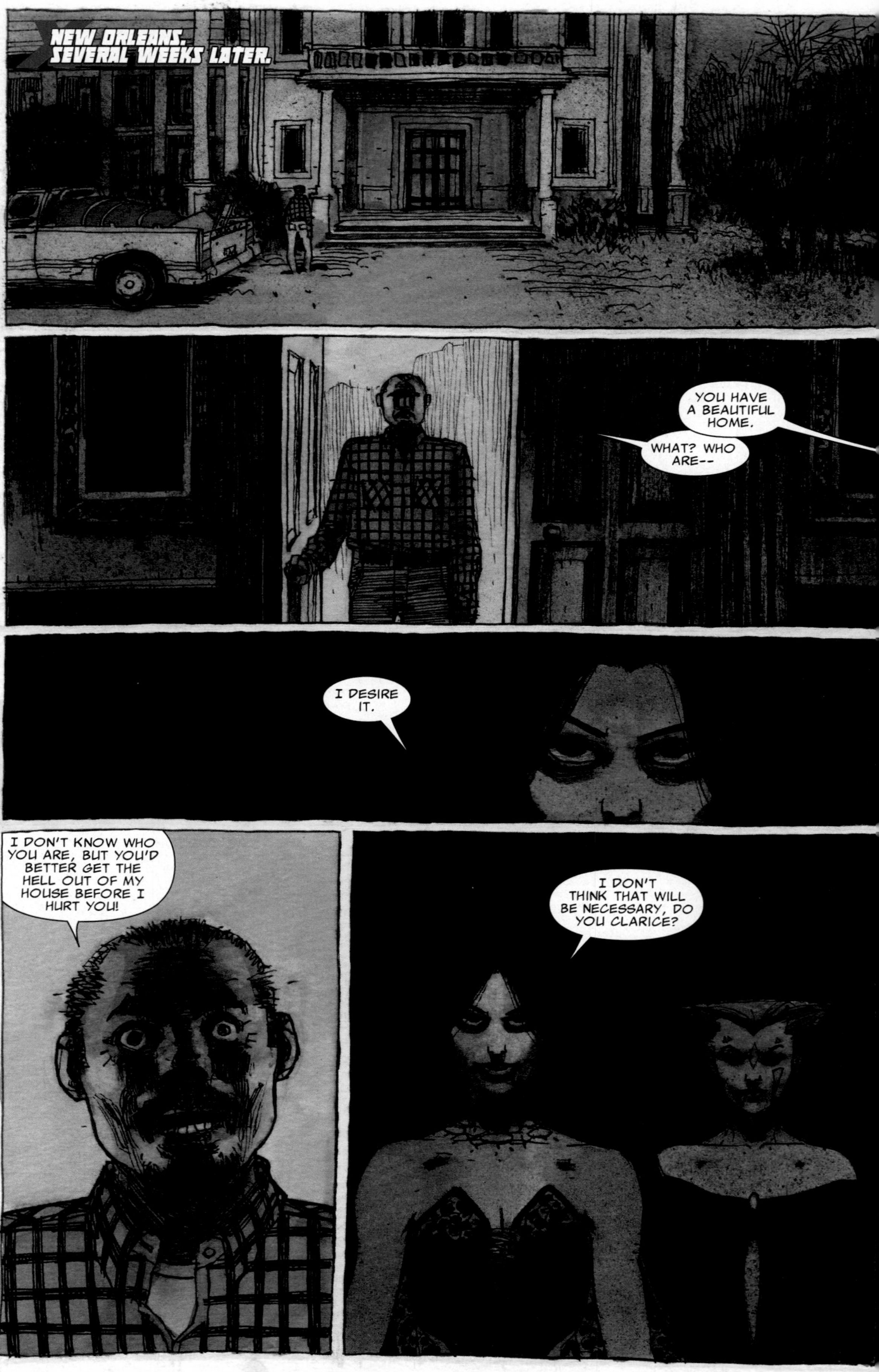
NEW ORLEANS.
SEVERAL WEEKS LATER.
YOU HAVE A BEAUTIFUL HOME.
WHAT? WHO ARE--
I DESIRE IT.
I DON'T KNOW WHO YOU ARE, BUT YOU'D BETTER GET THE HELL OUT OF MY HOUSE BEFORE I HURT YOU!
I DON'T THINK THAT WILL BE NECESSARY, DO YOU CLARICE?

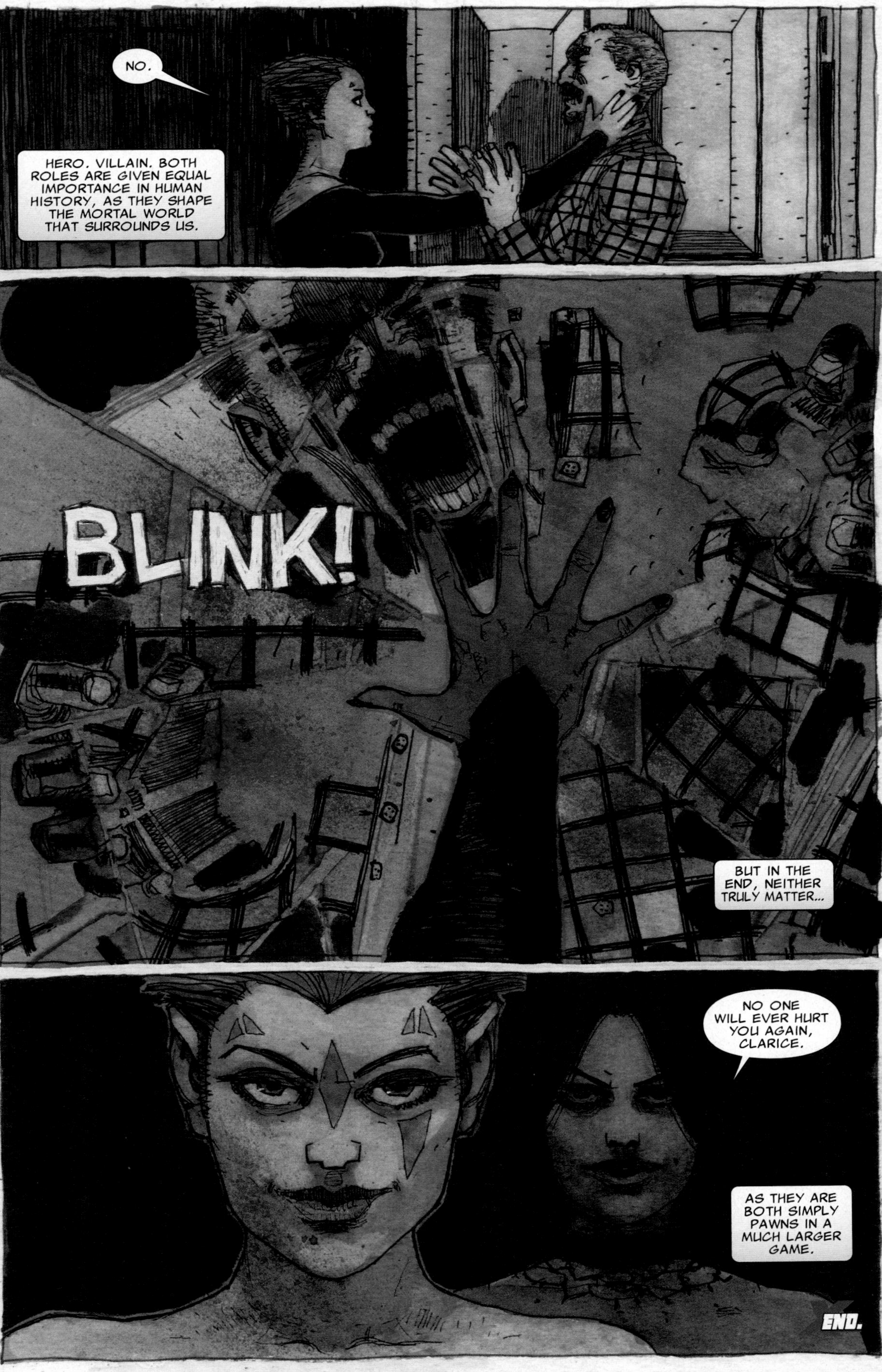
NO.
HERO. VILLAIN. BOTH ROLES ARE GIVEN EQUAL IMPORTANCE IN HUMAN HISTORY, AS THEY SHAPE THE MORTAL WORLD THAT SURROUNDS US.
BLINK!
BUT IN THE END, NEITHER TRULY MATTER...
NO ONE WILL EVER HURT YOU AGAIN, CLARICE.
AS THEY ARE BOTH SIMPLY PAWNS IN A MUCH LARGER GAME.
END.

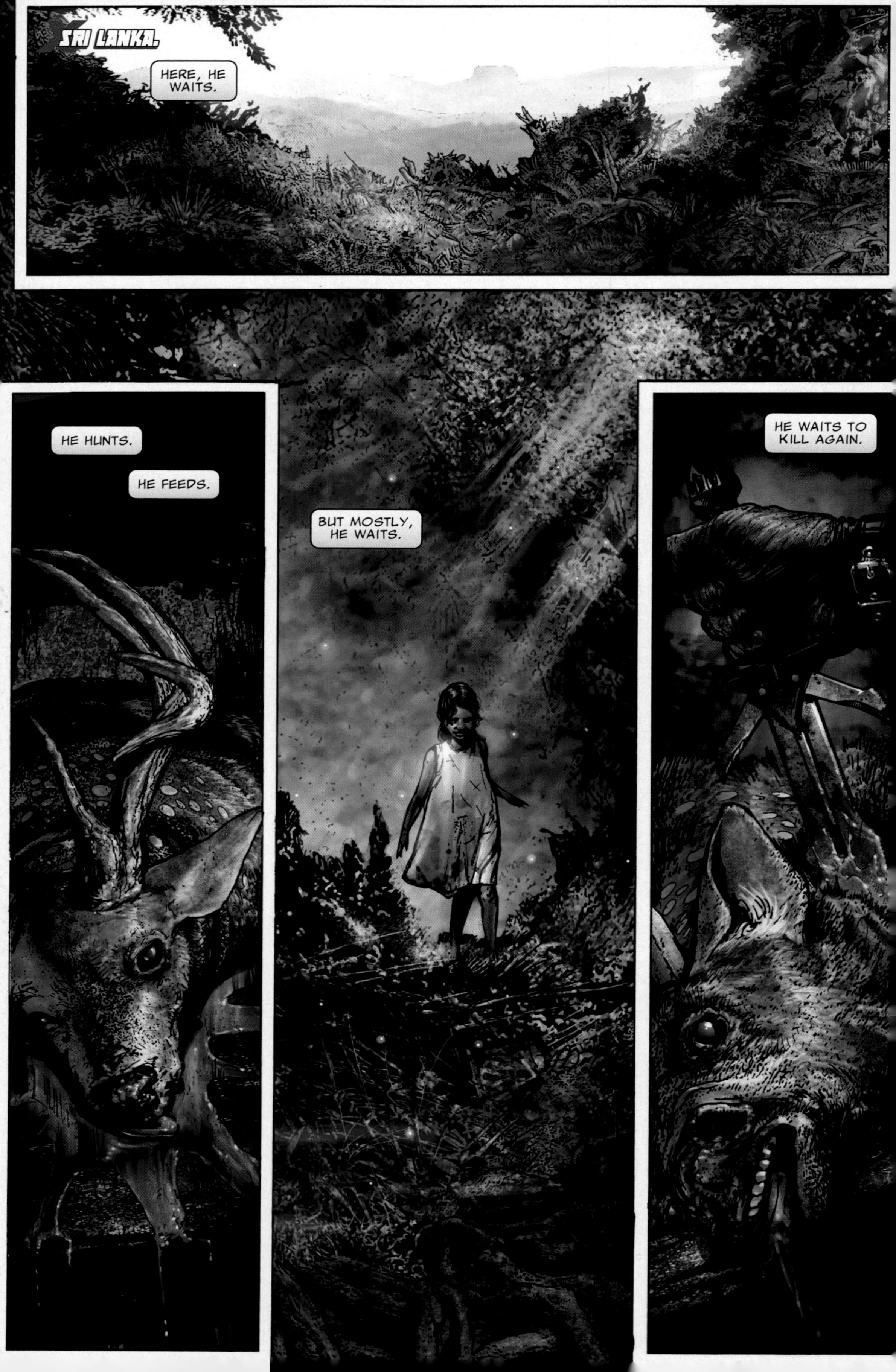
SRI LANKA.
HERE, HE WAITS.
HE HUNTS.
HE FEEDS.
BUT MOSTLY, HE WAITS.
HE WAITS TO KILL AGAIN.

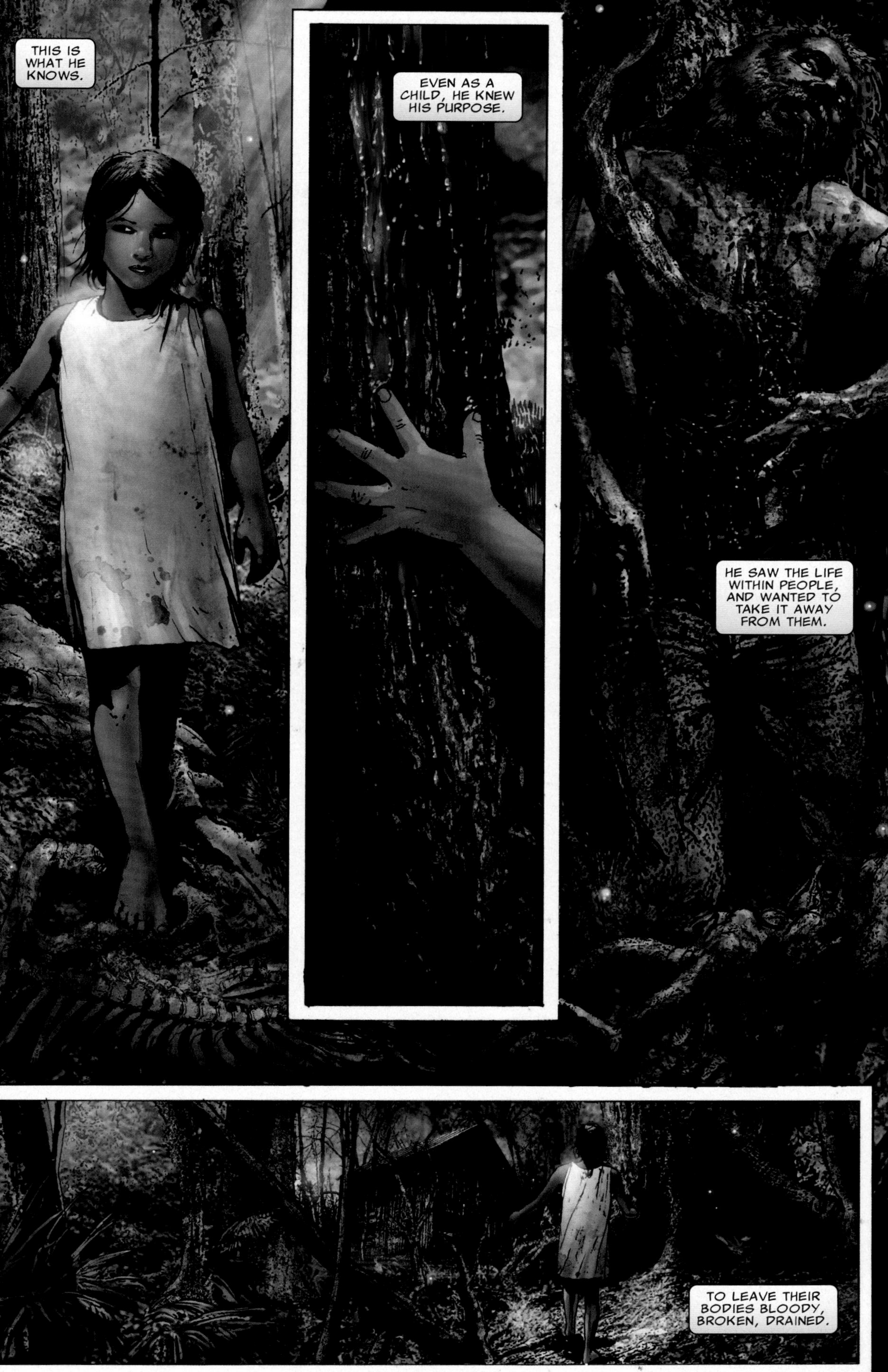
THIS IS WHAT HE KNOWS.
EVEN AS A CHILD, HE KNEW HIS PURPOSE.
HE SAW THE LIFE WITHIN PEOPLE, AND WANTED TO TAKE IT AWAY FROM THEM.
TO LEAVE THEIR BODIES BLOODY, BROKEN, DRAINED.

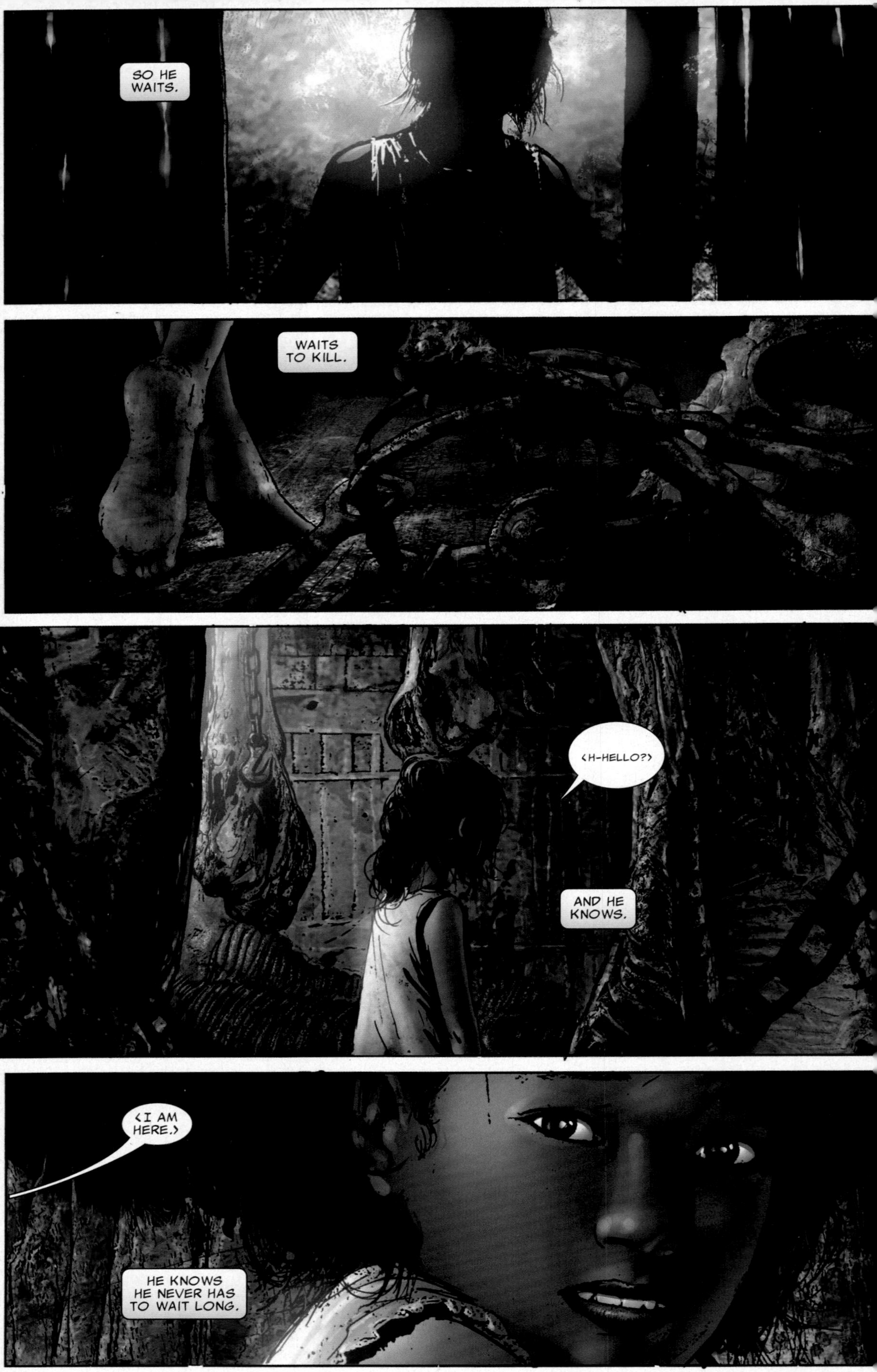
SO HE WAITS.
WAITS TO KILL.
‹H-HELLO?›
AND HE KNOWS.
‹I AM HERE.›
HE KNOWS HE NEVER HAS TO WAIT LONG.

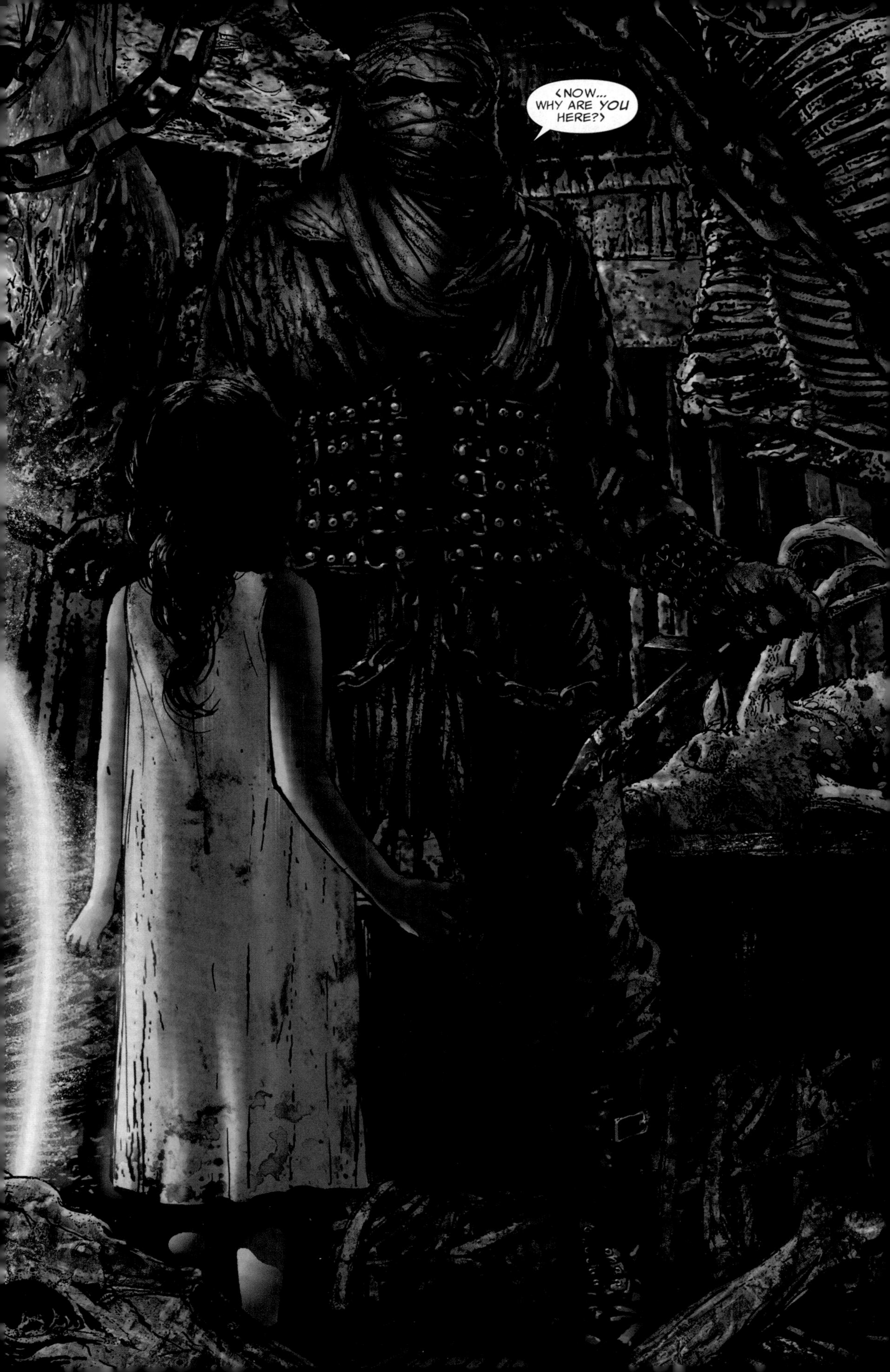
‹NOW... WHY ARE YOU HERE?›

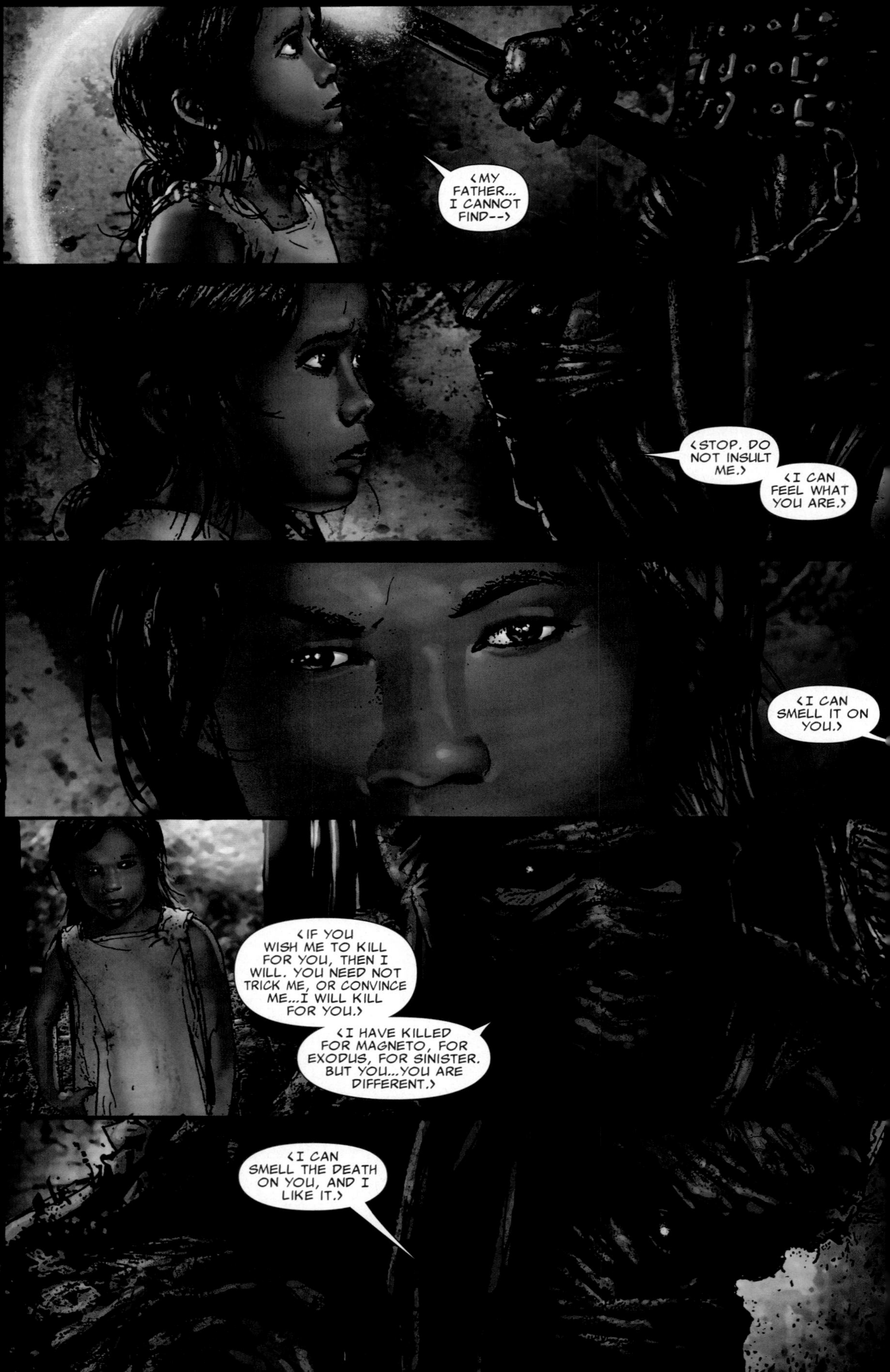
‹MY FATHER... I CANNOT FIND--›
‹STOP. DO NOT INSULT ME.›
‹I CAN FEEL WHAT YOU ARE.›
‹I CAN SMELL IT ON YOU.›
‹IF YOU WISH ME TO KILL FOR YOU, THEN I WILL. YOU NEED NOT TRICK ME, OR CONVINCE ME...I WILL KILL FOR YOU.›
‹I HAVE KILLED FOR MAGNETO, FOR EXODUS, FOR SINISTER. BUT YOU...YOU ARE DIFFERENT.›
‹I CAN SMELL THE DEATH ON YOU, AND I LIKE IT.›

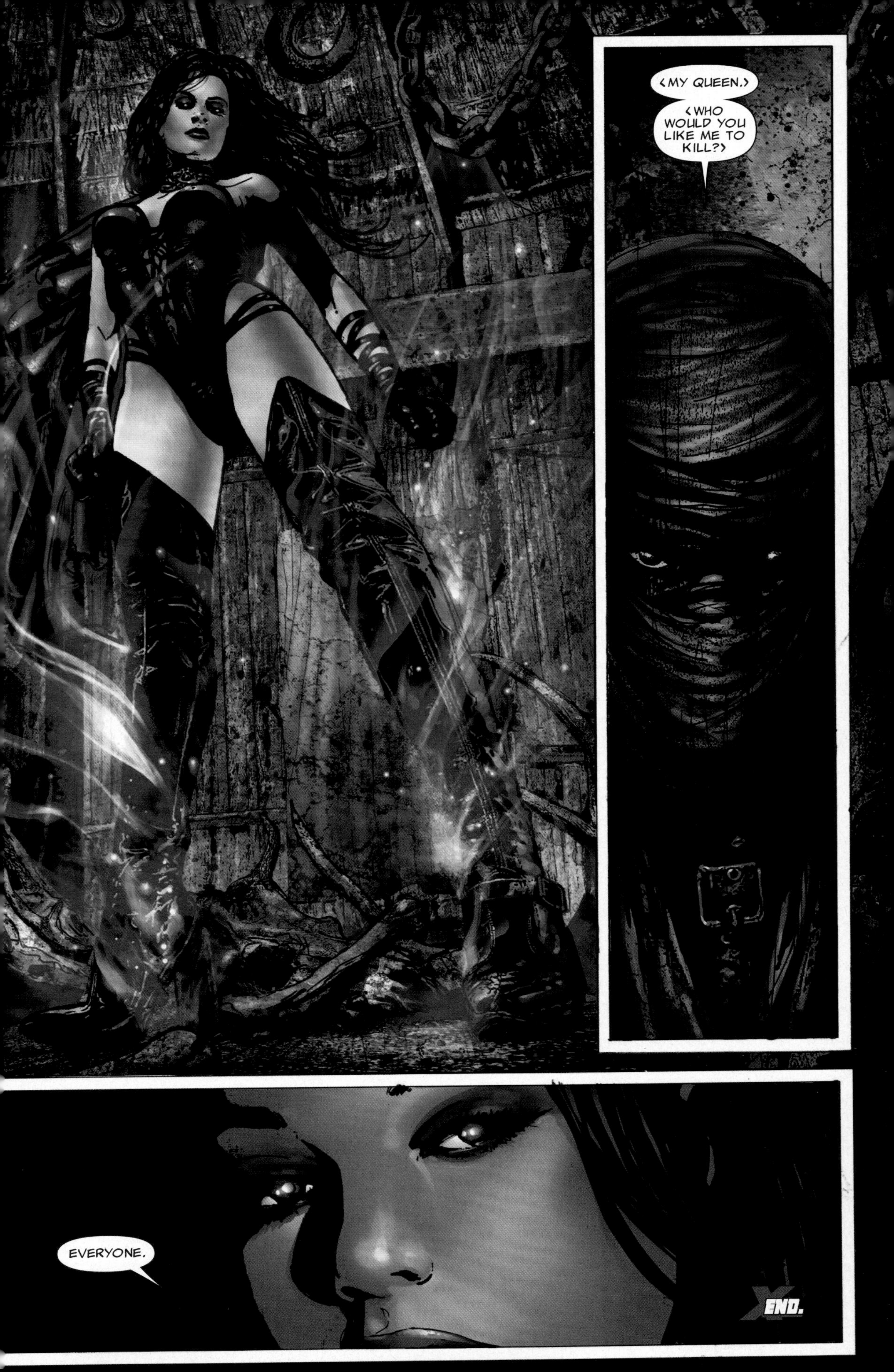
‹MY QUEEN.›
‹WHO WOULD YOU LIKE ME TO KILL?›
EVERYONE.
END.

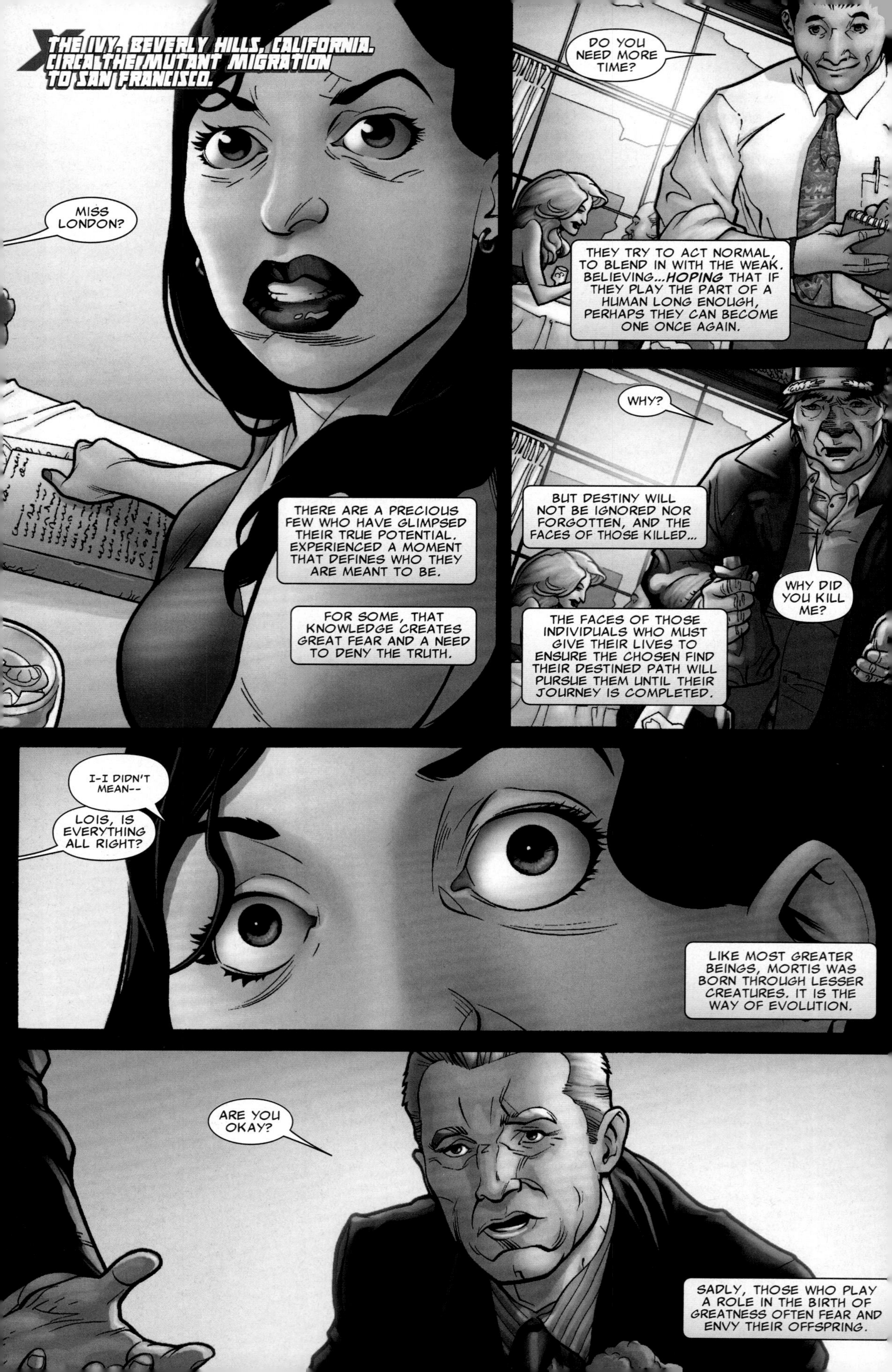
THE IVY, BEVERLY HILLS, CALIFORNIA. CIRCA THE MUTANT MIGRATION TO SAN FRANCISCO.
MISS LONDON?
THERE ARE A PRECIOUS FEW WHO HAVE GLIMPSED THEIR TRUE POTENTIAL. EXPERIENCED A MOMENT THAT DEFINES WHO THEY ARE MEANT TO BE.
FOR SOME, THAT KNOWLEDGE CREATES GREAT FEAR AND A NEED TO DENY THE TRUTH.
DO YOU NEED MORE TIME?
THEY TRY TO ACT NORMAL, TO BLEND IN WITH THE WEAK. BELIEVING...*HOPING* THAT IF THEY PLAY THE PART OF A HUMAN LONG ENOUGH, PERHAPS THEY CAN BECOME ONE ONCE AGAIN.
WHY?
BUT DESTINY WILL NOT BE IGNORED NOR FORGOTTEN, AND THE FACES OF THOSE KILLED...
WHY DID YOU KILL ME?
THE FACES OF THOSE INDIVIDUALS WHO MUST GIVE THEIR LIVES TO ENSURE THE CHOSEN FIND THEIR DESTINED PATH WILL PURSUE THEM UNTIL THEIR JOURNEY IS COMPLETED.
I-I DIDN'T MEAN--
LOIS, IS EVERYTHING ALL RIGHT?
LIKE MOST GREATER BEINGS, MORTIS WAS BORN THROUGH LESSER CREATURES. IT IS THE WAY OF EVOLUTION.
ARE YOU OKAY?
SADLY, THOSE WHO PLAY A ROLE IN THE BIRTH OF GREATNESS OFTEN FEAR AND ENVY THEIR OFFSPRING.

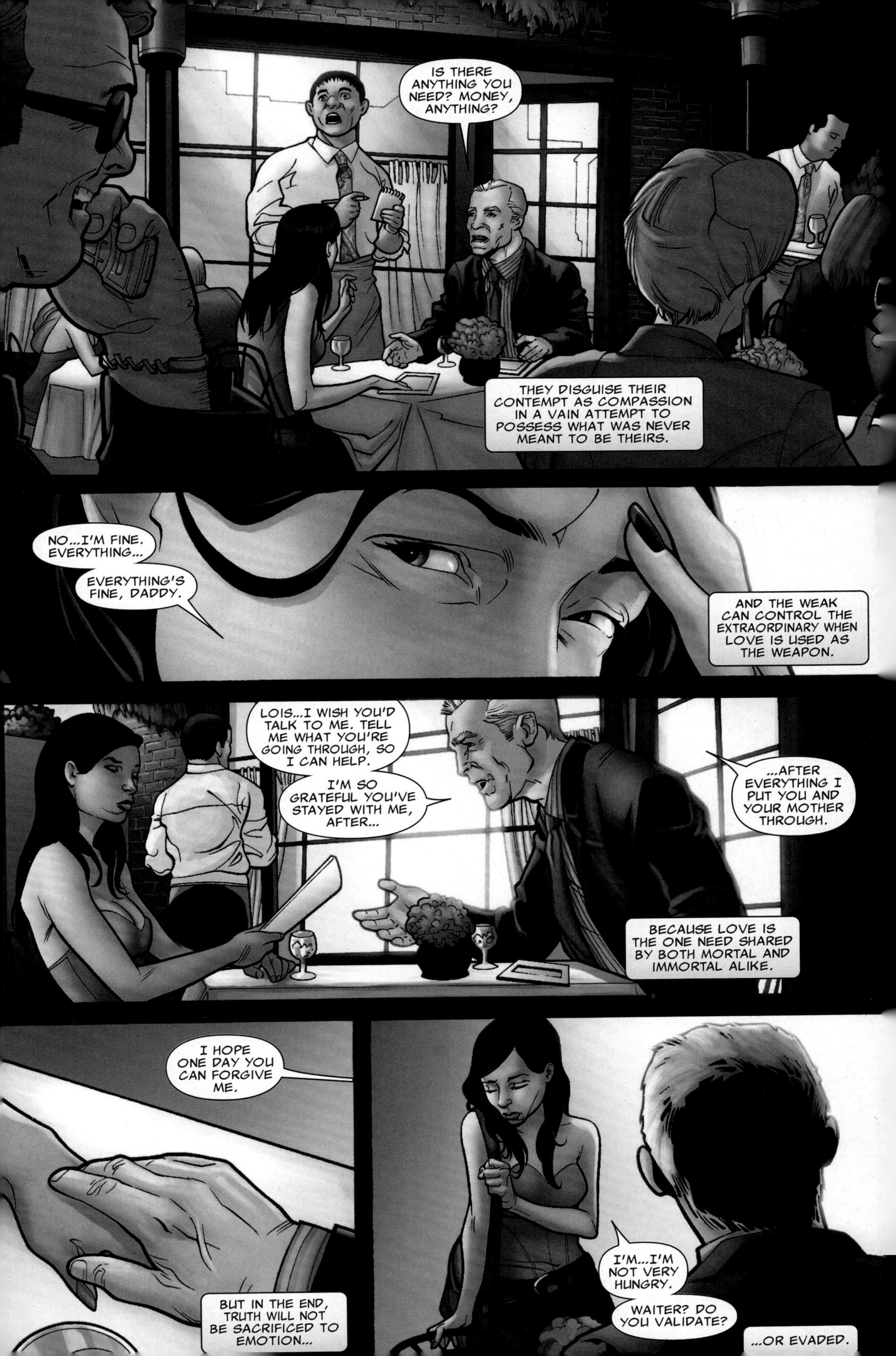
IS THERE ANYTHING YOU NEED? MONEY, ANYTHING?
THEY DISGUISE THEIR CONTEMPT AS COMPASSION IN A VAIN ATTEMPT TO POSSESS WHAT WAS NEVER MEANT TO BE THEIRS.
NO...I'M FINE. EVERYTHING...
EVERYTHING'S FINE, DADDY.
AND THE WEAK CAN CONTROL THE EXTRAORDINARY WHEN LOVE IS USED AS THE WEAPON.
LOIS...I WISH YOU'D TALK TO ME. TELL ME WHAT YOU'RE GOING THROUGH, SO I CAN HELP.
I'M SO GRATEFUL YOU'VE STAYED WITH ME, AFTER...
...AFTER EVERYTHING I PUT YOU AND YOUR MOTHER THROUGH.
BECAUSE LOVE IS THE ONE NEED SHARED BY BOTH MORTAL AND IMMORTAL ALIKE.
I HOPE ONE DAY YOU CAN FORGIVE ME.
BUT IN THE END, TRUTH WILL NOT BE SACRIFICED TO EMOTION...
I'M...I'M NOT VERY HUNGRY.
WAITER? DO YOU VALIDATE?
...OR EVADED.

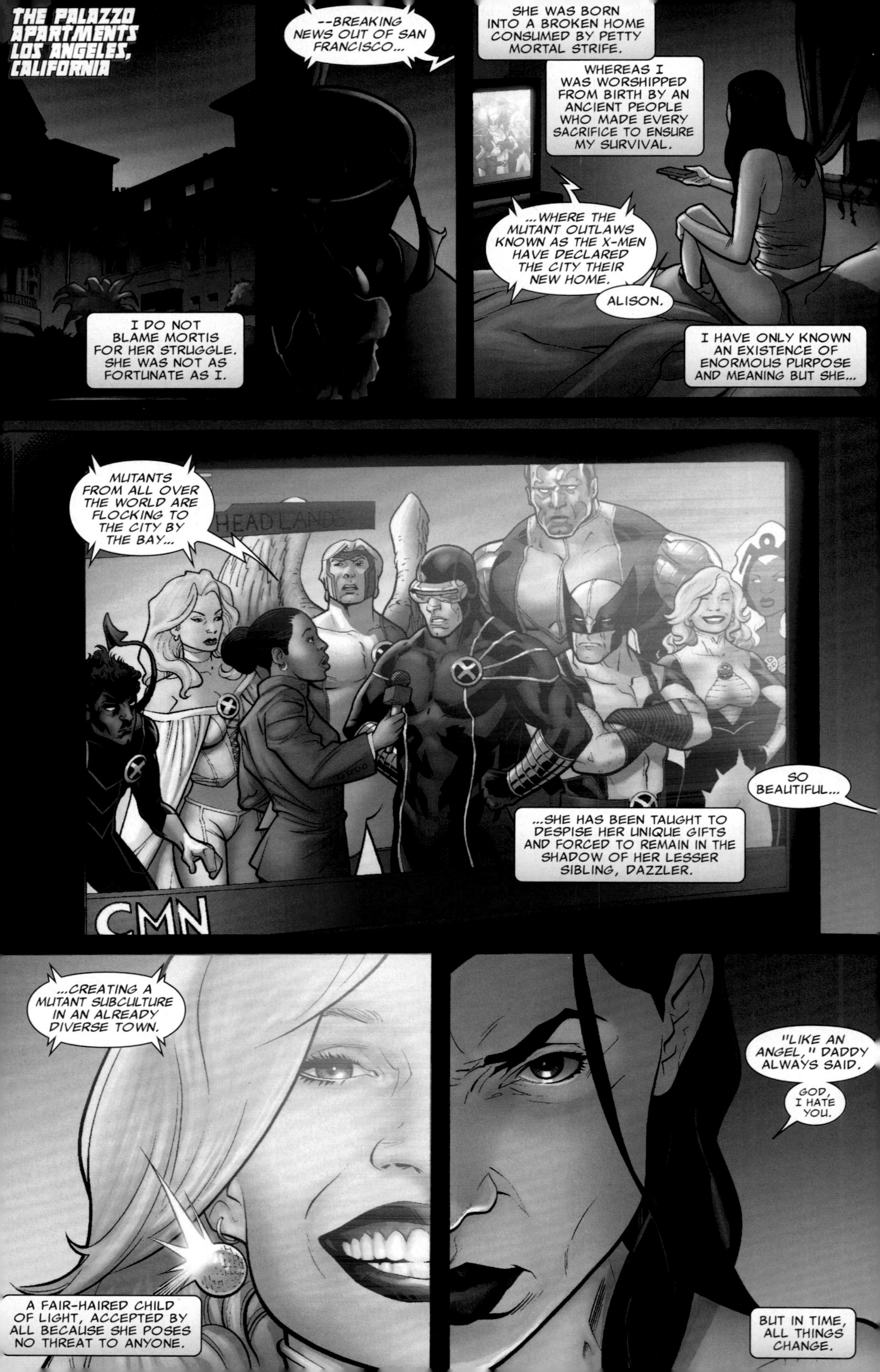
THE PALAZZO APARTMENTS LOS ANGELES, CALIFORNIA
--BREAKING NEWS OUT OF SAN FRANCISCO...
I DO NOT BLAME MORTIS FOR HER STRUGGLE. SHE WAS NOT AS FORTUNATE AS I.
SHE WAS BORN INTO A BROKEN HOME CONSUMED BY PETTY MORTAL STRIFE.
WHEREAS I WAS WORSHIPPED FROM BIRTH BY AN ANCIENT PEOPLE WHO MADE EVERY SACRIFICE TO ENSURE MY SURVIVAL.
...WHERE THE MUTANT OUTLAWS KNOWN AS THE X-MEN HAVE DECLARED THE CITY THEIR NEW HOME.
ALISON.
I HAVE ONLY KNOWN AN EXISTENCE OF ENORMOUS PURPOSE AND MEANING BUT SHE...
MUTANTS FROM ALL OVER THE WORLD ARE FLOCKING TO THE CITY BY THE BAY...
HEADLANDS
SO BEAUTIFUL...
...SHE HAS BEEN TAUGHT TO DESPISE HER UNIQUE GIFTS AND FORCED TO REMAIN IN THE SHADOW OF HER LESSER SIBLING, DAZZLER.
CMN
...CREATING A MUTANT SUBCULTURE IN AN ALREADY DIVERSE TOWN.
A FAIR-HAIRED CHILD OF LIGHT, ACCEPTED BY ALL BECAUSE SHE POSES NO THREAT TO ANYONE.
"LIKE AN ANGEL," DADDY ALWAYS SAID.
GOD, I HATE YOU.
BUT IN TIME, ALL THINGS CHANGE.

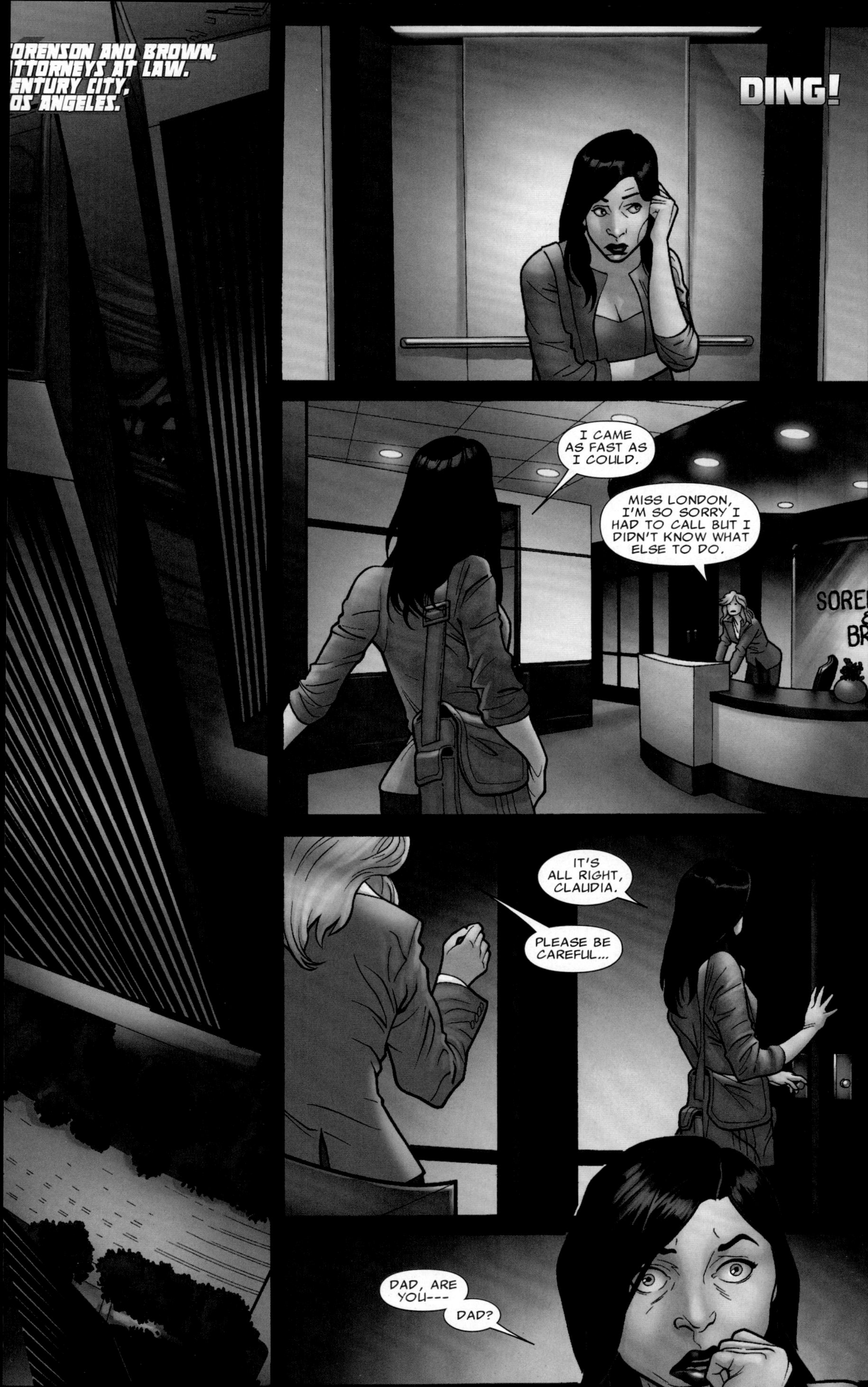
ORENSON AND BROWN,
TTORNEYS AT LAW.
ENTURY CITY,
OS ANGELES.
DING!
I CAME AS FAST AS I COULD.
MISS LONDON, I'M SO SORRY I HAD TO CALL BUT I DIDN'T KNOW WHAT ELSE TO DO.
IT'S ALL RIGHT, CLAUDIA.
PLEASE BE CAREFUL...
DAD, ARE YOU---
DAD?

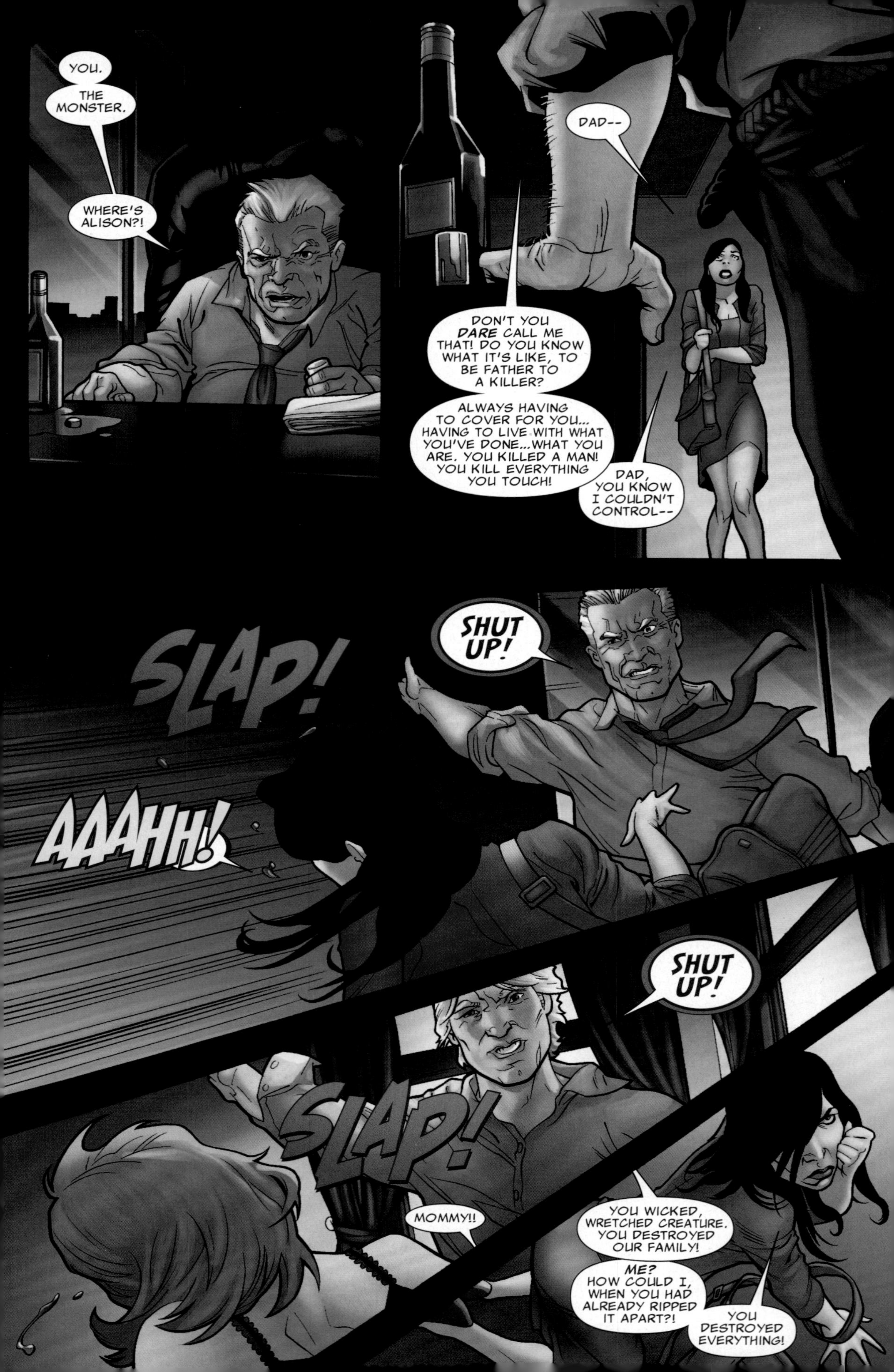
YOU.
THE MONSTER.
WHERE'S ALISON?!
DAD--
DON'T YOU DARE CALL ME THAT! DO YOU KNOW WHAT IT'S LIKE, TO BE FATHER TO A KILLER?
ALWAYS HAVING TO COVER FOR YOU... HAVING TO LIVE WITH WHAT YOU'VE DONE...WHAT YOU ARE. YOU KILLED A MAN! YOU KILL EVERYTHING YOU TOUCH!
DAD, YOU KNOW I COULDN'T CONTROL--
SLAP!
SHUT UP!
AAAHH!
SHUT UP!
SLAP!
MOMMY!!
YOU WICKED, WRETCHED CREATURE. YOU DESTROYED OUR FAMILY!
ME? HOW COULD I, WHEN YOU HAD ALREADY RIPPED IT APART?!
YOU DESTROYED EVERYTHING!

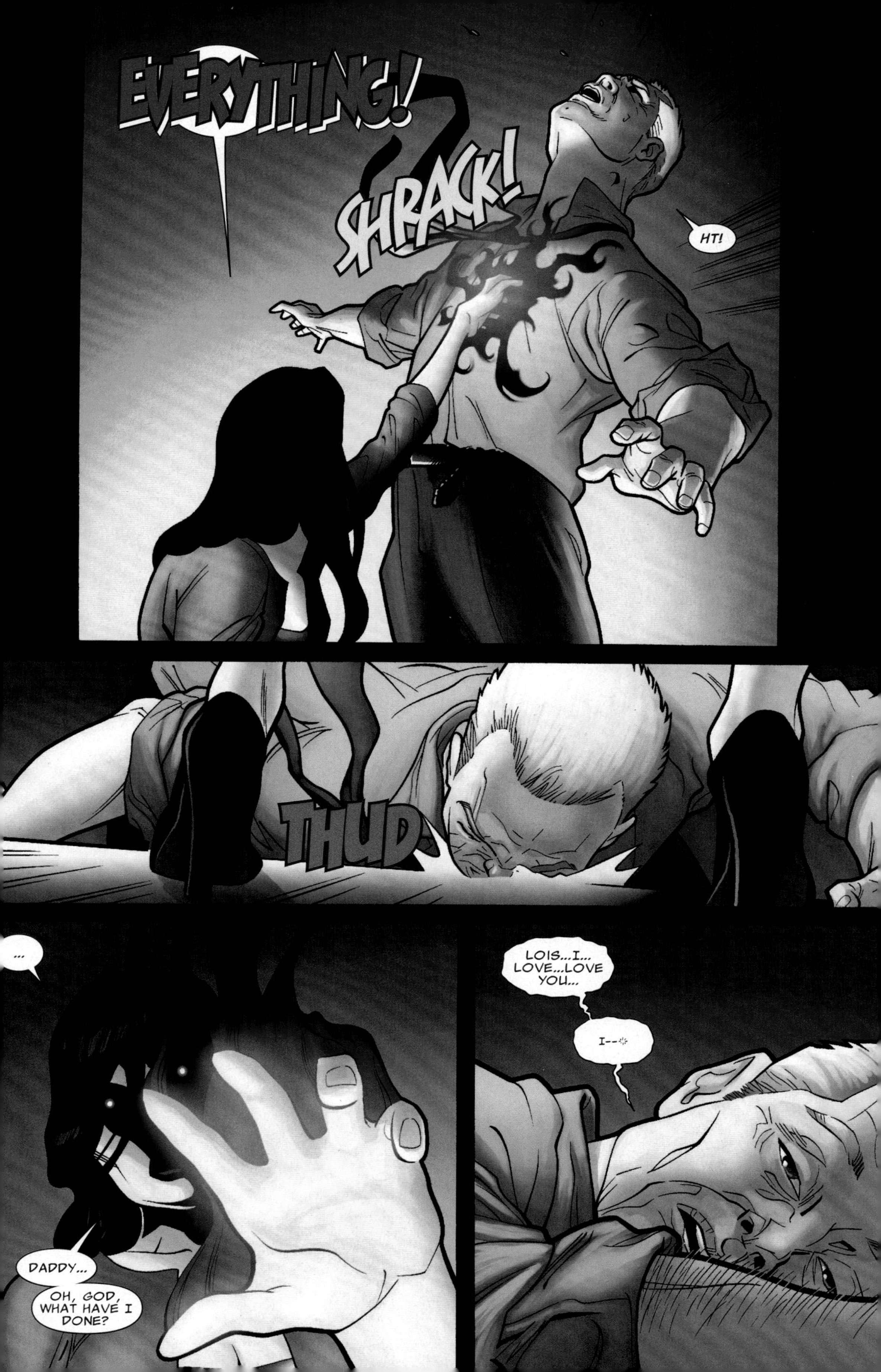
EVERYTHING!
SHRACK!
HT!
THUD
...
DADDY...
OH, GOD, WHAT HAVE I DONE?
LOIS...I... LOVE...LOVE YOU...
I--

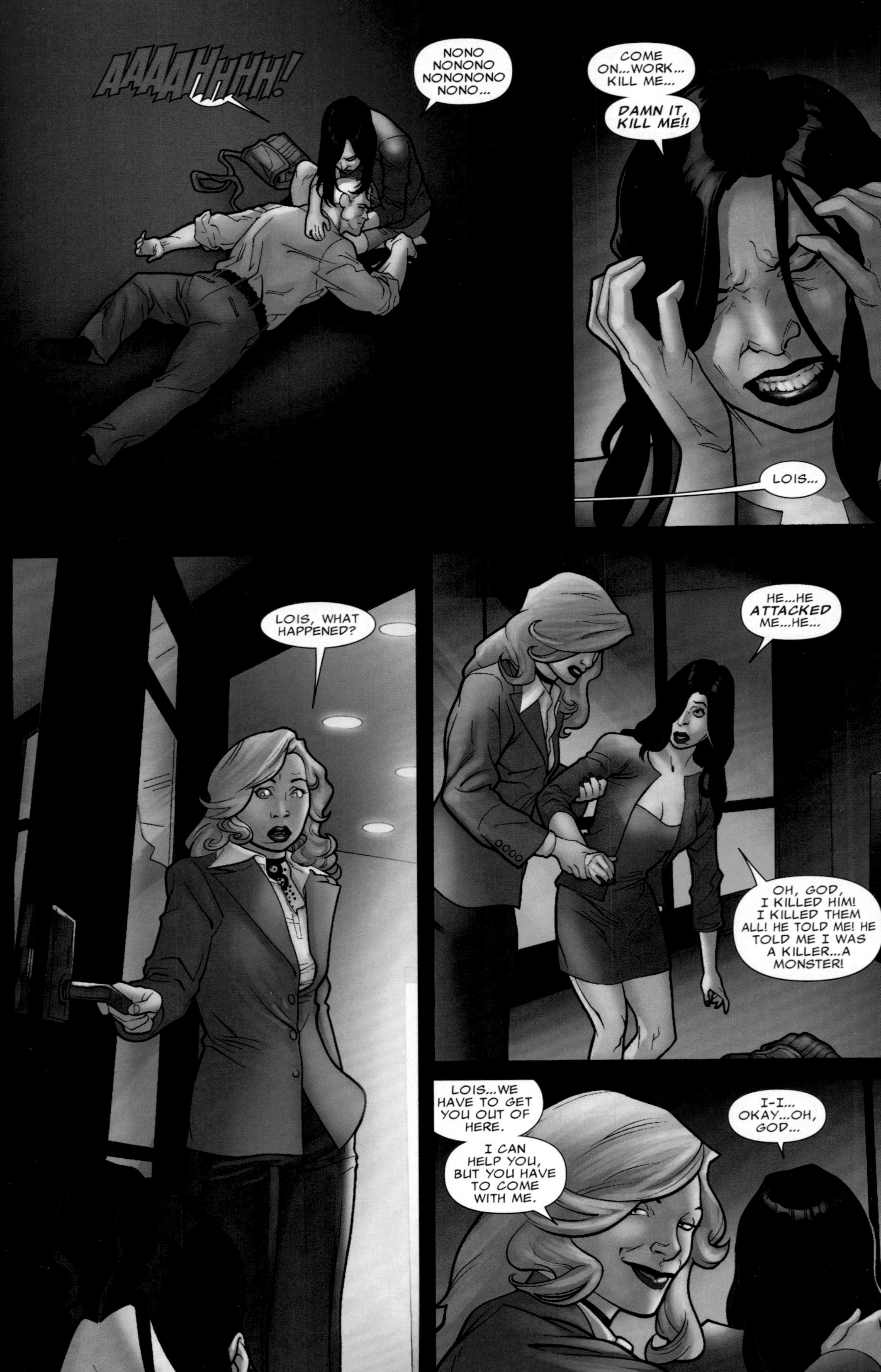
AAAAHHHH!
NONO NONONO NONONONO NONO...
COME ON...WORK... KILL ME...
DAMN IT, KILL ME!!
LOIS...
LOIS, WHAT HAPPENED?
HE...HE ATTACKED ME...HE...
OH, GOD, I KILLED HIM! I KILLED THEM ALL! HE TOLD ME! HE TOLD ME I WAS A KILLER...A MONSTER!
LOIS...WE HAVE TO GET YOU OUT OF HERE.
I CAN HELP YOU, BUT YOU HAVE TO COME WITH ME.
I-I... OKAY...OH, GOD...

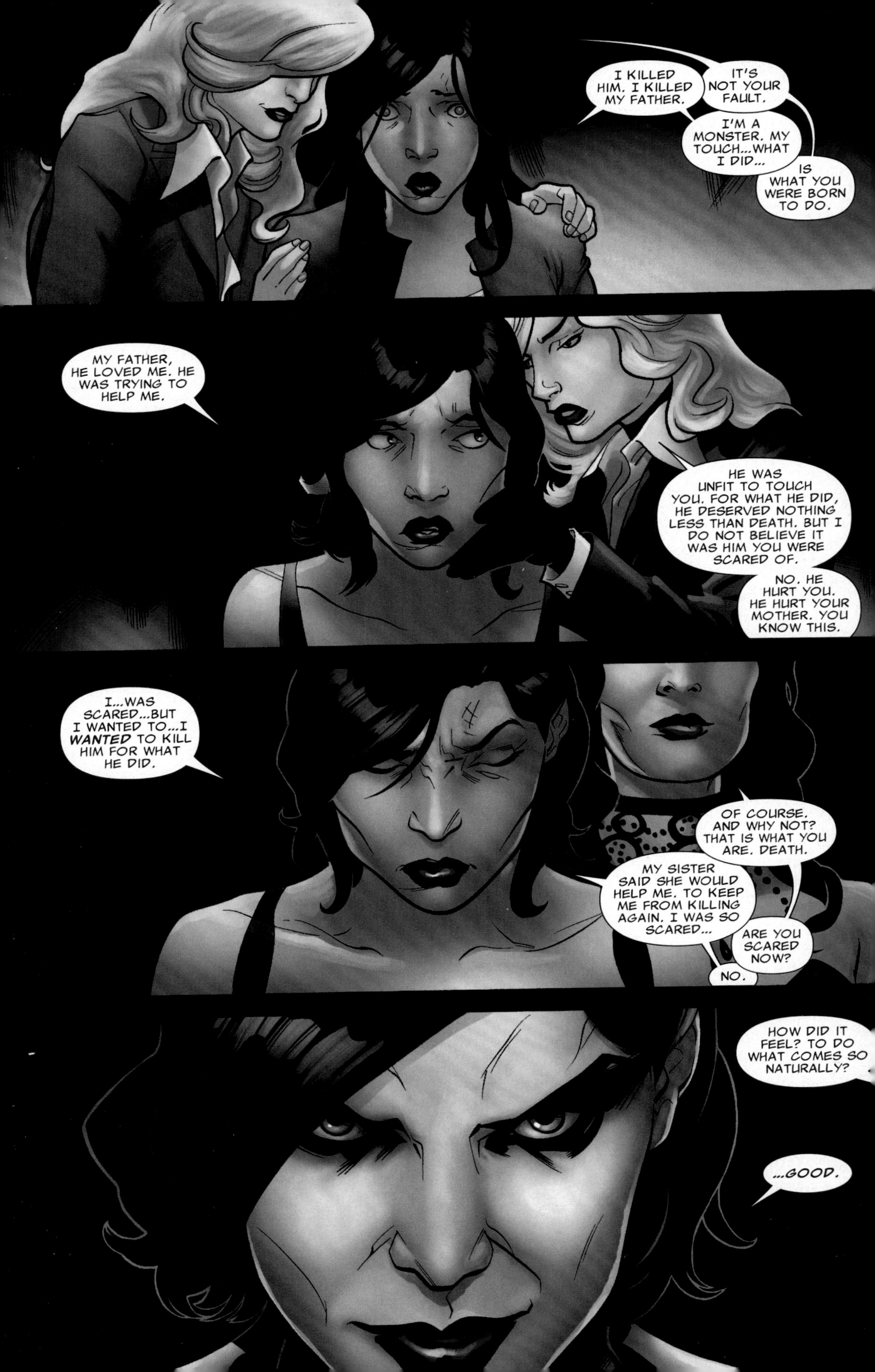
I KILLED HIM. I KILLED MY FATHER.
IT'S NOT YOUR FAULT.
I'M A MONSTER. MY TOUCH...WHAT I DID...
IS WHAT YOU WERE BORN TO DO.
MY FATHER, HE LOVED ME. HE WAS TRYING TO HELP ME.
HE WAS UNFIT TO TOUCH YOU. FOR WHAT HE DID, HE DESERVED NOTHING LESS THAN DEATH. BUT I DO NOT BELIEVE IT WAS HIM YOU WERE SCARED OF.
NO. HE HURT YOU. HE HURT YOUR MOTHER. YOU KNOW THIS.
I...WAS SCARED...BUT I WANTED TO...I *WANTED* TO KILL HIM FOR WHAT HE DID.
OF COURSE. AND WHY NOT? THAT IS WHAT YOU ARE. DEATH.
MY SISTER SAID SHE WOULD HELP ME. TO KEEP ME FROM KILLING AGAIN. I WAS SO SCARED...
ARE YOU SCARED NOW?
NO.
HOW DID IT FEEL? TO DO WHAT COMES SO NATURALLY?
...*GOOD*.

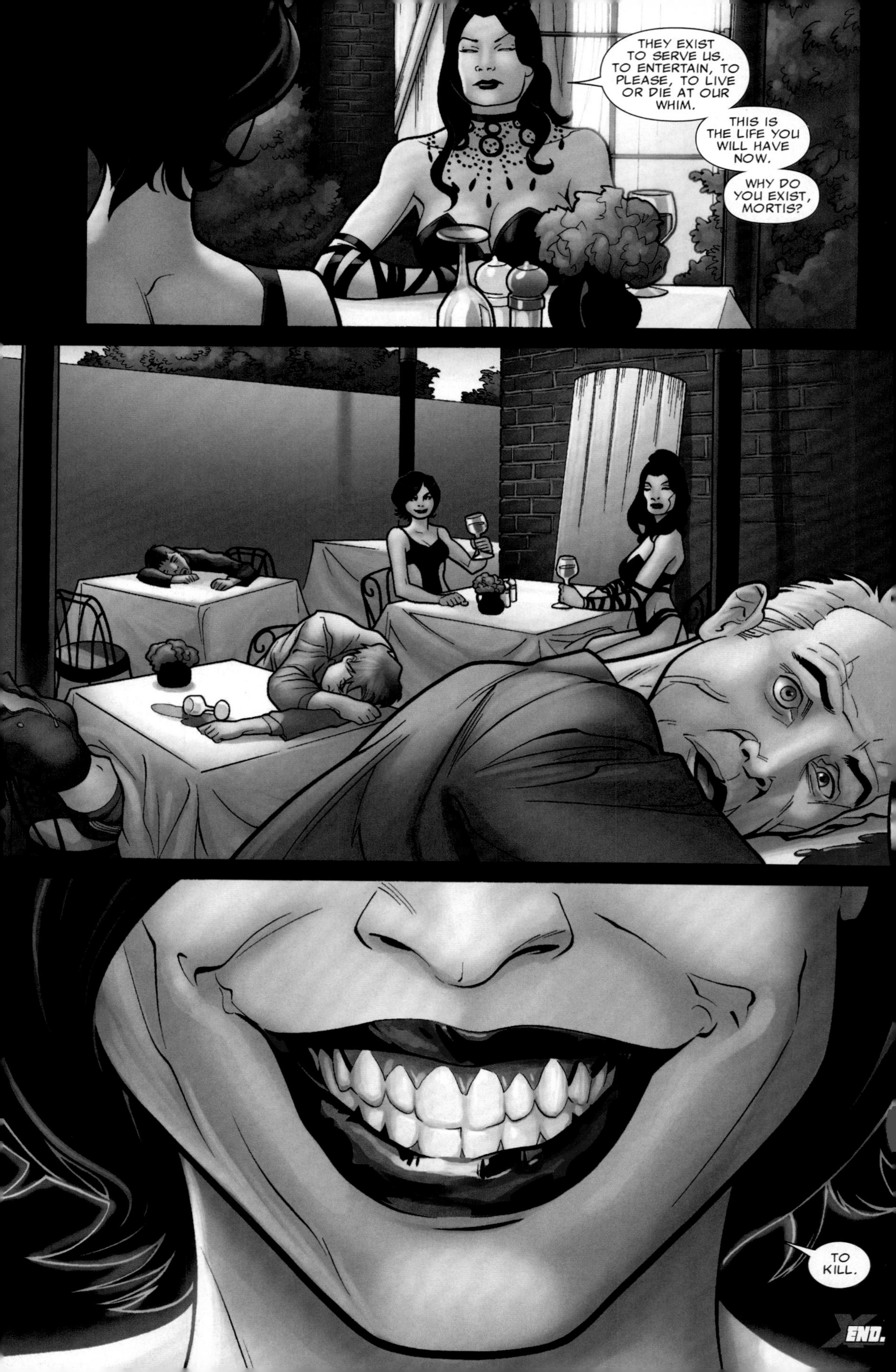
THEY EXIST TO SERVE US. TO ENTERTAIN, TO PLEASE, TO LIVE OR DIE AT OUR WHIM.
THIS IS THE LIFE YOU WILL HAVE NOW.
WHY DO YOU EXIST, MORTIS?
TO KILL.
END.

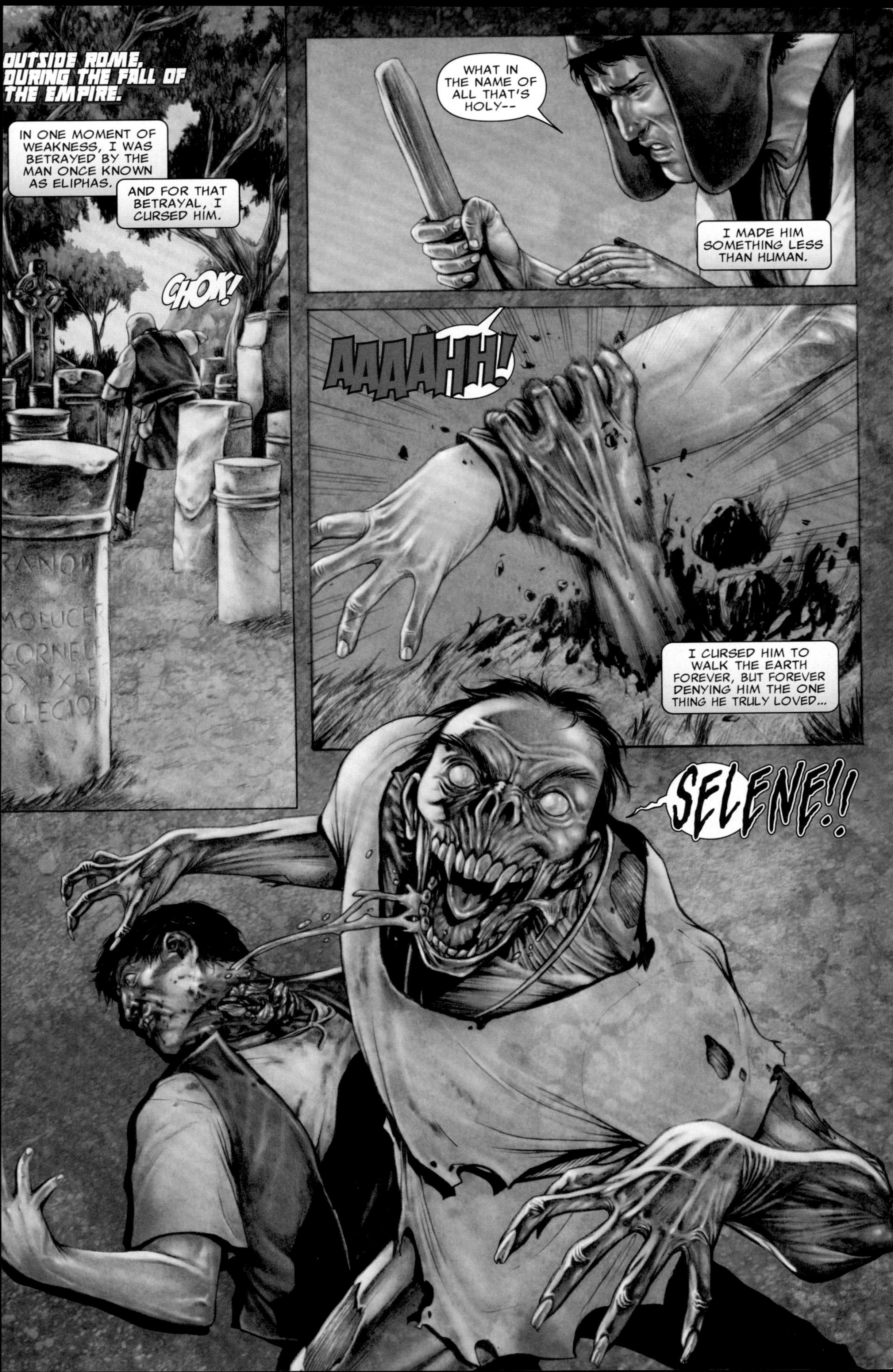
OUTSIDE ROME, DURING THE FALL OF THE EMPIRE.
IN ONE MOMENT OF WEAKNESS, I WAS BETRAYED BY THE MAN ONCE KNOWN AS ELIPHAS.
AND FOR THAT BETRAYAL, I CURSED HIM.
CHOK!
WHAT IN THE NAME OF ALL THAT'S HOLY--
I MADE HIM SOMETHING LESS THAN HUMAN.
AAAAHH!
I CURSED HIM TO WALK THE EARTH FOREVER, BUT FOREVER DENYING HIM THE ONE THING HE TRULY LOVED...
SELENE!!

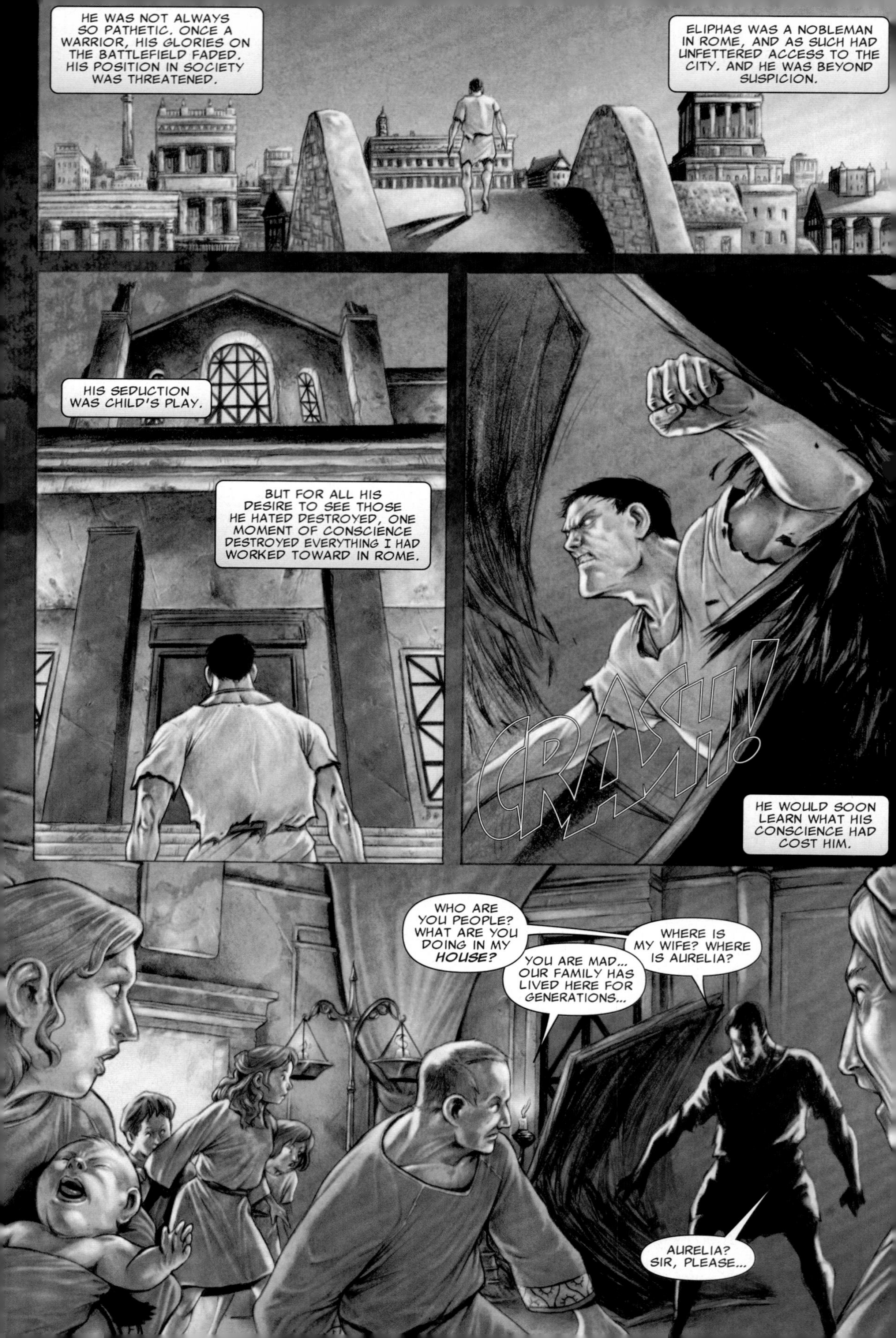
HE WAS NOT ALWAYS SO PATHETIC. ONCE A WARRIOR, HIS GLORIES ON THE BATTLEFIELD FADED. HIS POSITION IN SOCIETY WAS THREATENED.
ELIPHAS WAS A NOBLEMAN IN ROME, AND AS SUCH HAD UNFETTERED ACCESS TO THE CITY. AND HE WAS BEYOND SUSPICION.
HIS SEDUCTION WAS CHILD'S PLAY.
BUT FOR ALL HIS DESIRE TO SEE THOSE HE HATED DESTROYED, ONE MOMENT OF CONSCIENCE DESTROYED EVERYTHING I HAD WORKED TOWARD IN ROME.
CRASH!
HE WOULD SOON LEARN WHAT HIS CONSCIENCE HAD COST HIM.
WHO ARE YOU PEOPLE? WHAT ARE YOU DOING IN MY *HOUSE?*
WHERE IS MY WIFE? WHERE IS AURELIA?
YOU ARE MAD... OUR FAMILY HAS LIVED HERE FOR GENERATIONS...
AURELIA? SIR, PLEASE...

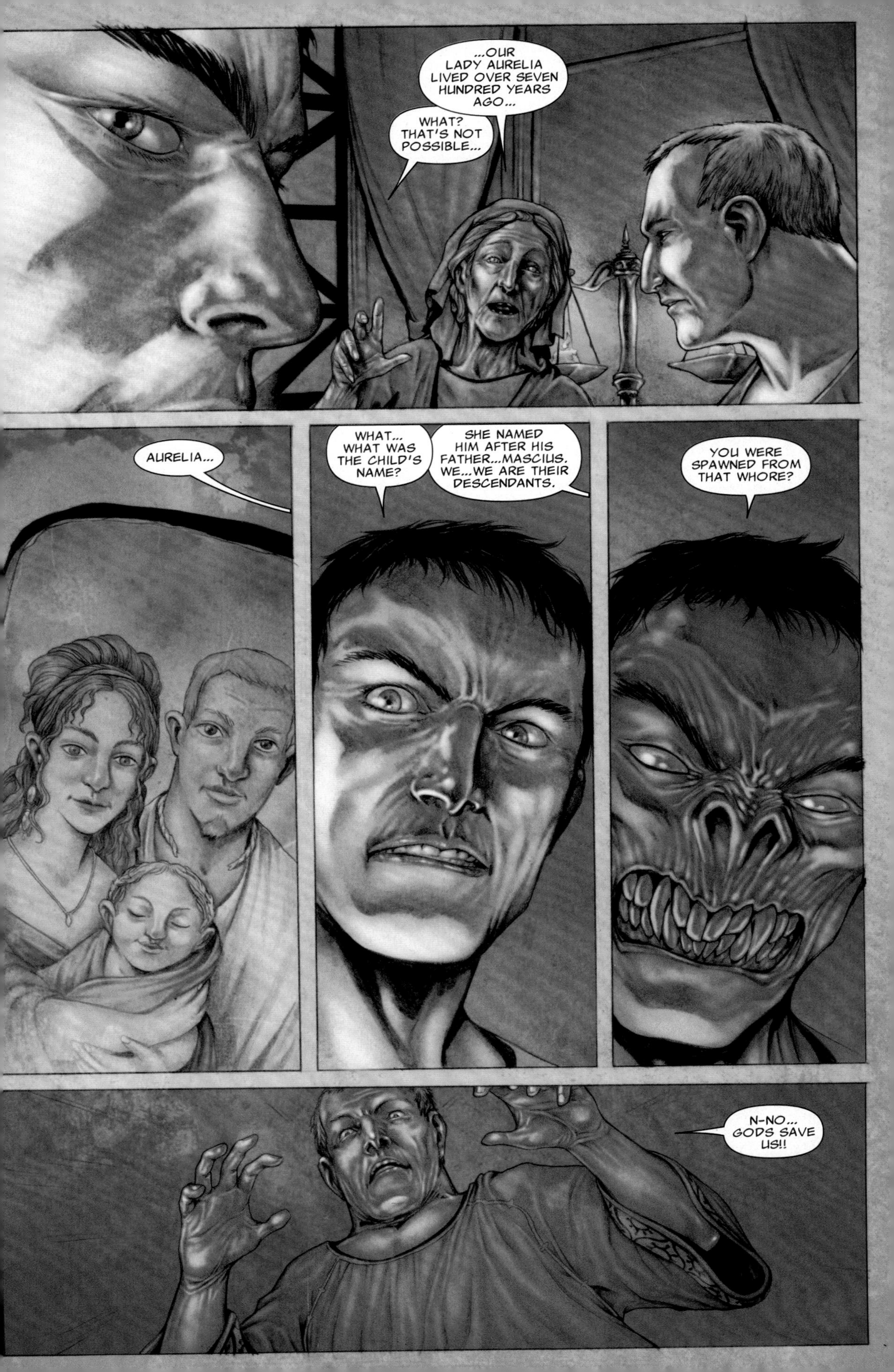
...OUR LADY AURELIA LIVED OVER SEVEN HUNDRED YEARS AGO...
WHAT? THAT'S NOT POSSIBLE...
AURELIA...
WHAT... WHAT WAS THE CHILD'S NAME?
SHE NAMED HIM AFTER HIS FATHER...MASCIUS. WE...WE ARE THEIR DESCENDANTS.
YOU WERE SPAWNED FROM THAT WHORE?
N-NO... GODS SAVE US!!

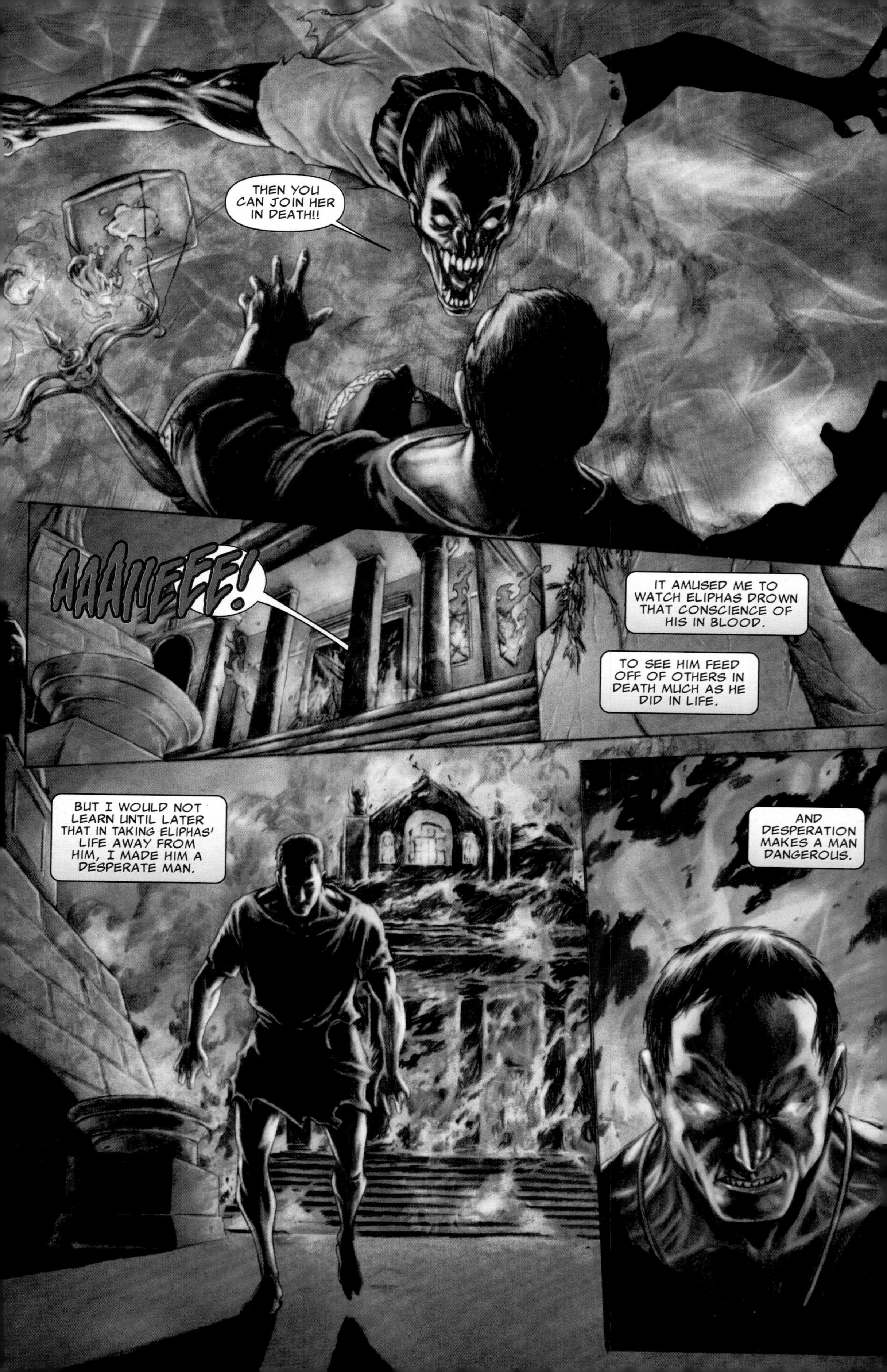
THEN YOU CAN JOIN HER IN DEATH!!
AAAAIEEEE!
IT AMUSED ME TO WATCH ELIPHAS DROWN THAT CONSCIENCE OF HIS IN BLOOD.
TO SEE HIM FEED OFF OF OTHERS IN DEATH MUCH AS HE DID IN LIFE.
BUT I WOULD NOT LEARN UNTIL LATER THAT IN TAKING ELIPHAS' LIFE AWAY FROM HIM, I MADE HIM A DESPERATE MAN.
AND DESPERATION MAKES A MAN DANGEROUS.

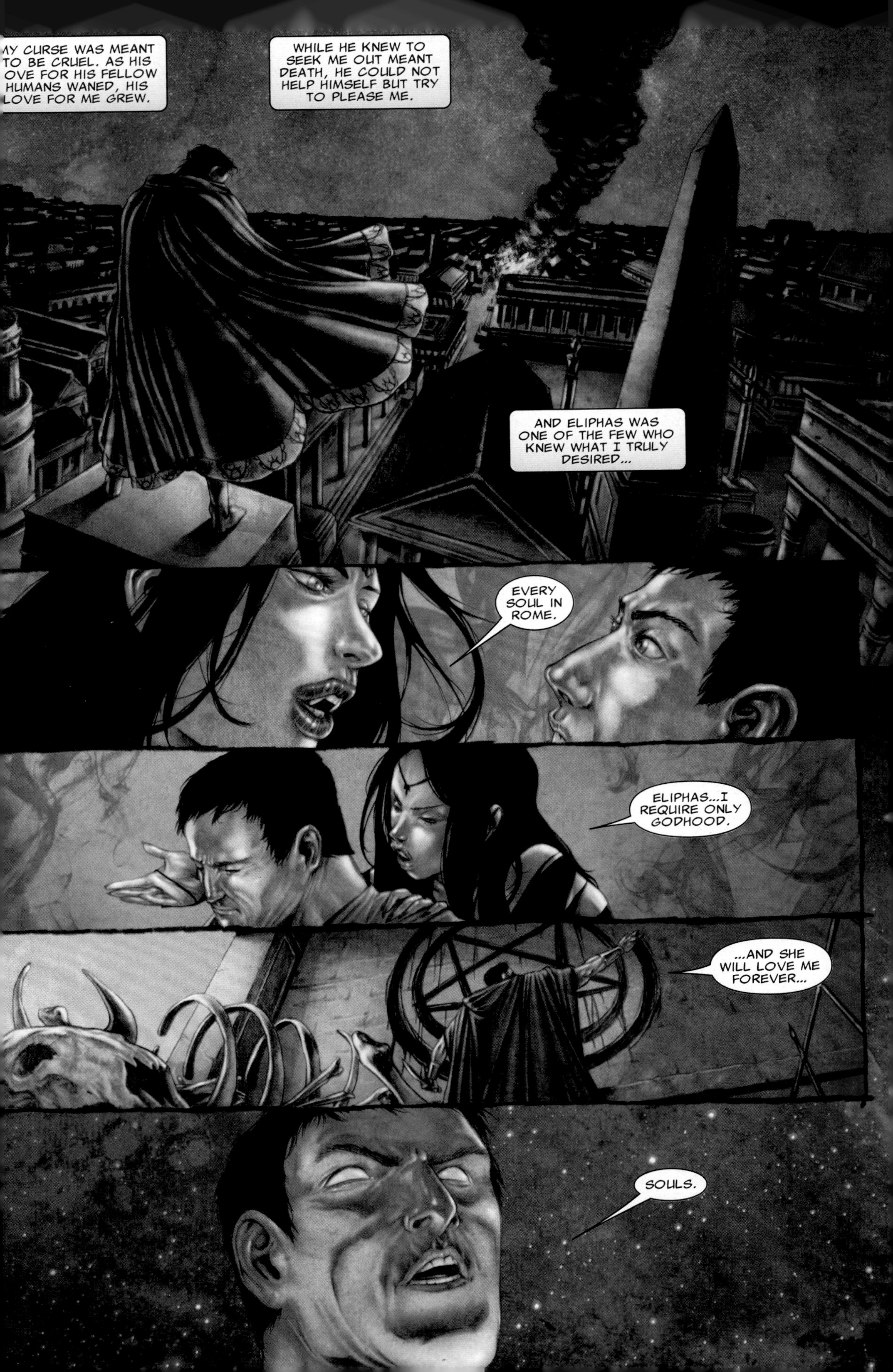
MY CURSE WAS MEANT TO BE CRUEL. AS HIS LOVE FOR HIS FELLOW HUMANS WANED, HIS LOVE FOR ME GREW.
WHILE HE KNEW TO SEEK ME OUT MEANT DEATH, HE COULD NOT HELP HIMSELF BUT TRY TO PLEASE ME.
AND ELIPHAS WAS ONE OF THE FEW WHO KNEW WHAT I TRULY DESIRED...
EVERY SOUL IN ROME.
ELIPHAS...I REQUIRE ONLY GODHOOD.
...AND SHE WILL LOVE ME FOREVER...
SOULS.

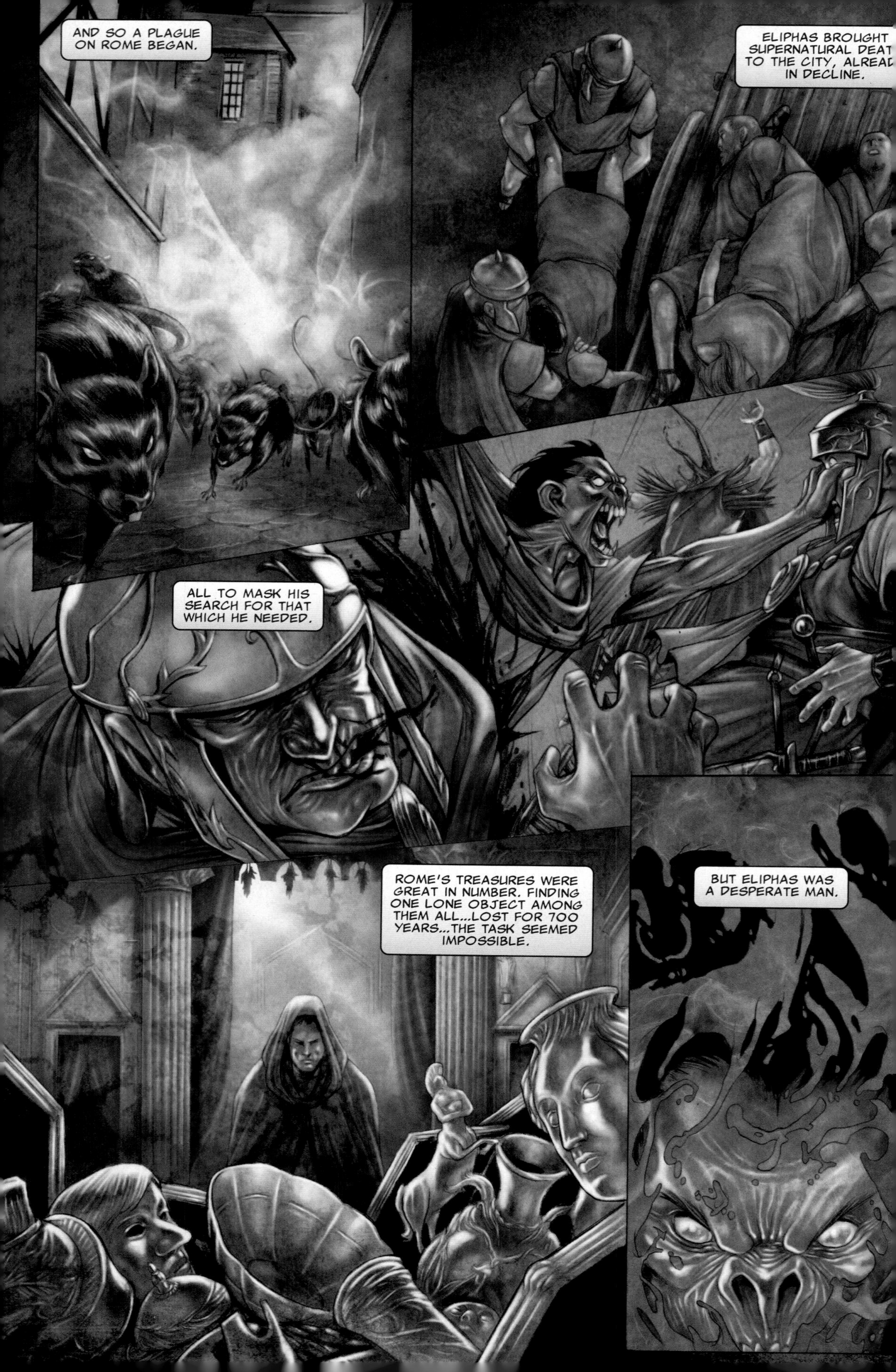
AND SO A PLAGUE ON ROME BEGAN.
ELIPHAS BROUGHT SUPERNATURAL DEAT TO THE CITY, ALREAD IN DECLINE.
ALL TO MASK HIS SEARCH FOR THAT WHICH HE NEEDED.
ROME'S TREASURES WERE GREAT IN NUMBER. FINDING ONE LONE OBJECT AMONG THEM ALL...LOST FOR 700 YEARS...THE TASK SEEMED IMPOSSIBLE.
BUT ELIPHAS WAS A DESPERATE MAN.

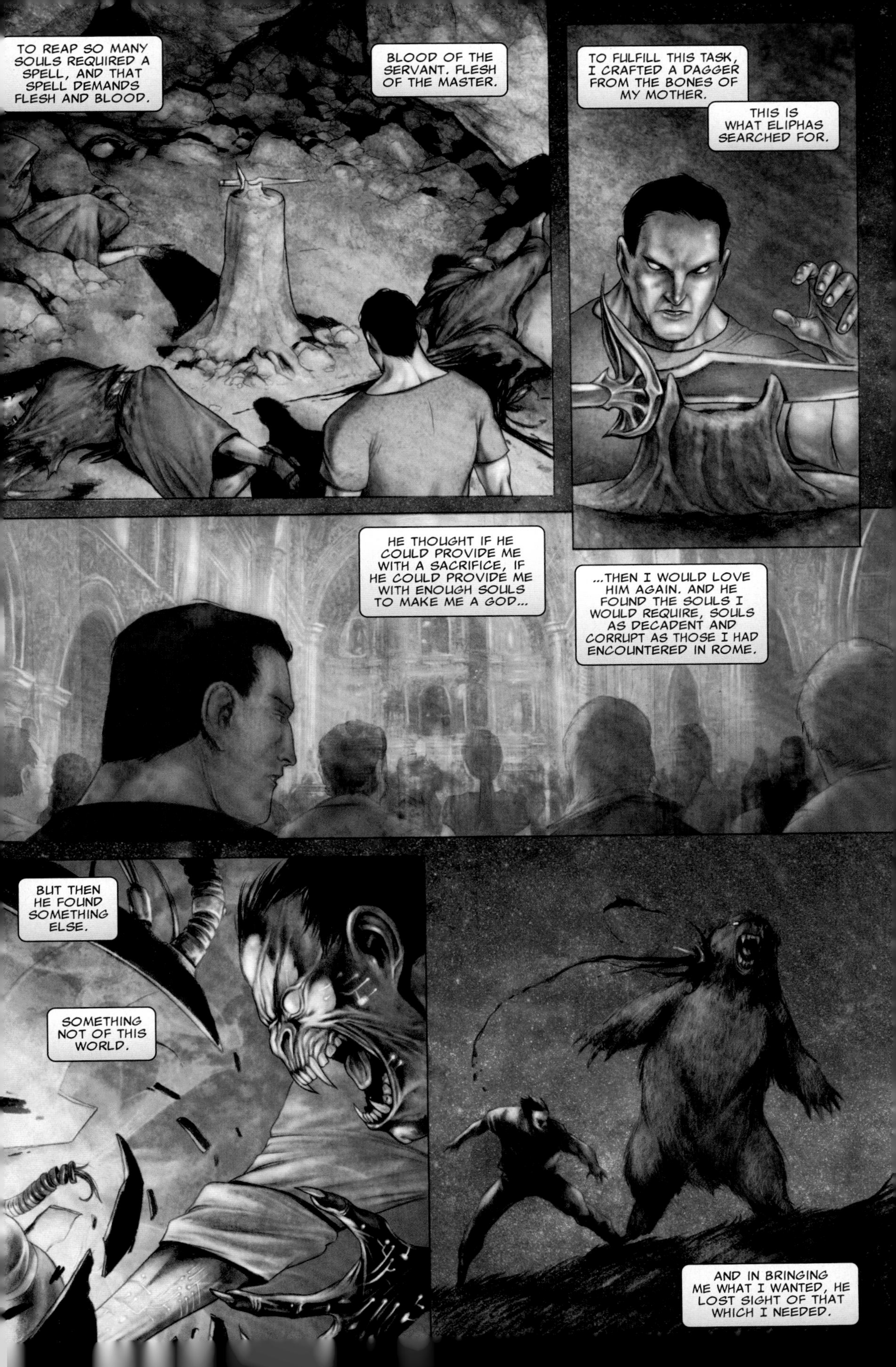
TO REAP SO MANY SOULS REQUIRED A SPELL, AND THAT SPELL DEMANDS FLESH AND BLOOD.
BLOOD OF THE SERVANT. FLESH OF THE MASTER.
TO FULFILL THIS TASK, I CRAFTED A DAGGER FROM THE BONES OF MY MOTHER.
THIS IS WHAT ELIPHAS SEARCHED FOR.
HE THOUGHT IF HE COULD PROVIDE ME WITH A SACRIFICE, IF HE COULD PROVIDE ME WITH ENOUGH SOULS TO MAKE ME A GOD...
...THEN I WOULD LOVE HIM AGAIN. AND HE FOUND THE SOULS I WOULD REQUIRE, SOULS AS DECADENT AND CORRUPT AS THOSE I HAD ENCOUNTERED IN ROME.
BUT THEN HE FOUND SOMETHING ELSE.
SOMETHING NOT OF THIS WORLD.
AND IN BRINGING ME WHAT I WANTED, HE LOST SIGHT OF THAT WHICH I NEEDED.

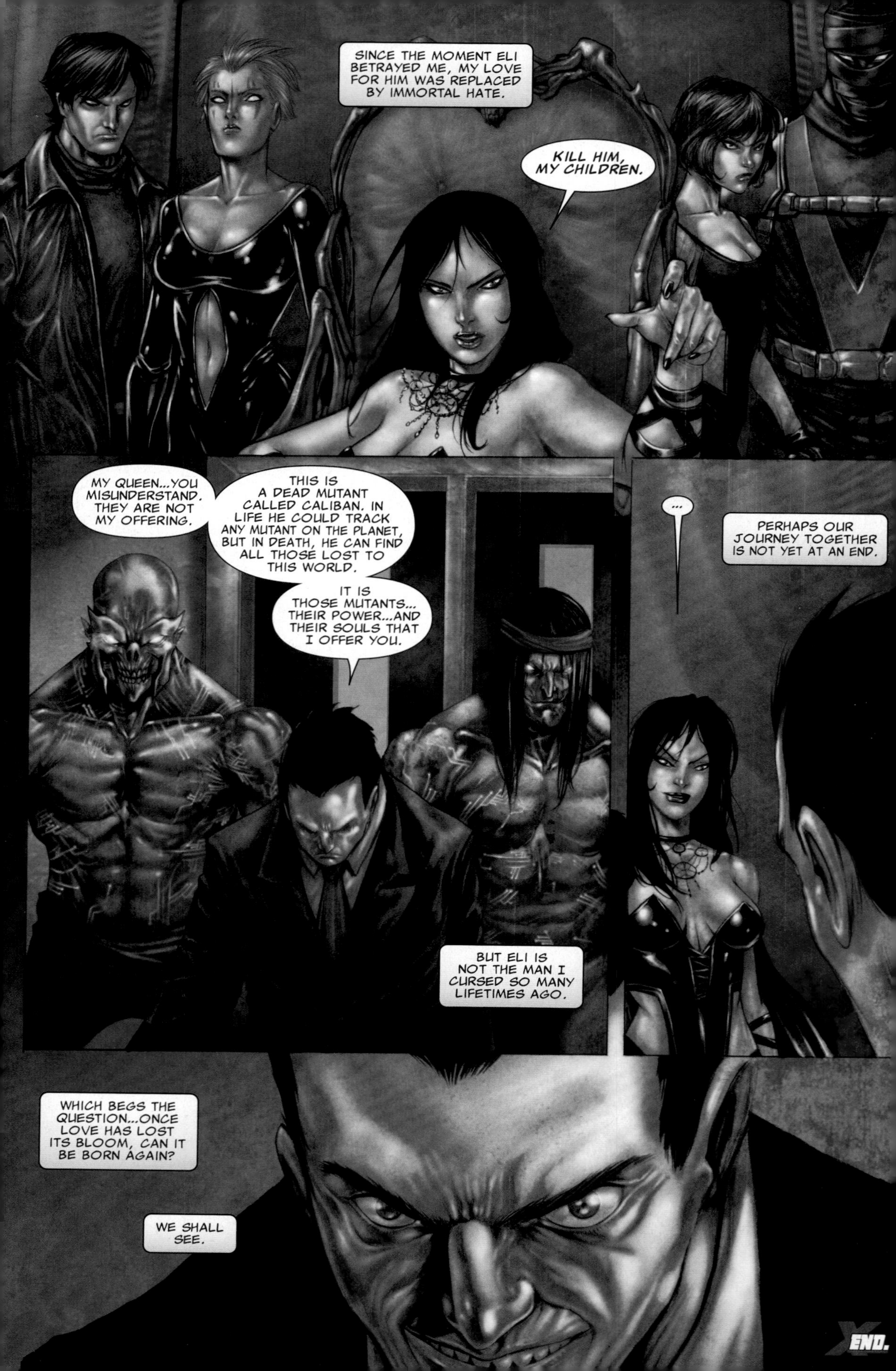
SINCE THE MOMENT ELI BETRAYED ME, MY LOVE FOR HIM WAS REPLACED BY IMMORTAL HATE.
KILL HIM, MY CHILDREN.
MY QUEEN...YOU MISUNDERSTAND. THEY ARE NOT MY OFFERING.
THIS IS A DEAD MUTANT CALLED CALIBAN. IN LIFE HE COULD TRACK ANY MUTANT ON THE PLANET, BUT IN DEATH, HE CAN FIND ALL THOSE LOST TO THIS WORLD.
IT IS THOSE MUTANTS... THEIR POWER...AND THEIR SOULS THAT I OFFER YOU.
BUT ELI IS NOT THE MAN I CURSED SO MANY LIFETIMES AGO.
...
PERHAPS OUR JOURNEY TOGETHER IS NOT YET AT AN END.
WHICH BEGS THE QUESTION...ONCE LOVE HAS LOST ITS BLOOM, CAN IT BE BORN AGAIN?
WE SHALL SEE.
END.

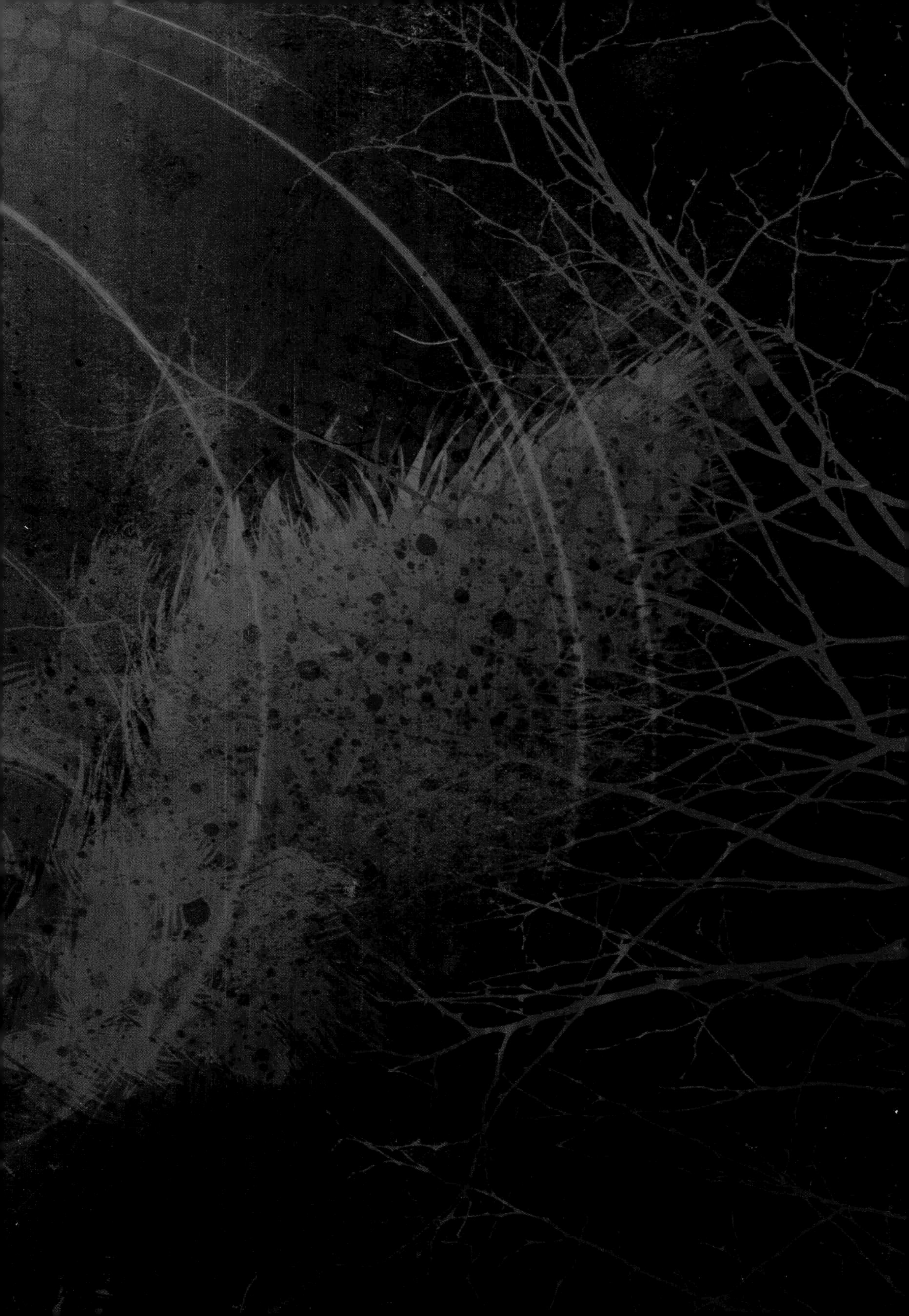

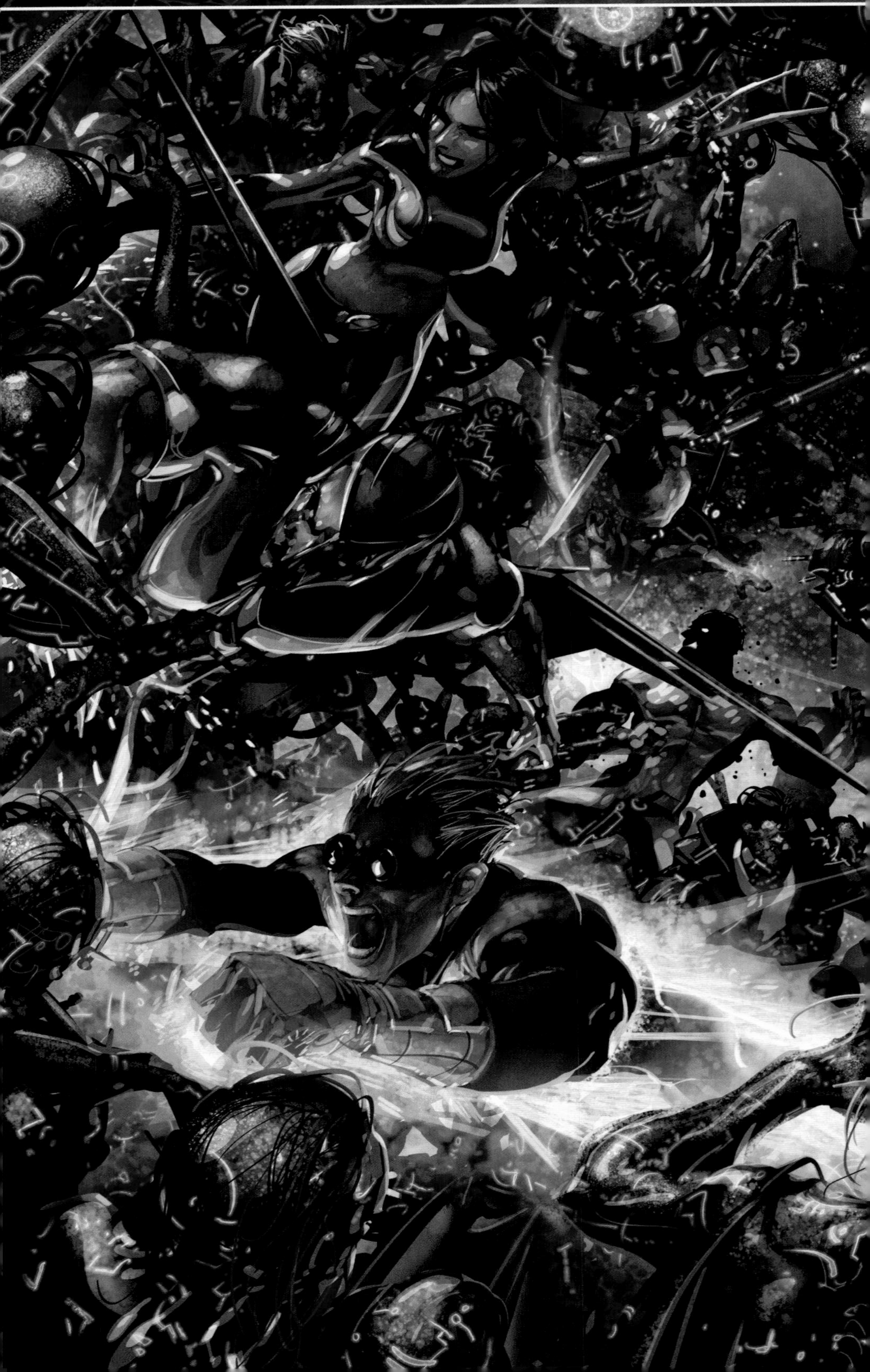

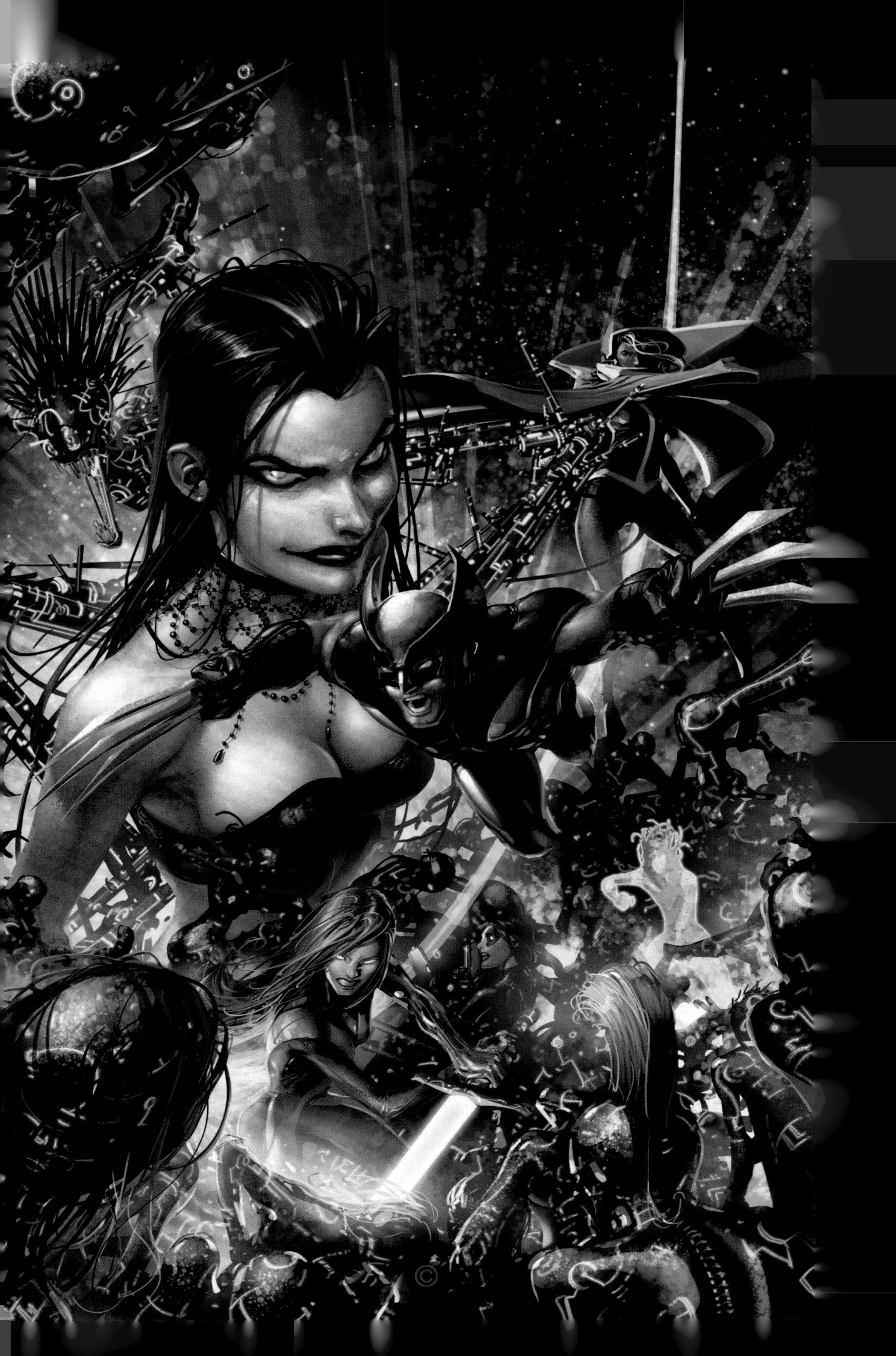

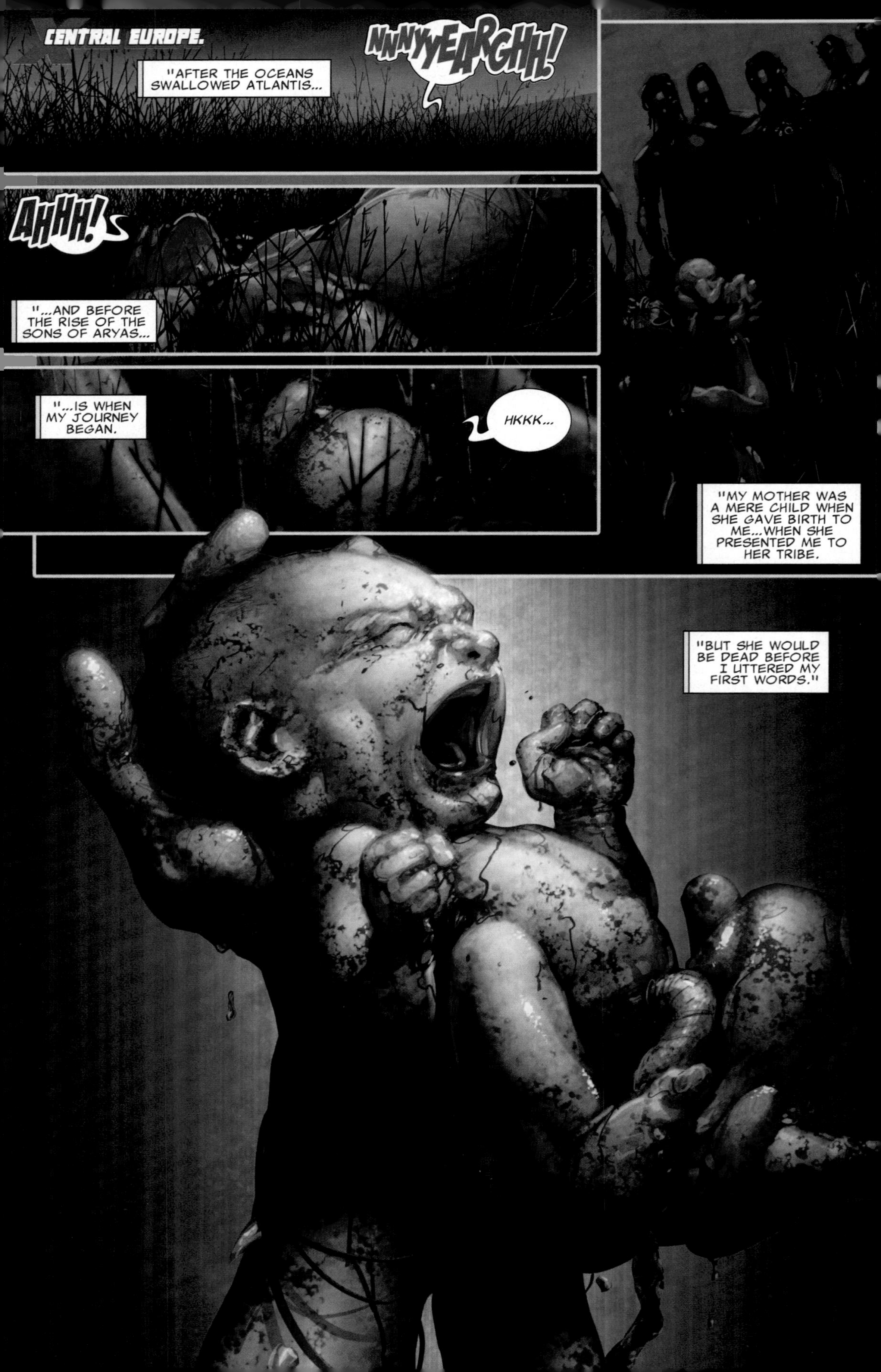
CENTRAL EUROPE.
"AFTER THE OCEANS SWALLOWED ATLANTIS...
NNNYYYEARGHH!
AHHH!
"...AND BEFORE THE RISE OF THE SONS OF ARYAS...
"...IS WHEN MY JOURNEY BEGAN.
HKKK...
"MY MOTHER WAS A MERE CHILD WHEN SHE GAVE BIRTH TO ME...WHEN SHE PRESENTED ME TO HER TRIBE.
"BUT SHE WOULD BE DEAD BEFORE I UTTERED MY FIRST WORDS."

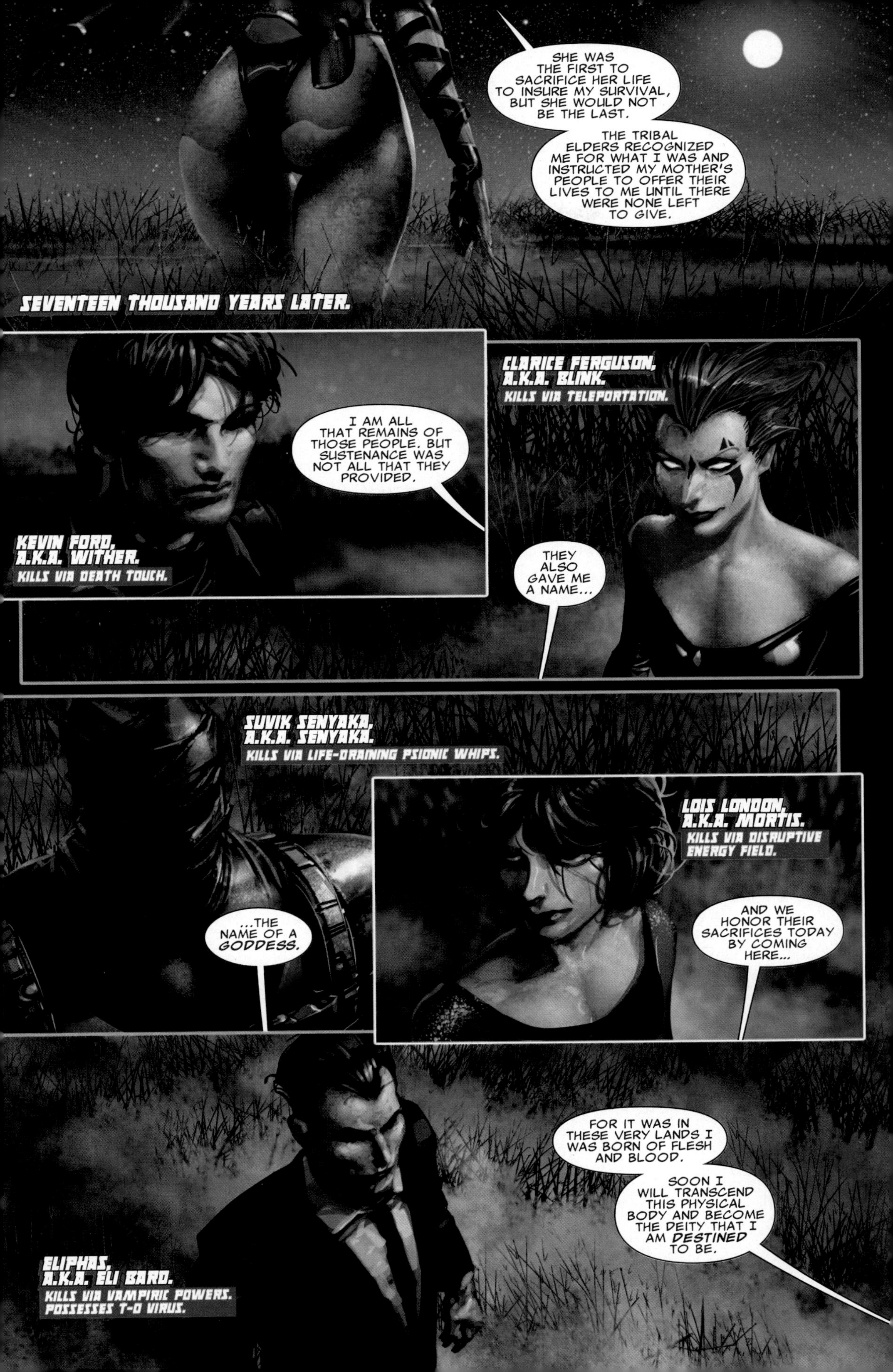
SHE WAS THE FIRST TO SACRIFICE HER LIFE TO INSURE MY SURVIVAL, BUT SHE WOULD NOT BE THE LAST.
THE TRIBAL ELDERS RECOGNIZED ME FOR WHAT I WAS AND INSTRUCTED MY MOTHER'S PEOPLE TO OFFER THEIR LIVES TO ME UNTIL THERE WERE NONE LEFT TO GIVE.
SEVENTEEN THOUSAND YEARS LATER.
I AM ALL THAT REMAINS OF THOSE PEOPLE. BUT SUSTENANCE WAS NOT ALL THAT THEY PROVIDED.
KEVIN FORD, A.K.A. WITHER.
KILLS VIA DEATH TOUCH.
CLARICE FERGUSON, A.K.A. BLINK.
KILLS VIA TELEPORTATION.
THEY ALSO GAVE ME A NAME...
SUVIK SENYAKA, A.K.A. SENYAKA.
KILLS VIA LIFE-DRAINING PSIONIC WHIPS.
...THE NAME OF A GODDESS.
LOIS LONDON, A.K.A. MORTIS.
KILLS VIA DISRUPTIVE ENERGY FIELD.
AND WE HONOR THEIR SACRIFICES TODAY BY COMING HERE...
FOR IT WAS IN THESE VERY LANDS I WAS BORN OF FLESH AND BLOOD.
SOON I WILL TRANSCEND THIS PHYSICAL BODY AND BECOME THE DEITY THAT I AM DESTINED TO BE.
ELIPHAS, A.K.A. ELI BARD.
KILLS VIA VAMPIRIC POWERS. POSSESSES T-O VIRUS.

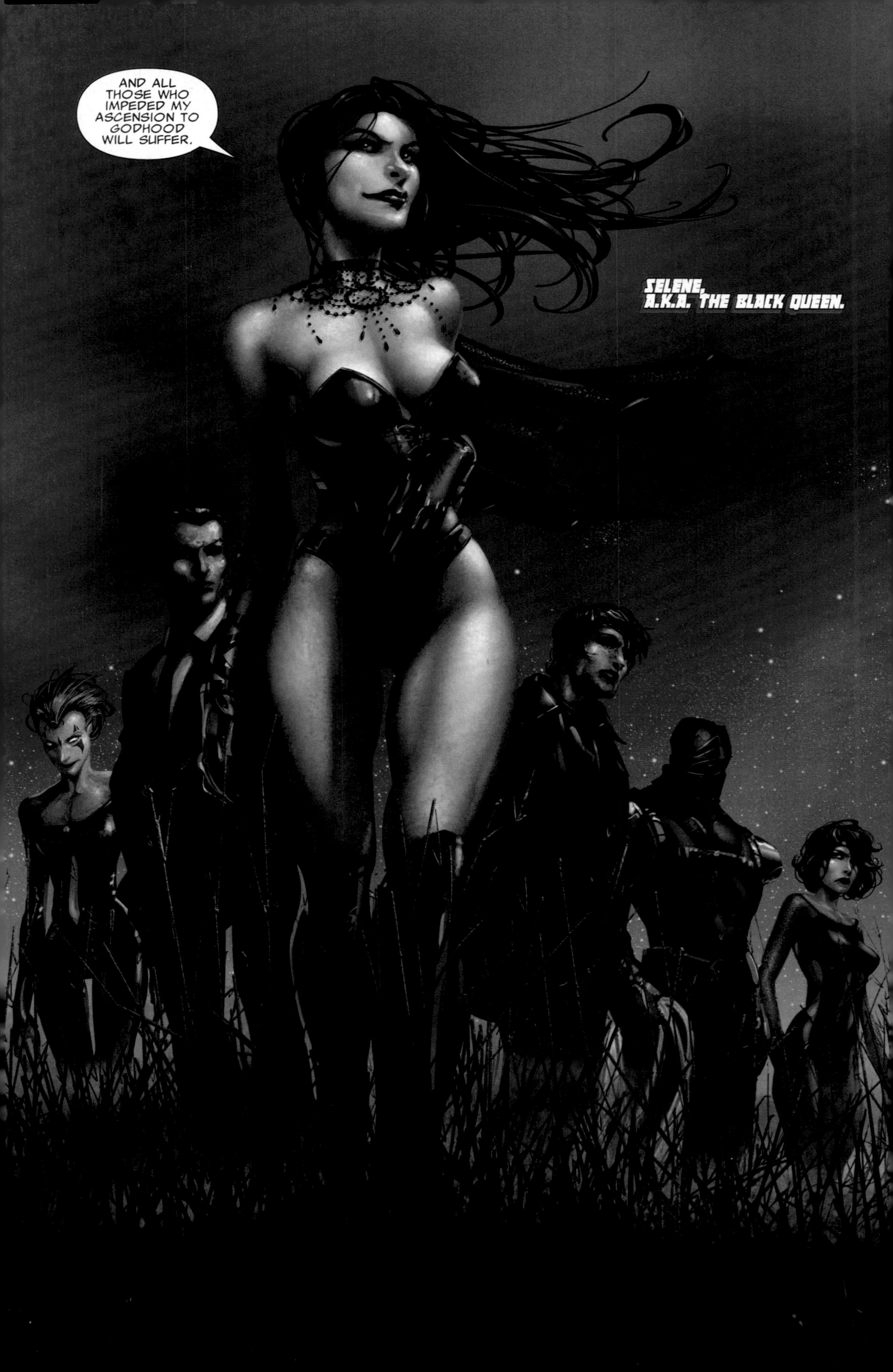
AND ALL THOSE WHO IMPEDED MY ASCENSION TO GODHOOD WILL SUFFER.
SELENE, A.K.A. THE BLACK QUEEN.

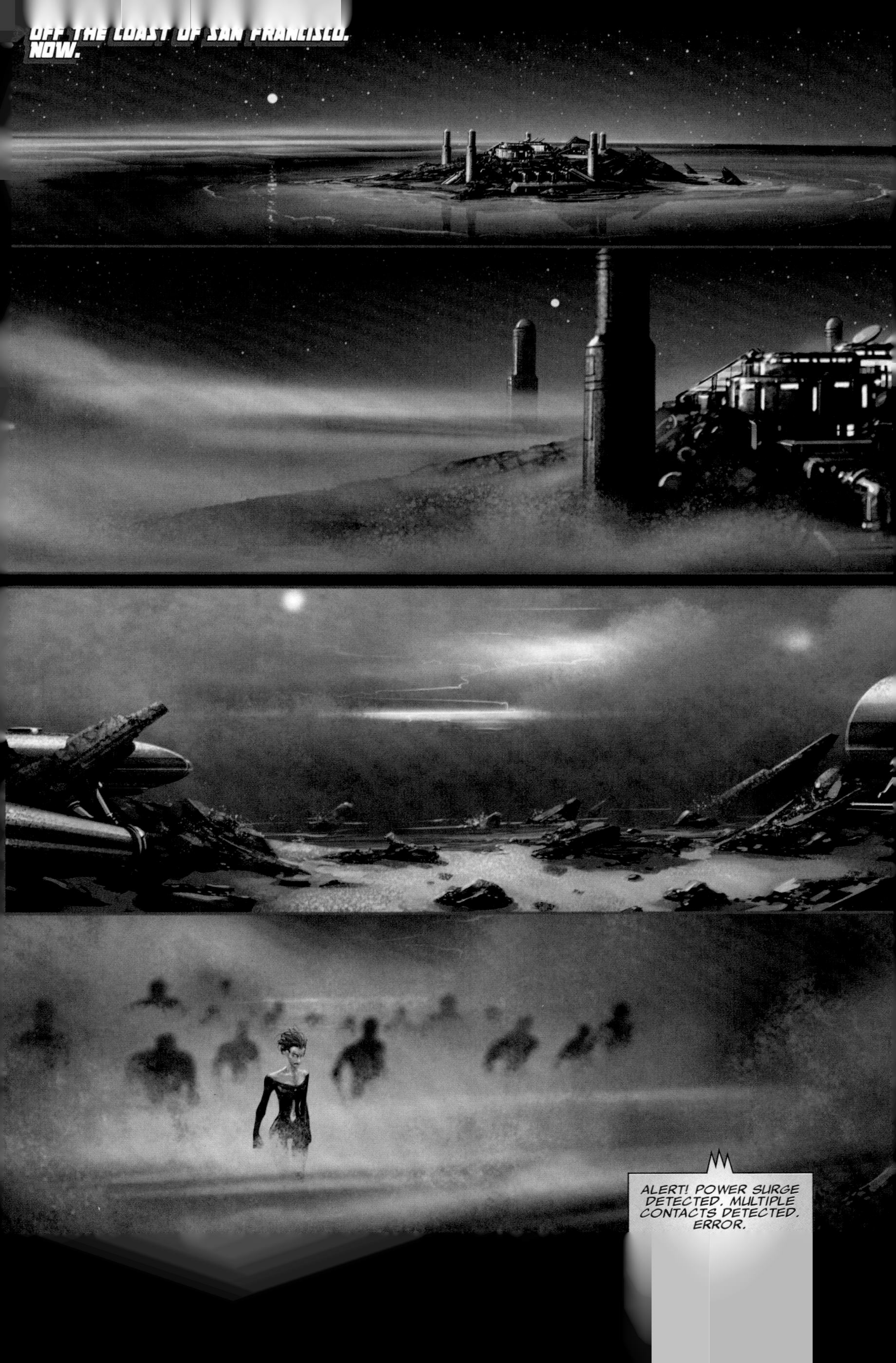
OFF THE COAST OF SAN FRANCISCO.
NOW.
ALERT! POWER SURGE DETECTED. MULTIPLE CONTACTS DETECTED. ERROR.

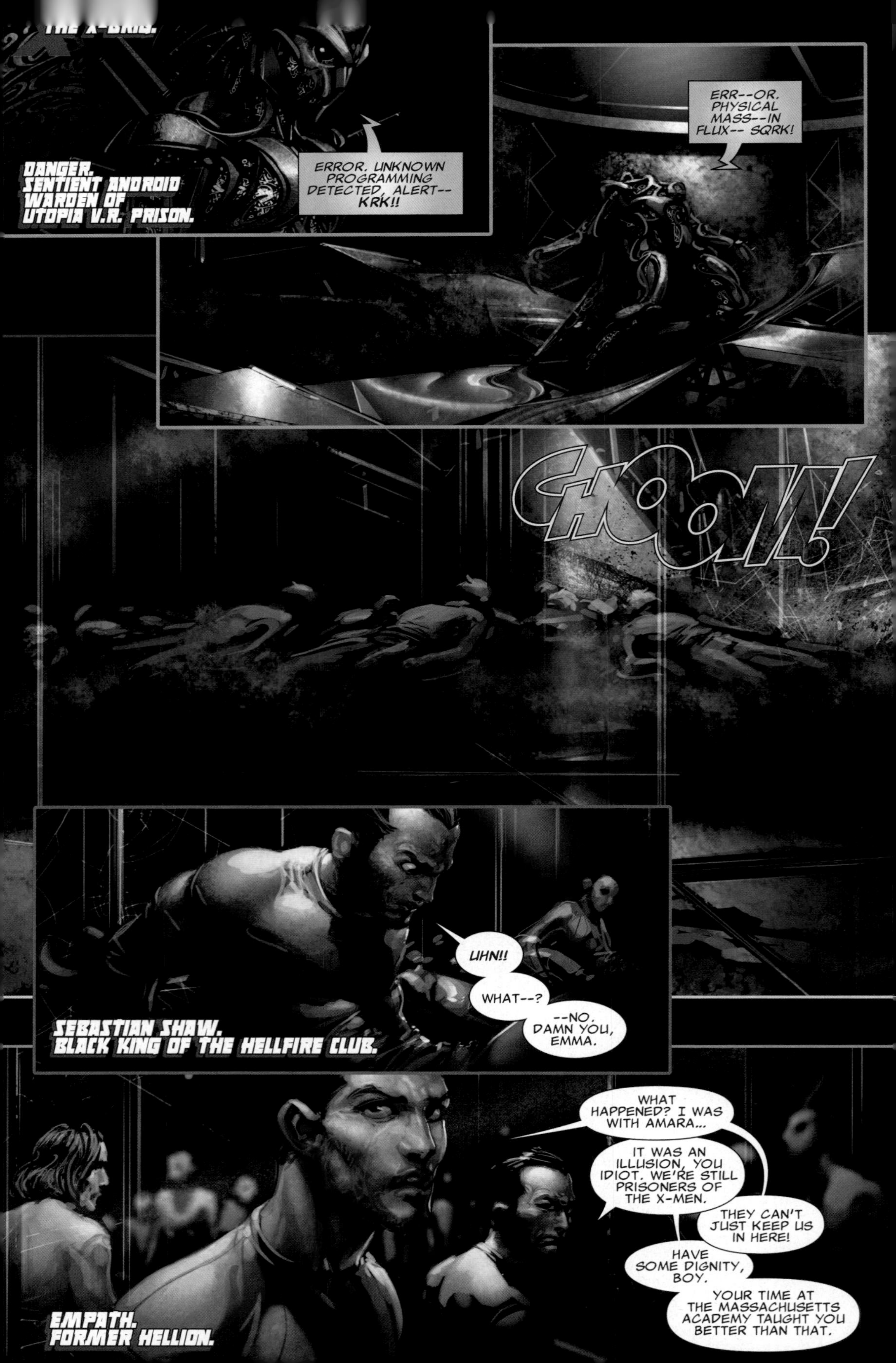
DANGER. SENTIENT ANDROID WARDEN OF UTOPIA V.R. PRISON.
ERROR. UNKNOWN PROGRAMMING DETECTED. ALERT-- KRK!!
ERR--OR. PHYSICAL MASS--IN FLUX-- SQRK!
CHOOM!
SEBASTIAN SHAW. BLACK KING OF THE HELLFIRE CLUB.
UHN!!
WHAT--?
--NO. DAMN YOU, EMMA.
EMPATH. FORMER HELLION.
WHAT HAPPENED? I WAS WITH AMARA...
IT WAS AN ILLUSION, YOU IDIOT. WE'RE STILL PRISONERS OF THE X-MEN.
THEY CAN'T JUST KEEP US IN HERE!
HAVE SOME DIGNITY, BOY.
YOUR TIME AT THE MASSACHUSETTS ACADEMY TAUGHT YOU BETTER THAN THAT.

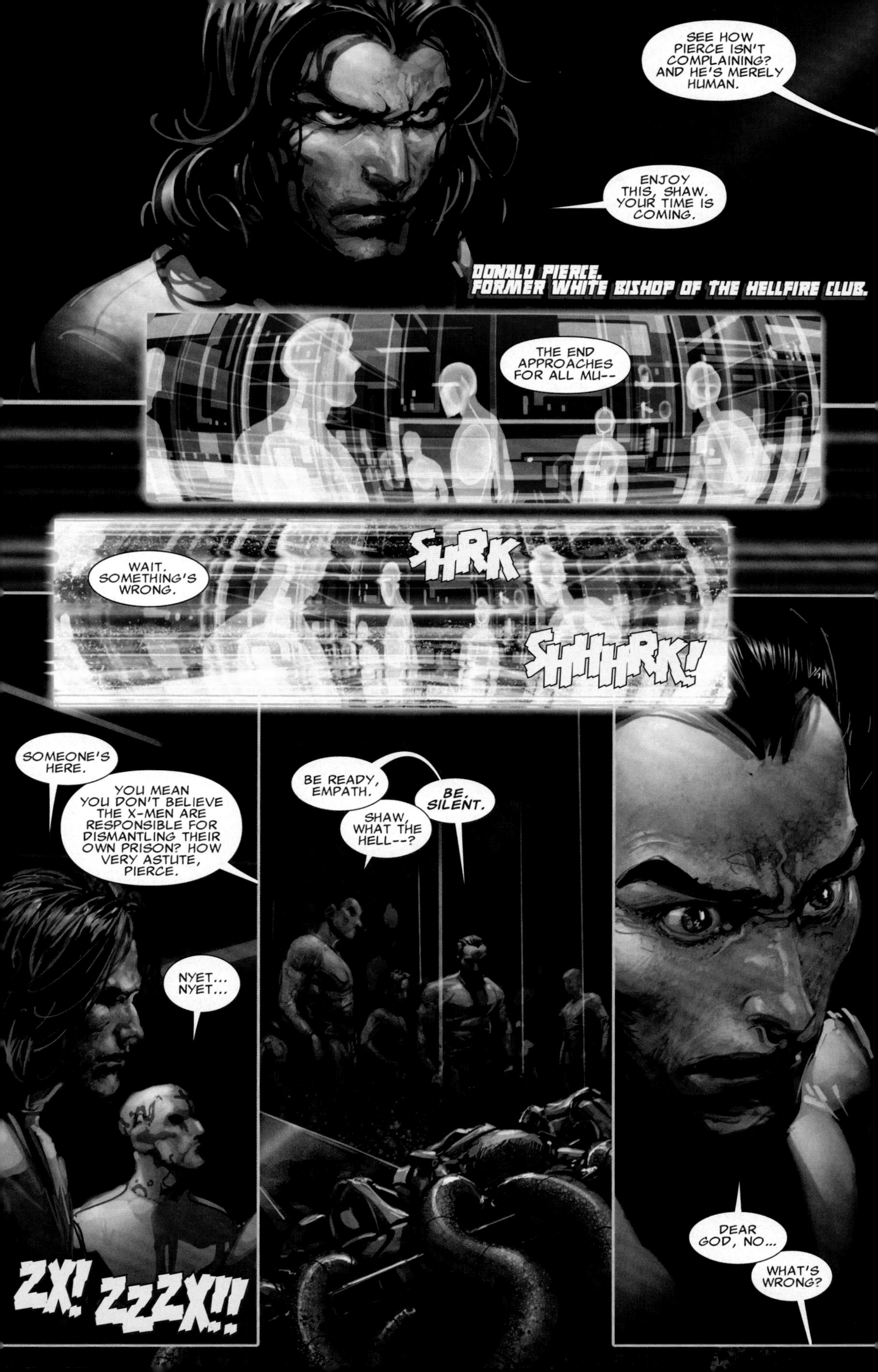
SEE HOW PIERCE ISN'T COMPLAINING? AND HE'S MERELY HUMAN.
ENJOY THIS, SHAW. YOUR TIME IS COMING.
DONALD PIERCE. FORMER WHITE BISHOP OF THE HELLFIRE CLUB.
THE END APPROACHES FOR ALL MU--
WAIT. SOMETHING'S WRONG.
SHRK
SHHHRK!
SOMEONE'S HERE.
YOU MEAN YOU DON'T BELIEVE THE X-MEN ARE RESPONSIBLE FOR DISMANTLING THEIR OWN PRISON? HOW VERY ASTUTE, PIERCE.
NYET... NYET...
ZX! ZZZX!!
BE READY, EMPATH.
BE. SILENT.
SHAW, WHAT THE HELL--?
DEAR GOD, NO...
WHAT'S WRONG?

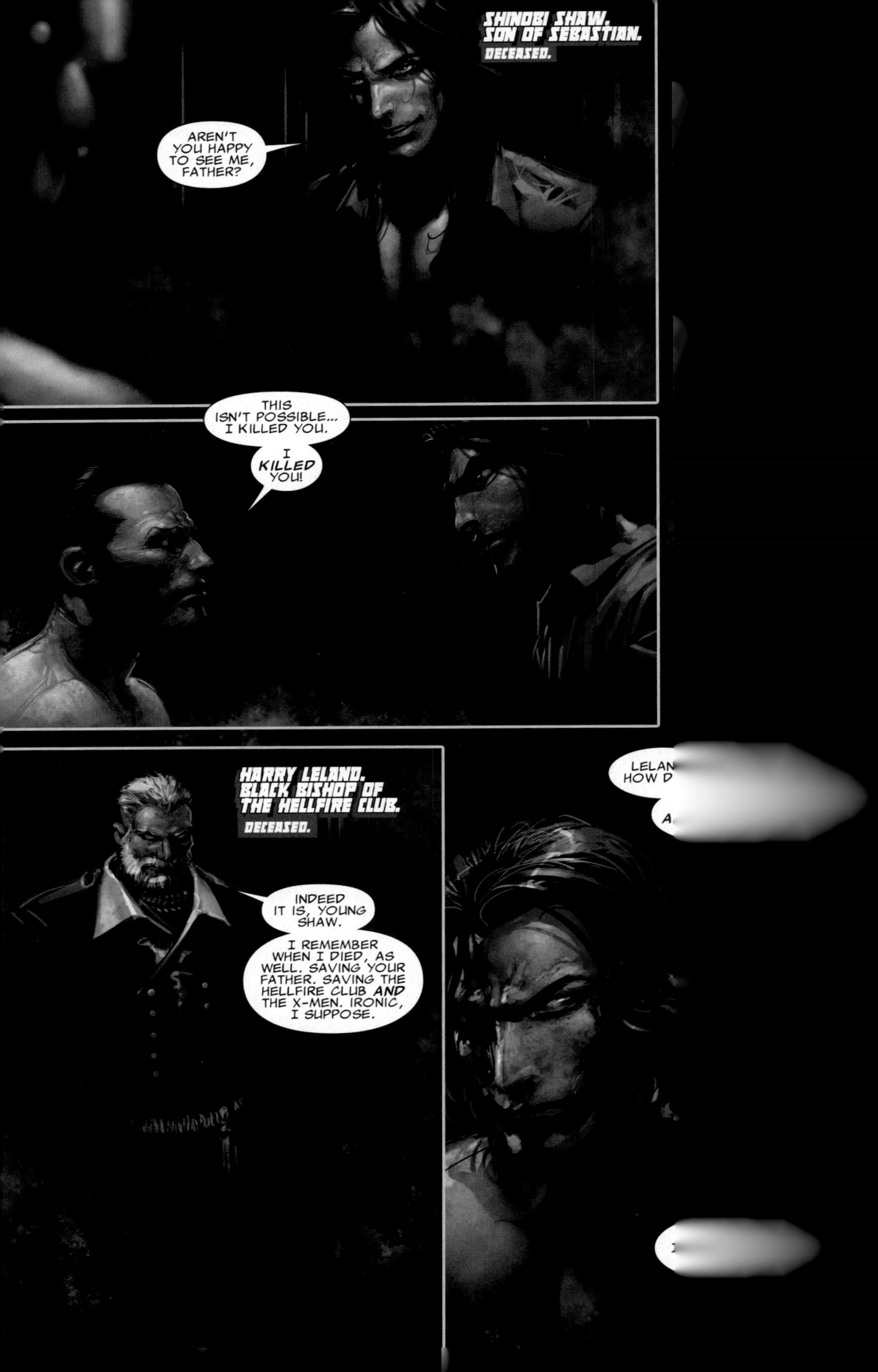
SHINOBI SHAW. SON OF SEBASTIAN.
DECEASED.
AREN'T YOU HAPPY TO SEE ME, FATHER?
THIS ISN'T POSSIBLE... I KILLED YOU.
I *KILLED* YOU!
HARRY LELAND. BLACK BISHOP OF THE HELLFIRE CLUB.
DECEASED.
INDEED IT IS, YOUNG SHAW.
I REMEMBER WHEN I DIED, AS WELL. SAVING YOUR FATHER. SAVING THE HELLFIRE CLUB *AND* THE X-MEN. IRONIC, I SUPPOSE.

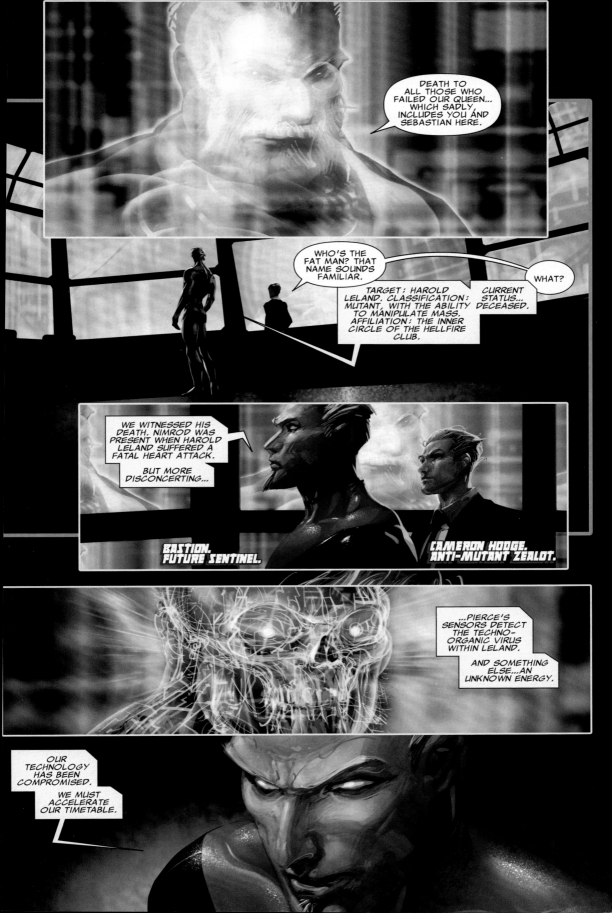

DEATH TO ALL THOSE WHO FAILED OUR QUEEN... WHICH SADLY INCLUDES YOU AND SEBASTIAN HERE.

WHO'S THE FAT MAN? THAT NAME SOUNDS FAMILIAR.

TARGET: HAROLD LELAND. CLASSIFICATION: MUTANT, WITH THE ABILITY TO MANIPULATE MASS. AFFILIATION: THE INNER CIRCLE OF THE HELLFIRE CLUB.

CURRENT STATUS... DECEASED.

WHAT?

WE WITNESSED HIS DEATH. NIMROD WAS PRESENT WHEN HAROLD LELAND SUFFERED A FATAL HEART ATTACK.

BUT MORE DISCONCERTING...

BASTION. FUTURE SENTINEL.

CAMERON HODGE. ANTI-MUTANT ZEALOT.

...PIERCE'S SENSORS DETECT THE TECHNO-ORGANIC VIRUS WITHIN LELAND..

AND SOMETHING ELSE...AN UNKNOWN ENERGY.

OUR TECHNOLOGY HAS BEEN COMPROMISED.

WE MUST ACCELERATE OUR TIMETABLE.

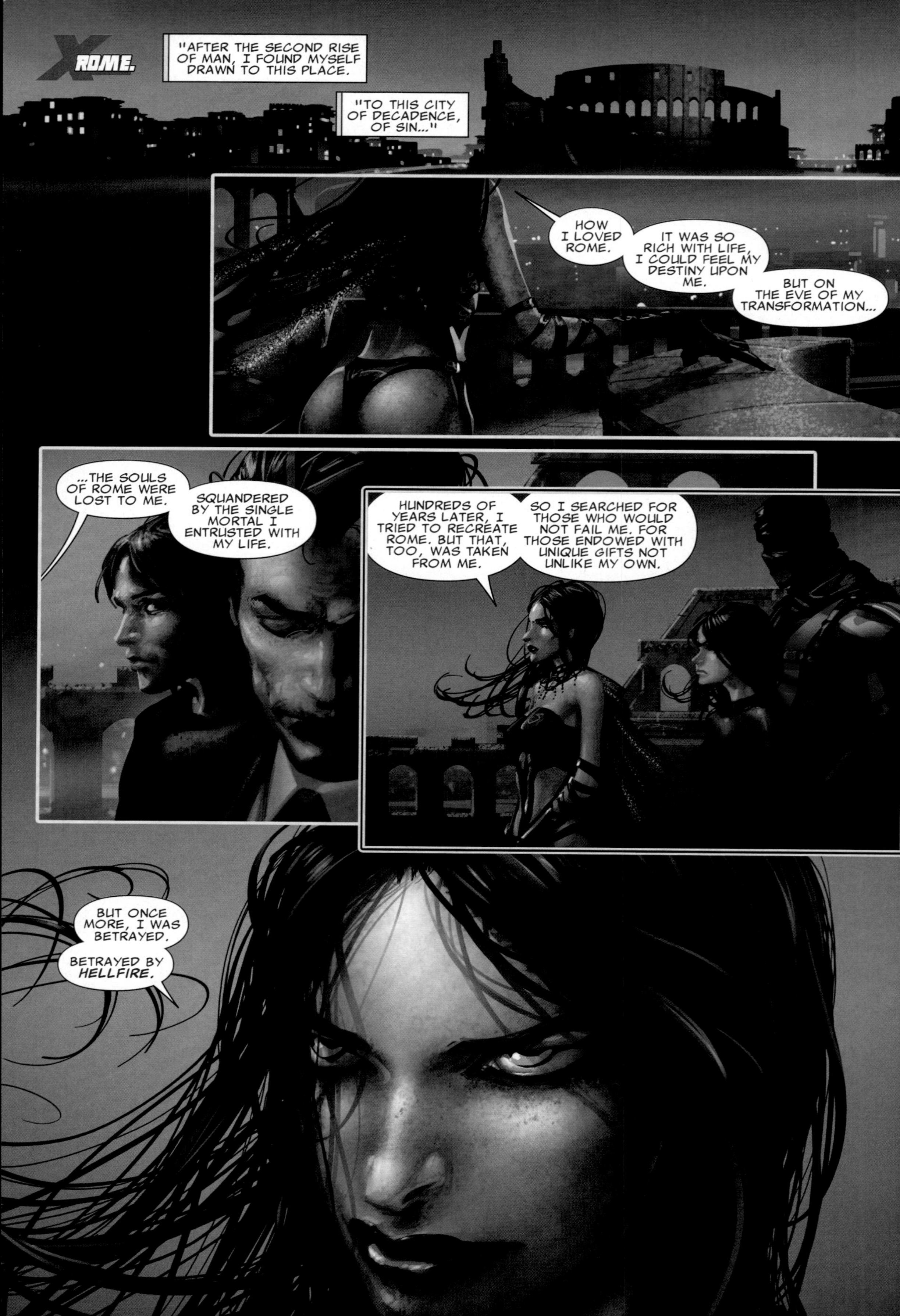
ROME.
"AFTER THE SECOND RISE OF MAN, I FOUND MYSELF DRAWN TO THIS PLACE.
"TO THIS CITY OF DECADENCE, OF SIN..."
HOW I LOVED ROME.
IT WAS SO RICH WITH LIFE, I COULD FEEL MY DESTINY UPON ME.
BUT ON THE EVE OF MY TRANSFORMATION...
...THE SOULS OF ROME WERE LOST TO ME.
SQUANDERED BY THE SINGLE MORTAL I ENTRUSTED WITH MY LIFE.
HUNDREDS OF YEARS LATER, I TRIED TO RECREATE ROME. BUT THAT, TOO, WAS TAKEN FROM ME.
SO I SEARCHED FOR THOSE WHO WOULD NOT FAIL ME. FOR THOSE ENDOWED WITH UNIQUE GIFTS NOT UNLIKE MY OWN.
BUT ONCE MORE, I WAS BETRAYED.
BETRAYED BY HELLFIRE.

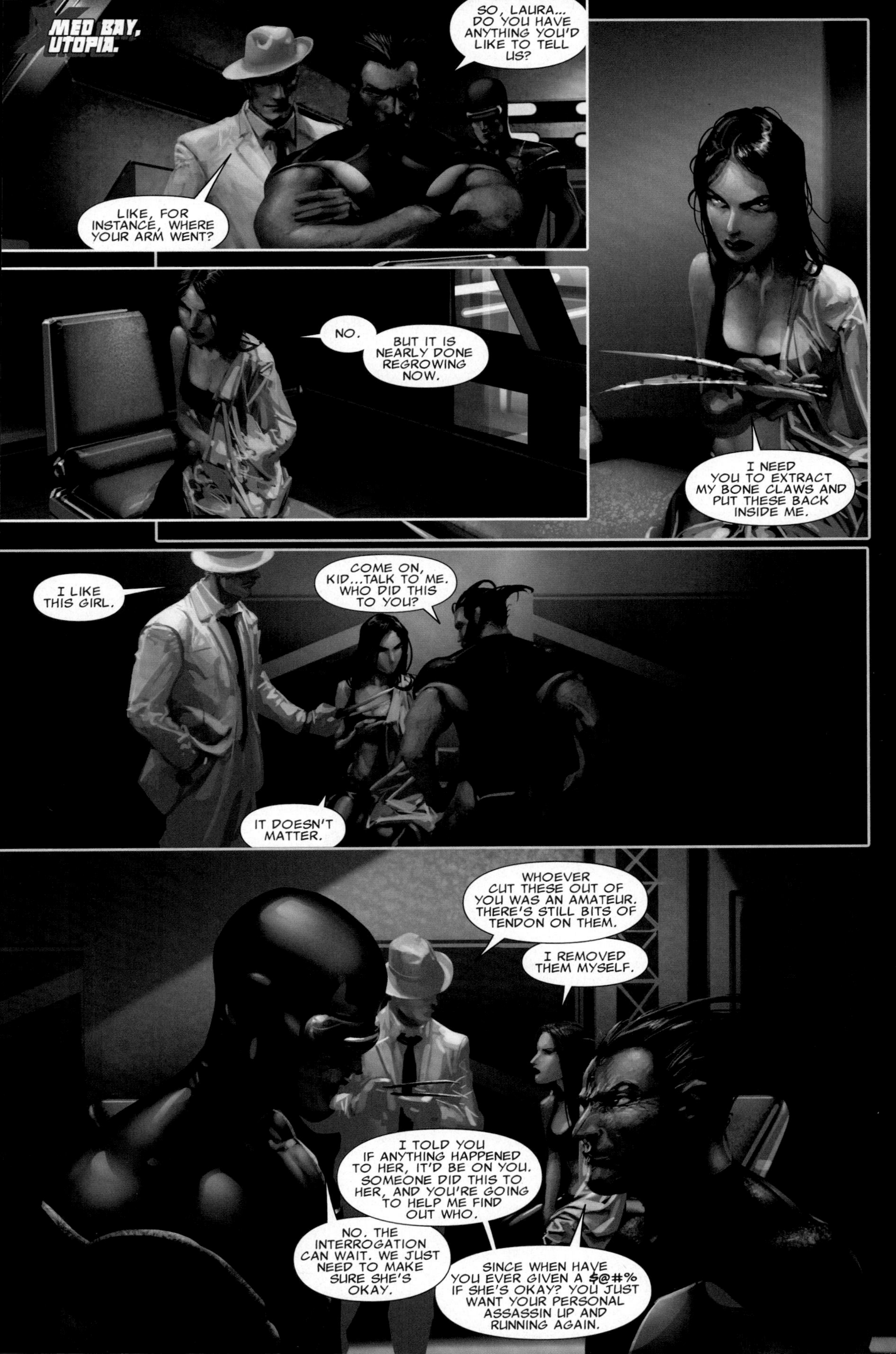
MED BAY, UTOPIA.
SO, LAURA... DO YOU HAVE ANYTHING YOU'D LIKE TO TELL US?
LIKE, FOR INSTANCE, WHERE YOUR ARM WENT?
NO.
BUT IT IS NEARLY DONE REGROWING NOW.
I NEED YOU TO EXTRACT MY BONE CLAWS AND PUT THESE BACK INSIDE ME.
I LIKE THIS GIRL.
COME ON, KID...TALK TO ME. WHO DID THIS TO YOU?
IT DOESN'T MATTER.
WHOEVER CUT THESE OUT OF YOU WAS AN AMATEUR. THERE'S STILL BITS OF TENDON ON THEM.
I REMOVED THEM MYSELF.
I TOLD YOU IF ANYTHING HAPPENED TO HER, IT'D BE ON YOU. SOMEONE DID THIS TO HER, AND YOU'RE GOING TO HELP ME FIND OUT WHO.
NO. THE INTERROGATION CAN WAIT. WE JUST NEED TO MAKE SURE SHE'S OKAY.
SINCE WHEN HAVE YOU EVER GIVEN A $@#% IF SHE'S OKAY? YOU JUST WANT YOUR PERSONAL ASSASSIN UP AND RUNNING AGAIN.

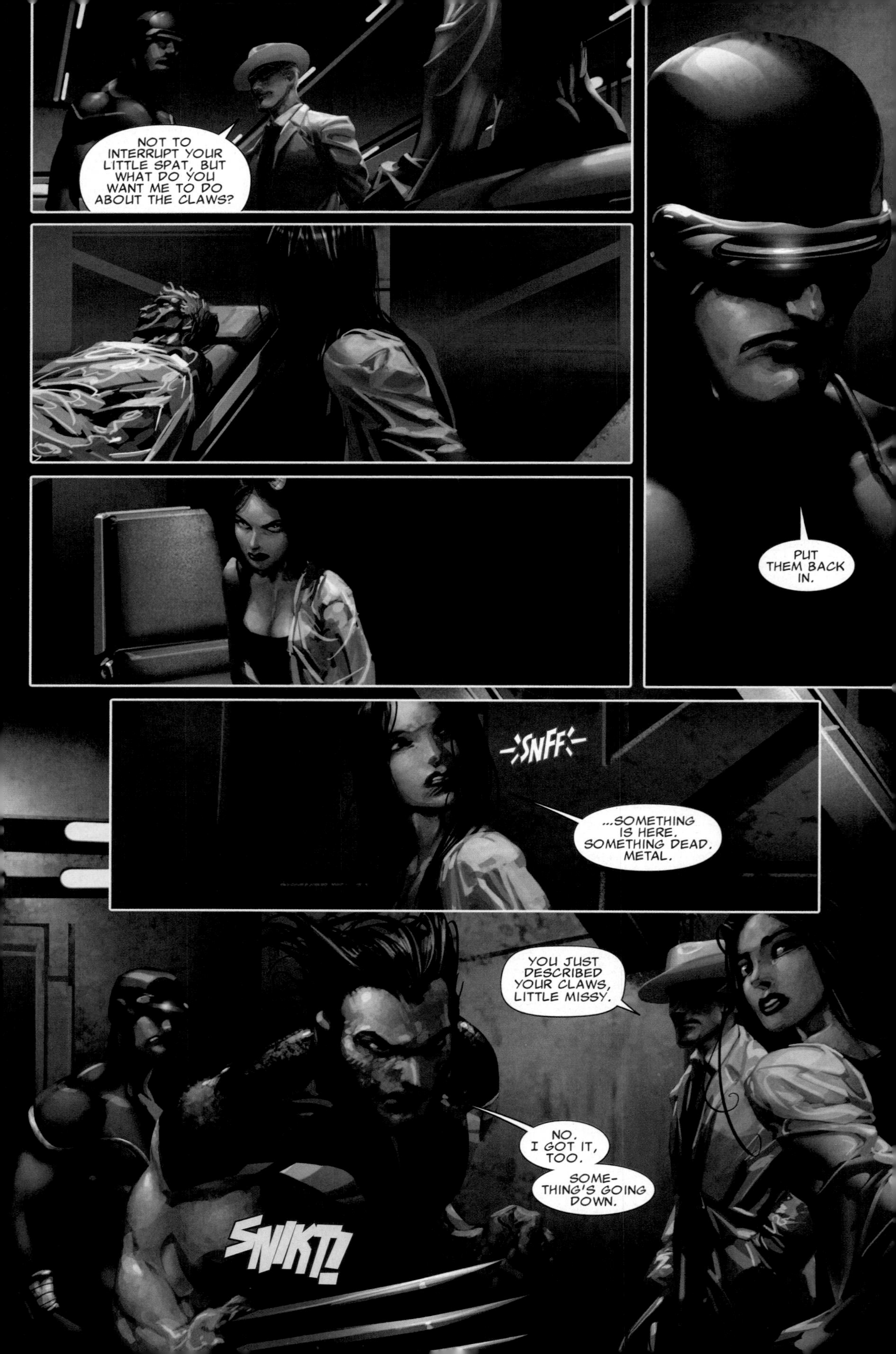
NOT TO INTERRUPT YOUR LITTLE SPAT, BUT WHAT DO YOU WANT ME TO DO ABOUT THE CLAWS?
PUT THEM BACK IN.
SNFF
...SOMETHING IS HERE. SOMETHING DEAD. METAL.
YOU JUST DESCRIBED YOUR CLAWS, LITTLE MISSY.
NO. I GOT IT, TOO.
SOME-THING'S GOING DOWN.
SNIKT!

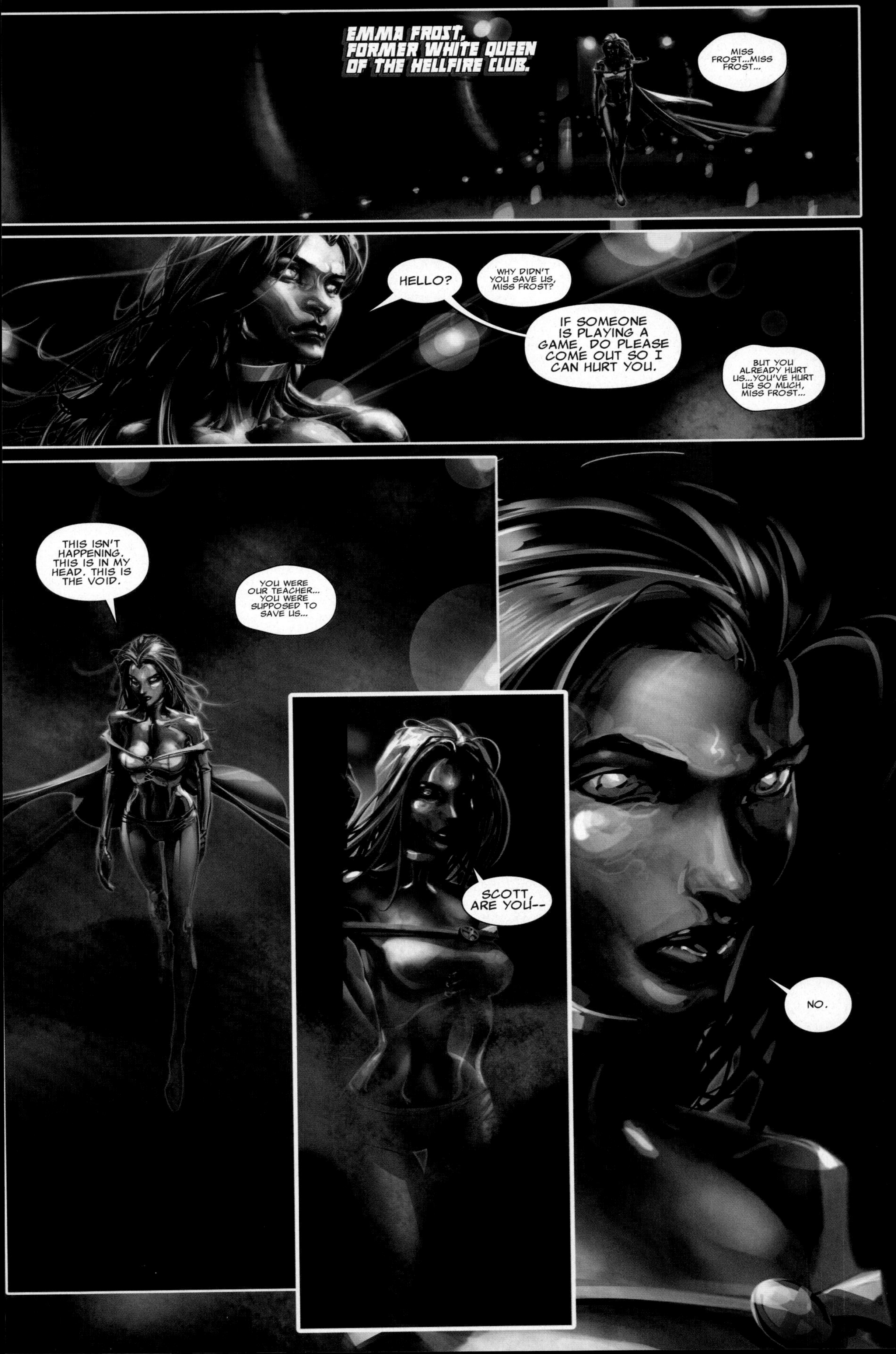
EMMA FROST, FORMER WHITE QUEEN OF THE HELLFIRE CLUB.
MISS FROST...MISS FROST...
HELLO?
WHY DIDN'T YOU SAVE US, MISS FROST?
IF SOMEONE IS PLAYING A GAME, DO PLEASE COME OUT SO I CAN HURT YOU.
BUT YOU ALREADY HURT US...YOU'VE HURT US SO MUCH, MISS FROST...
THIS ISN'T HAPPENING. THIS IS IN MY HEAD. THIS IS THE VOID.
YOU WERE OUR TEACHER... YOU WERE SUPPOSED TO SAVE US...
SCOTT, ARE YOU--
NO.

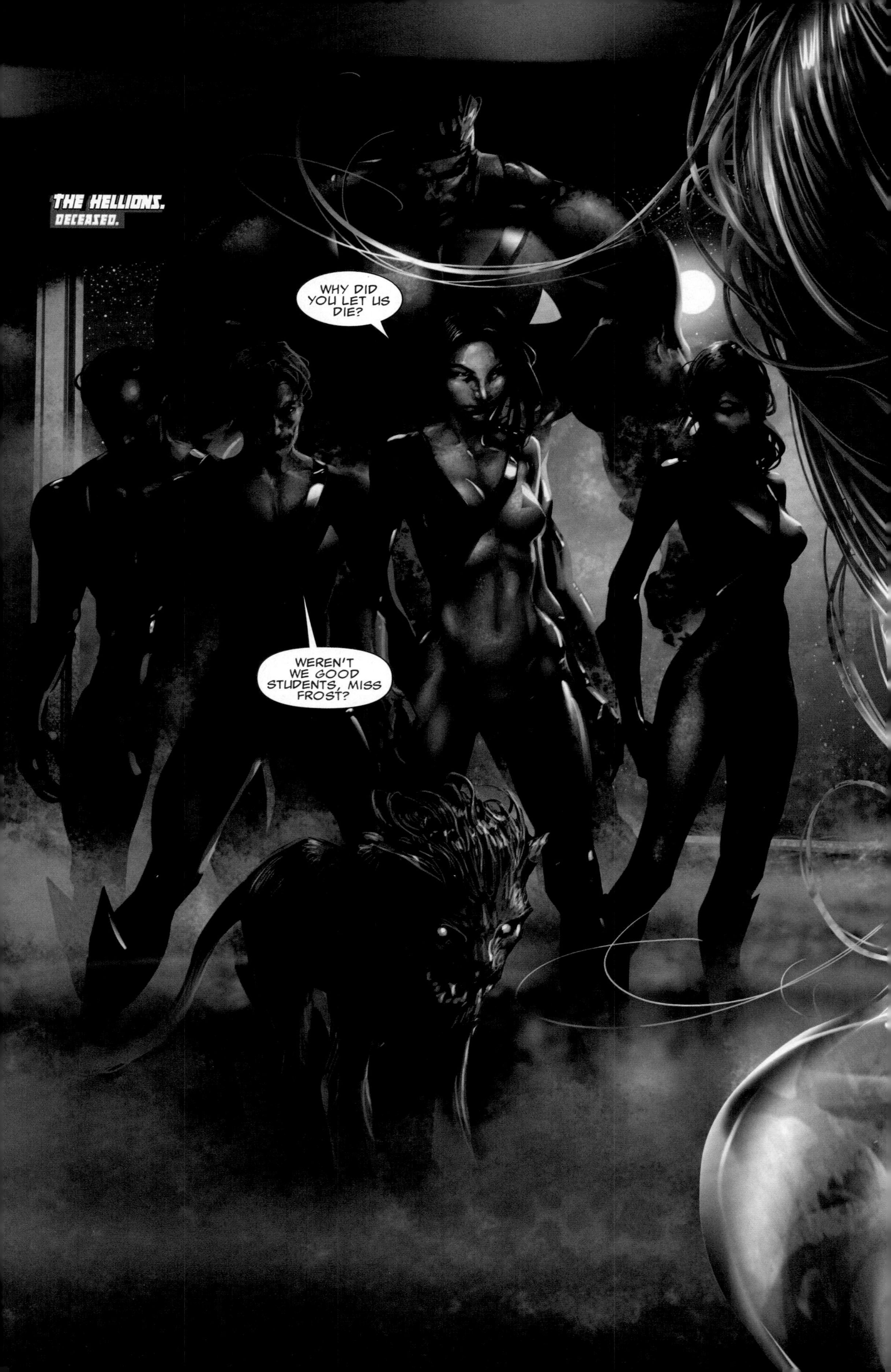
THE HELLIONS.
DECEASED.
WHY DID YOU LET US DIE?
WEREN'T WE GOOD STUDENTS, MISS FROST?

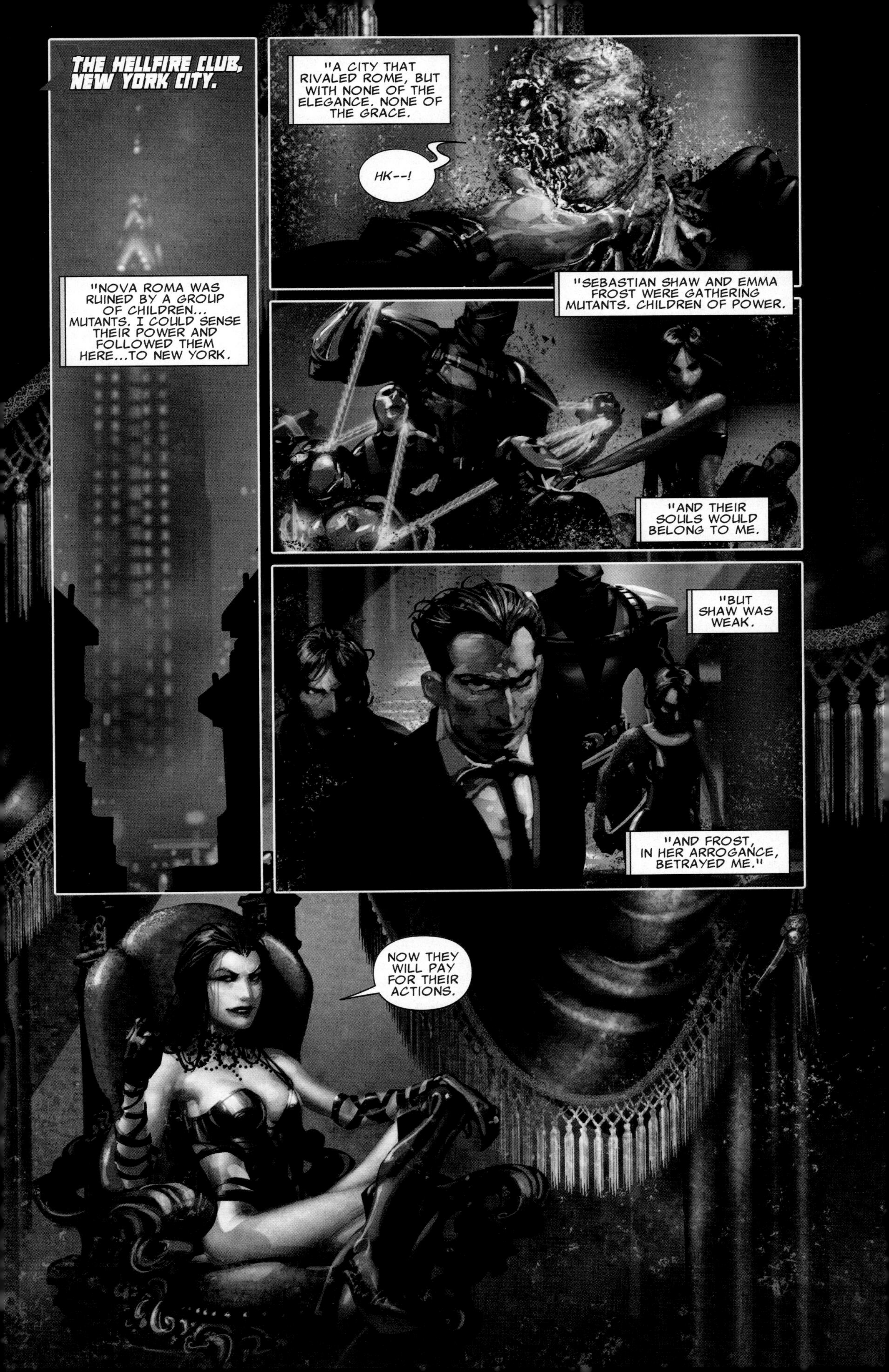
THE HELLFIRE CLUB, NEW YORK CITY.
"A CITY THAT RIVALED ROME, BUT WITH NONE OF THE ELEGANCE. NONE OF THE GRACE.
HK--!
"NOVA ROMA WAS RUINED BY A GROUP OF CHILDREN... MUTANTS. I COULD SENSE THEIR POWER AND FOLLOWED THEM HERE...TO NEW YORK.
"SEBASTIAN SHAW AND EMMA FROST WERE GATHERING MUTANTS. CHILDREN OF POWER.
"AND THEIR SOULS WOULD BELONG TO ME.
"BUT SHAW WAS WEAK.
"AND FROST, IN HER ARROGANCE, BETRAYED ME."
NOW THEY WILL PAY FOR THEIR ACTIONS.

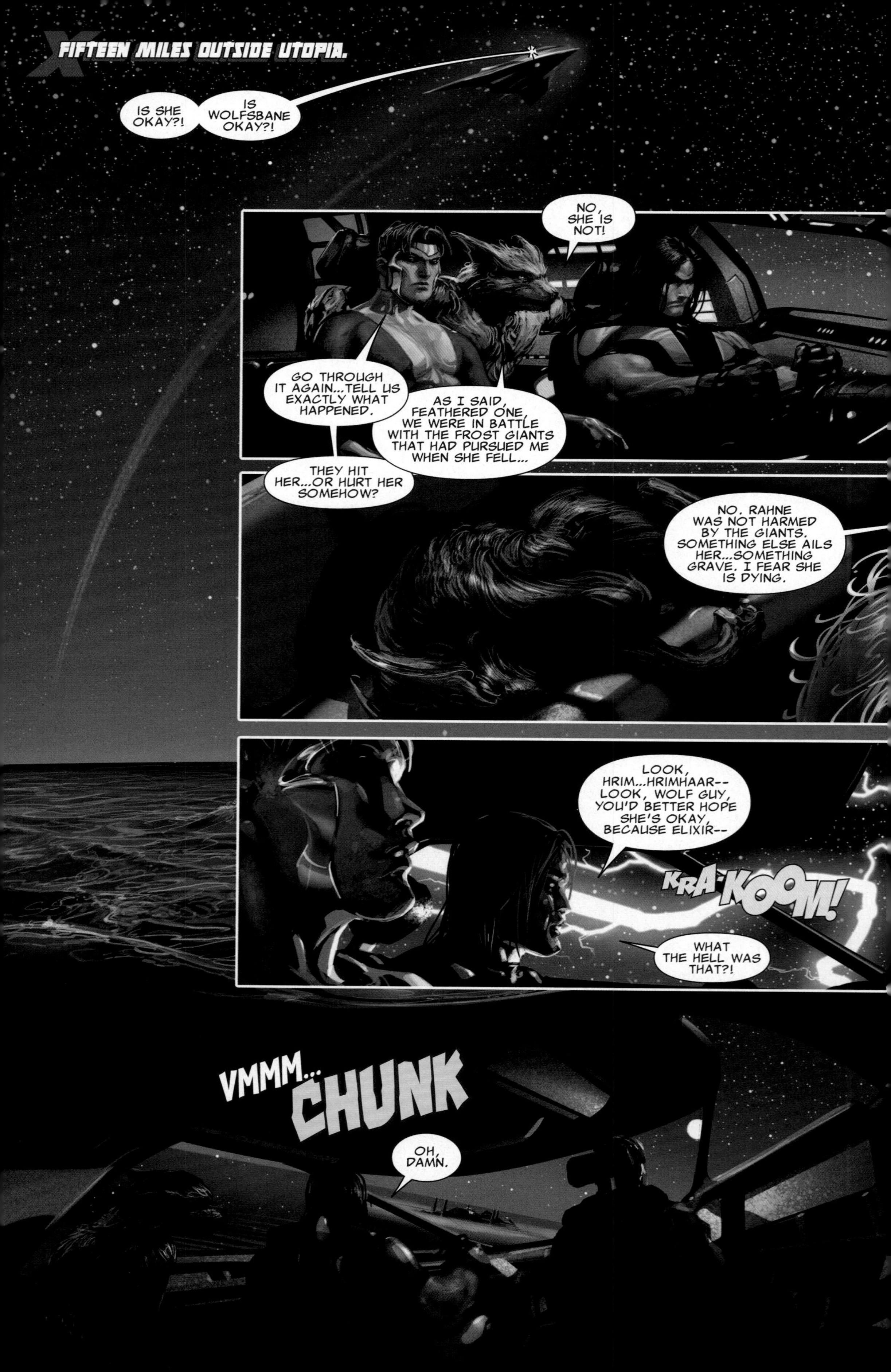
FIFTEEN MILES OUTSIDE UTOPIA.
IS SHE OKAY?!
IS WOLFSBANE OKAY?!
NO, SHE IS NOT!
GO THROUGH IT AGAIN...TELL US EXACTLY WHAT HAPPENED.
AS I SAID, FEATHERED ONE, WE WERE IN BATTLE WITH THE FROST GIANTS THAT HAD PURSUED ME WHEN SHE FELL...
THEY HIT HER...OR HURT HER SOMEHOW?
NO. RAHNE WAS NOT HARMED BY THE GIANTS. SOMETHING ELSE AILS HER...SOMETHING GRAVE. I FEAR SHE IS DYING.
LOOK, HRIM...HRIMHAAR-- LOOK, WOLF GUY, YOU'D BETTER HOPE SHE'S OKAY, BECAUSE ELIXIR--
KRA-KOOM!
WHAT THE HELL WAS THAT?!
VMMM... CHUNK
OH, DAMN.

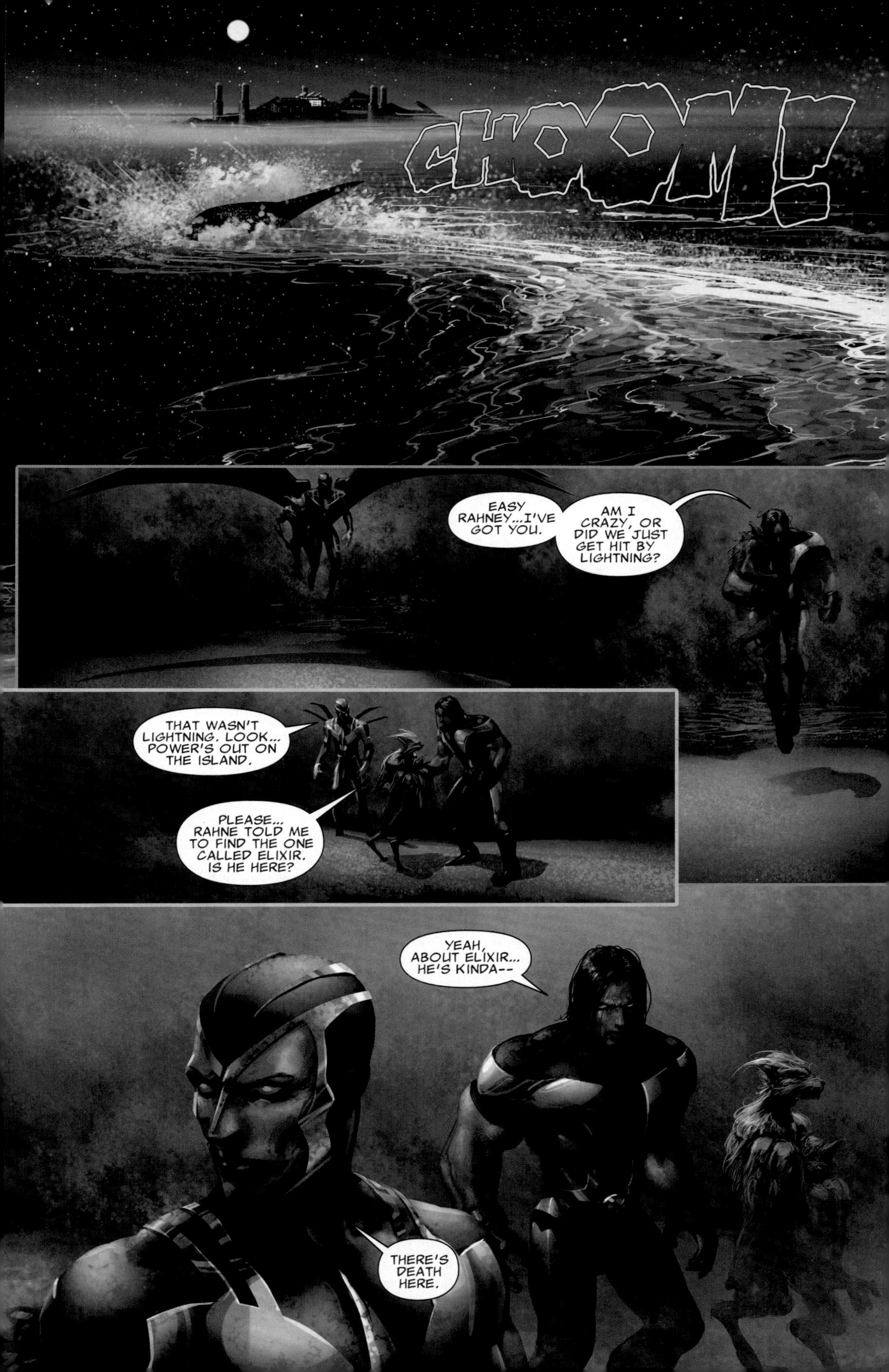
CHOOM!
EASY RAHNEY...I'VE GOT YOU.
AM I CRAZY, OR DID WE JUST GET HIT BY LIGHTNING?
THAT WASN'T LIGHTNING. LOOK... POWER'S OUT ON THE ISLAND.
PLEASE... RAHNE TOLD ME TO FIND THE ONE CALLED ELIXIR. IS HE HERE?
YEAH, ABOUT ELIXIR... HE'S KINDA--
THERE'S DEATH HERE.

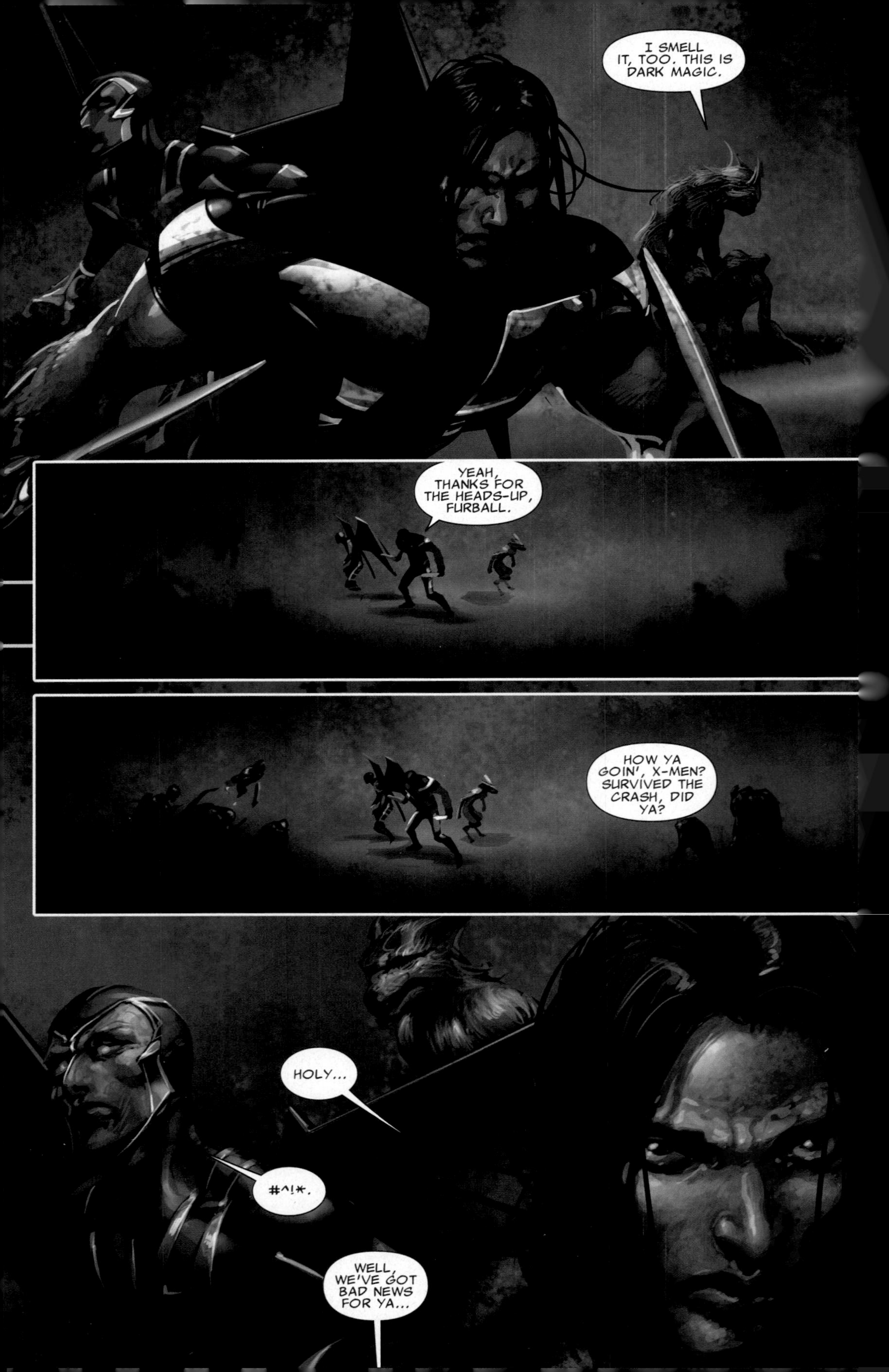
I SMELL IT, TOO. THIS IS DARK MAGIC.
YEAH, THANKS FOR THE HEADS-UP, FURBALL.
HOW YA GOIN', X-MEN? SURVIVED THE CRASH, DID YA?
HOLY...
#^!*.
WELL, WE'VE GOT BAD NEWS FOR YA...

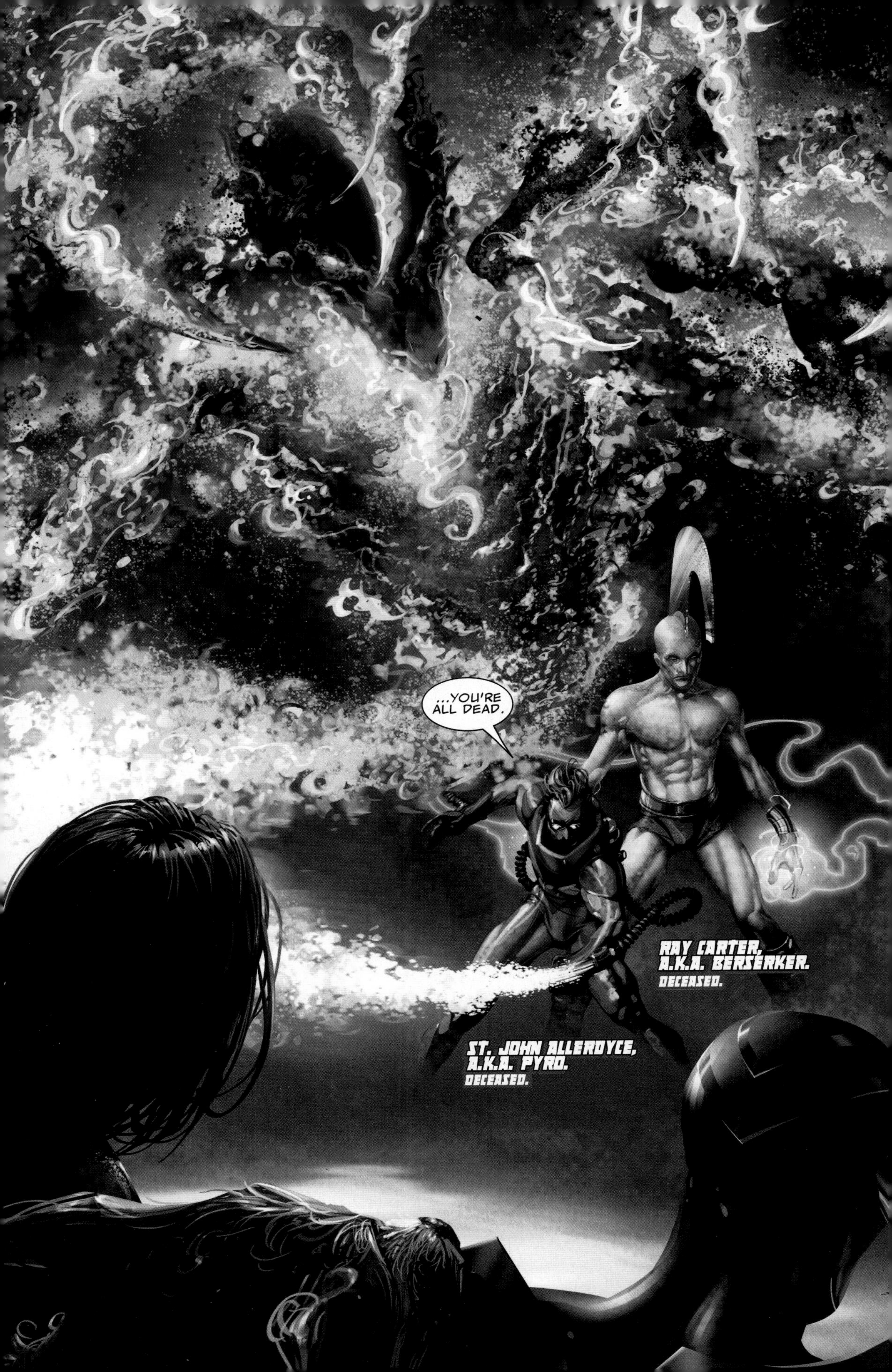
...YOU'RE ALL DEAD.
RAY CARTER, A.K.A. BERSERKER.
DECEASED.
ST. JOHN ALLERDYCE, A.K.A. PYRO.
DECEASED.

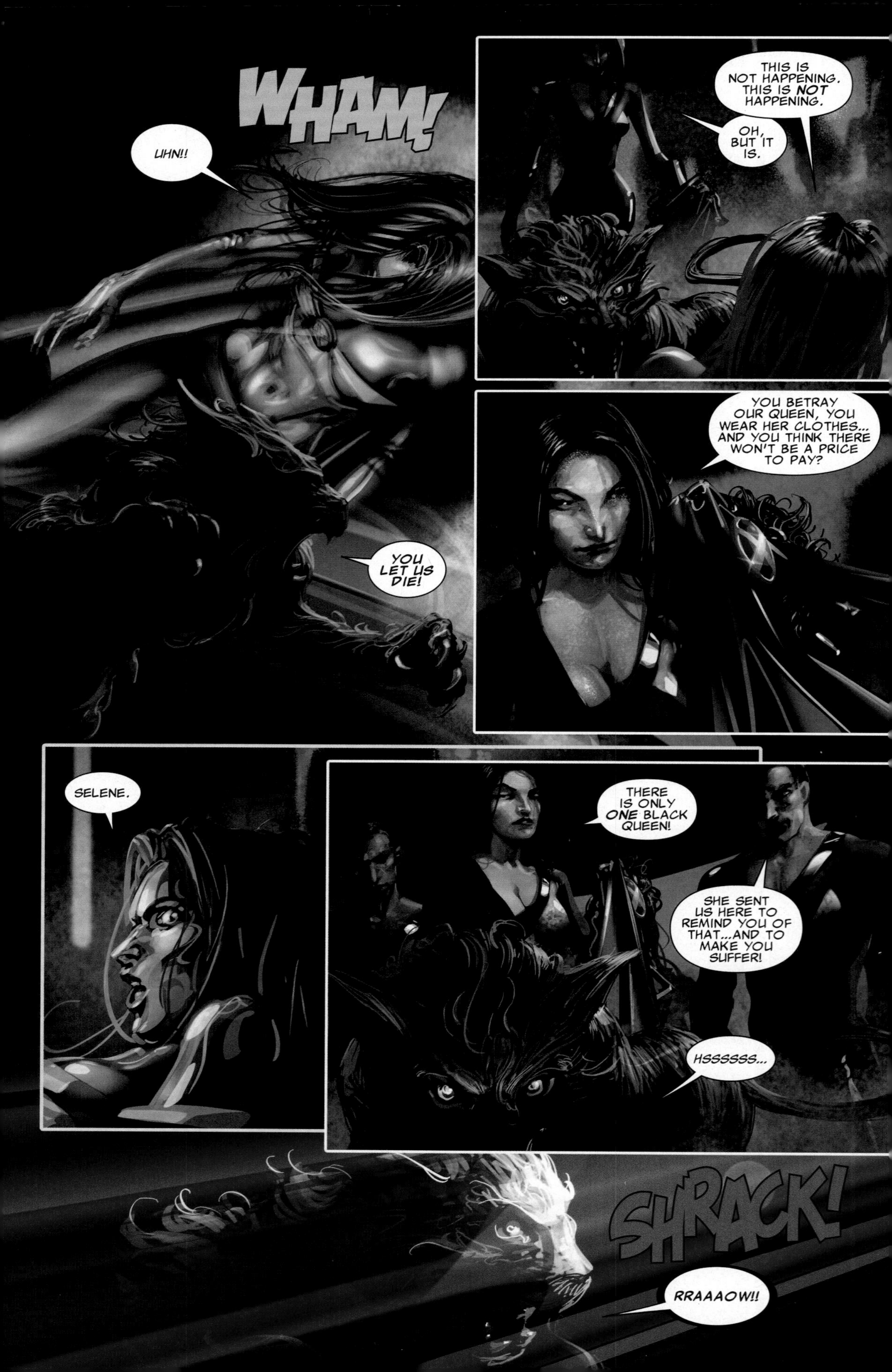
WHAM!
UHN!!
YOU LET US DIE!
THIS IS NOT HAPPENING. THIS IS NOT HAPPENING.
OH, BUT IT IS.
YOU BETRAY OUR QUEEN, YOU WEAR HER CLOTHES... AND YOU THINK THERE WON'T BE A PRICE TO PAY?
SELENE.
THERE IS ONLY ONE BLACK QUEEN!
SHE SENT US HERE TO REMIND YOU OF THAT...AND TO MAKE YOU SUFFER!
HSSSSSS...
SHRACK!
RRAAAOW!!

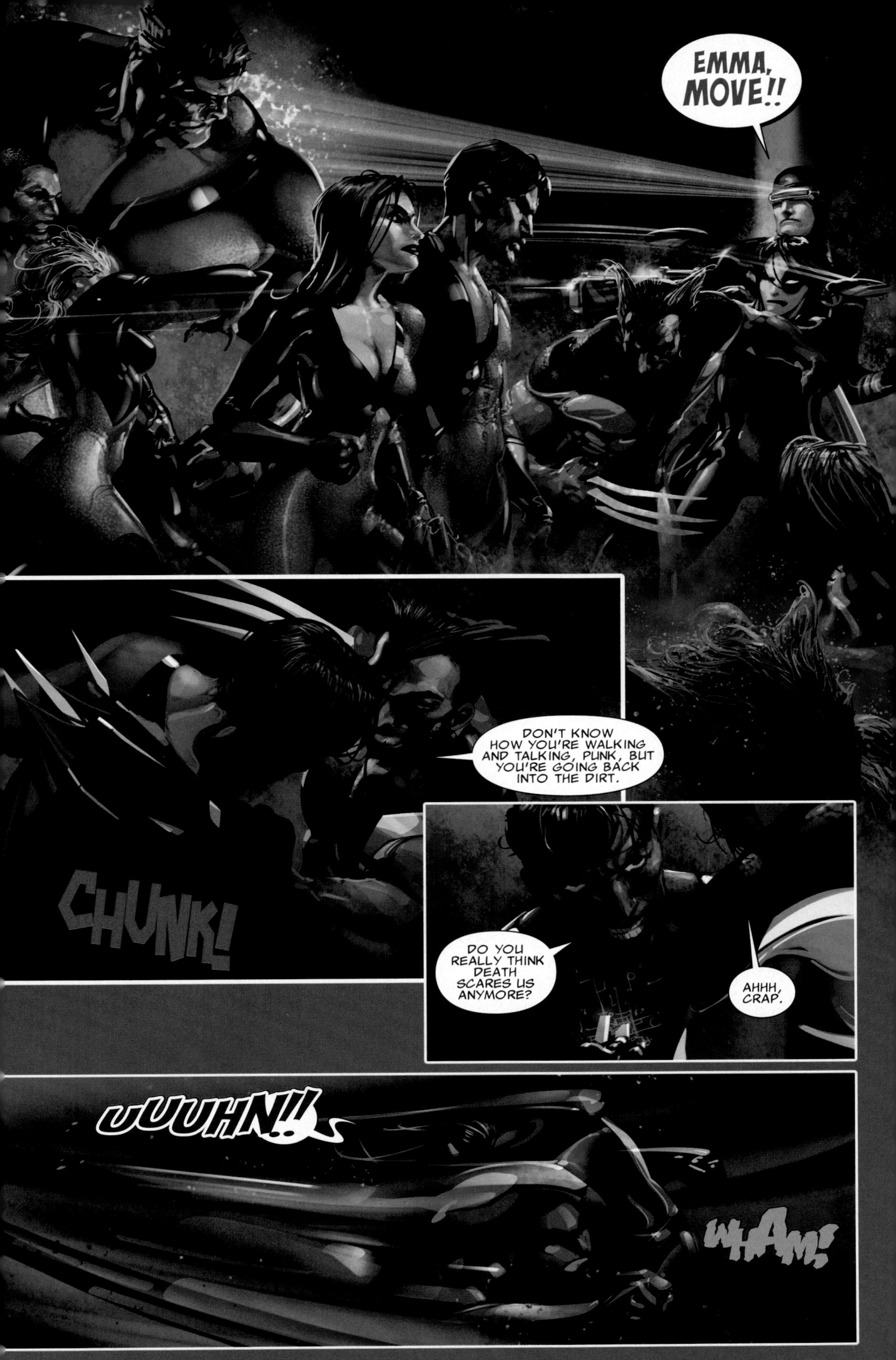
EMMA, MOVE!!
DON'T KNOW HOW YOU'RE WALKING AND TALKING, PUNK, BUT YOU'RE GOING BACK INTO THE DIRT.
CHUNK!
DO YOU REALLY THINK DEATH SCARES US ANYMORE?
AHHH, CRAP.
UUUHN!!
WHAM!

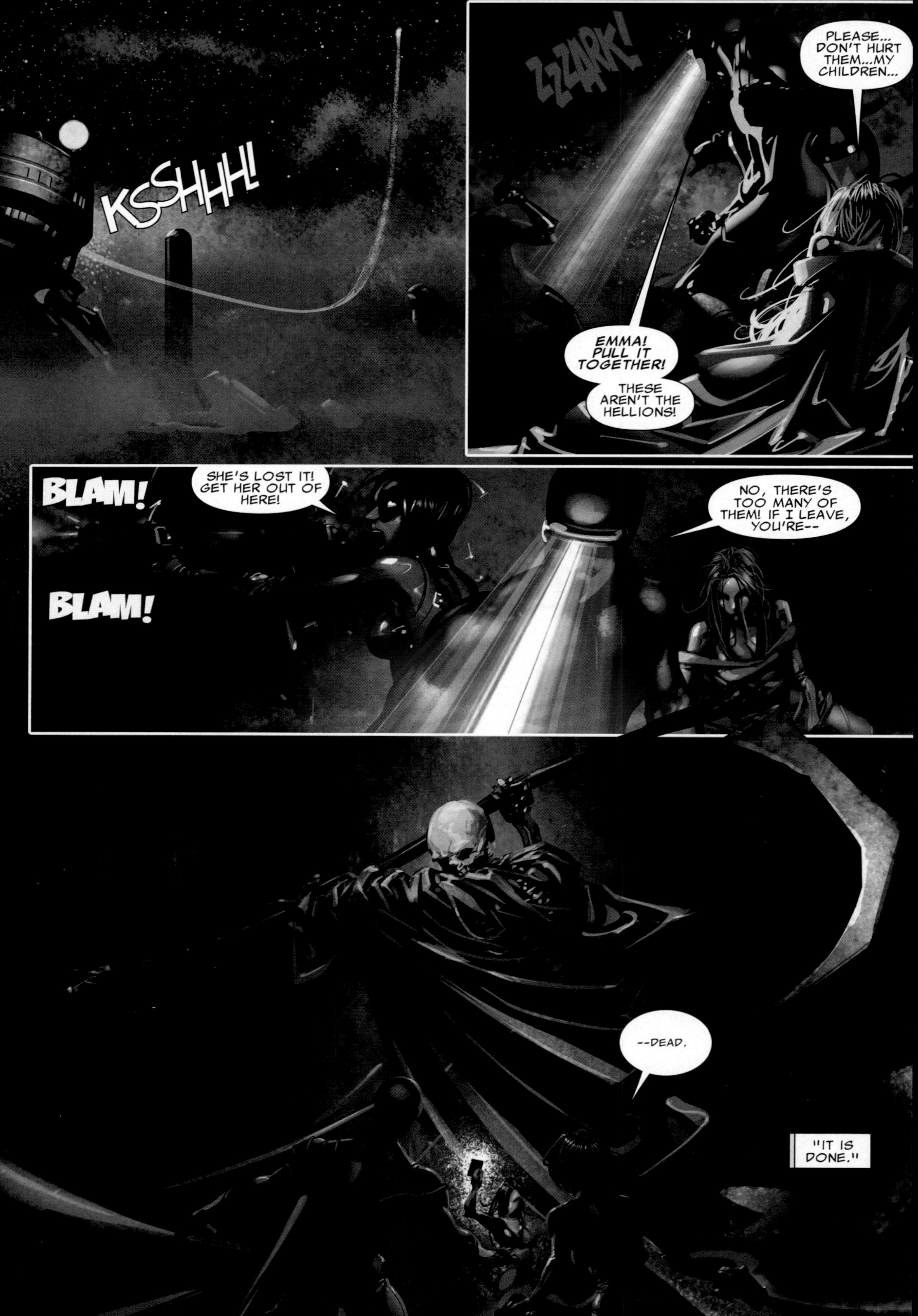
KSSHHH!
ZZZARK!
PLEASE... DON'T HURT THEM...MY CHILDREN...
EMMA! PULL IT TOGETHER!
THESE AREN'T THE HELLIONS!
BLAM!
SHE'S LOST IT! GET HER OUT OF HERE!
BLAM!
NO, THERE'S TOO MANY OF THEM! IF I LEAVE, YOU'RE--
--DEAD.
"IT IS DONE."

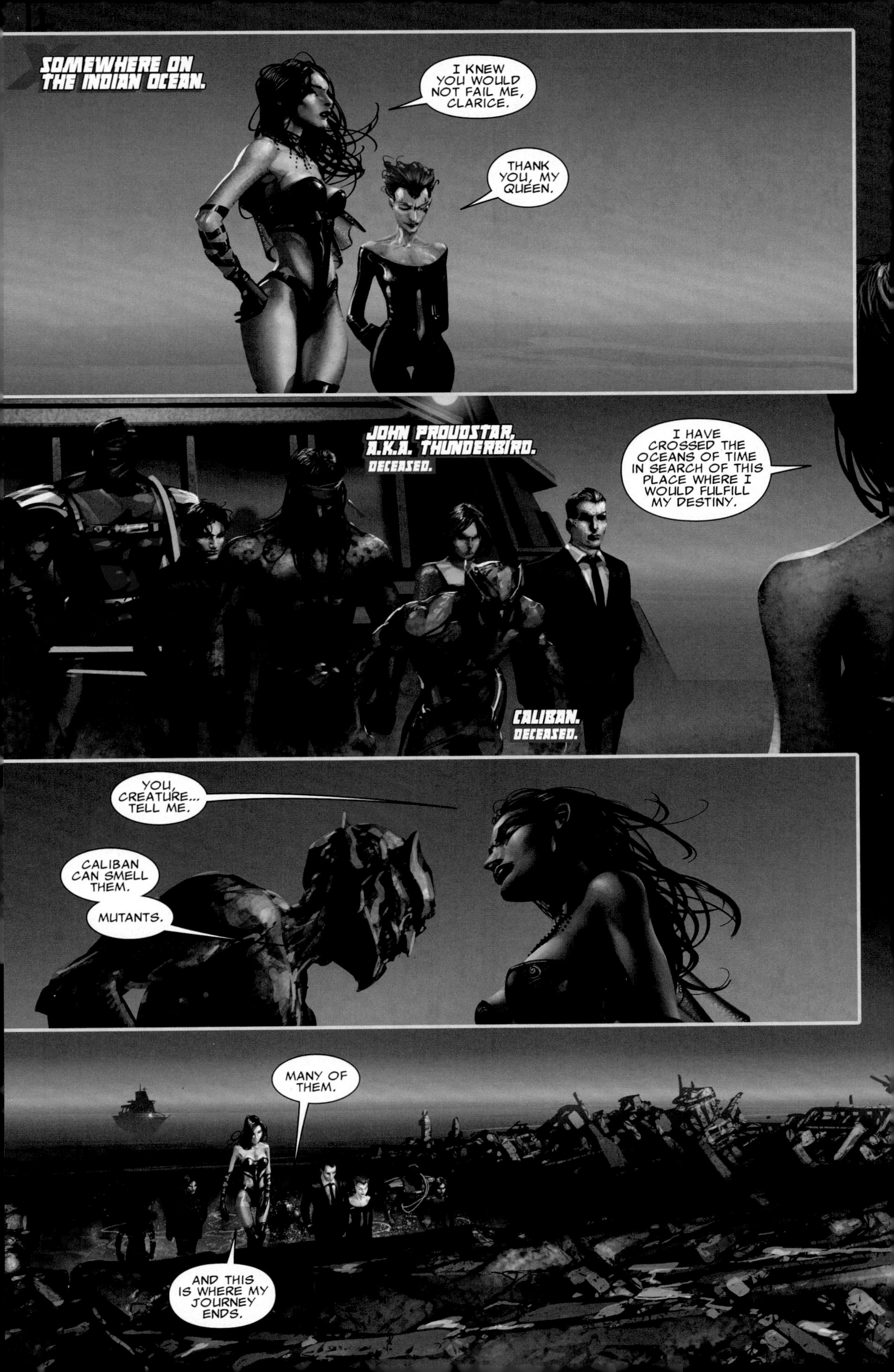
SOMEWHERE ON THE INDIAN OCEAN.
I KNEW YOU WOULD NOT FAIL ME, CLARICE.
THANK YOU, MY QUEEN.
JOHN PROUDSTAR, A.K.A. THUNDERBIRD.
DECEASED.
I HAVE CROSSED THE OCEANS OF TIME IN SEARCH OF THIS PLACE WHERE I WOULD FULFILL MY DESTINY.
CALIBAN.
DECEASED.
YOU, CREATURE... TELL ME.
CALIBAN CAN SMELL THEM.
MUTANTS.
MANY OF THEM.
AND THIS IS WHERE MY JOURNEY ENDS.

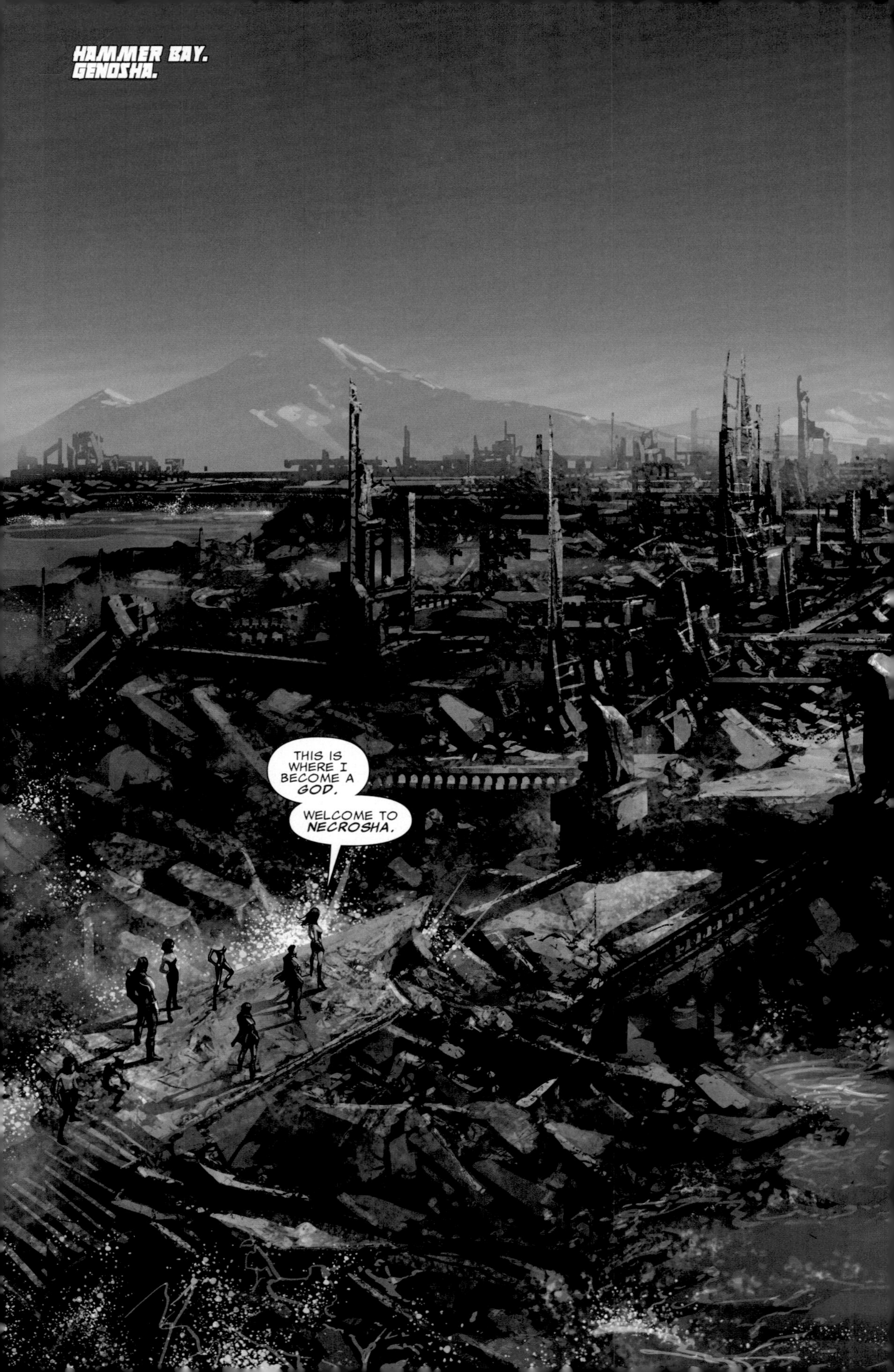
HAMMER BAY.
GENOSHA.
THIS IS WHERE I BECOME A GOD.
WELCOME TO NECROSHA.

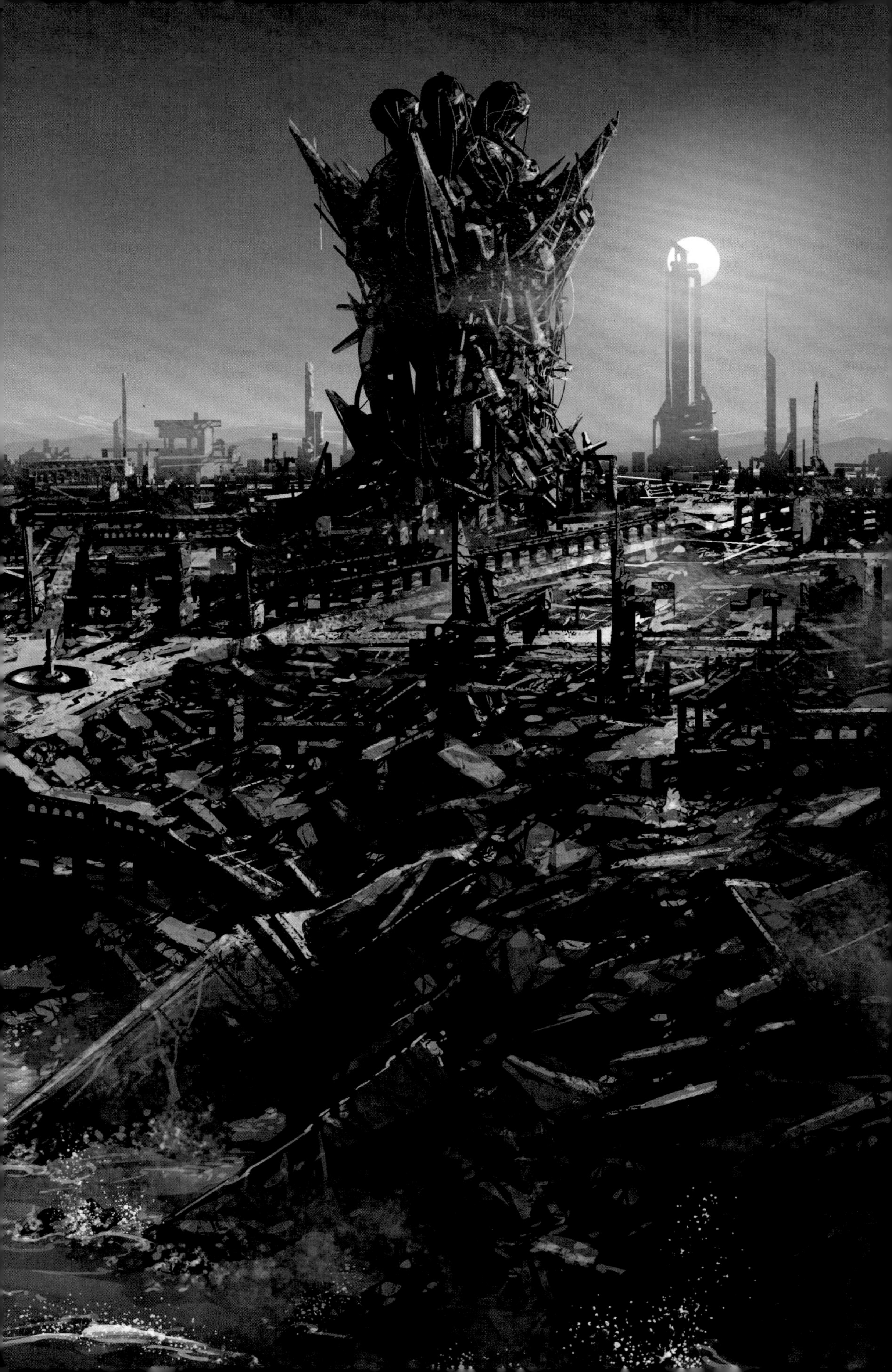

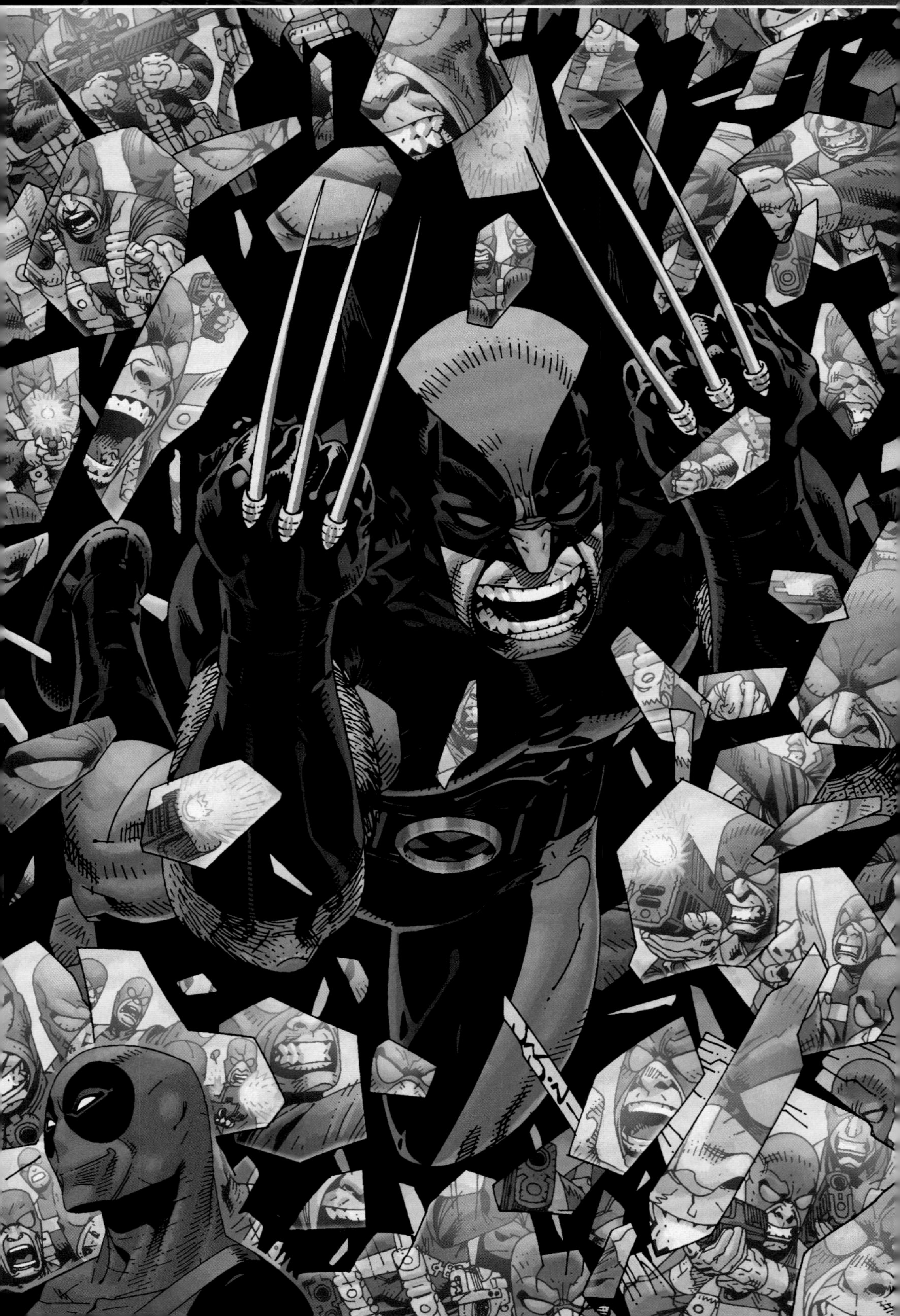

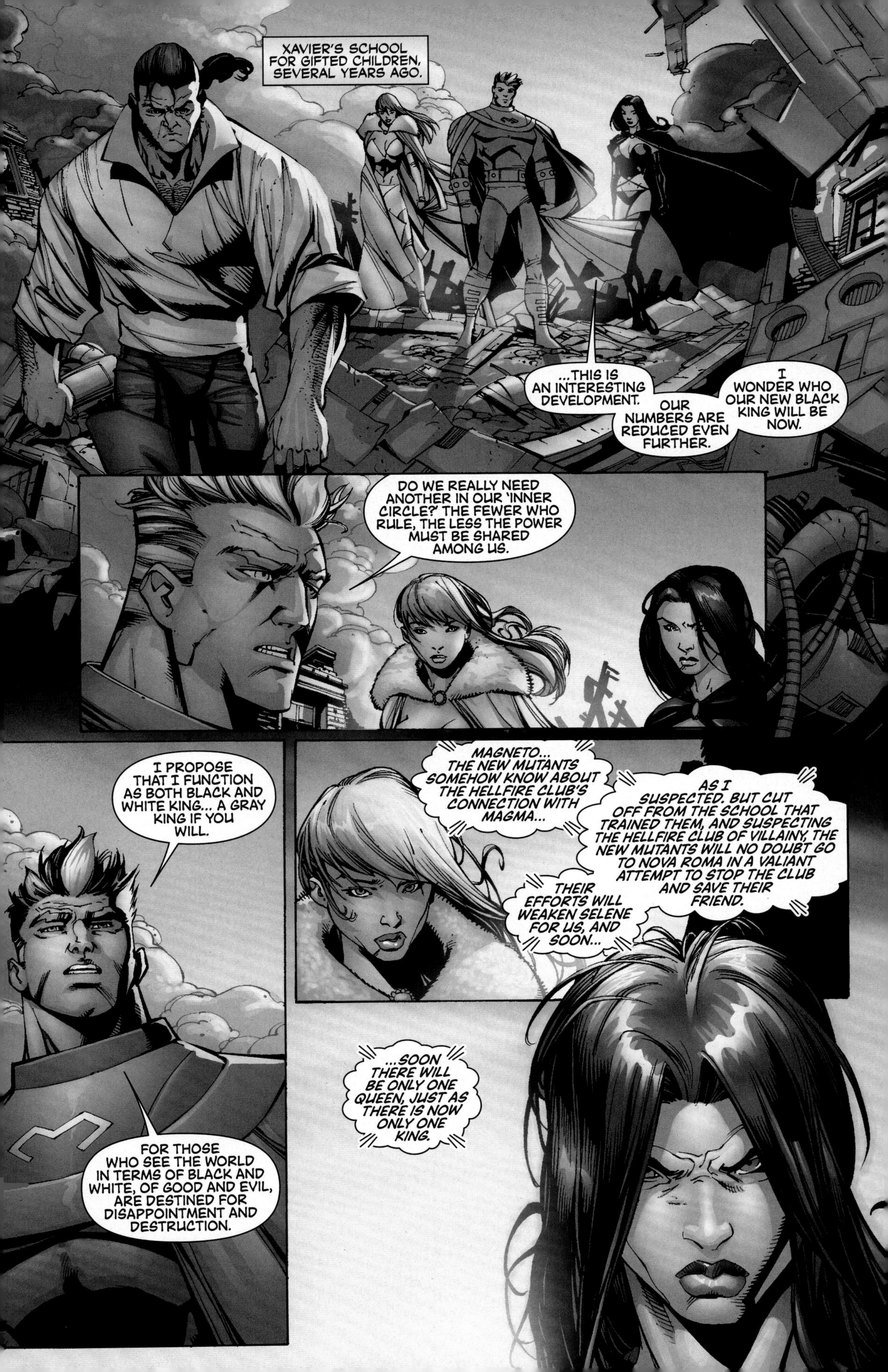
XAVIER'S SCHOOL FOR GIFTED CHILDREN, SEVERAL YEARS AGO.
...THIS IS AN INTERESTING DEVELOPMENT.
OUR NUMBERS ARE REDUCED EVEN FURTHER.
I WONDER WHO OUR NEW BLACK KING WILL BE NOW.
DO WE REALLY NEED ANOTHER IN OUR 'INNER CIRCLE?' THE FEWER WHO RULE, THE LESS THE POWER MUST BE SHARED AMONG US.
I PROPOSE THAT I FUNCTION AS BOTH BLACK AND WHITE KING... A GRAY KING IF YOU WILL.
FOR THOSE WHO SEE THE WORLD IN TERMS OF BLACK AND WHITE, OF GOOD AND EVIL, ARE DESTINED FOR DISAPPOINTMENT AND DESTRUCTION.
MAGNETO... THE NEW MUTANTS SOMEHOW KNOW ABOUT THE HELLFIRE CLUB'S CONNECTION WITH MAGMA...
AS I SUSPECTED. BUT CUT OFF FROM THE SCHOOL THAT TRAINED THEM, AND SUSPECTING THE HELLFIRE CLUB OF VILLAINY, THE NEW MUTANTS WILL NO DOUBT GO TO NOVA ROMA IN A VALIANT ATTEMPT TO STOP THE CLUB AND SAVE THEIR FRIEND.
THEIR EFFORTS WILL WEAKEN SELENE FOR US, AND SOON...
...SOON THERE WILL BE ONLY ONE QUEEN, JUST AS THERE IS NOW ONLY ONE KING.

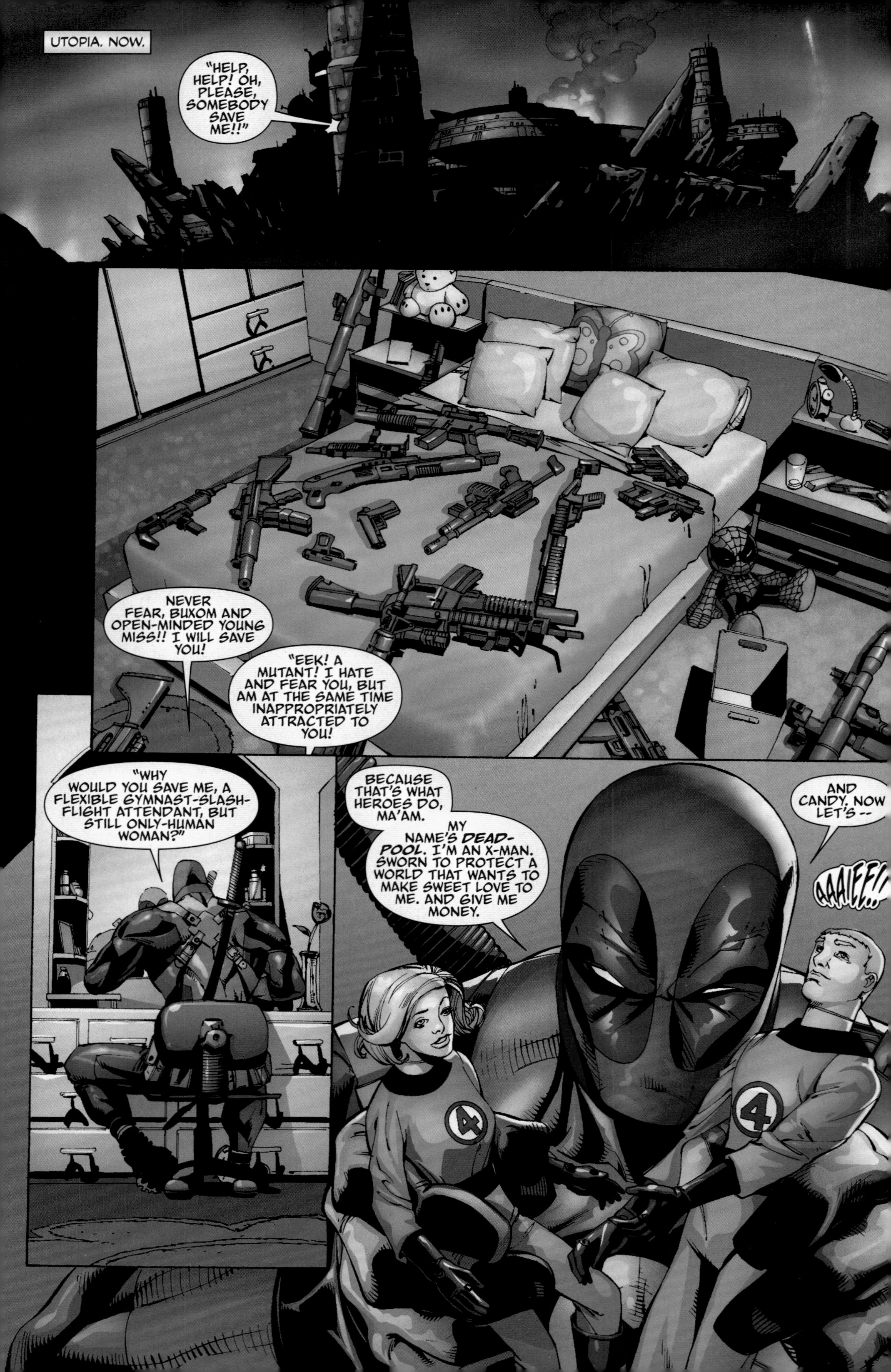
UTOPIA. NOW.
"HELP, HELP! OH, PLEASE, SOMEBODY SAVE ME!!"
NEVER FEAR, BUXOM AND OPEN-MINDED YOUNG MISS!! I WILL SAVE YOU!
"EEK! A MUTANT! I HATE AND FEAR YOU, BUT AM AT THE SAME TIME INAPPROPRIATELY ATTRACTED TO YOU!
"WHY WOULD YOU SAVE ME, A FLEXIBLE GYMNAST-SLASH-FLIGHT ATTENDANT, BUT STILL ONLY-HUMAN WOMAN?"
BECAUSE THAT'S WHAT HEROES DO, MA'AM.
MY NAME'S *DEADPOOL*. I'M AN X-MAN. SWORN TO PROTECT A WORLD THAT WANTS TO MAKE SWEET LOVE TO ME. AND GIVE ME MONEY.
AND CANDY. NOW LET'S --
AAAIEE!!

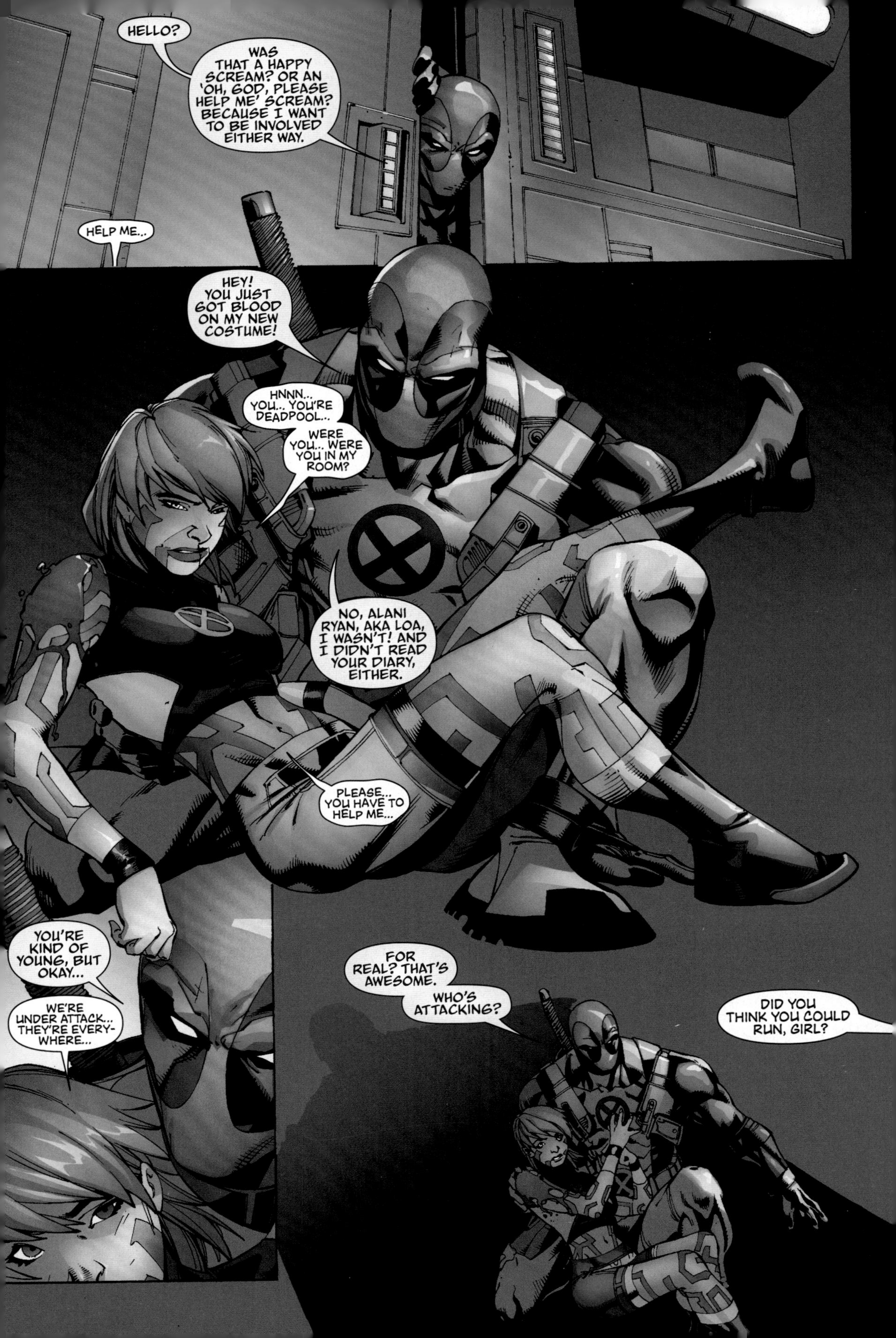
HELLO?
WAS THAT A HAPPY SCREAM? OR AN 'OH, GOD, PLEASE HELP ME' SCREAM? BECAUSE I WANT TO BE INVOLVED EITHER WAY.
HELP ME...
HEY! YOU JUST GOT BLOOD ON MY NEW COSTUME!
HNNN... YOU... YOU'RE DEADPOOL...
WERE YOU... WERE YOU IN MY ROOM?
NO, ALANI RYAN, AKA LOA, I WASN'T! AND I DIDN'T READ YOUR DIARY, EITHER.
PLEASE... YOU HAVE TO HELP ME...
YOU'RE KIND OF YOUNG, BUT OKAY...
WE'RE UNDER ATTACK... THEY'RE EVERYWHERE...
FOR REAL? THAT'S AWESOME.
WHO'S ATTACKING?
DID YOU THINK YOU COULD RUN, GIRL?

DELGADO. CORTEZ. MELLENCAMP.
ACOLYTES. ALL DECEASED.
WE ASKED YOU A QUESTION... WHERE IS THE GRAY KING?
WHERE IS MAGNETO?
UNDEADPOOL

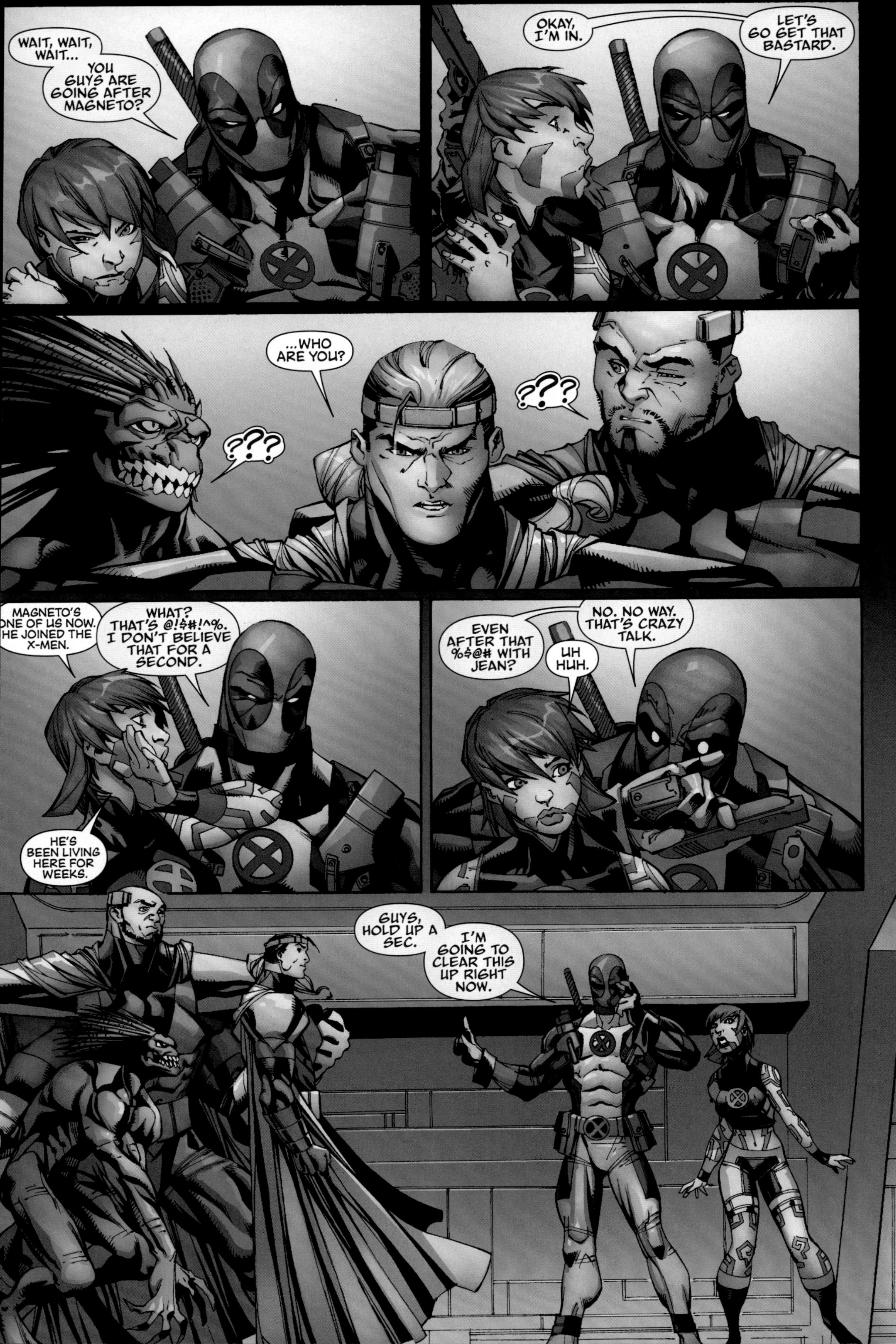
WAIT, WAIT, WAIT... YOU GUYS ARE GOING AFTER MAGNETO?
OKAY, I'M IN.
LET'S GO GET THAT BASTARD.
...WHO ARE YOU?
???
???
MAGNETO'S ONE OF US NOW. HE JOINED THE X-MEN.
WHAT? THAT'S @!$#!^%. I DON'T BELIEVE THAT FOR A SECOND.
HE'S BEEN LIVING HERE FOR WEEKS.
EVEN AFTER THAT %$@# WITH JEAN?
UH HUH.
NO. NO WAY. THAT'S CRAZY TALK.
GUYS, HOLD UP A SEC.
I'M GOING TO CLEAR THIS UP RIGHT NOW.

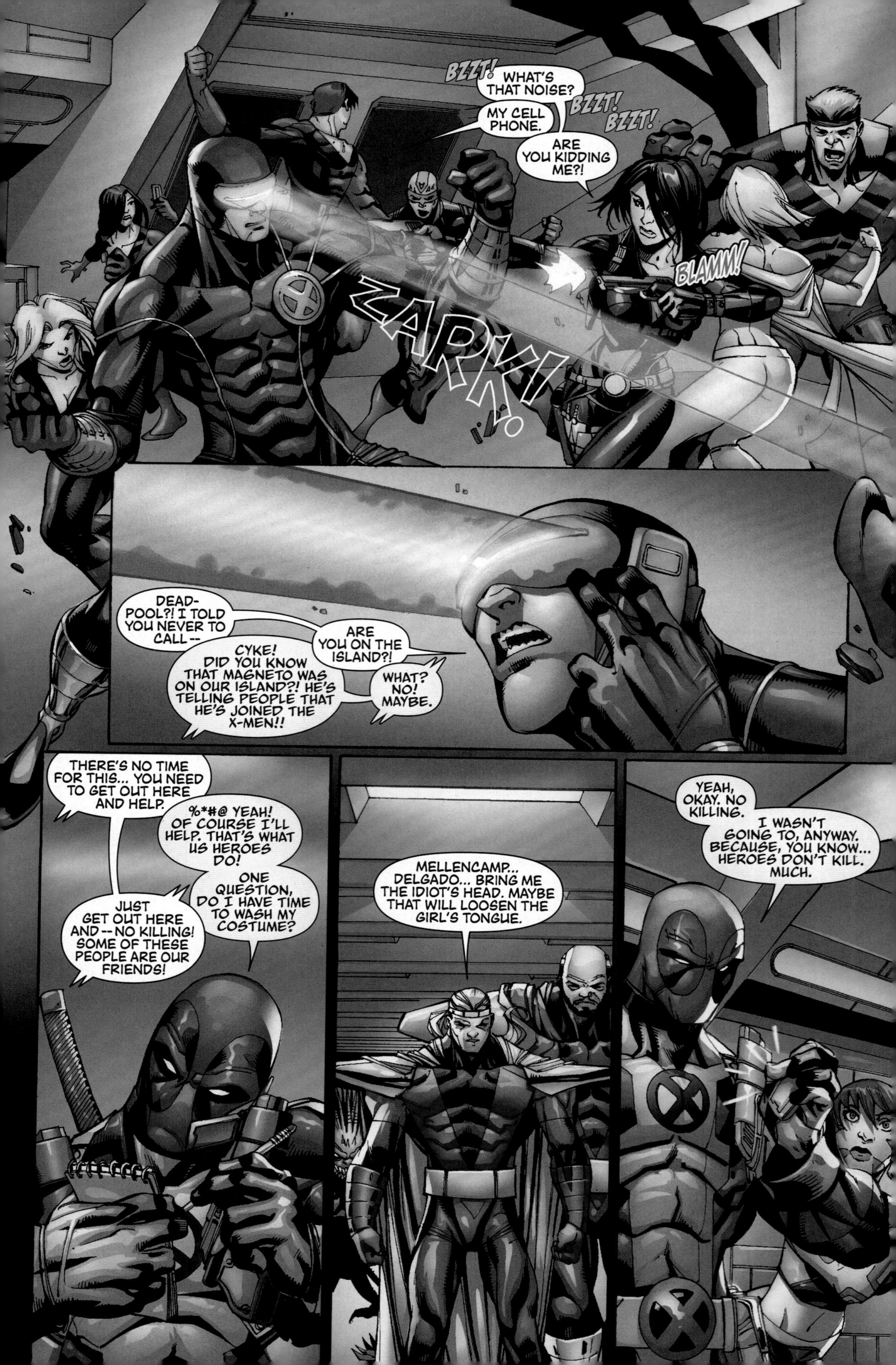
BZZT!
WHAT'S THAT NOISE?
MY CELL PHONE.
BZZT! BZZT!
ARE YOU KIDDING ME?!
BLAMM!
ZARK!
DEAD-POOL?! I TOLD YOU NEVER TO CALL --
ARE YOU ON THE ISLAND?!
CYKE! DID YOU KNOW THAT MAGNETO WAS ON OUR ISLAND?! HE'S TELLING PEOPLE THAT HE'S JOINED THE X-MEN!!
WHAT? NO! MAYBE.
THERE'S NO TIME FOR THIS... YOU NEED TO GET OUT HERE AND HELP.
%*#@ YEAH! OF COURSE I'LL HELP. THAT'S WHAT US HEROES DO!
ONE QUESTION, DO I HAVE TIME TO WASH MY COSTUME?
JUST GET OUT HERE AND -- NO KILLING! SOME OF THESE PEOPLE ARE OUR FRIENDS!
MELLENCAMP... DELGADO... BRING ME THE IDIOT'S HEAD. MAYBE THAT WILL LOOSEN THE GIRL'S TONGUE.
YEAH, OKAY. NO KILLING.
I WASN'T GOING TO, ANYWAY. BECAUSE, YOU KNOW... HEROES DON'T KILL. MUCH.

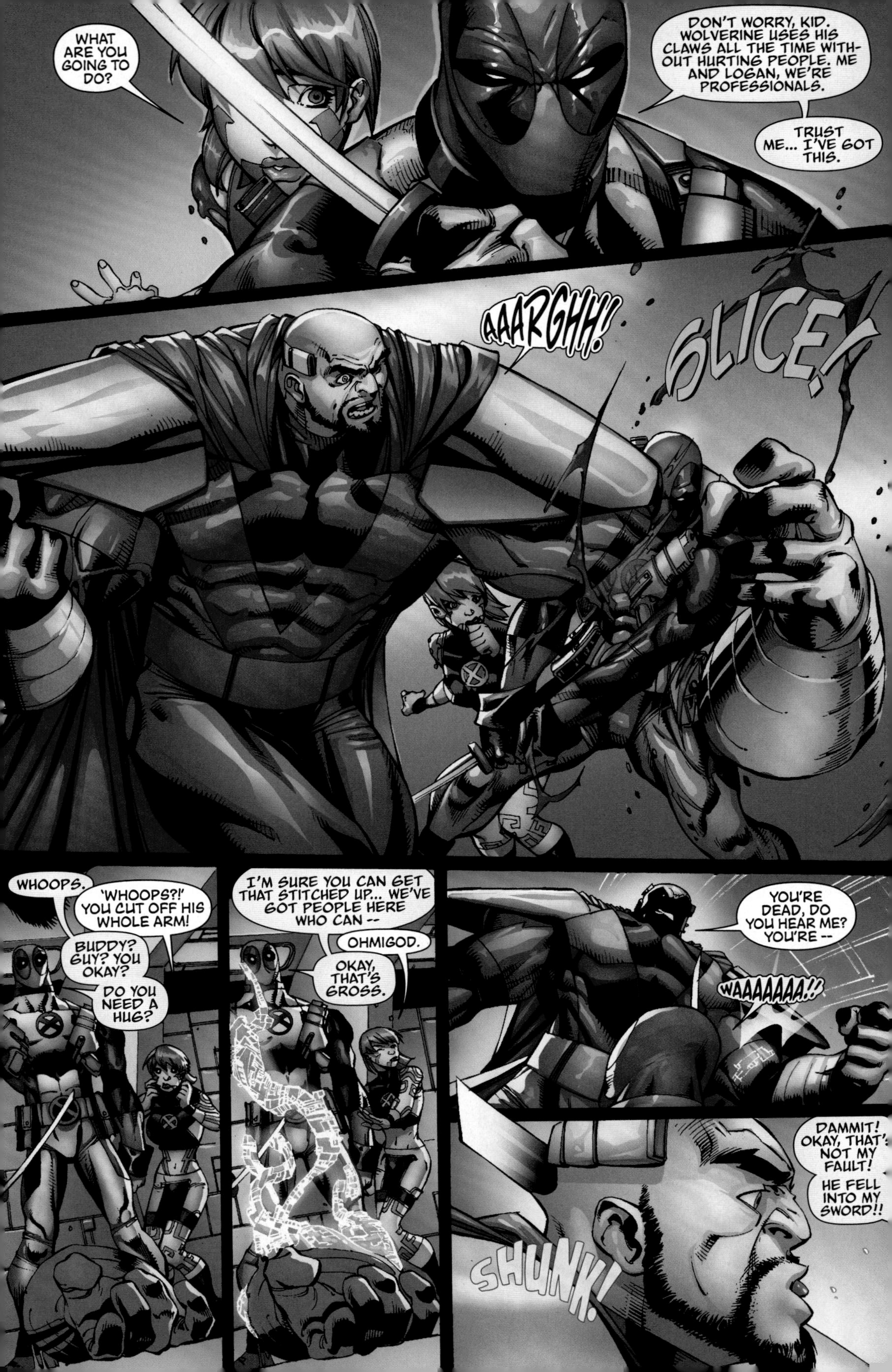
WHAT ARE YOU GOING TO DO?
DON'T WORRY, KID. WOLVERINE USES HIS CLAWS ALL THE TIME WITH-OUT HURTING PEOPLE. ME AND LOGAN, WE'RE PROFESSIONALS.
TRUST ME... I'VE GOT THIS.
AAARGHH!
SLICE!
WHOOPS.
'WHOOPS?!' YOU CUT OFF HIS WHOLE ARM!
BUDDY? GUY? YOU OKAY?
DO YOU NEED A HUG?
I'M SURE YOU CAN GET THAT STITCHED UP... WE'VE GOT PEOPLE HERE WHO CAN --
OHMIGOD.
OKAY, THAT'S GROSS.
YOU'RE DEAD, DO YOU HEAR ME? YOU'RE --
WAAAAAAA!!
SHUNK!
DAMMIT! OKAY, THAT'S NOT MY FAULT!
HE FELL INTO MY SWORD!!

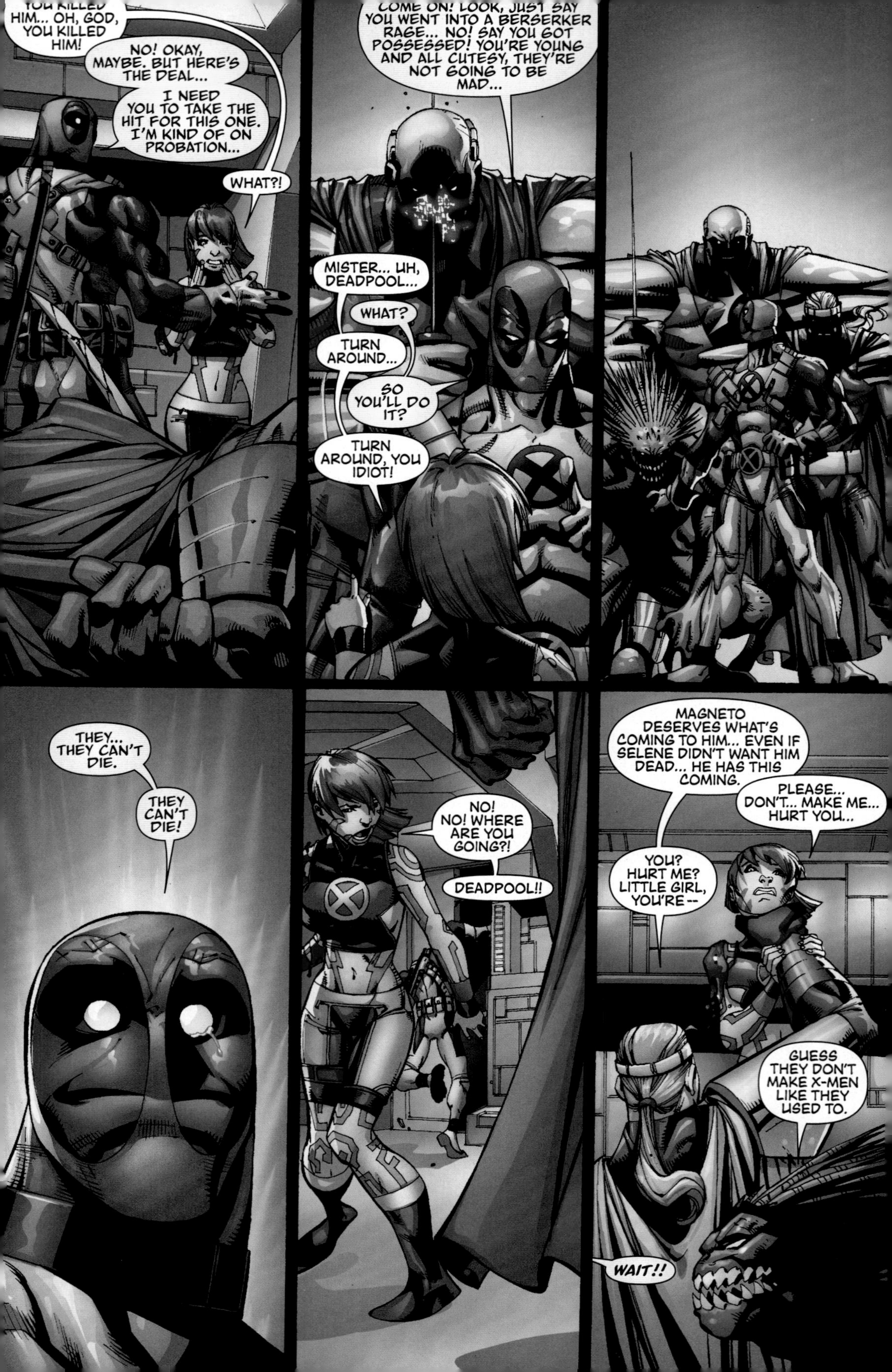
YOU KILLED HIM... OH, GOD, YOU KILLED HIM!
NO! OKAY, MAYBE. BUT HERE'S THE DEAL...
I NEED YOU TO TAKE THE HIT FOR THIS ONE. I'M KIND OF ON PROBATION...
WHAT?!
COME ON! LOOK, JUST SAY YOU WENT INTO A BERSERKER RAGE... NO! SAY YOU GOT POSSESSED! YOU'RE YOUNG AND ALL CUTESY, THEY'RE NOT GOING TO BE MAD...
MISTER... UH, DEADPOOL...
WHAT?
TURN AROUND...
SO YOU'LL DO IT?
TURN AROUND, YOU IDIOT!
THEY... THEY CAN'T DIE.
THEY CAN'T DIE!
NO! NO! WHERE ARE YOU GOING?!
DEADPOOL!!
MAGNETO DESERVES WHAT'S COMING TO HIM... EVEN IF SELENE DIDN'T WANT HIM DEAD... HE HAS THIS COMING.
PLEASE... DON'T... MAKE ME... HURT YOU...
YOU? HURT ME? LITTLE GIRL, YOU'RE --
GUESS THEY DON'T MAKE X-MEN LIKE THEY USED TO.
WAIT!!

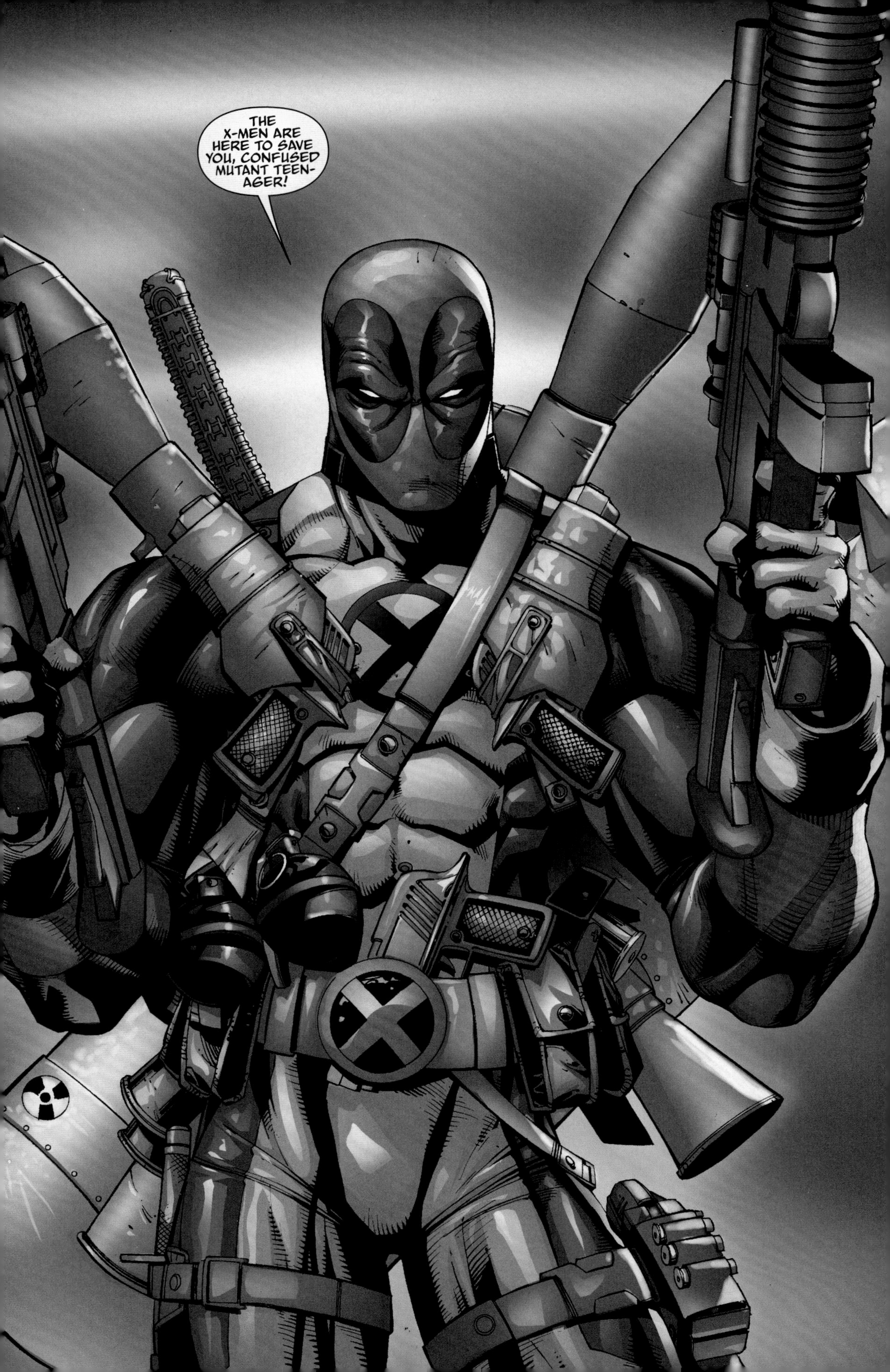
THE X-MEN ARE HERE TO SAVE YOU, CONFUSED MUTANT TEEN-AGER!

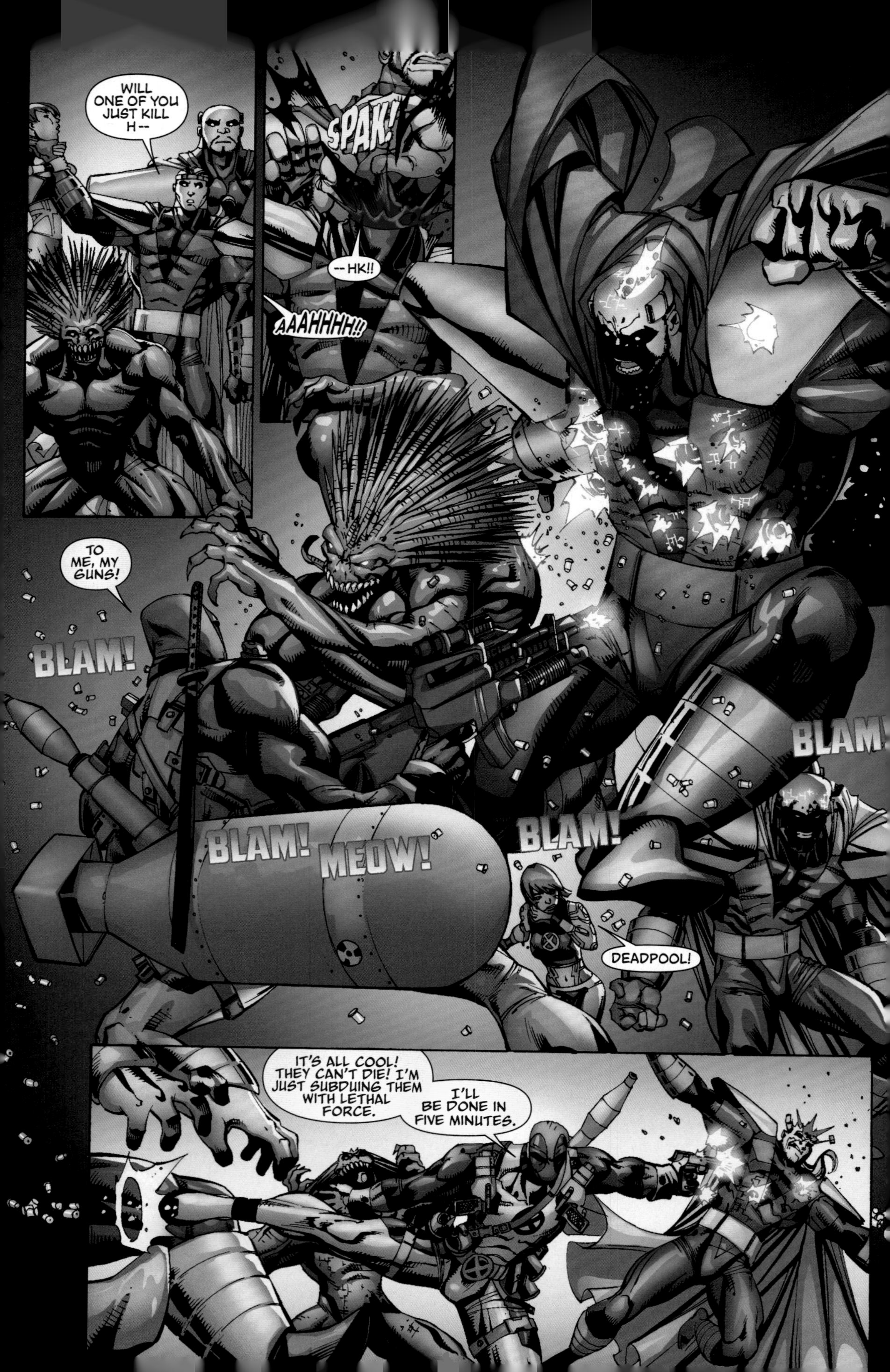
WILL ONE OF YOU JUST KILL H--
SPAK!
--HK!!
AAAHHHH!!
TO ME, MY GUNS!
BLAM!
BLAM!
BLAM!
MEOW!
BLAM!
DEADPOOL!
IT'S ALL COOL! THEY CAN'T DIE! I'M JUST SUBDUING THEM WITH LETHAL FORCE.
I'LL BE DONE IN FIVE MINUTES.

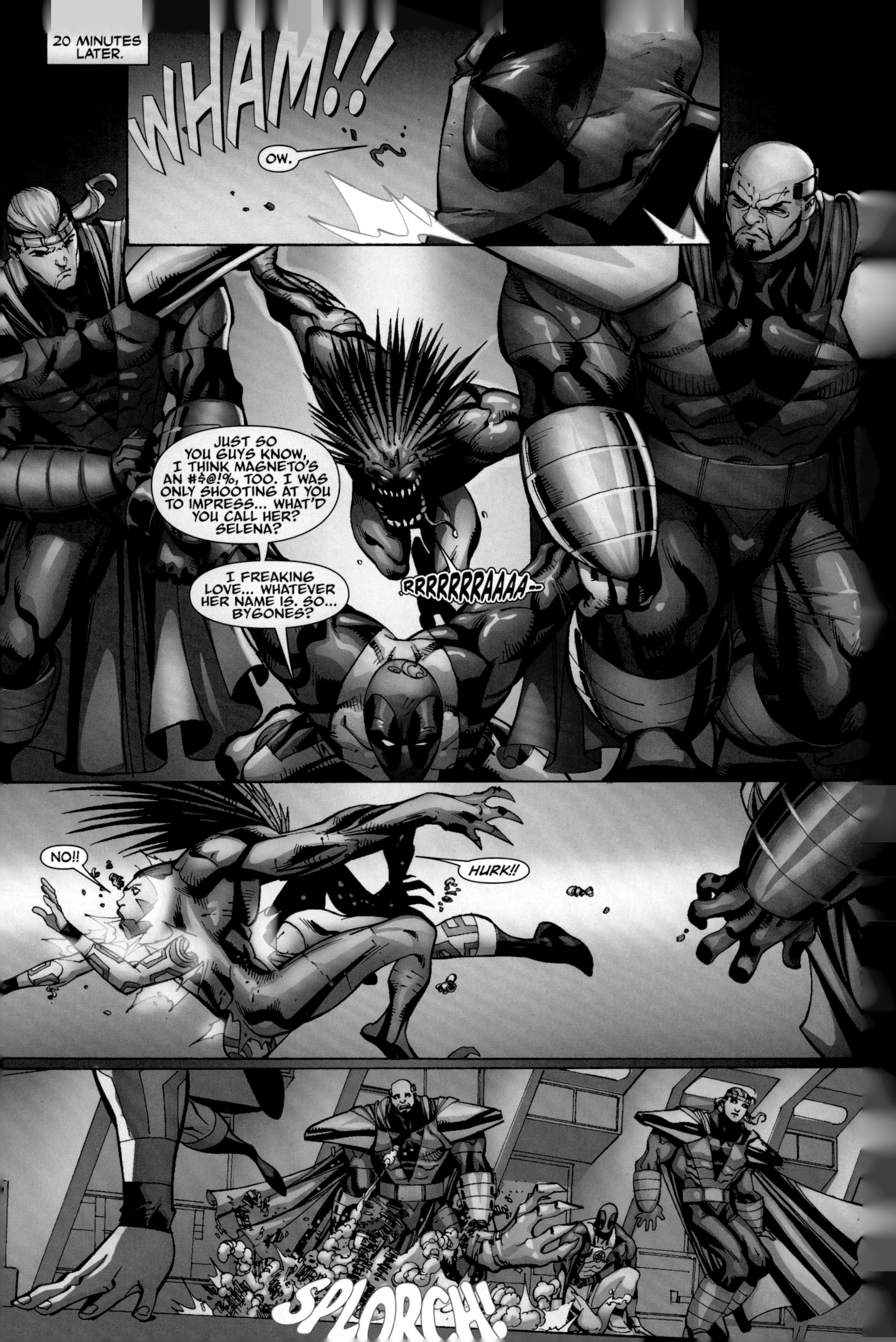
20 MINUTES LATER.
WHAM!!
OW.
JUST SO YOU GUYS KNOW, I THINK MAGNETO'S AN #$@!%, TOO. I WAS ONLY SHOOTING AT YOU TO IMPRESS... WHAT'D YOU CALL HER? SELENA?
I FREAKING LOVE... WHATEVER HER NAME IS. SO... BYGONES?
RRRRRRRAAAA--
NO!!
HURK!!
SPLORCH!

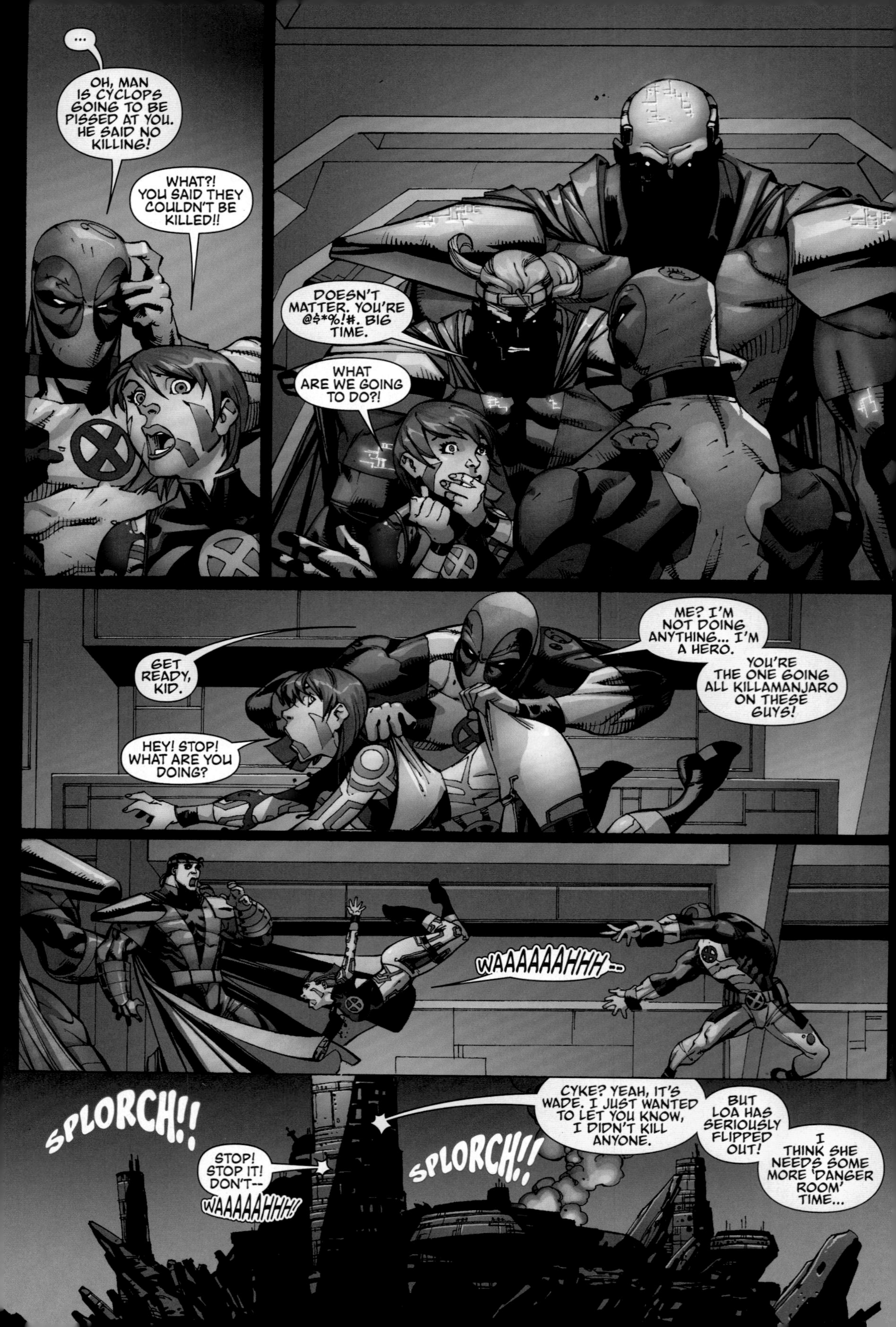
...
OH, MAN IS CYCLOPS GOING TO BE PISSED AT YOU. HE SAID NO KILLING!
WHAT?! YOU SAID THEY COULDN'T BE KILLED!!
DOESN'T MATTER. YOU'RE @$*%!#. BIG TIME.
WHAT ARE WE GOING TO DO?!
GET READY, KID.
ME? I'M NOT DOING ANYTHING... I'M A HERO.
YOU'RE THE ONE GOING ALL KILLAMANJARO ON THESE GUYS!
HEY! STOP! WHAT ARE YOU DOING?
WAAAAAAHHH--
SPLORCH!!
STOP! STOP IT! DON'T--
WAAAAAHHH!
CYKE? YEAH, IT'S WADE. I JUST WANTED TO LET YOU KNOW, I DIDN'T KILL ANYONE.
SPLORCH!!
BUT LOA HAS SERIOUSLY FLIPPED OUT!
I THINK SHE NEEDS SOME MORE 'DANGER ROOM' TIME...

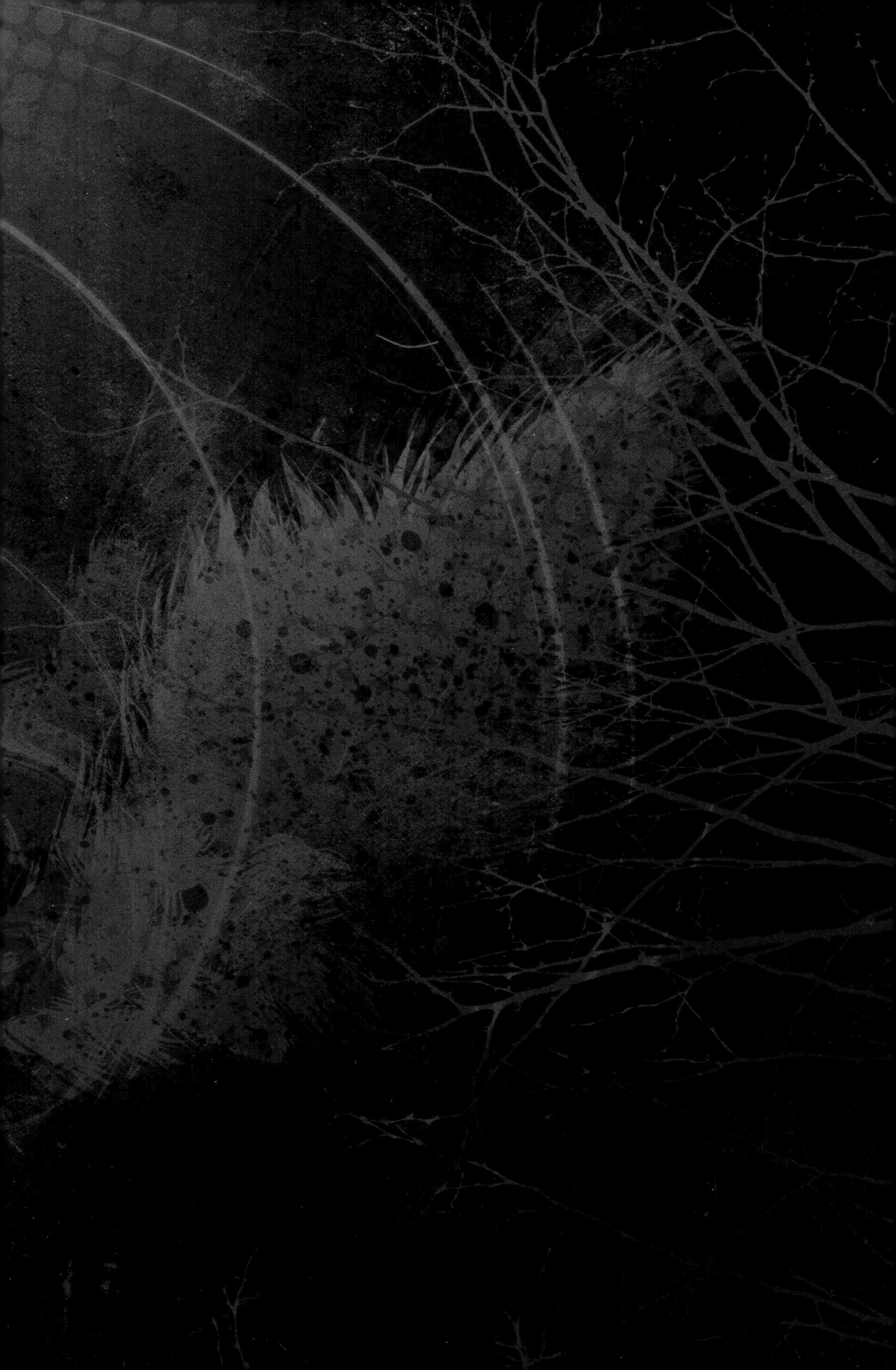

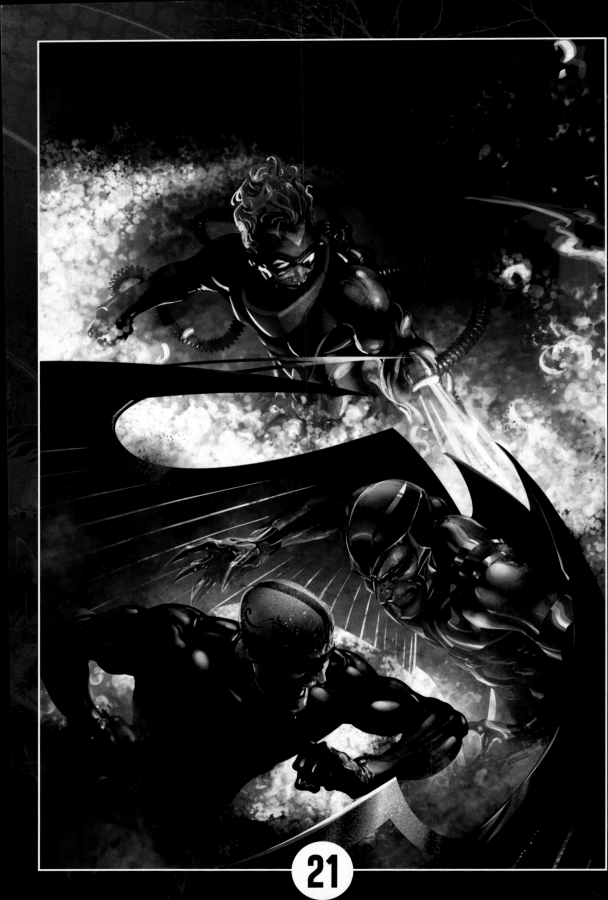

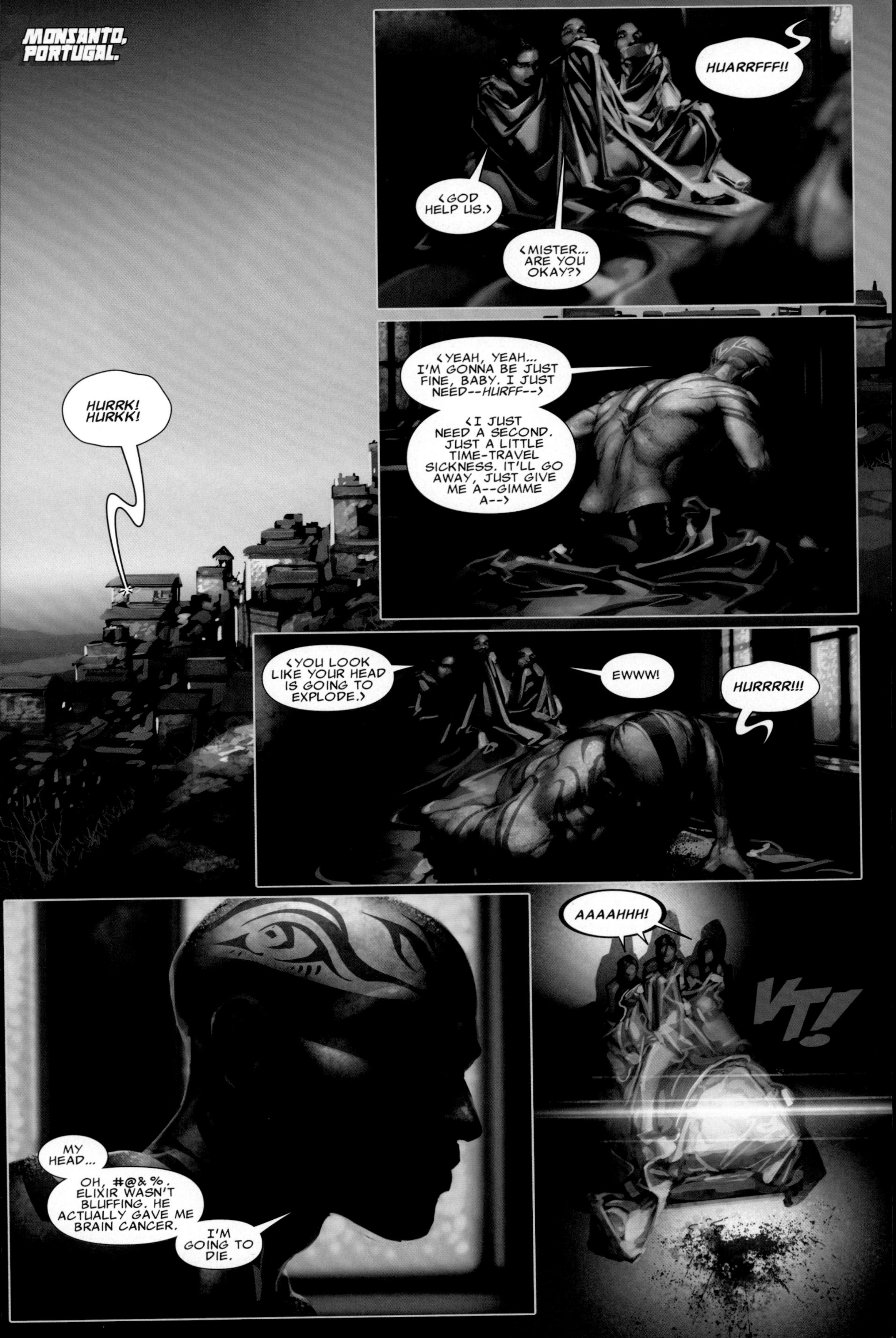
MONSANTO, PORTUGAL.
HUARRFFF!!
‹GOD HELP US.›
‹MISTER... ARE YOU OKAY?›
HURRK! HURKK!
‹YEAH, YEAH... I'M GONNA BE JUST FINE, BABY. I JUST NEED--HURFF--›
‹I JUST NEED A SECOND. JUST A LITTLE TIME-TRAVEL SICKNESS. IT'LL GO AWAY, JUST GIVE ME A--GIMME A--›
‹YOU LOOK LIKE YOUR HEAD IS GOING TO EXPLODE.›
EWWW!
HURRRR!!!
MY HEAD...
OH, #@&%. ELIXIR WASN'T BLUFFING. HE ACTUALLY GAVE ME BRAIN CANCER.
I'M GOING TO DIE.
AAAAHHH!
VT!

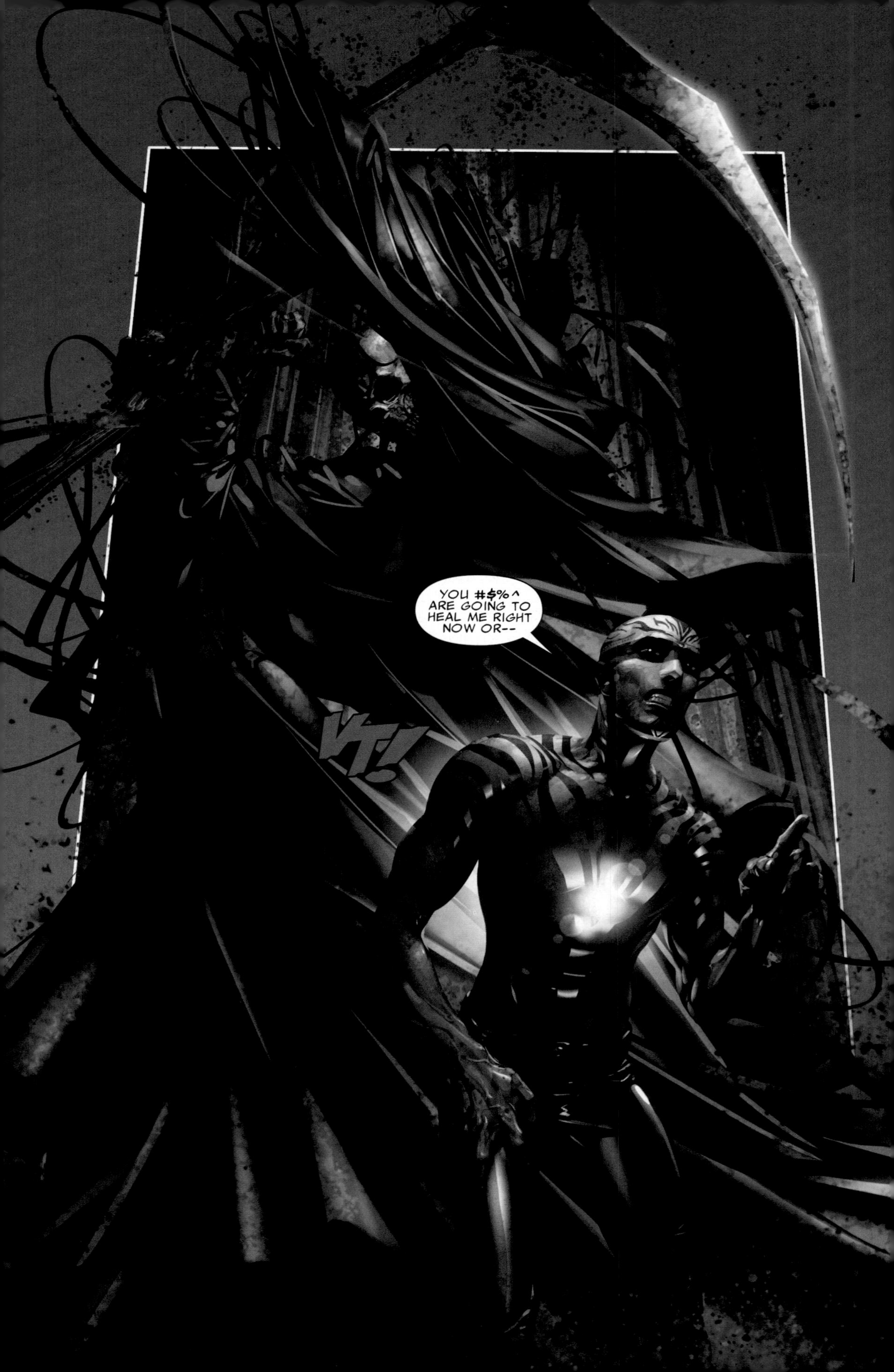
YOU #$%^ ARE GOING TO HEAL ME RIGHT NOW OR--
VT!

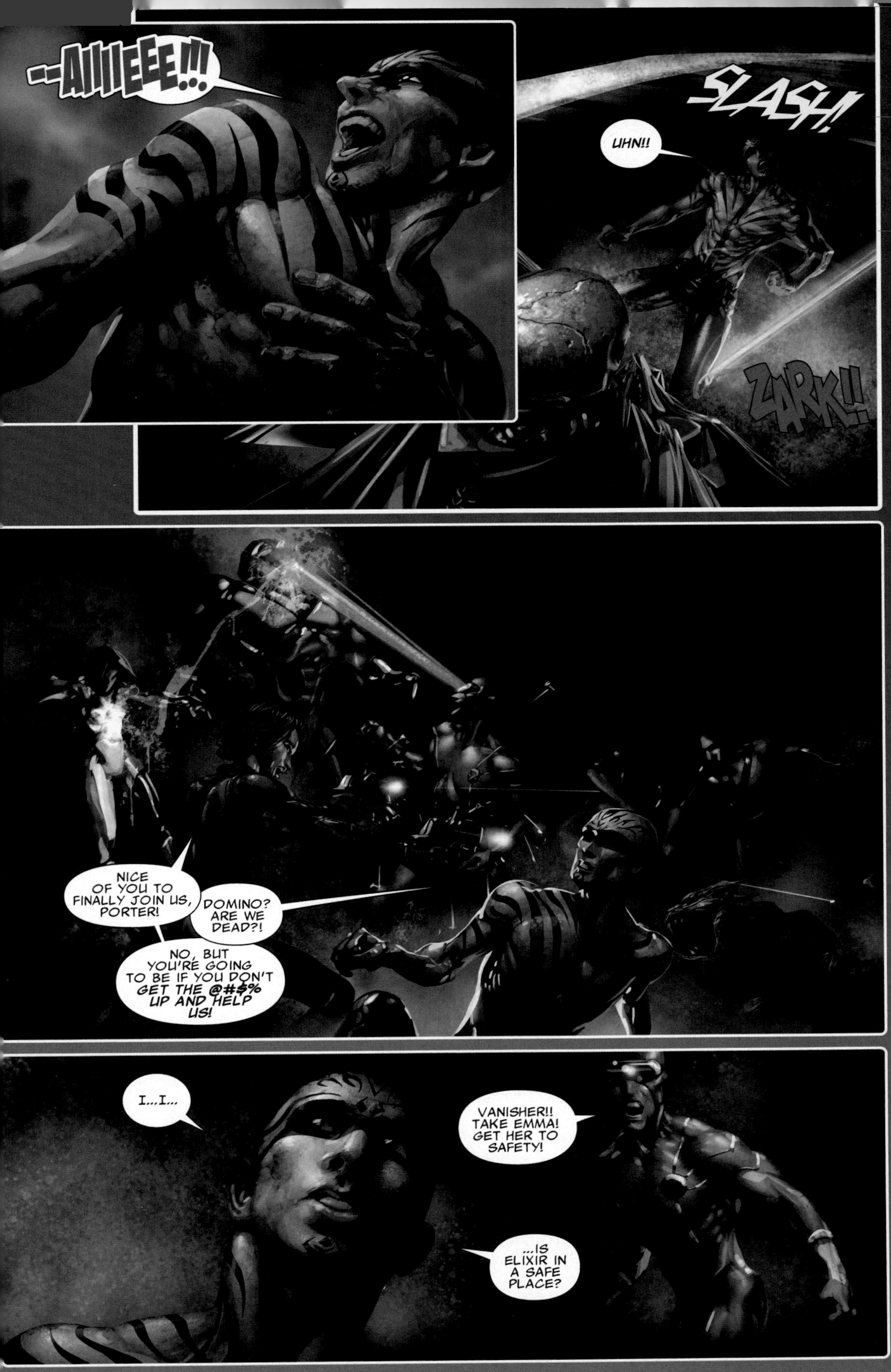
--AIIIIEEE!!!
SLASH!
UHN!!
ZARK!!!
NICE OF YOU TO FINALLY JOIN US, PORTER!
DOMINO? ARE WE DEAD?!
NO, BUT YOU'RE GOING TO BE IF YOU DON'T GET THE @#$% UP AND HELP US!
I...I...
VANISHER!! TAKE EMMA! GET HER TO SAFETY!
...IS ELIXIR IN A SAFE PLACE?

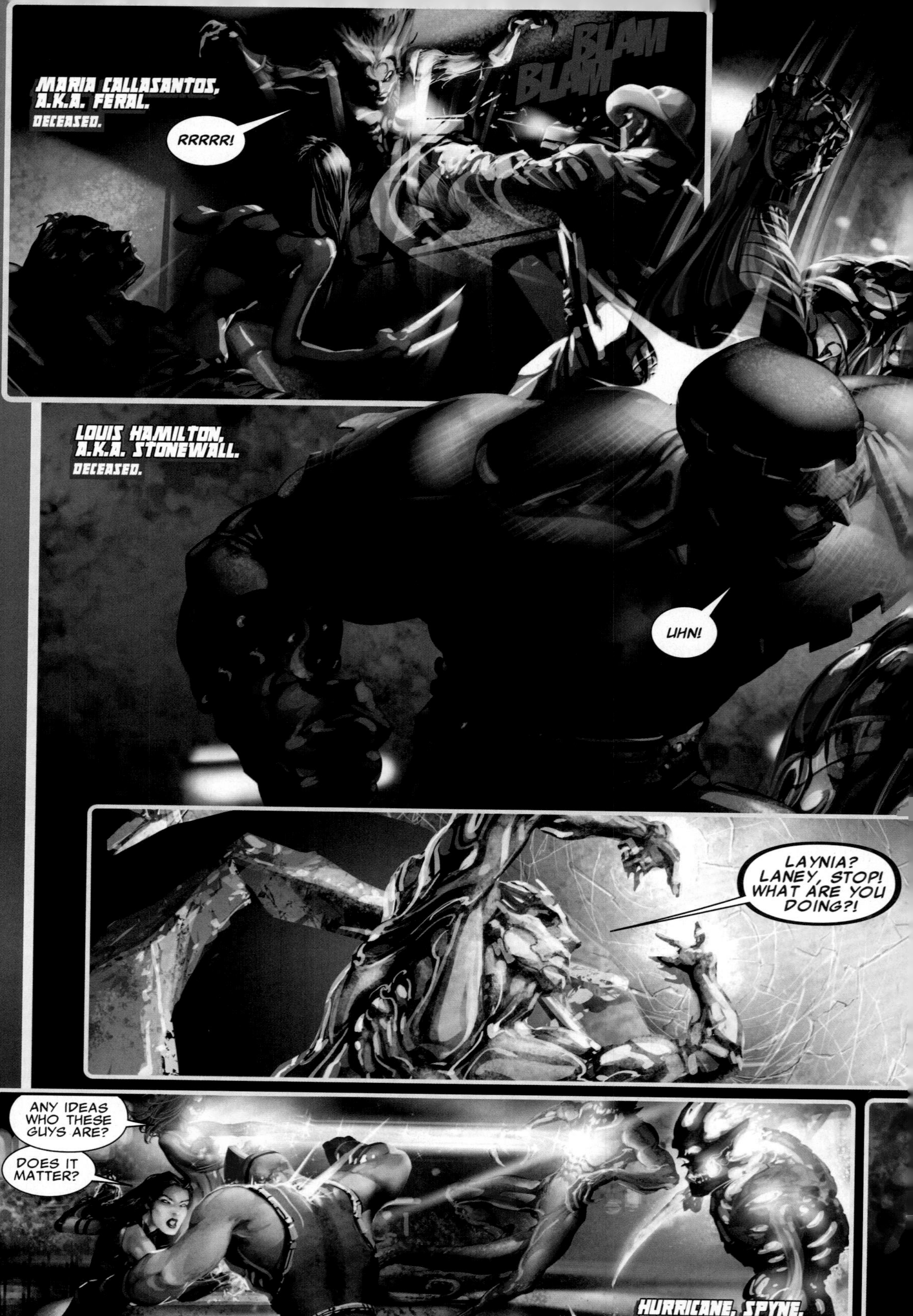
BLAM
BLAM
MARIA CALLASANTOS, A.K.A. FERAL.
DECEASED.
RRRRR!
LOUIS HAMILTON, A.K.A. STONEWALL.
DECEASED.
UHN!
LAYNIA? LANEY, STOP! WHAT ARE YOU DOING?!
ANY IDEAS WHO THESE GUYS ARE?
DOES IT MATTER?
HURRICANE, SPYNE, AND DEADBOLT. IDENTITIES UNKNOWN.
DECEASED.

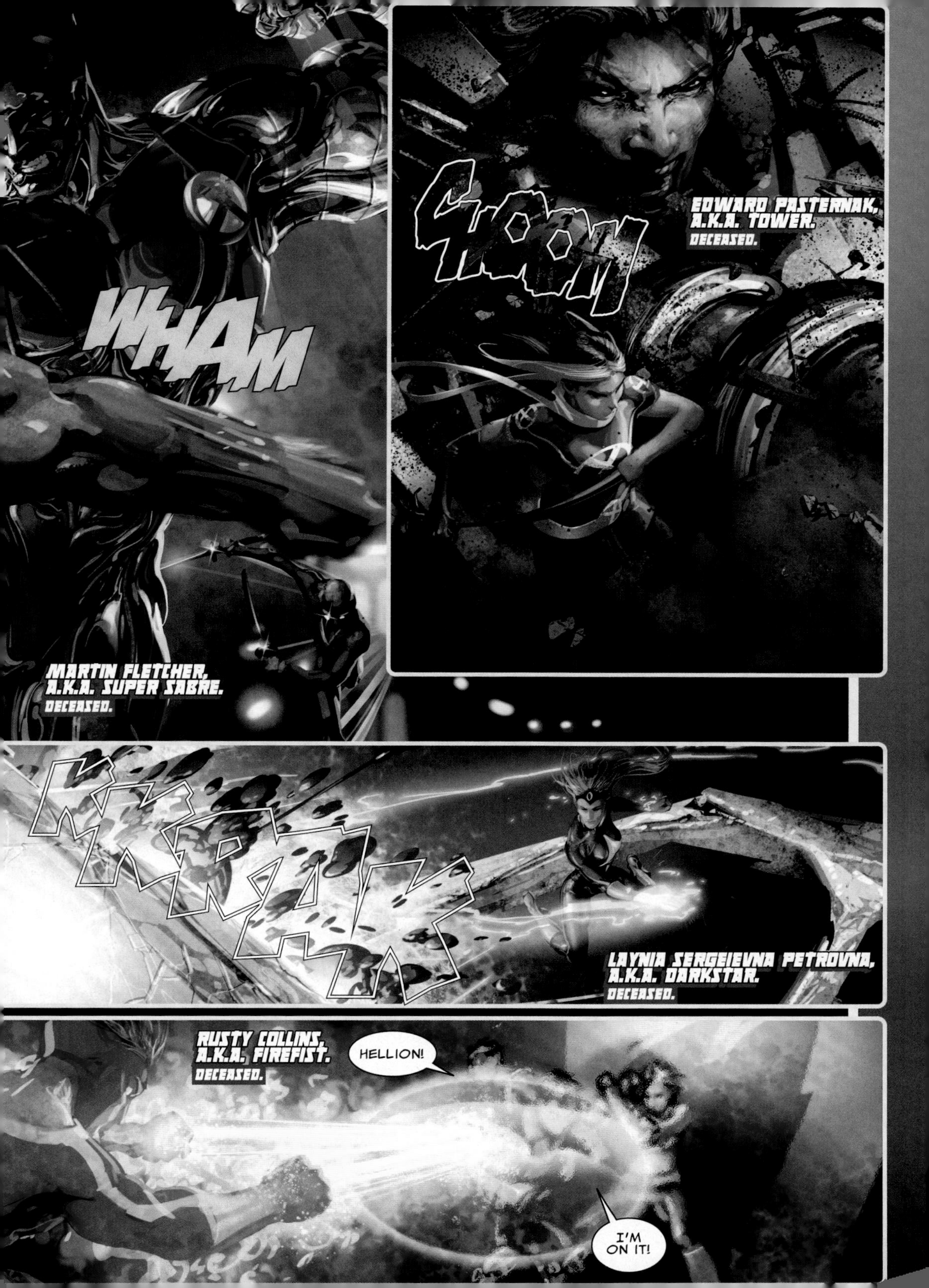

WHAM
MARTIN FLETCHER, A.K.A. SUPER SABRE.
DECEASED.
CHOOM
EDWARD PASTERNAK, A.K.A. TOWER.
DECEASED.
LAYNIA SERGEIEVNA PETROVNA, A.K.A. DARKSTAR.
DECEASED.
RUSTY COLLINS, A.K.A. FIREFIST.
DECEASED.
HELLION!
I'M ON IT!

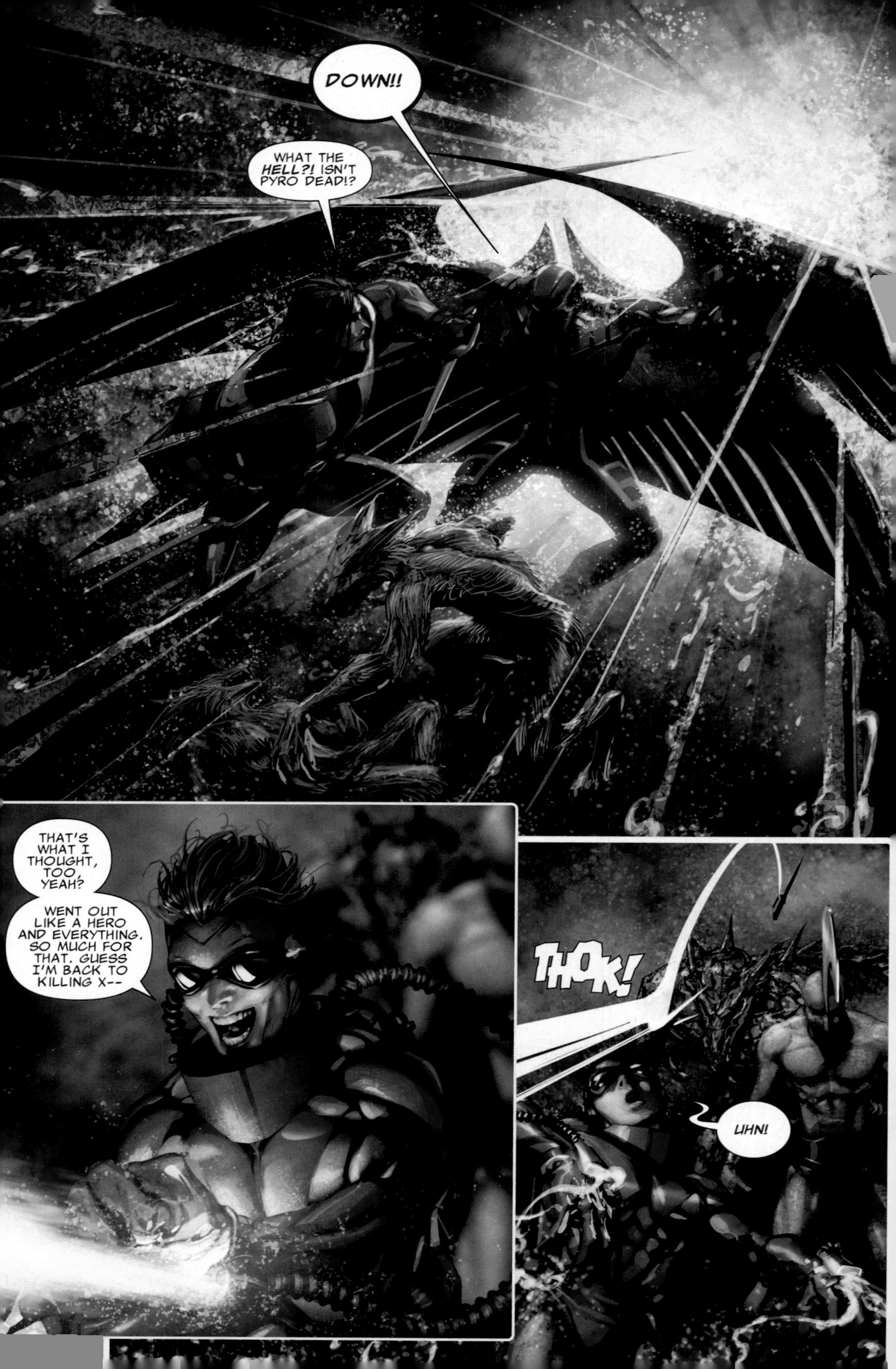
DOWN!!
WHAT THE HELL?! ISN'T PYRO DEAD!?
THAT'S WHAT I THOUGHT, TOO, YEAH?
WENT OUT LIKE A HERO AND EVERYTHING. SO MUCH FOR THAT. GUESS I'M BACK TO KILLING X--
THOK!
UHN!

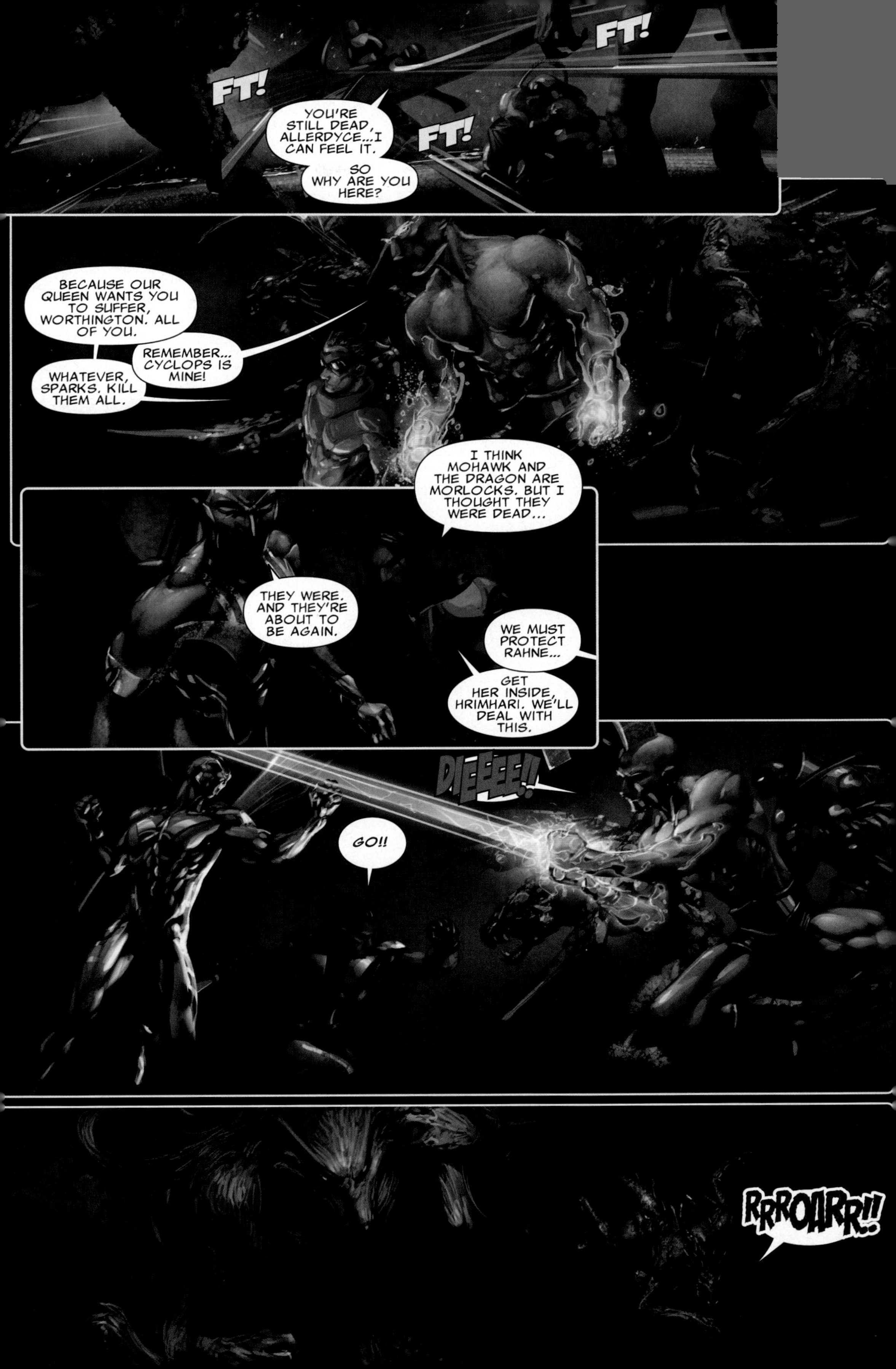
FT!
FT!
FT!
YOU'RE STILL DEAD, ALLERDYCE...I CAN FEEL IT.
SO WHY ARE YOU HERE?
BECAUSE OUR QUEEN WANTS YOU TO SUFFER, WORTHINGTON. ALL OF YOU.
WHATEVER, SPARKS. KILL THEM ALL.
REMEMBER... CYCLOPS IS MINE!
I THINK MOHAWK AND THE DRAGON ARE MORLOCKS. BUT I THOUGHT THEY WERE DEAD...
THEY WERE. AND THEY'RE ABOUT TO BE AGAIN.
WE MUST PROTECT RAHNE...
GET HER INSIDE, HRIMHARI. WE'LL DEAL WITH THIS.
DIEEEE!!
GO!!
RRROARR!!

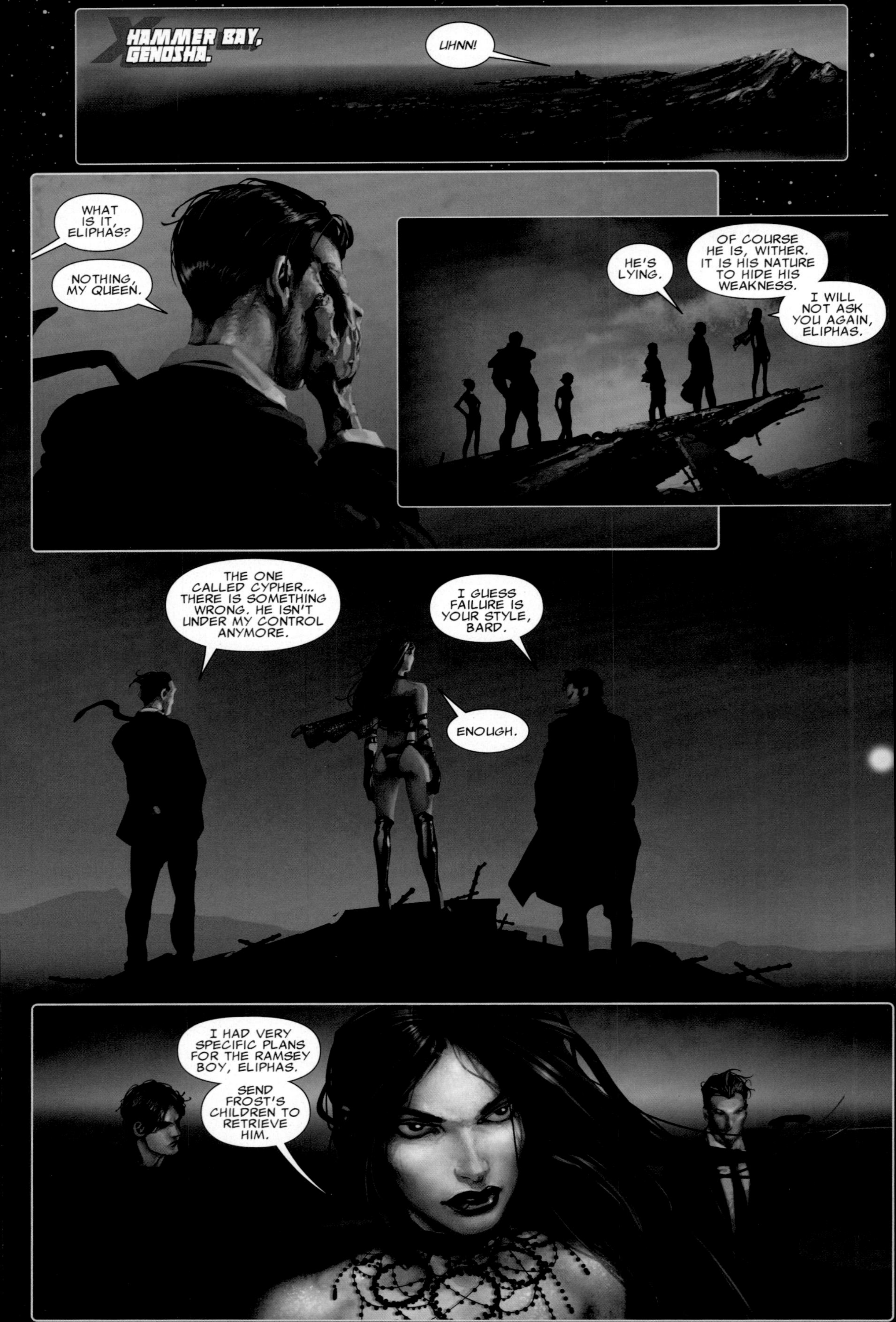
HAMMER BAY, GENOSHA.
UHNN!
WHAT IS IT, ELIPHAS?
NOTHING, MY QUEEN.
HE'S LYING.
OF COURSE HE IS, WITHER. IT IS HIS NATURE TO HIDE HIS WEAKNESS.
I WILL NOT ASK YOU AGAIN, ELIPHAS.
THE ONE CALLED CYPHER... THERE IS SOMETHING WRONG. HE ISN'T UNDER MY CONTROL ANYMORE.
I GUESS FAILURE IS YOUR STYLE, BARD.
ENOUGH.
I HAD VERY SPECIFIC PLANS FOR THE RAMSEY BOY, ELIPHAS.
SEND FROST'S CHILDREN TO RETRIEVE HIM.

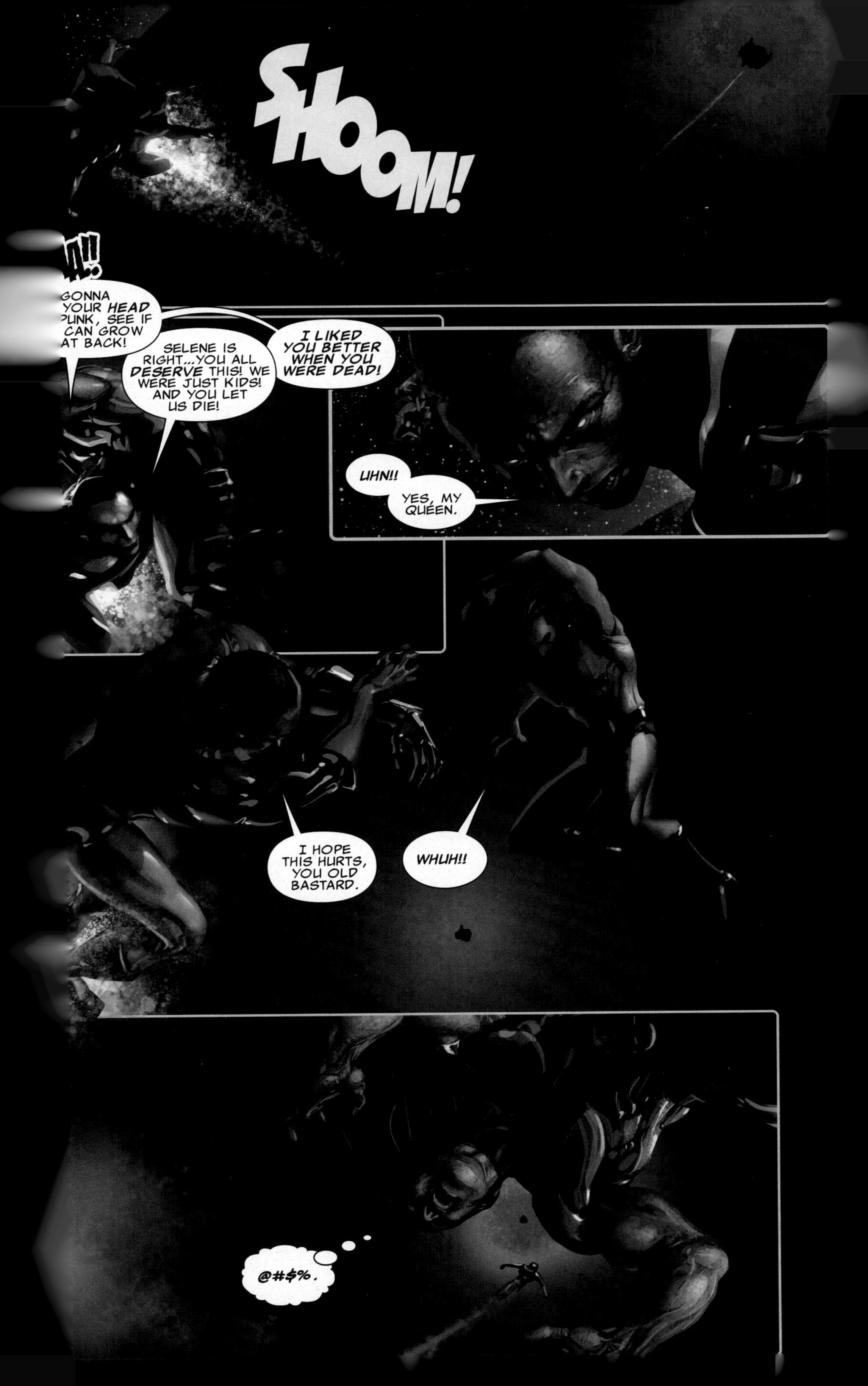
SHOOM!
GONNA YOUR HEAD PUNK, SEE IF CAN GROW AT BACK!
SELENE IS RIGHT...YOU ALL DESERVE THIS! WE WERE JUST KIDS! AND YOU LET US DIE!
I LIKED YOU BETTER WHEN YOU WERE DEAD!
UHN!!
YES, MY QUEEN.
I HOPE THIS HURTS, YOU OLD BASTARD.
WHUH!!
@#$%.

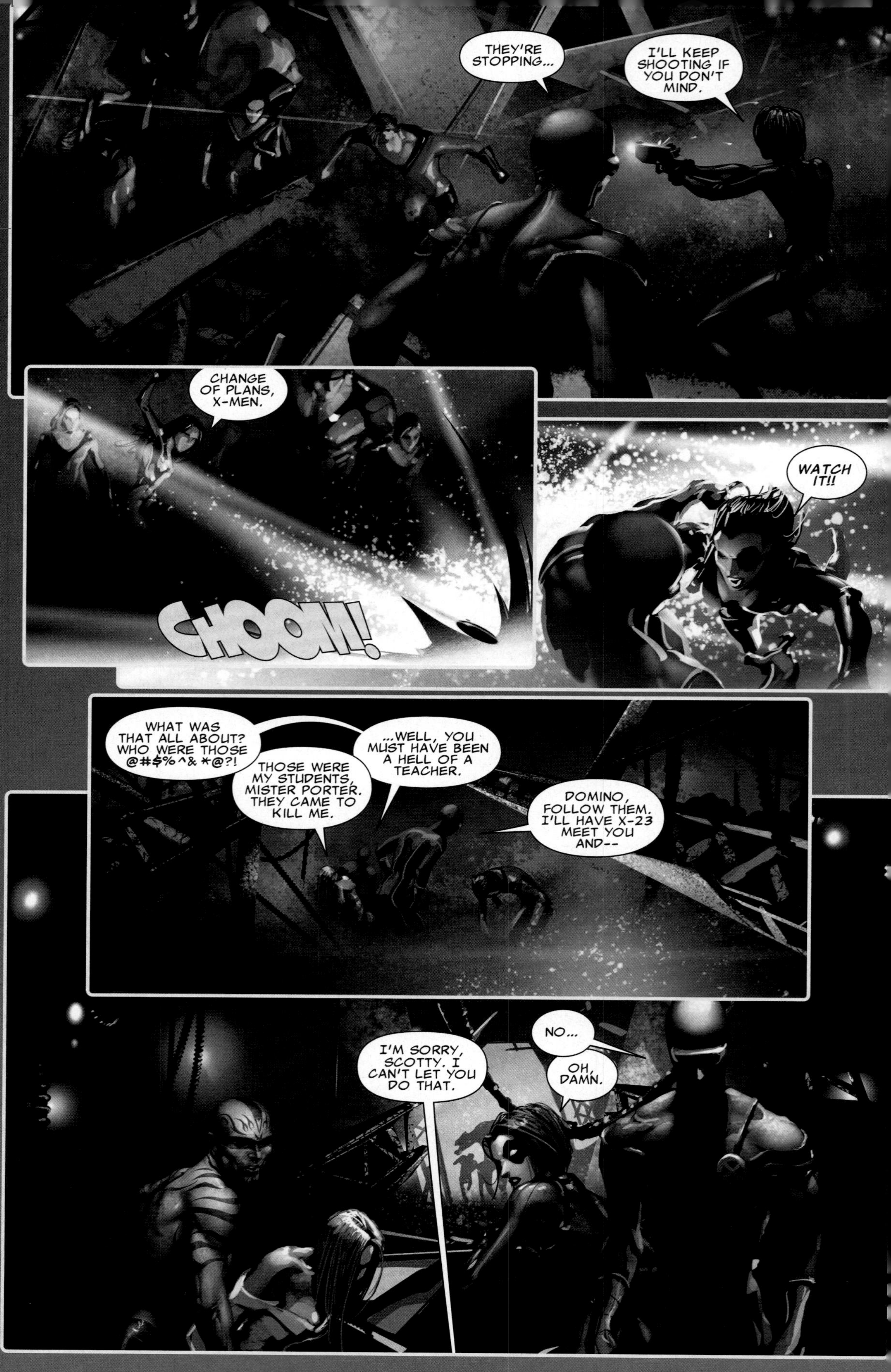

THEY'RE STOPPING...
I'LL KEEP SHOOTING IF YOU DON'T MIND.
CHANGE OF PLANS, X-MEN.
CHOOM!
WATCH IT!!
WHAT WAS THAT ALL ABOUT? WHO WERE THOSE @#$%^& *@?!
THOSE WERE MY STUDENTS, MISTER PORTER. THEY CAME TO KILL ME.
...WELL, YOU MUST HAVE BEEN A HELL OF A TEACHER.
DOMINO, FOLLOW THEM. I'LL HAVE X-23 MEET YOU AND--
I'M SORRY, SCOTTY. I CAN'T LET YOU DO THAT.
NO...
OH, DAMN.

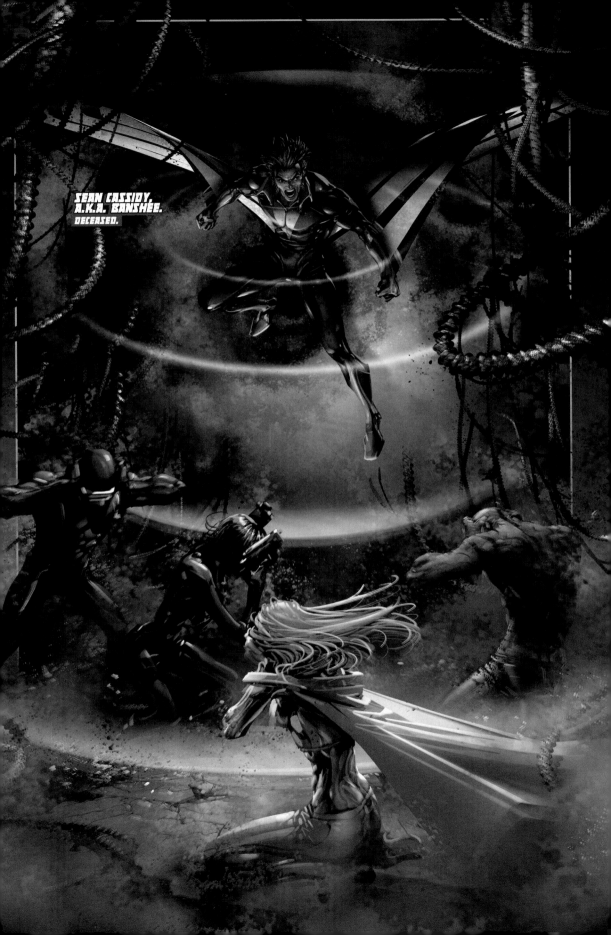

SEAN CASSIDY,
A.K.A. BANSHEE.
DECEASED.

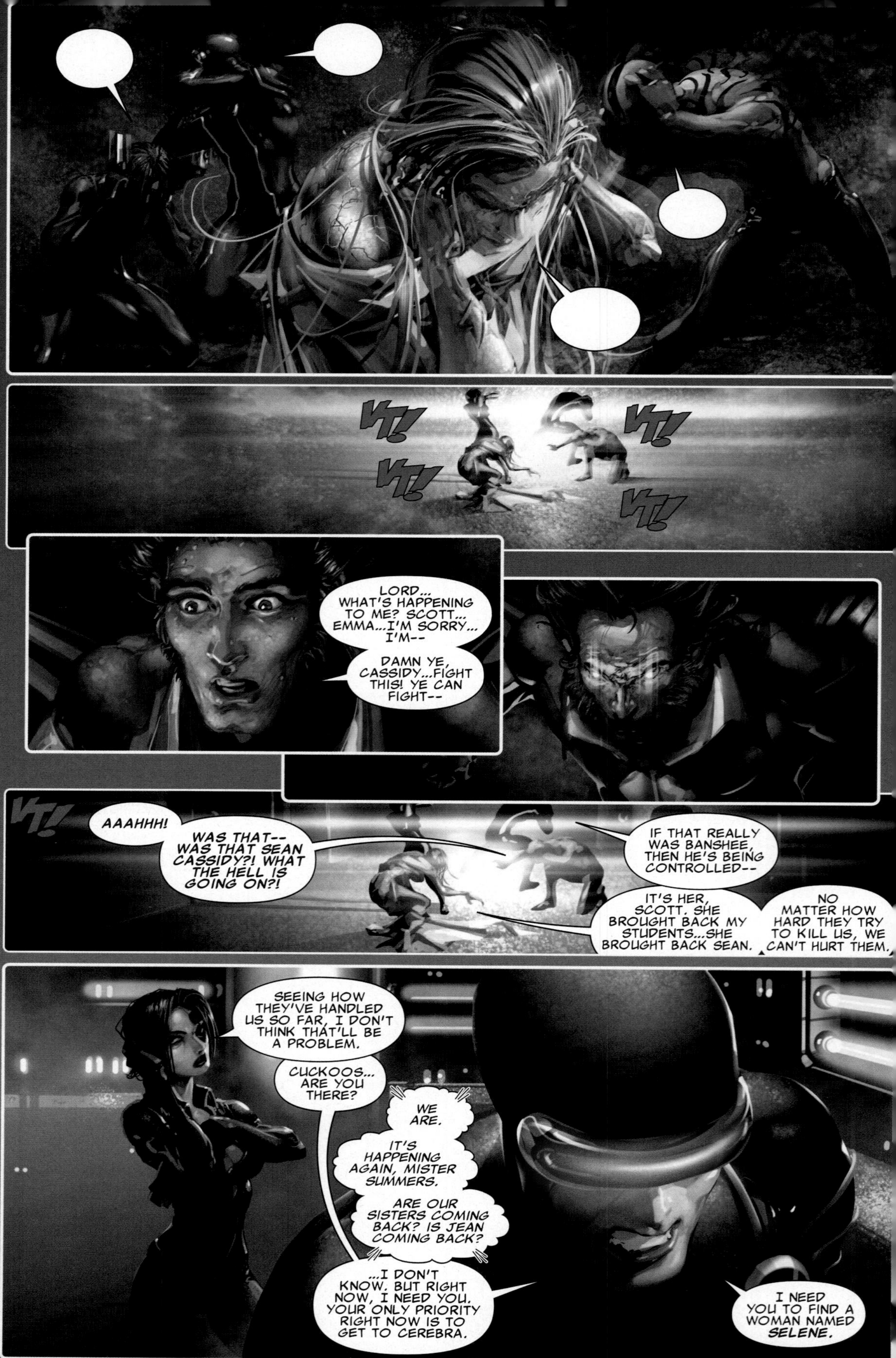
VT!
VT!
VT!
VT!
LORD... WHAT'S HAPPENING TO ME? SCOTT... EMMA...I'M SORRY... I'M--
DAMN YE, CASSIDY...FIGHT THIS! YE CAN FIGHT--
VT!
AAAHHH!
WAS THAT-- WAS THAT SEAN CASSIDY?! WHAT THE HELL IS GOING ON?!
IF THAT REALLY WAS BANSHEE, THEN HE'S BEING CONTROLLED--
IT'S HER, SCOTT. SHE BROUGHT BACK MY STUDENTS...SHE BROUGHT BACK SEAN.
NO MATTER HOW HARD THEY TRY TO KILL US, WE CAN'T HURT THEM.
SEEING HOW THEY'VE HANDLED US SO FAR, I DON'T THINK THAT'LL BE A PROBLEM.
CUCKOOS... ARE YOU THERE?
WE ARE.
IT'S HAPPENING AGAIN, MISTER SUMMERS.
ARE OUR SISTERS COMING BACK? IS JEAN COMING BACK?
...I DON'T KNOW. BUT RIGHT NOW, I NEED YOU. YOUR ONLY PRIORITY RIGHT NOW IS TO GET TO CEREBRA.
I NEED YOU TO FIND A WOMAN NAMED SELENE.

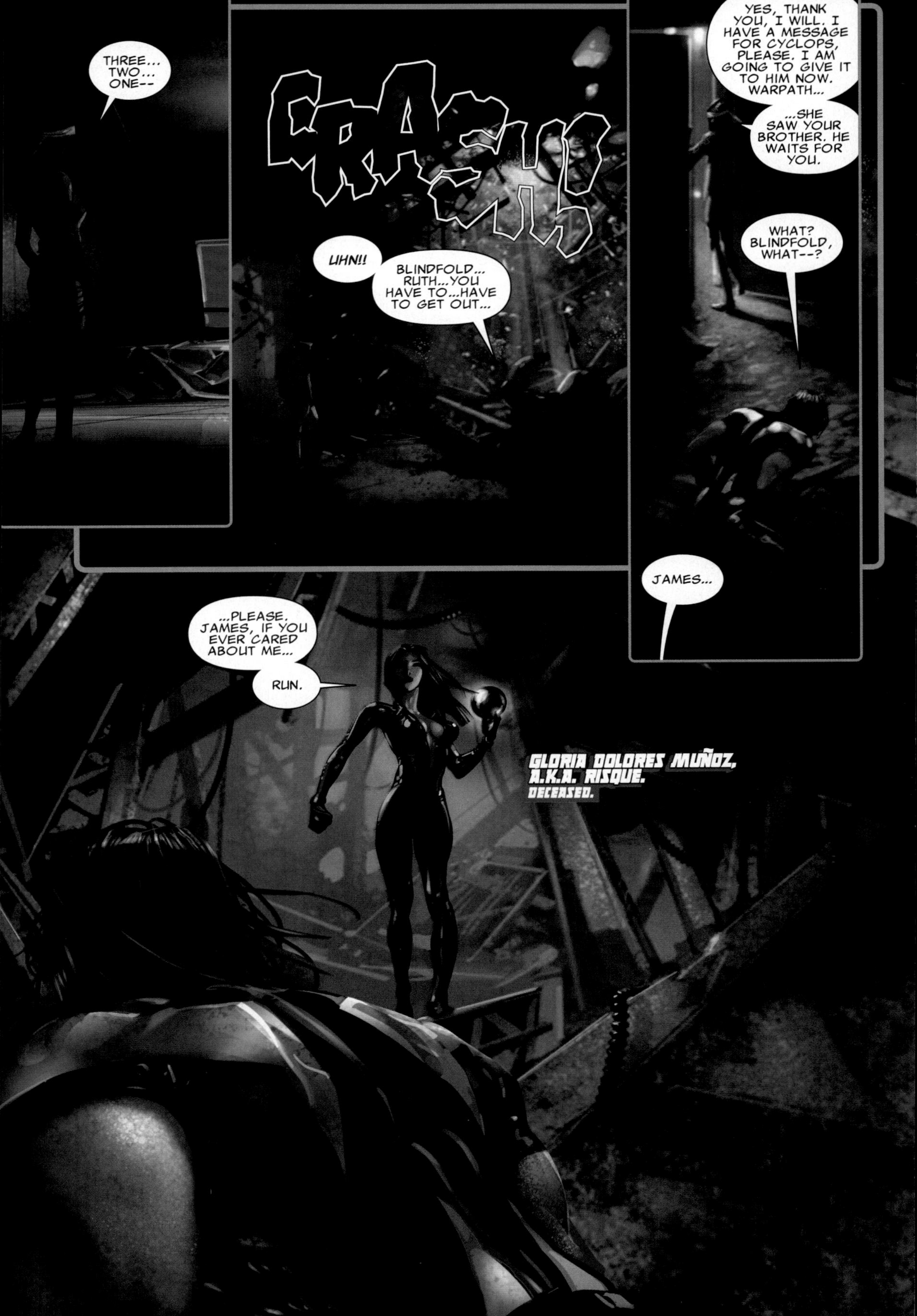
THREE... TWO... ONE--
CRASH
UHN!!
BLINDFOLD... RUTH...YOU HAVE TO...HAVE TO GET OUT...
YES, THANK YOU, I WILL. I HAVE A MESSAGE FOR CYCLOPS, PLEASE. I AM GOING TO GIVE IT TO HIM NOW. WARPATH...
...SHE SAW YOUR BROTHER. HE WAITS FOR YOU.
WHAT? BLINDFOLD, WHAT--?
JAMES...
...PLEASE. JAMES, IF YOU EVER CARED ABOUT ME...
RUN.
GLORIA DOLORES MUÑOZ, A.K.A. RISQUE.
DECEASED.

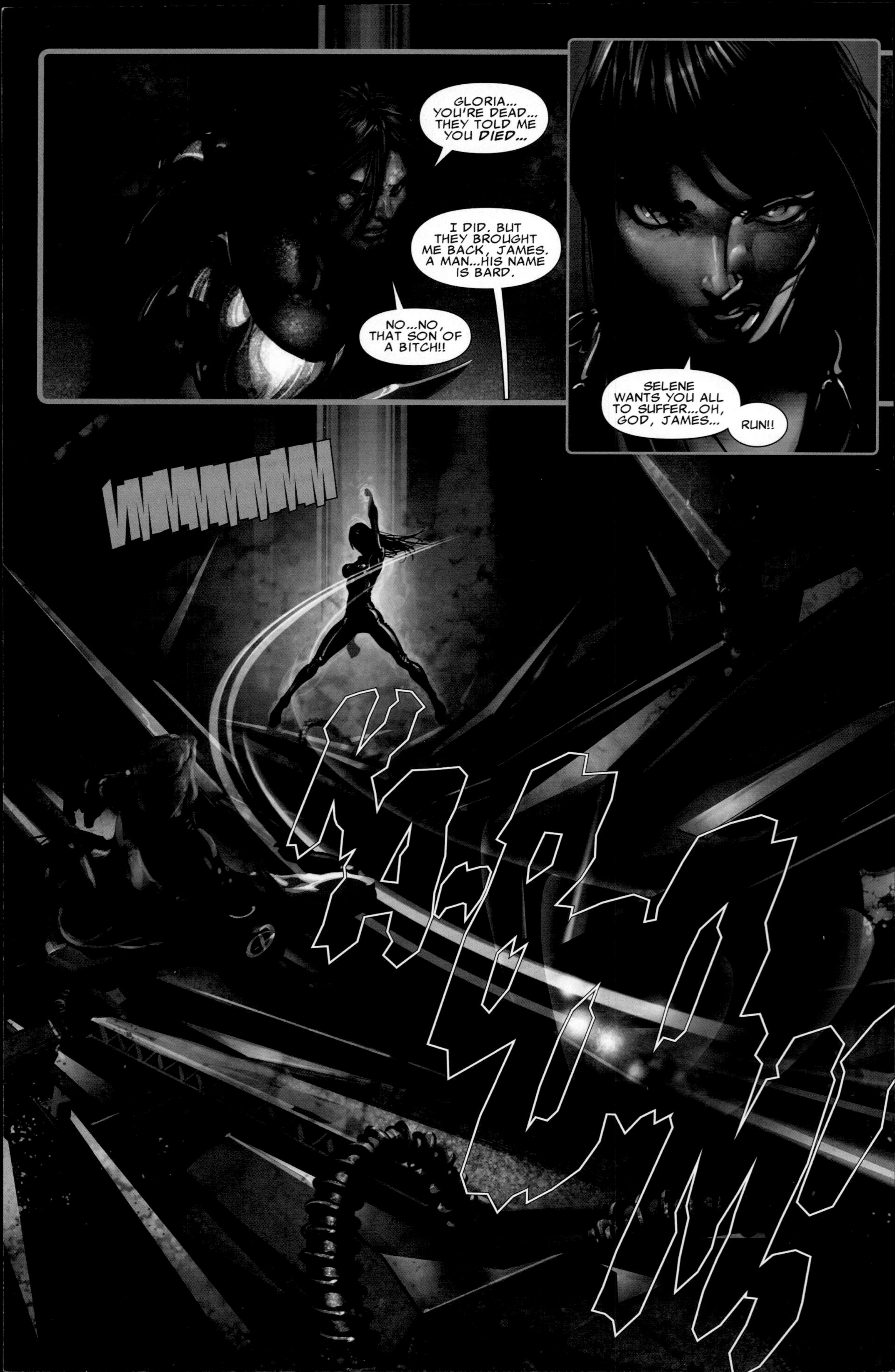
GLORIA... YOU'RE DEAD... THEY TOLD ME YOU **DIED...**
I DID. BUT THEY BROUGHT ME BACK, JAMES. A MAN...HIS NAME IS BARD.
NO...NO, THAT SON OF A BITCH!!
SELENE WANTS YOU ALL TO SUFFER...OH, GOD, JAMES...
RUN!!
VMMMMMMM

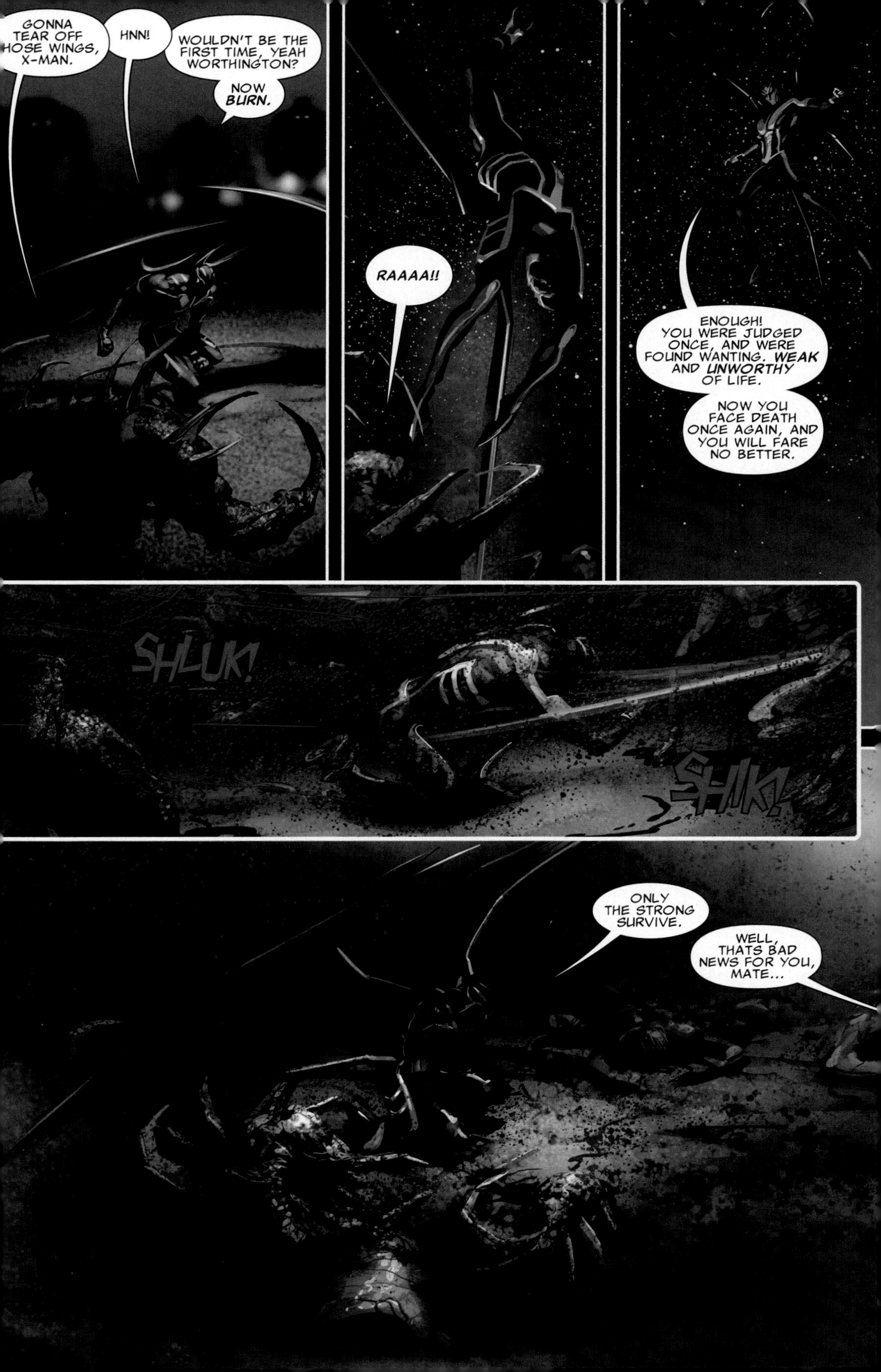

GONNA TEAR OFF THOSE WINGS, X-MAN.
HNN!
WOULDN'T BE THE FIRST TIME, YEAH WORTHINGTON?
NOW BURN.
RAAAA!!
ENOUGH! YOU WERE JUDGED ONCE, AND WERE FOUND WANTING. WEAK AND UNWORTHY OF LIFE.
NOW YOU FACE DEATH ONCE AGAIN, AND YOU WILL FARE NO BETTER.
SHLUK!
SHIK!
ONLY THE STRONG SURVIVE.
WELL, THATS BAD NEWS FOR YOU, MATE...

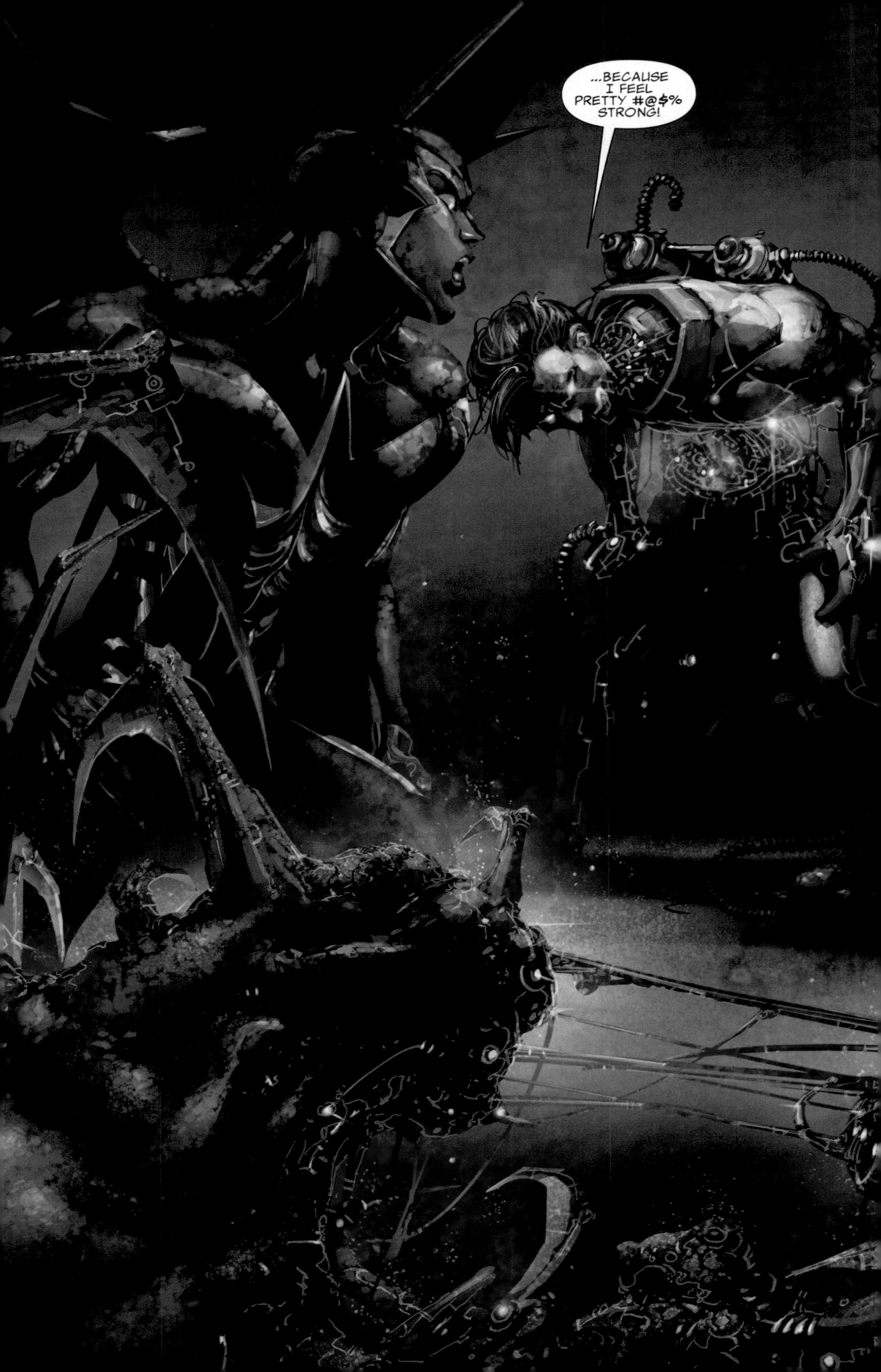
...BECAUSE I FEEL PRETTY #@$% STRONG!

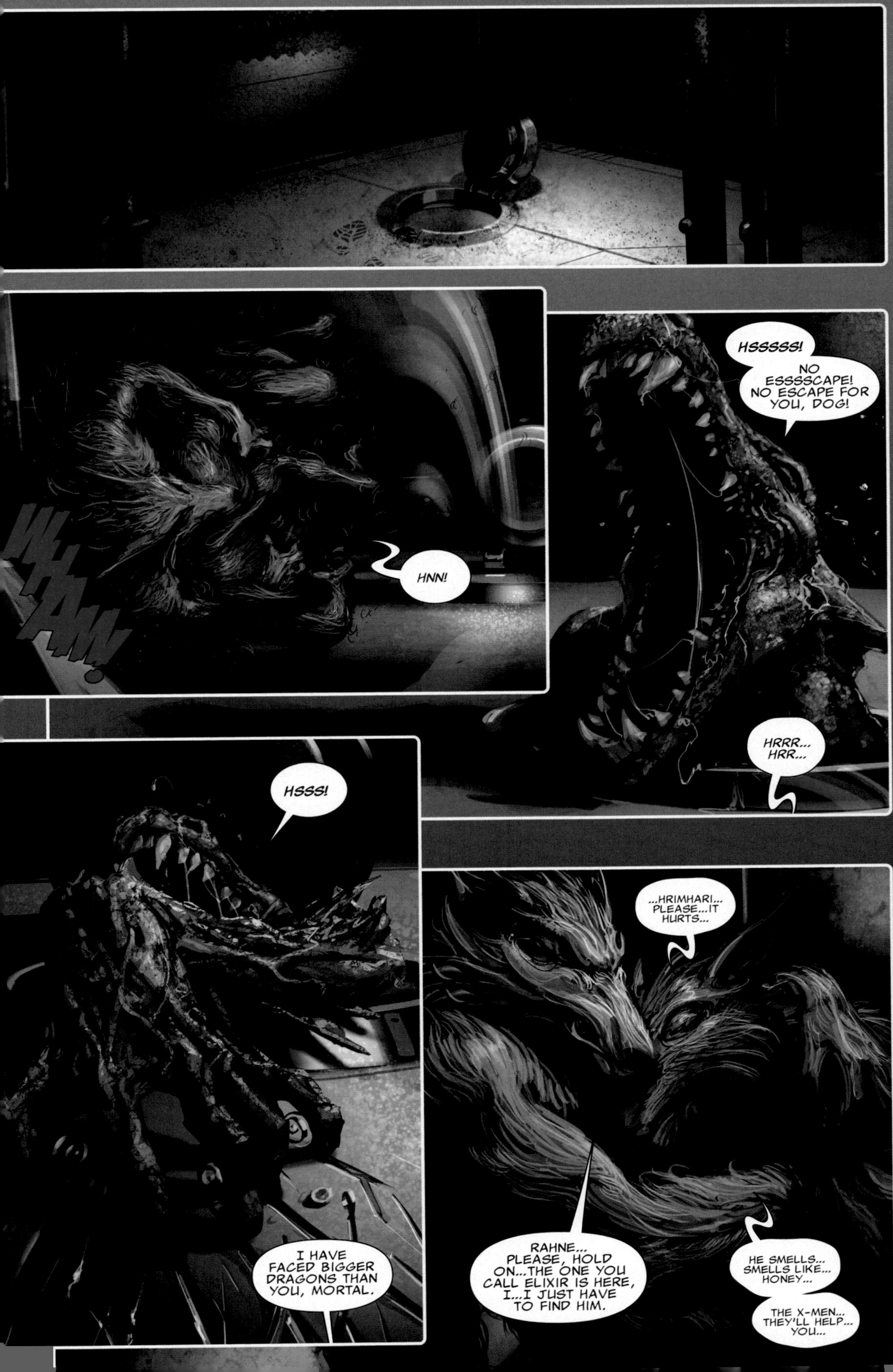
WHAM!
HNN!
HSSSSS!
NO ESSSSCAPE! NO ESCAPE FOR YOU, DOG!
HRRR... HRR...
HSSS!
I HAVE FACED BIGGER DRAGONS THAN YOU, MORTAL.
...HRIMHARI... PLEASE...IT HURTS...
RAHNE... PLEASE, HOLD ON...THE ONE YOU CALL ELIXIR IS HERE, I...I JUST HAVE TO FIND HIM.
HE SMELLS... SMELLS LIKE... HONEY...
THE X-MEN... THEY'LL HELP... YOU...

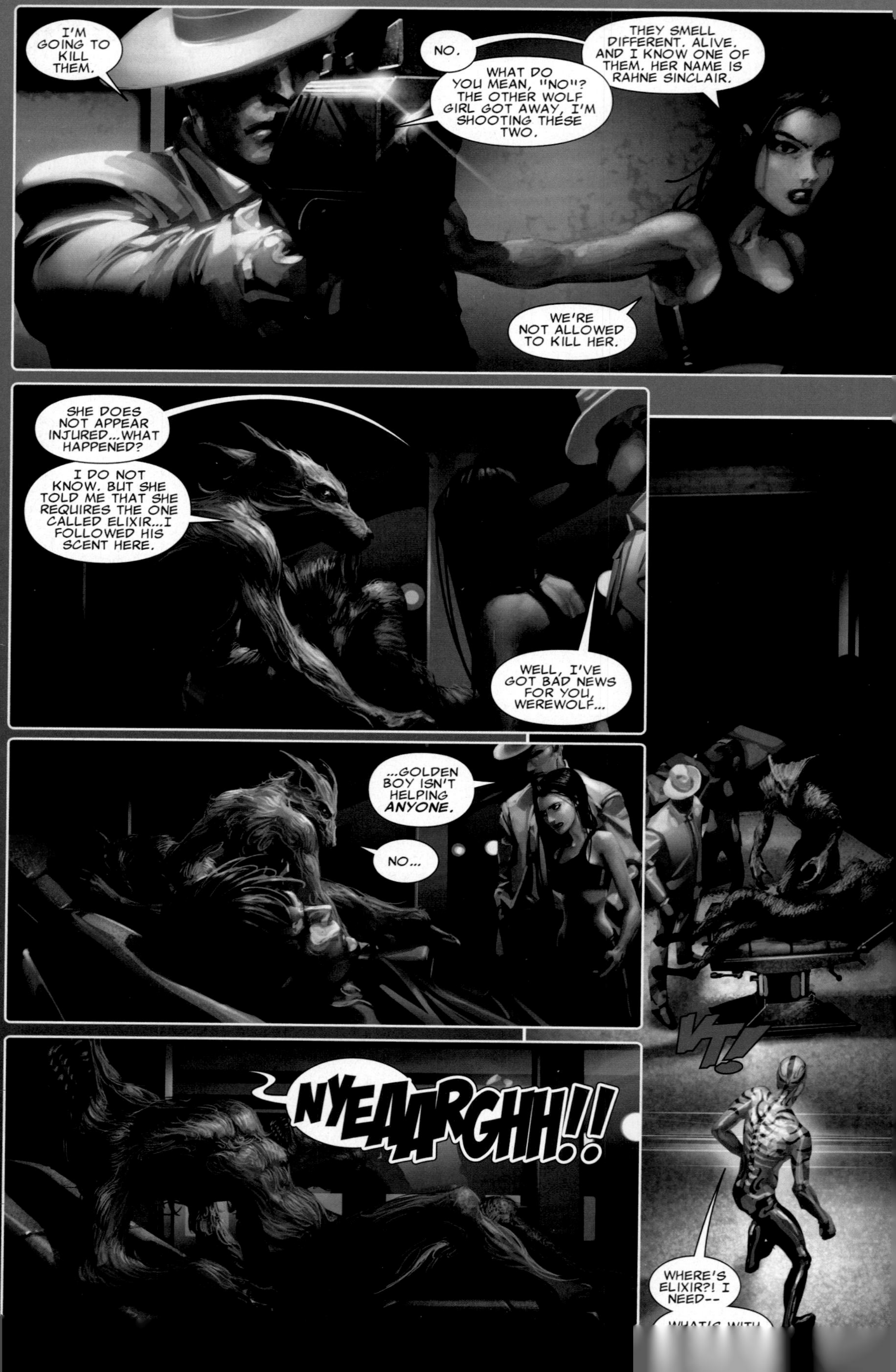
I'M GOING TO KILL THEM.
NO.
WHAT DO YOU MEAN, "NO"? THE OTHER WOLF GIRL GOT AWAY, I'M SHOOTING THESE TWO.
THEY SMELL DIFFERENT. ALIVE. AND I KNOW ONE OF THEM. HER NAME IS RAHNE SINCLAIR.
WE'RE NOT ALLOWED TO KILL HER.
SHE DOES NOT APPEAR INJURED...WHAT HAPPENED?
I DO NOT KNOW. BUT SHE TOLD ME THAT SHE REQUIRES THE ONE CALLED ELIXIR...I FOLLOWED HIS SCENT HERE.
WELL, I'VE GOT BAD NEWS FOR YOU, WEREWOLF...
...GOLDEN BOY ISN'T HELPING ANYONE.
NO...
NYEAAARGHH!!
VT!
WHERE'S ELIXIR?! I NEED--

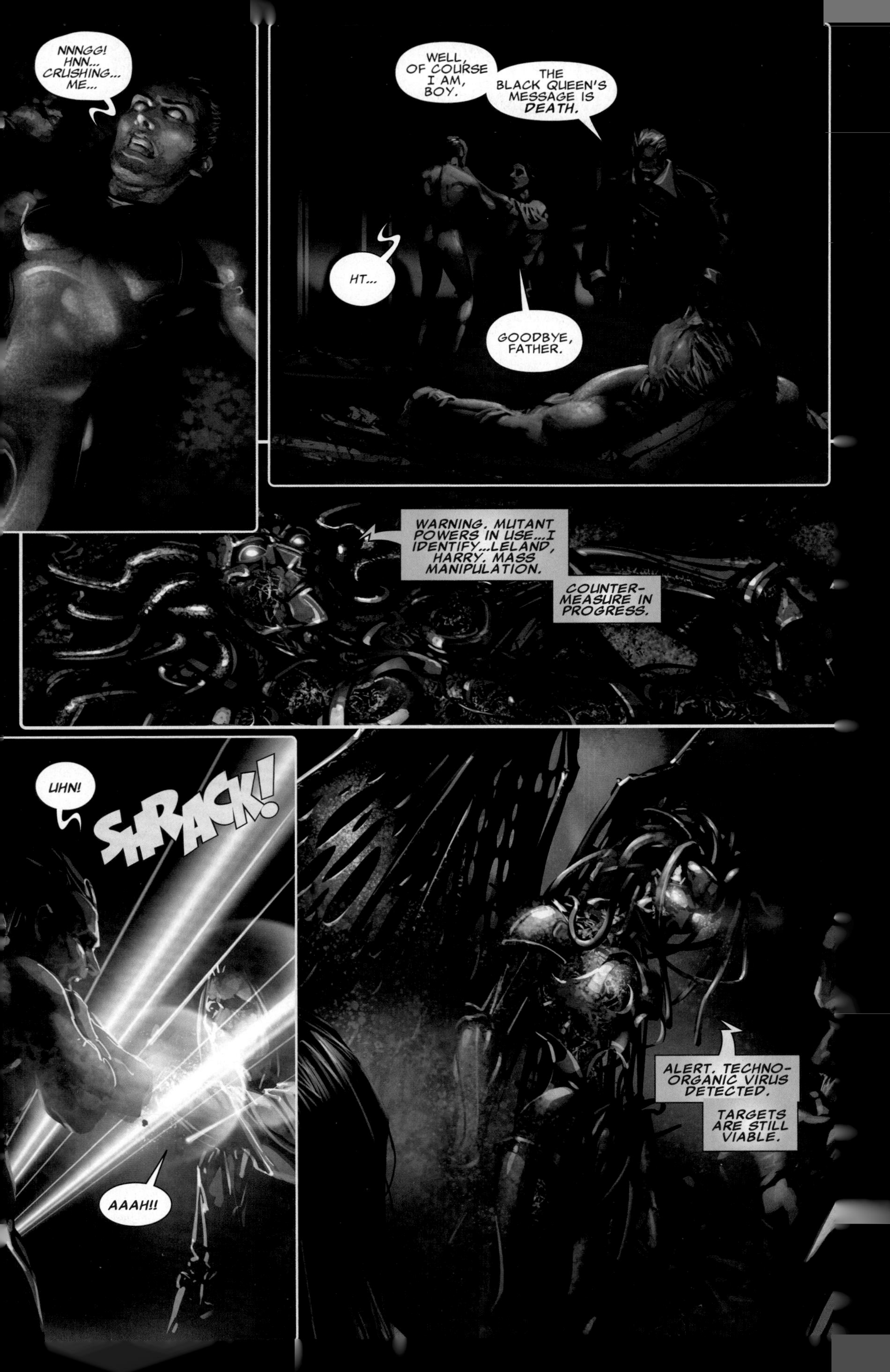
NNNGG! HNN... CRUSHING... ME...
WELL, OF COURSE I AM, BOY.
THE BLACK QUEEN'S MESSAGE IS DEATH.
HT...
GOODBYE, FATHER.
WARNING. MUTANT POWERS IN USE...I IDENTIFY...LELAND, HARRY. MASS MANIPULATION.
COUNTER-MEASURE IN PROGRESS.
UHN!
SHRACK!
AAAH!!
ALERT. TECHNO-ORGANIC VIRUS DETECTED.
TARGETS ARE STILL VIABLE.

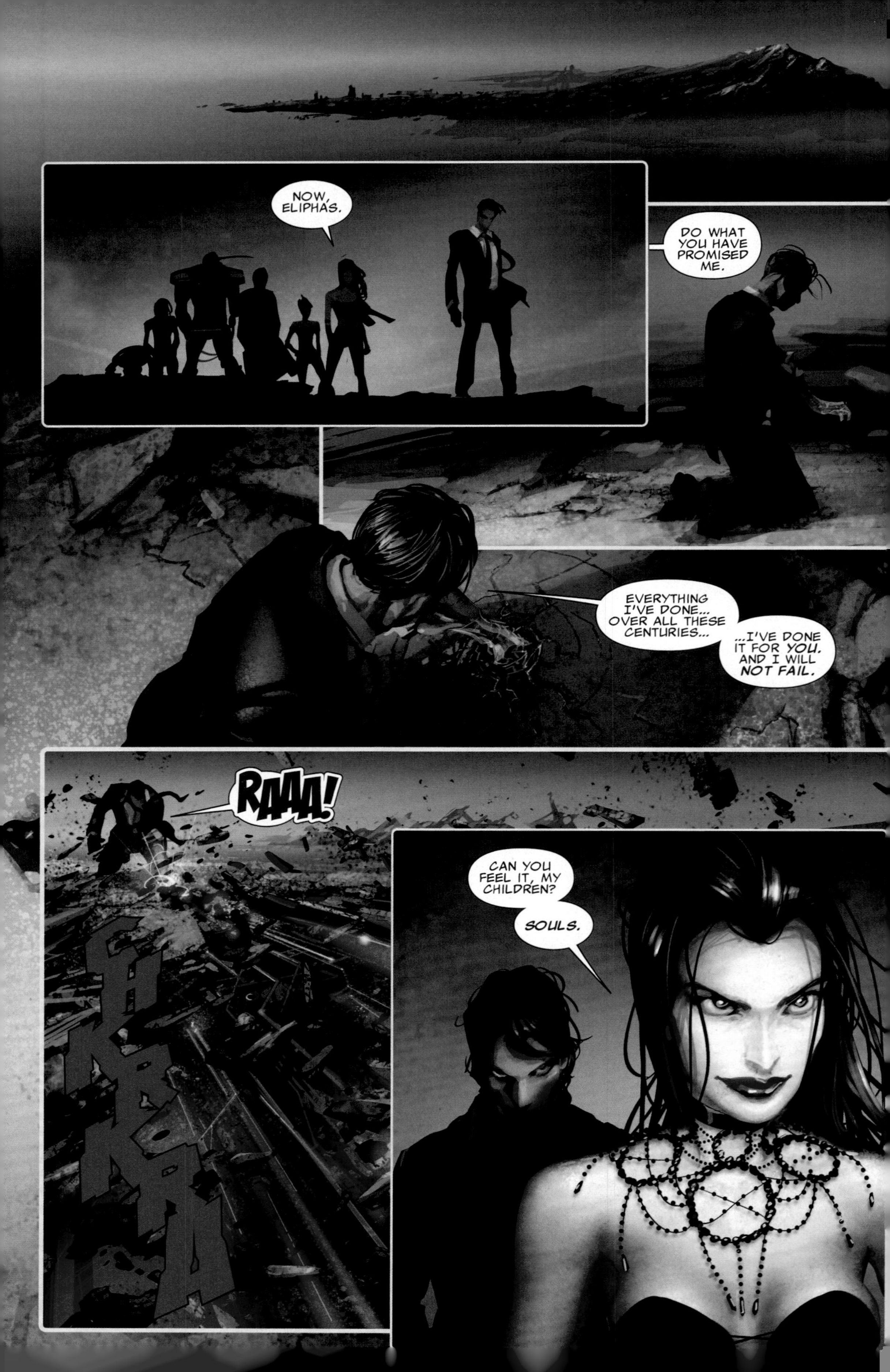
NOW, ELIPHAS.
DO WHAT YOU HAVE PROMISED ME.
EVERYTHING I'VE DONE... OVER ALL THESE CENTURIES...
...I'VE DONE IT FOR *YOU*. AND I WILL *NOT FAIL*.
RAAAA!
CAN YOU FEEL IT, MY CHILDREN?
SOULS.

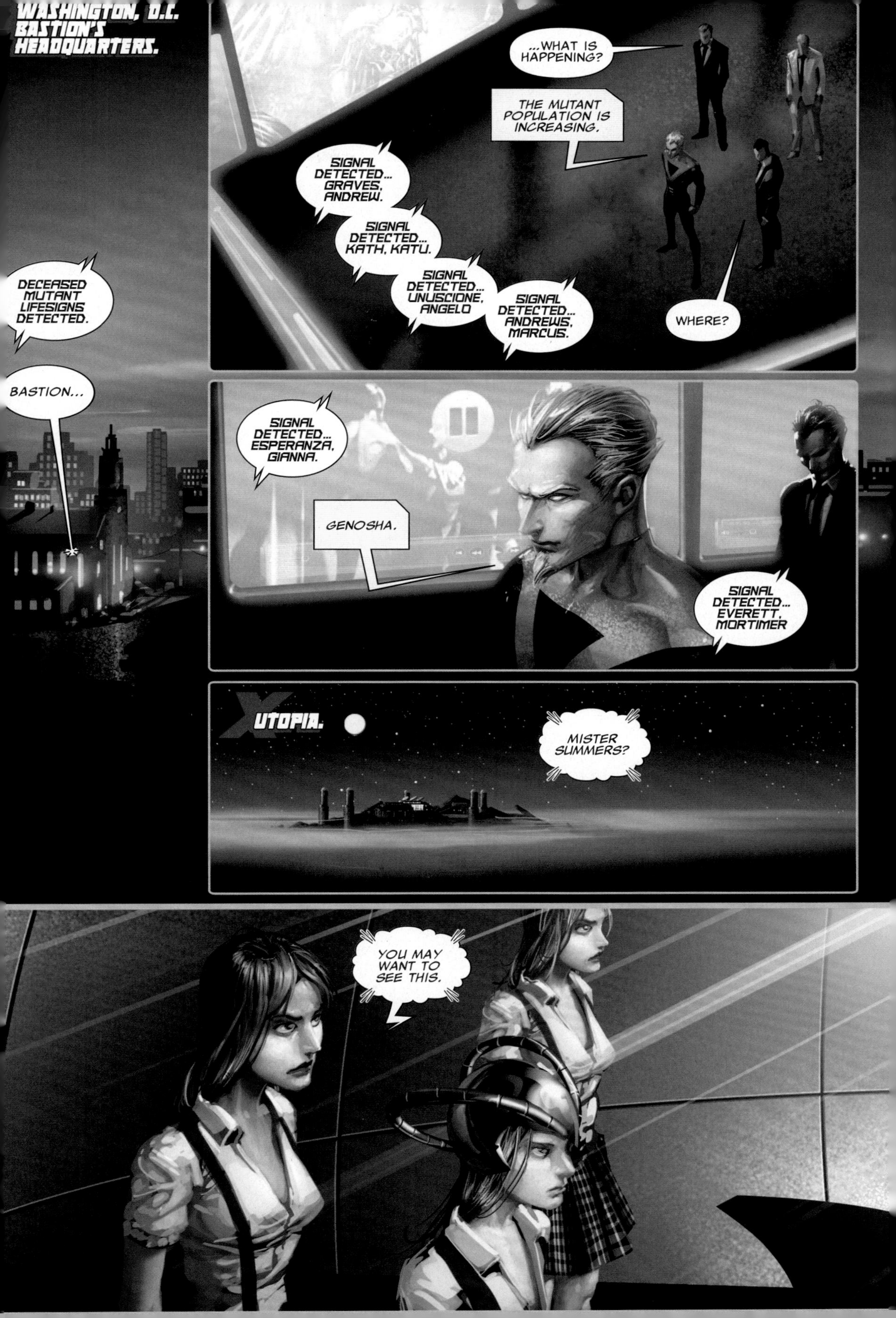
WASHINGTON, D.C. BASTION'S HEADQUARTERS.
DECEASED MUTANT LIFESIGNS DETECTED.
BASTION...
...WHAT IS HAPPENING?
THE MUTANT POPULATION IS INCREASING.
SIGNAL DETECTED... GRAVES, ANDREW.
SIGNAL DETECTED... KATH, KATU.
SIGNAL DETECTED... UNUSCIONE, ANGELO
SIGNAL DETECTED... ANDREWS, MARCUS.
WHERE?
SIGNAL DETECTED... ESPERANZA, GIANNA.
GENOSHA.
SIGNAL DETECTED... EVERETT, MORTIMER
UTOPIA.
MISTER SUMMERS?
YOU MAY WANT TO SEE THIS.

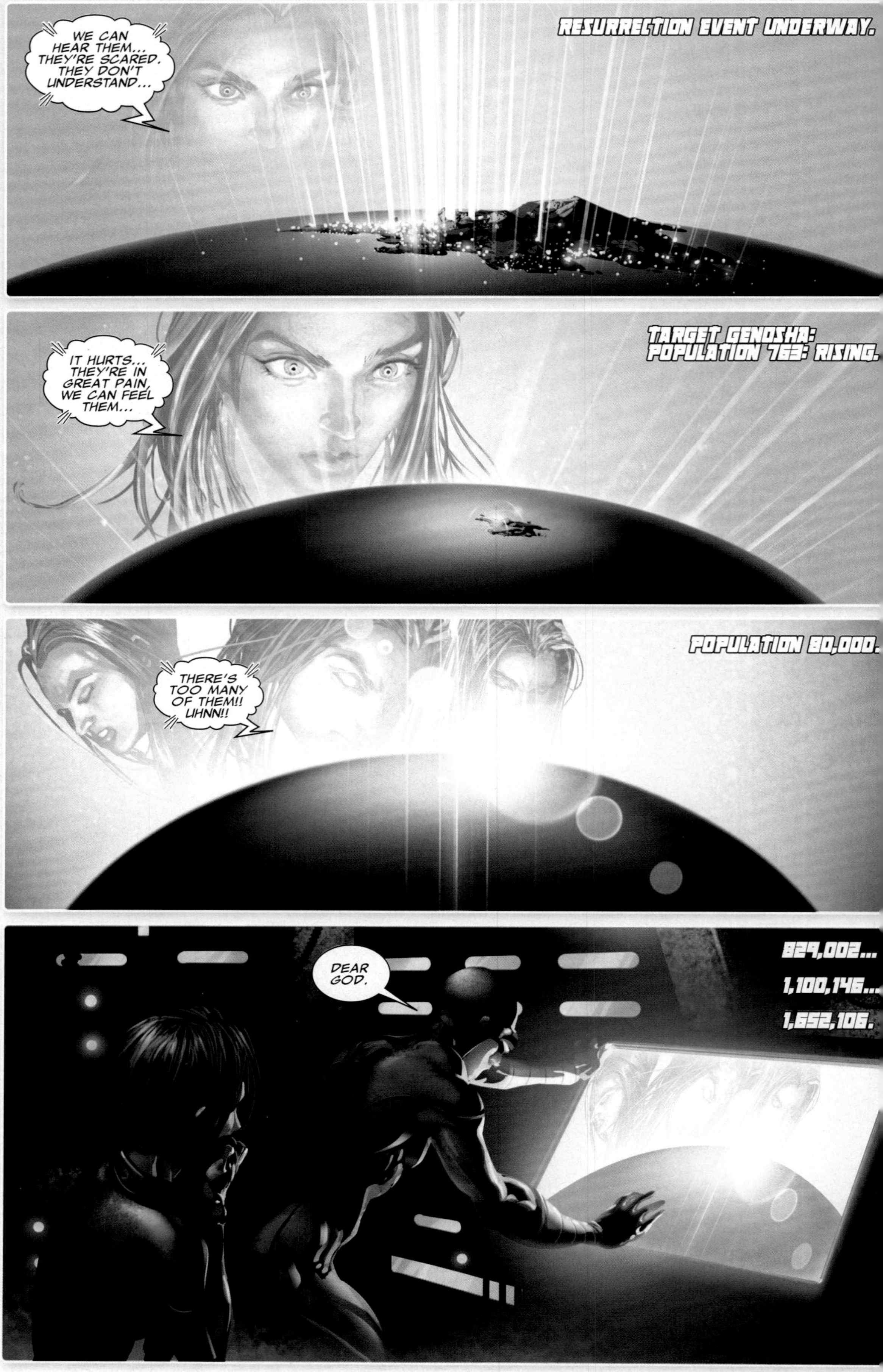
RESURRECTION EVENT UNDERWAY.
WE CAN HEAR THEM... THEY'RE SCARED. THEY DON'T UNDERSTAND...
TARGET GENOSHA: POPULATION 763: RISING.
IT HURTS... THEY'RE IN GREAT PAIN, WE CAN FEEL THEM...
POPULATION 80,000.
THERE'S TOO MANY OF THEM!! UHNN!!
829,002...
1,100,146...
1,652,106.
DEAR GOD.

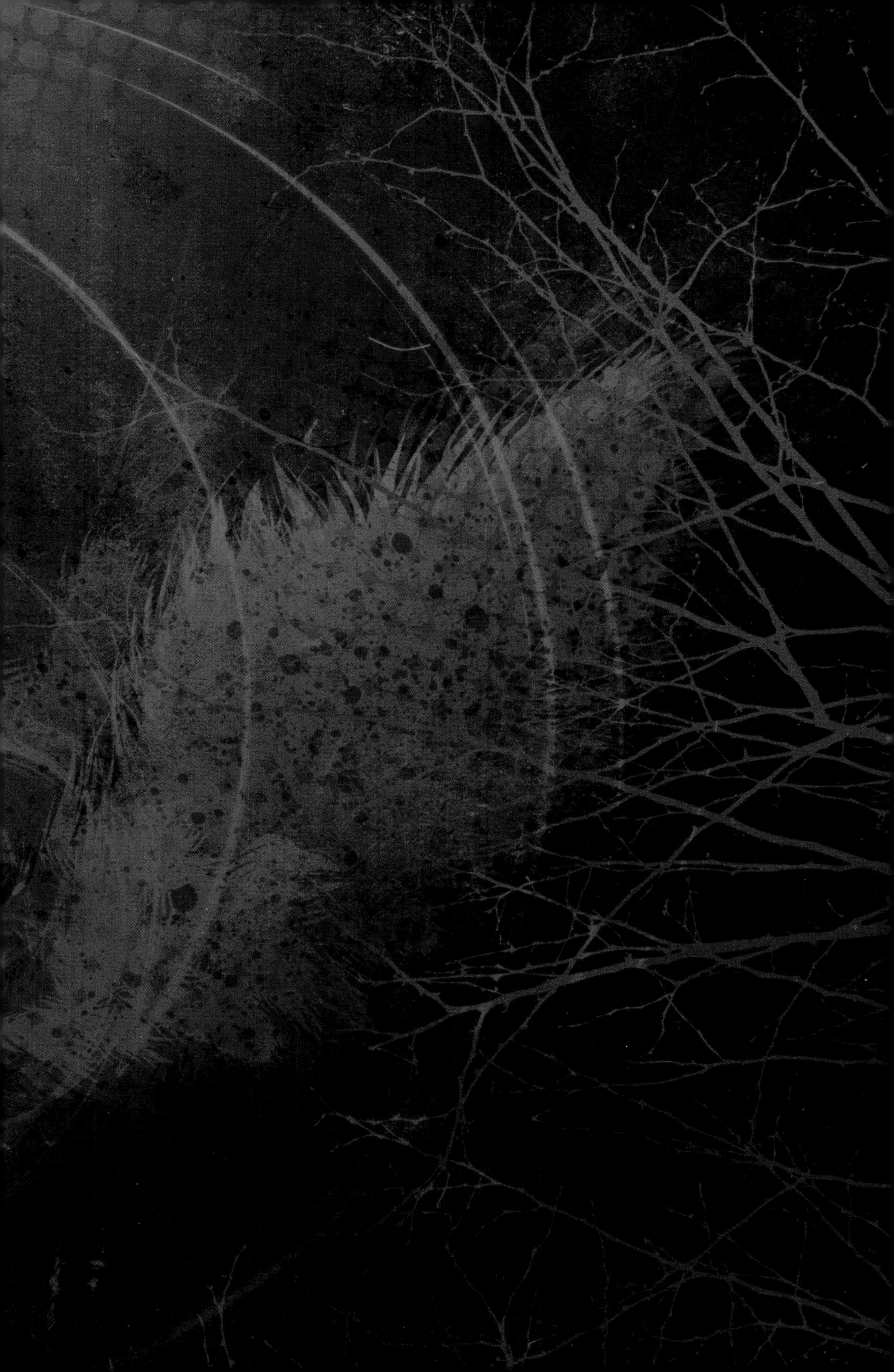

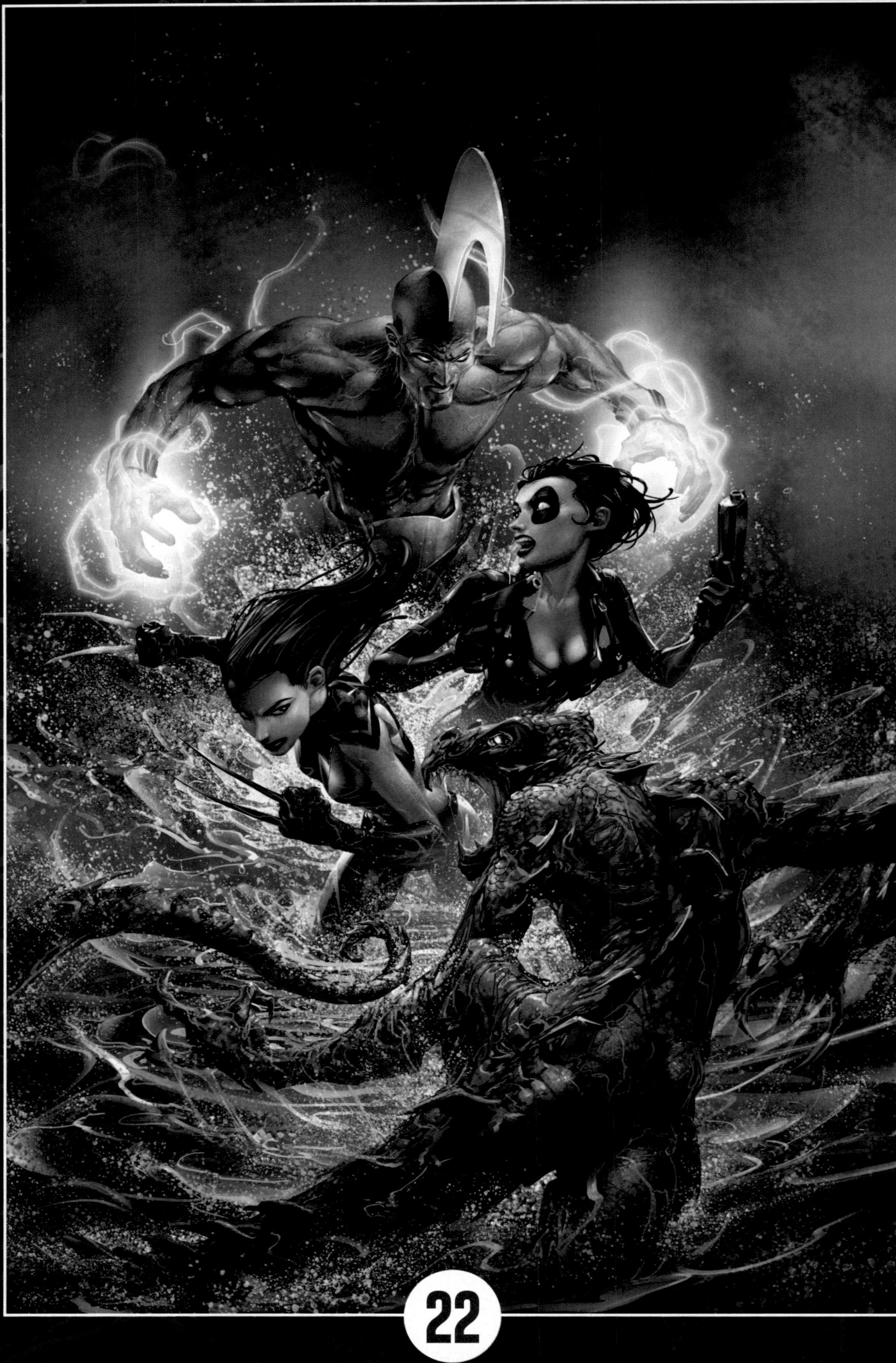
22

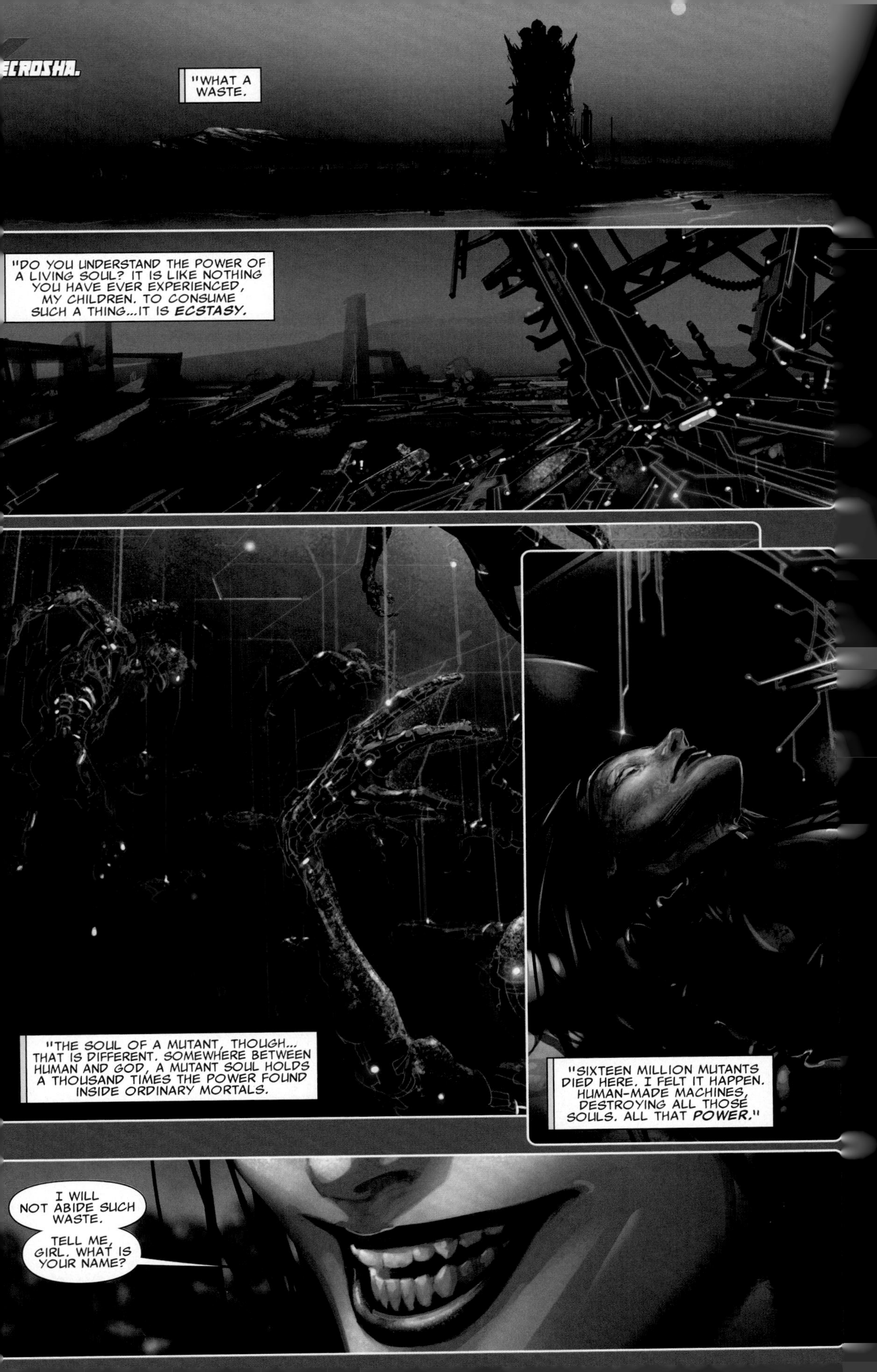
ECROSHA.
"WHAT A WASTE.
"DO YOU UNDERSTAND THE POWER OF A LIVING SOUL? IT IS LIKE NOTHING YOU HAVE EVER EXPERIENCED, MY CHILDREN. TO CONSUME SUCH A THING...IT IS ECSTASY.
"THE SOUL OF A MUTANT, THOUGH... THAT IS DIFFERENT. SOMEWHERE BETWEEN HUMAN AND GOD, A MUTANT SOUL HOLDS A THOUSAND TIMES THE POWER FOUND INSIDE ORDINARY MORTALS.
"SIXTEEN MILLION MUTANTS DIED HERE. I FELT IT HAPPEN. HUMAN-MADE MACHINES, DESTROYING ALL THOSE SOULS. ALL THAT POWER."
I WILL NOT ABIDE SUCH WASTE.
TELL ME, GIRL. WHAT IS YOUR NAME?

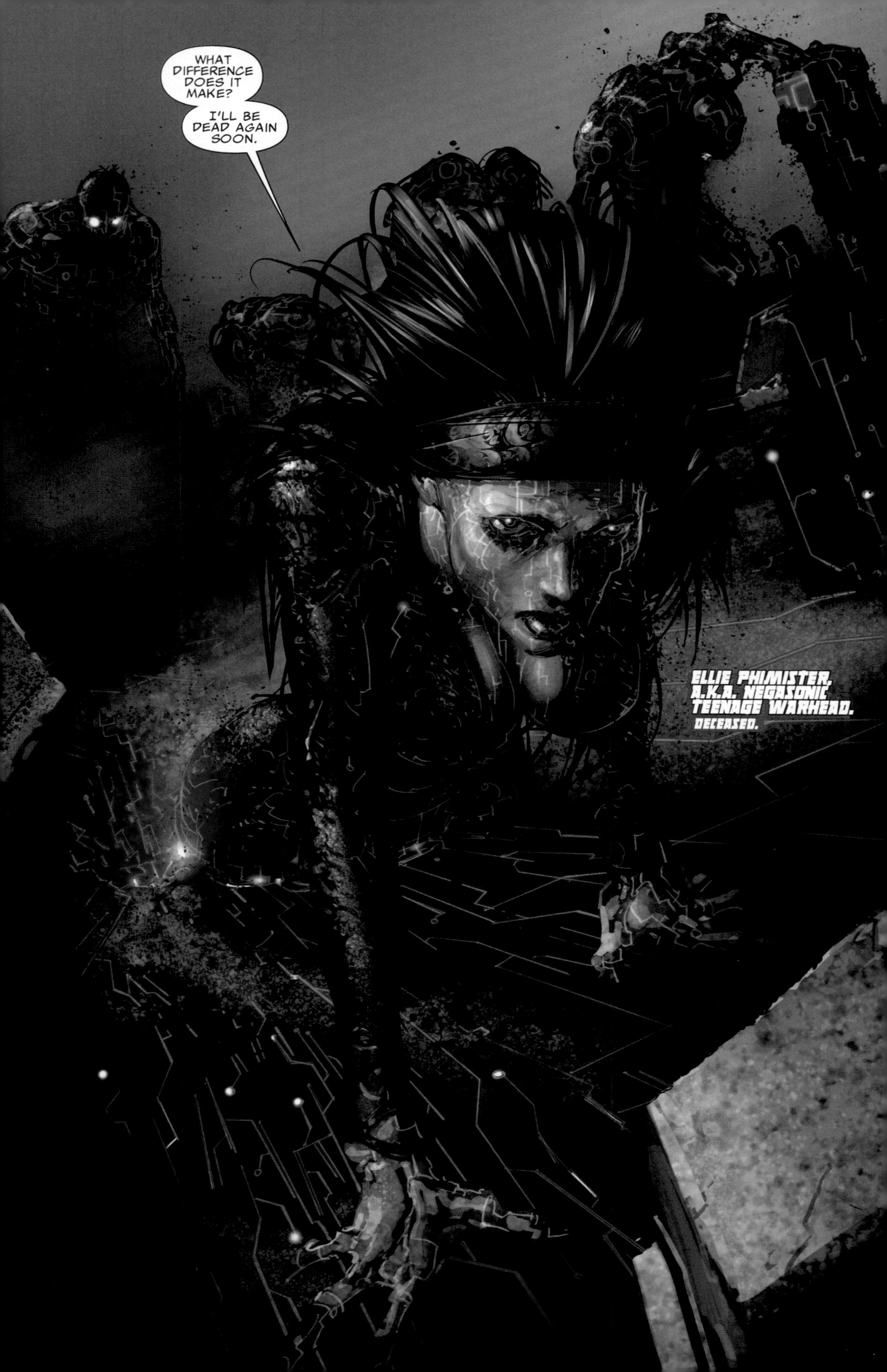
WHAT DIFFERENCE DOES IT MAKE?
I'LL BE DEAD AGAIN SOON.
ELLIE PHIMISTER, A.K.A. NEGASONIC TEENAGE WARHEAD.
DECEASED.

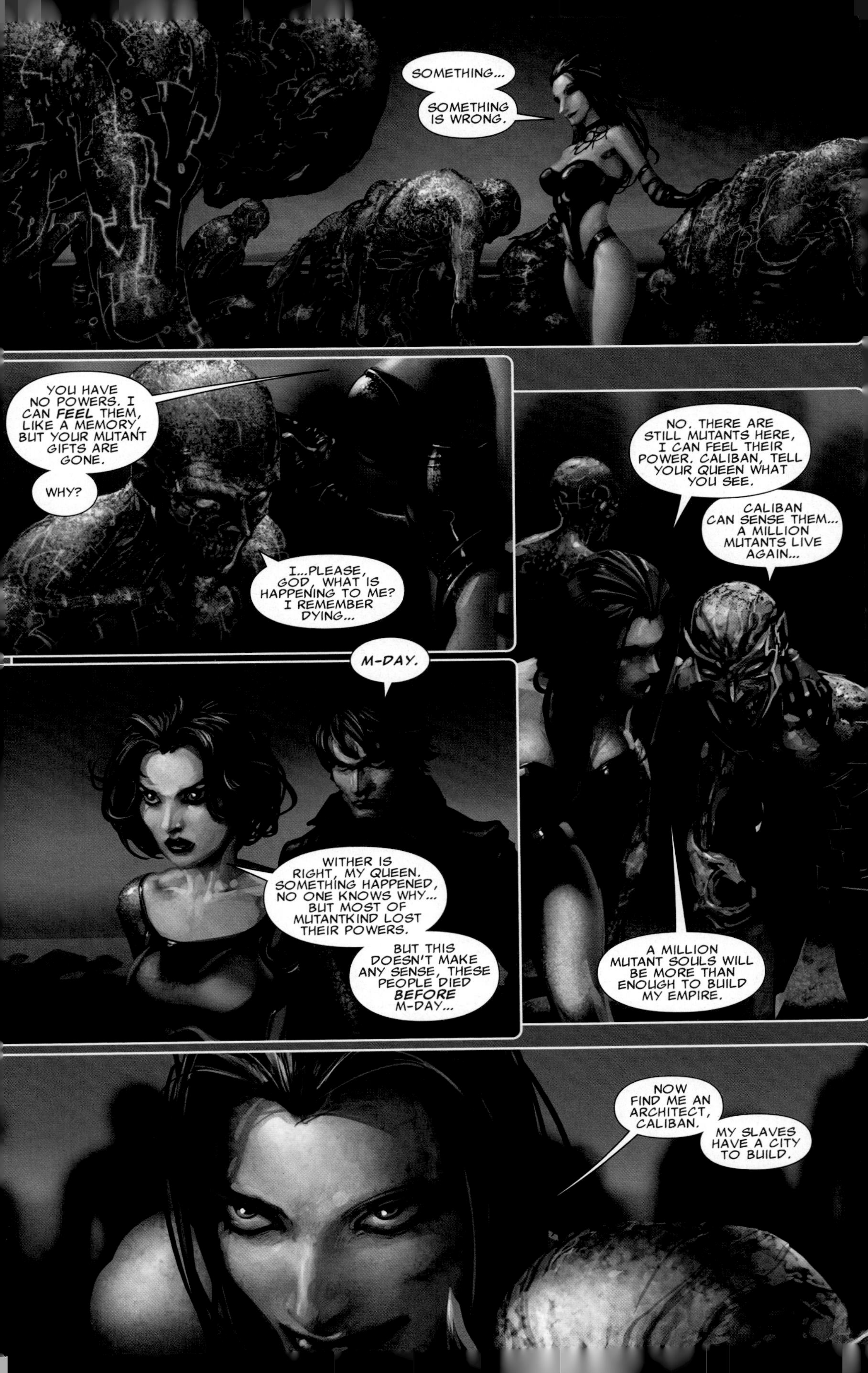
SOMETHING...
SOMETHING IS WRONG.
YOU HAVE NO POWERS. I CAN FEEL THEM, LIKE A MEMORY, BUT YOUR MUTANT GIFTS ARE GONE.
WHY?
I...PLEASE, GOD, WHAT IS HAPPENING TO ME? I REMEMBER DYING...
NO. THERE ARE STILL MUTANTS HERE, I CAN FEEL THEIR POWER. CALIBAN, TELL YOUR QUEEN WHAT YOU SEE.
CALIBAN CAN SENSE THEM... A MILLION MUTANTS LIVE AGAIN...
M-DAY.
WITHER IS RIGHT, MY QUEEN. SOMETHING HAPPENED, NO ONE KNOWS WHY... BUT MOST OF MUTANTKIND LOST THEIR POWERS.
BUT THIS DOESN'T MAKE ANY SENSE, THESE PEOPLE DIED BEFORE M-DAY...
A MILLION MUTANT SOULS WILL BE MORE THAN ENOUGH TO BUILD MY EMPIRE.
NOW FIND ME AN ARCHITECT, CALIBAN.
MY SLAVES HAVE A CITY TO BUILD.

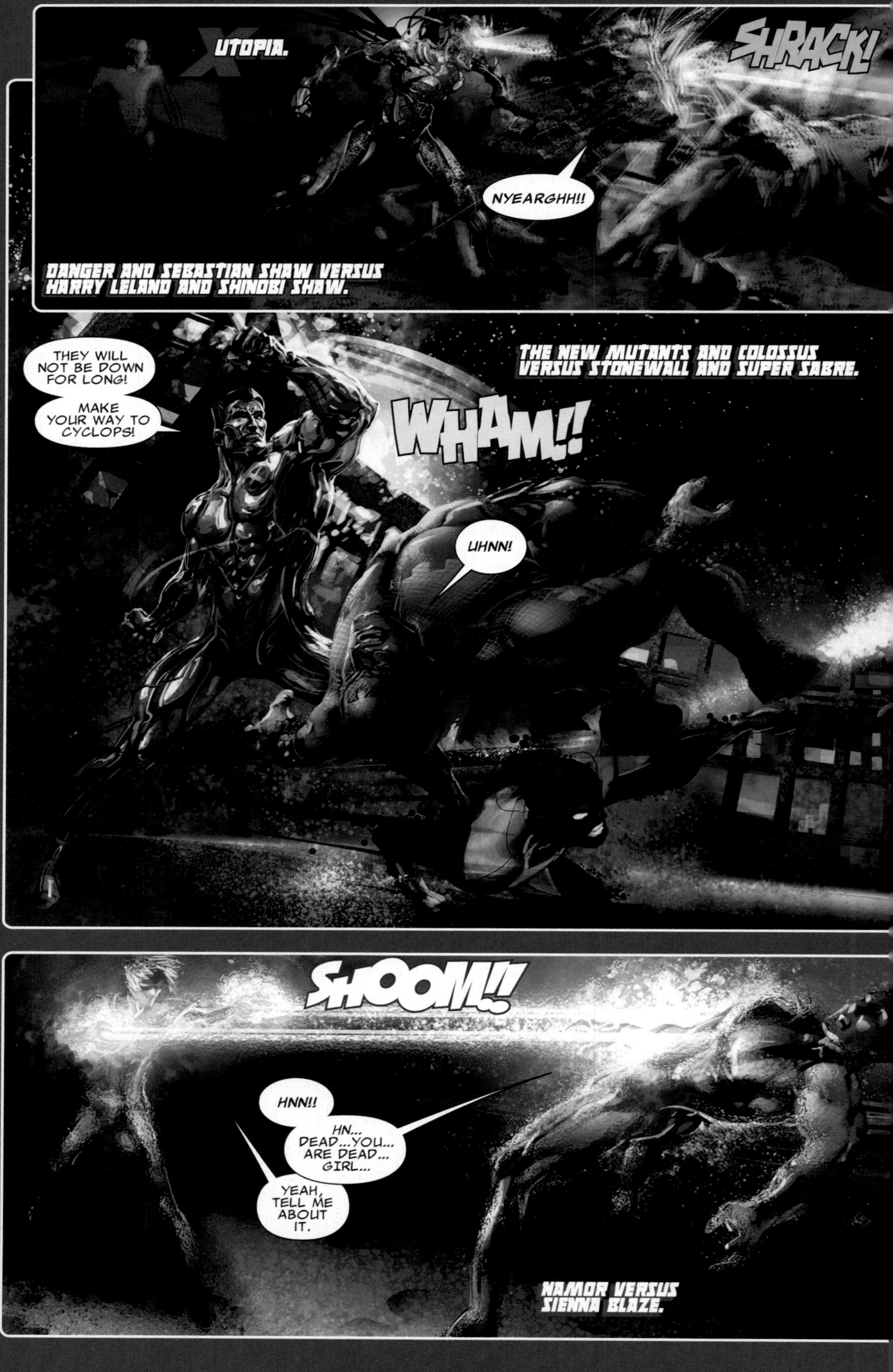
UTOPIA.
SHRACK!
NYEARGHH!!
DANGER AND SEBASTIAN SHAW VERSUS HARRY LELAND AND SHINOBI SHAW.
THE NEW MUTANTS AND COLOSSUS VERSUS STONEWALL AND SUPER SABRE.
THEY WILL NOT BE DOWN FOR LONG!
MAKE YOUR WAY TO CYCLOPS!
WHAM!!
UHNN!
SHOOM!!
HNN!!
HN... DEAD...YOU... ARE DEAD... GIRL...
YEAH, TELL ME ABOUT IT.
NAMOR VERSUS SIENNA BLAZE.

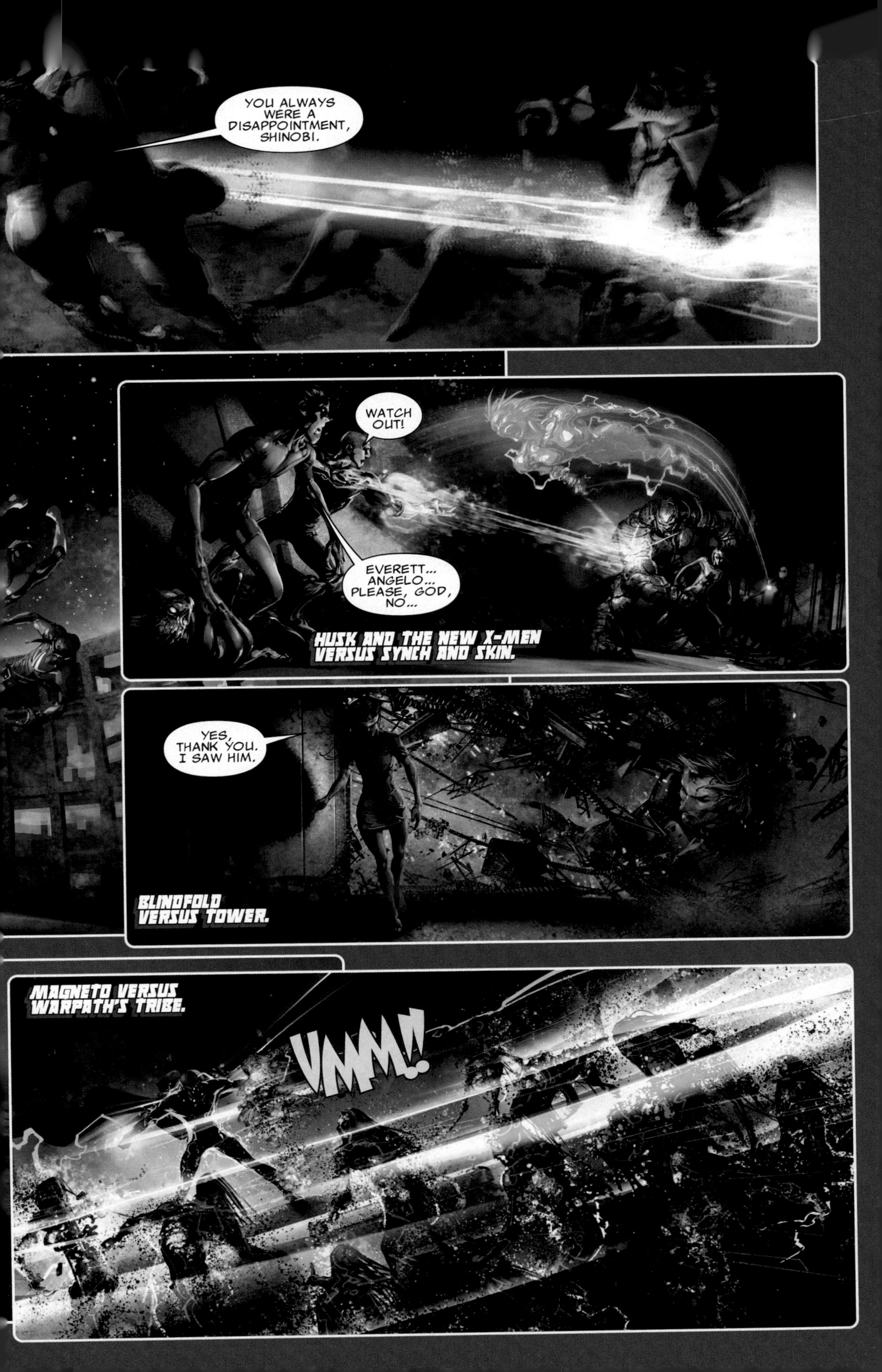
YOU ALWAYS WERE A DISAPPOINTMENT, SHINOBI.
WATCH OUT!
EVERETT... ANGELO... PLEASE, GOD, NO...
HUSK AND THE NEW X-MEN VERSUS SYNCH AND SKIN.
YES, THANK YOU. I SAW HIM.
BLINDFOLD VERSUS TOWER.
MAGNETO VERSUS WARPATH'S TRIBE.
VMM!!

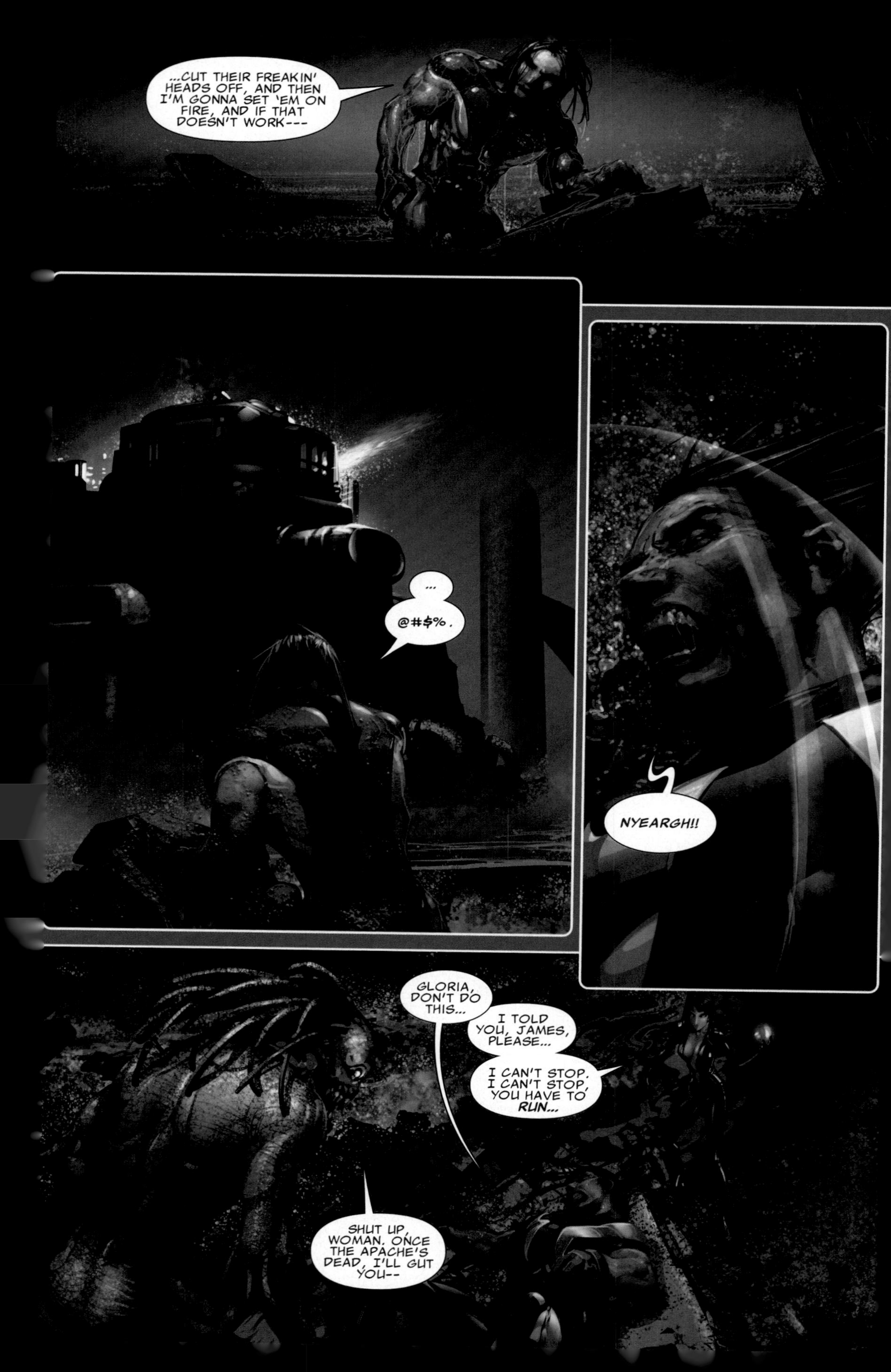
...CUT THEIR FREAKIN' HEADS OFF, AND THEN I'M GONNA SET 'EM ON FIRE, AND IF THAT DOESN'T WORK---
...
@#$%.
NYEARGH!!
GLORIA, DON'T DO THIS...
I TOLD YOU, JAMES, PLEASE...
I CAN'T STOP. I CAN'T STOP, YOU HAVE TO RUN...
SHUT UP, WOMAN. ONCE THE APACHE'S DEAD, I'LL GUT YOU--

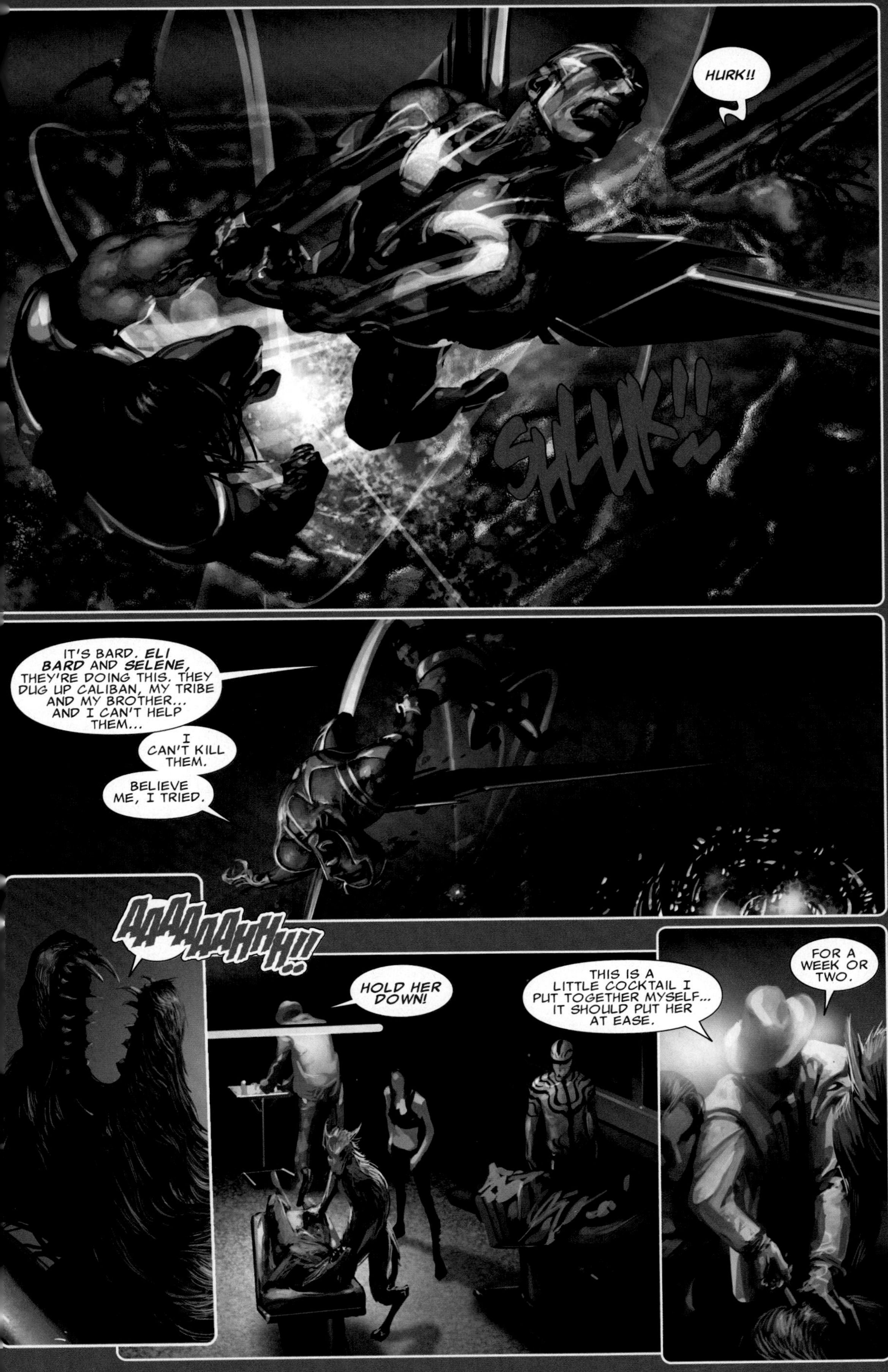
HURK!!
SHLUK!!
IT'S BARD. ELI BARD AND SELENE, THEY'RE DOING THIS. THEY DUG UP CALIBAN, MY TRIBE AND MY BROTHER... AND I CAN'T HELP THEM...
I CAN'T KILL THEM.
BELIEVE ME, I TRIED.
AAAAAAAHHHH!!!
HOLD HER DOWN!
THIS IS A LITTLE COCKTAIL I PUT TOGETHER MYSELF... IT SHOULD PUT HER AT EASE.
FOR A WEEK OR TWO.

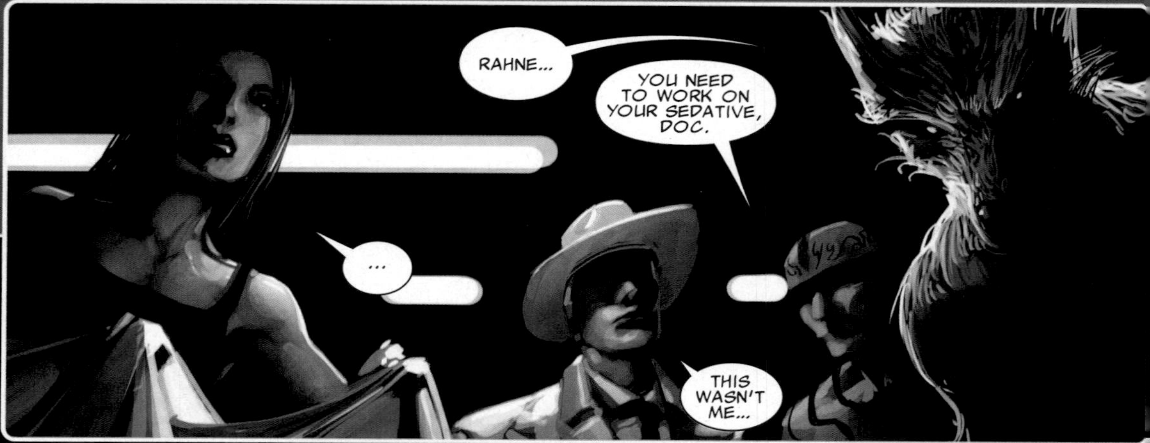
RAHNE...
YOU NEED TO WORK ON YOUR SEDATIVE, DOC.
...
THIS WASN'T ME...

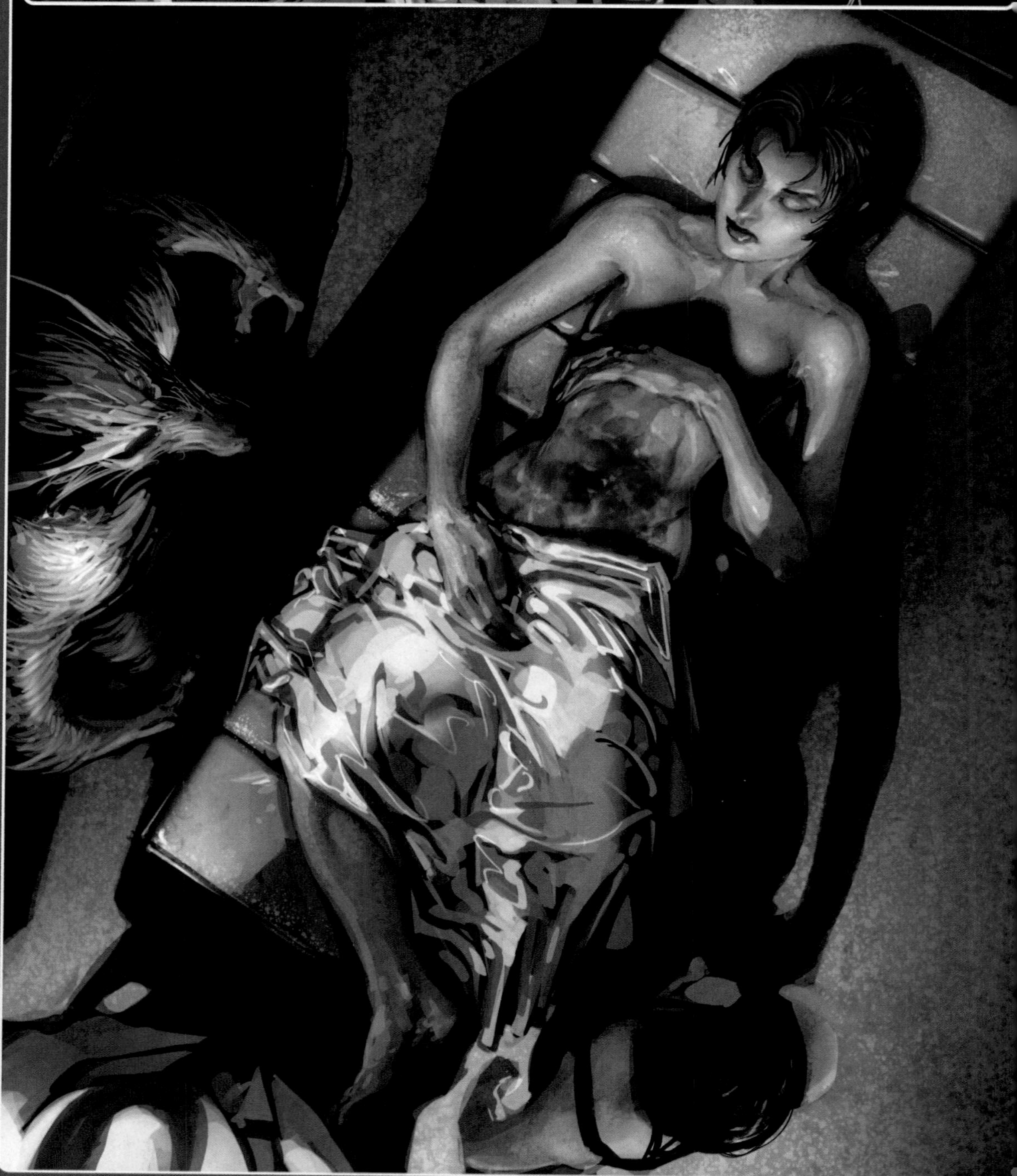

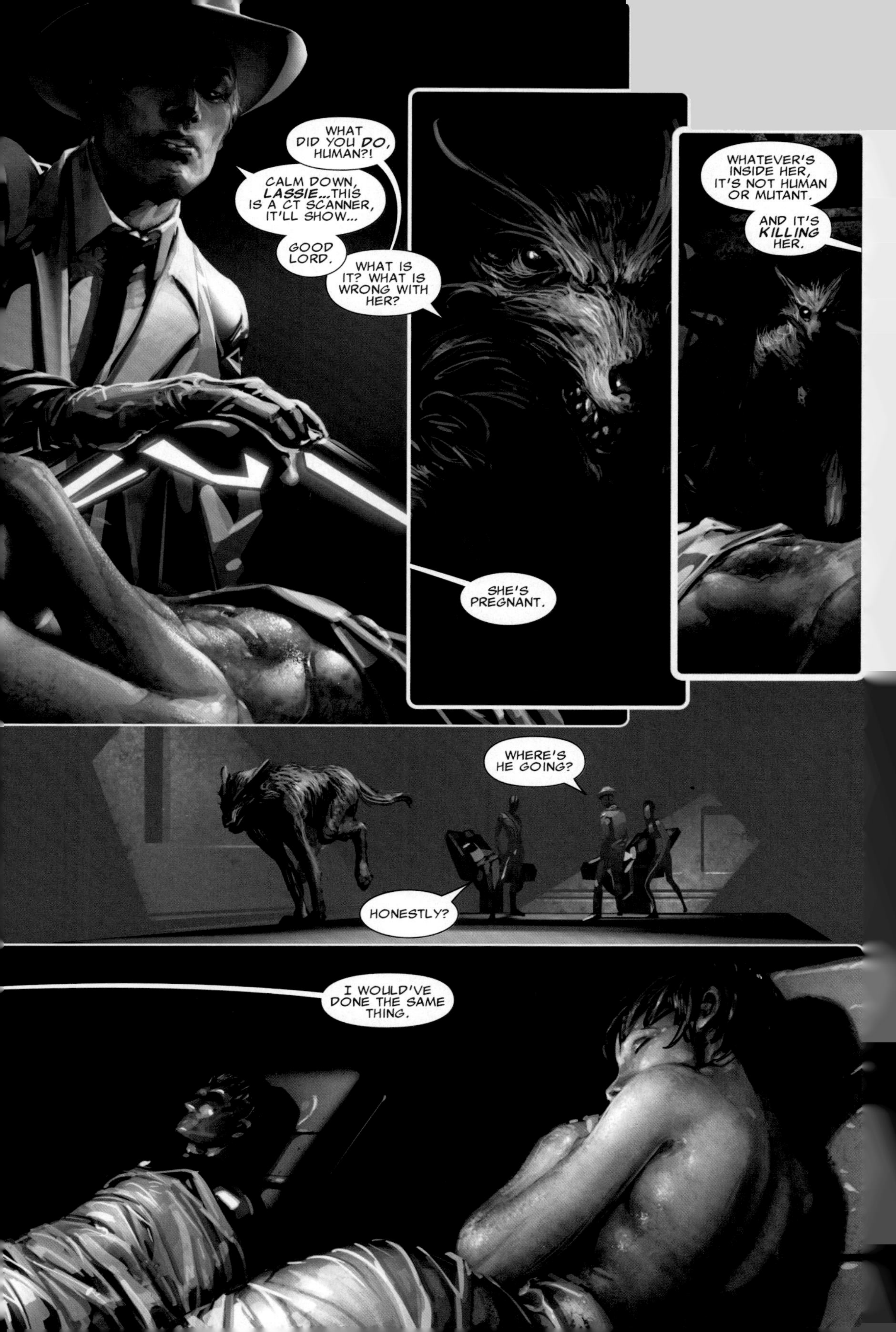
WHAT DID YOU DO, HUMAN?!
CALM DOWN, LASSIE...THIS IS A CT SCANNER, IT'LL SHOW...
GOOD LORD.
WHAT IS IT? WHAT IS WRONG WITH HER?
SHE'S PREGNANT.
WHATEVER'S INSIDE HER, IT'S NOT HUMAN OR MUTANT.
AND IT'S KILLING HER.
WHERE'S HE GOING?
HONESTLY?
I WOULD'VE DONE THE SAME THING.

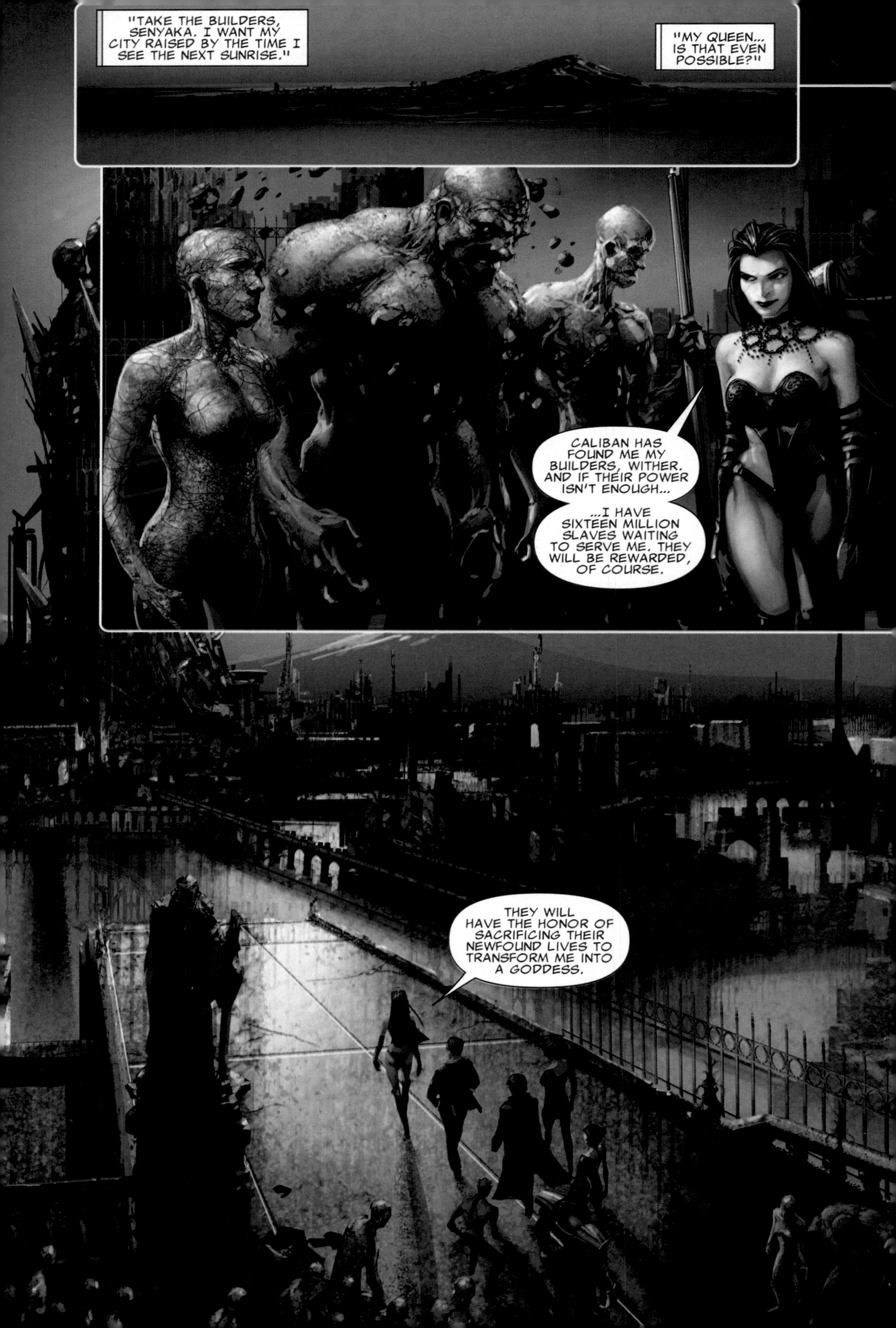
"TAKE THE BUILDERS, SENYAKA. I WANT MY CITY RAISED BY THE TIME I SEE THE NEXT SUNRISE."
"MY QUEEN... IS THAT EVEN POSSIBLE?"
CALIBAN HAS FOUND ME MY BUILDERS, WITHER. AND IF THEIR POWER ISN'T ENOUGH...
...I HAVE SIXTEEN MILLION SLAVES WAITING TO SERVE ME. THEY WILL BE REWARDED, OF COURSE.
THEY WILL HAVE THE HONOR OF SACRIFICING THEIR NEWFOUND LIVES TO TRANSFORM ME INTO A GODDESS.

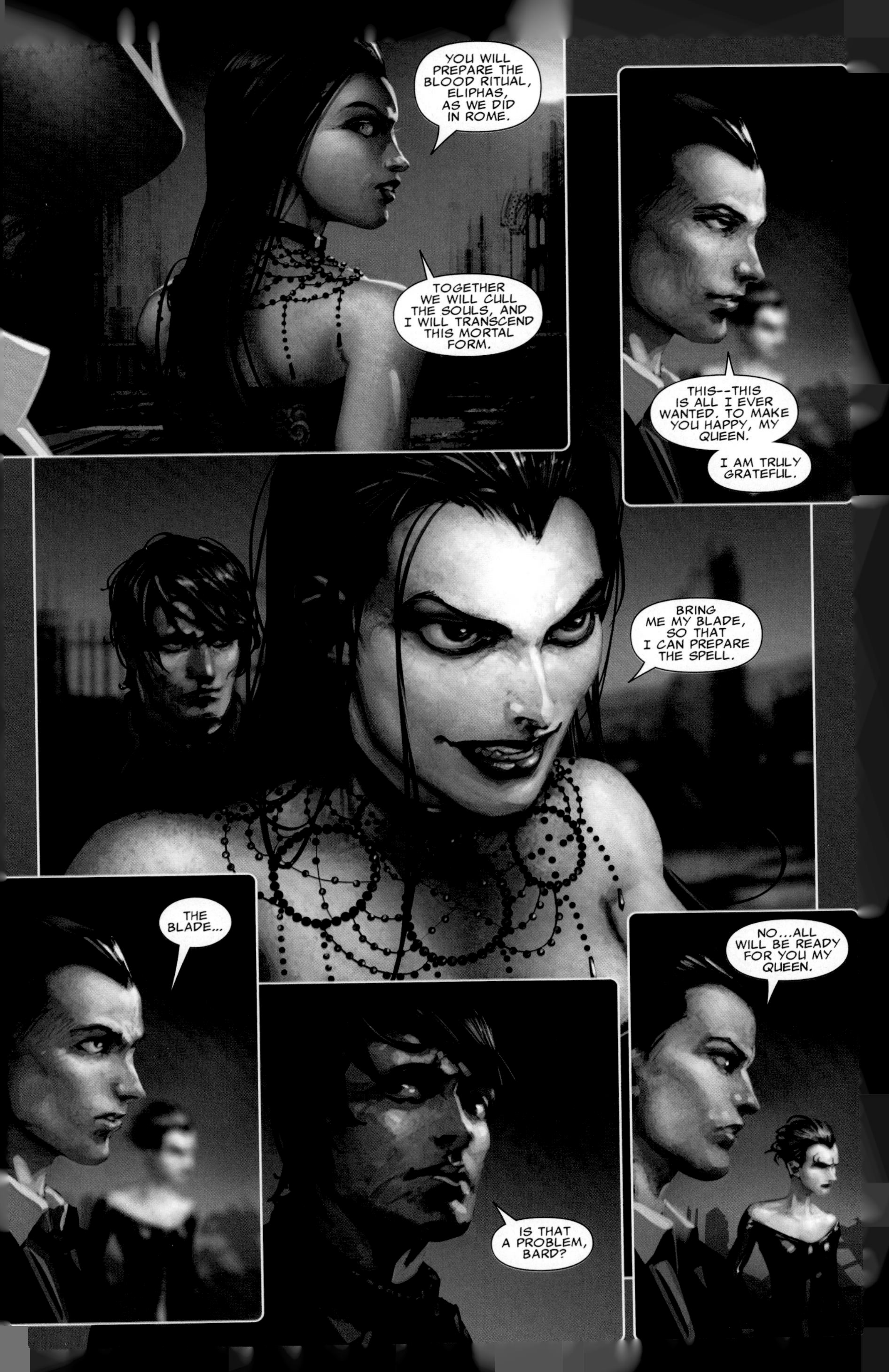

YOU WILL PREPARE THE BLOOD RITUAL, ELIPHAS, AS WE DID IN ROME.
TOGETHER WE WILL CULL THE SOULS, AND I WILL TRANSCEND THIS MORTAL FORM.
THIS--THIS IS ALL I EVER WANTED. TO MAKE YOU HAPPY, MY QUEEN.
I AM TRULY GRATEFUL.
BRING ME MY BLADE, SO THAT I CAN PREPARE THE SPELL.
THE BLADE...
IS THAT A PROBLEM, BARD?
NO...ALL WILL BE READY FOR YOU MY QUEEN.

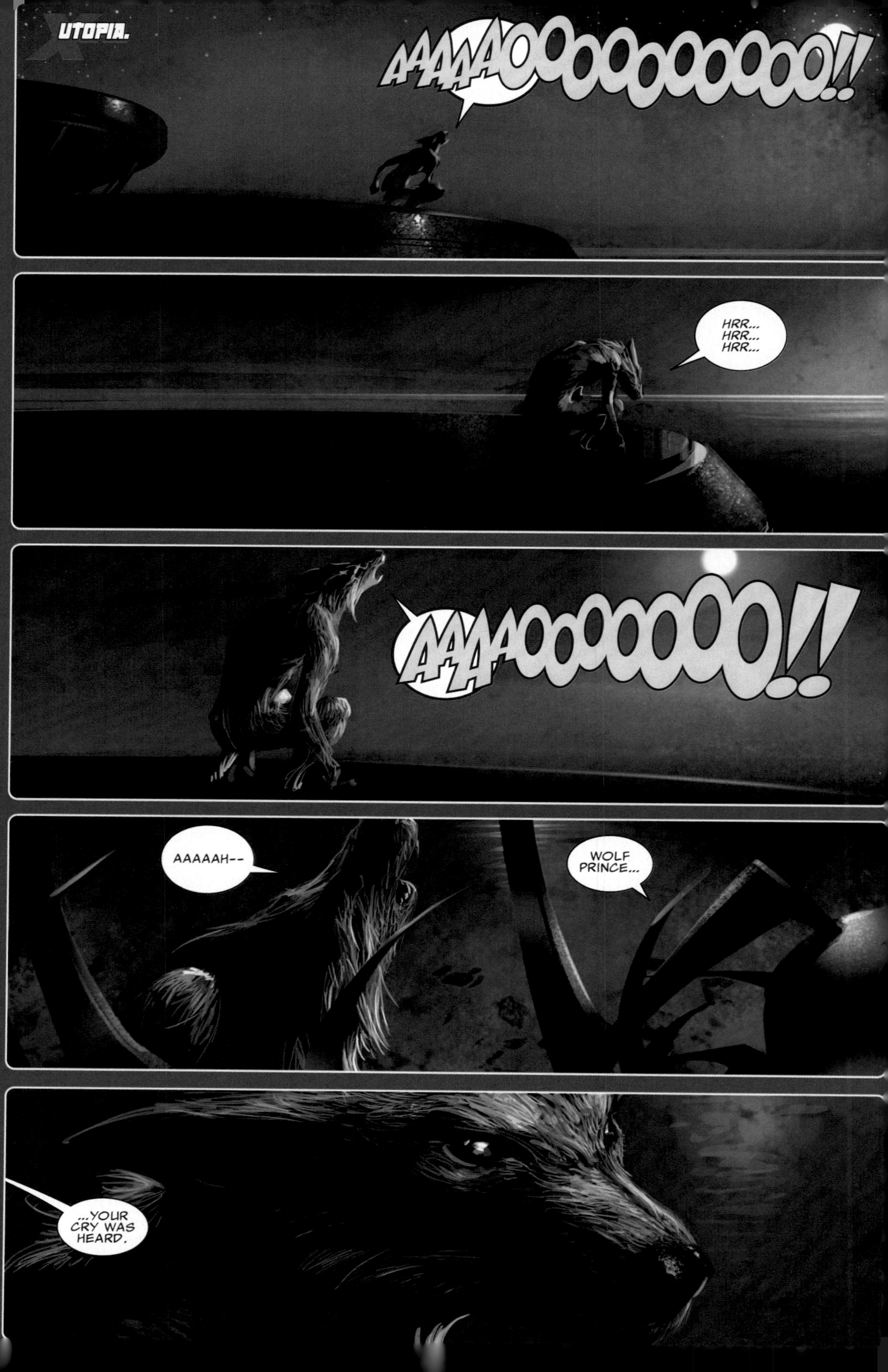
UTOPIA.
AAAAAOOOOOOOOOOOO!!
HRR... HRR... HRR...
AAAAOOOOOOOO!!
AAAAAH--
WOLF PRINCE...
...YOUR CRY WAS HEARD.

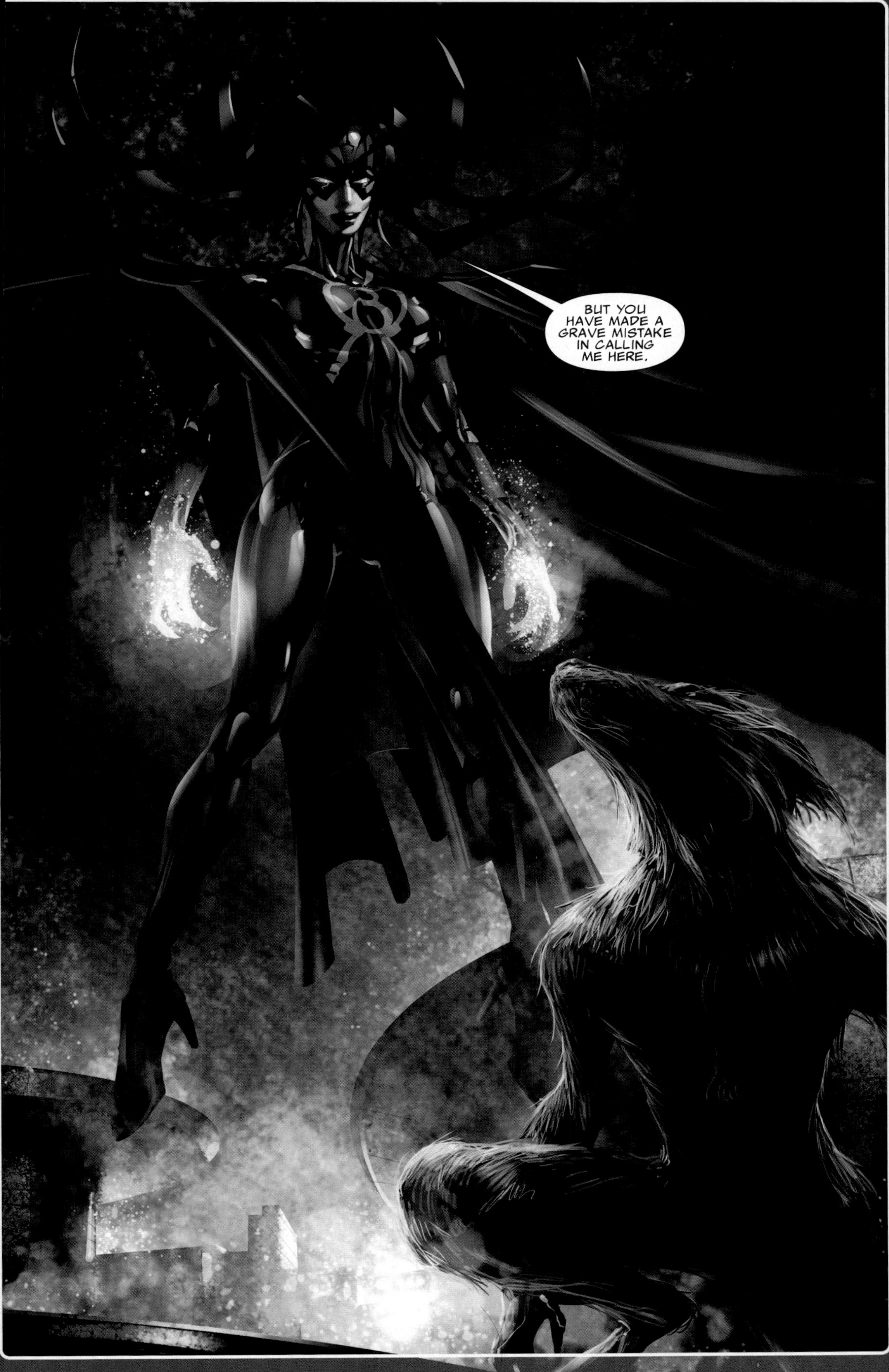
BUT YOU HAVE MADE A GRAVE MISTAKE IN CALLING ME HERE.

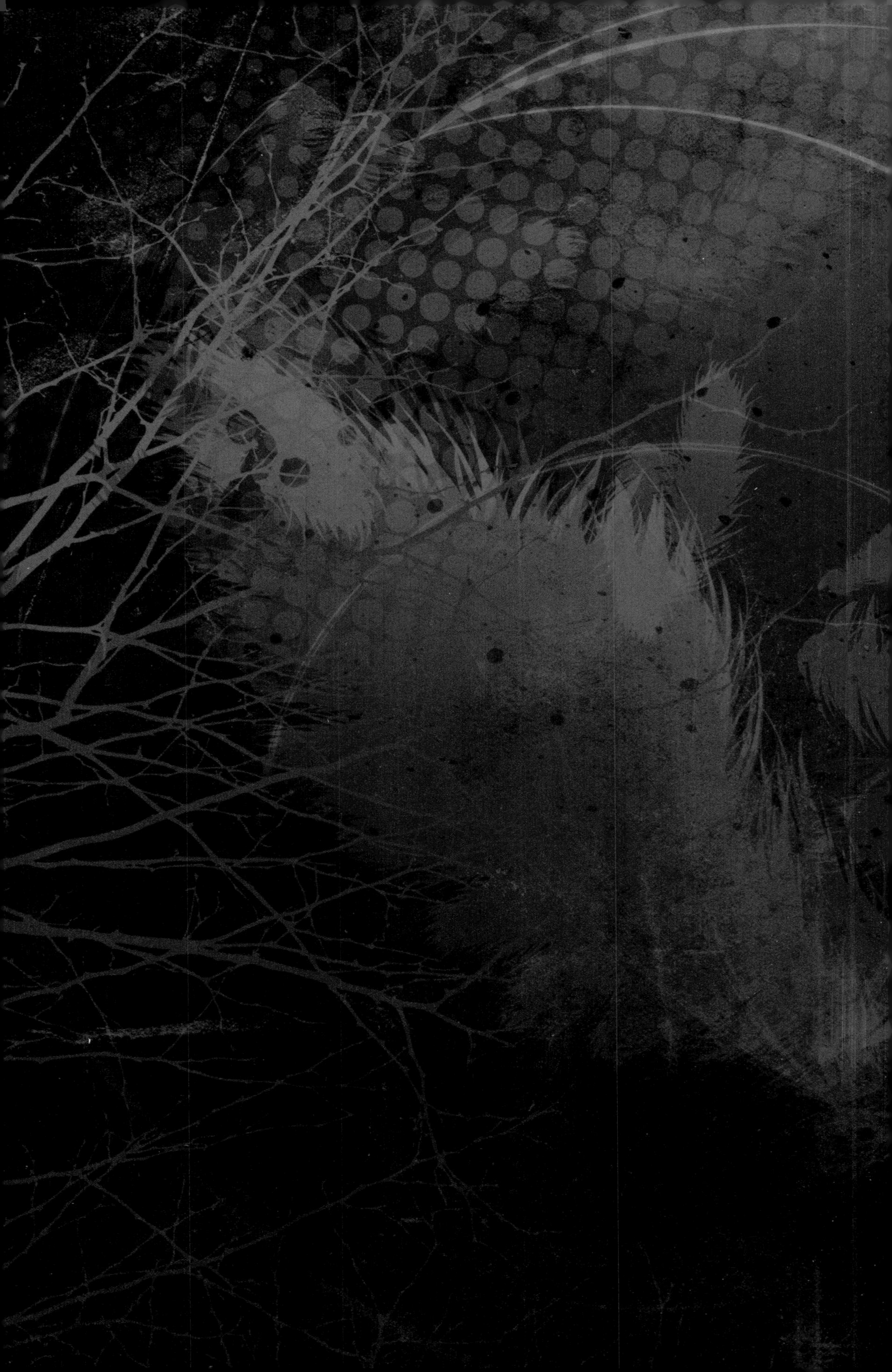

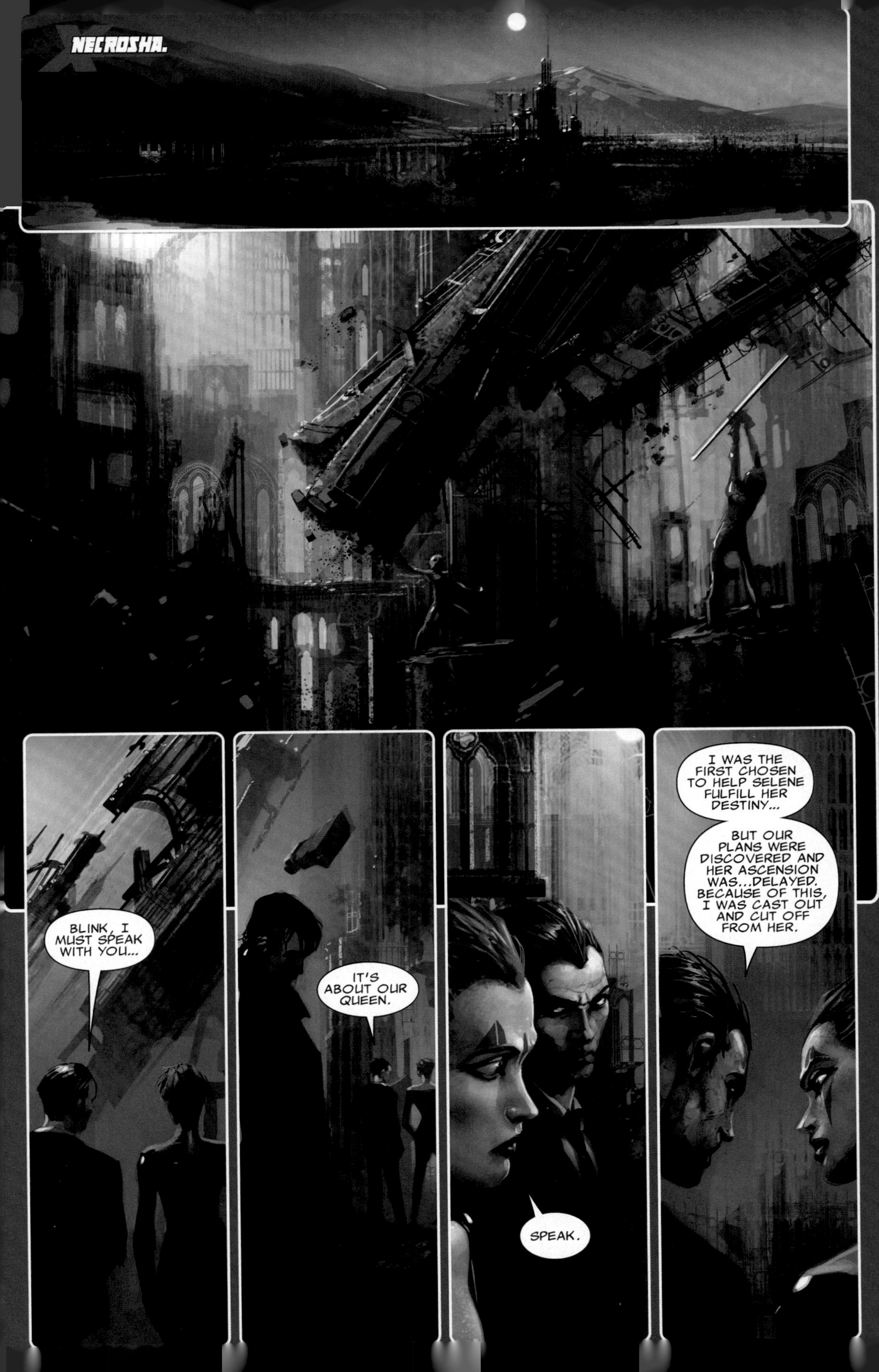
NECROSHA.
BLINK, I MUST SPEAK WITH YOU...
IT'S ABOUT OUR QUEEN.
SPEAK.
I WAS THE FIRST CHOSEN TO HELP SELENE FULFILL HER DESTINY...
BUT OUR PLANS WERE DISCOVERED AND HER ASCENSION WAS...DELAYED. BECAUSE OF THIS, I WAS CAST OUT AND CUT OFF FROM HER.

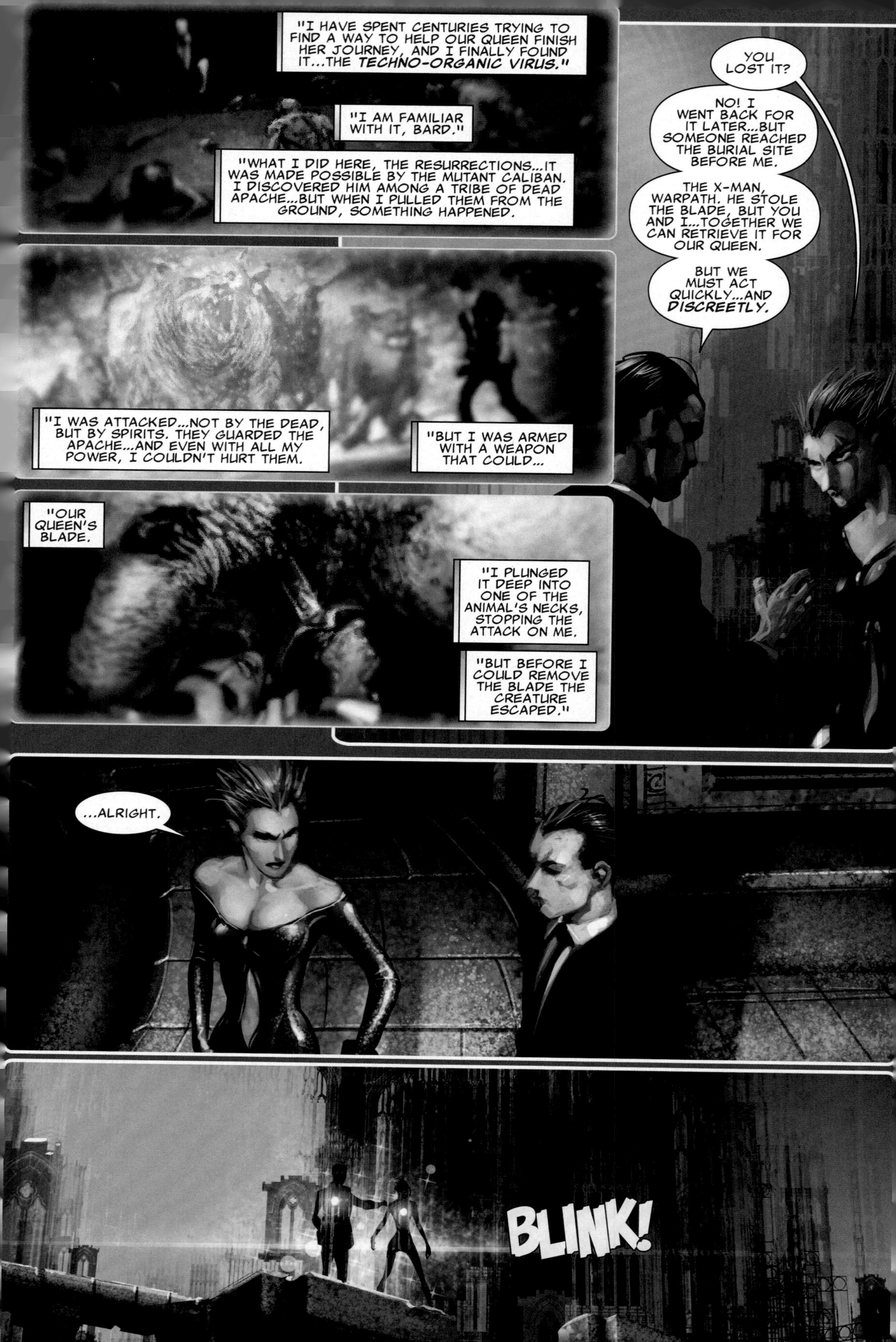
"I HAVE SPENT CENTURIES TRYING TO FIND A WAY TO HELP OUR QUEEN FINISH HER JOURNEY, AND I FINALLY FOUND IT...THE TECHNO-ORGANIC VIRUS."
"I AM FAMILIAR WITH IT, BARD."
"WHAT I DID HERE, THE RESURRECTIONS...IT WAS MADE POSSIBLE BY THE MUTANT CALIBAN. I DISCOVERED HIM AMONG A TRIBE OF DEAD APACHE...BUT WHEN I PULLED THEM FROM THE GROUND, SOMETHING HAPPENED.
"I WAS ATTACKED...NOT BY THE DEAD, BUT BY SPIRITS. THEY GUARDED THE APACHE...AND EVEN WITH ALL MY POWER, I COULDN'T HURT THEM.
"BUT I WAS ARMED WITH A WEAPON THAT COULD...
"OUR QUEEN'S BLADE.
"I PLUNGED IT DEEP INTO ONE OF THE ANIMAL'S NECKS, STOPPING THE ATTACK ON ME.
"BUT BEFORE I COULD REMOVE THE BLADE THE CREATURE ESCAPED."
YOU LOST IT?
NO! I WENT BACK FOR IT LATER...BUT SOMEONE REACHED THE BURIAL SITE BEFORE ME.
THE X-MAN, WARPATH. HE STOLE THE BLADE, BUT YOU AND I...TOGETHER WE CAN RETRIEVE IT FOR OUR QUEEN.
BUT WE MUST ACT QUICKLY...AND DISCREETLY.
...ALRIGHT.
BLINK!

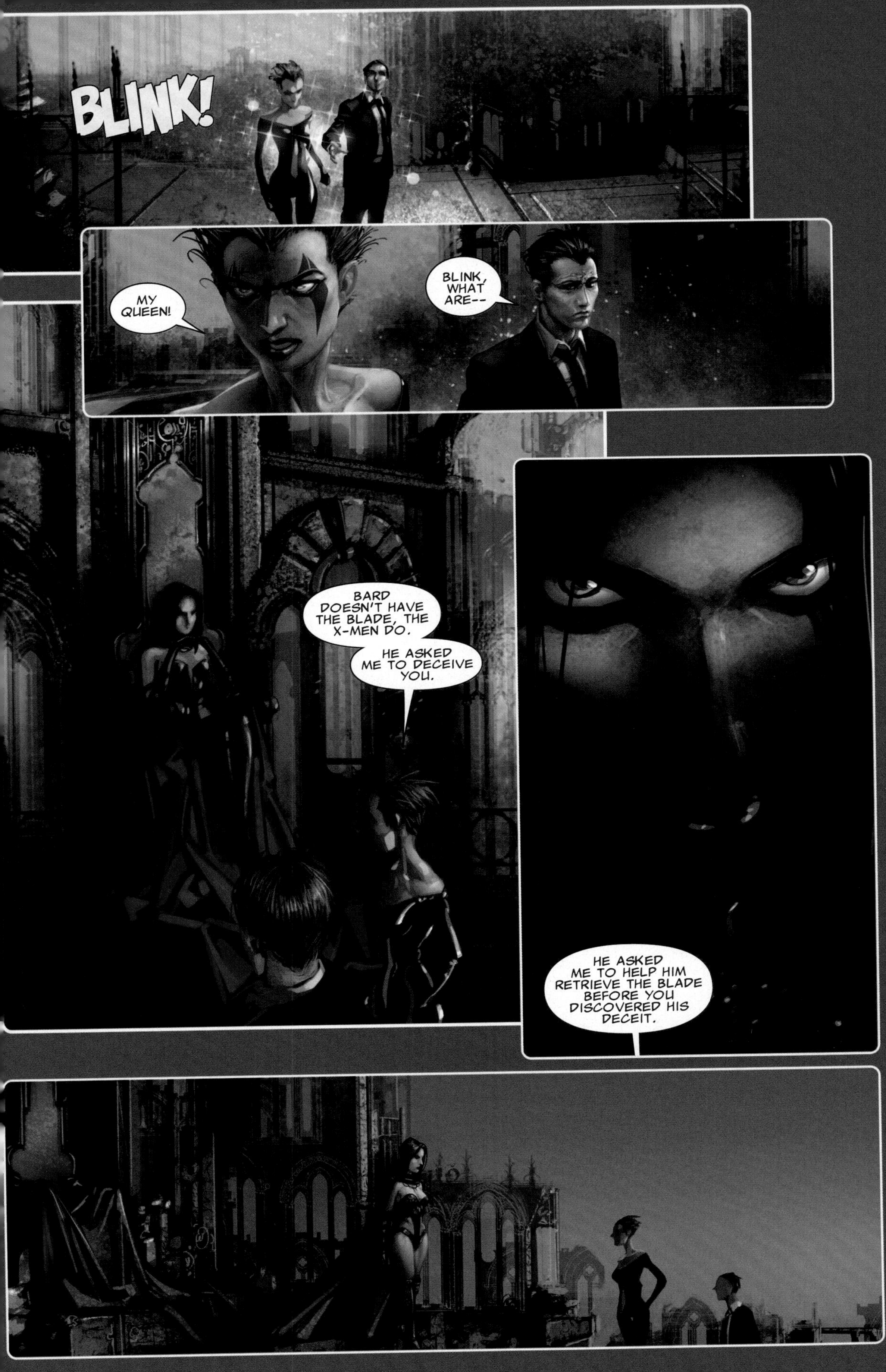
BLINK!
MY QUEEN!
BLINK, WHAT ARE--
BARD DOESN'T HAVE THE BLADE, THE X-MEN DO.
HE ASKED ME TO DECEIVE YOU.
HE ASKED ME TO HELP HIM RETRIEVE THE BLADE BEFORE YOU DISCOVERED HIS DECEIT.

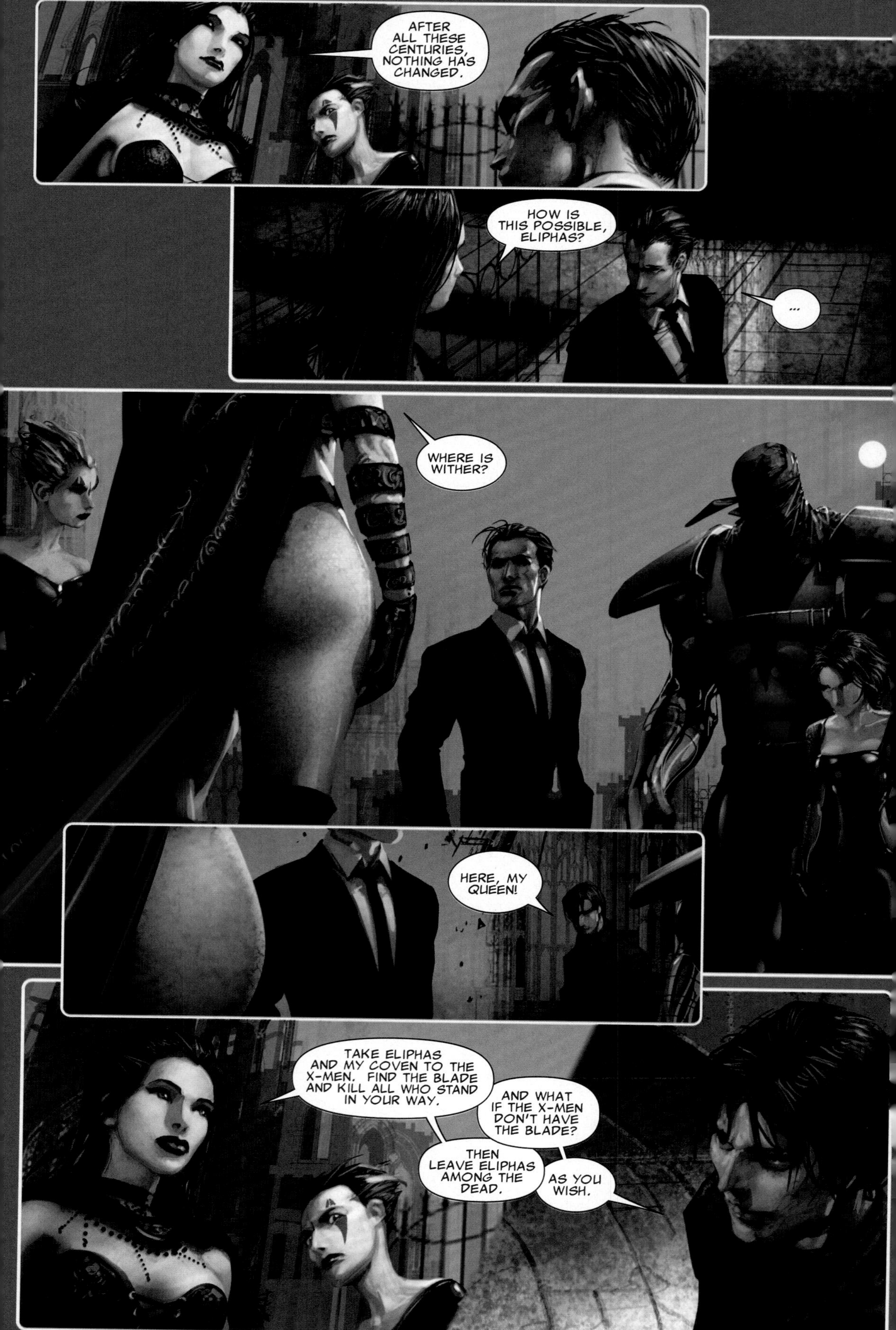
AFTER ALL THESE CENTURIES, NOTHING HAS CHANGED.
HOW IS THIS POSSIBLE, ELIPHAS?
...
WHERE IS WITHER?
HERE, MY QUEEN!
TAKE ELIPHAS AND MY COVEN TO THE X-MEN. FIND THE BLADE AND KILL ALL WHO STAND IN YOUR WAY.
AND WHAT IF THE X-MEN DON'T HAVE THE BLADE?
THEN LEAVE ELIPHAS AMONG THE DEAD.
AS YOU WISH.

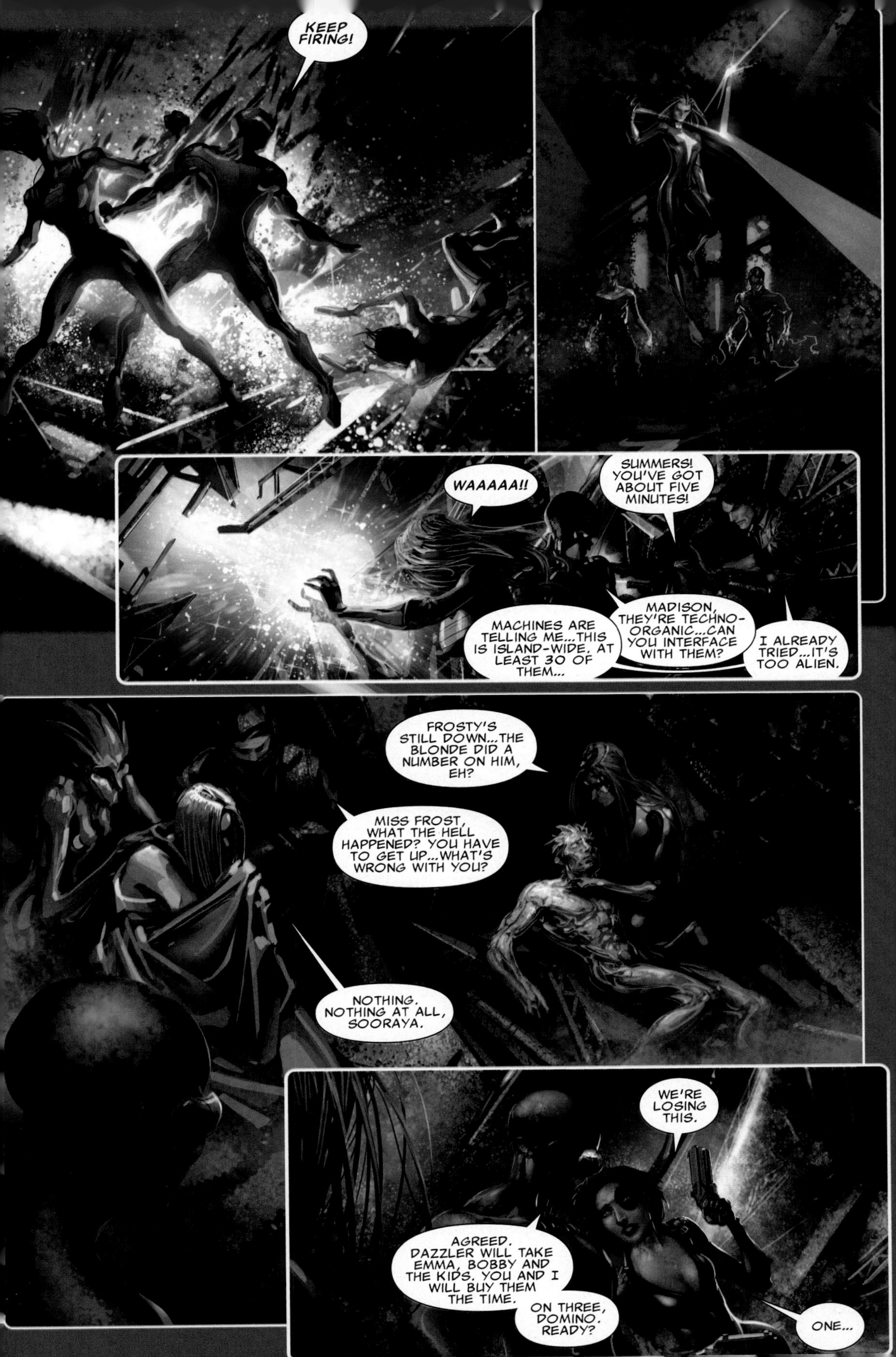
KEEP FIRING!
WAAAAA!!
SUMMERS! YOU'VE GOT ABOUT FIVE MINUTES!
MACHINES ARE TELLING ME...THIS IS ISLAND-WIDE. AT LEAST 30 OF THEM...
MADISON, THEY'RE TECHNO-ORGANIC...CAN YOU INTERFACE WITH THEM?
I ALREADY TRIED...IT'S TOO ALIEN.
FROSTY'S STILL DOWN...THE BLONDE DID A NUMBER ON HIM, EH?
MISS FROST, WHAT THE HELL HAPPENED? YOU HAVE TO GET UP...WHAT'S WRONG WITH YOU?
NOTHING. NOTHING AT ALL, SOORAYA.
WE'RE LOSING THIS.
AGREED. DAZZLER WILL TAKE EMMA, BOBBY AND THE KIDS. YOU AND I WILL BUY THEM THE TIME.
ON THREE, DOMINO. READY?
ONE...

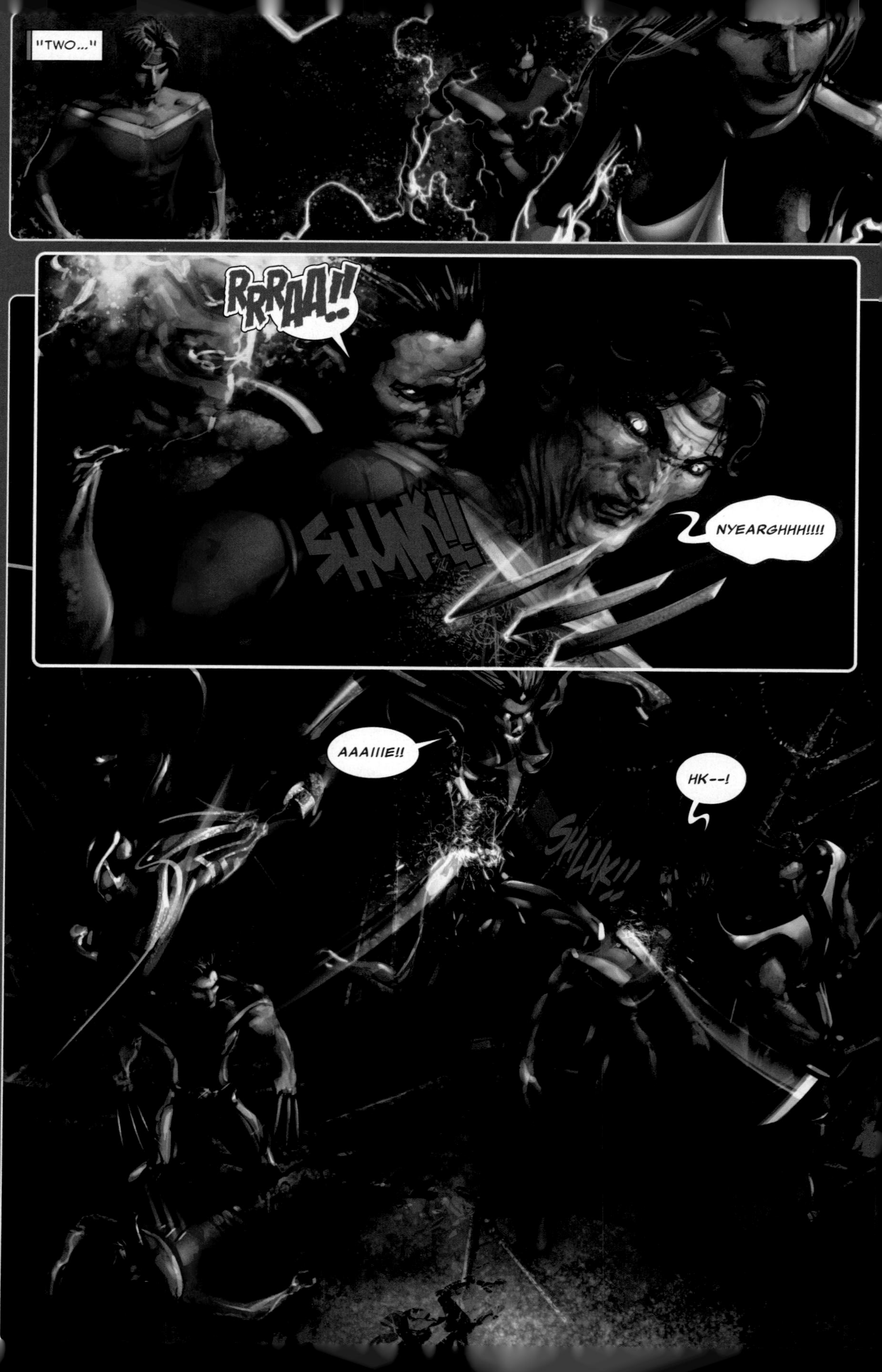
"TWO..."
RRRAA!!
SHUK!!
NYEARGHHH!!!!
AAAIIIE!!
HK--!
SHUK!!

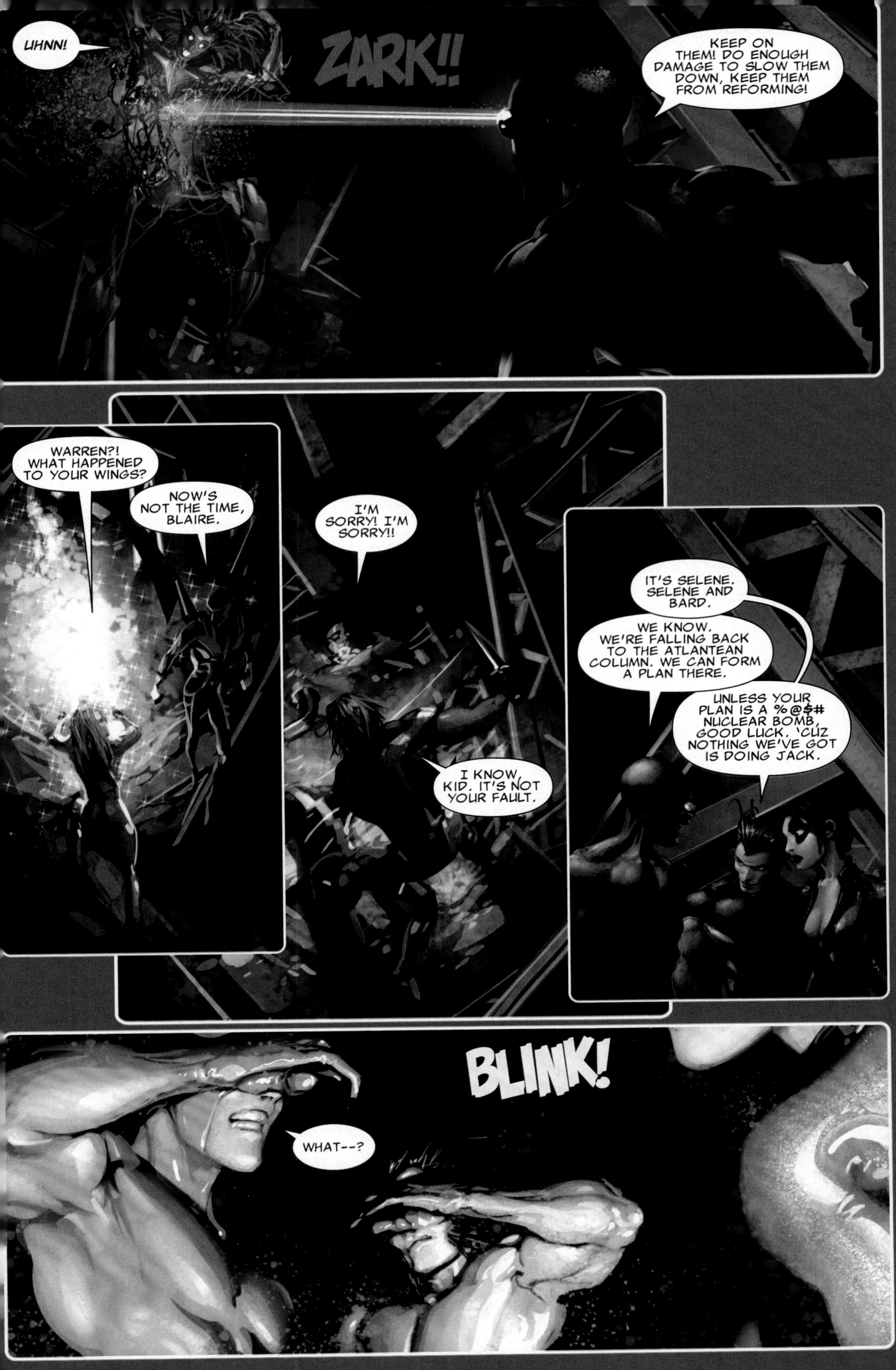

UHNN!
ZARK!!
KEEP ON THEM! DO ENOUGH DAMAGE TO SLOW THEM DOWN, KEEP THEM FROM REFORMING!
WARREN?! WHAT HAPPENED TO YOUR WINGS?
NOW'S NOT THE TIME, BLAIRE.
I'M SORRY! I'M SORRY!!
I KNOW, KID. IT'S NOT YOUR FAULT.
IT'S SELENE. SELENE AND BARD.
WE KNOW. WE'RE FALLING BACK TO THE ATLANTEAN COLUMN. WE CAN FORM A PLAN THERE.
UNLESS YOUR PLAN IS A %@$# NUCLEAR BOMB, GOOD LUCK. 'CUZ NOTHING WE'VE GOT IS DOING JACK.
BLINK!
WHAT--?

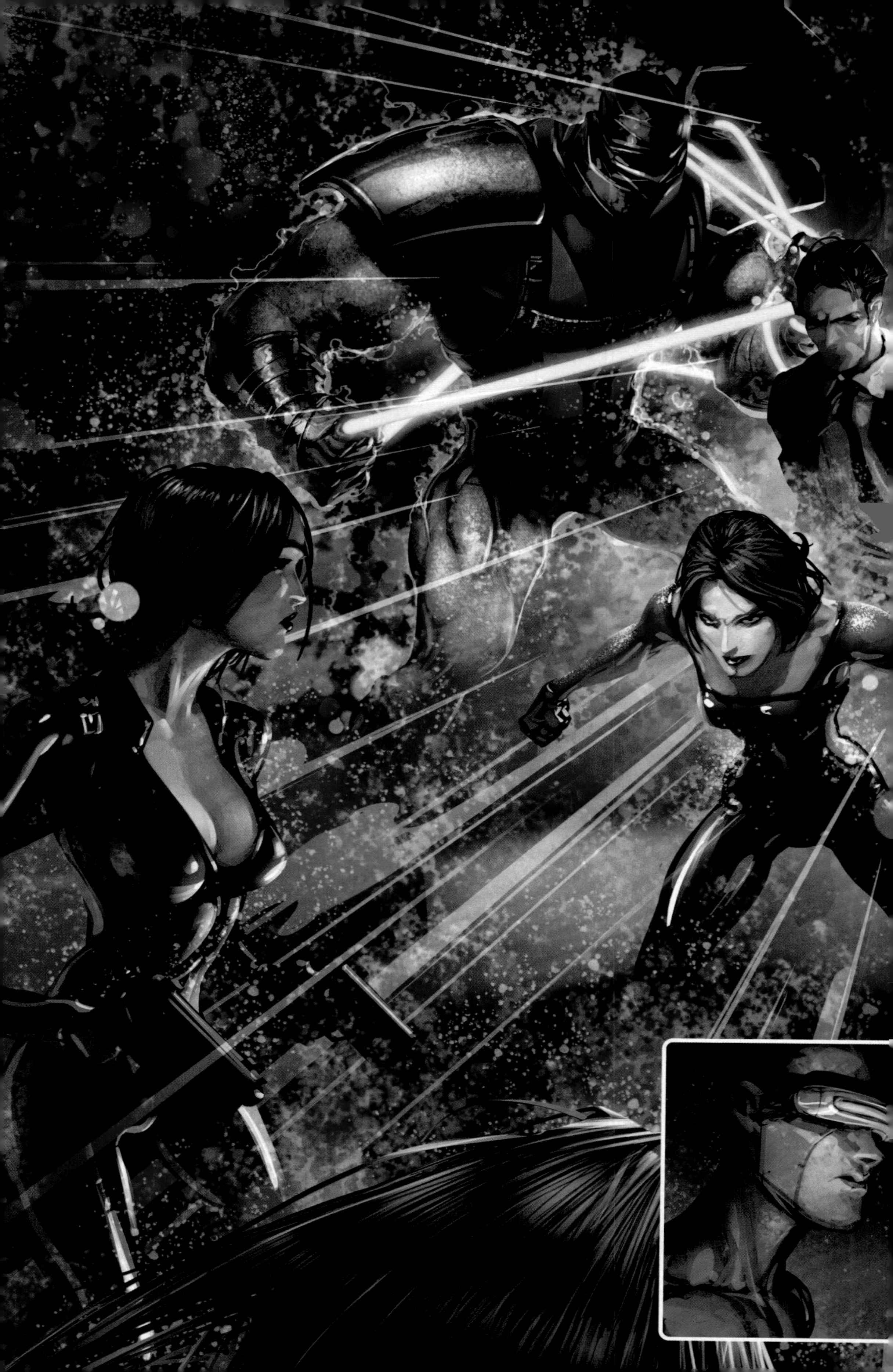

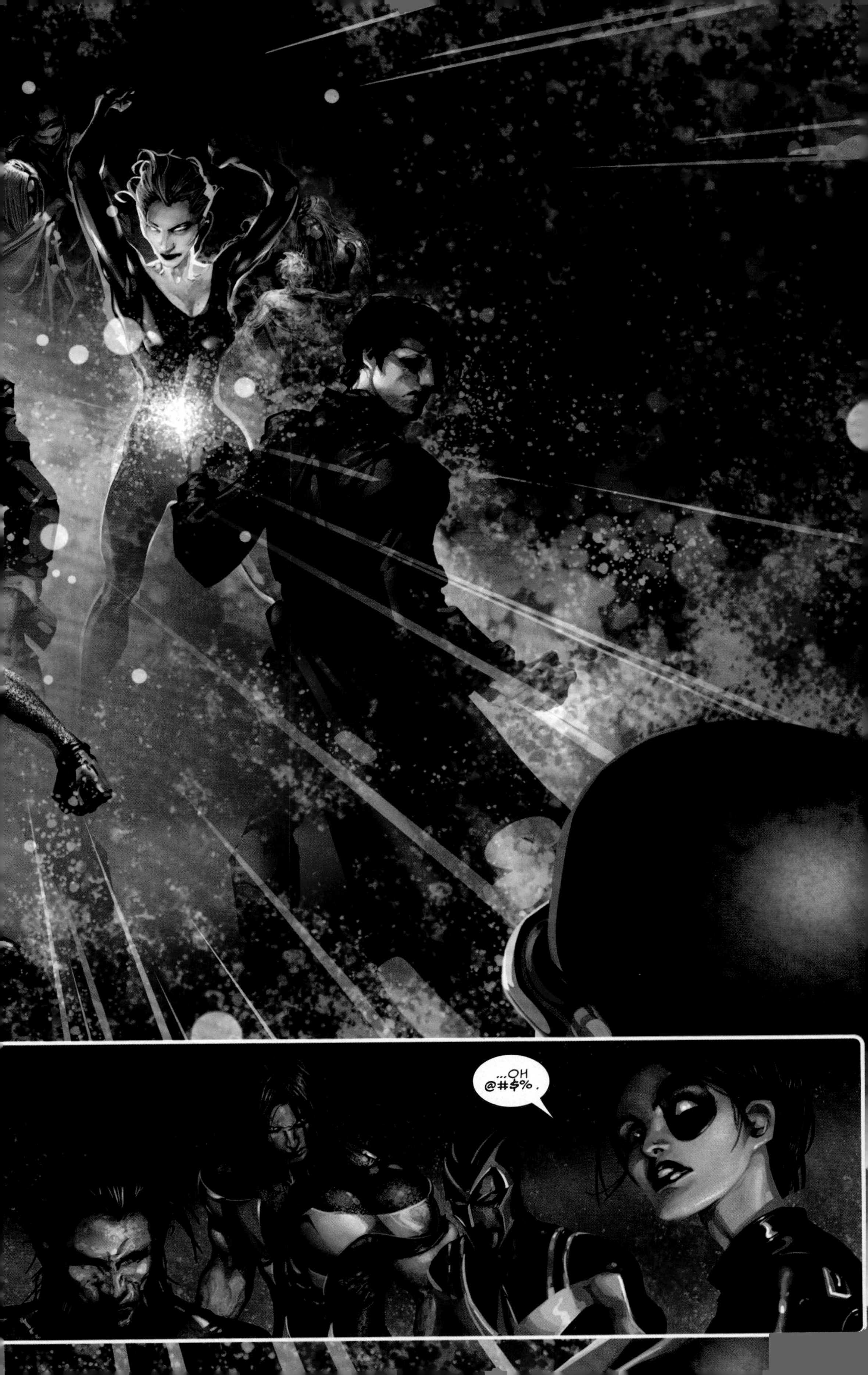
...OH
@#$%.

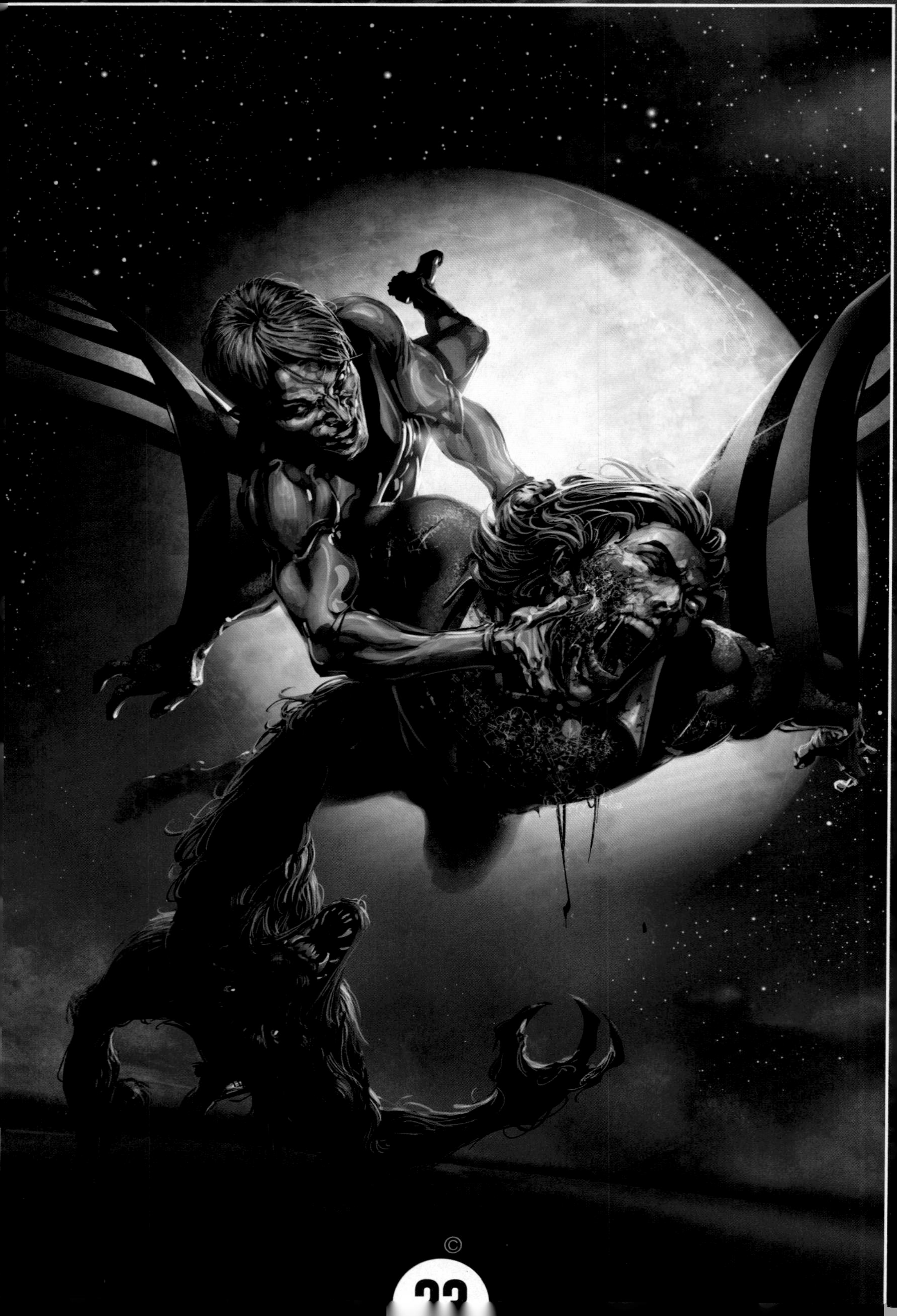

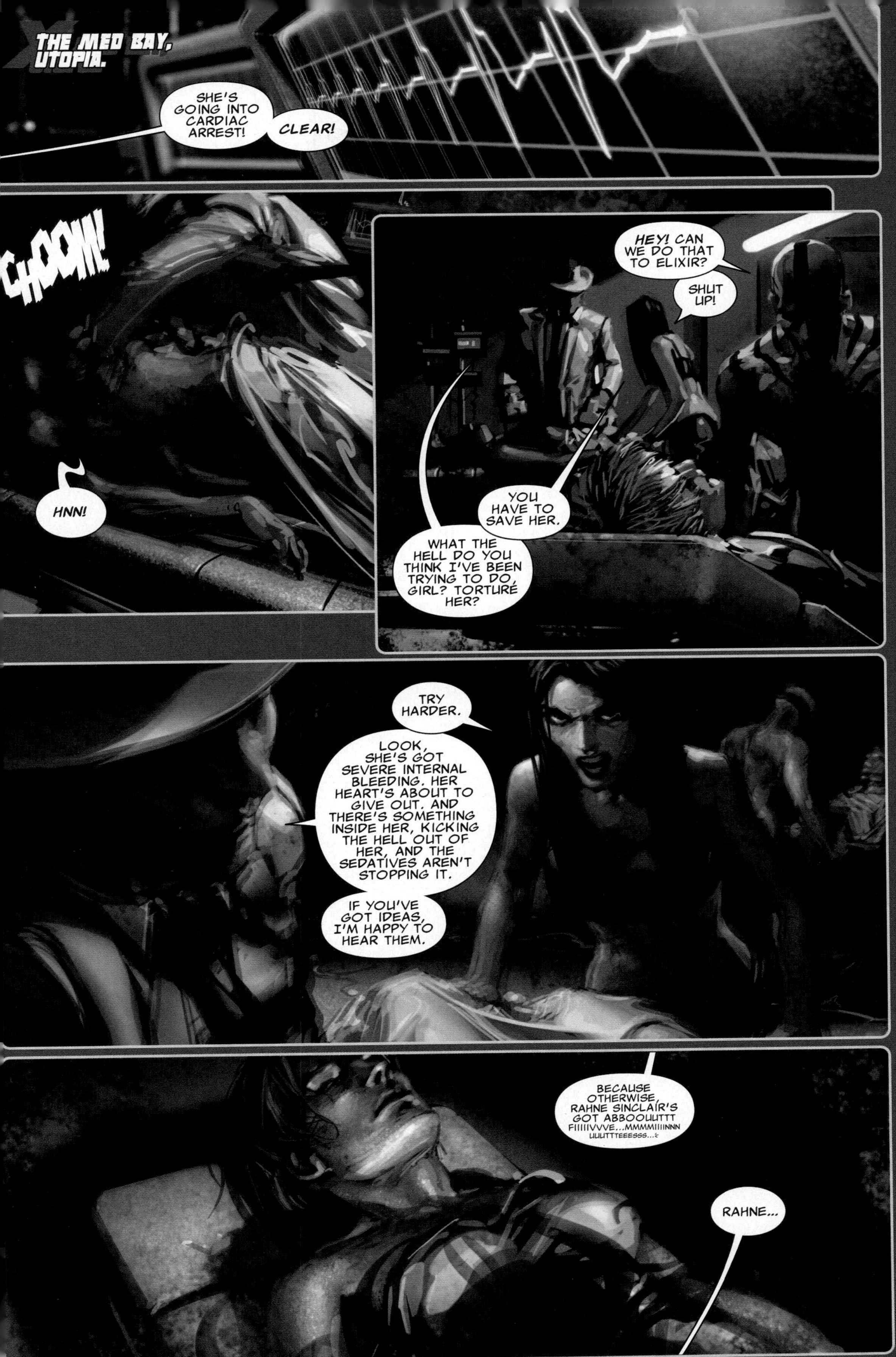

THE MED BAY, UTOPIA.
SHE'S GOING INTO CARDIAC ARREST!
CLEAR!
CHOOM!
HNN!
HEY! CAN WE DO THAT TO ELIXIR?
SHUT UP!
YOU HAVE TO SAVE HER.
WHAT THE HELL DO YOU THINK I'VE BEEN TRYING TO DO, GIRL? TORTURE HER?
TRY HARDER.
LOOK, SHE'S GOT SEVERE INTERNAL BLEEDING. HER HEART'S ABOUT TO GIVE OUT. AND THERE'S SOMETHING INSIDE HER, KICKING THE HELL OUT OF HER, AND THE SEDATIVES AREN'T STOPPING IT.
IF YOU'VE GOT IDEAS, I'M HAPPY TO HEAR THEM.
BECAUSE OTHERWISE, RAHNE SINCLAIR'S GOT ABBOOUUTTT FIIIIIVVVE...MMMMIIIINNN UUUTTTEEEESSS...
RAHNE...

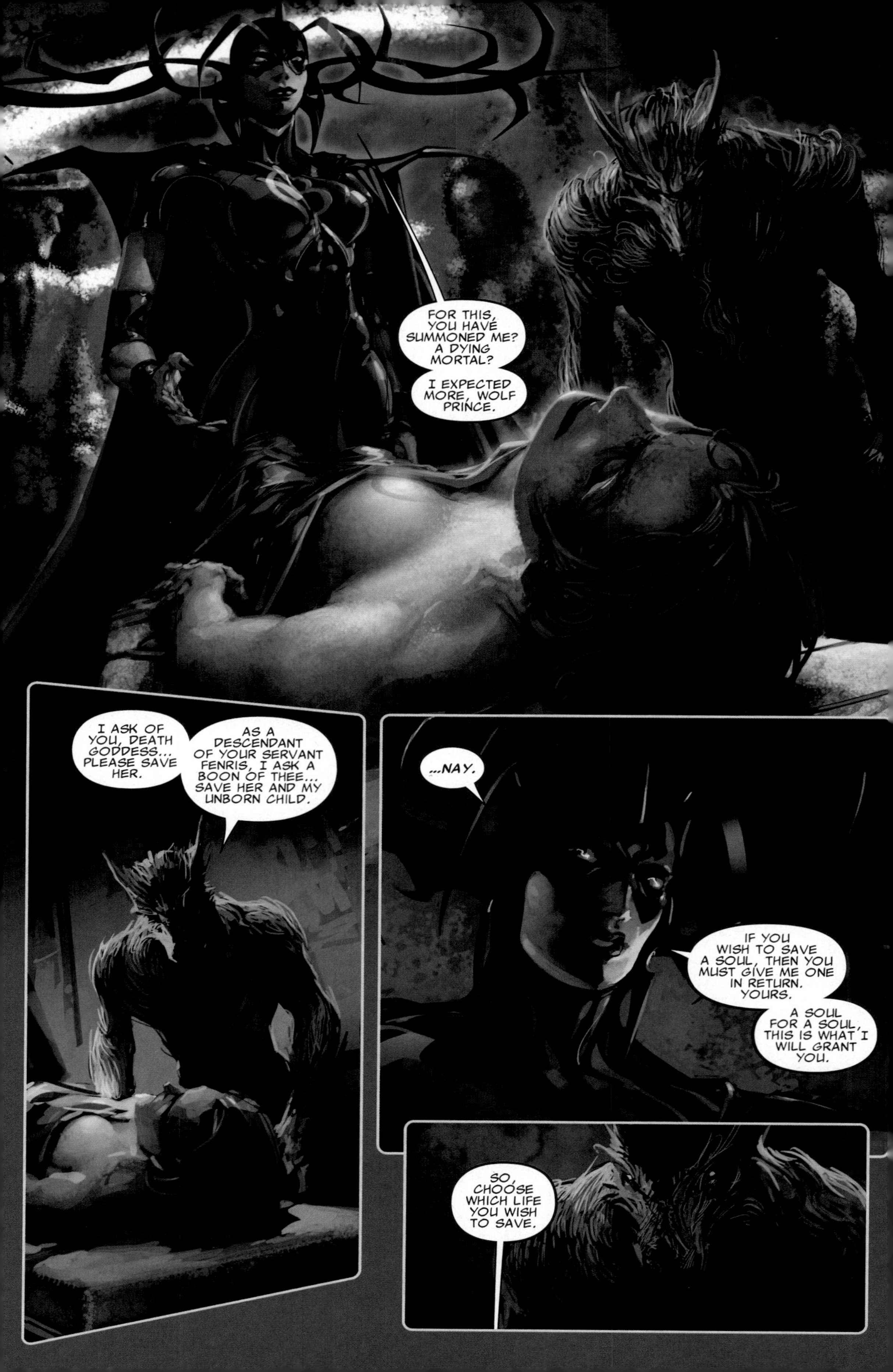
FOR THIS, YOU HAVE SUMMONED ME? A DYING MORTAL?
I EXPECTED MORE, WOLF PRINCE.
I ASK OF YOU, DEATH GODDESS... PLEASE SAVE HER.
AS A DESCENDANT OF YOUR SERVANT FENRIS, I ASK A BOON OF THEE... SAVE HER AND MY UNBORN CHILD.
...NAY.
IF YOU WISH TO SAVE A SOUL, THEN YOU MUST GIVE ME ONE IN RETURN. YOURS.
A SOUL FOR A SOUL, THIS IS WHAT I WILL GRANT YOU.
SO, CHOOSE WHICH LIFE YOU WISH TO SAVE.

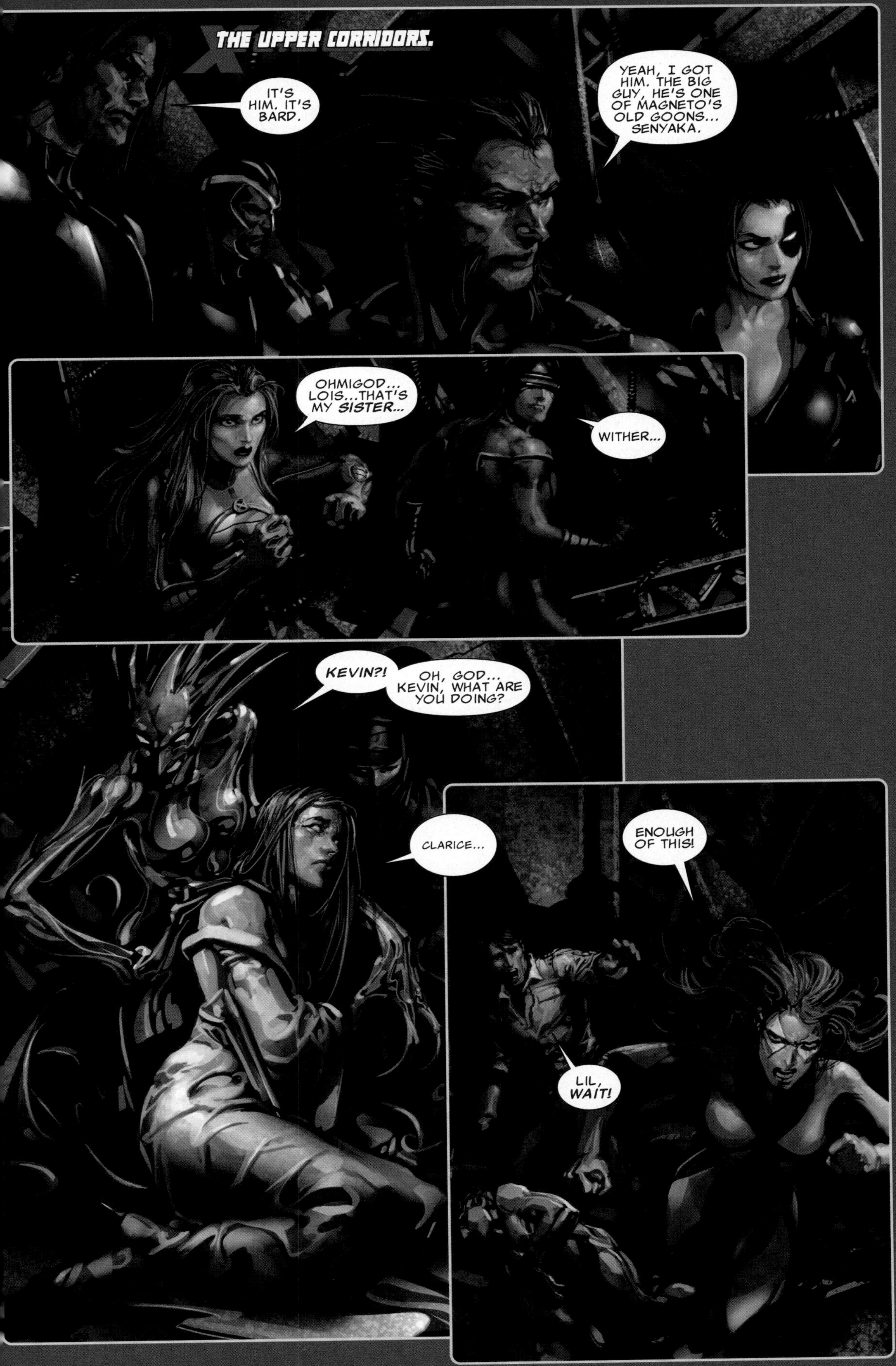
THE UPPER CORRIDORS.
IT'S HIM. IT'S BARD.
YEAH, I GOT HIM. THE BIG GUY, HE'S ONE OF MAGNETO'S OLD GOONS... SENYAKA.
OHMIGOD... LOIS...THAT'S MY SISTER...
WITHER...
KEVIN?!
OH, GOD... KEVIN, WHAT ARE YOU DOING?
CLARICE...
ENOUGH OF THIS!
LIL, WAIT!

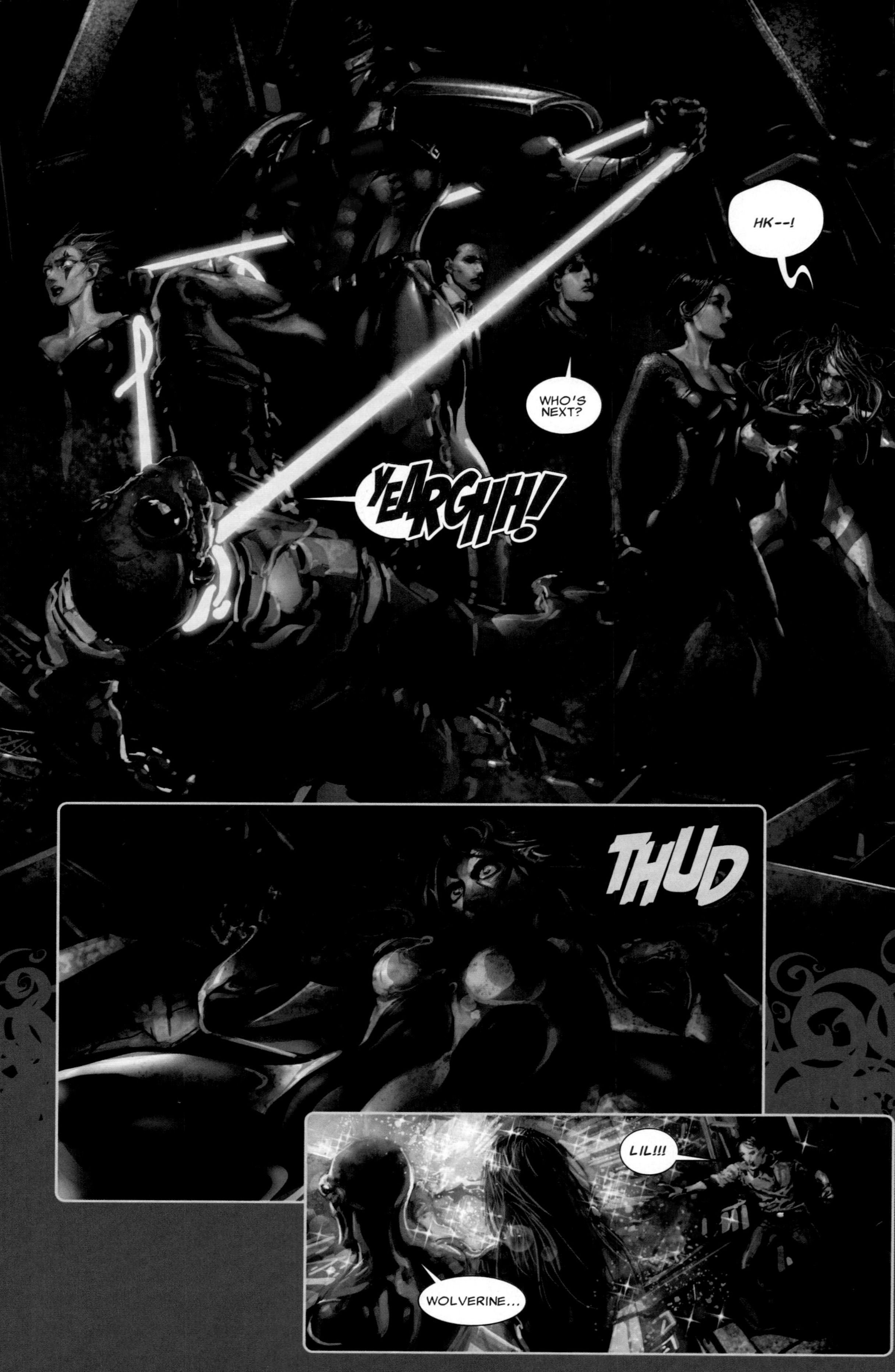
HK--!
WHO'S NEXT?
YEARGHH!
THUD
LIL!!!
WOLVERINE...

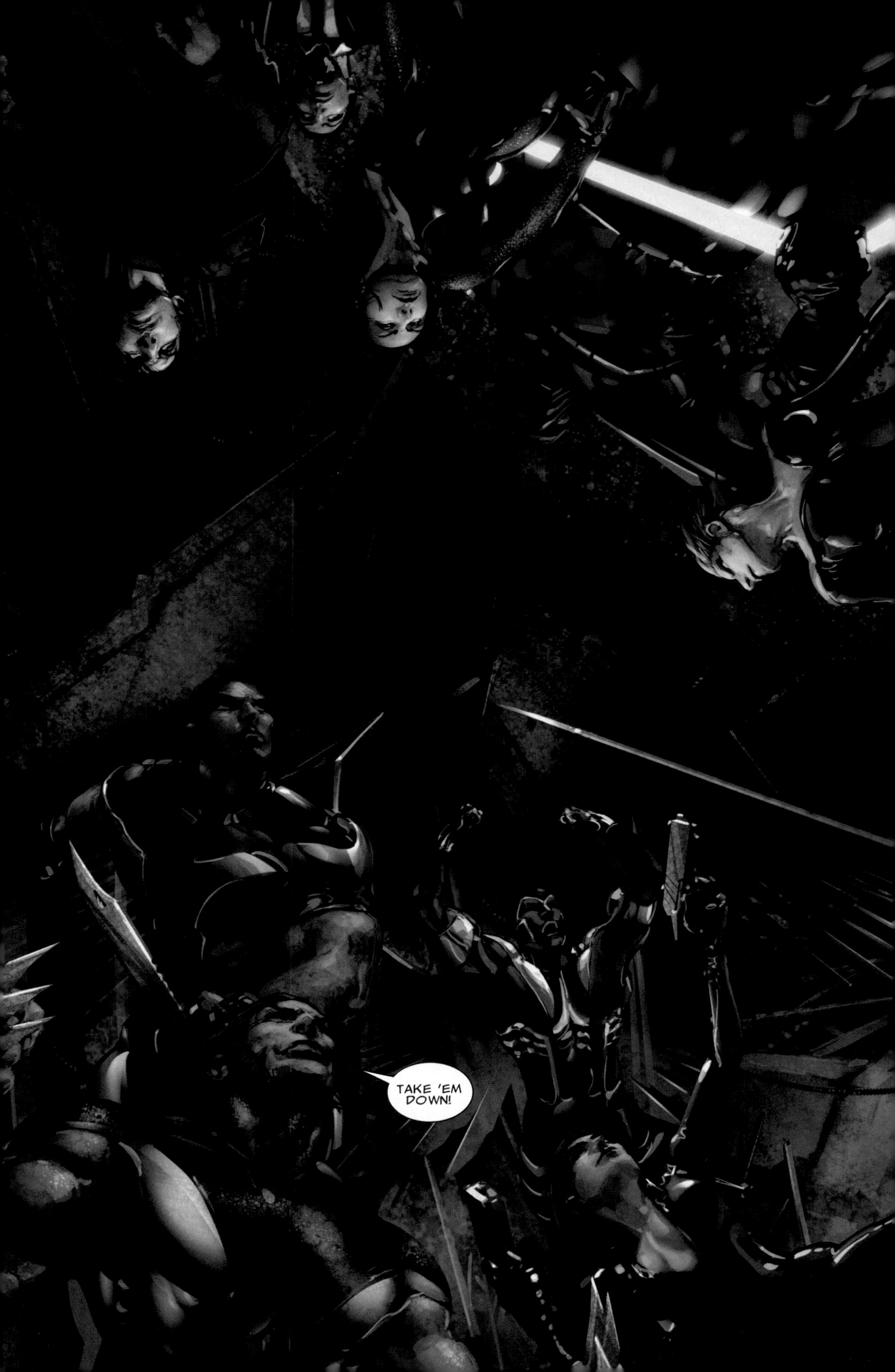
TAKE 'EM DOWN!

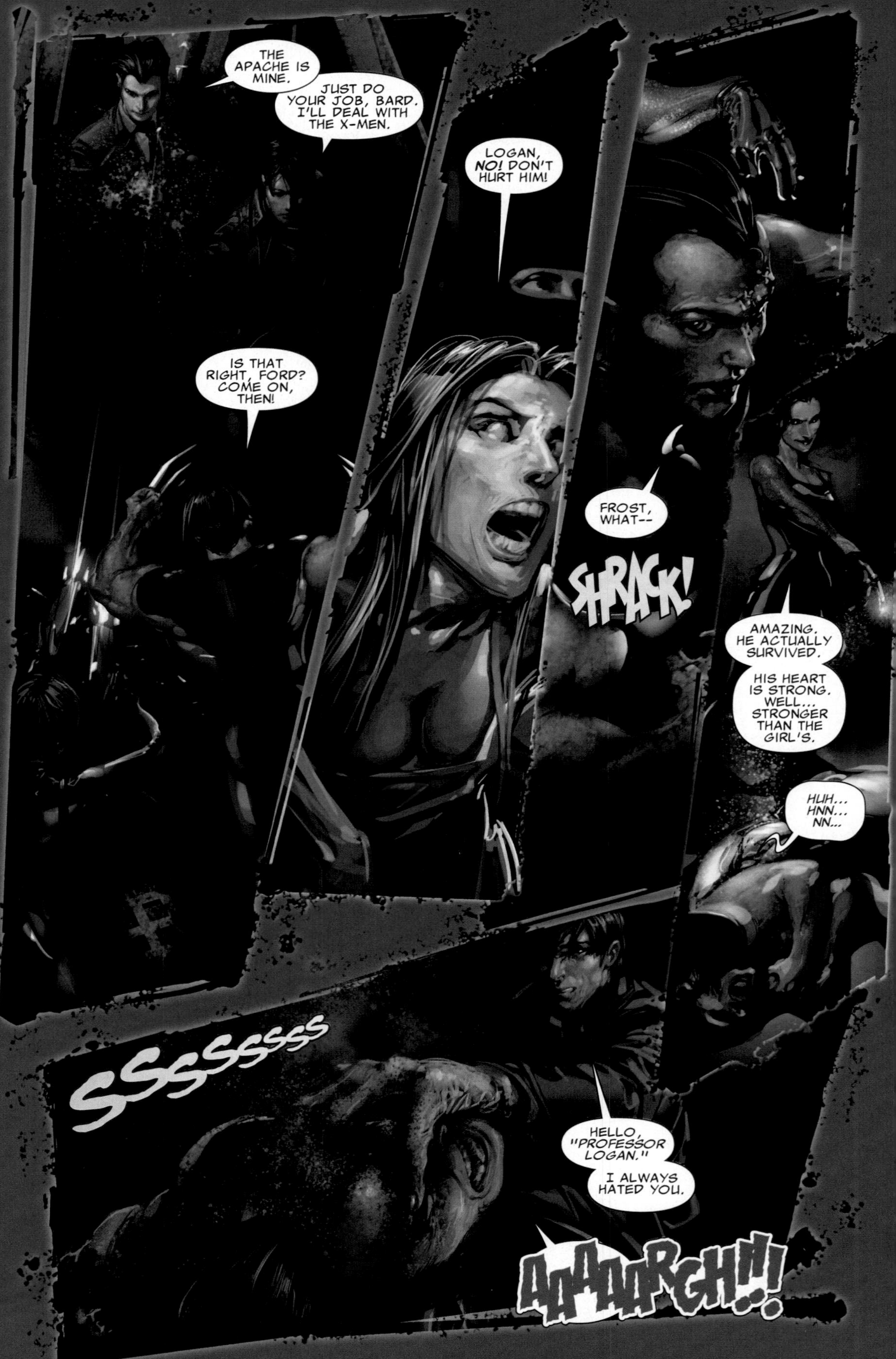
THE APACHE IS MINE.
JUST DO YOUR JOB, BARD. I'LL DEAL WITH THE X-MEN.
IS THAT RIGHT, FORD? COME ON, THEN!
LOGAN, NO! DON'T HURT HIM!
FROST, WHAT--
SHRACK!
AMAZING. HE ACTUALLY SURVIVED.
HIS HEART IS STRONG. WELL... STRONGER THAN THE GIRL'S.
HUH... HNN... NN...
SSSSSSSS
HELLO, "PROFESSOR LOGAN."
I ALWAYS HATED YOU.
AAAAARGH!!!

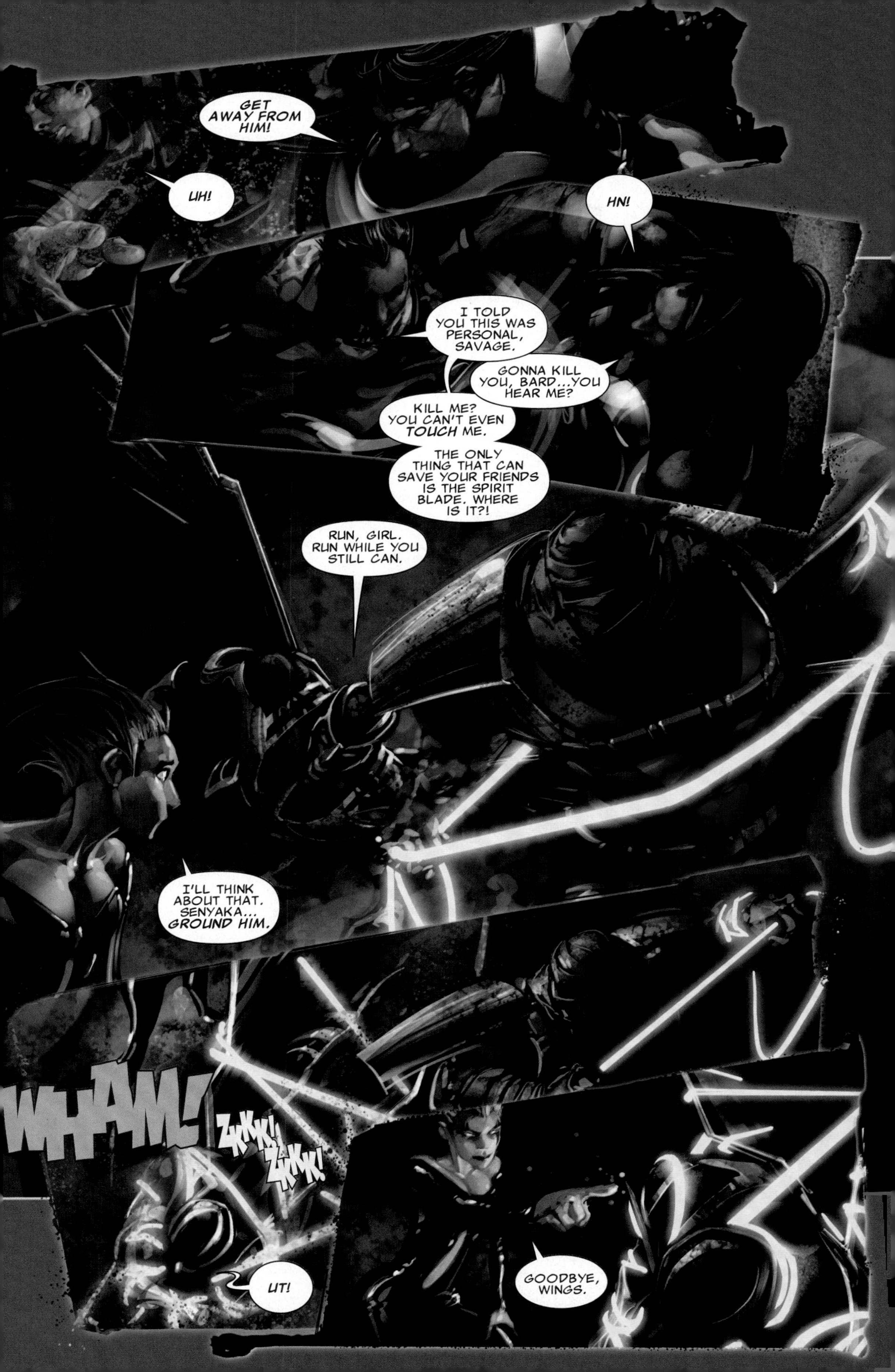
GET AWAY FROM HIM!
UH!
HN!
I TOLD YOU THIS WAS PERSONAL, SAVAGE.
GONNA KILL YOU, BARD...YOU HEAR ME?
KILL ME? YOU CAN'T EVEN *TOUCH* ME.
THE ONLY THING THAT CAN SAVE YOUR FRIENDS IS THE SPIRIT BLADE. WHERE IS IT?!
RUN, GIRL. RUN WHILE YOU STILL CAN.
I'LL THINK ABOUT THAT. SENYAKA... *GROUND HIM.*
WHAM!
ZKKK! ZKKK!
UT!
GOODBYE, WINGS.

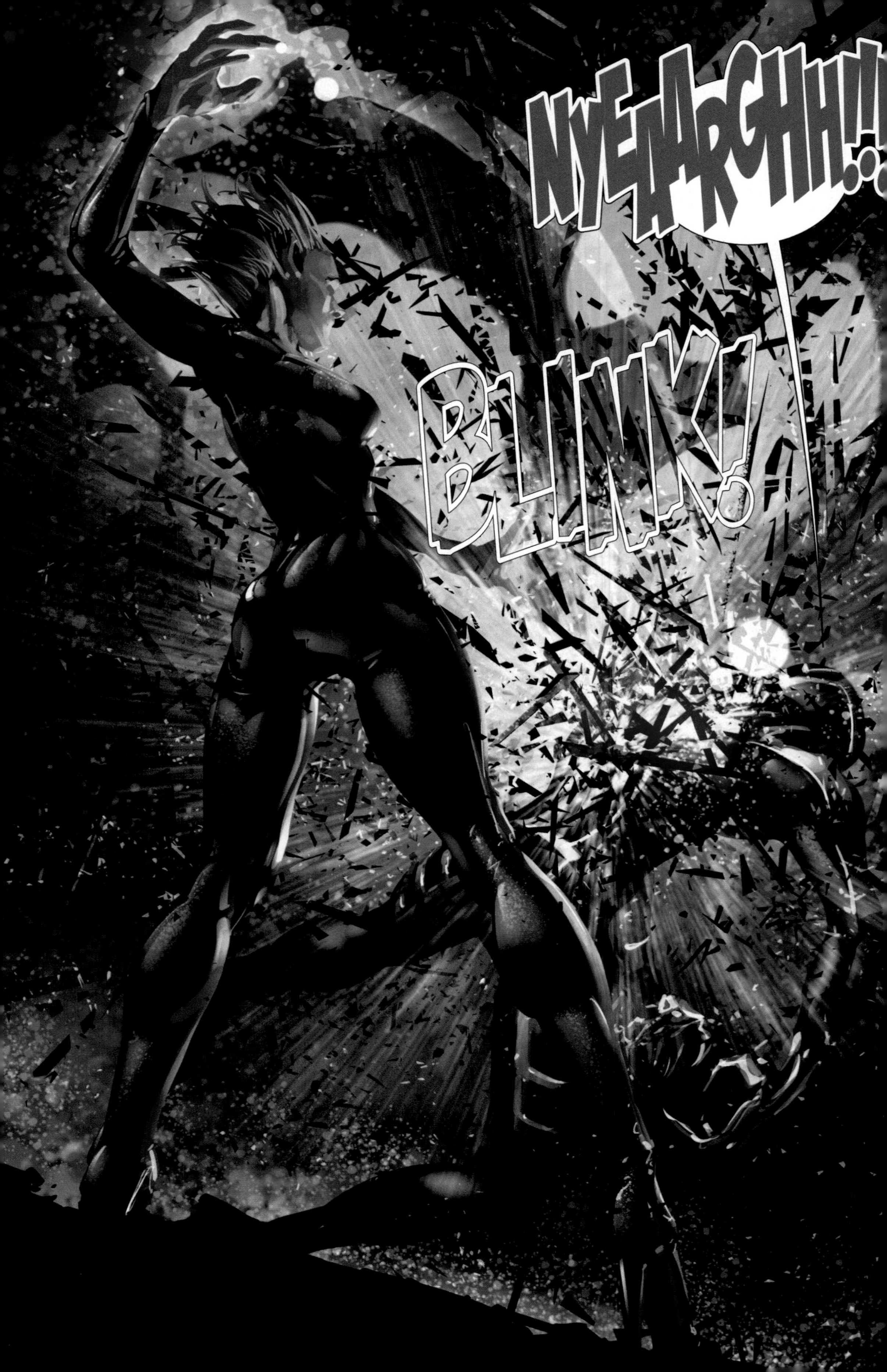
NYEAARGHH!!
BLINK!

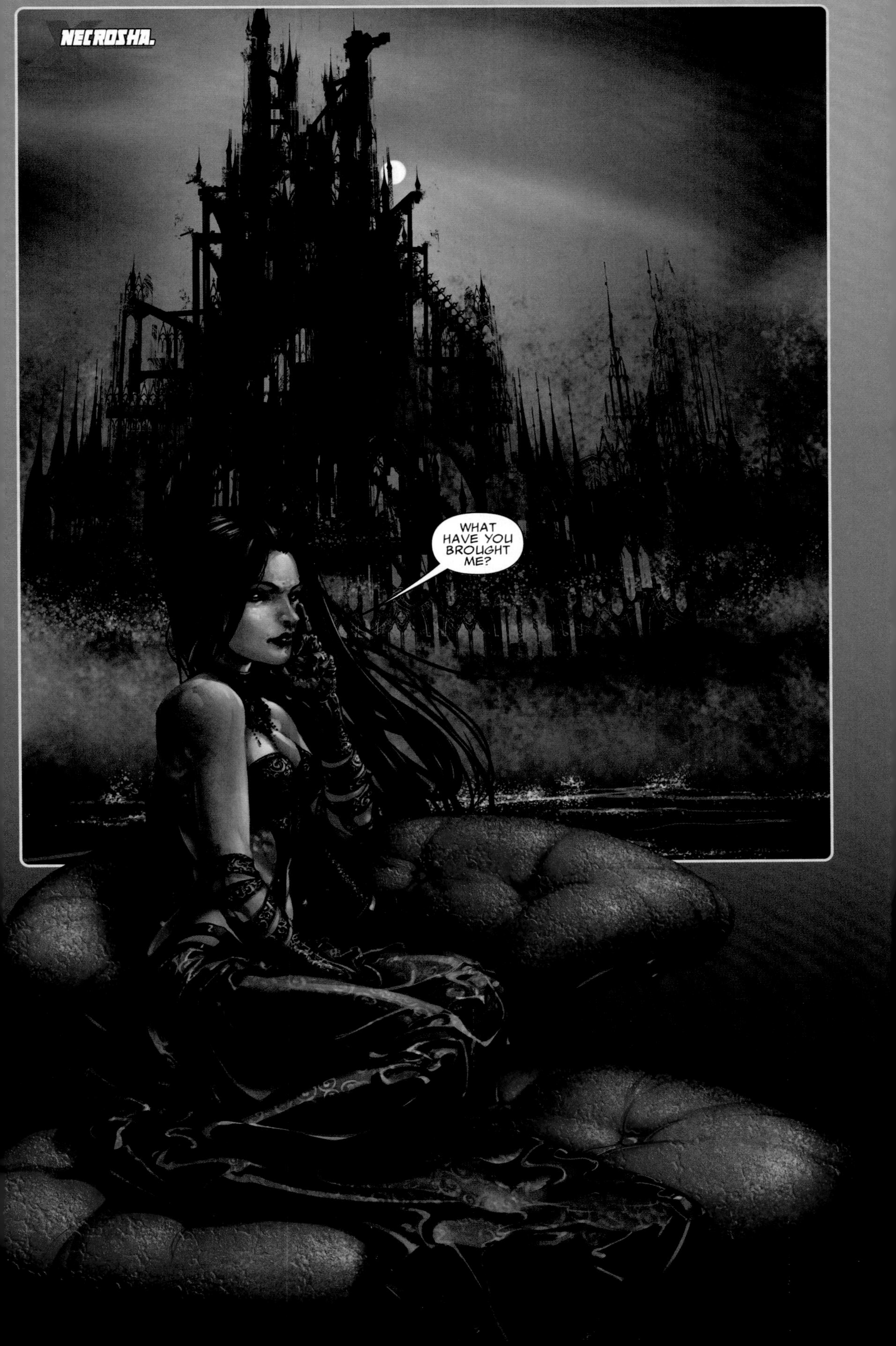
NECROSHA.
WHAT HAVE YOU BROUGHT ME?

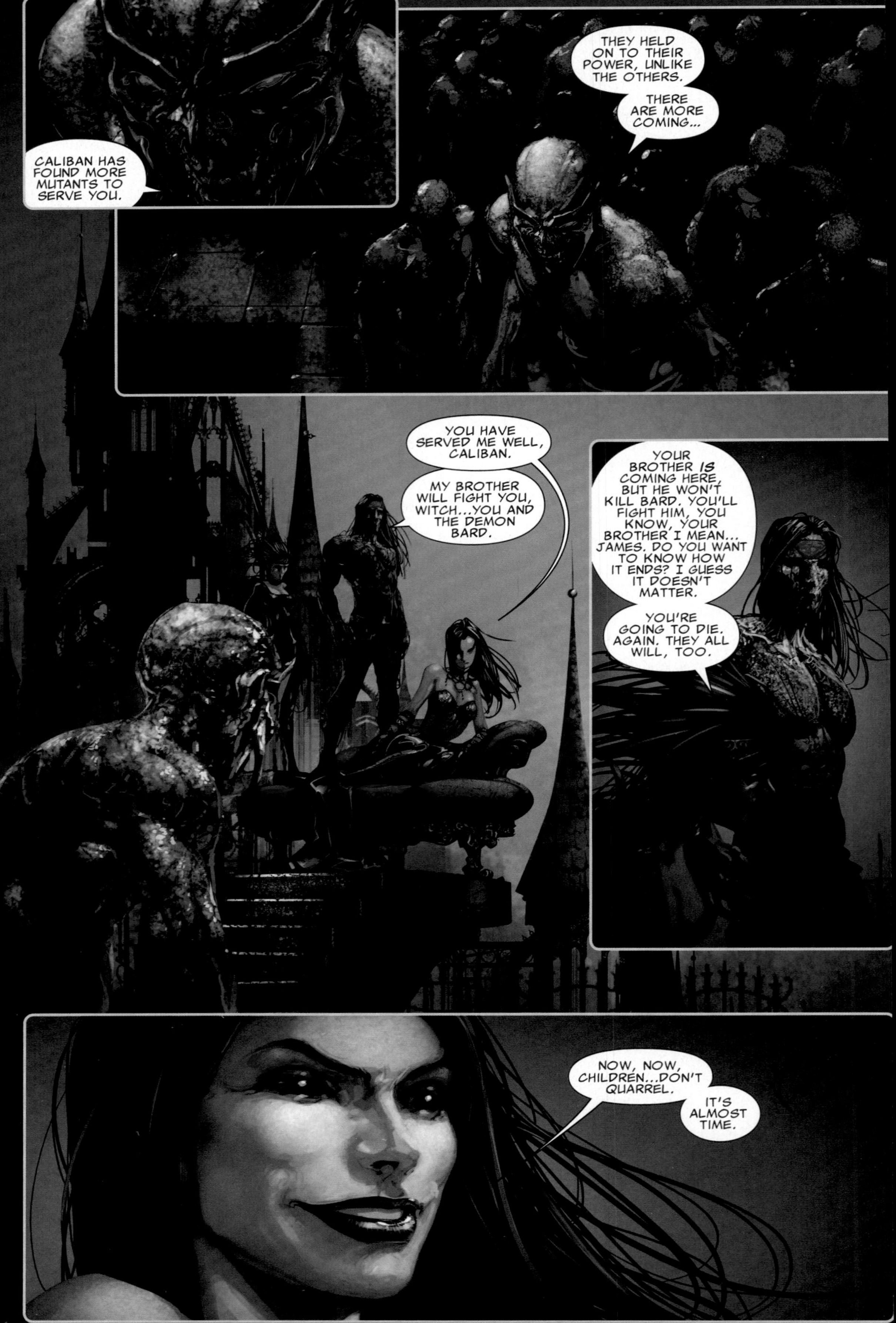
CALIBAN HAS FOUND MORE MUTANTS TO SERVE YOU.
THEY HELD ON TO THEIR POWER, UNLIKE THE OTHERS.
THERE ARE MORE COMING...
YOU HAVE SERVED ME WELL, CALIBAN.
MY BROTHER WILL FIGHT YOU, WITCH...YOU AND THE DEMON BARD.
YOUR BROTHER *IS* COMING HERE, BUT HE WON'T KILL BARD. YOU'LL FIGHT HIM, YOU KNOW, YOUR BROTHER I MEAN... JAMES. DO YOU WANT TO KNOW HOW IT ENDS? I GUESS IT DOESN'T MATTER.
YOU'RE GOING TO DIE. AGAIN. THEY ALL WILL, TOO.
NOW, NOW, CHILDREN...DON'T QUARREL.
IT'S ALMOST TIME.

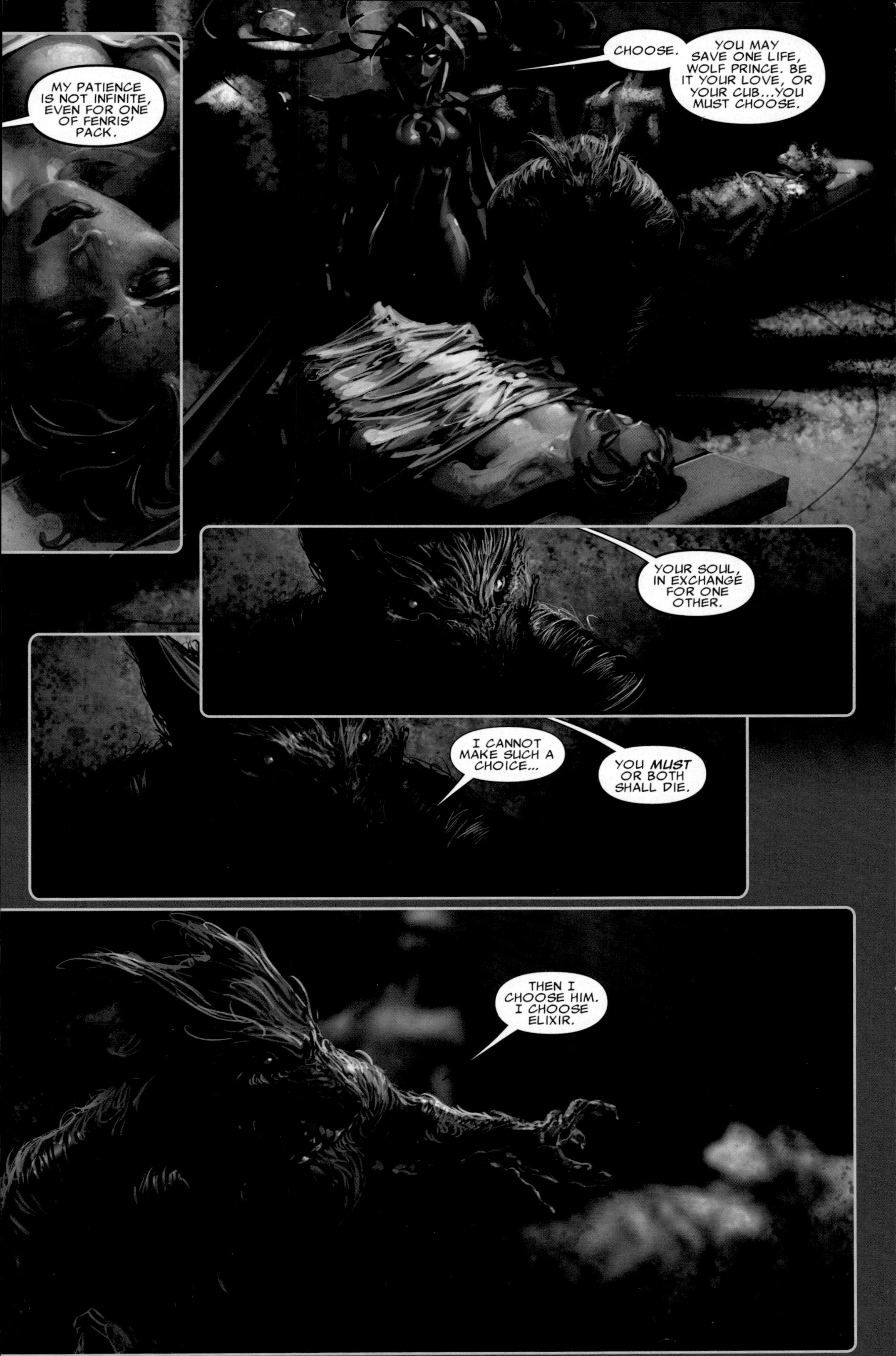
MY PATIENCE IS NOT INFINITE, EVEN FOR ONE OF FENRIS' PACK.
CHOOSE.
YOU MAY SAVE ONE LIFE, WOLF PRINCE. BE IT YOUR LOVE, OR YOUR CUB...YOU MUST CHOOSE.
YOUR SOUL, IN EXCHANGE FOR ONE OTHER.
I CANNOT MAKE SUCH A CHOICE...
YOU **MUST** OR BOTH SHALL DIE.
THEN I CHOOSE HIM. I CHOOSE ELIXIR.

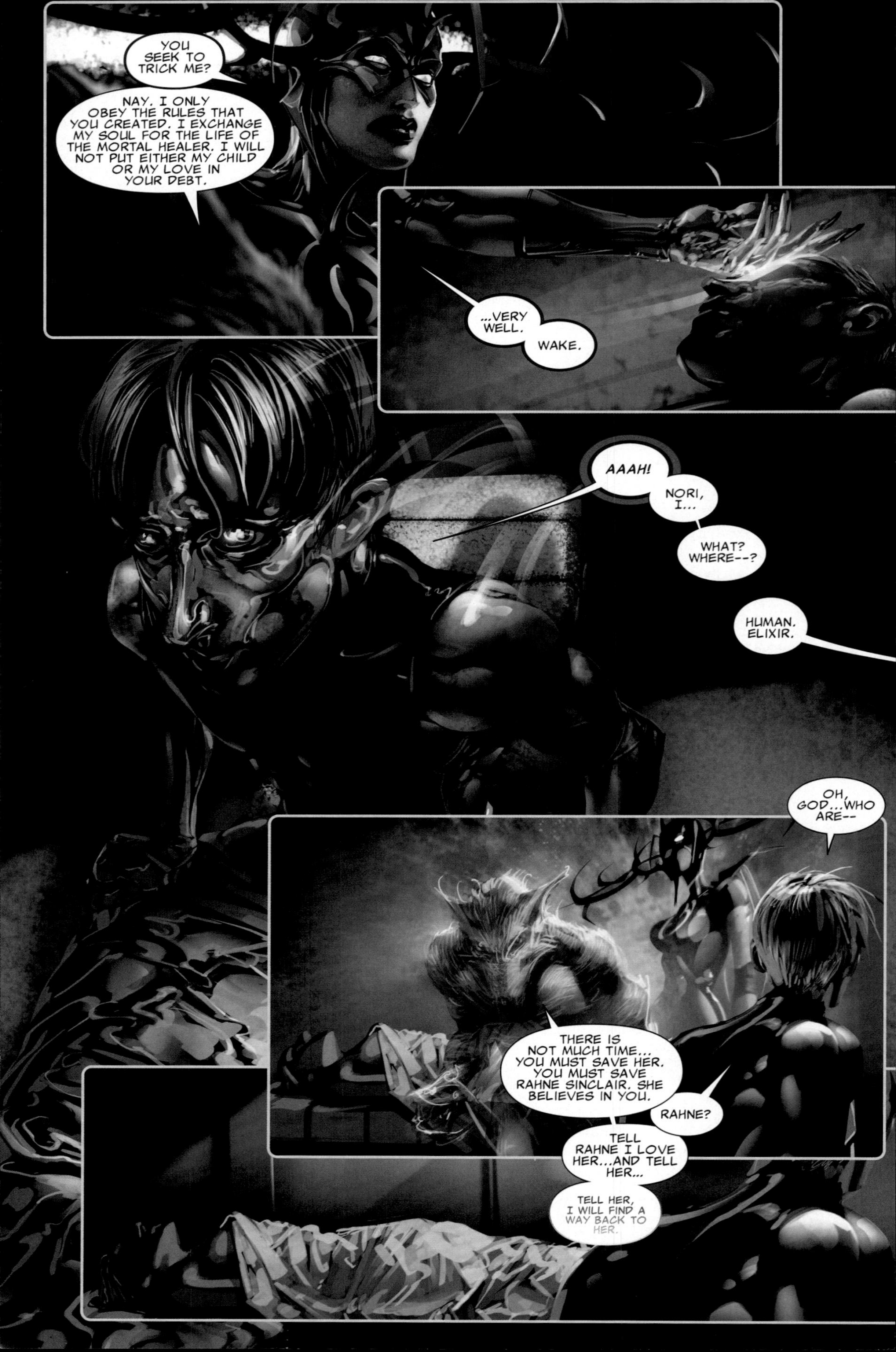
YOU SEEK TO TRICK ME?
NAY. I ONLY OBEY THE RULES THAT YOU CREATED. I EXCHANGE MY SOUL FOR THE LIFE OF THE MORTAL HEALER. I WILL NOT PUT EITHER MY CHILD OR MY LOVE IN YOUR DEBT.
...VERY WELL.
WAKE.
AAAH!
NORI, I...
WHAT? WHERE--?
HUMAN. ELIXIR.
OH, GOD...WHO ARE--
THERE IS NOT MUCH TIME... YOU MUST SAVE HER. YOU MUST SAVE RAHNE SINCLAIR. SHE BELIEVES IN YOU.
RAHNE?
TELL RAHNE I LOVE HER...AND TELL HER...
TELL HER, I WILL FIND A WAY BACK TO HER.

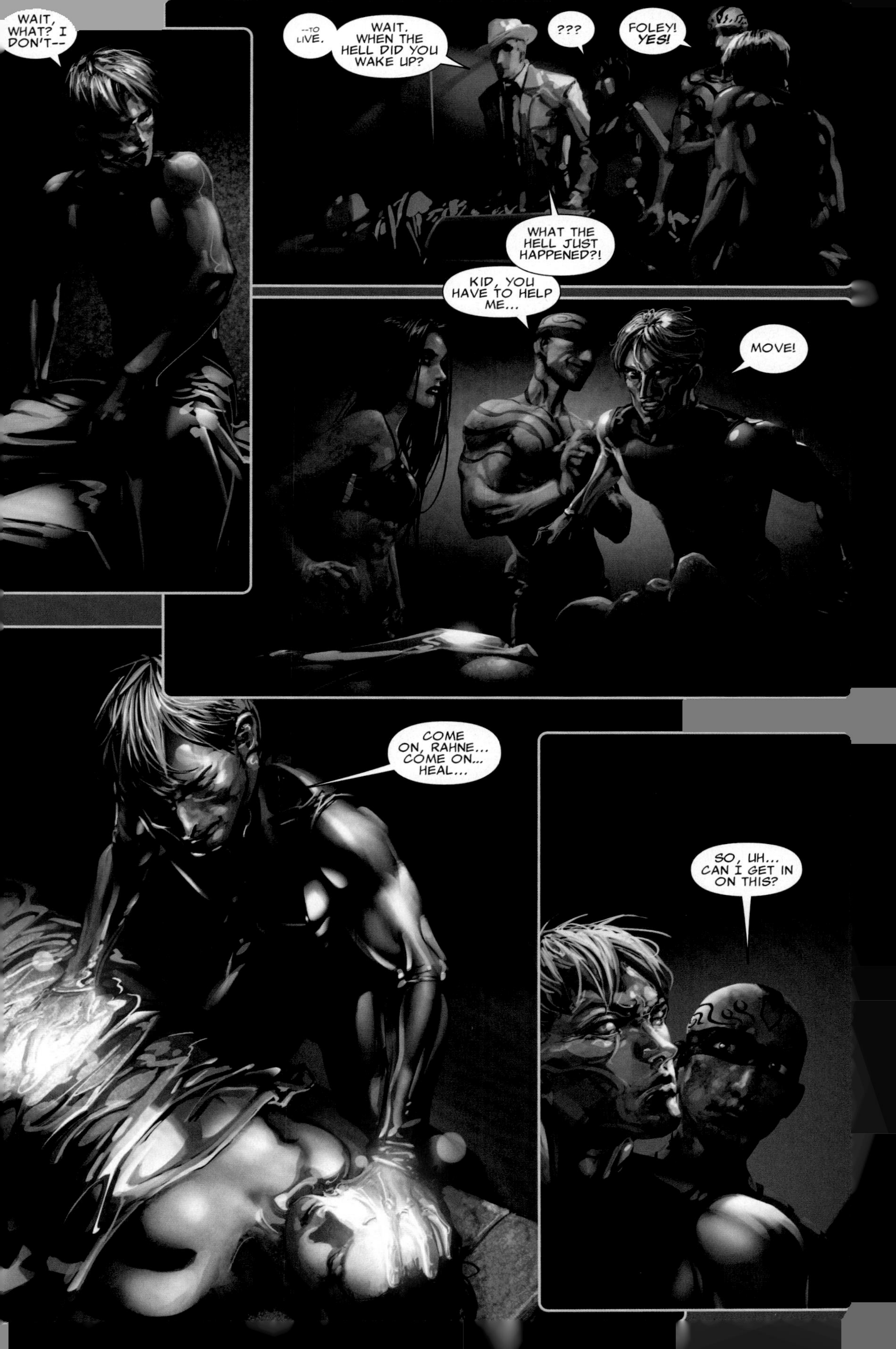
WAIT, WHAT? I DON'T--
--TO LIVE.
WAIT. WHEN THE HELL DID YOU WAKE UP?
???
FOLEY! YES!
WHAT THE HELL JUST HAPPENED?!
KID, YOU HAVE TO HELP ME...
MOVE!
COME ON, RAHNE... COME ON... HEAL...
SO, UH... CAN I GET IN ON THIS?

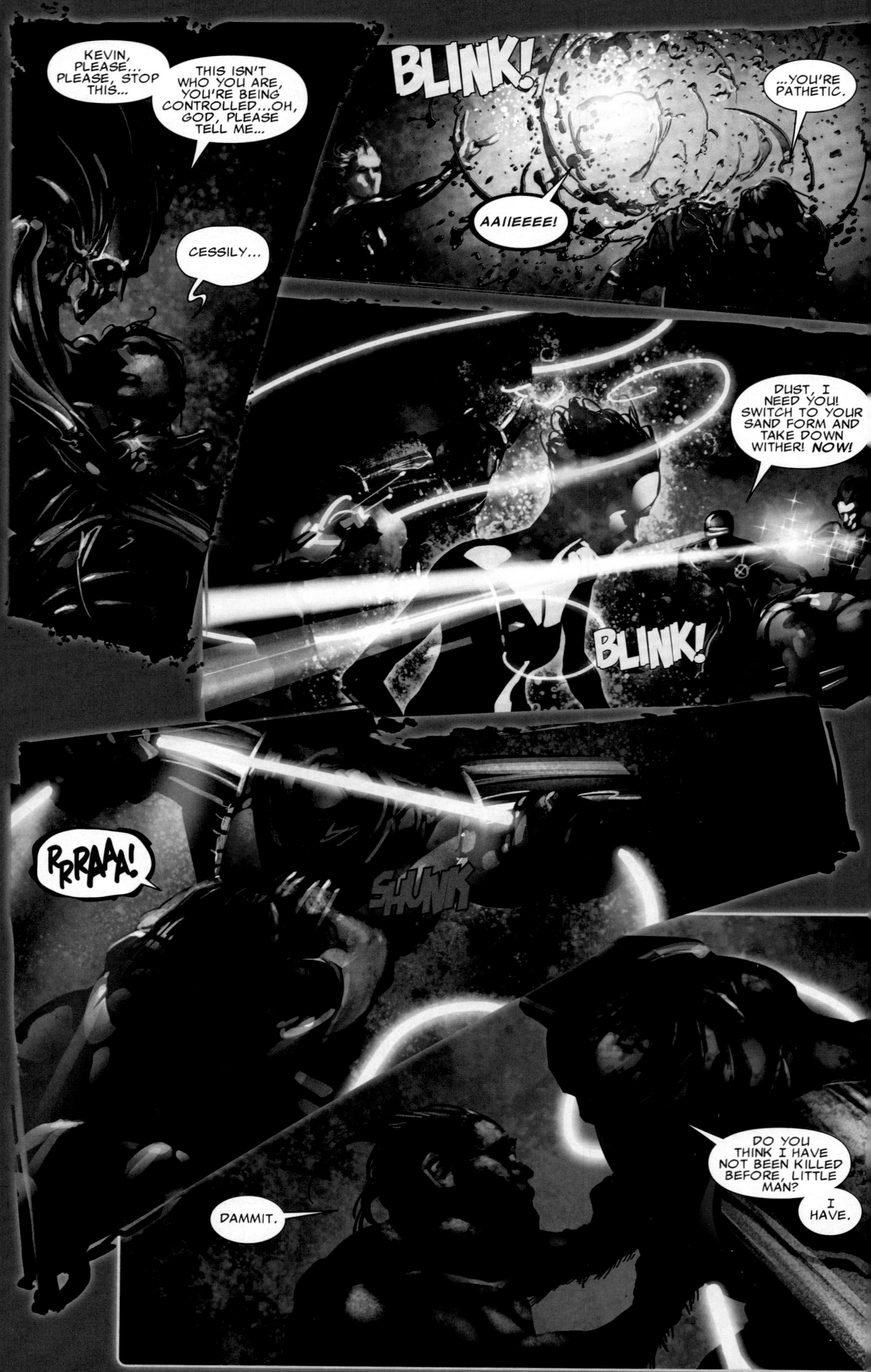
KEVIN, PLEASE... PLEASE, STOP THIS...
THIS ISN'T WHO YOU ARE, YOU'RE BEING CONTROLLED...OH, GOD, PLEASE TELL ME...
CESSILY...
BLINK!
...YOU'RE PATHETIC.
AAIIEEEE!
DUST, I NEED YOU! SWITCH TO YOUR SAND FORM AND TAKE DOWN WITHER! NOW!
BLINK!
RRRAAA!
SHUNK
DO YOU THINK I HAVE NOT BEEN KILLED BEFORE, LITTLE MAN?
I HAVE.
DAMMIT.

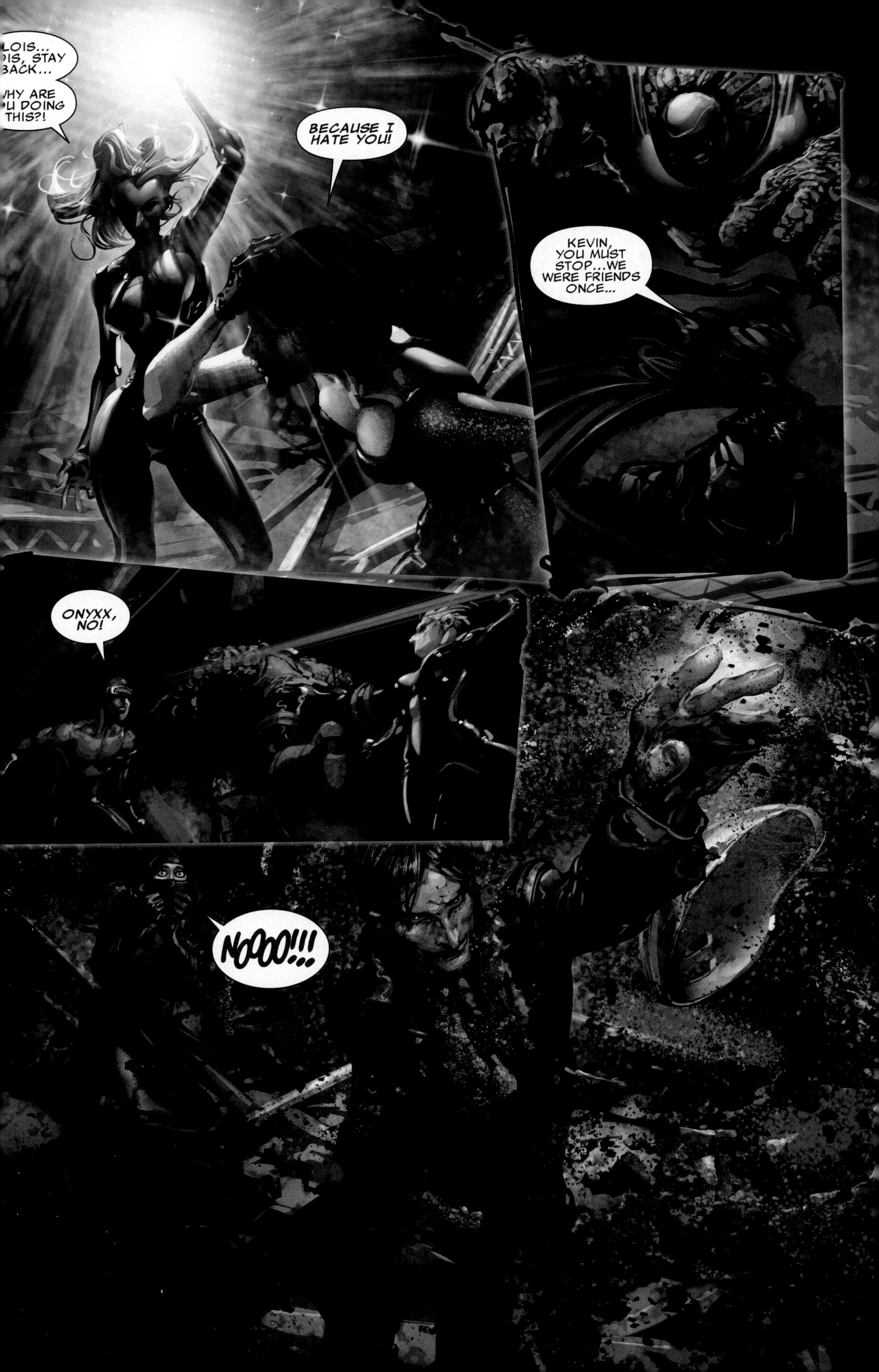
LOIS... OIS, STAY BACK...
HY ARE U DOING THIS?!
BECAUSE I HATE YOU!
KEVIN, YOU MUST STOP...WE WERE FRIENDS ONCE...
ONYXX, NO!
NOOOO!!!

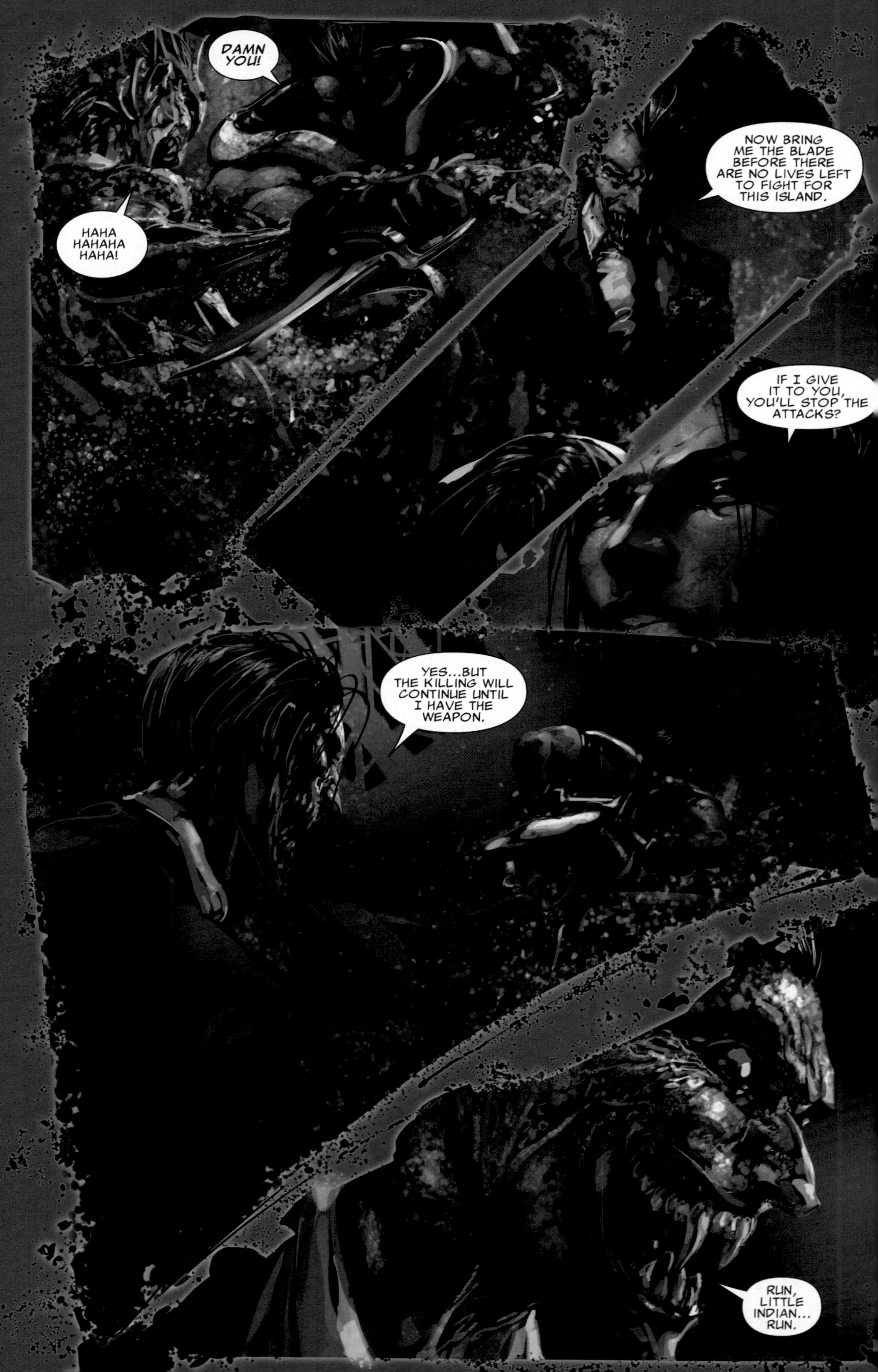
DAMN YOU!
HAHA HAHAHA HAHA!
NOW BRING ME THE BLADE BEFORE THERE ARE NO LIVES LEFT TO FIGHT FOR THIS ISLAND.
IF I GIVE IT TO YOU, YOU'LL STOP THE ATTACKS?
YES...BUT THE KILLING WILL CONTINUE UNTIL I HAVE THE WEAPON.
RUN, LITTLE INDIAN... RUN.

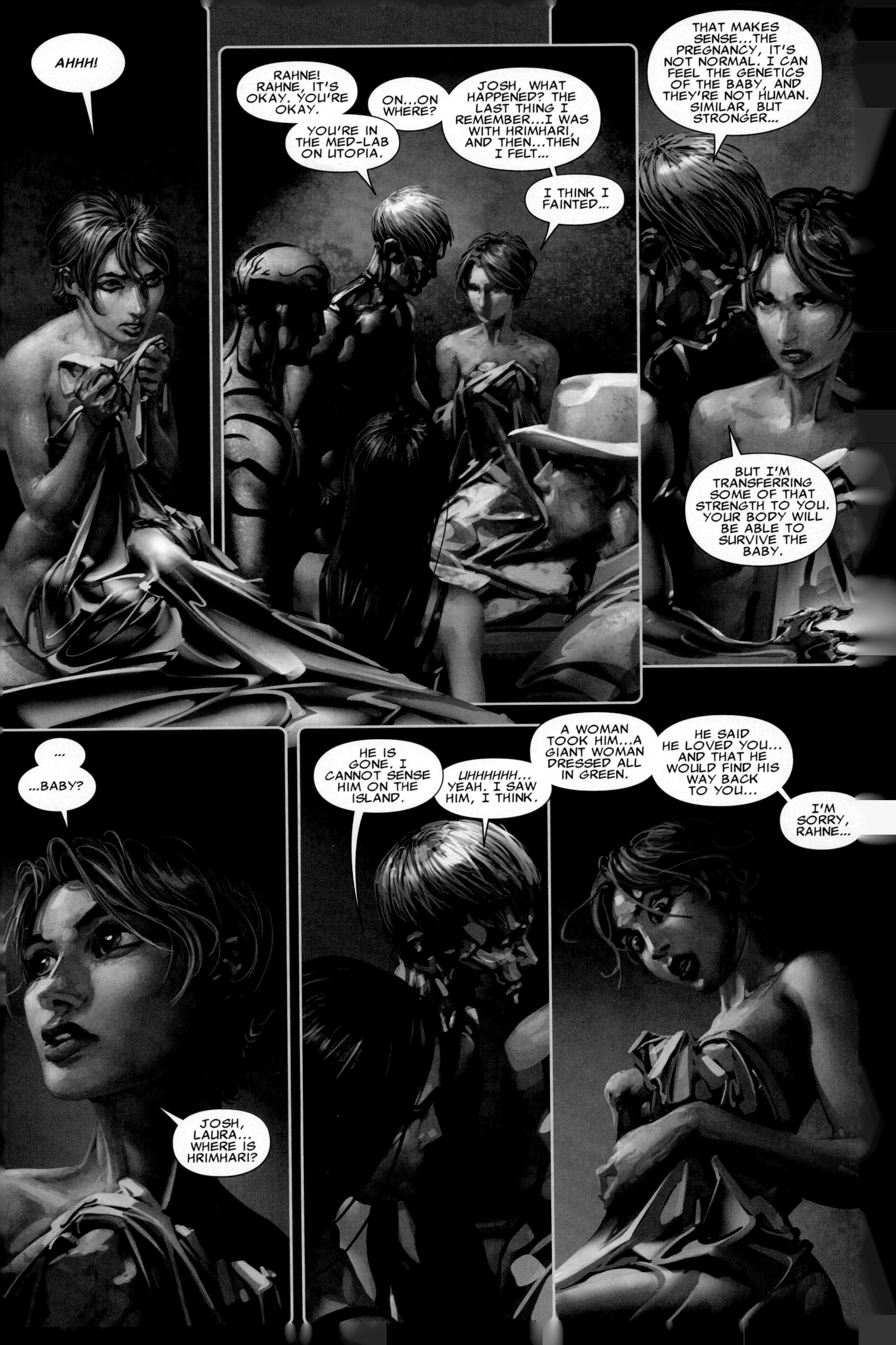
AHHH!
RAHNE! RAHNE, IT'S OKAY. YOU'RE OKAY.
ON...ON WHERE?
YOU'RE IN THE MED-LAB ON UTOPIA.
JOSH, WHAT HAPPENED? THE LAST THING I REMEMBER...I WAS WITH HRIMHARI, AND THEN...THEN I FELT...
I THINK I FAINTED...
THAT MAKES SENSE...THE PREGNANCY, IT'S NOT NORMAL. I CAN FEEL THE GENETICS OF THE BABY, AND THEY'RE NOT HUMAN. SIMILAR, BUT STRONGER...
BUT I'M TRANSFERRING SOME OF THAT STRENGTH TO YOU. YOUR BODY WILL BE ABLE TO SURVIVE THE BABY.
...
...BABY?
JOSH, LAURA... WHERE IS HRIMHARI?
HE IS GONE. I CANNOT SENSE HIM ON THE ISLAND.
UHHHHHH... YEAH. I SAW HIM, I THINK.
A WOMAN TOOK HIM...A GIANT WOMAN DRESSED ALL IN GREEN.
HE SAID HE LOVED YOU... AND THAT HE WOULD FIND HIS WAY BACK TO YOU...
I'M SORRY, RAHNE...

UHNN!

THOOM!

COME ON...
COME ON...
WHERE--

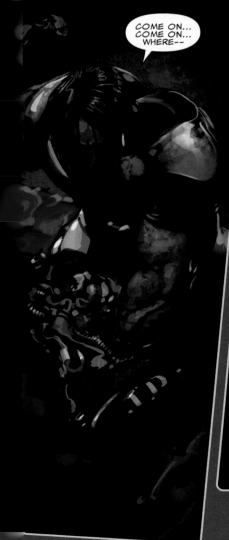

GOT
YOU.

YOU WANT
THIS KNIFE, BARD?
I'M GONNA PUT IT
RIGHT IN YOUR
DAMN--

BLINK!

--HEAD?!

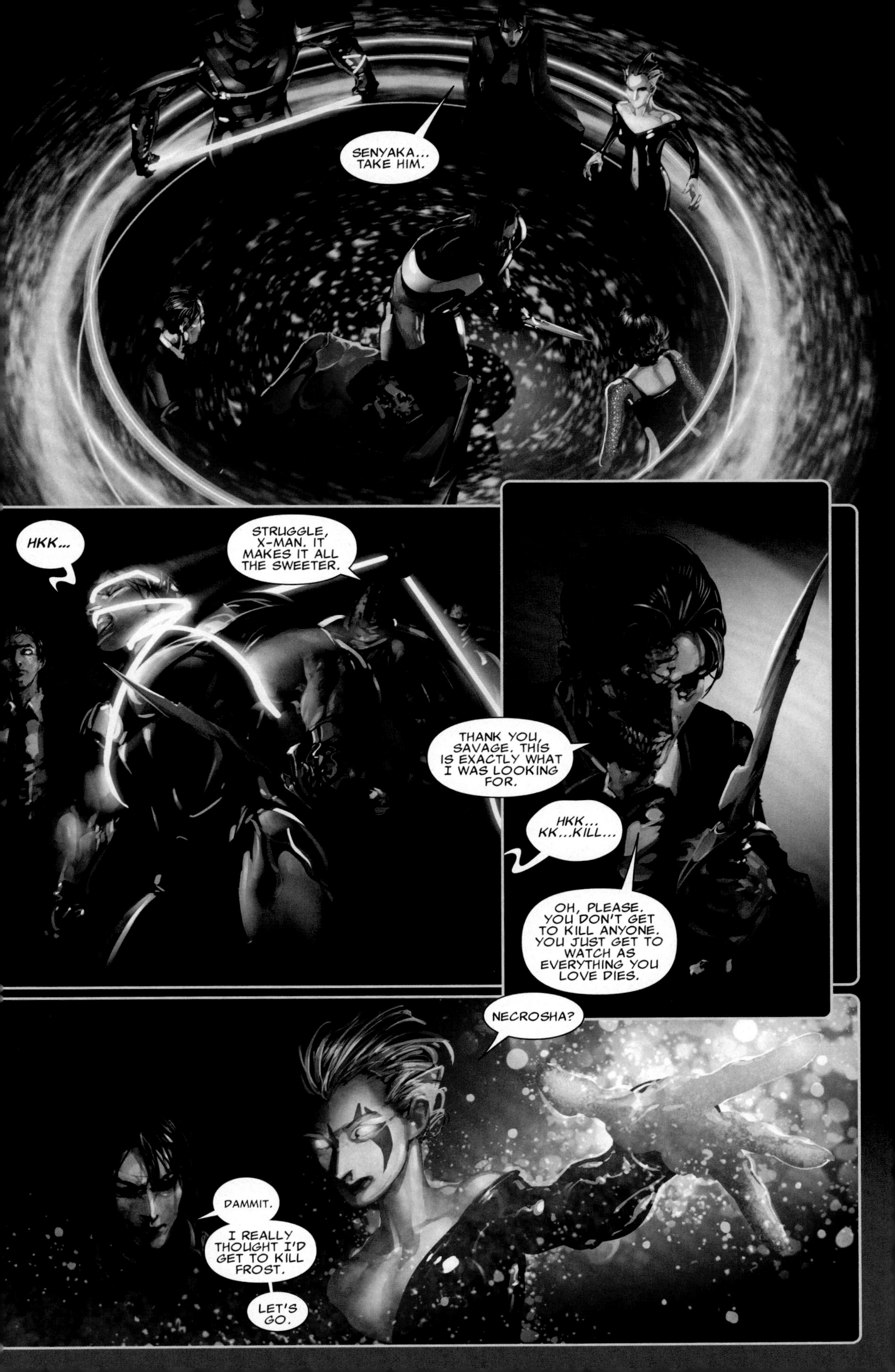
SENYAKA... TAKE HIM.
HKK...
STRUGGLE, X-MAN. IT MAKES IT ALL THE SWEETER.
THANK YOU, SAVAGE. THIS IS EXACTLY WHAT I WAS LOOKING FOR.
HKK... KK...KILL...
OH, PLEASE. YOU DON'T GET TO KILL ANYONE. YOU JUST GET TO WATCH AS EVERYTHING YOU LOVE DIES.
NECROSHA?
DAMMIT.
I REALLY THOUGHT I'D GET TO KILL FROST.
LET'S GO.

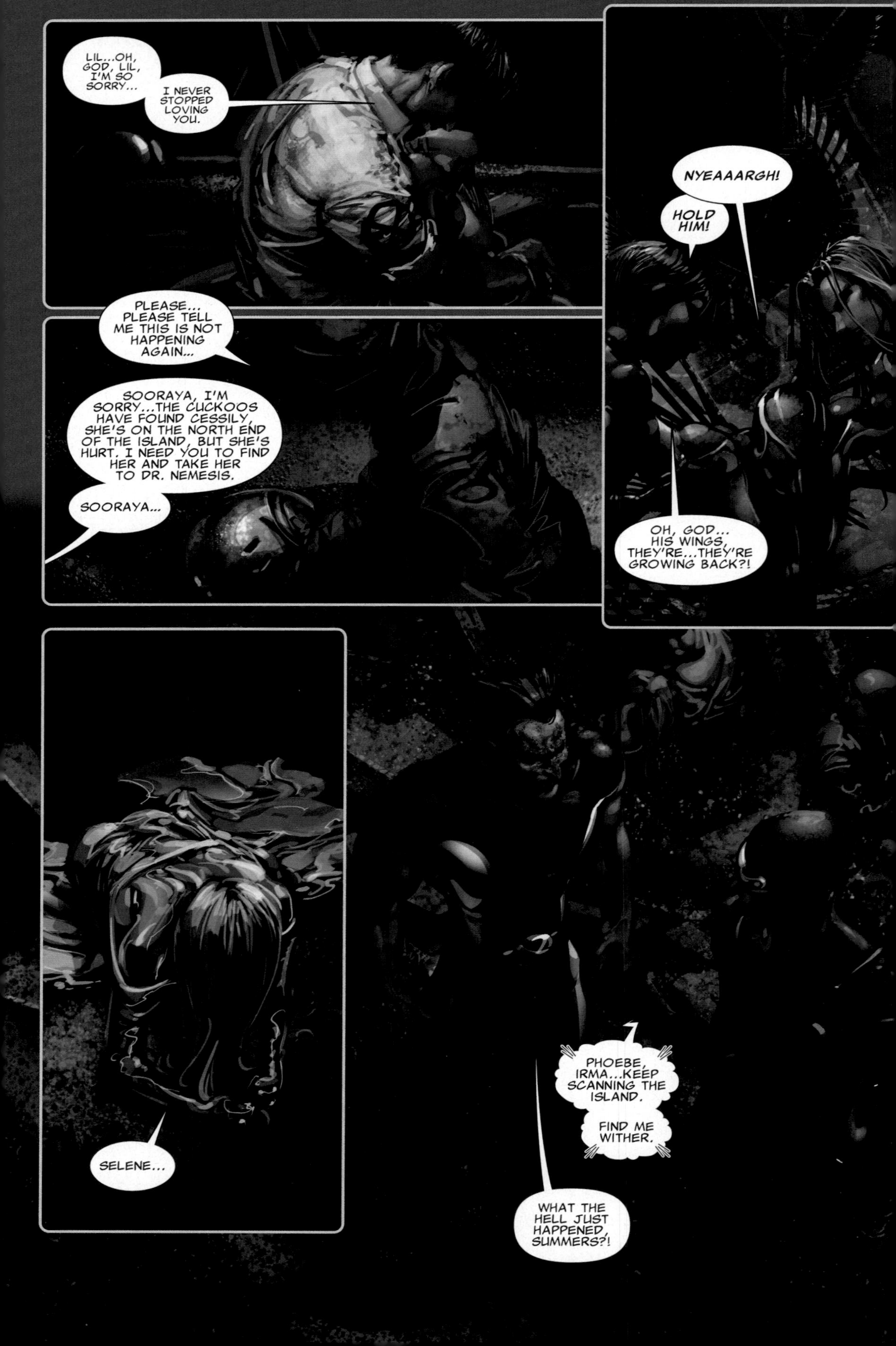

LIL...OH, GOD, LIL, I'M SO SORRY...
I NEVER STOPPED LOVING YOU.
NYEAAARGH!
HOLD HIM!
OH, GOD... HIS WINGS, THEY'RE...THEY'RE GROWING BACK?!
PLEASE... PLEASE TELL ME THIS IS NOT HAPPENING AGAIN...
SOORAYA, I'M SORRY...THE CUCKOOS HAVE FOUND CESSILY, SHE'S ON THE NORTH END OF THE ISLAND, BUT SHE'S HURT. I NEED YOU TO FIND HER AND TAKE HER TO DR. NEMESIS.
SOORAYA...
SELENE...
PHOEBE, IRMA...KEEP SCANNING THE ISLAND.
FIND ME WITHER.
WHAT THE HELL JUST HAPPENED, SUMMERS?!

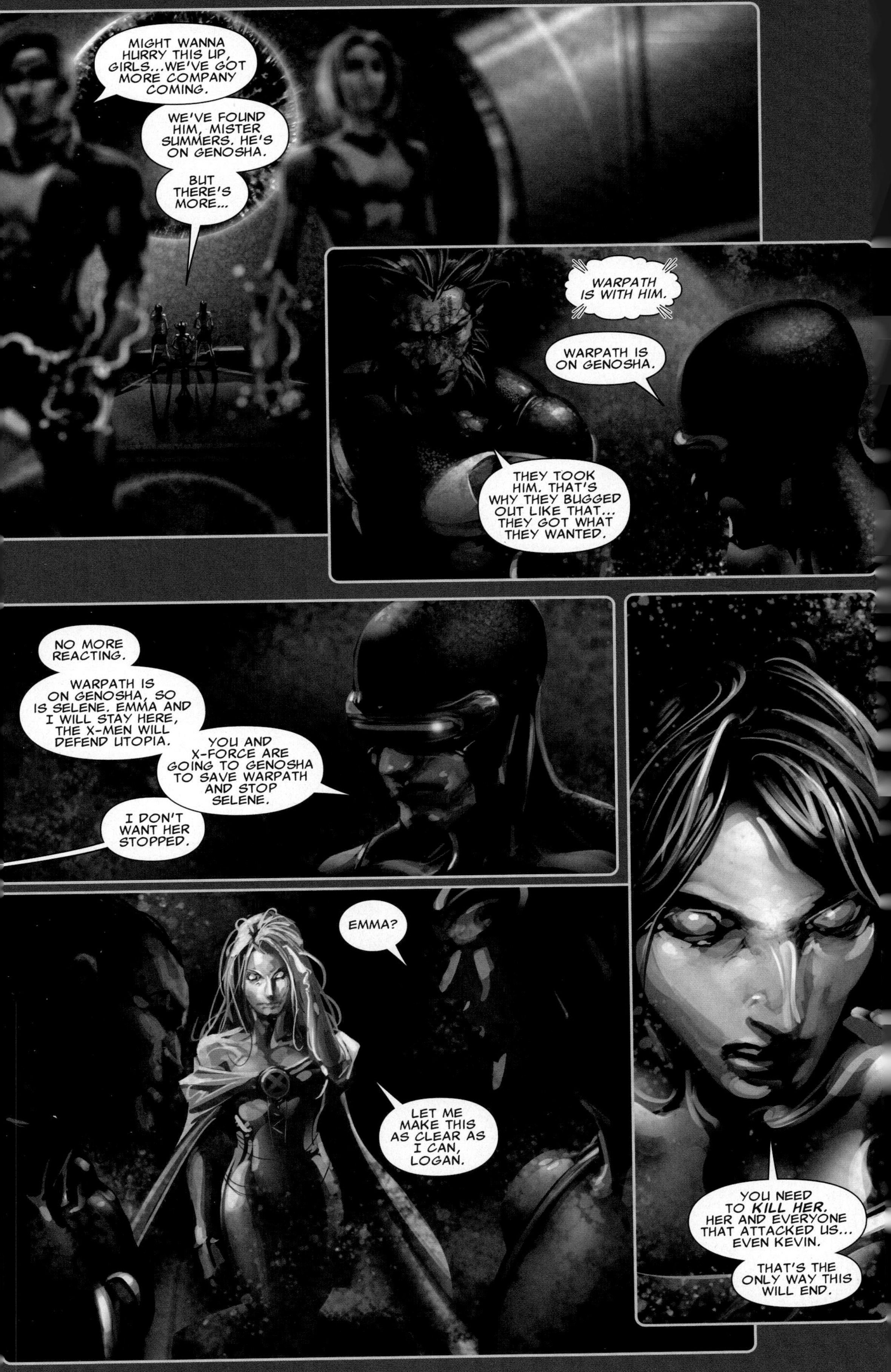
MIGHT WANNA HURRY THIS UP, GIRLS...WE'VE GOT MORE COMPANY COMING.
WE'VE FOUND HIM, MISTER SUMMERS. HE'S ON GENOSHA.
BUT THERE'S MORE...
WARPATH IS WITH HIM.
WARPATH IS ON GENOSHA.
THEY TOOK HIM. THAT'S WHY THEY BUGGED OUT LIKE THAT... THEY GOT WHAT THEY WANTED.
NO MORE REACTING.
WARPATH IS ON GENOSHA, SO IS SELENE. EMMA AND I WILL STAY HERE, THE X-MEN WILL DEFEND UTOPIA.
YOU AND X-FORCE ARE GOING TO GENOSHA TO SAVE WARPATH AND STOP SELENE.
I DON'T WANT HER STOPPED.
YOU NEED TO KILL HER. HER AND EVERYONE THAT ATTACKED US... EVEN KEVIN.
THAT'S THE ONLY WAY THIS WILL END.
EMMA?
LET ME MAKE THIS AS CLEAR AS I CAN, LOGAN.

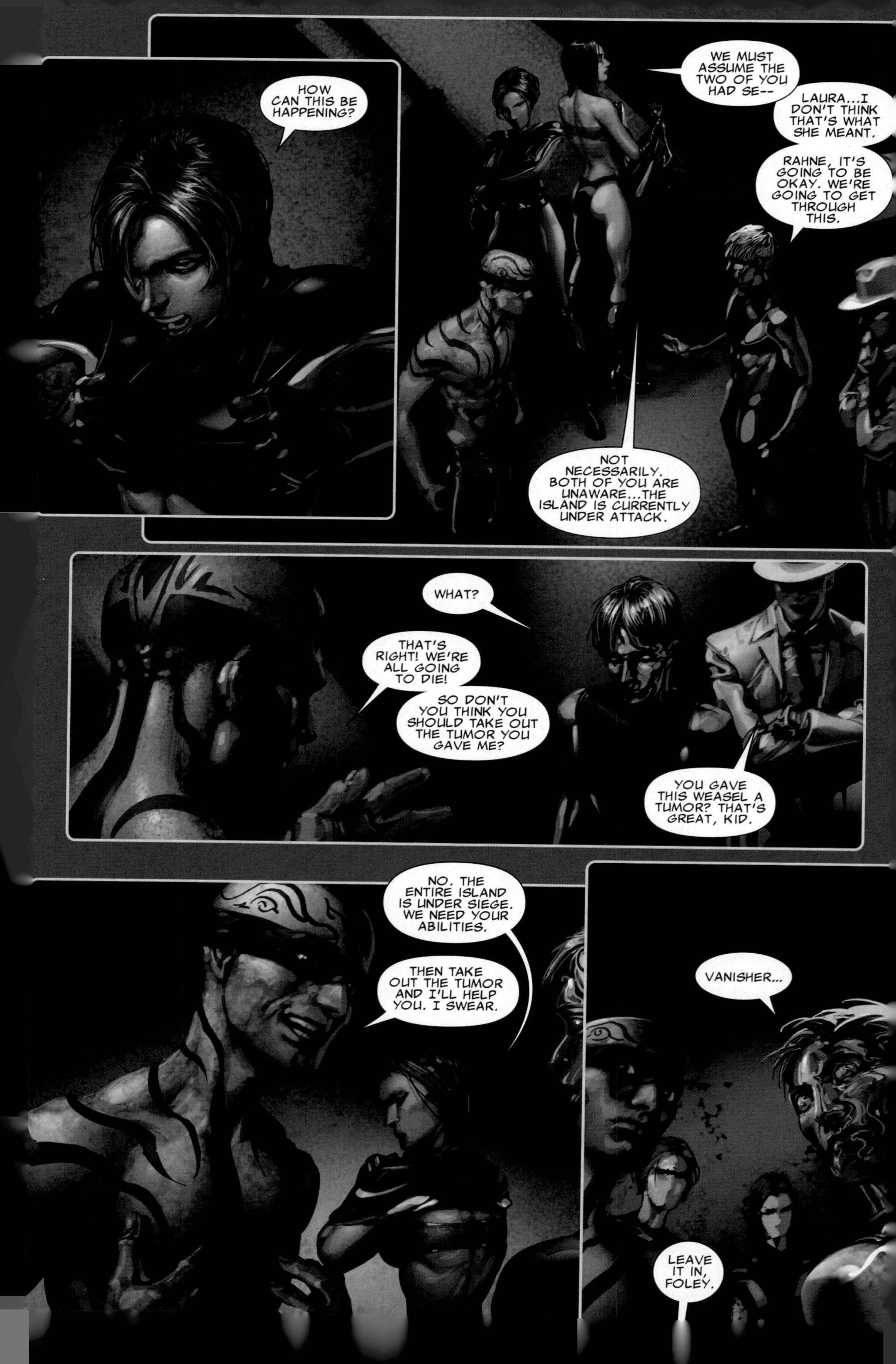
HOW CAN THIS BE HAPPENING?
WE MUST ASSUME THE TWO OF YOU HAD SE--
LAURA...I DON'T THINK THAT'S WHAT SHE MEANT.
RAHNE, IT'S GOING TO BE OKAY. WE'RE GOING TO GET THROUGH THIS.
NOT NECESSARILY. BOTH OF YOU ARE UNAWARE...THE ISLAND IS CURRENTLY UNDER ATTACK.
WHAT?
THAT'S RIGHT! WE'RE ALL GOING TO DIE!
SO DON'T YOU THINK YOU SHOULD TAKE OUT THE TUMOR YOU GAVE ME?
YOU GAVE THIS WEASEL A TUMOR? THAT'S GREAT, KID.
NO. THE ENTIRE ISLAND IS UNDER SIEGE. WE NEED YOUR ABILITIES.
THEN TAKE OUT THE TUMOR AND I'LL HELP YOU. I SWEAR.
VANISHER...
LEAVE IT IN, FOLEY.

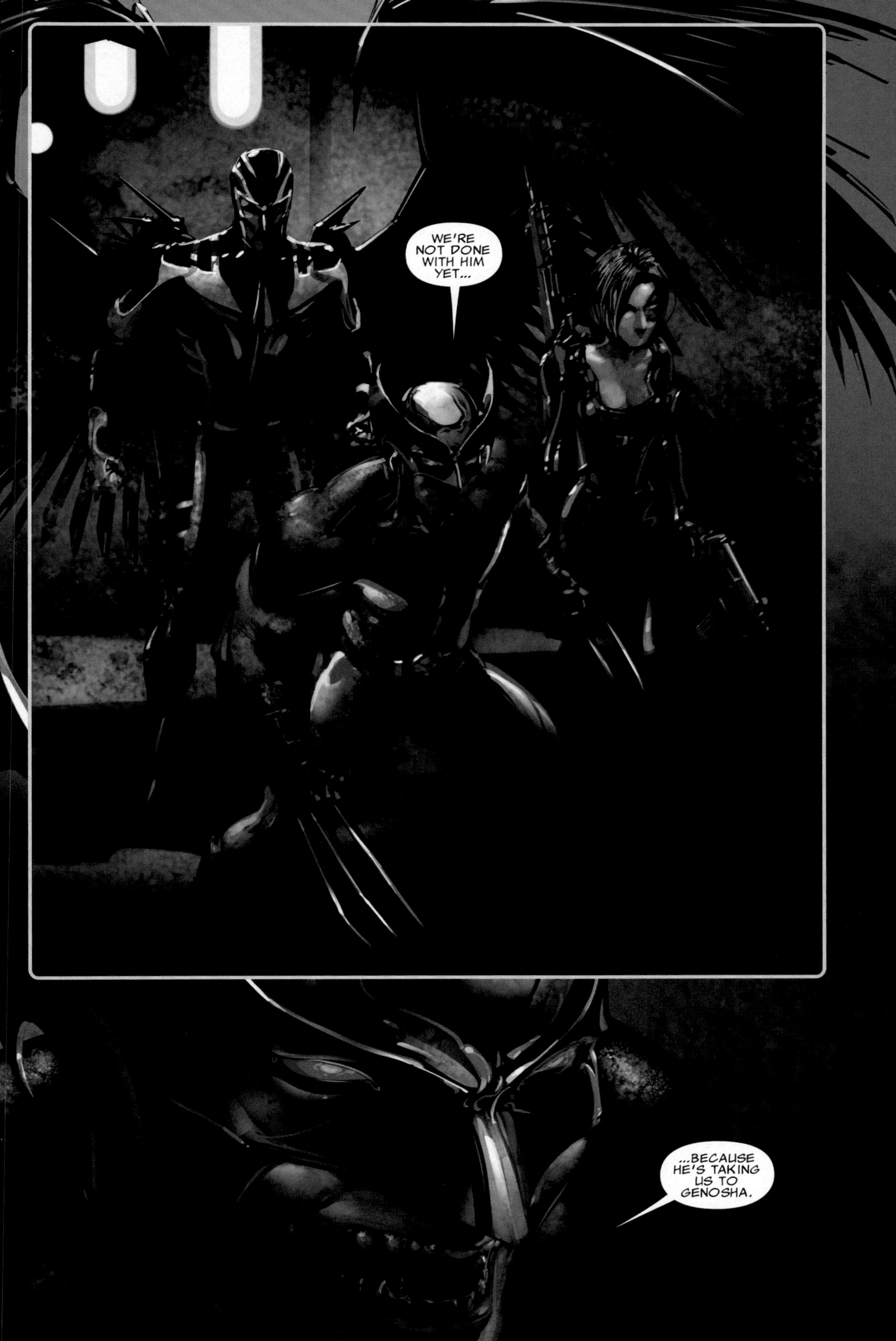
WE'RE NOT DONE WITH HIM YET...
...BECAUSE HE'S TAKING US TO GENOSHA.

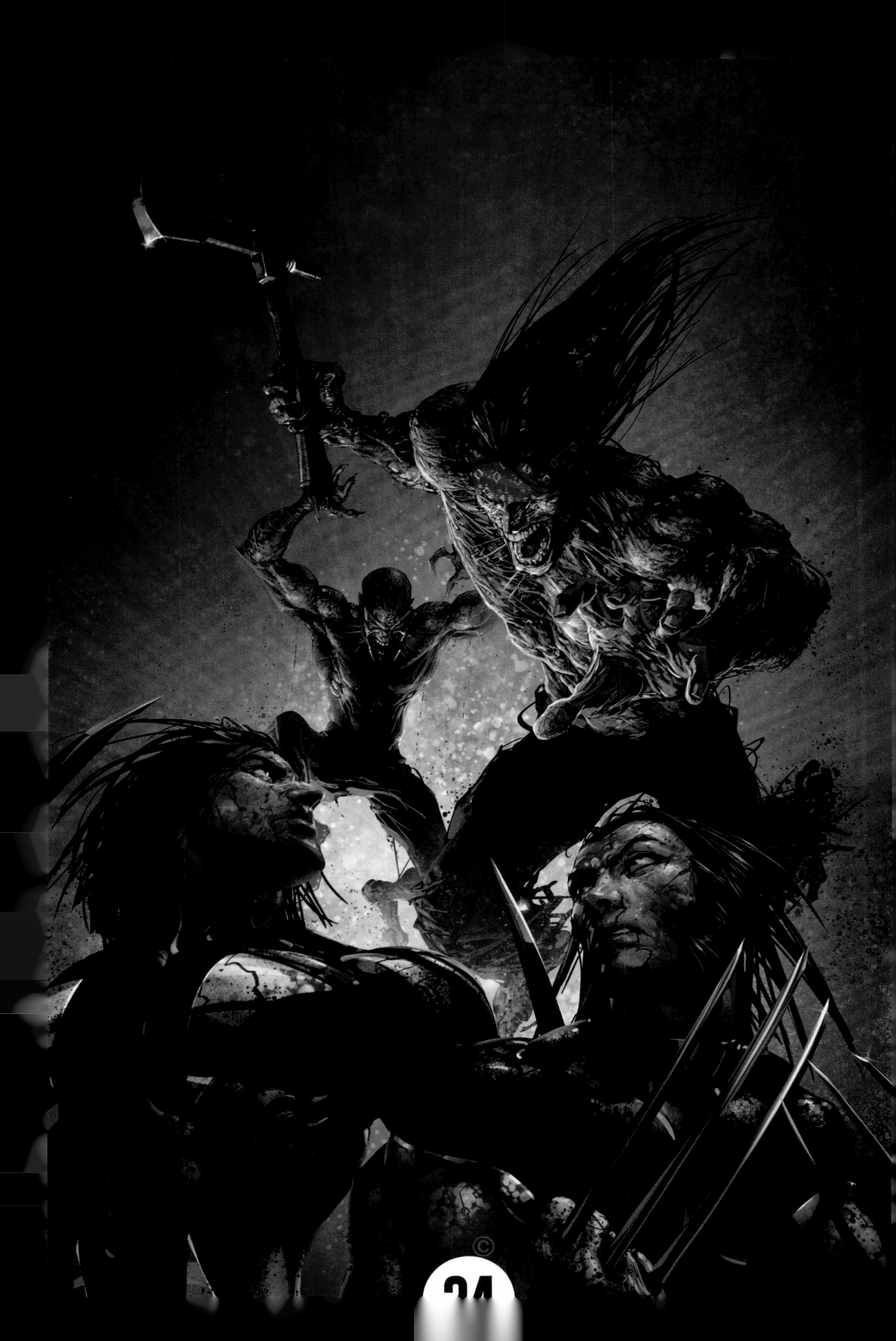

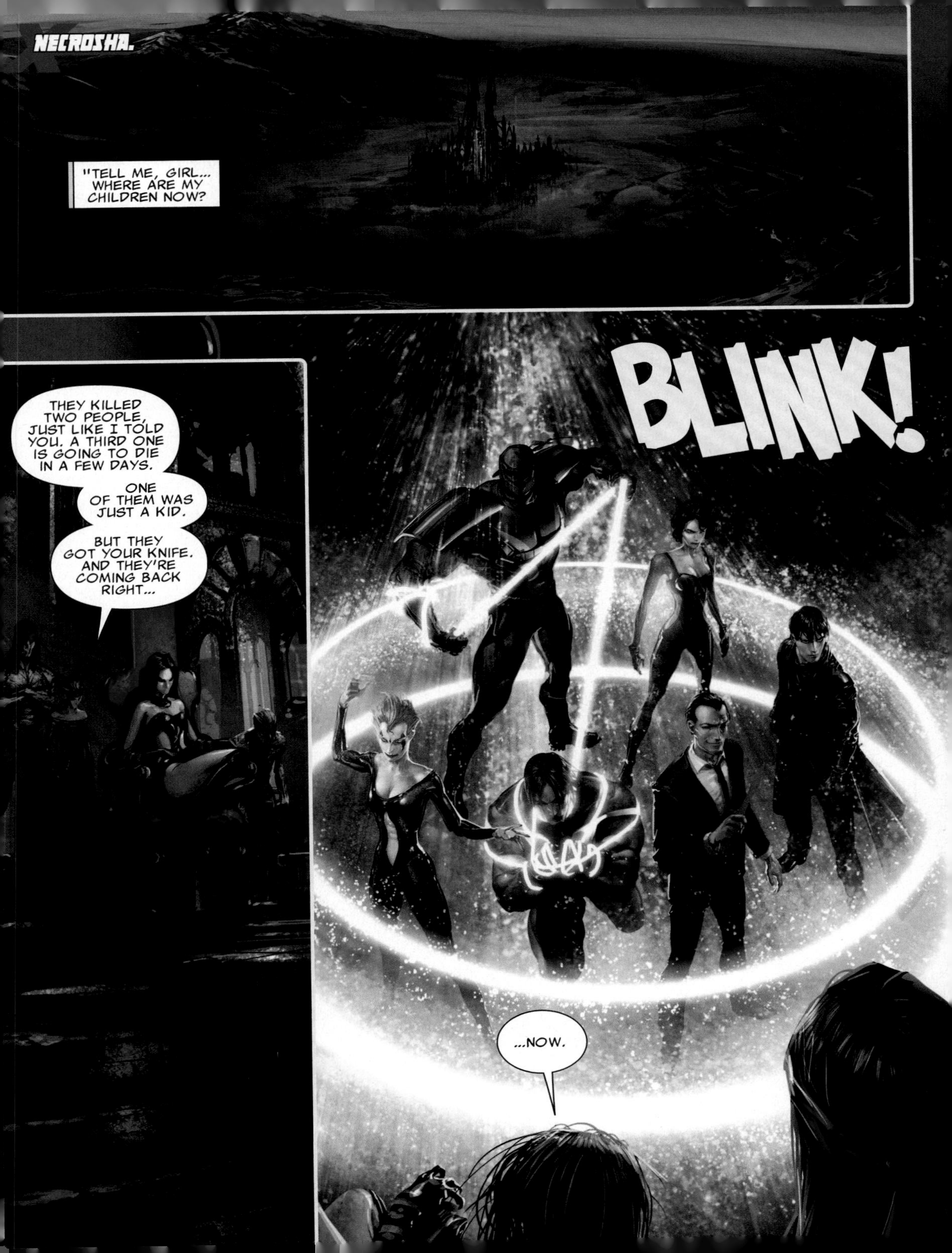
NECROSHA.
"TELL ME, GIRL... WHERE ARE MY CHILDREN NOW?
THEY KILLED TWO PEOPLE, JUST LIKE I TOLD YOU. A THIRD ONE IS GOING TO DIE IN A FEW DAYS.
ONE OF THEM WAS JUST A KID.
BUT THEY GOT YOUR KNIFE. AND THEY'RE COMING BACK RIGHT...
BLINK!
...NOW.

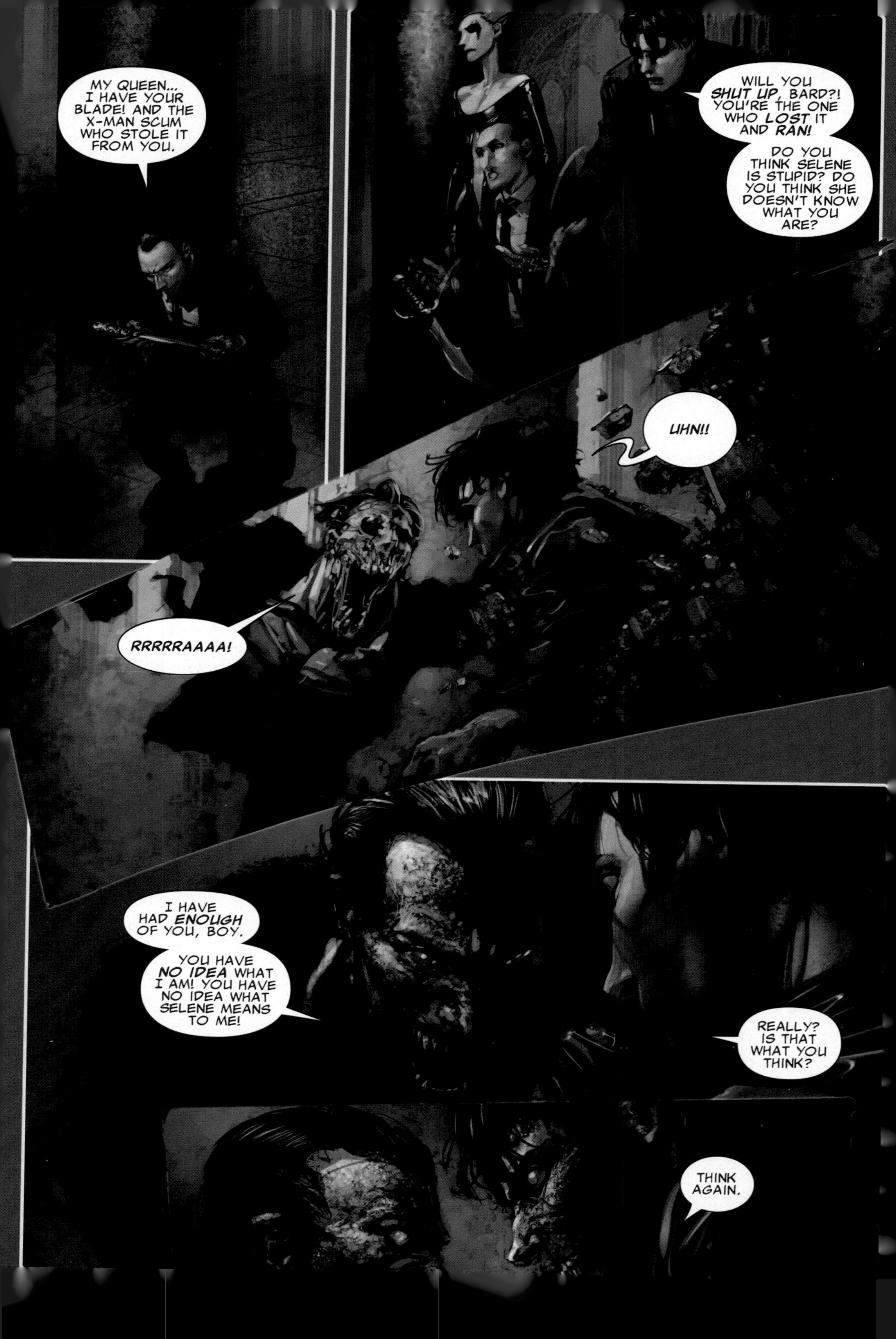
MY QUEEN... I HAVE YOUR BLADE! AND THE X-MAN SCUM WHO STOLE IT FROM YOU.
WILL YOU SHUT UP, BARD?! YOU'RE THE ONE WHO LOST IT AND RAN!
DO YOU THINK SELENE IS STUPID? DO YOU THINK SHE DOESN'T KNOW WHAT YOU ARE?
UHN!!
RRRRRAAAA!
I HAVE HAD ENOUGH OF YOU, BOY.
YOU HAVE NO IDEA WHAT I AM! YOU HAVE NO IDEA WHAT SELENE MEANS TO ME!
REALLY? IS THAT WHAT YOU THINK?
THINK AGAIN.

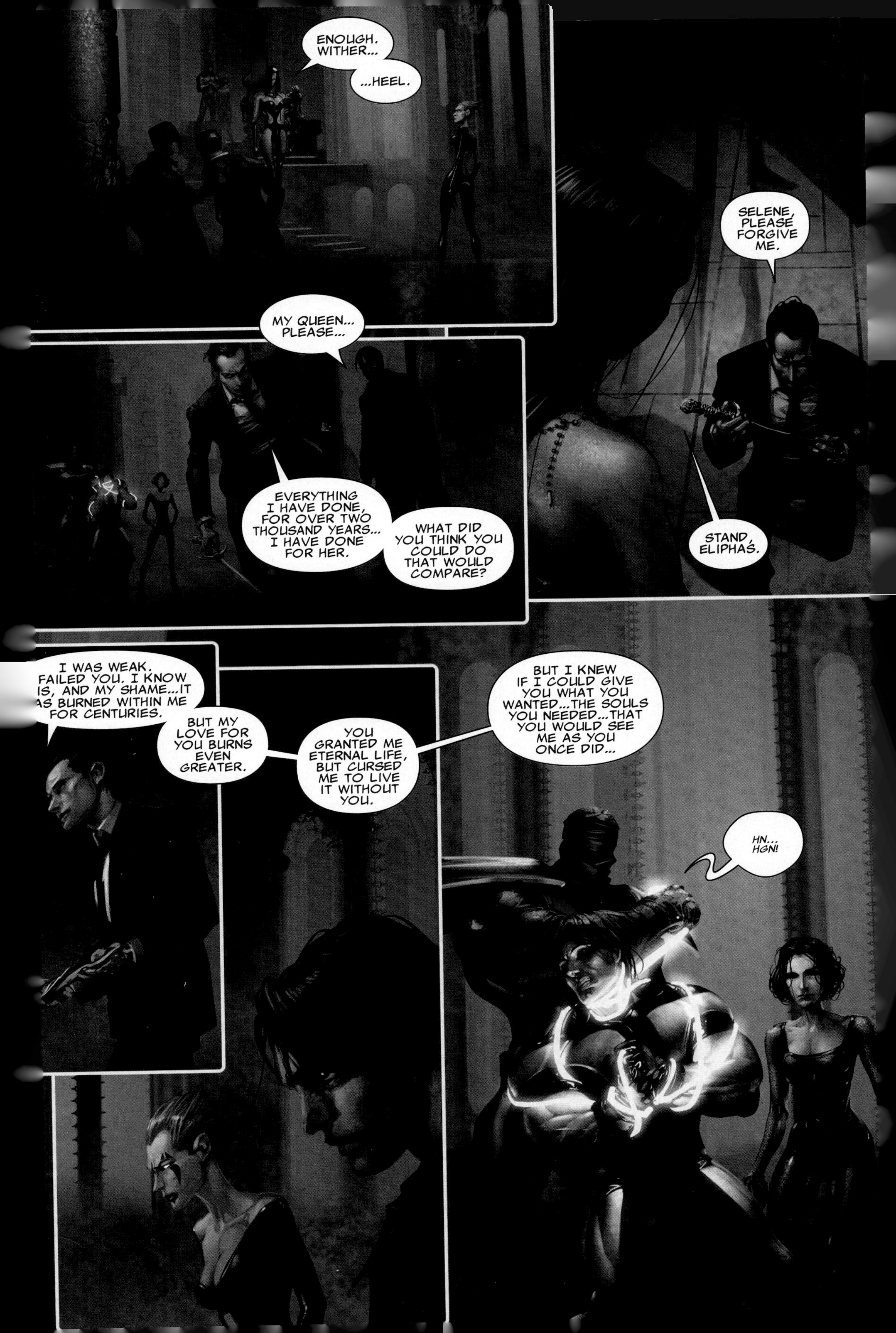
ENOUGH. WITHER...
...HEEL.
MY QUEEN... PLEASE...
EVERYTHING I HAVE DONE, FOR OVER TWO THOUSAND YEARS... I HAVE DONE FOR HER.
WHAT DID YOU THINK YOU COULD DO THAT WOULD COMPARE?
SELENE, PLEASE FORGIVE ME.
STAND, ELIPHAS.
I WAS WEAK. FAILED YOU. I KNOW IS, AND MY SHAME...IT AS BURNED WITHIN ME FOR CENTURIES.
BUT MY LOVE FOR YOU BURNS EVEN GREATER.
YOU GRANTED ME ETERNAL LIFE, BUT CURSED ME TO LIVE IT WITHOUT YOU.
BUT I KNEW IF I COULD GIVE YOU WHAT YOU WANTED...THE SOULS YOU NEEDED...THAT YOU WOULD SEE ME AS YOU ONCE DID...
HN... HGN!

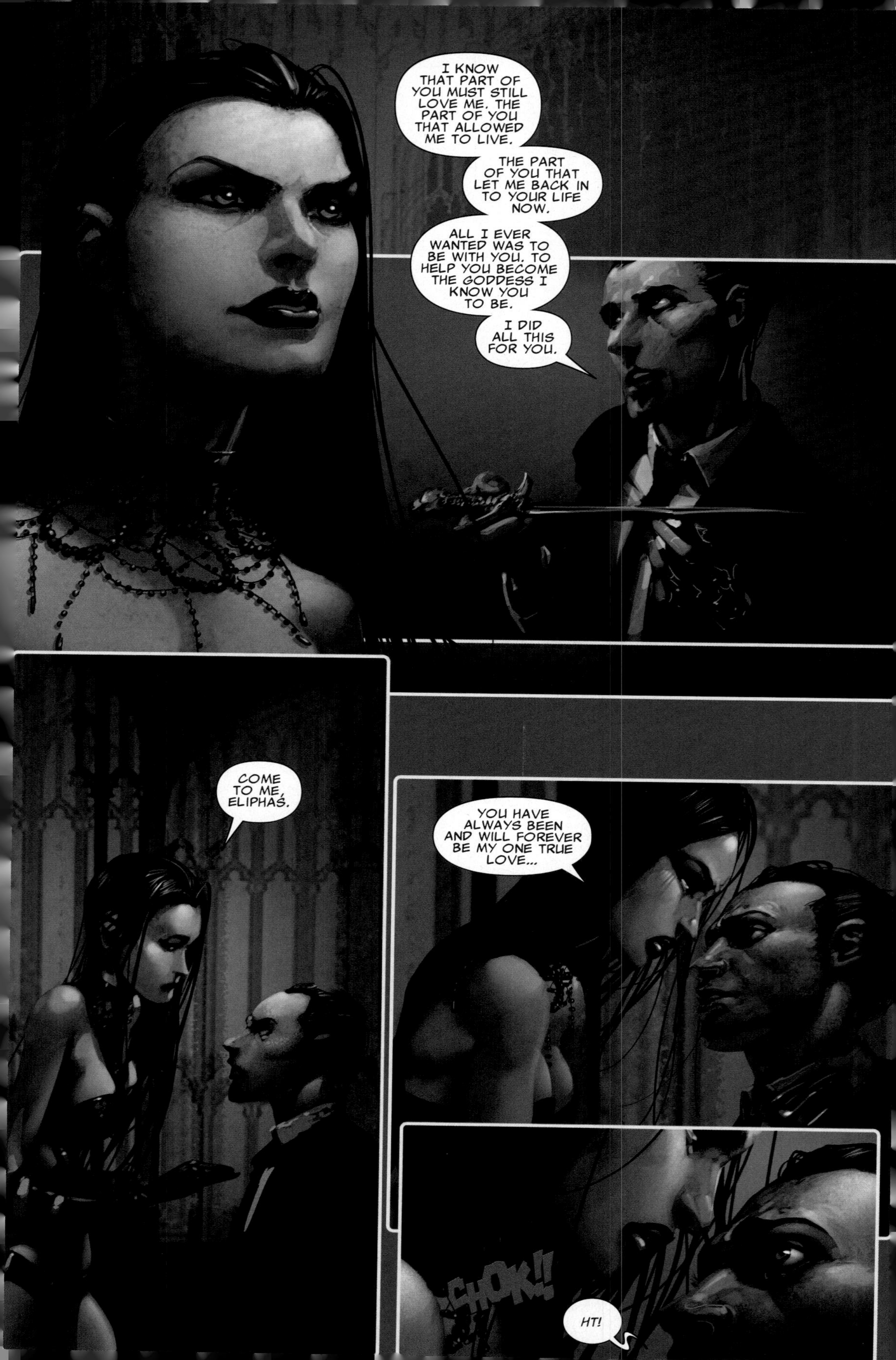
I KNOW THAT PART OF YOU MUST STILL LOVE ME. THE PART OF YOU THAT ALLOWED ME TO LIVE.
THE PART OF YOU THAT LET ME BACK IN TO YOUR LIFE NOW.
ALL I EVER WANTED WAS TO BE WITH YOU. TO HELP YOU BECOME THE GODDESS I KNOW YOU TO BE.
I DID ALL THIS FOR YOU.
COME TO ME, ELIPHAS.
YOU HAVE ALWAYS BEEN AND WILL FOREVER BE MY ONE TRUE LOVE...
CHOK!!
HT!

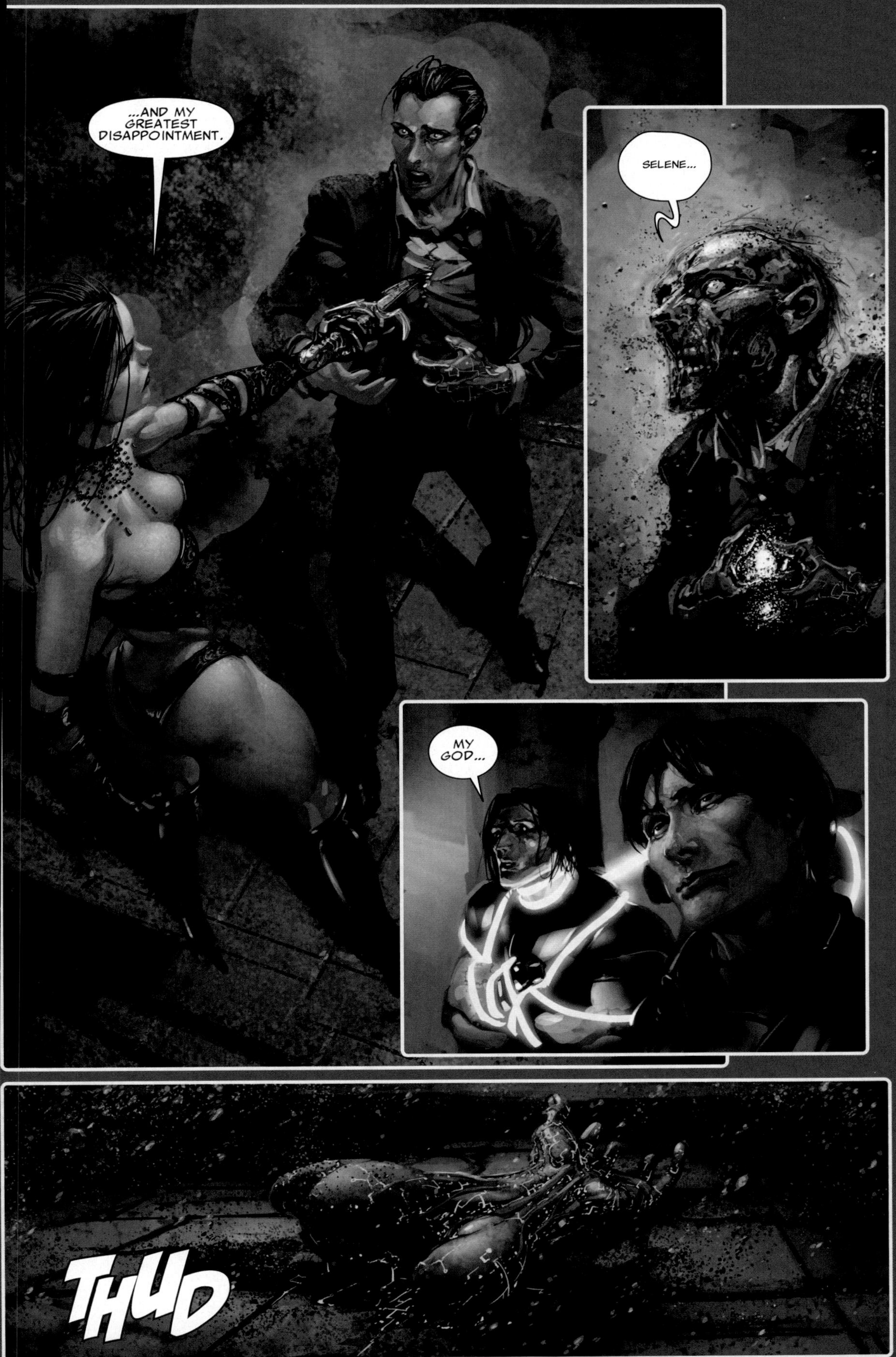
...AND MY GREATEST DISAPPOINTMENT.
SELENE...
MY GOD...
THUD

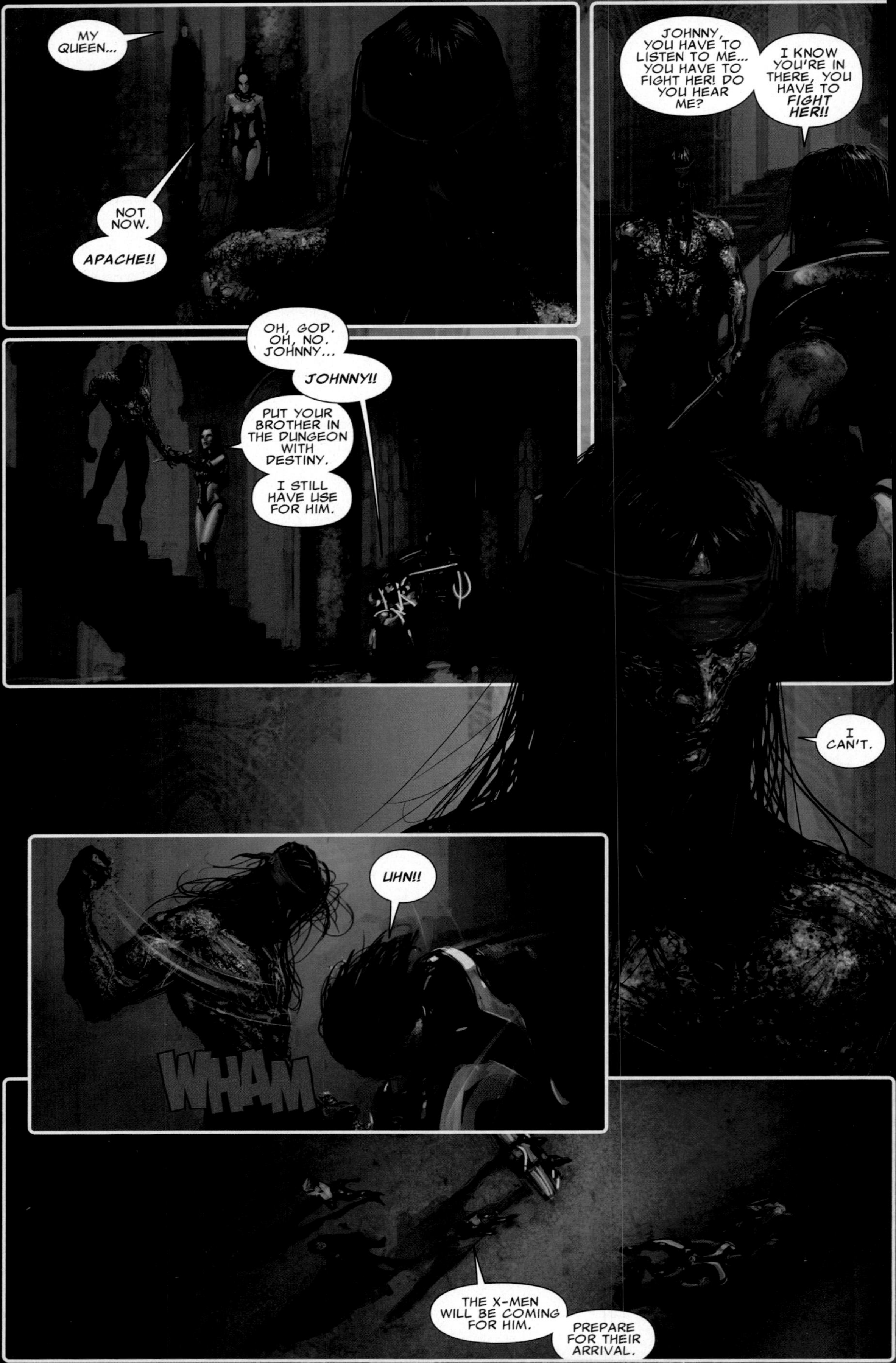
MY QUEEN...
NOT NOW.
APACHE!!
JOHNNY, YOU HAVE TO LISTEN TO ME... YOU HAVE TO FIGHT HER! DO YOU HEAR ME?
I KNOW YOU'RE IN THERE, YOU HAVE TO FIGHT HER!!
OH, GOD. OH, NO. JOHNNY...
JOHNNY!!
PUT YOUR BROTHER IN THE DUNGEON WITH DESTINY.
I STILL HAVE USE FOR HIM.
I CAN'T.
UHN!!
WHAM
THE X-MEN WILL BE COMING FOR HIM.
PREPARE FOR THEIR ARRIVAL.

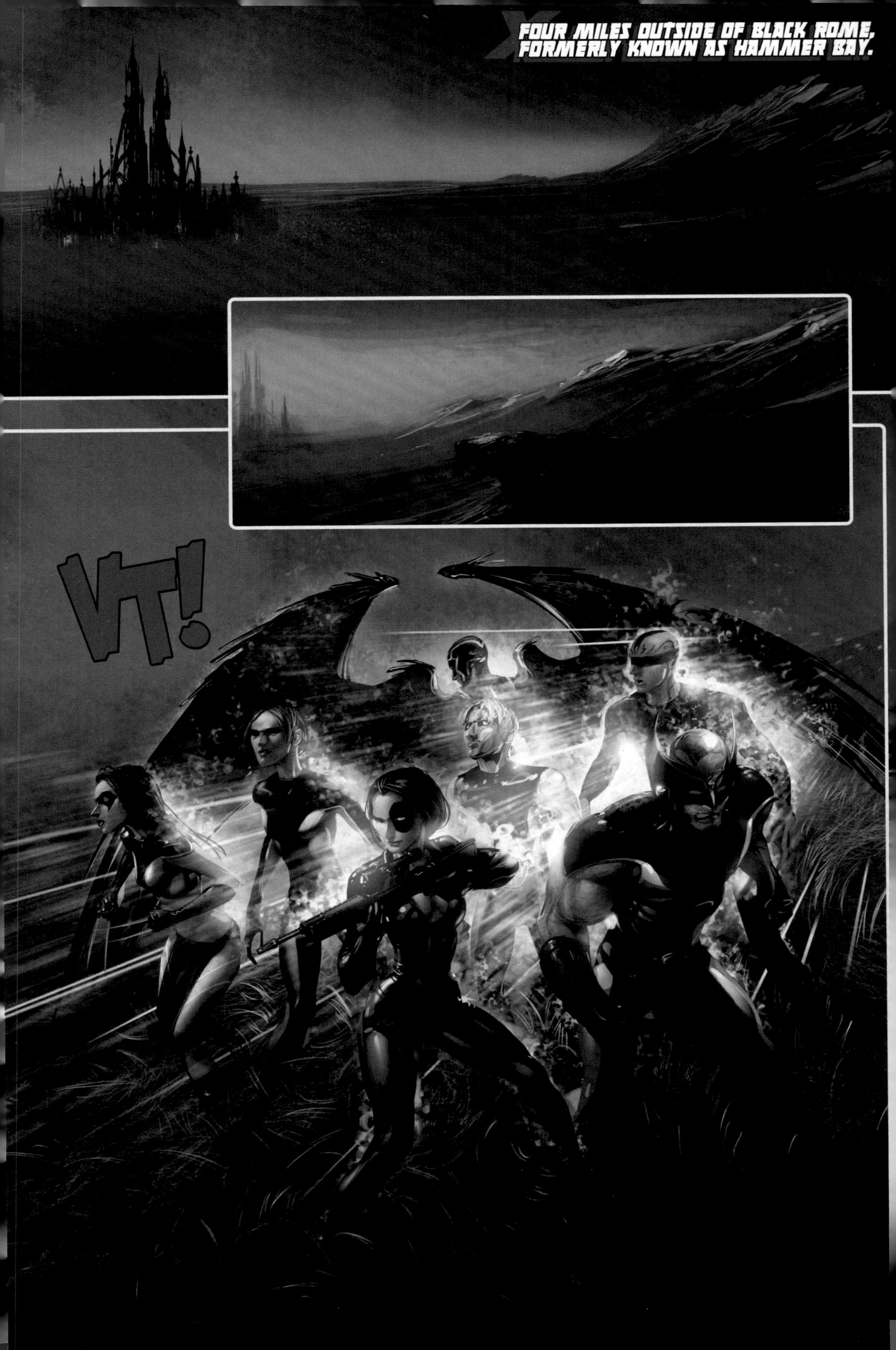
FOUR MILES OUTSIDE OF BLACK ROME, FORMERLY KNOWN AS HAMMER BAY.
VT!

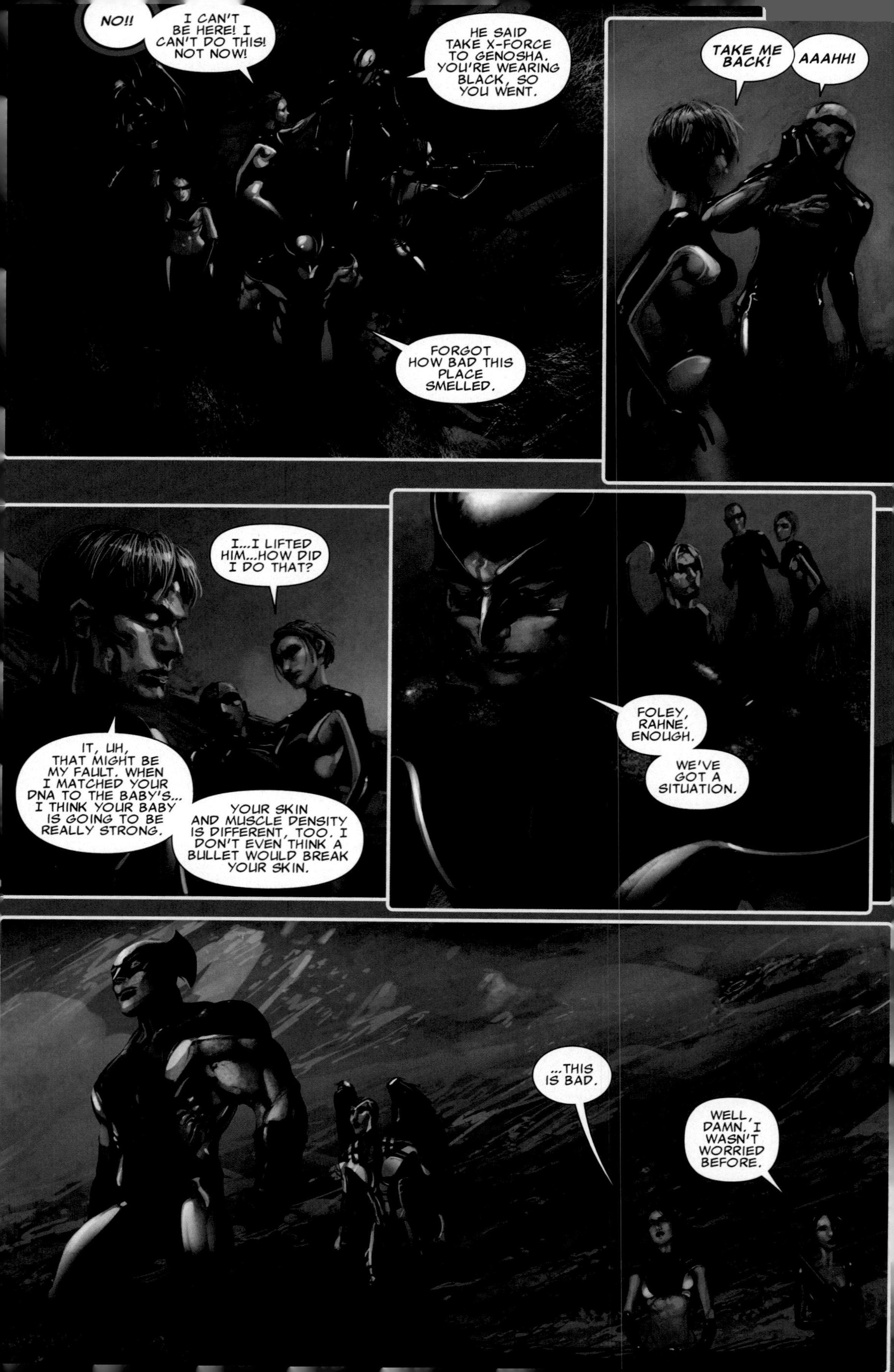
NO!!
I CAN'T BE HERE! I CAN'T DO THIS! NOT NOW!
HE SAID TAKE X-FORCE TO GENOSHA. YOU'RE WEARING BLACK, SO YOU WENT.
FORGOT HOW BAD THIS PLACE SMELLED.
TAKE ME BACK!
AAAHH!
I...I LIFTED HIM...HOW DID I DO THAT?
IT, UH, THAT MIGHT BE MY FAULT. WHEN I MATCHED YOUR DNA TO THE BABY'S... I THINK YOUR BABY IS GOING TO BE REALLY STRONG.
YOUR SKIN AND MUSCLE DENSITY IS DIFFERENT, TOO. I DON'T EVEN THINK A BULLET WOULD BREAK YOUR SKIN.
FOLEY, RAHNE. ENOUGH.
WE'VE GOT A SITUATION.
...THIS IS BAD.
WELL, DAMN. I WASN'T WORRIED BEFORE.

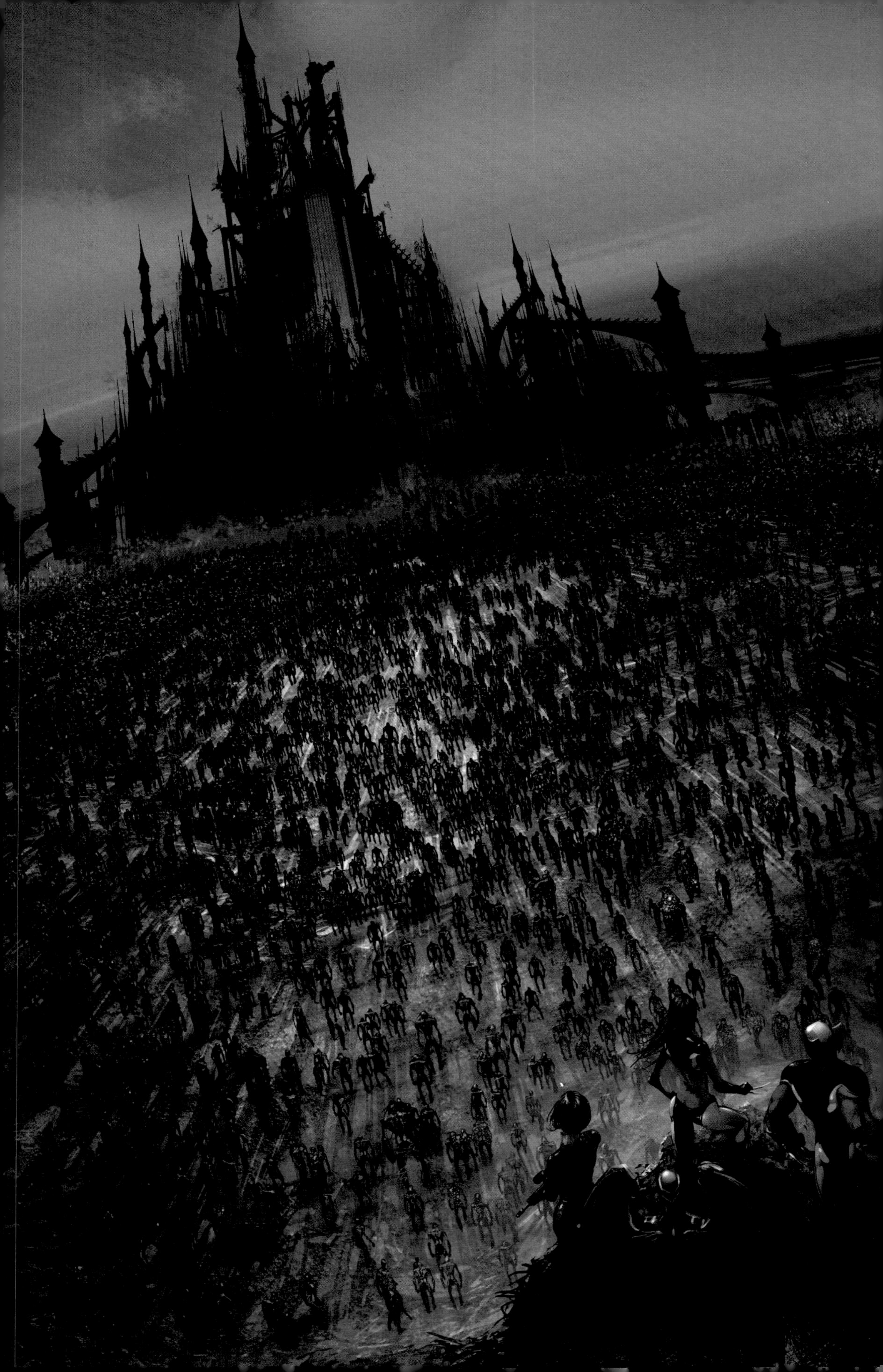

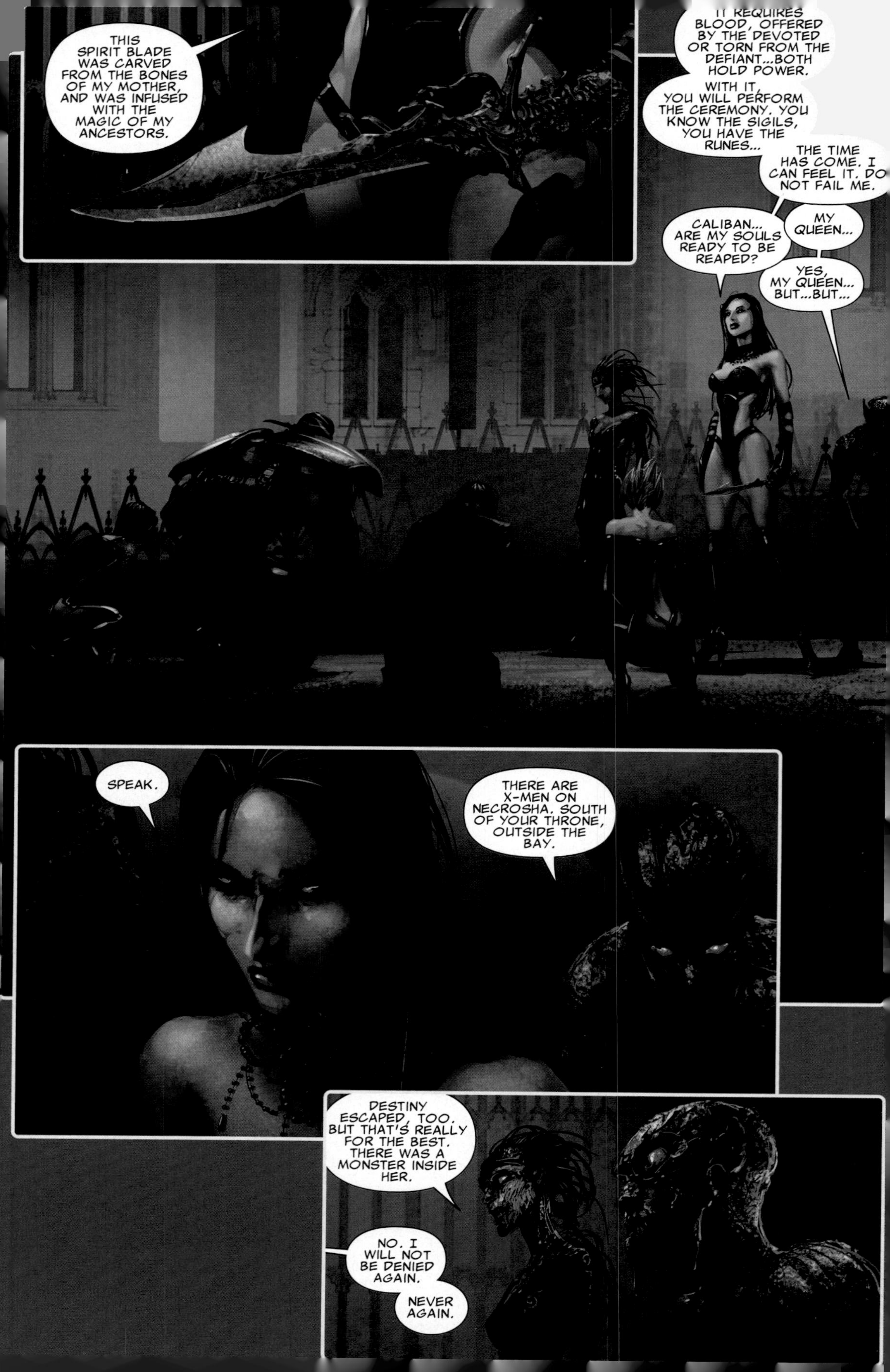
THIS SPIRIT BLADE WAS CARVED FROM THE BONES OF MY MOTHER, AND WAS INFUSED WITH THE MAGIC OF MY ANCESTORS.
IT REQUIRES BLOOD, OFFERED BY THE DEVOTED OR TORN FROM THE DEFIANT...BOTH HOLD POWER.
WITH IT, YOU WILL PERFORM THE CEREMONY. YOU KNOW THE SIGILS, YOU HAVE THE RUNES...
THE TIME HAS COME. I CAN FEEL IT. DO NOT FAIL ME.
MY QUEEN...
CALIBAN... ARE MY SOULS READY TO BE REAPED?
YES, MY QUEEN... BUT...BUT...
SPEAK.
THERE ARE X-MEN ON NECROSHA. SOUTH OF YOUR THRONE, OUTSIDE THE BAY.
DESTINY ESCAPED, TOO. BUT THAT'S REALLY FOR THE BEST. THERE WAS A MONSTER INSIDE HER.
NO. I WILL NOT BE DENIED AGAIN.
NEVER AGAIN.

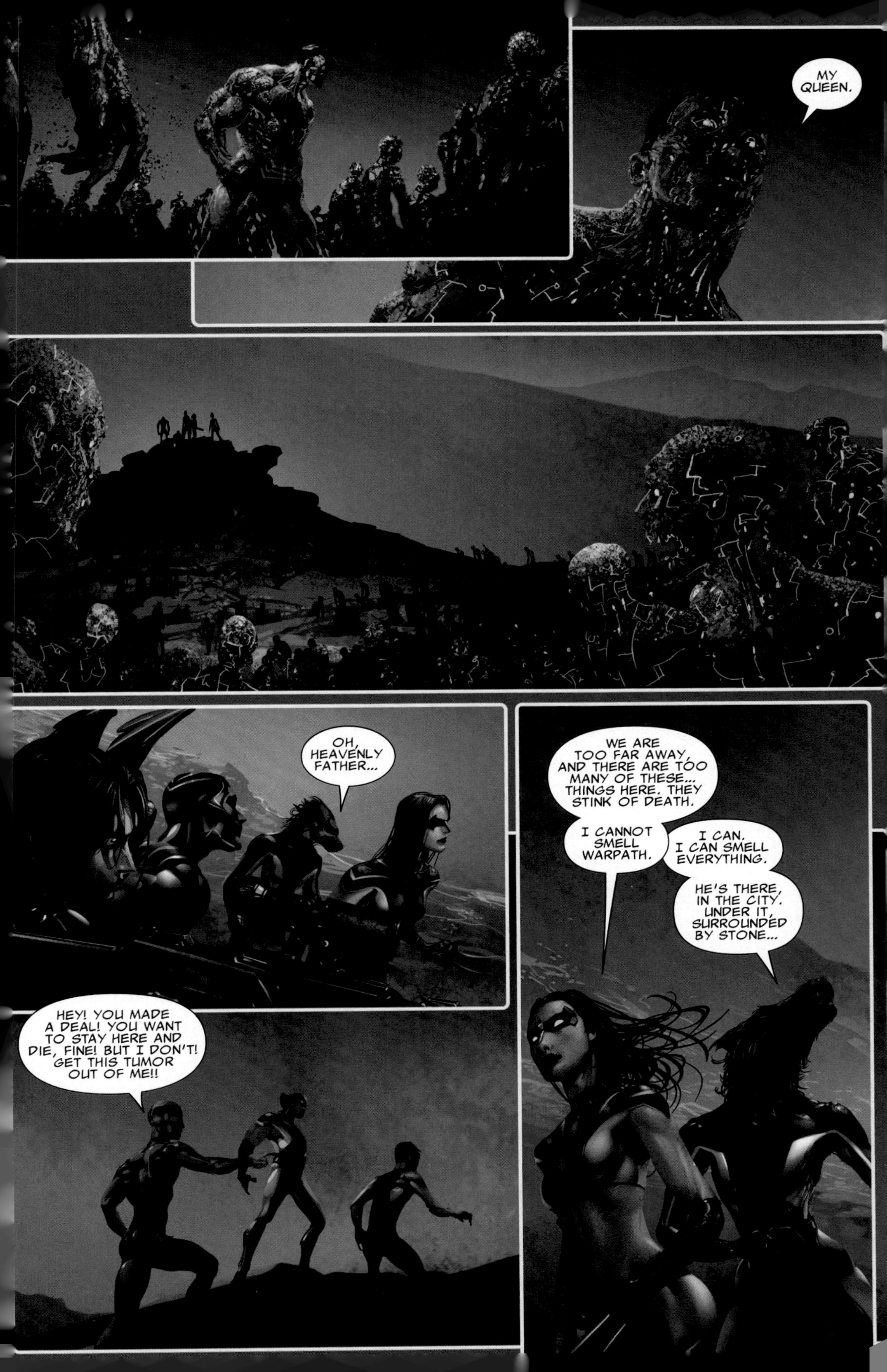
MY QUEEN.
OH, HEAVENLY FATHER...
WE ARE TOO FAR AWAY, AND THERE ARE TOO MANY OF THESE... THINGS HERE. THEY STINK OF DEATH.
I CANNOT SMELL WARPATH.
I CAN. I CAN SMELL EVERYTHING.
HE'S THERE, IN THE CITY. UNDER IT, SURROUNDED BY STONE...
HEY! YOU MADE A DEAL! YOU WANT TO STAY HERE AND DIE, FINE! BUT I DON'T! GET THIS TUMOR OUT OF ME!!

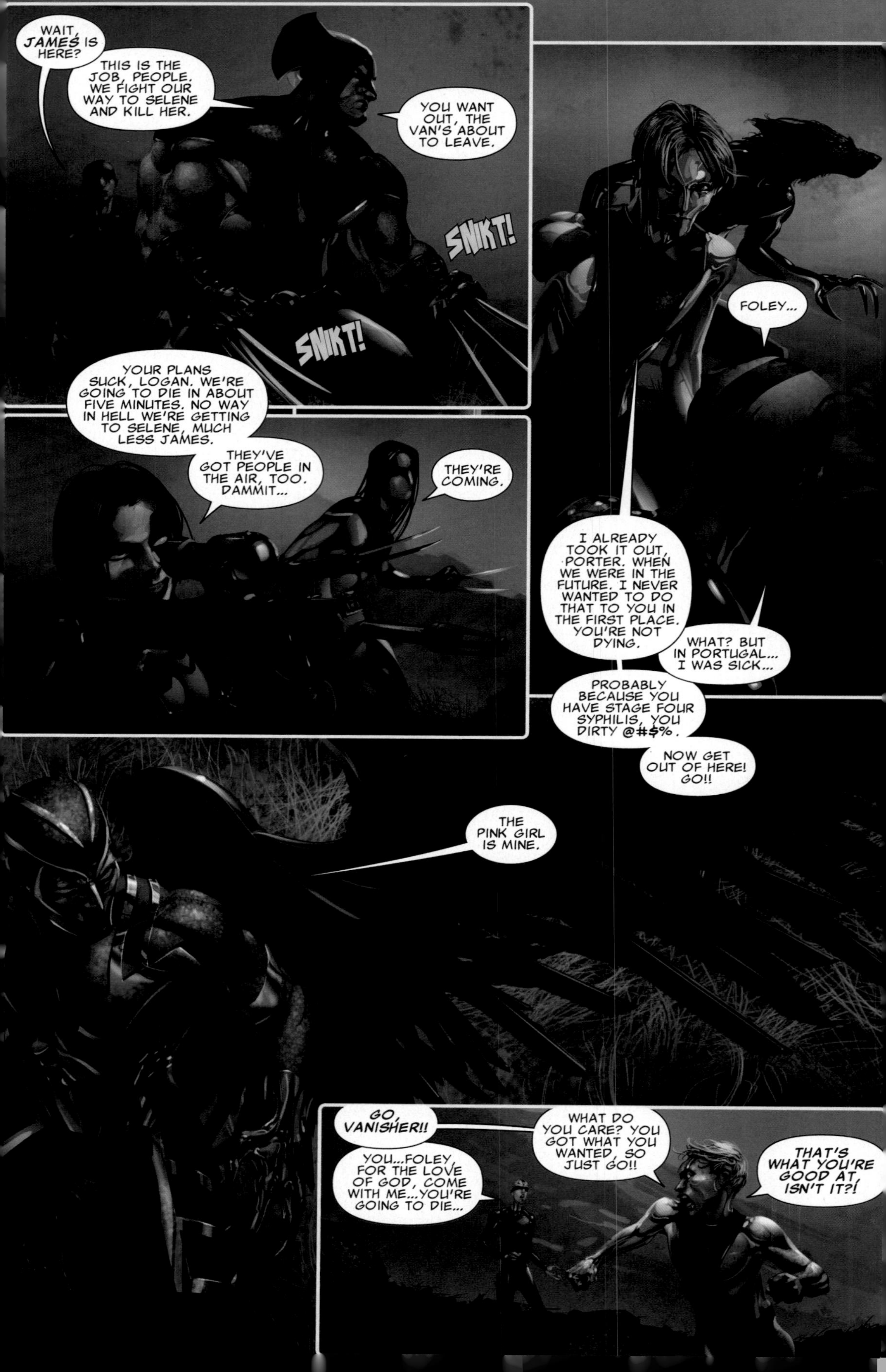
WAIT, JAMES IS HERE?
THIS IS THE JOB, PEOPLE. WE FIGHT OUR WAY TO SELENE AND KILL HER.
YOU WANT OUT, THE VAN'S ABOUT TO LEAVE.
SNIKT!
SNIKT!
YOUR PLANS SUCK, LOGAN. WE'RE GOING TO DIE IN ABOUT FIVE MINUTES. NO WAY IN HELL WE'RE GETTING TO SELENE, MUCH LESS JAMES.
THEY'VE GOT PEOPLE IN THE AIR, TOO. DAMMIT...
THEY'RE COMING.
FOLEY...
I ALREADY TOOK IT OUT, PORTER. WHEN WE WERE IN THE FUTURE. I NEVER WANTED TO DO THAT TO YOU IN THE FIRST PLACE. YOU'RE NOT DYING.
WHAT? BUT IN PORTUGAL... I WAS SICK...
PROBABLY BECAUSE YOU HAVE STAGE FOUR SYPHILIS, YOU DIRTY @#$%.
NOW GET OUT OF HERE! GO!!
THE PINK GIRL IS MINE.
GO, VANISHER!!
YOU...FOLEY, FOR THE LOVE OF GOD, COME WITH ME...YOU'RE GOING TO DIE...
WHAT DO YOU CARE? YOU GOT WHAT YOU WANTED, SO JUST GO!!
THAT'S WHAT YOU'RE GOOD AT, ISN'T IT?!

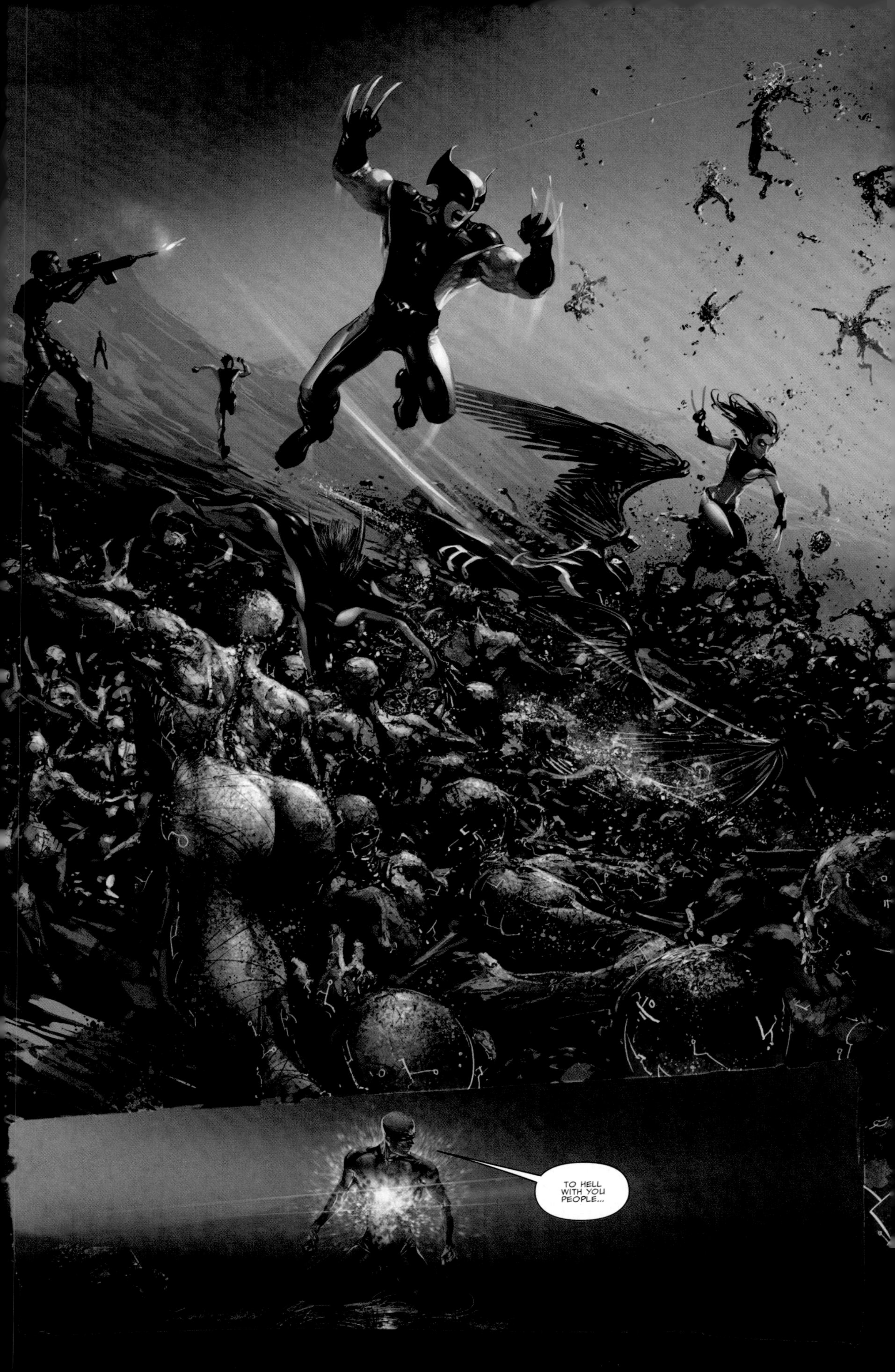
TO HELL WITH YOU PEOPLE...

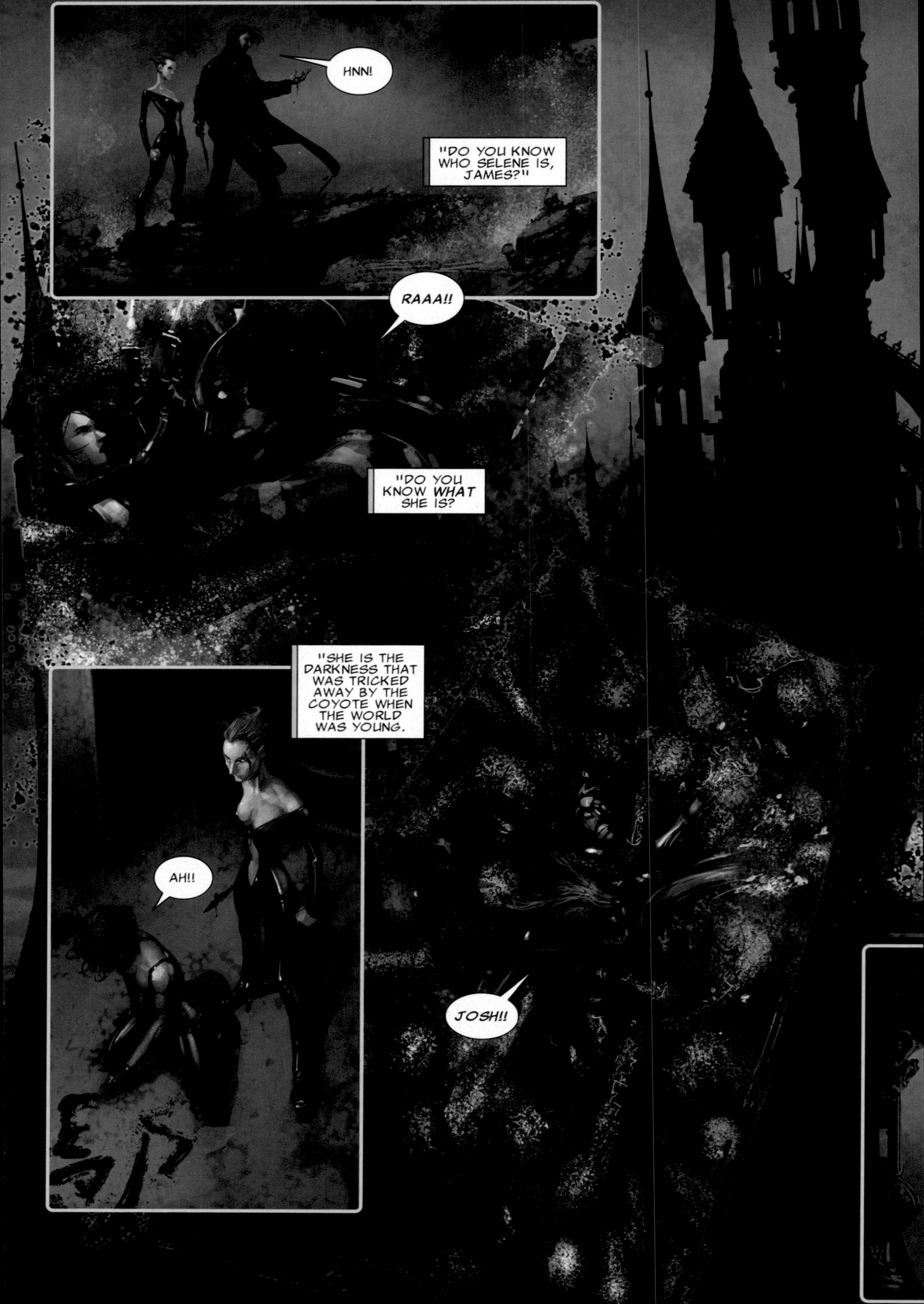
HNN!
"DO YOU KNOW WHO SELENE IS, JAMES?"
RAAA!!
"DO YOU KNOW WHAT SHE IS?
"SHE IS THE DARKNESS THAT WAS TRICKED AWAY BY THE COYOTE WHEN THE WORLD WAS YOUNG.
AH!!
JOSH!!

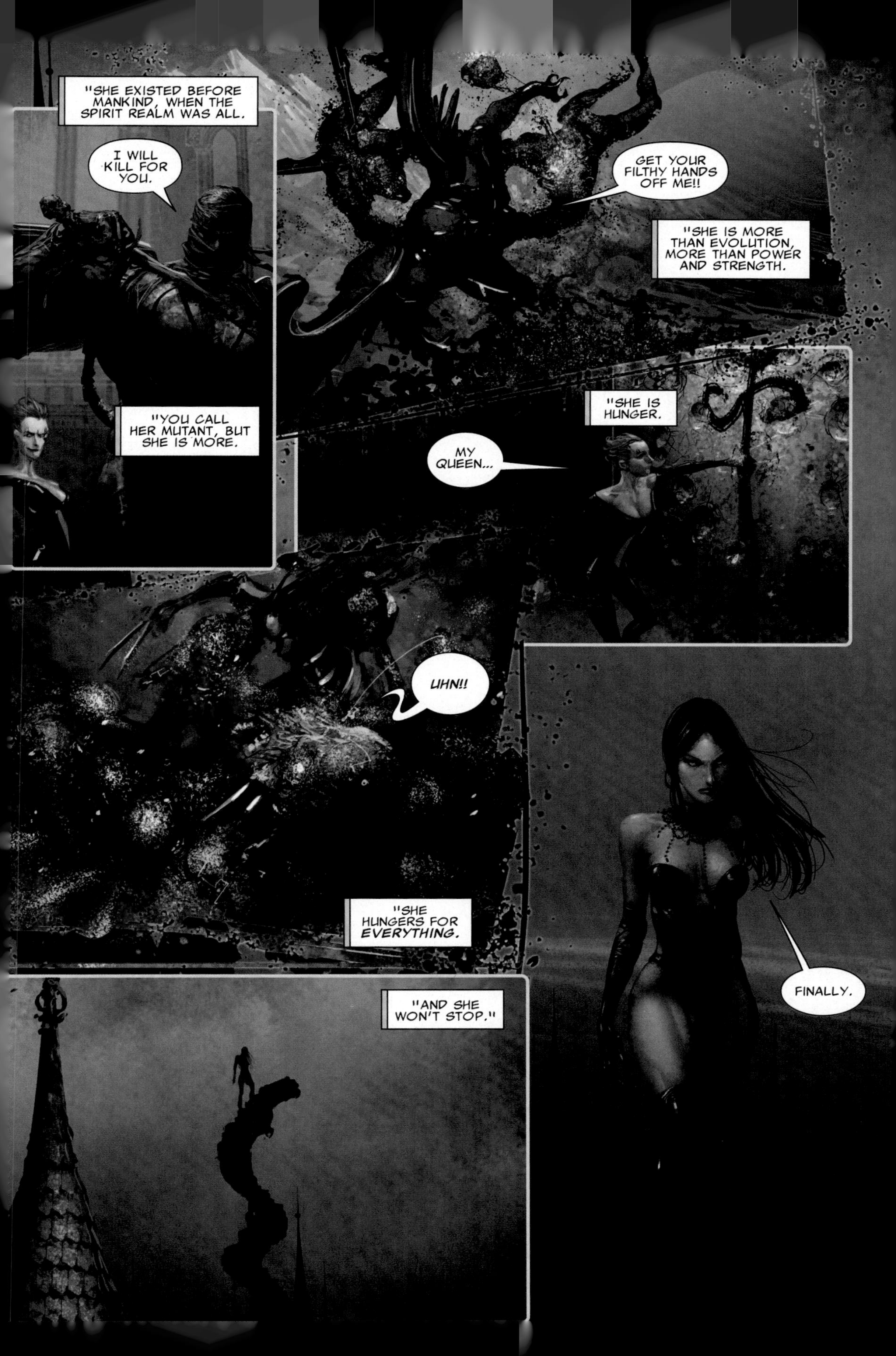
"SHE EXISTED BEFORE MANKIND, WHEN THE SPIRIT REALM WAS ALL.
I WILL KILL FOR YOU.
GET YOUR FILTHY HANDS OFF ME!!
"SHE IS MORE THAN EVOLUTION, MORE THAN POWER AND STRENGTH.
"YOU CALL HER MUTANT, BUT SHE IS MORE.
"SHE IS HUNGER.
MY QUEEN...
UHN!!
"SHE HUNGERS FOR EVERYTHING.
"AND SHE WON'T STOP."
FINALLY.

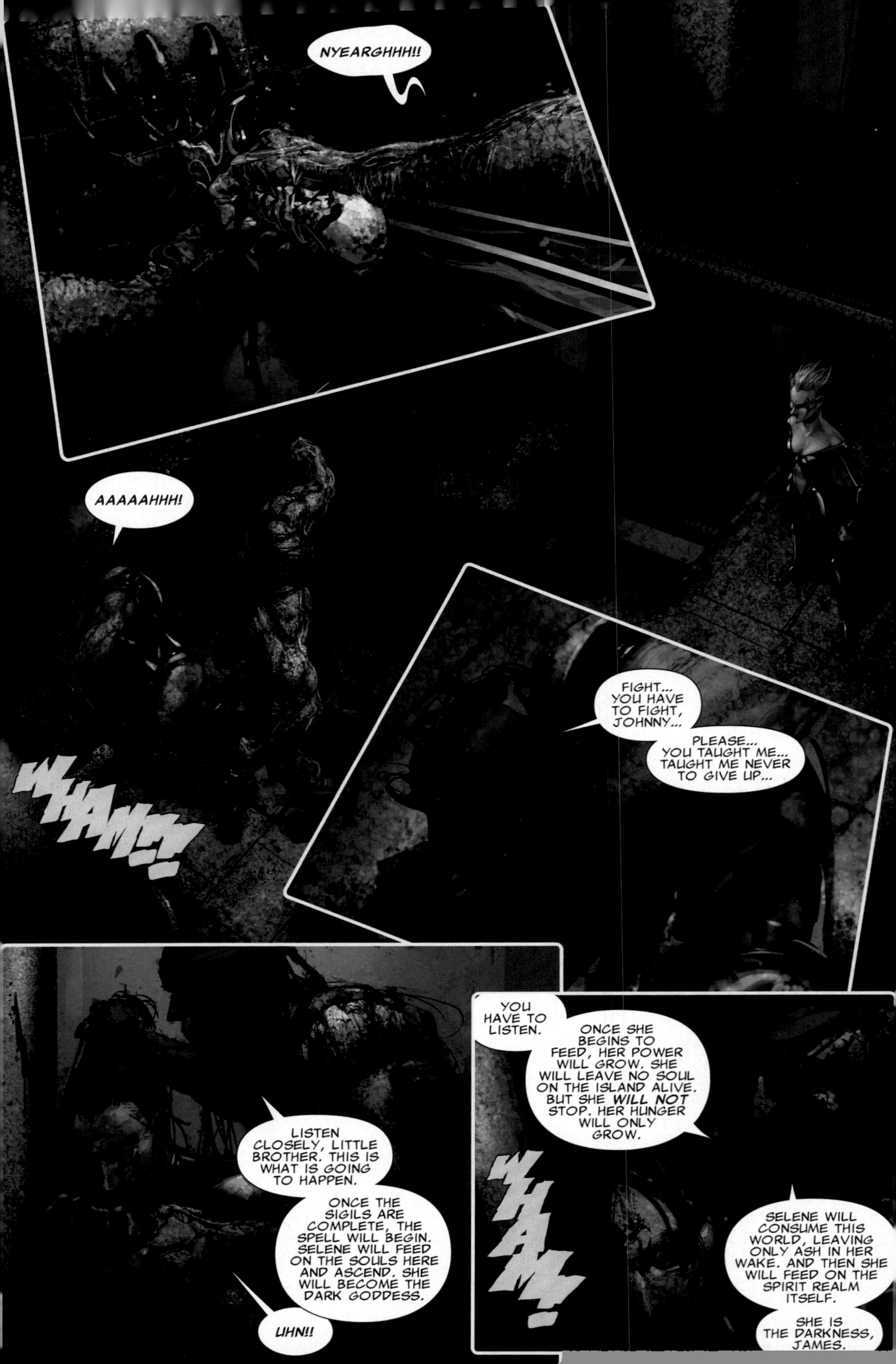
NYEARGHHH!!
AAAAAHHH!
WHAM!!
FIGHT... YOU HAVE TO FIGHT, JOHNNY...
PLEASE... YOU TAUGHT ME... TAUGHT ME NEVER TO GIVE UP...
LISTEN CLOSELY, LITTLE BROTHER. THIS IS WHAT IS GOING TO HAPPEN.
ONCE THE SIGILS ARE COMPLETE, THE SPELL WILL BEGIN. SELENE WILL FEED ON THE SOULS HERE AND ASCEND. SHE WILL BECOME THE DARK GODDESS.
UHN!!
YOU HAVE TO LISTEN.
ONCE SHE BEGINS TO FEED, HER POWER WILL GROW. SHE WILL LEAVE NO SOUL ON THE ISLAND ALIVE. BUT SHE WILL NOT STOP. HER HUNGER WILL ONLY GROW.
WHAM!
SELENE WILL CONSUME THIS WORLD, LEAVING ONLY ASH IN HER WAKE. AND THEN SHE WILL FEED ON THE SPIRIT REALM ITSELF.
SHE IS THE DARKNESS, JAMES.

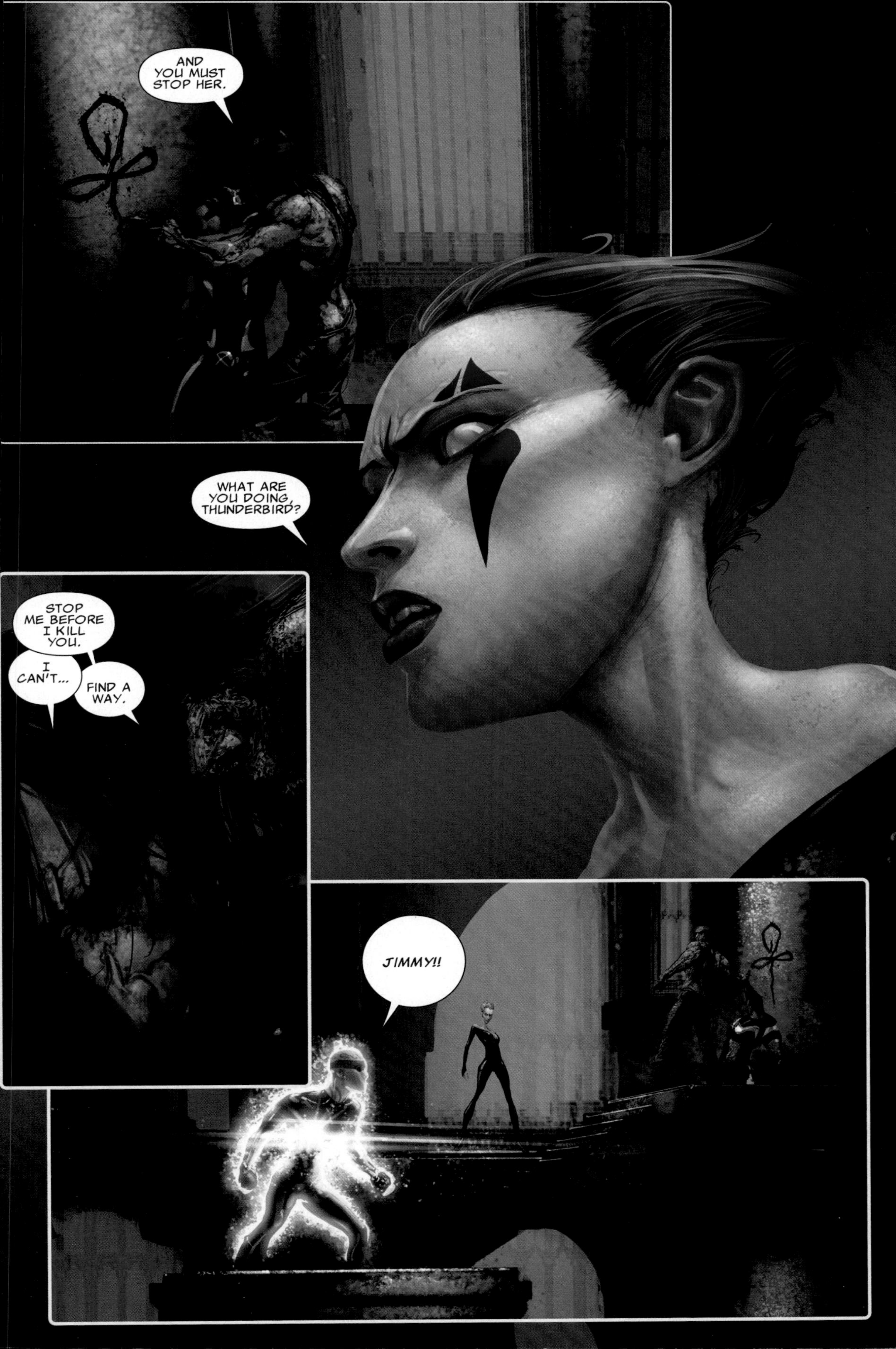
AND YOU MUST STOP HER.
WHAT ARE YOU DOING, THUNDERBIRD?
STOP ME BEFORE I KILL YOU.
I CAN'T...
FIND A WAY.
JIMMY!!

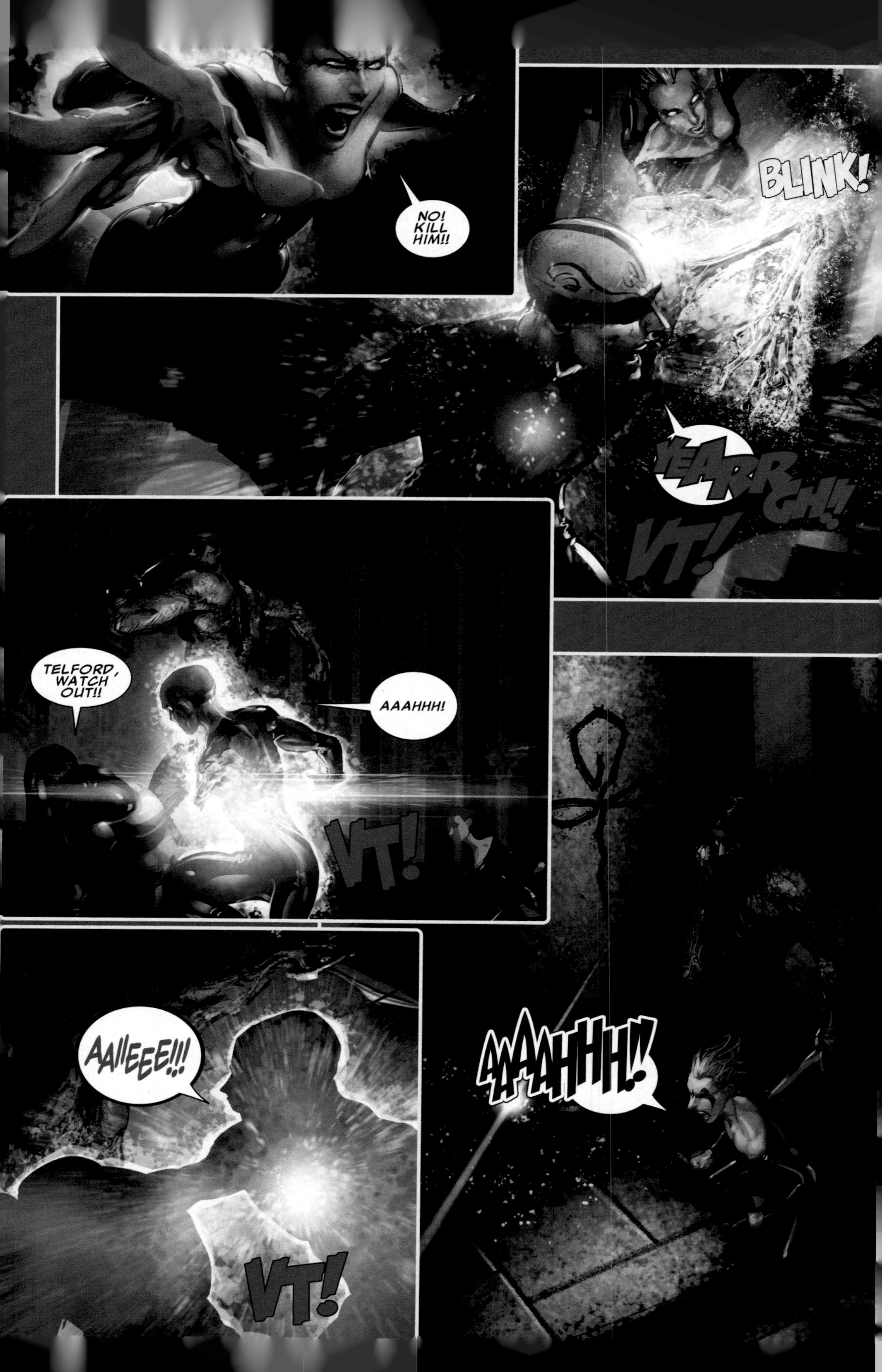
NO! KILL HIM!!
BLINK!
YEARRRGH!!
VT!
TELFORD, WATCH OUT!!
AAAHHH!
VT!
AAIIEEE!!!
VT!
AAAAHHH!!

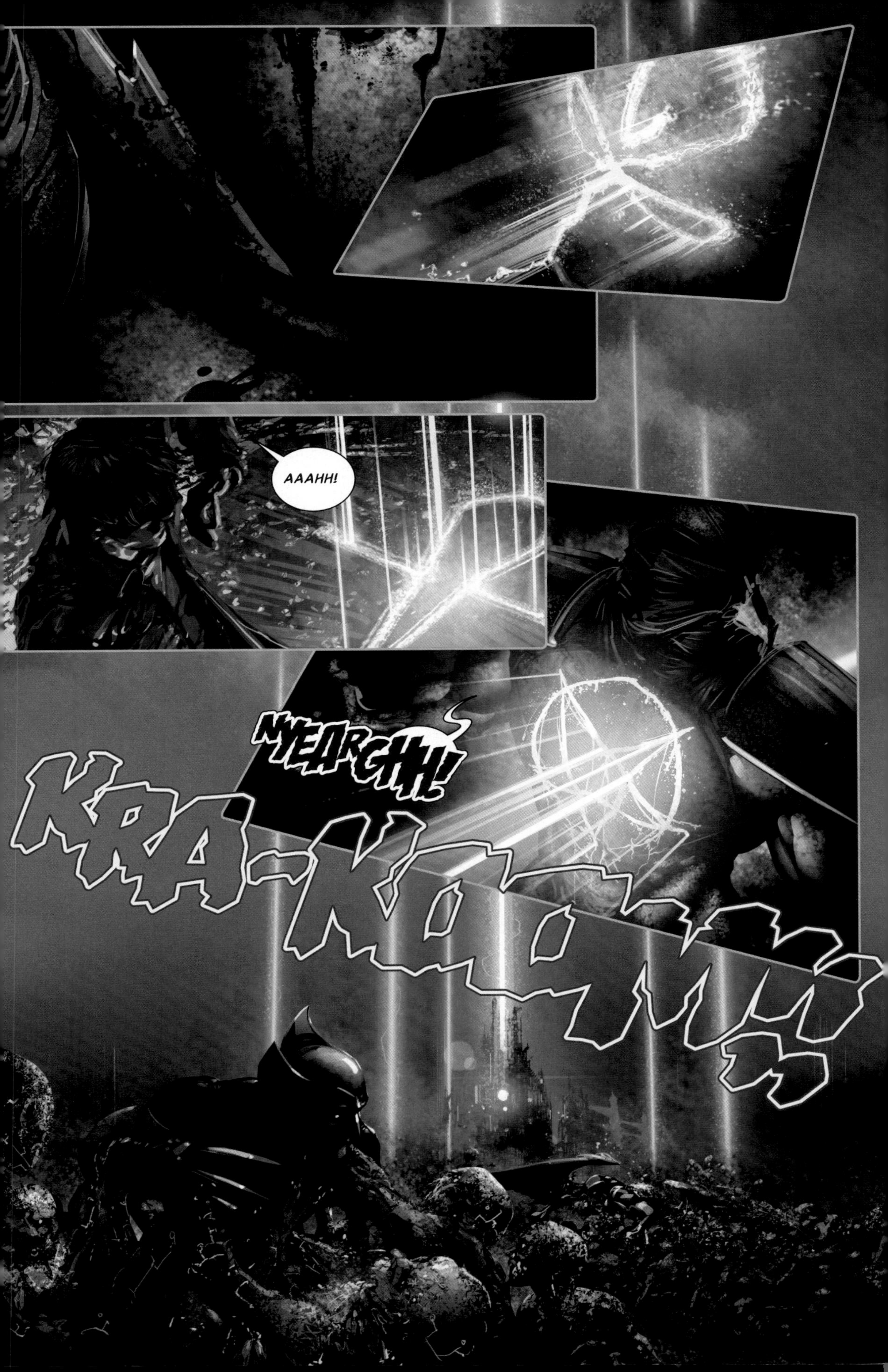
AAAHH!
NYEARGHH!
KRA-KOOOM!

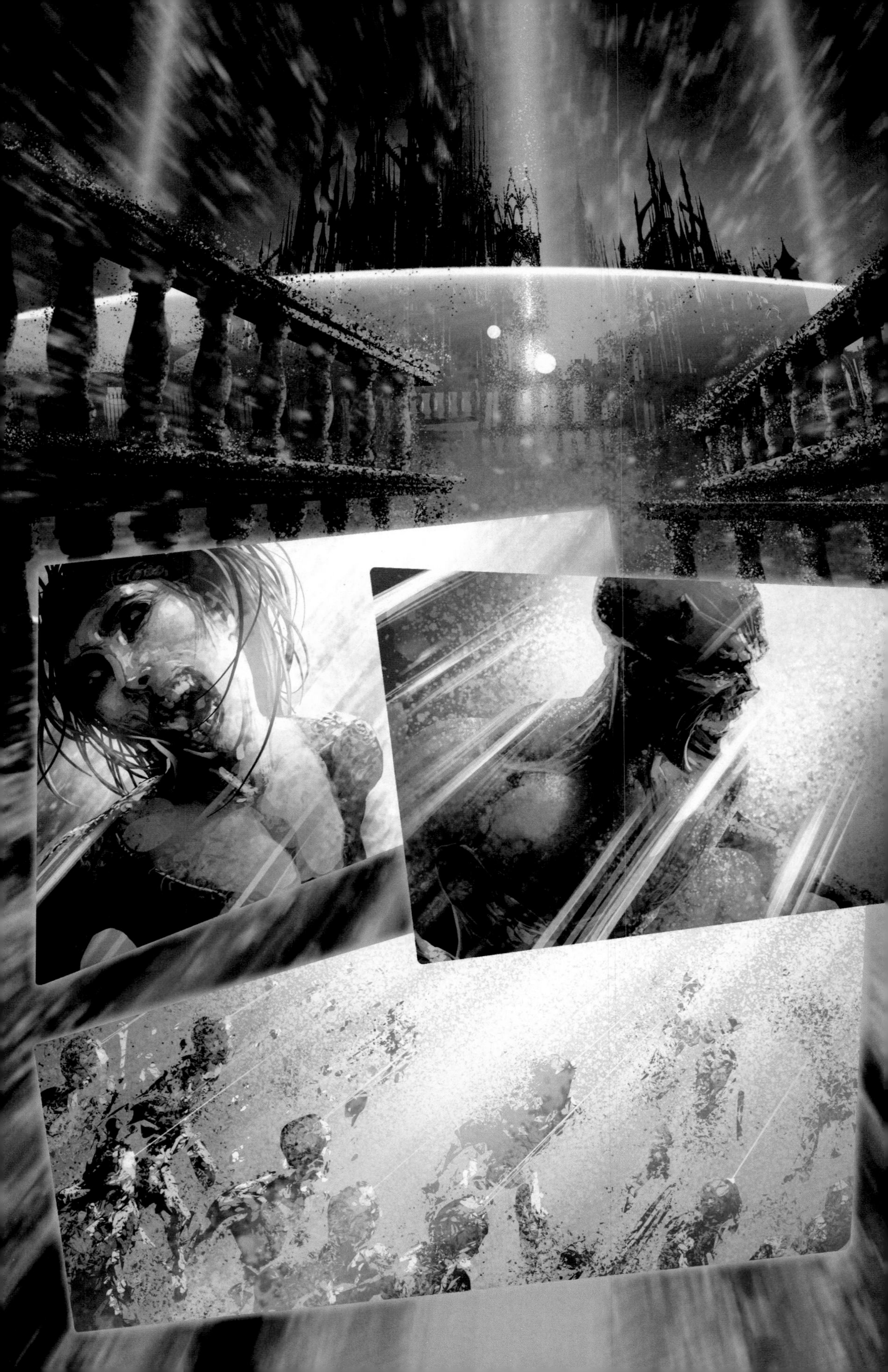

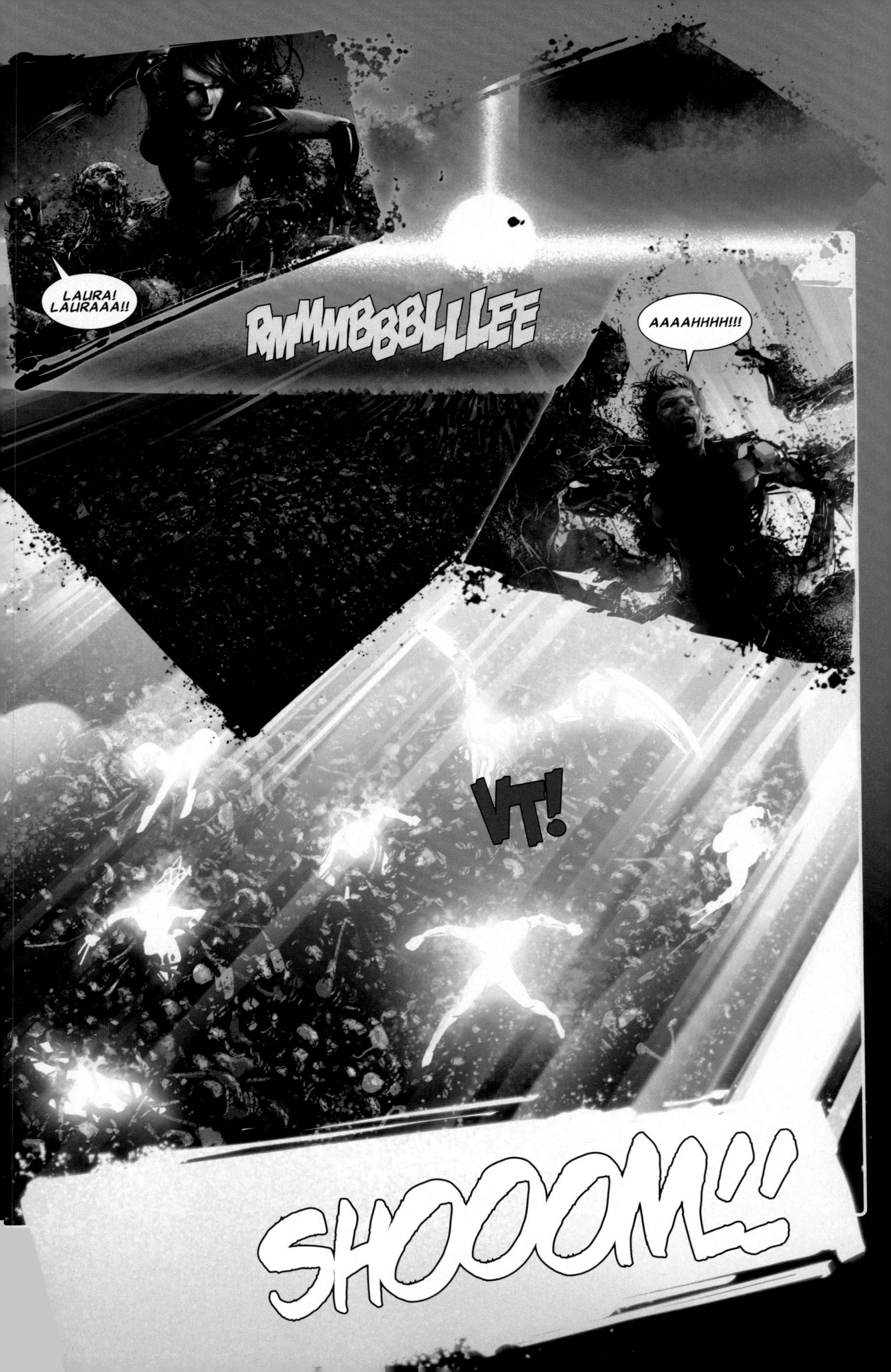
LAURA! LAURAAA!!
RMMMBBBLLLEE
AAAAHHHH!!!
VT!
SHOOOM!!

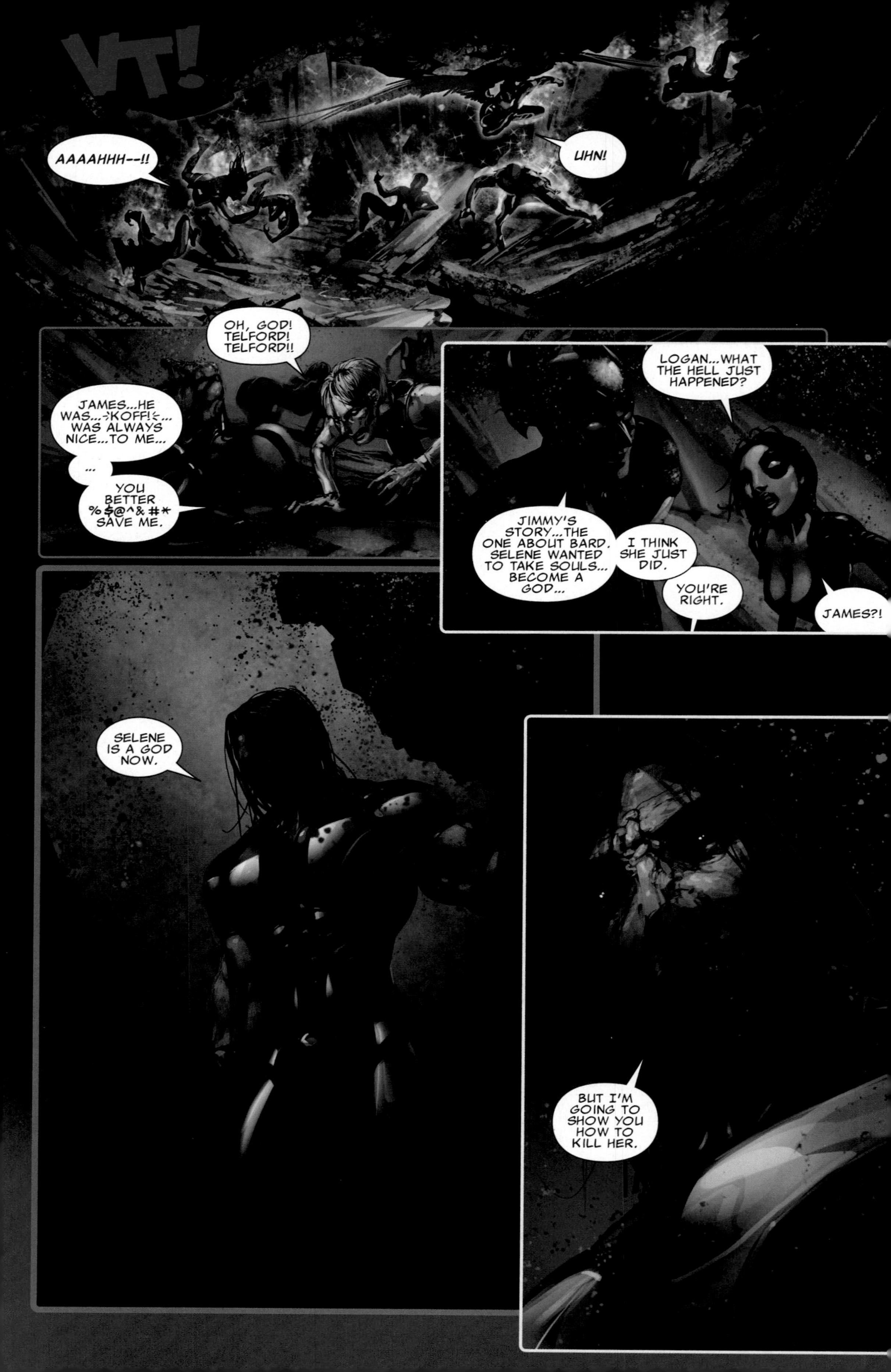
VT!
AAAAHHH--!!
UHN!
OH, GOD! TELFORD! TELFORD!!
JAMES...HE WAS...*KOFF!*... WAS ALWAYS NICE...TO ME...
...
YOU BETTER %$@^& #* SAVE ME.
LOGAN...WHAT THE HELL JUST HAPPENED?
JIMMY'S STORY...THE ONE ABOUT BARD. SELENE WANTED TO TAKE SOULS... BECOME A GOD...
I THINK SHE JUST DID.
YOU'RE RIGHT.
JAMES?!
SELENE IS A GOD NOW.
BUT I'M GOING TO SHOW YOU HOW TO KILL HER.

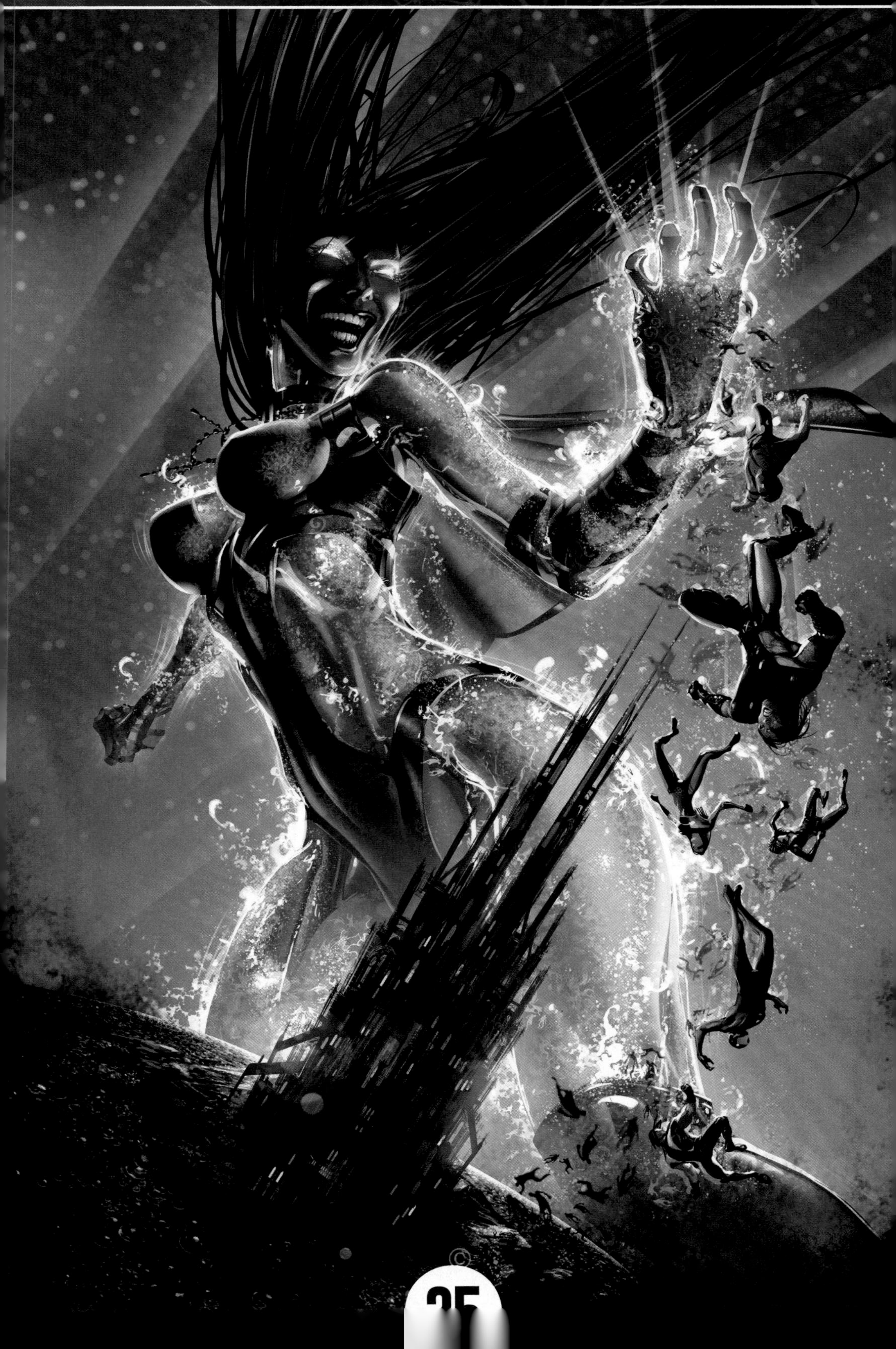

THE FORMER NATION OF GENOSHA.

MY BROTHER TOLD ME WHAT WOULD HAPPEN.

JOHNNY IS CONNECTED TO SELENE. AND SELENE'S CONNECTED TO *EVERYTHING* NOW.

LOS ANGELES. DR. STEPHEN STRANGE.

STEPHEN! *STEPHEN!*

HE SAID THE SORCERERS WOULD FEEL IT.

UHN!!

LATVERIA. DOCTOR DOOM.

HNNN... HNN...

THAT HER ASCENSION TO POWER WOULD BE LIKE SETTING OFF A BOMB IN THE SPIRIT REALM.

NEW ORLEANS. DOCTOR VOODOO.

NYEARGHHH!

AND THOSE WITH THE POWER TO DO SOMETHING ABOUT IT WOULD BE HIT THE HARDEST.

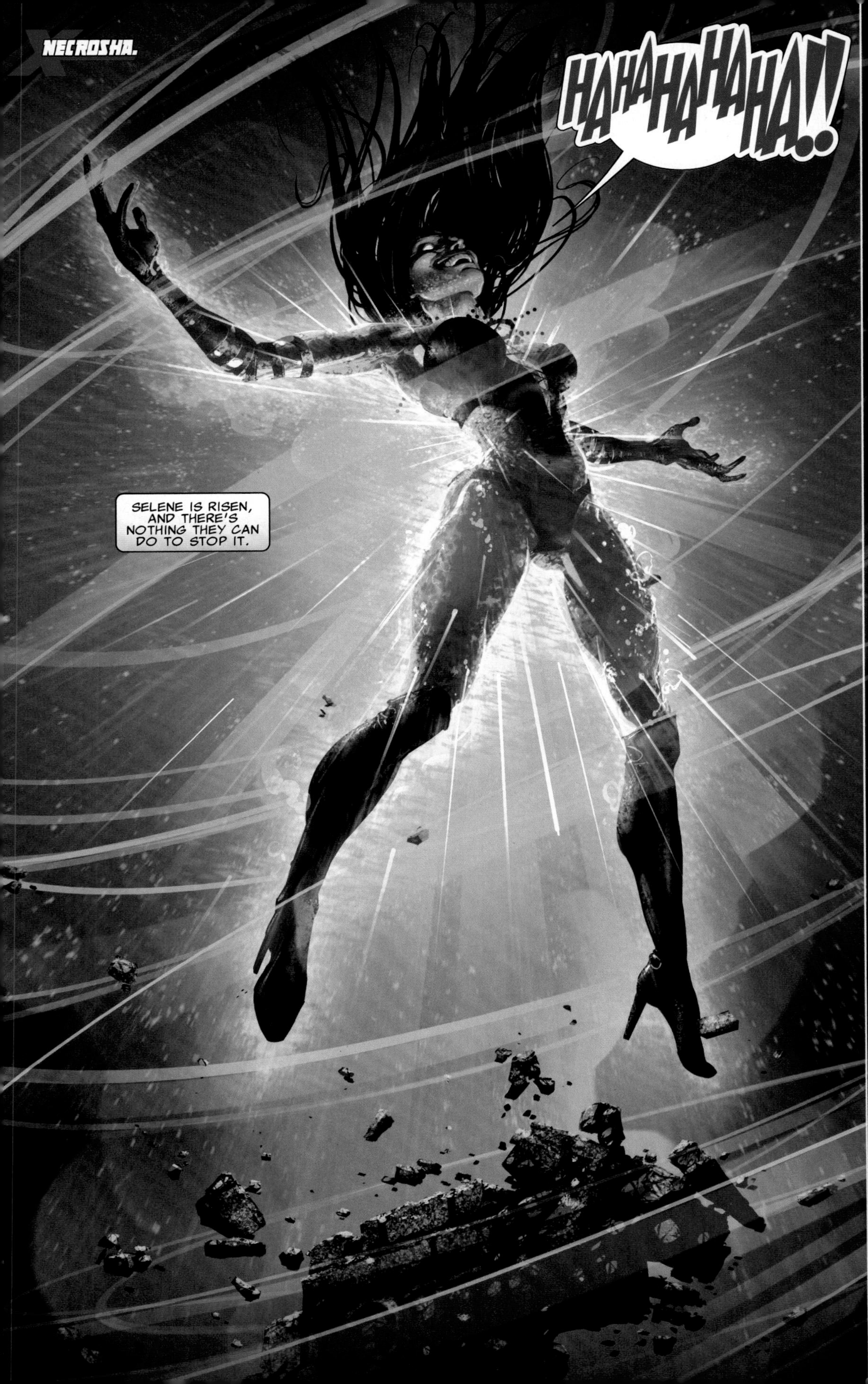
HAHAHAHAHAHA!!
SELENE IS RISEN, AND THERE'S NOTHING THEY CAN DO TO STOP IT.

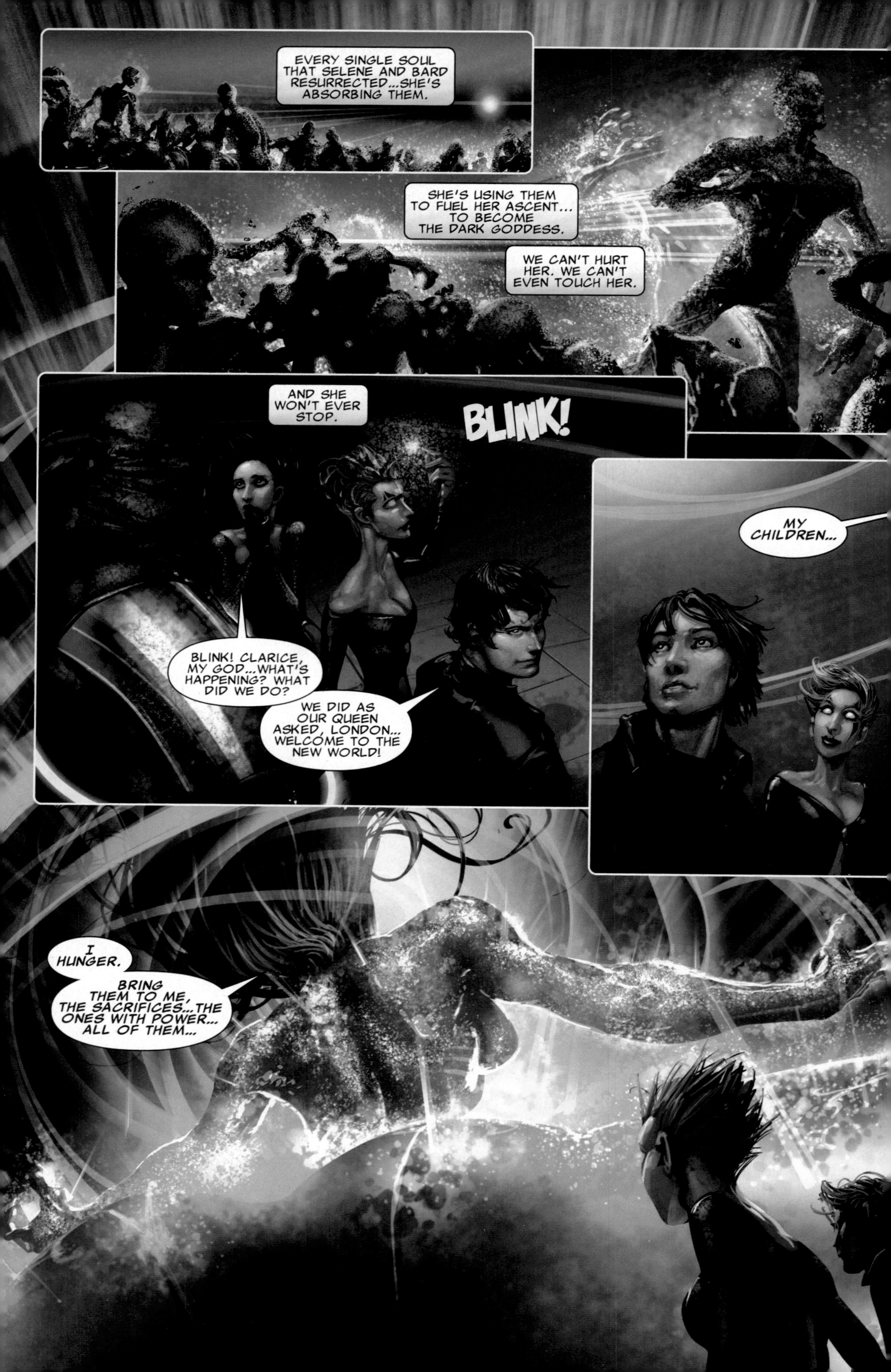
EVERY SINGLE SOUL THAT SELENE AND BARD RESURRECTED...SHE'S ABSORBING THEM.
SHE'S USING THEM TO FUEL HER ASCENT... TO BECOME THE DARK GODDESS.
WE CAN'T HURT HER. WE CAN'T EVEN TOUCH HER.
AND SHE WON'T EVER STOP.
BLINK!
BLINK! CLARICE, MY GOD...WHAT'S HAPPENING? WHAT DID WE DO?
WE DID AS OUR QUEEN ASKED, LONDON... WELCOME TO THE NEW WORLD!
MY CHILDREN...
I HUNGER.
BRING THEM TO ME, THE SACRIFICES...THE ONES WITH POWER... ALL OF THEM...

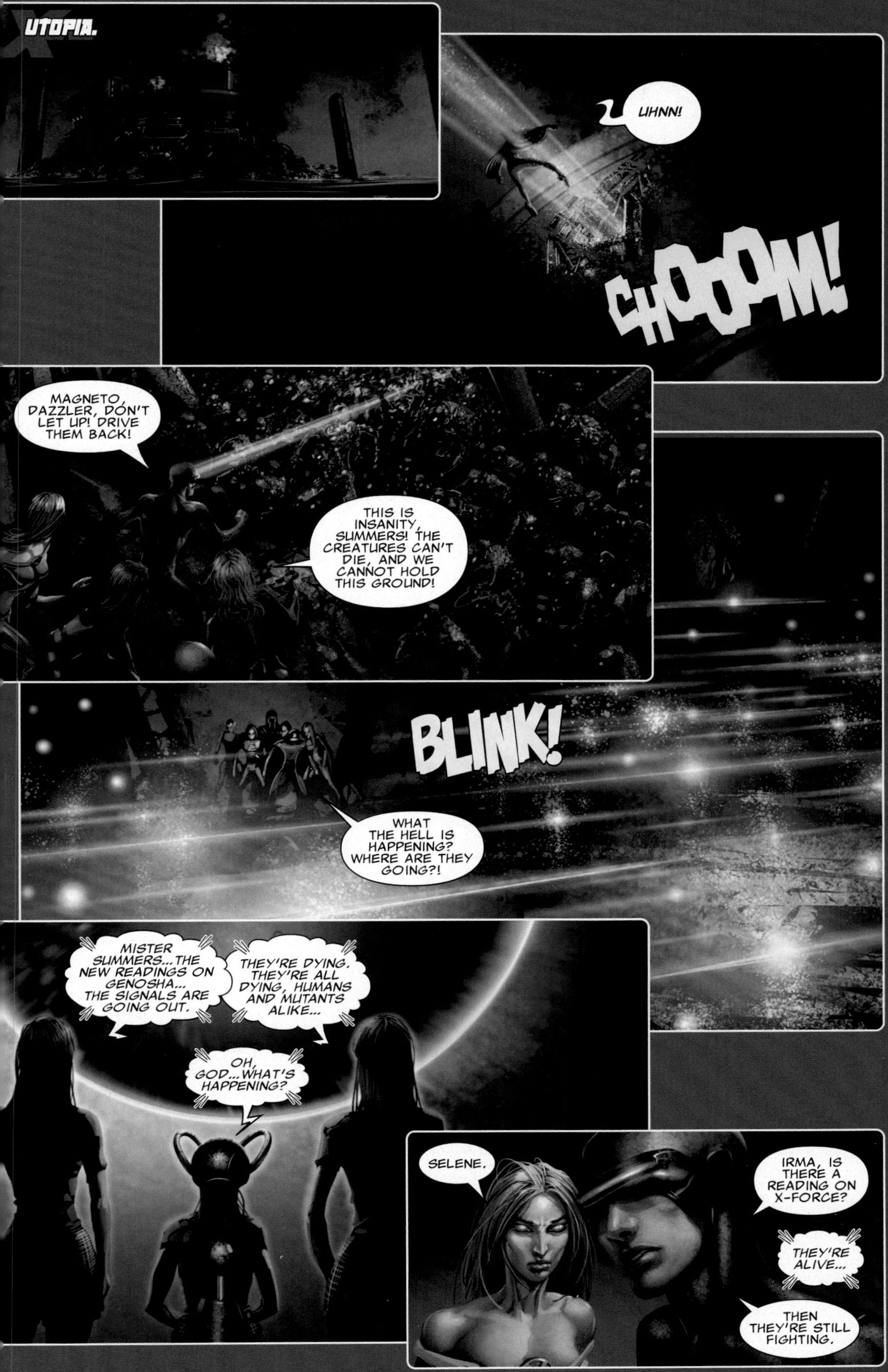
UTOPIA.
UHNN!
CHOOOM!
MAGNETO, DAZZLER, DON'T LET UP! DRIVE THEM BACK!
THIS IS INSANITY, SUMMERS! THE CREATURES CAN'T DIE, AND WE CANNOT HOLD THIS GROUND!
BLINK!
WHAT THE HELL IS HAPPENING? WHERE ARE THEY GOING?!
MISTER SUMMERS...THE NEW READINGS ON GENOSHA... THE SIGNALS ARE GOING OUT.
THEY'RE DYING. THEY'RE ALL DYING, HUMANS AND MUTANTS ALIKE...
OH, GOD...WHAT'S HAPPENING?
SELENE.
IRMA, IS THERE A READING ON X-FORCE?
THEY'RE ALIVE...
THEN THEY'RE STILL FIGHTING.

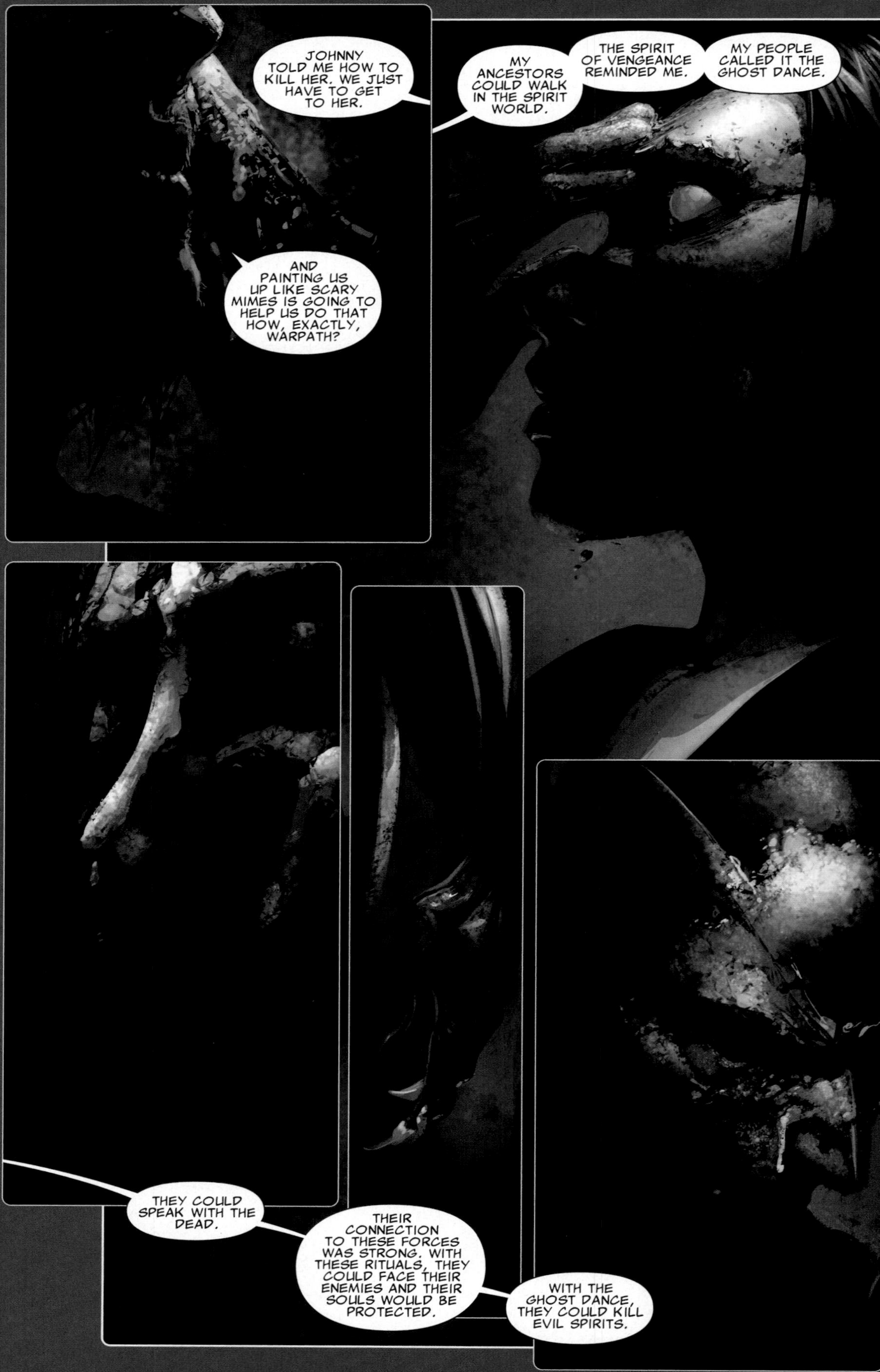
JOHNNY TOLD ME HOW TO KILL HER. WE JUST HAVE TO GET TO HER.
MY ANCESTORS COULD WALK IN THE SPIRIT WORLD.
THE SPIRIT OF VENGEANCE REMINDED ME.
MY PEOPLE CALLED IT THE GHOST DANCE.
AND PAINTING US UP LIKE SCARY MIMES IS GOING TO HELP US DO THAT HOW, EXACTLY, WARPATH?
THEY COULD SPEAK WITH THE DEAD.
THEIR CONNECTION TO THESE FORCES WAS STRONG. WITH THESE RITUALS, THEY COULD FACE THEIR ENEMIES AND THEIR SOULS WOULD BE PROTECTED.
WITH THE GHOST DANCE, THEY COULD KILL EVIL SPIRITS.

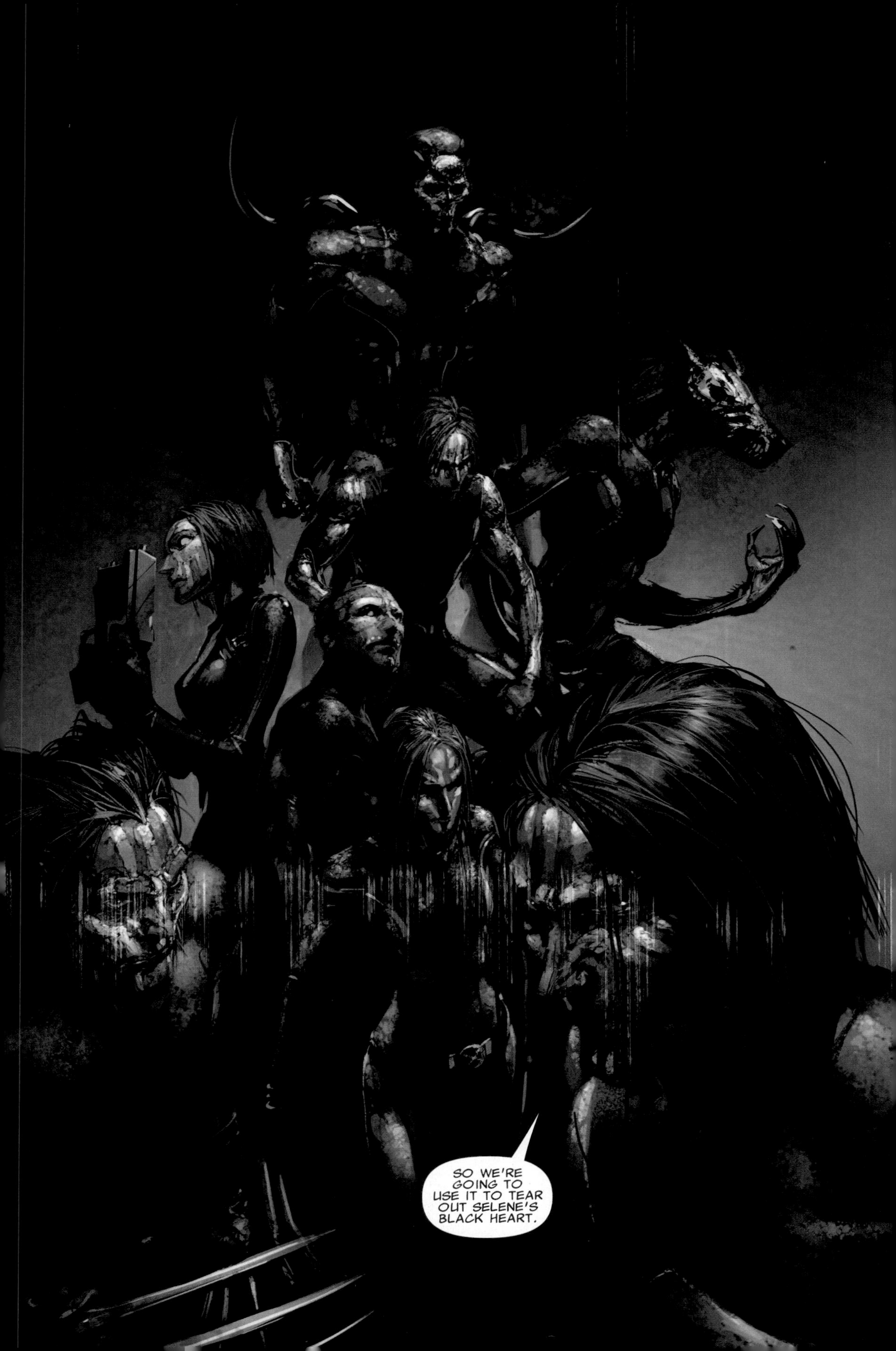
SO WE'RE GOING TO USE IT TO TEAR OUT SELENE'S BLACK HEART.

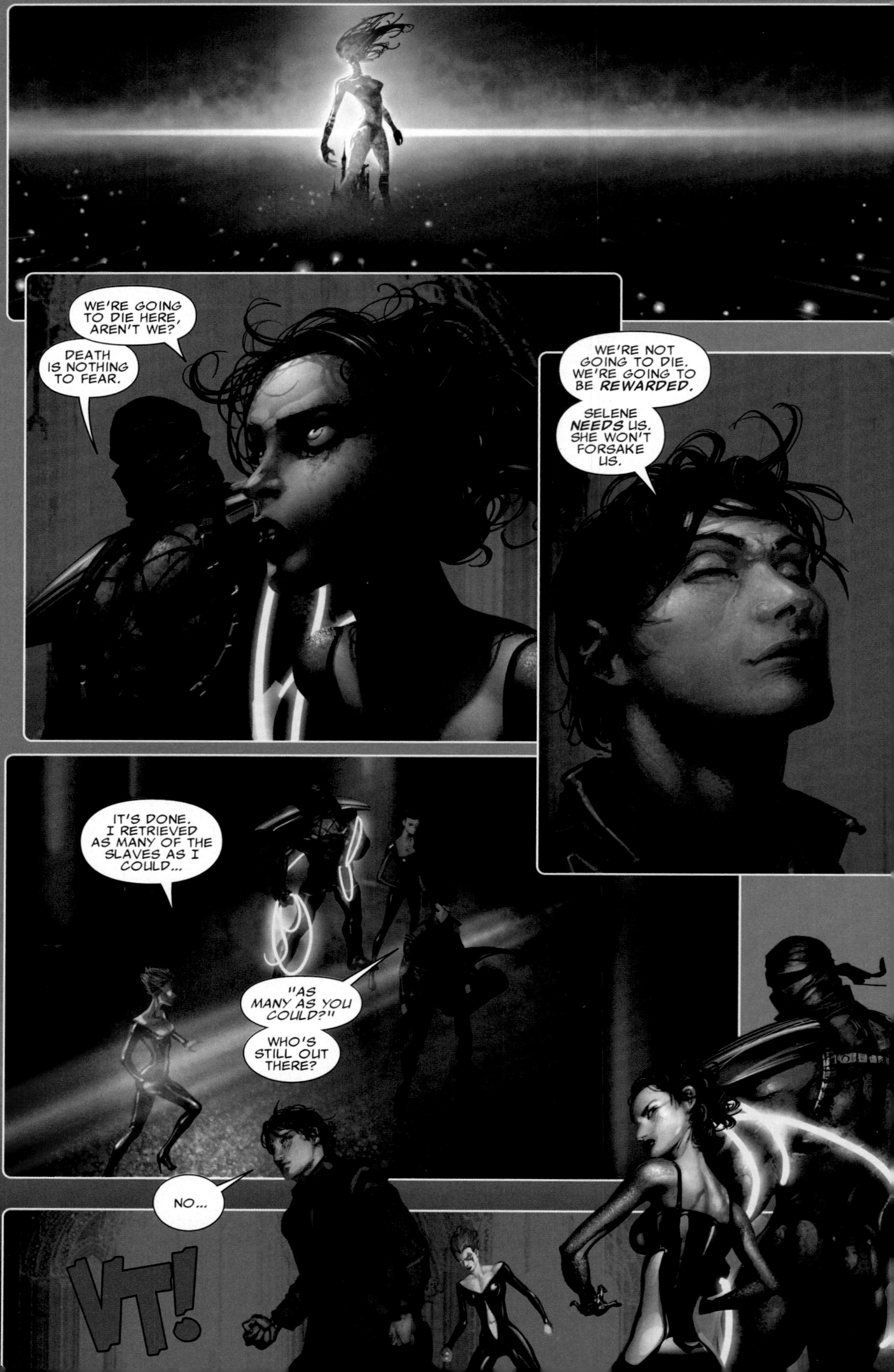
WE'RE GOING TO DIE HERE, AREN'T WE?
DEATH IS NOTHING TO FEAR.
WE'RE NOT GOING TO DIE. WE'RE GOING TO BE **REWARDED.**
SELENE **NEEDS** US. SHE WON'T FORSAKE US.
IT'S DONE. I RETRIEVED AS MANY OF THE SLAVES AS I COULD...
"AS MANY AS YOU COULD?"
WHO'S STILL OUT THERE?
NO...
VT!

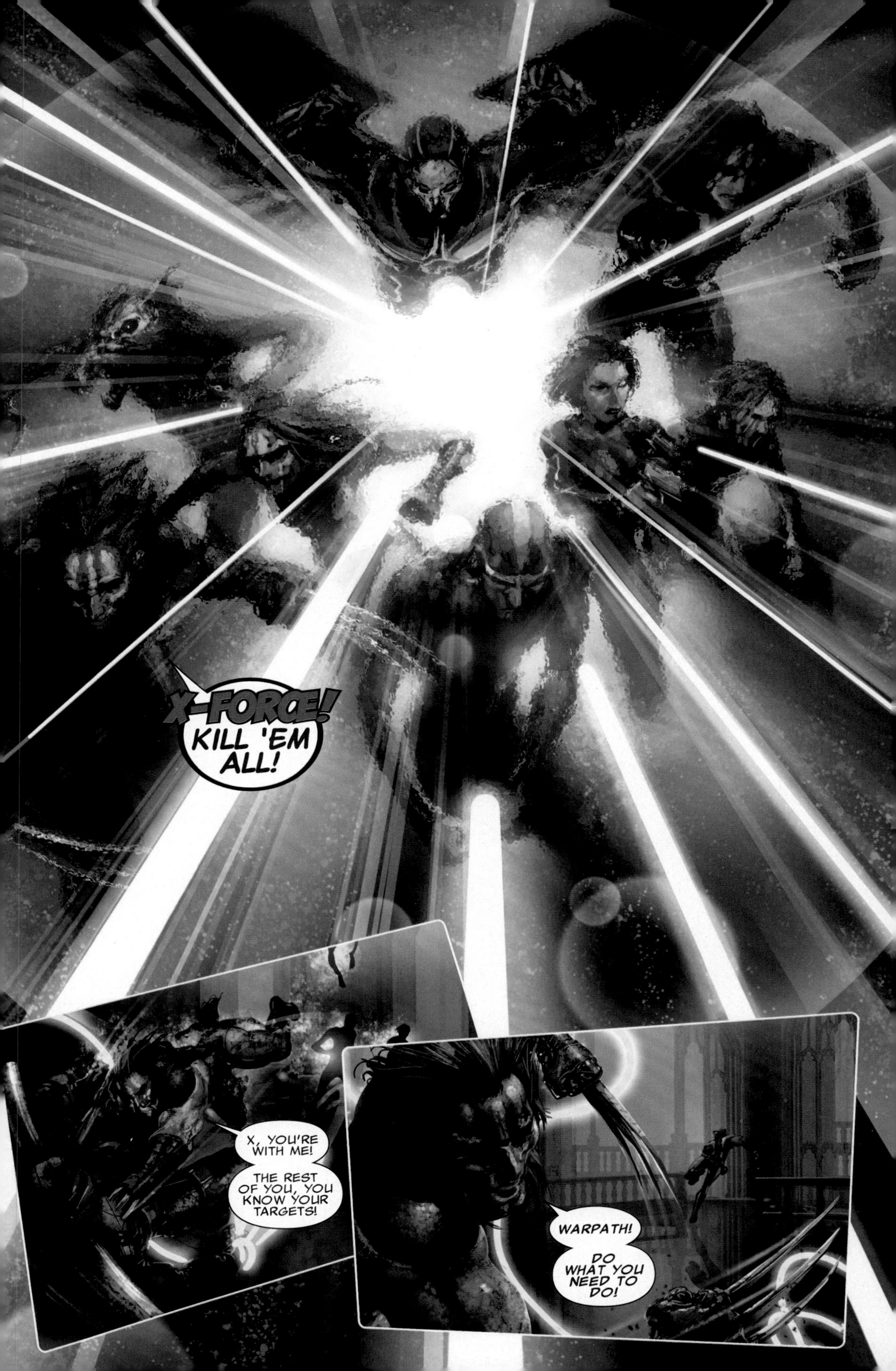
X-FORCE! KILL 'EM ALL!
X, YOU'RE WITH ME!
THE REST OF YOU, YOU KNOW YOUR TARGETS!
WARPATH!
DO WHAT YOU NEED TO DO!

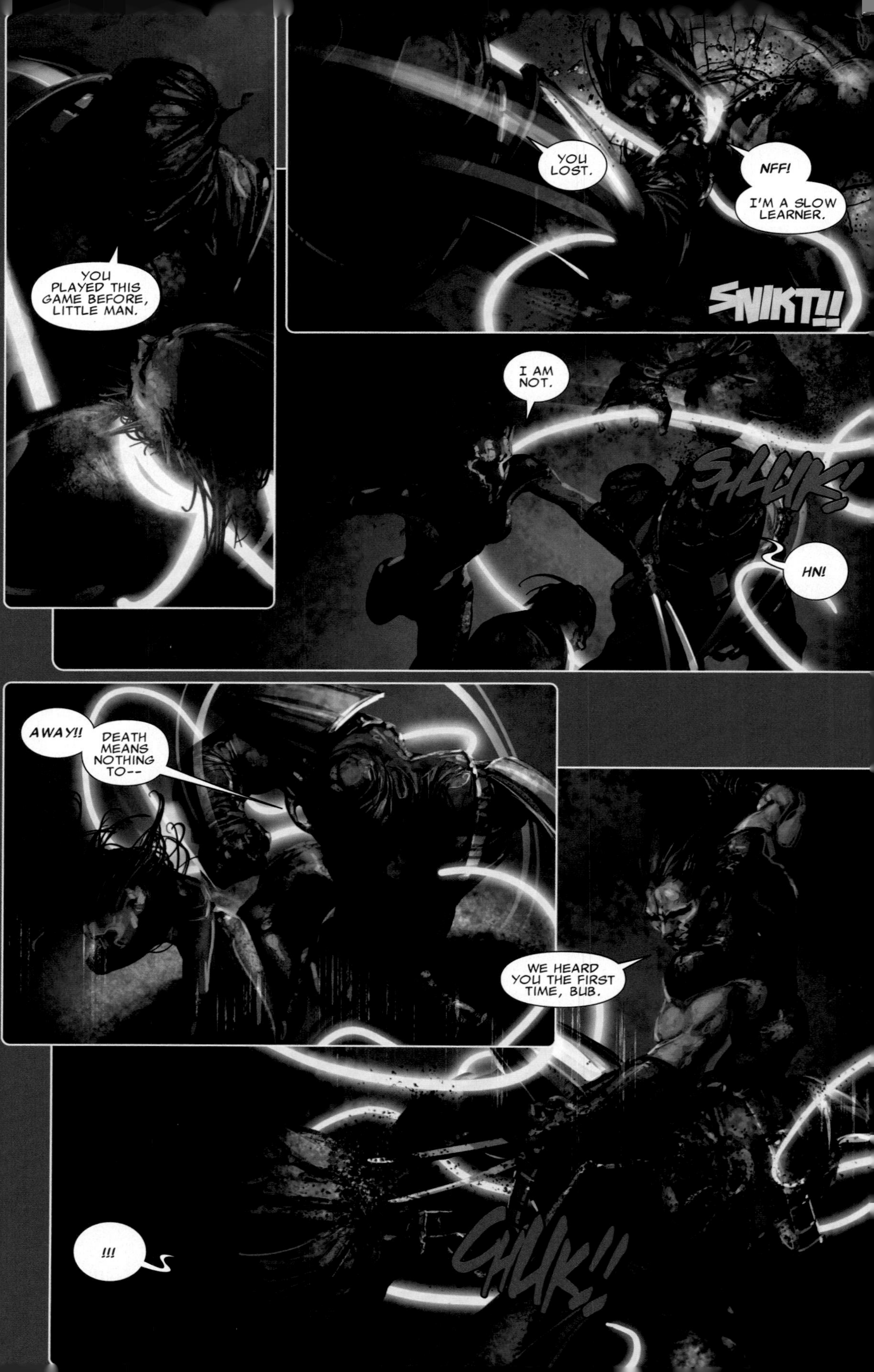
YOU PLAYED THIS GAME BEFORE, LITTLE MAN.
YOU LOST.
NFF!
I'M A SLOW LEARNER.
SNIKT!!
I AM NOT.
SHLUK!
HN!
AWAY!!
DEATH MEANS NOTHING TO--
WE HEARD YOU THE FIRST TIME, BUB.
!!!
CHUK!!

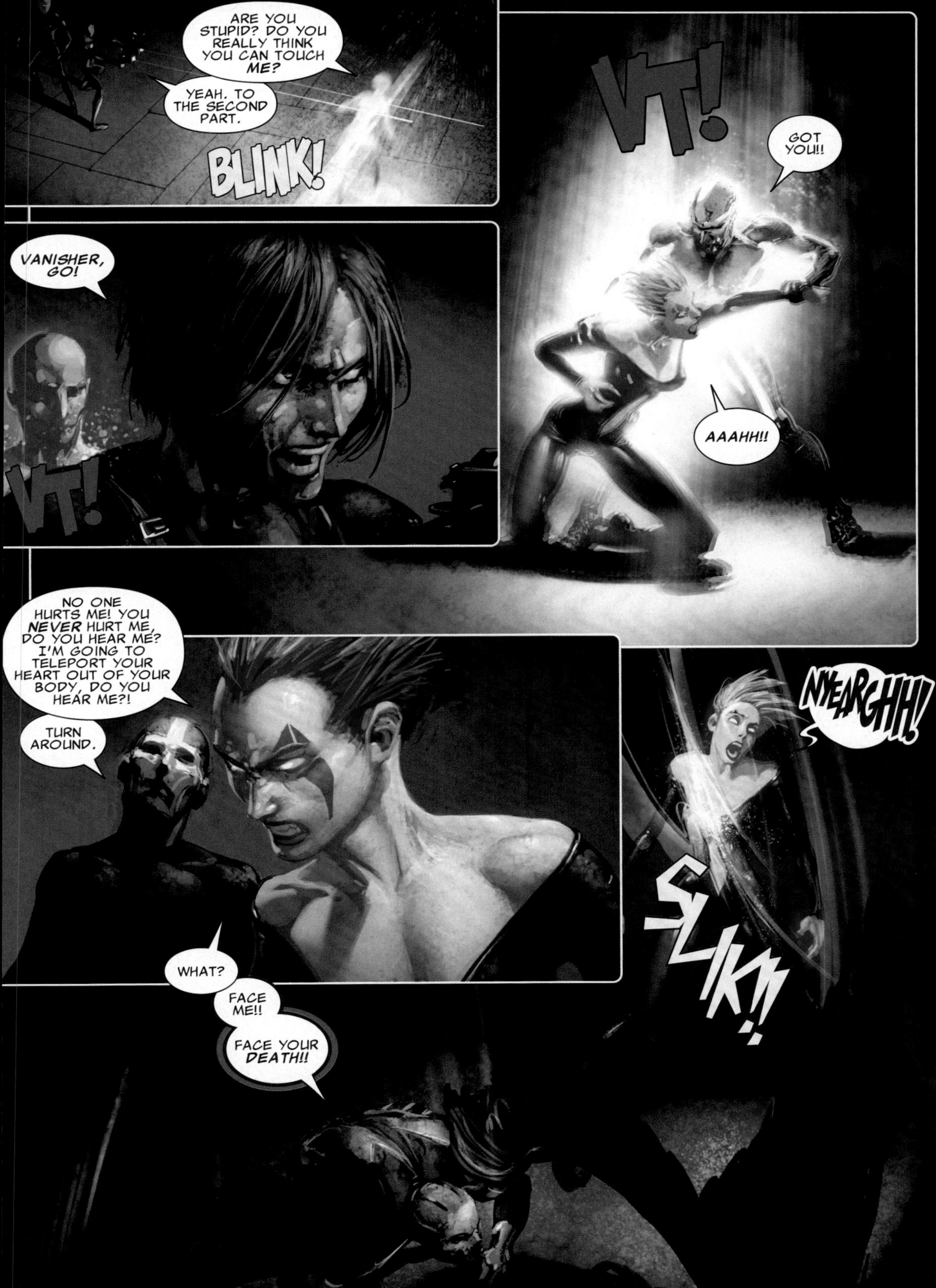

ARE YOU STUPID? DO YOU REALLY THINK YOU CAN TOUCH ME?
YEAH. TO THE SECOND PART.
BLINK!
VT!
GOT YOU!!
AAAHH!!
VANISHER, GO!
VT!
NO ONE HURTS ME! YOU NEVER HURT ME, DO YOU HEAR ME? I'M GOING TO TELEPORT YOUR HEART OUT OF YOUR BODY, DO YOU HEAR ME?!
TURN AROUND.
WHAT?
FACE ME!!
FACE YOUR DEATH!!
NYEARGHH!
SLIK!!

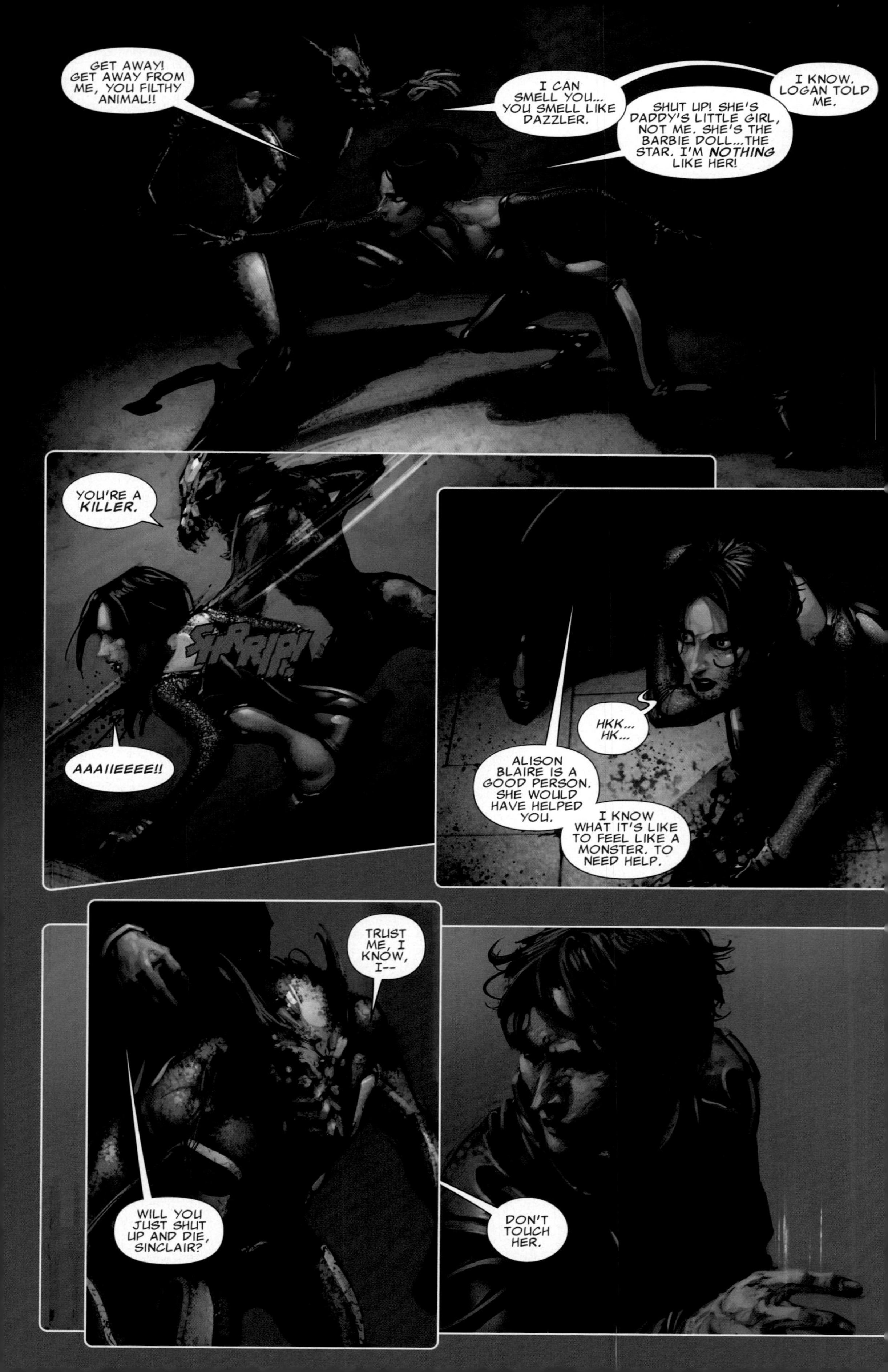
GET AWAY! GET AWAY FROM ME, YOU FILTHY ANIMAL!!
I CAN SMELL YOU... YOU SMELL LIKE DAZZLER.
I KNOW. LOGAN TOLD ME.
SHUT UP! SHE'S DADDY'S LITTLE GIRL, NOT ME. SHE'S THE BARBIE DOLL...THE STAR. I'M NOTHING LIKE HER!
YOU'RE A KILLER.
SHRRIP!
AAAIIEEEE!!
HKK... HK...
ALISON BLAIRE IS A GOOD PERSON. SHE WOULD HAVE HELPED YOU.
I KNOW WHAT IT'S LIKE TO FEEL LIKE A MONSTER. TO NEED HELP.
TRUST ME, I KNOW, I--
WILL YOU JUST SHUT UP AND DIE, SINCLAIR?
DON'T TOUCH HER.

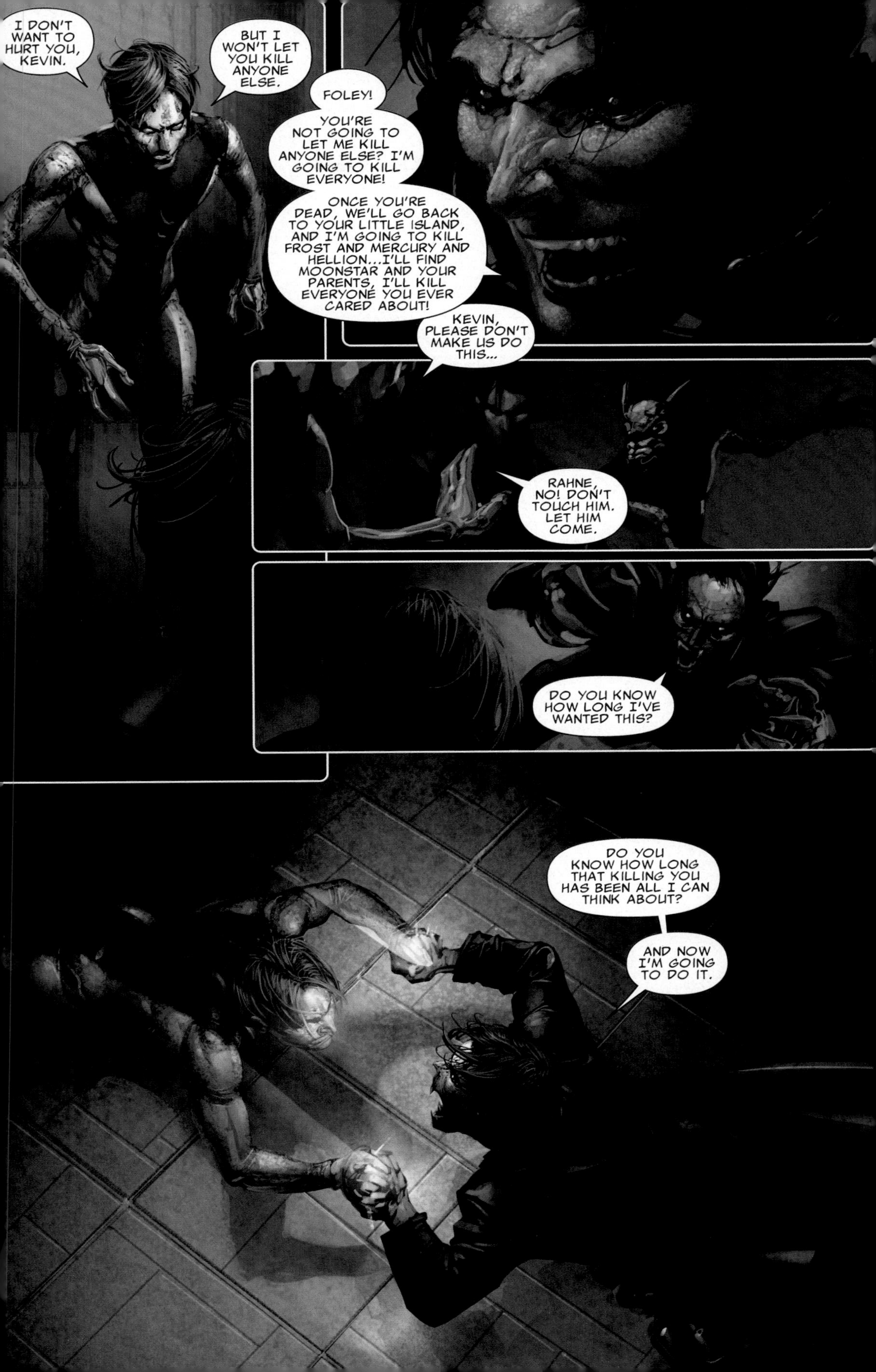
I DON'T WANT TO HURT YOU, KEVIN.
BUT I WON'T LET YOU KILL ANYONE ELSE.
FOLEY!
YOU'RE NOT GOING TO LET ME KILL ANYONE ELSE? I'M GOING TO KILL EVERYONE!
ONCE YOU'RE DEAD, WE'LL GO BACK TO YOUR LITTLE ISLAND, AND I'M GOING TO KILL FROST AND MERCURY AND HELLION...I'LL FIND MOONSTAR AND YOUR PARENTS, I'LL KILL EVERYONE YOU EVER CARED ABOUT!
KEVIN, PLEASE DON'T MAKE US DO THIS...
RAHNE, NO! DON'T TOUCH HIM. LET HIM COME.
DO YOU KNOW HOW LONG I'VE WANTED THIS?
DO YOU KNOW HOW LONG THAT KILLING YOU HAS BEEN ALL I CAN THINK ABOUT?
AND NOW I'M GOING TO DO IT.

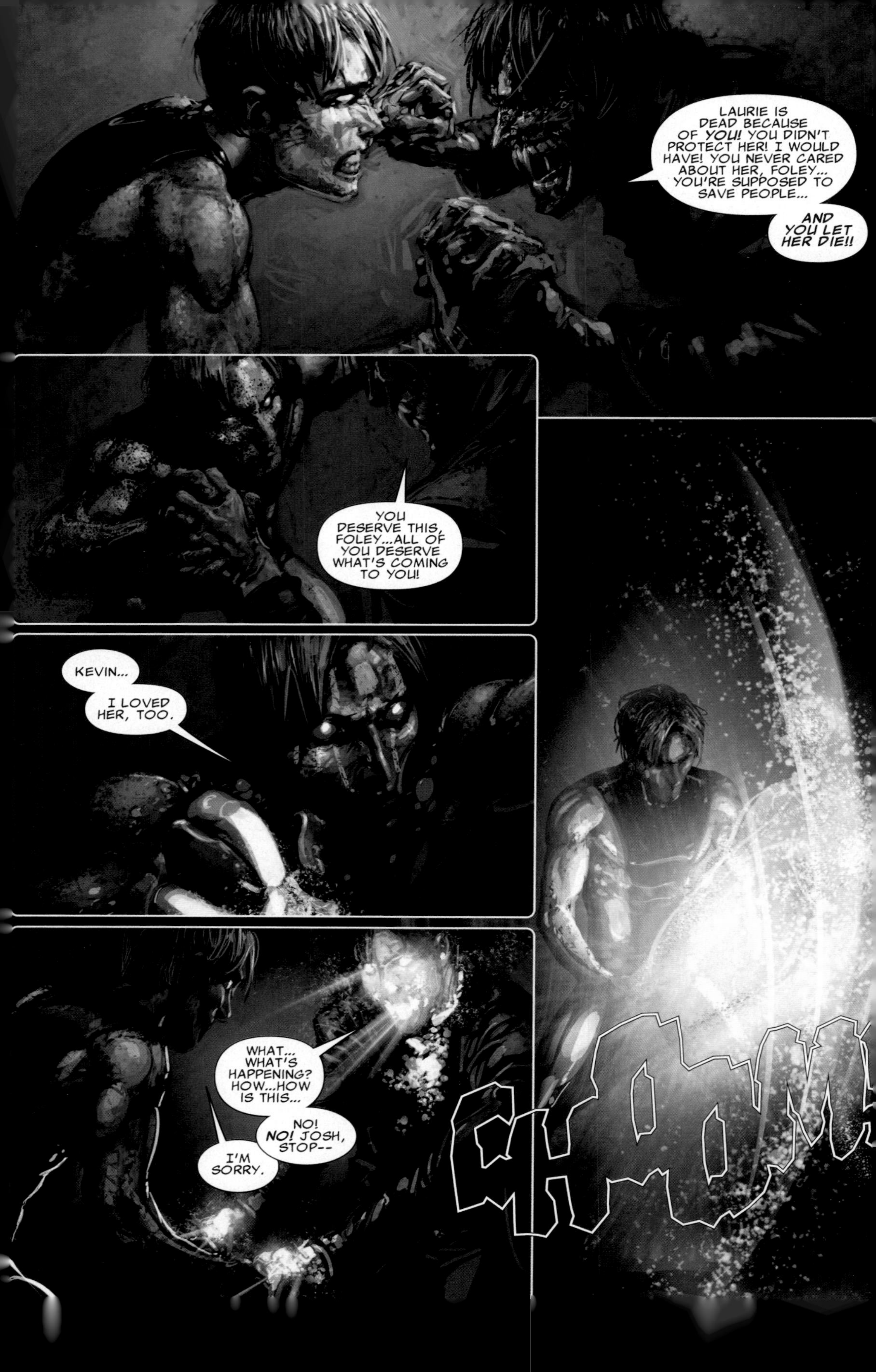
LAURIE IS DEAD BECAUSE OF YOU! YOU DIDN'T PROTECT HER! I WOULD HAVE! YOU NEVER CARED ABOUT HER, FOLEY... YOU'RE SUPPOSED TO SAVE PEOPLE...
AND YOU LET HER DIE!!
YOU DESERVE THIS, FOLEY...ALL OF YOU DESERVE WHAT'S COMING TO YOU!
KEVIN...
I LOVED HER, TOO.
WHAT... WHAT'S HAPPENING? HOW...HOW IS THIS...
NO! NO! JOSH, STOP--
I'M SORRY.

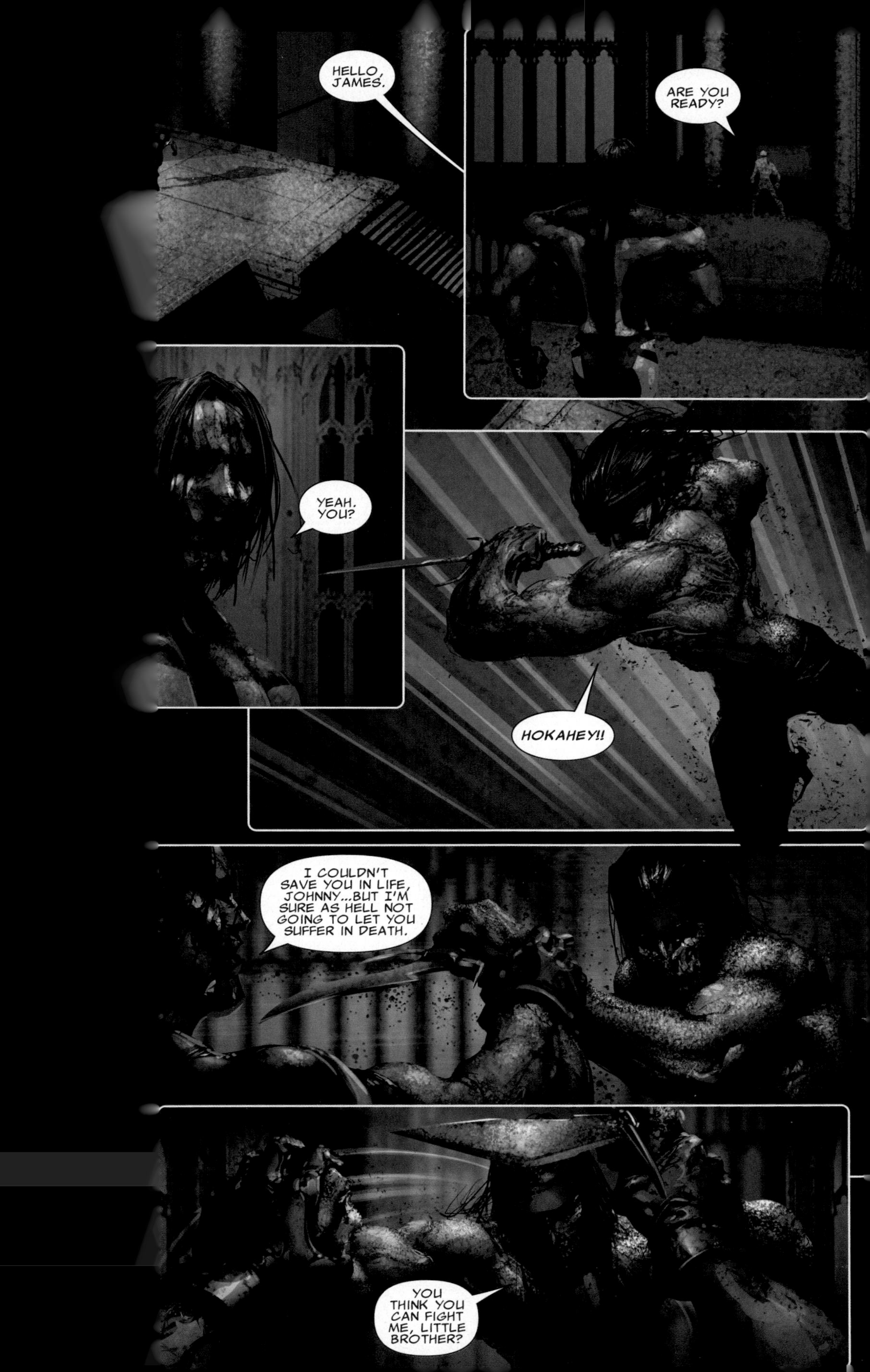
HELLO, JAMES.
ARE YOU READY?
YEAH. YOU?
HOKAHEY!!
I COULDN'T SAVE YOU IN LIFE, JOHNNY...BUT I'M SURE AS HELL NOT GOING TO LET YOU SUFFER IN DEATH.
YOU THINK YOU CAN FIGHT ME, LITTLE BROTHER?

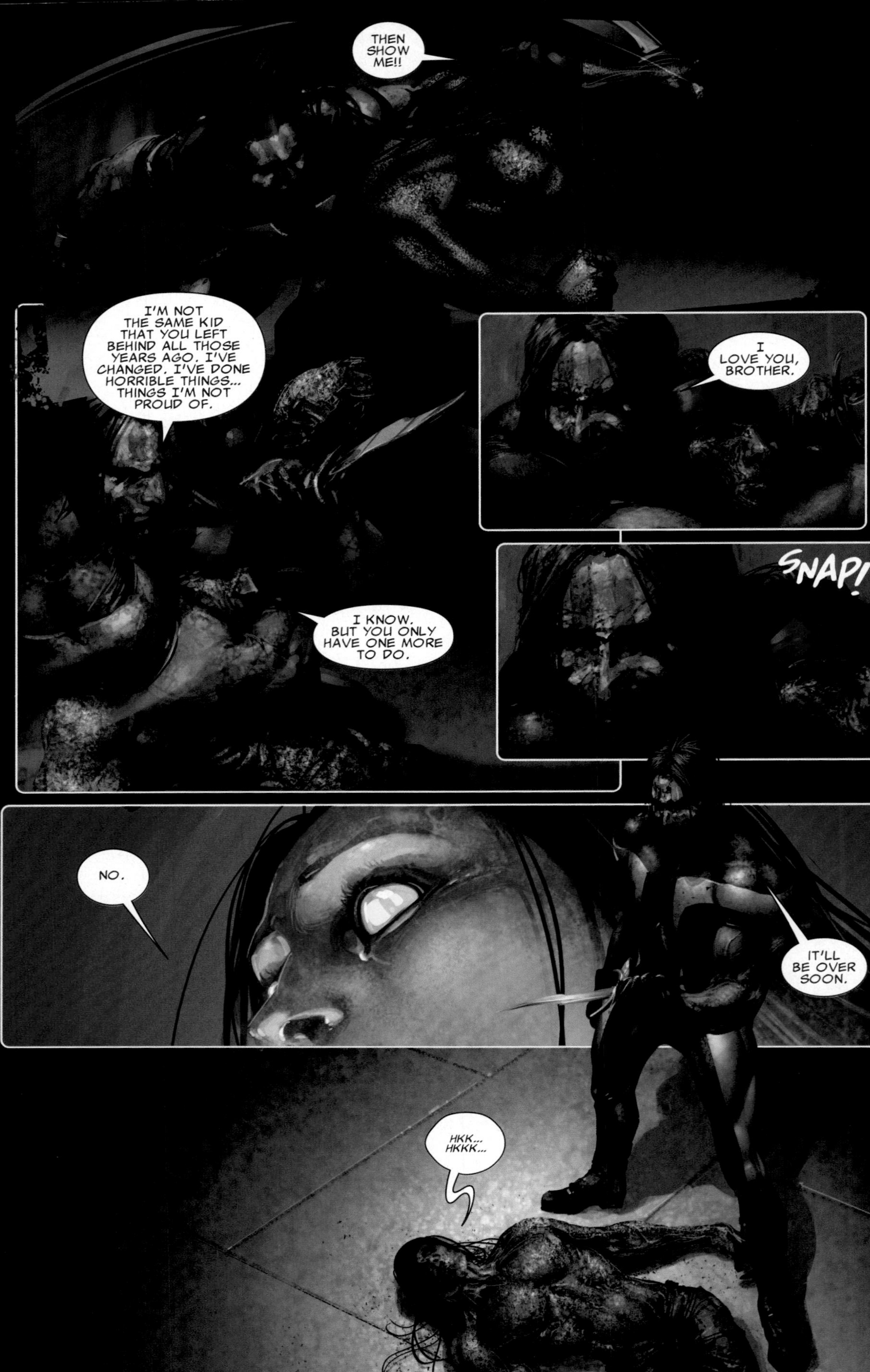
THEN SHOW ME!!
I'M NOT THE SAME KID THAT YOU LEFT BEHIND ALL THOSE YEARS AGO. I'VE CHANGED. I'VE DONE HORRIBLE THINGS... THINGS I'M NOT PROUD OF.
I KNOW. BUT YOU ONLY HAVE ONE MORE TO DO.
I LOVE YOU, BROTHER.
SNAP!
NO.
IT'LL BE OVER SOON.
HKK... HKKK...

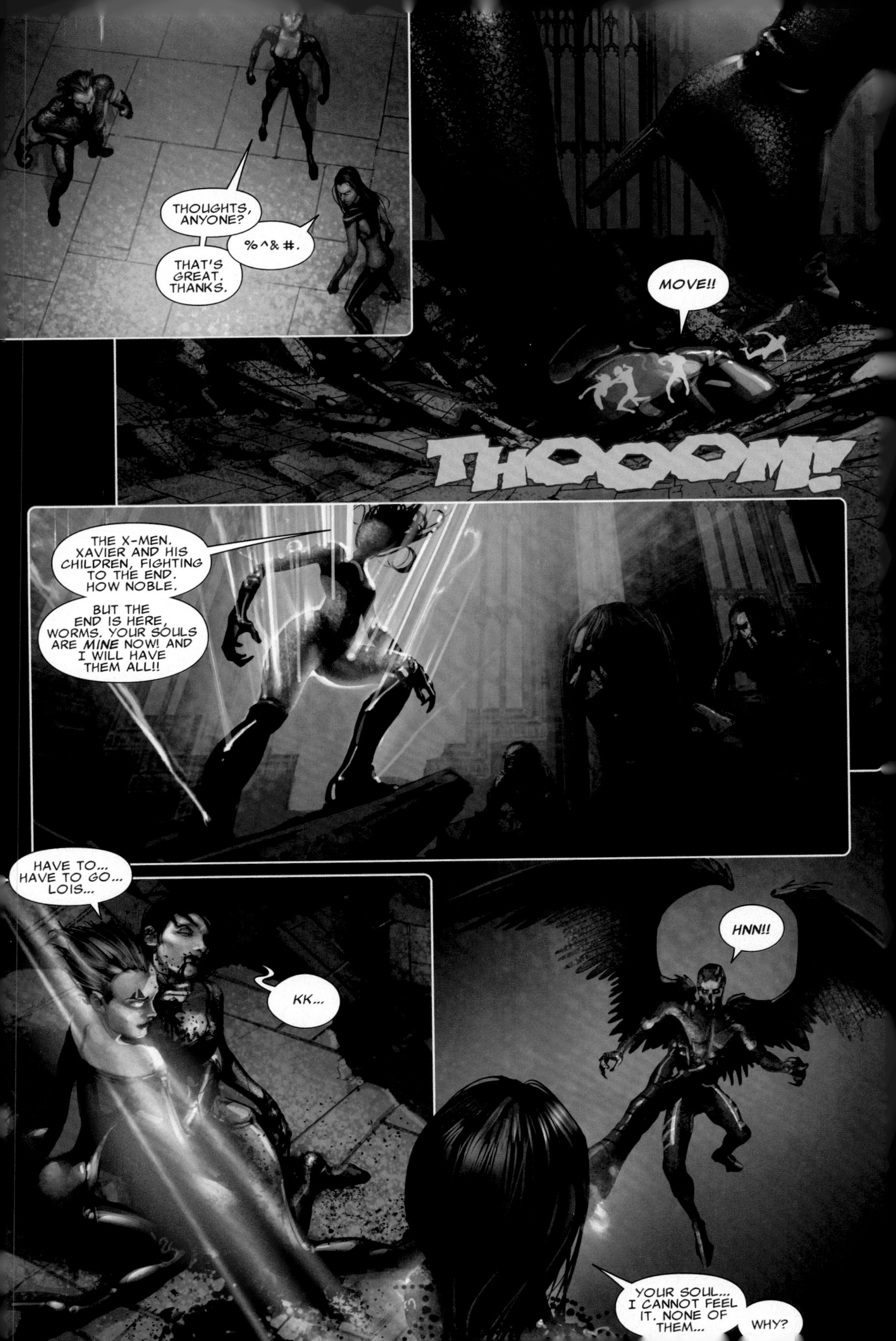
THOUGHTS, ANYONE?
%^&#.
THAT'S GREAT. THANKS.
MOVE!!
THOOOM!
THE X-MEN. XAVIER AND HIS CHILDREN, FIGHTING TO THE END. HOW NOBLE.
BUT THE END IS HERE, WORMS. YOUR SOULS ARE *MINE* NOW! AND I WILL HAVE THEM ALL!!
HAVE TO... HAVE TO GO... LOIS...
KK...
HNN!!
YOUR SOUL... I CANNOT FEEL IT. NONE OF THEM...
WHY?

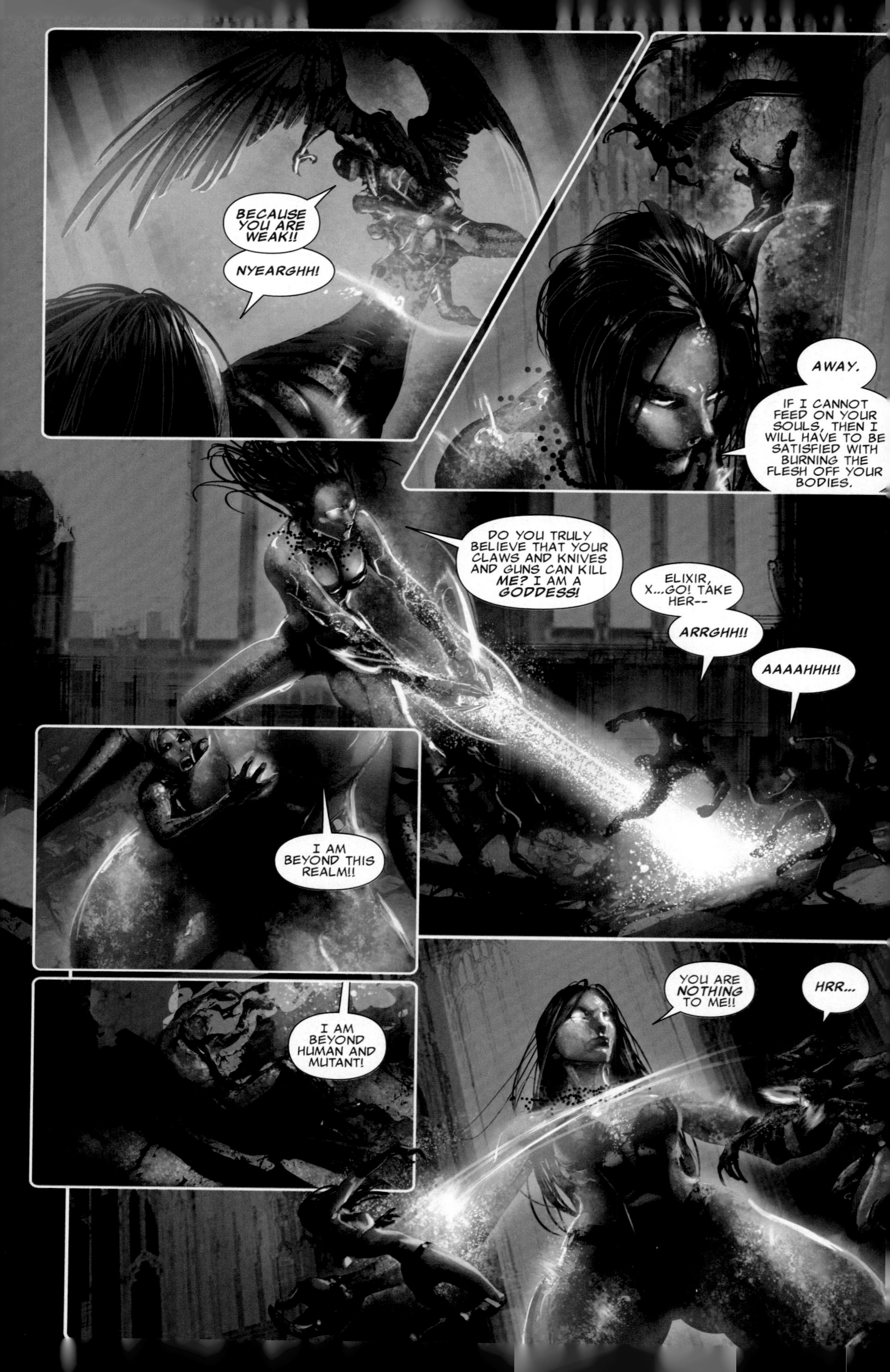
BECAUSE YOU ARE WEAK!!
NYEARGHH!
AWAY.
IF I CANNOT FEED ON YOUR SOULS, THEN I WILL HAVE TO BE SATISFIED WITH BURNING THE FLESH OFF YOUR BODIES.
DO YOU TRULY BELIEVE THAT YOUR CLAWS AND KNIVES AND GUNS CAN KILL ME? I AM A GODDESS!
ELIXIR, X...GO! TAKE HER--
ARRGHH!!
AAAAHHH!!
I AM BEYOND THIS REALM!!
I AM BEYOND HUMAN AND MUTANT!
YOU ARE NOTHING TO ME!!
HRR...

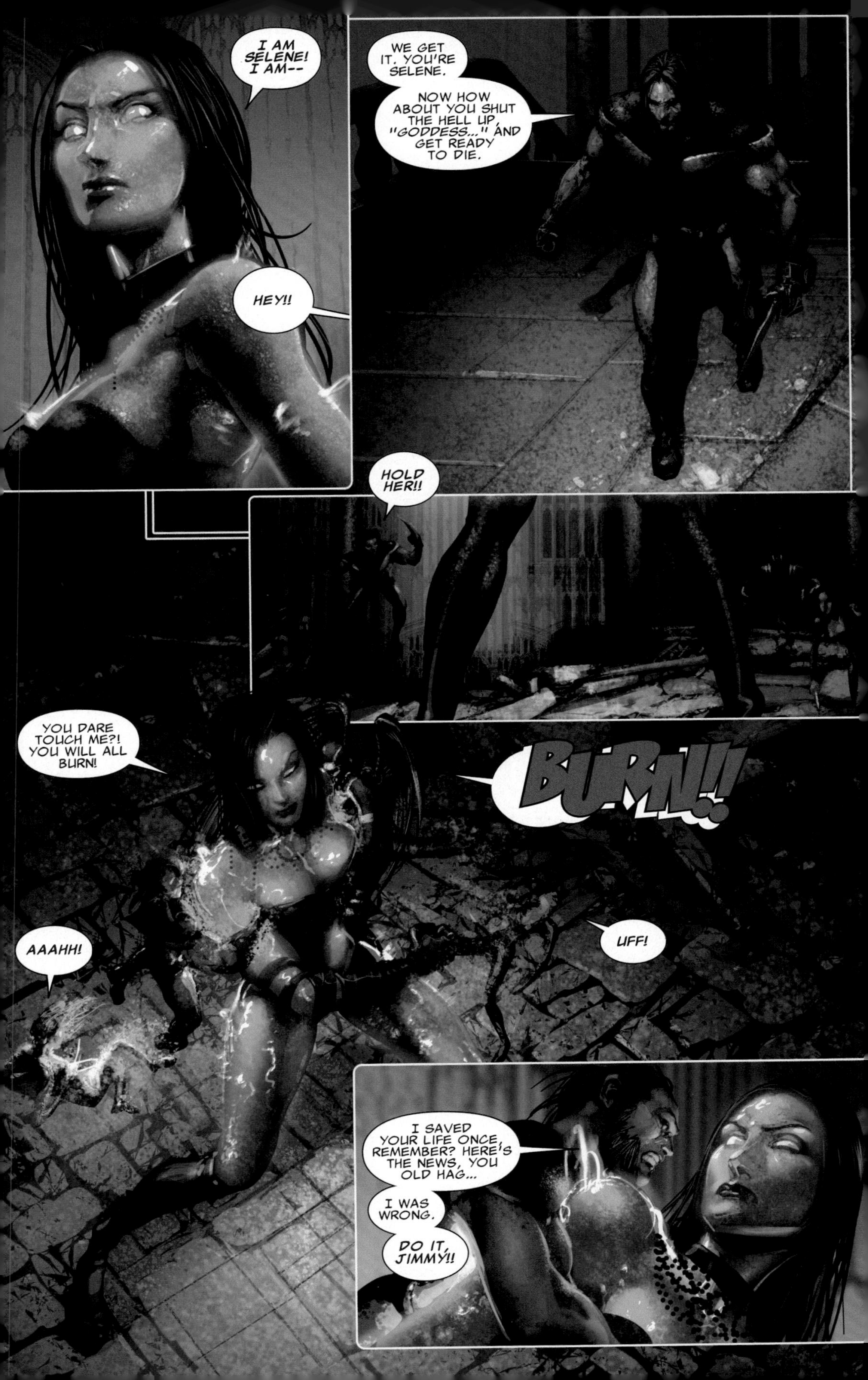
I AM SELENE! I AM--
WE GET IT. YOU'RE SELENE.
NOW HOW ABOUT YOU SHUT THE HELL UP, "GODDESS..." AND GET READY TO DIE.
HEY!!
HOLD HER!!
YOU DARE TOUCH ME?! YOU WILL ALL BURN!
BURN!!
AAAHH!
UFF!
I SAVED YOUR LIFE ONCE, REMEMBER? HERE'S THE NEWS, YOU OLD HAG...
I WAS WRONG.
DO IT, JIMMY!!

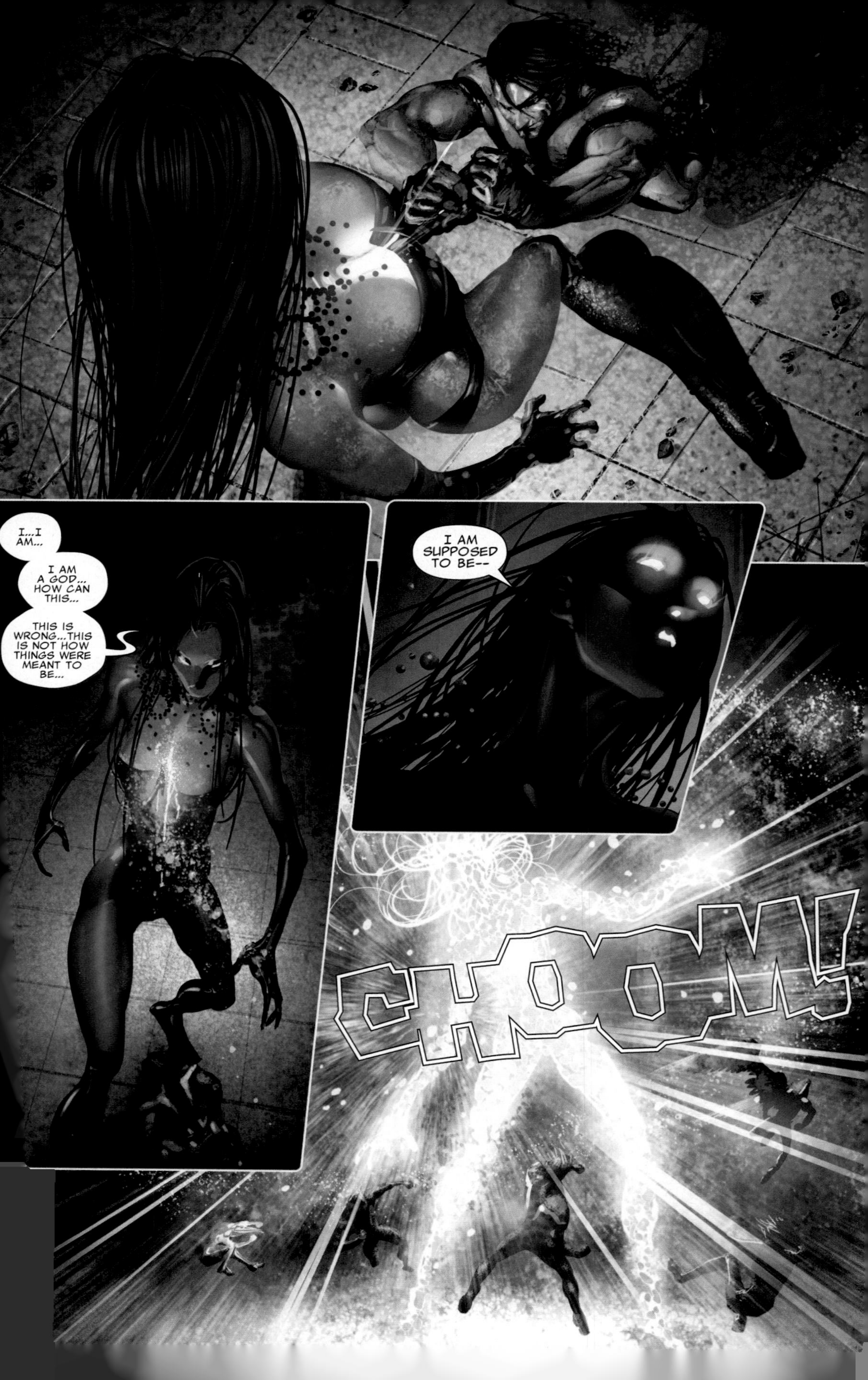
I...I AM...
I AM A GOD... HOW CAN THIS...
THIS IS WRONG...THIS IS NOT HOW THINGS WERE MEANT TO BE...
I AM SUPPOSED TO BE--
CHOOM!

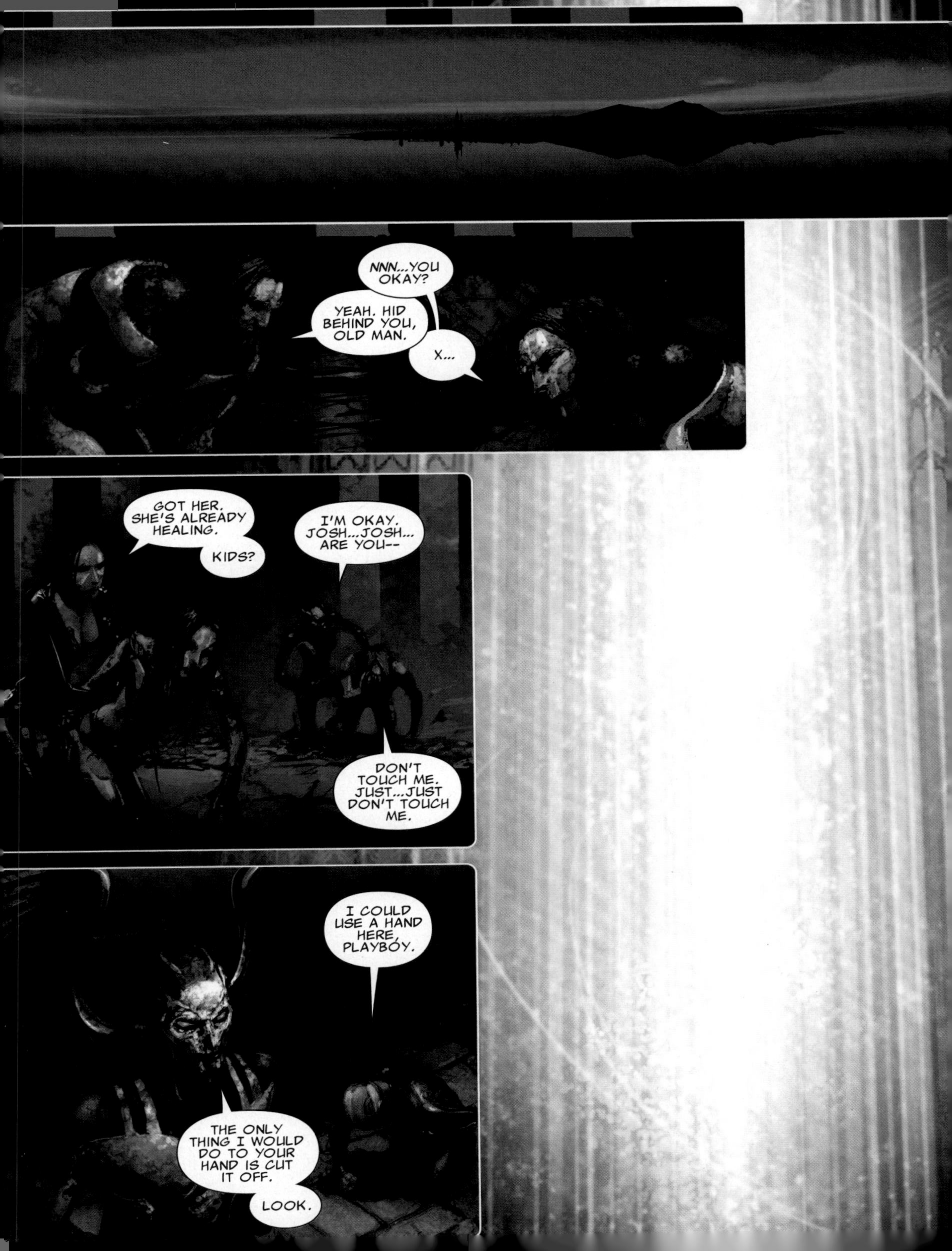
NNN...YOU OKAY?
YEAH. HID BEHIND YOU, OLD MAN.
X...
GOT HER. SHE'S ALREADY HEALING.
KIDS?
I'M OKAY. JOSH...JOSH... ARE YOU--
DON'T TOUCH ME. JUST...JUST DON'T TOUCH ME.
I COULD USE A HAND HERE, PLAYBOY.
THE ONLY THING I WOULD DO TO YOUR HAND IS CUT IT OFF.
LOOK.

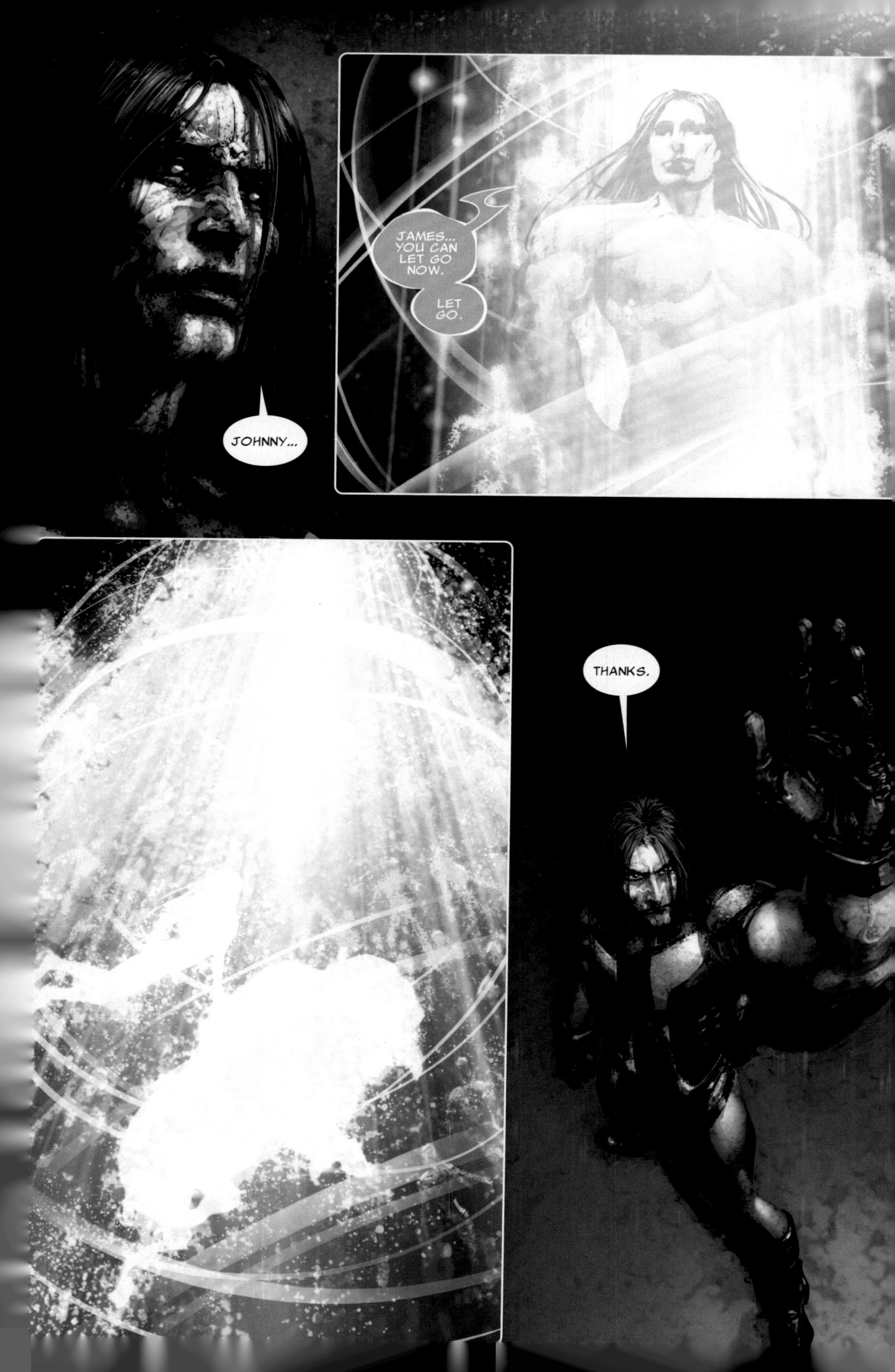
JOHNNY...
JAMES... YOU CAN LET GO NOW.
LET GO.
THANKS.

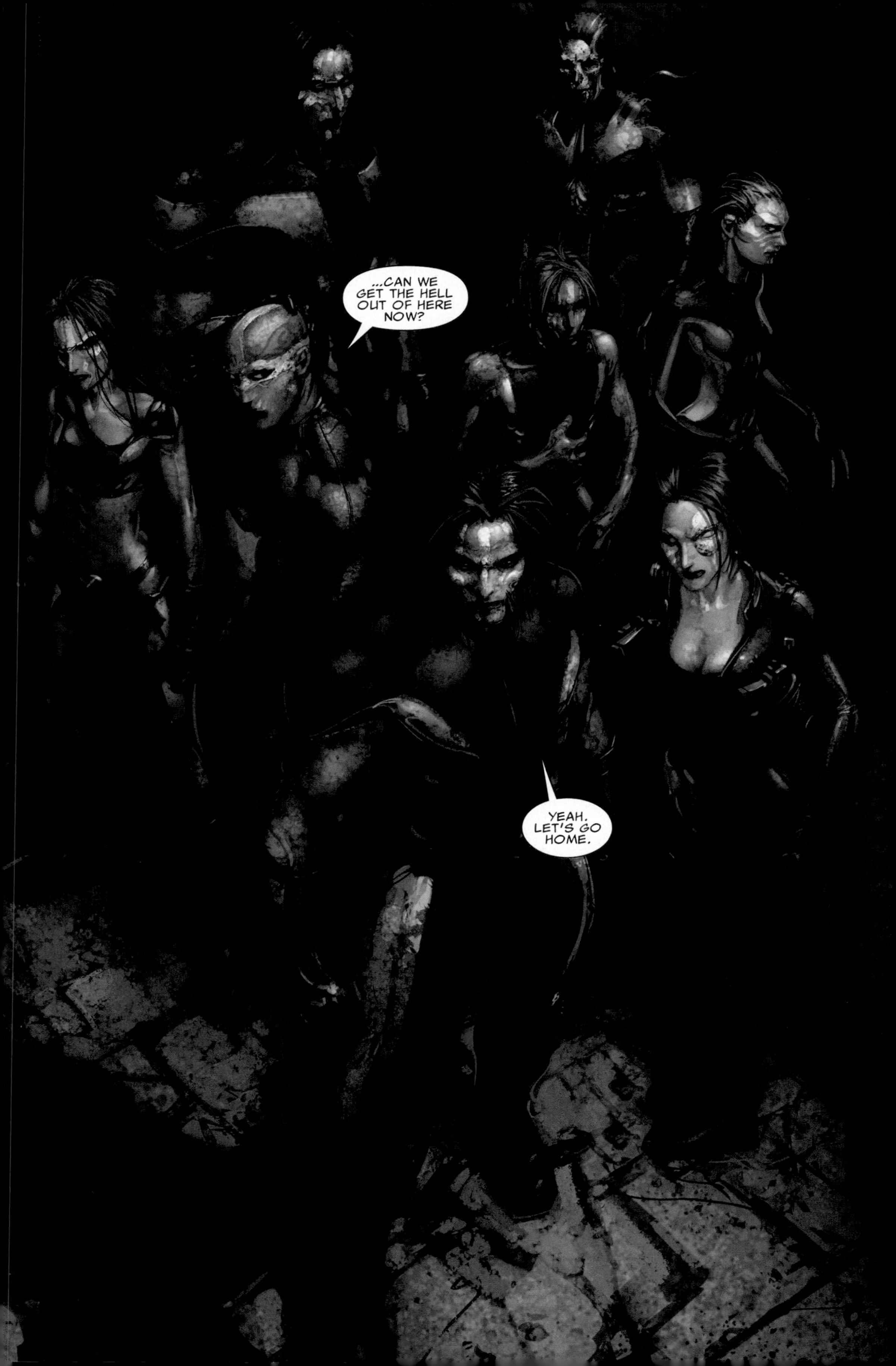
...CAN WE GET THE HELL OUT OF HERE NOW?
YEAH. LET'S GO HOME.

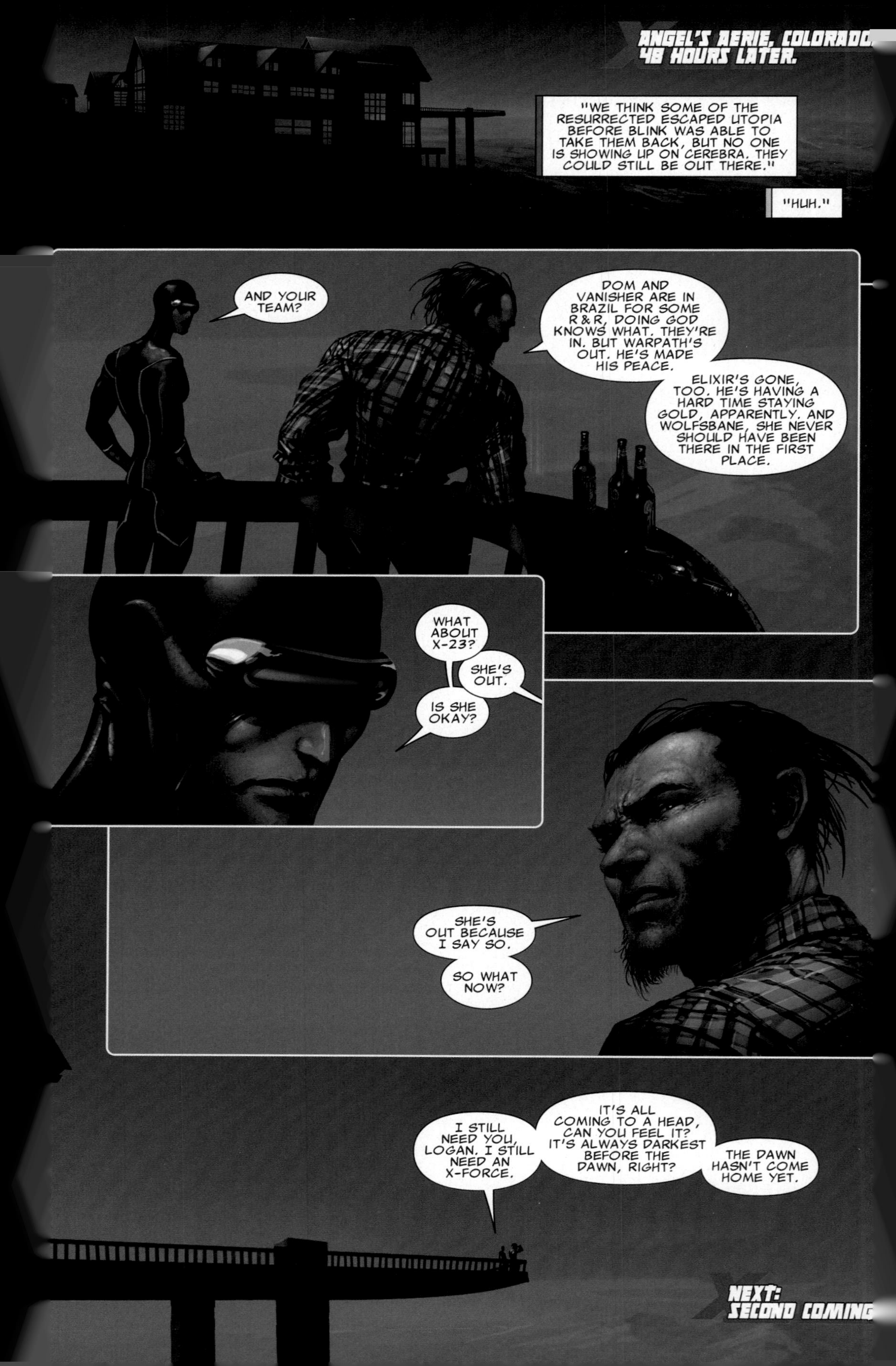
ANGEL'S AERIE, COLORADO
48 HOURS LATER.
"WE THINK SOME OF THE RESURRECTED ESCAPED UTOPIA BEFORE BLINK WAS ABLE TO TAKE THEM BACK, BUT NO ONE IS SHOWING UP ON CEREBRA. THEY COULD STILL BE OUT THERE."
"HUH."
AND YOUR TEAM?
DOM AND VANISHER ARE IN BRAZIL FOR SOME R & R, DOING GOD KNOWS WHAT. THEY'RE IN. BUT WARPATH'S OUT. HE'S MADE HIS PEACE.
ELIXIR'S GONE, TOO. HE'S HAVING A HARD TIME STAYING GOLD, APPARENTLY. AND WOLFSBANE, SHE NEVER SHOULD HAVE BEEN THERE IN THE FIRST PLACE.
WHAT ABOUT X-23?
SHE'S OUT.
IS SHE OKAY?
SHE'S OUT BECAUSE I SAY SO.
SO WHAT NOW?
I STILL NEED YOU, LOGAN. I STILL NEED AN X-FORCE.
IT'S ALL COMING TO A HEAD, CAN YOU FEEL IT? IT'S ALWAYS DARKEST BEFORE THE DAWN, RIGHT?
THE DAWN HASN'T COME HOME YET.
NEXT:
SECOND COMING

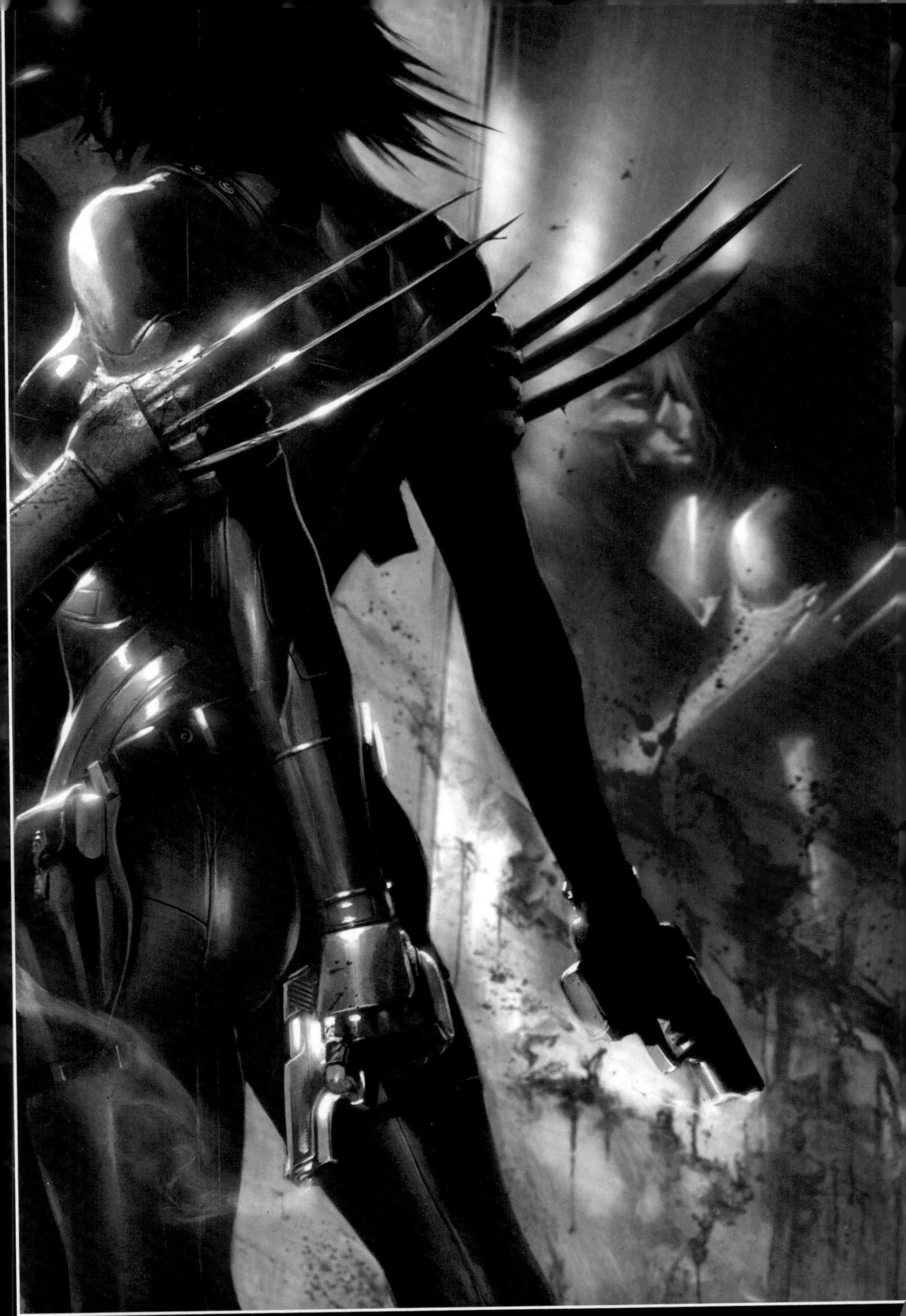

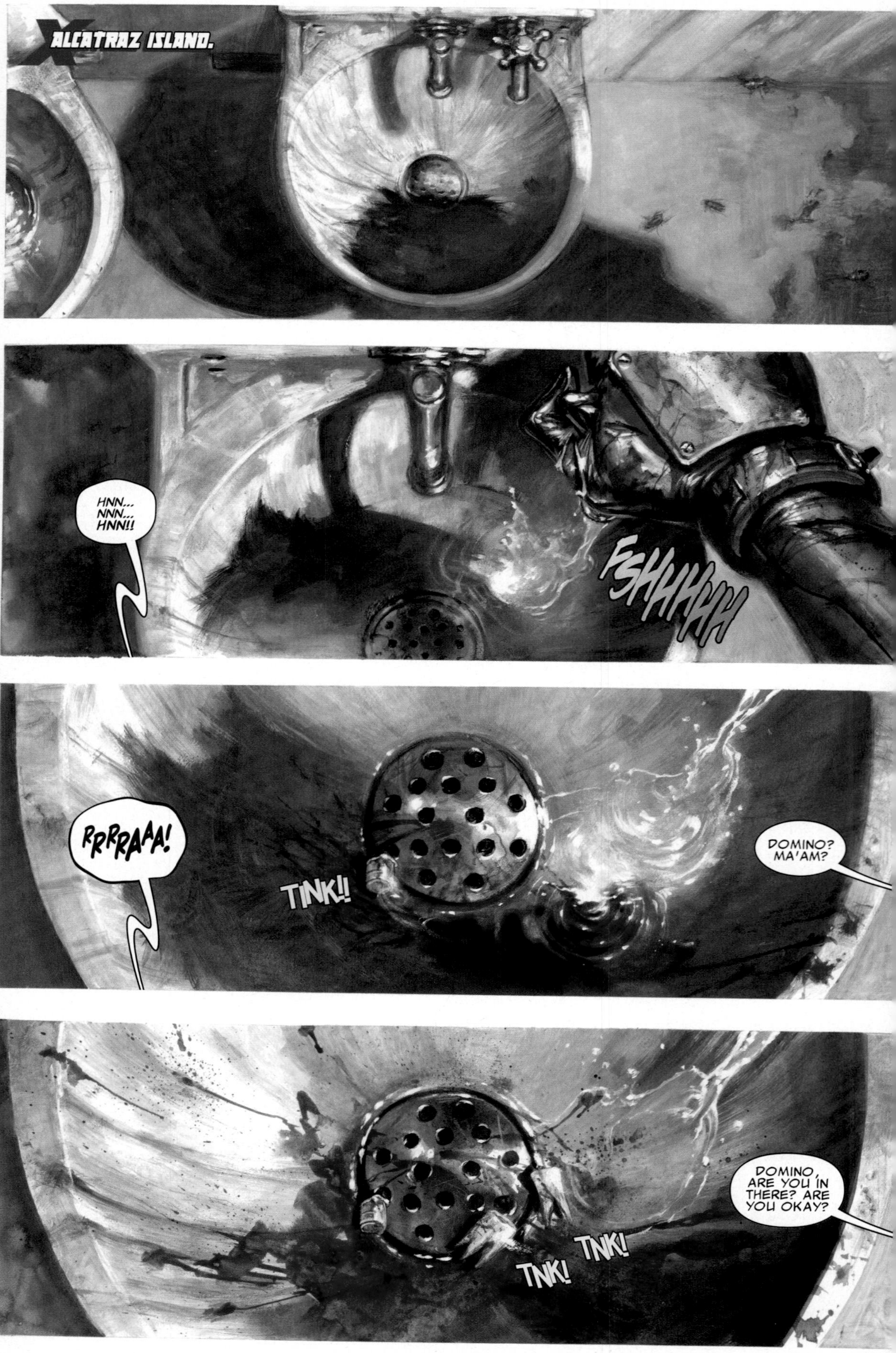
ALCATRAZ ISLAND.
HNN... NNN... HNN!!
FSHHHHHH
RRRRAAA!
TINK!!
DOMINO? MA'AM?
DOMINO, ARE YOU IN THERE? ARE YOU OKAY?
TNK! TNK!

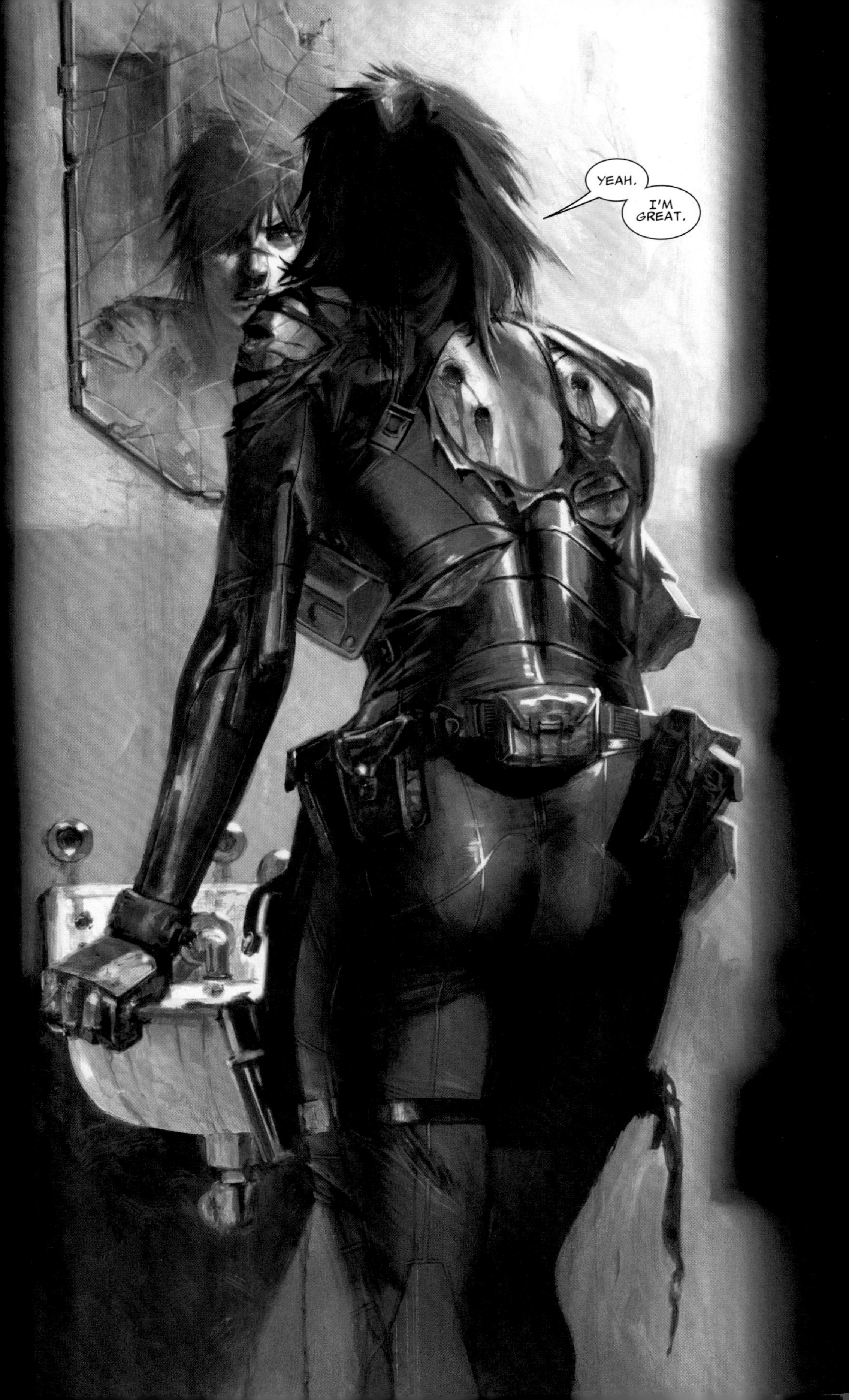
YEAH.
I'M GREAT.

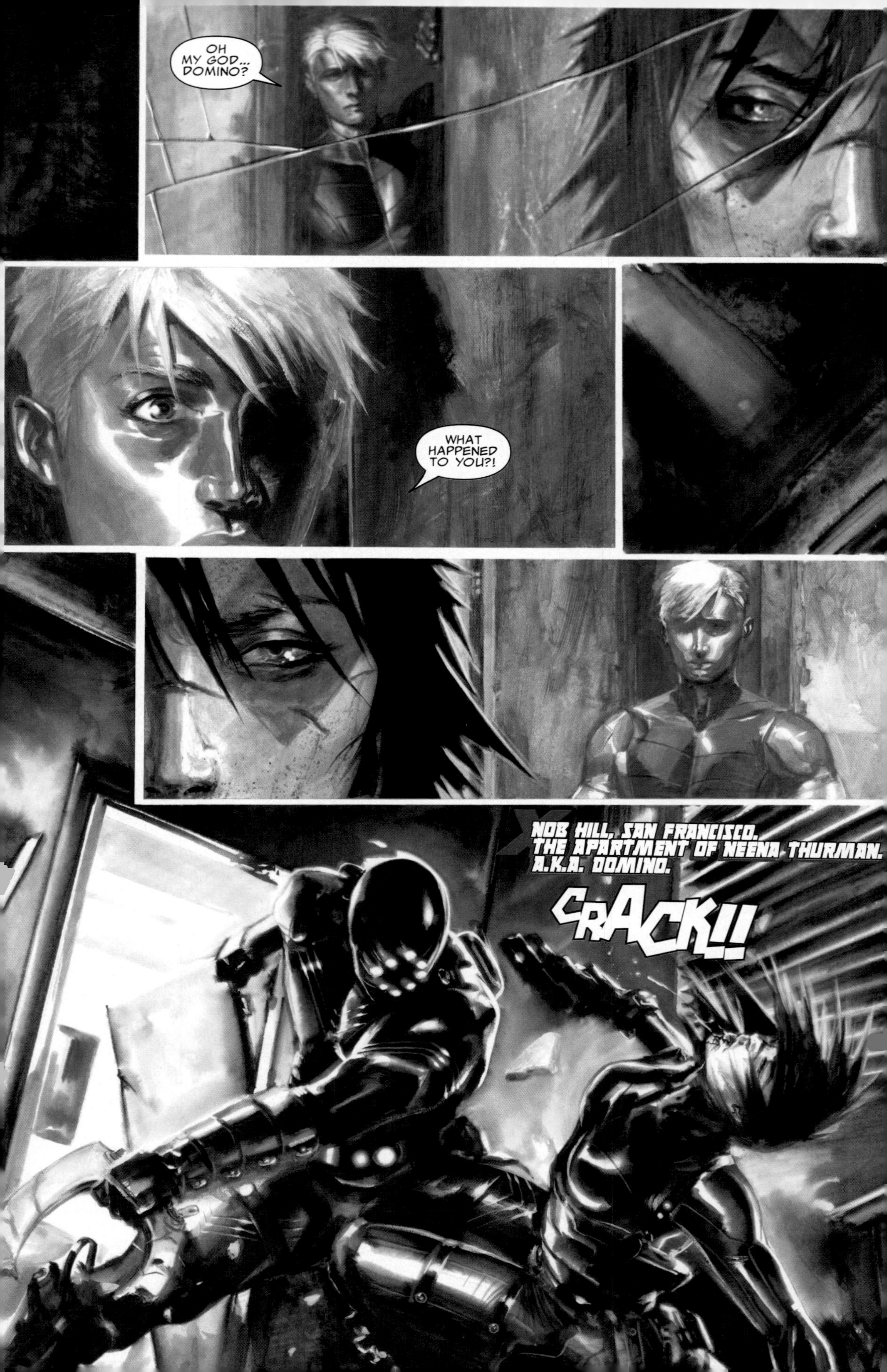

OH MY GOD... DOMINO?
WHAT HAPPENED TO YOU?!
NOB HILL, SAN FRANCISCO.
THE APARTMENT OF NEENA THURMAN.
A.K.A. DOMINO.
CRACK!!

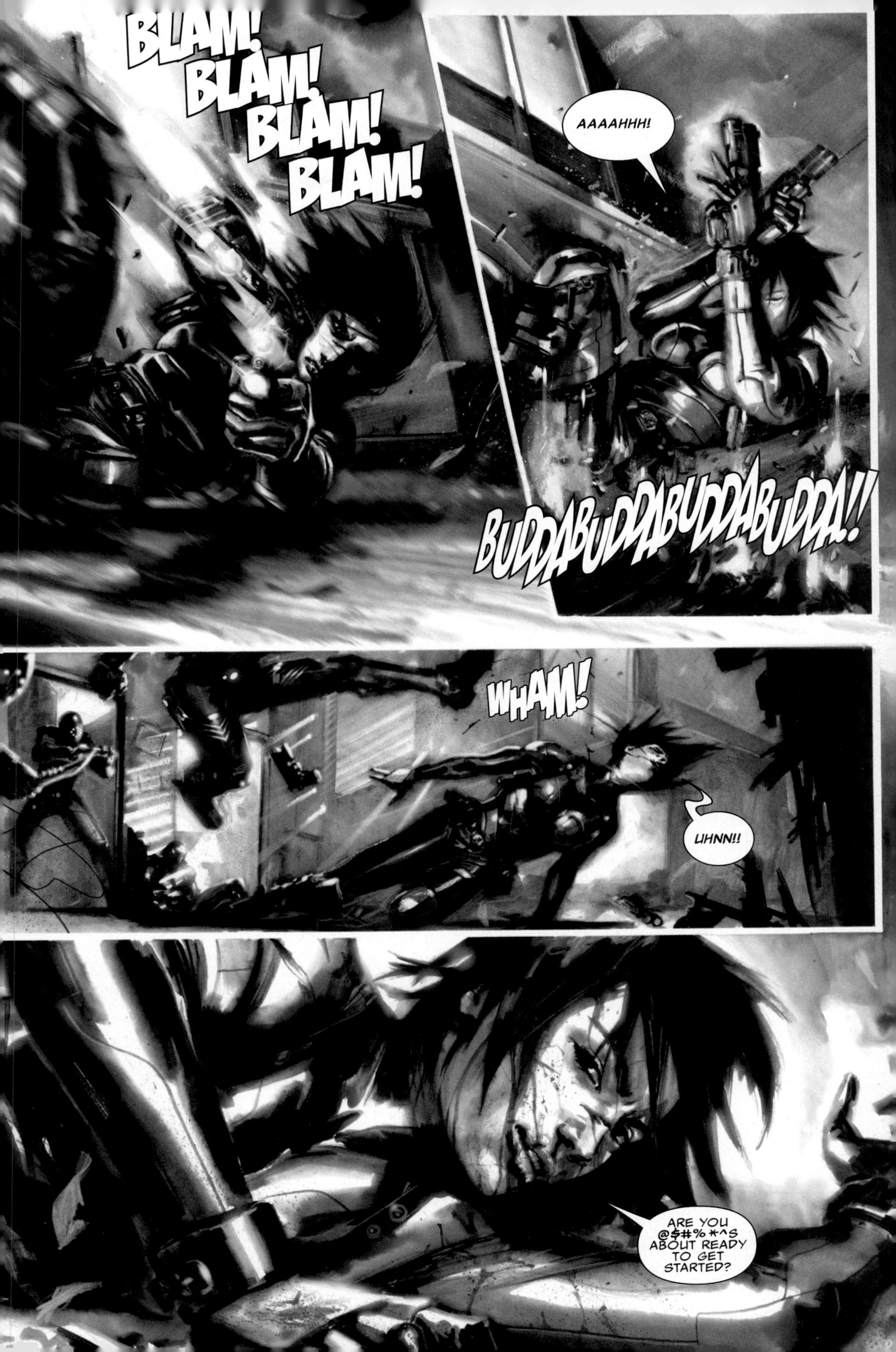
BLAM!
BLAM!
BLAM!
BLAM!
AAAAHHH!
BUDDABUDDABUDDABUDDA!!
WHAM!
UHNN!!
ARE YOU @$#% *^S ABOUT READY TO GET STARTED?

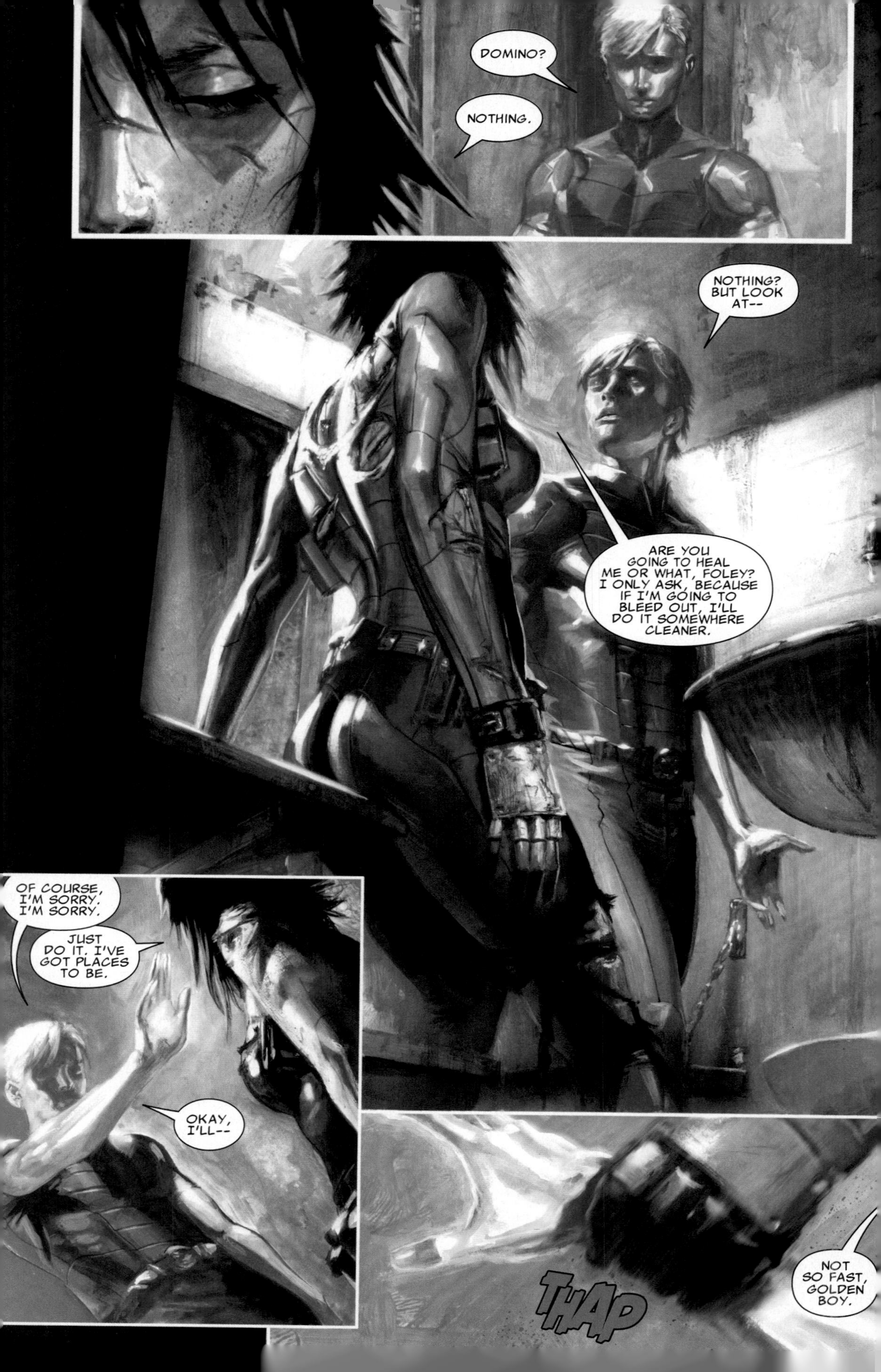
DOMINO?
NOTHING.
NOTHING? BUT LOOK AT--
ARE YOU GOING TO HEAL ME OR WHAT, FOLEY? I ONLY ASK, BECAUSE IF I'M GOING TO BLEED OUT, I'LL DO IT SOMEWHERE CLEANER.
OF COURSE, I'M SORRY. I'M SORRY.
JUST DO IT. I'VE GOT PLACES TO BE.
OKAY, I'LL--
THAP
NOT SO FAST, GOLDEN BOY.

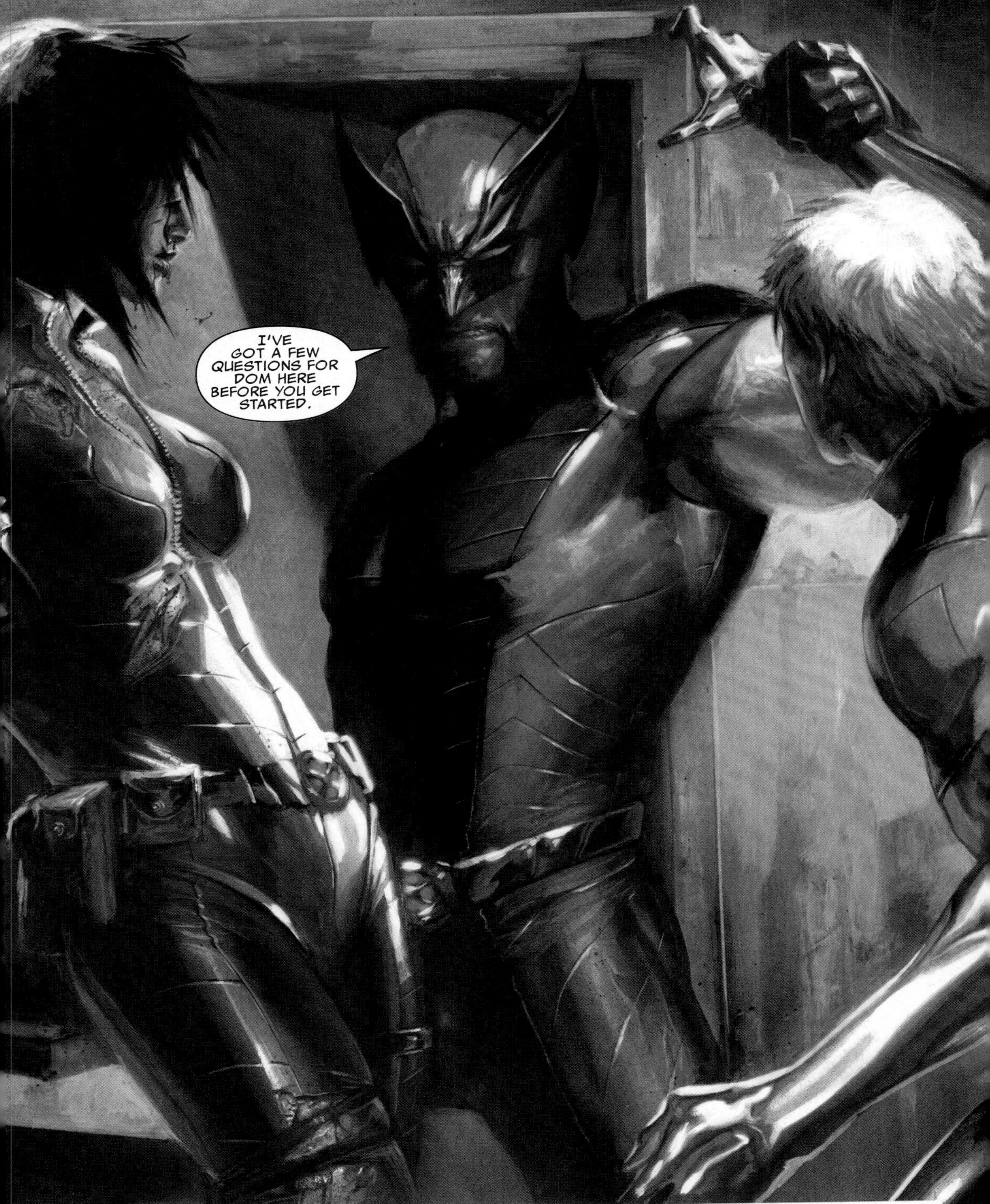
I'VE GOT A FEW QUESTIONS FOR DOM HERE BEFORE YOU GET STARTED.

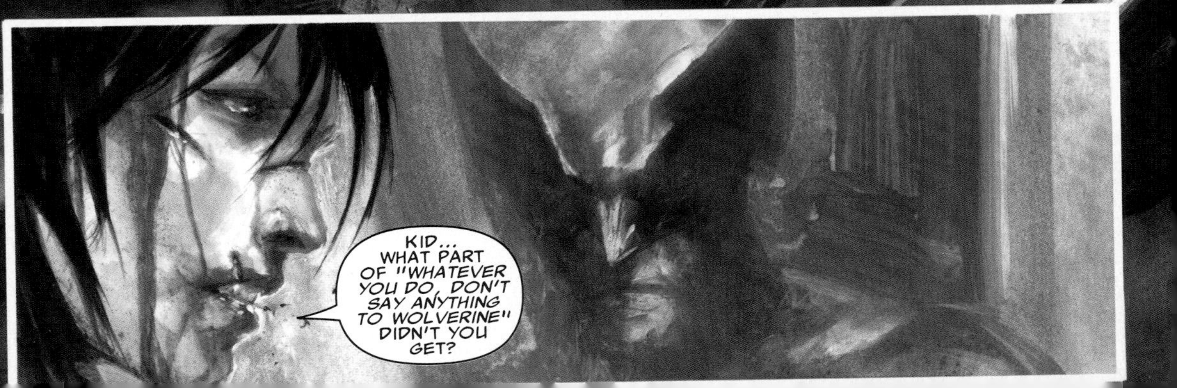
KID... WHAT PART OF "WHATEVER YOU DO, DON'T SAY ANYTHING TO WOLVERINE" DIDN'T YOU GET?

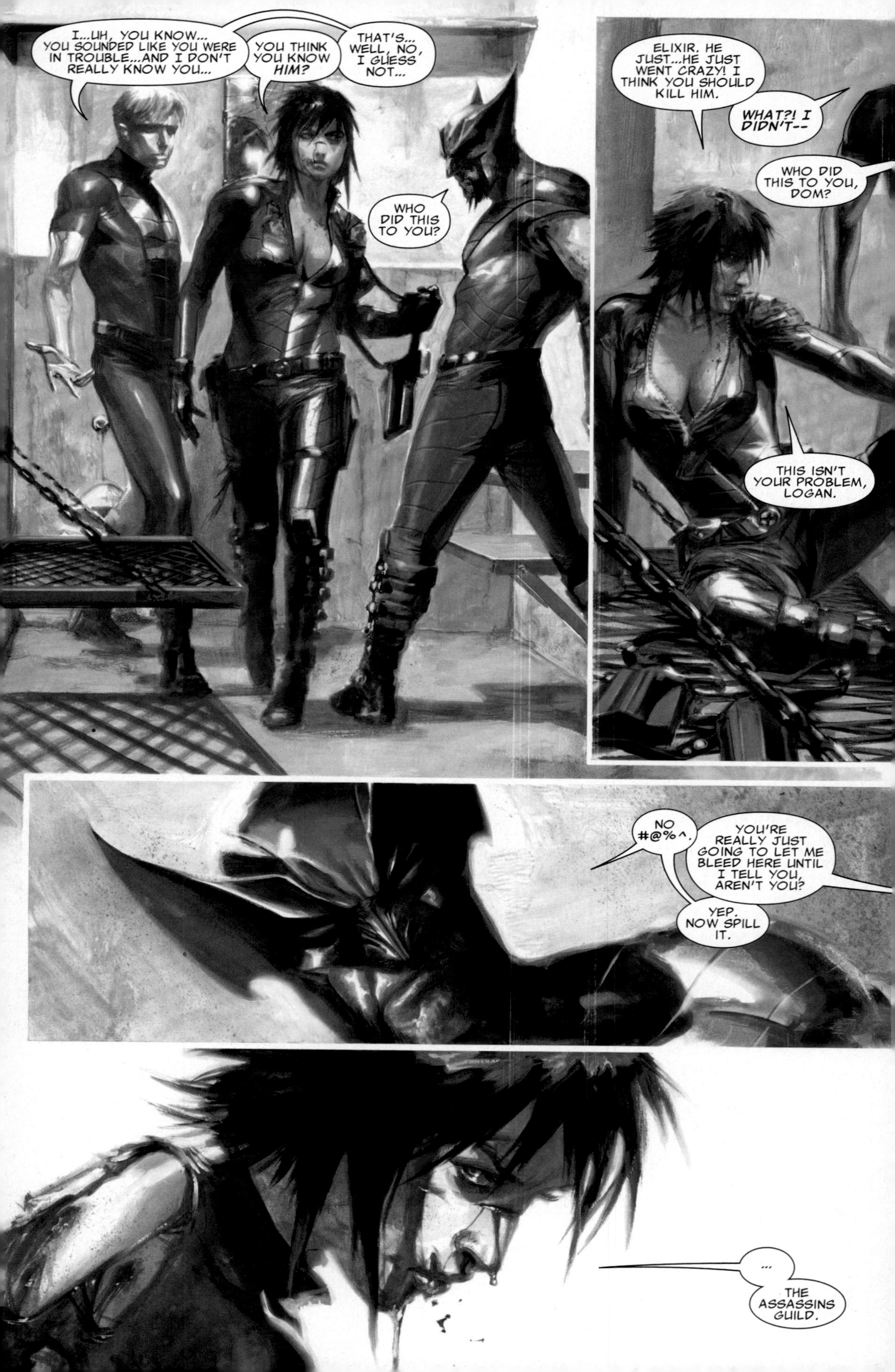

I...UH, YOU KNOW... YOU SOUNDED LIKE YOU WERE IN TROUBLE...AND I DON'T REALLY KNOW YOU...
YOU THINK YOU KNOW *HIM*?
THAT'S... WELL, NO, I GUESS NOT...
WHO DID THIS TO YOU?
ELIXIR. HE JUST...HE JUST WENT CRAZY! I THINK YOU SHOULD KILL HIM.
WHAT?! I DIDN'T--
WHO DID THIS TO YOU, DOM?
THIS ISN'T YOUR PROBLEM, LOGAN.
NO #@%^.
YOU'RE REALLY JUST GOING TO LET ME BLEED HERE UNTIL I TELL YOU, AREN'T YOU?
YEP. NOW SPILL IT.
...
THE ASSASSINS GUILD.

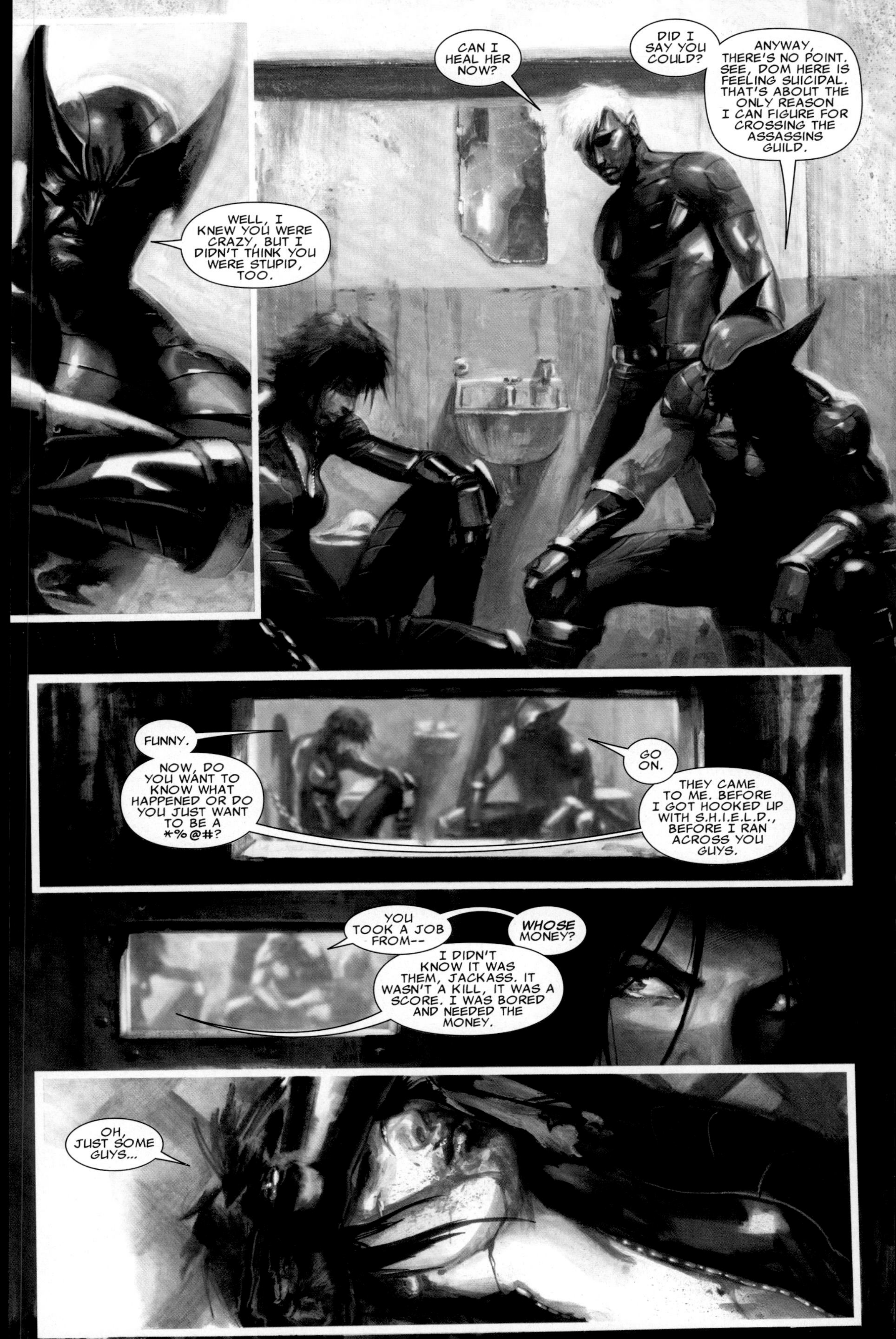
CAN I HEAL HER NOW?
DID I SAY YOU COULD?
ANYWAY, THERE'S NO POINT. SEE, DOM HERE IS FEELING SUICIDAL. THAT'S ABOUT THE ONLY REASON I CAN FIGURE FOR CROSSING THE ASSASSINS GUILD.
WELL, I KNEW YOU WERE CRAZY, BUT I DIDN'T THINK YOU WERE STUPID, TOO.
FUNNY.
NOW, DO YOU WANT TO KNOW WHAT HAPPENED OR DO YOU JUST WANT TO BE A *%@#?
GO ON.
THEY CAME TO ME. BEFORE I GOT HOOKED UP WITH S.H.I.E.L.D., BEFORE I RAN ACROSS YOU GUYS.
YOU TOOK A JOB FROM--
WHOSE MONEY?
I DIDN'T KNOW IT WAS THEM, JACKASS. IT WASN'T A KILL, IT WAS A SCORE. I WAS BORED AND NEEDED THE MONEY.
OH, JUST SOME GUYS...

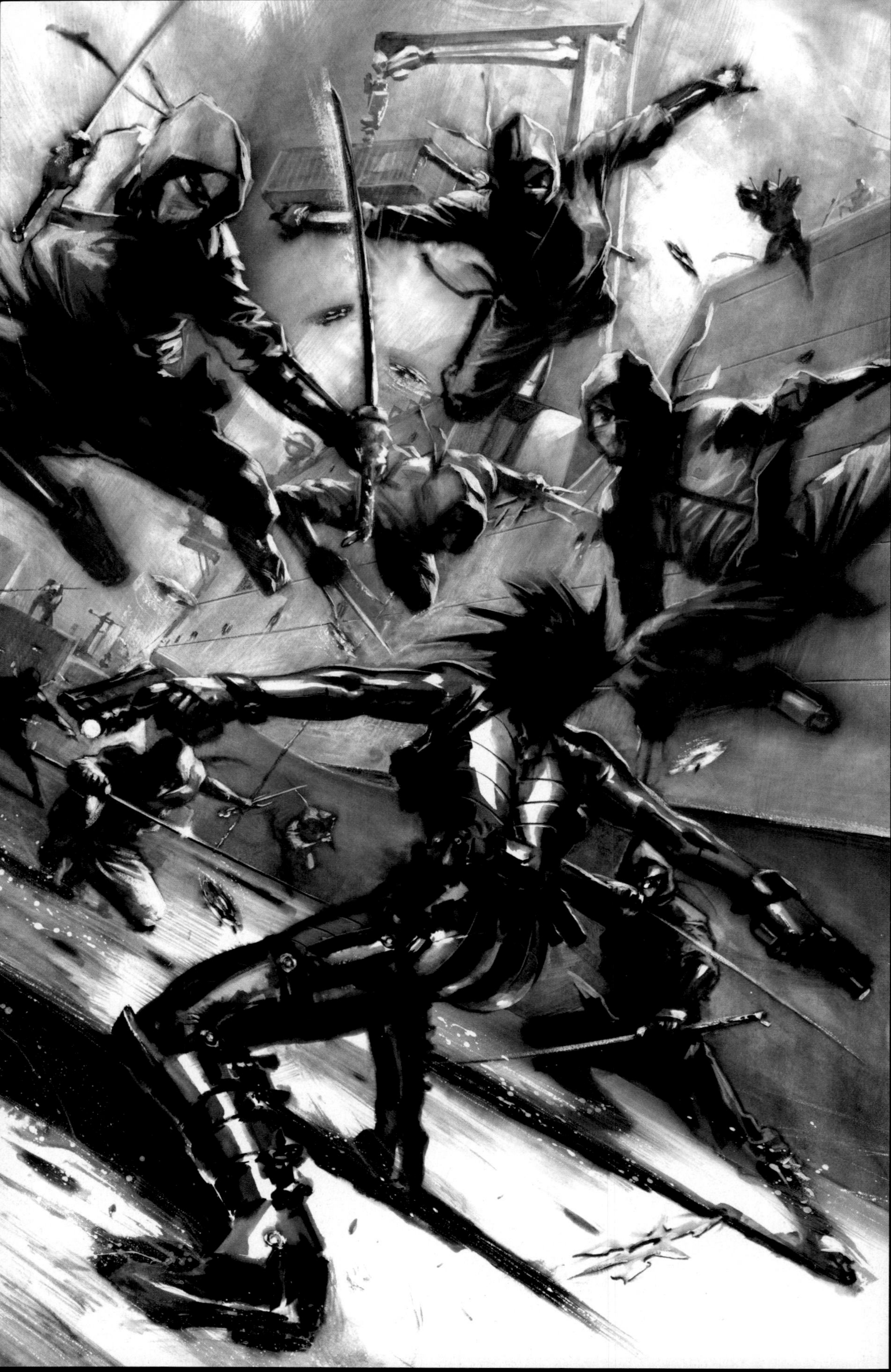

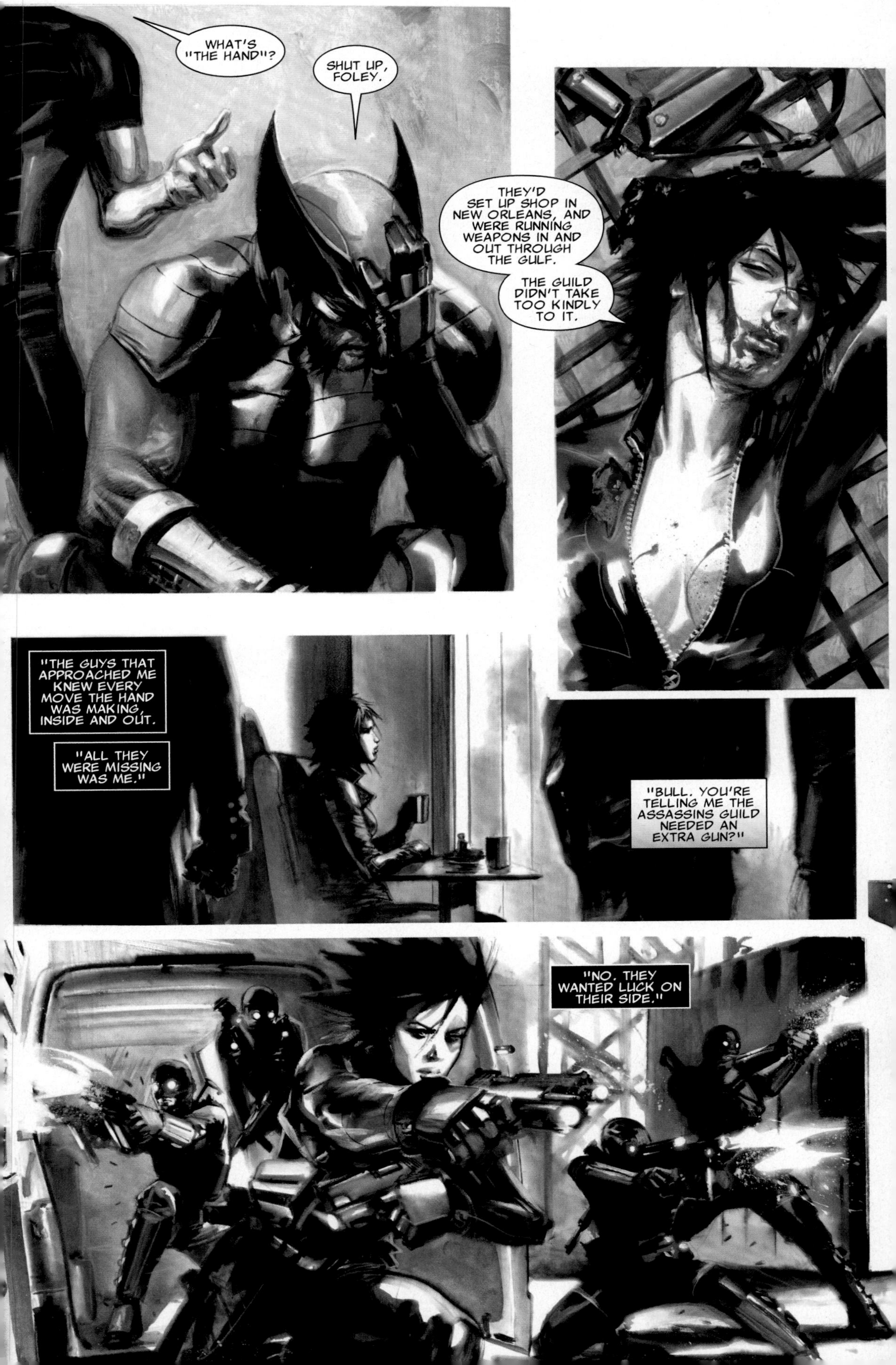
WHAT'S "THE HAND"?
SHUT UP, FOLEY.
THEY'D SET UP SHOP IN NEW ORLEANS, AND WERE RUNNING WEAPONS IN AND OUT THROUGH THE GULF.
THE GUILD DIDN'T TAKE TOO KINDLY TO IT.
"THE GUYS THAT APPROACHED ME KNEW EVERY MOVE THE HAND WAS MAKING, INSIDE AND OUT.
"ALL THEY WERE MISSING WAS ME."
"BULL. YOU'RE TELLING ME THE ASSASSINS GUILD NEEDED AN EXTRA GUN?"
"NO. THEY WANTED LUCK ON THEIR SIDE."

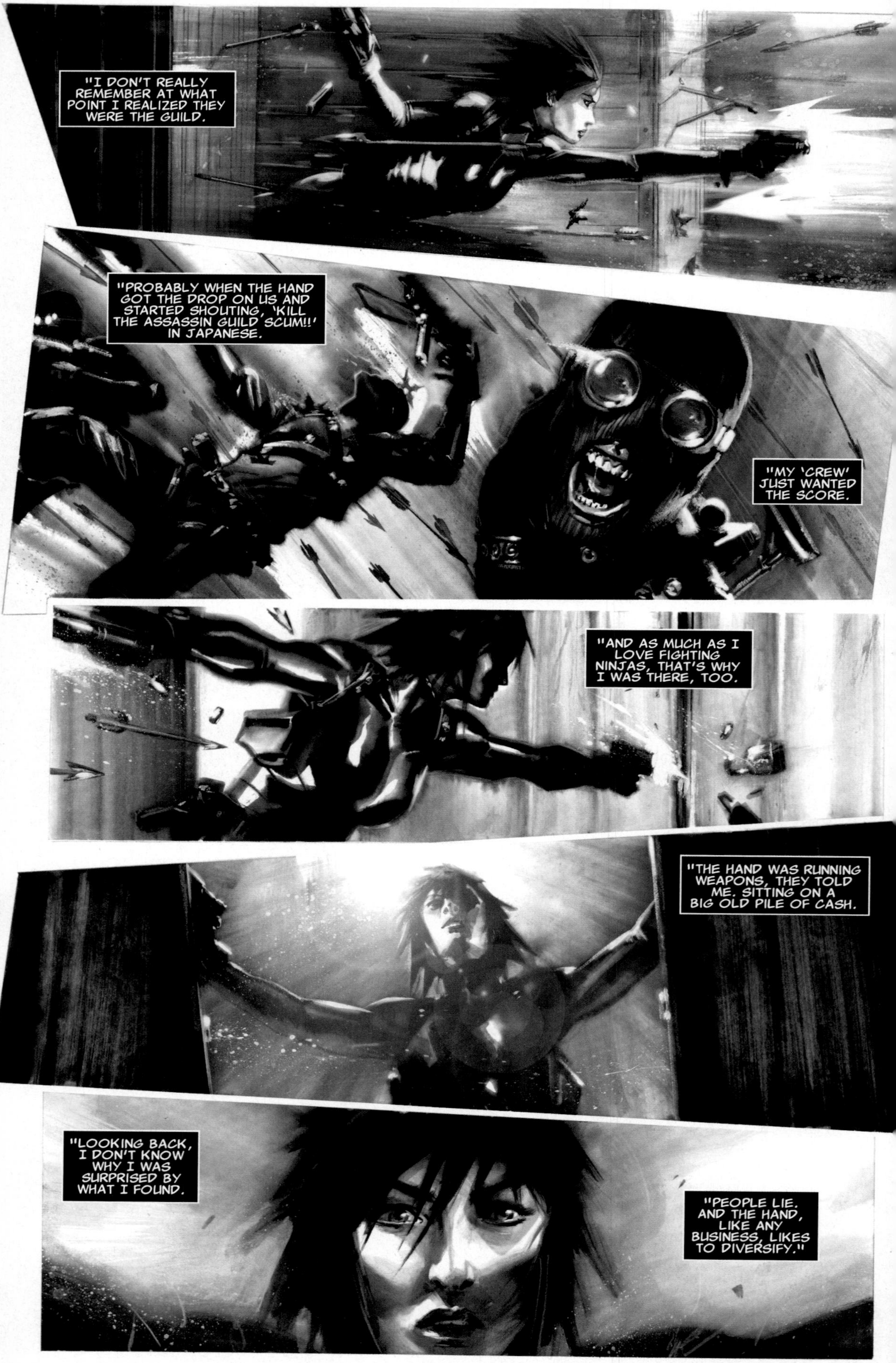
"I DON'T REALLY REMEMBER AT WHAT POINT I REALIZED THEY WERE THE GUILD.
"PROBABLY WHEN THE HAND GOT THE DROP ON US AND STARTED SHOUTING, 'KILL THE ASSASSIN GUILD SCUM!!' IN JAPANESE.
"MY 'CREW' JUST WANTED THE SCORE.
"AND AS MUCH AS I LOVE FIGHTING NINJAS, THAT'S WHY I WAS THERE, TOO.
"THE HAND WAS RUNNING WEAPONS, THEY TOLD ME. SITTING ON A BIG OLD PILE OF CASH.
"LOOKING BACK, I DON'T KNOW WHY I WAS SURPRISED BY WHAT I FOUND.
"PEOPLE LIE. AND THE HAND, LIKE ANY BUSINESS, LIKES TO DIVERSIFY."

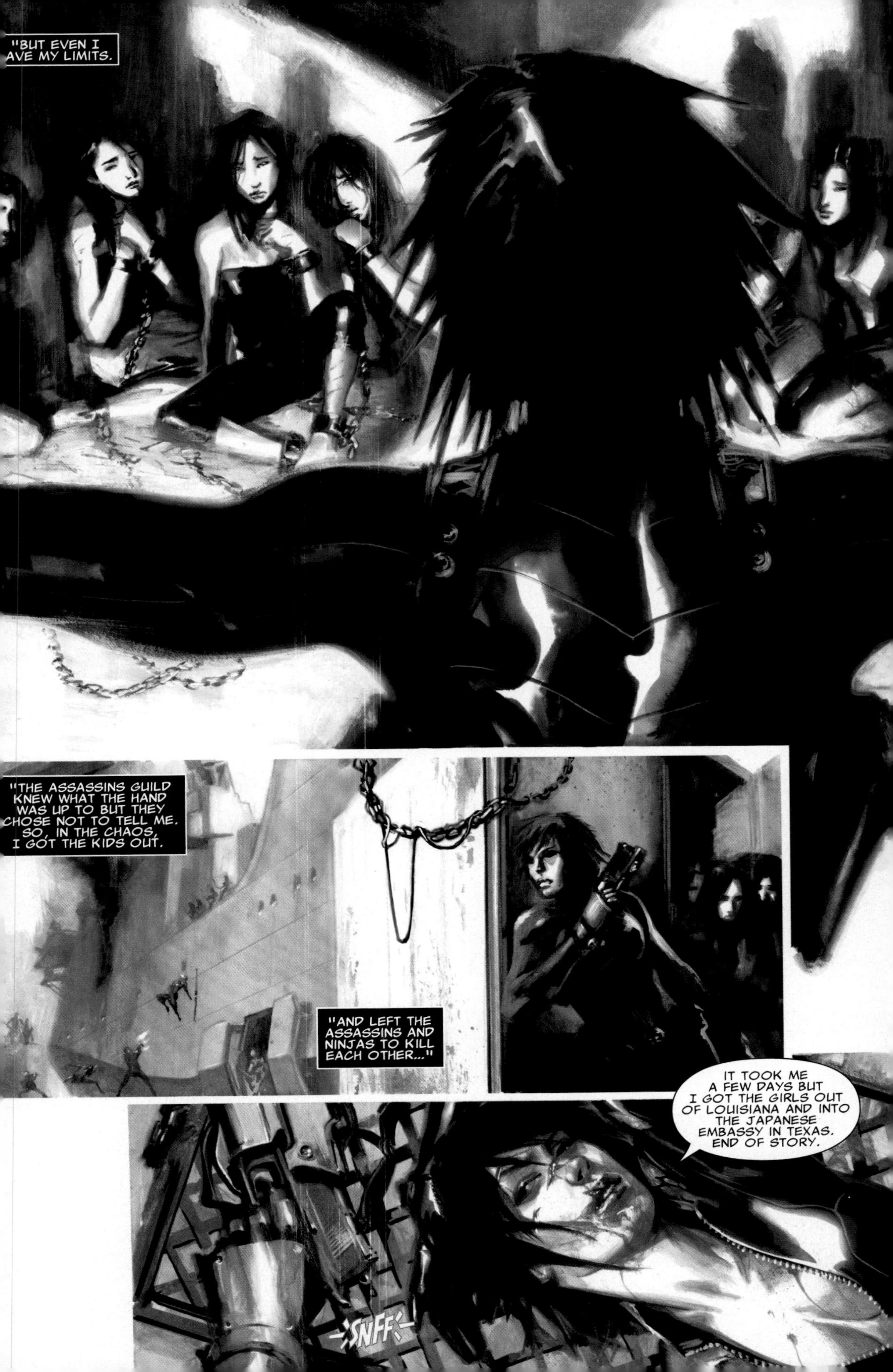
"BUT EVEN I
AVE MY LIMITS.
"THE ASSASSINS GUILD KNEW WHAT THE HAND WAS UP TO BUT THEY CHOSE NOT TO TELL ME. SO, IN THE CHAOS, I GOT THE KIDS OUT.
"AND LEFT THE ASSASSINS AND NINJAS TO KILL EACH OTHER..."
IT TOOK ME A FEW DAYS BUT I GOT THE GIRLS OUT OF LOUISIANA AND INTO THE JAPANESE EMBASSY IN TEXAS. END OF STORY.
SNFF

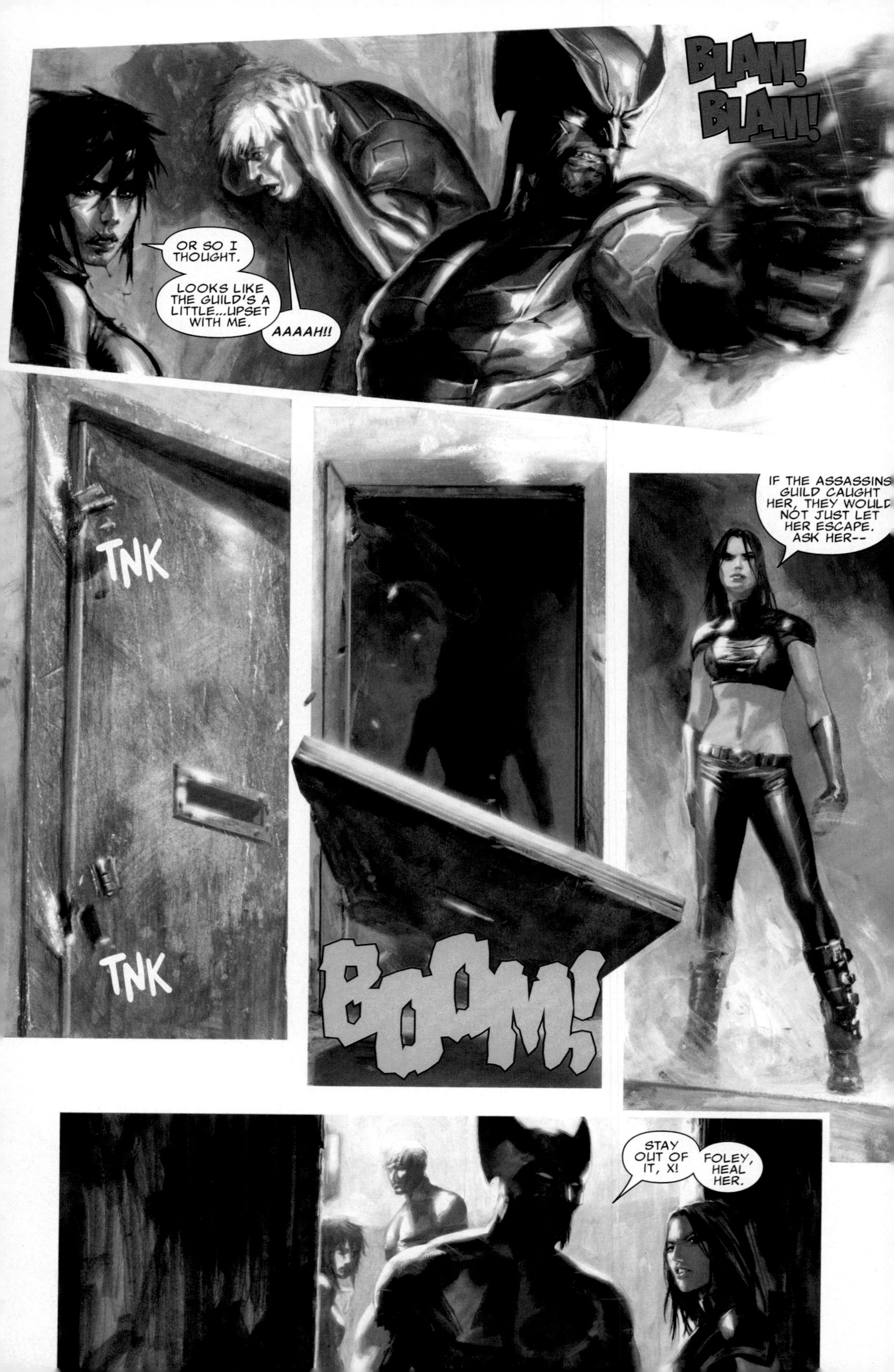
BLAM! BLAM!
OR SO I THOUGHT.
LOOKS LIKE THE GUILD'S A LITTLE...UPSET WITH ME.
AAAAH!!
TNK
TNK
BOOM!
IF THE ASSASSINS GUILD CAUGHT HER, THEY WOULD NOT JUST LET HER ESCAPE. ASK HER--
STAY OUT OF IT, X!
FOLEY, HEAL HER.

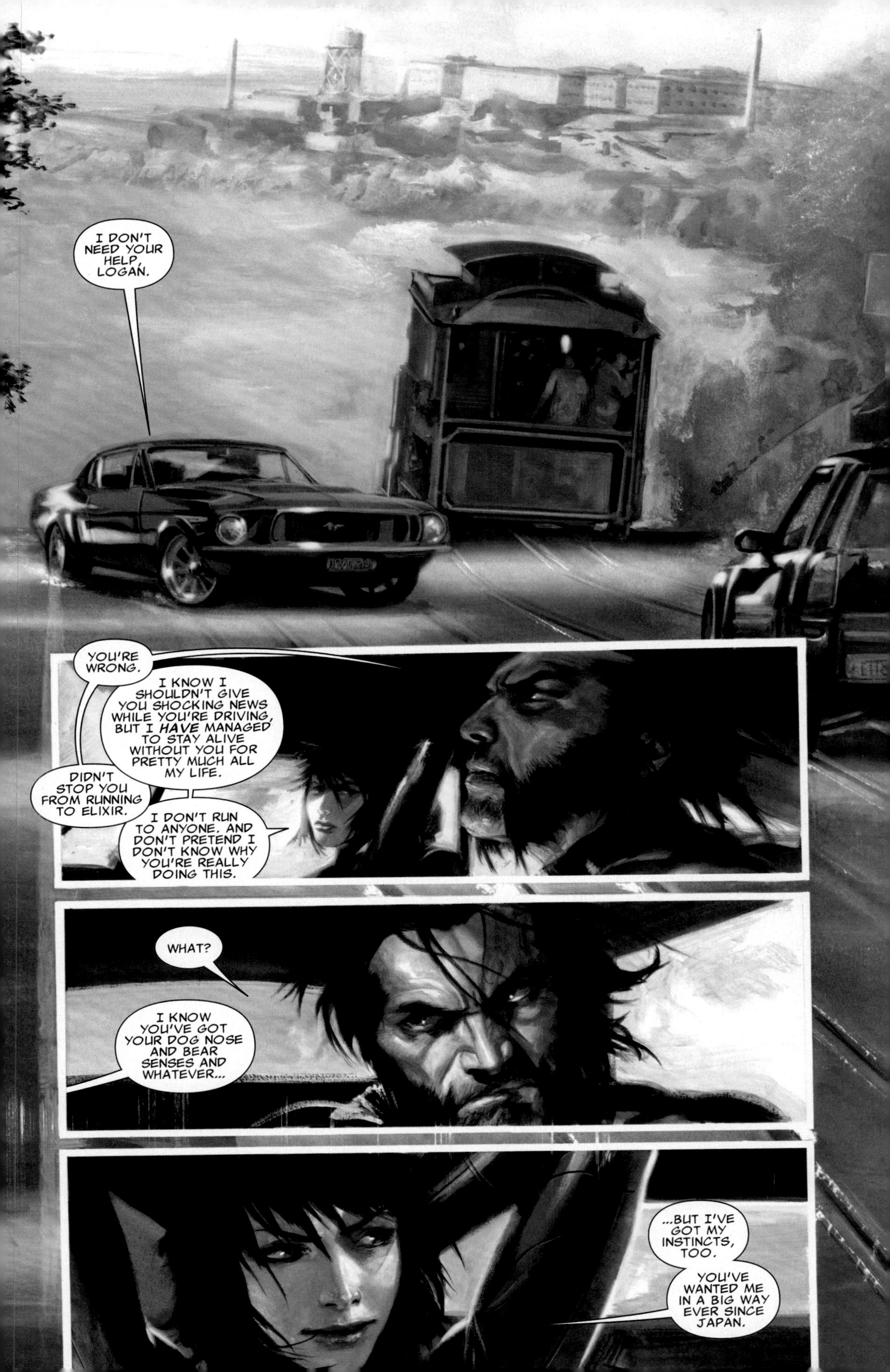

I DON'T NEED YOUR HELP, LOGAN.
YOU'RE WRONG.
I KNOW I SHOULDN'T GIVE YOU SHOCKING NEWS WHILE YOU'RE DRIVING, BUT I HAVE MANAGED TO STAY ALIVE WITHOUT YOU FOR PRETTY MUCH ALL MY LIFE.
DIDN'T STOP YOU FROM RUNNING TO ELIXIR.
I DON'T RUN TO ANYONE. AND DON'T PRETEND I DON'T KNOW WHY YOU'RE REALLY DOING THIS.
WHAT?
I KNOW YOU'VE GOT YOUR DOG NOSE AND BEAR SENSES AND WHATEVER...
...BUT I'VE GOT MY INSTINCTS, TOO.
YOU'VE WANTED ME IN A BIG WAY EVER SINCE JAPAN.

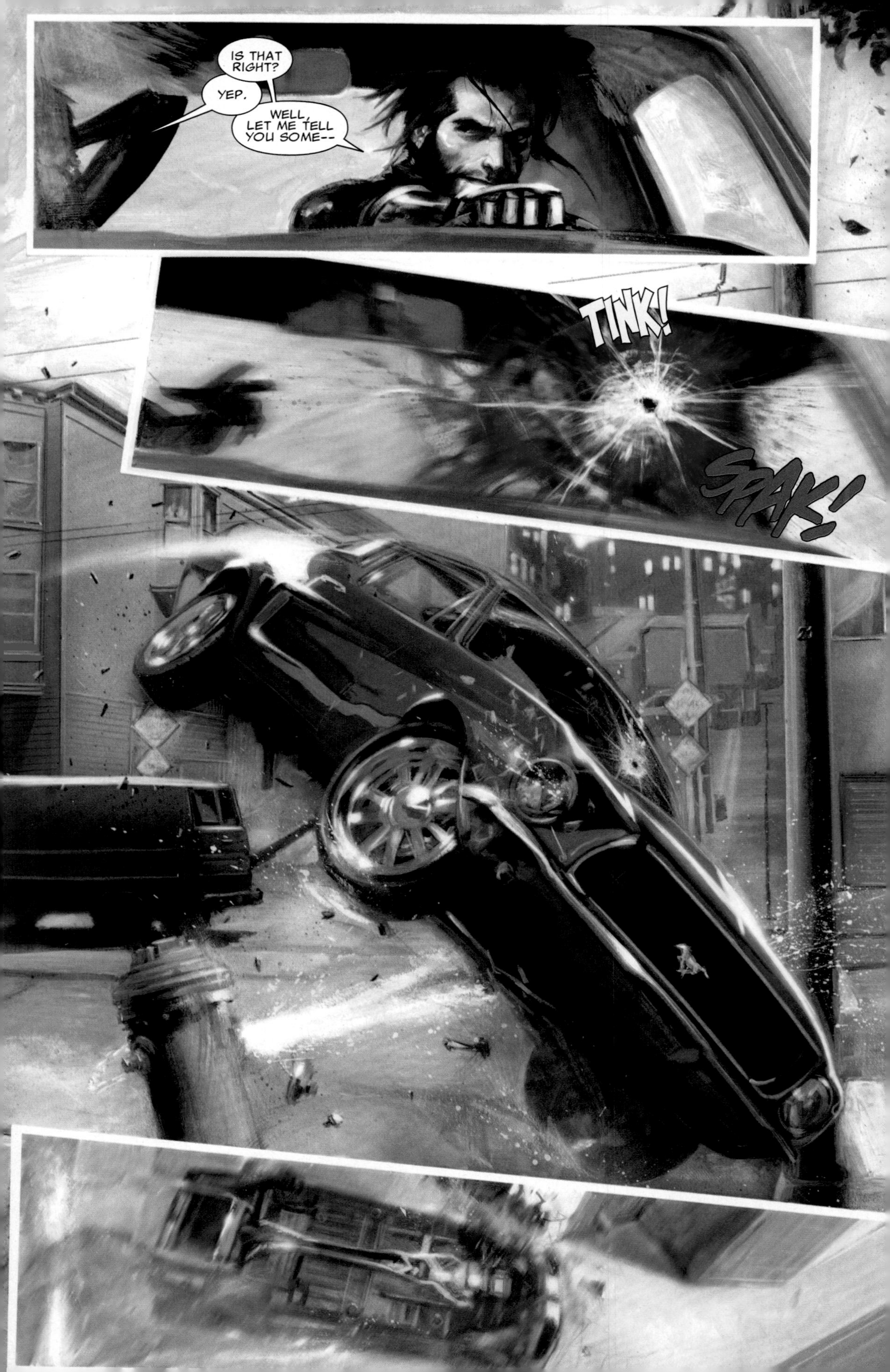
IS THAT RIGHT?
YEP.
WELL, LET ME TELL YOU SOME--
TINK!
SPAK!

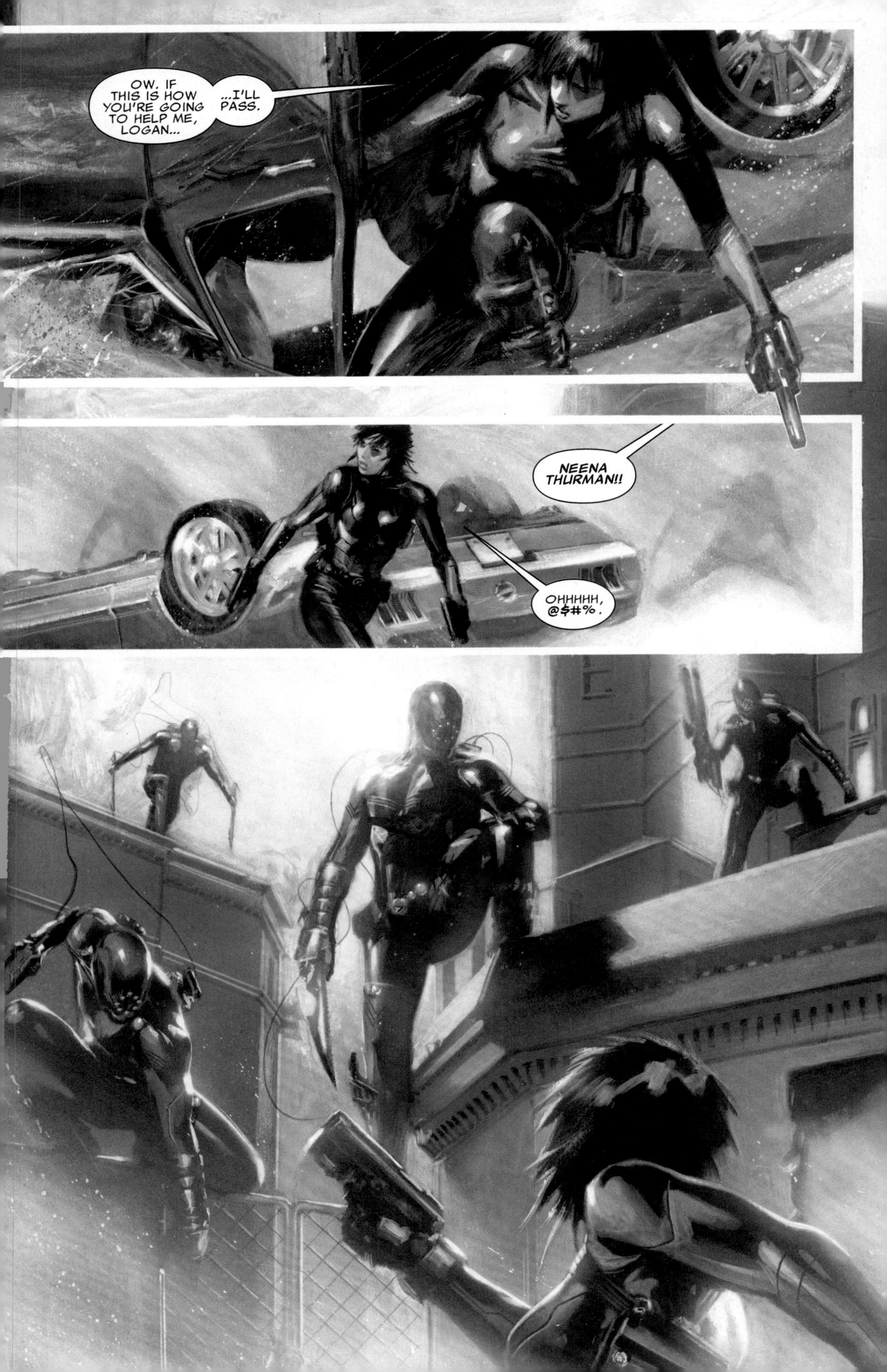
OW. IF THIS IS HOW YOU'RE GOING TO HELP ME, LOGAN...
...I'LL PASS.
NEENA THURMAN!!
OHHHHH, @$#%.

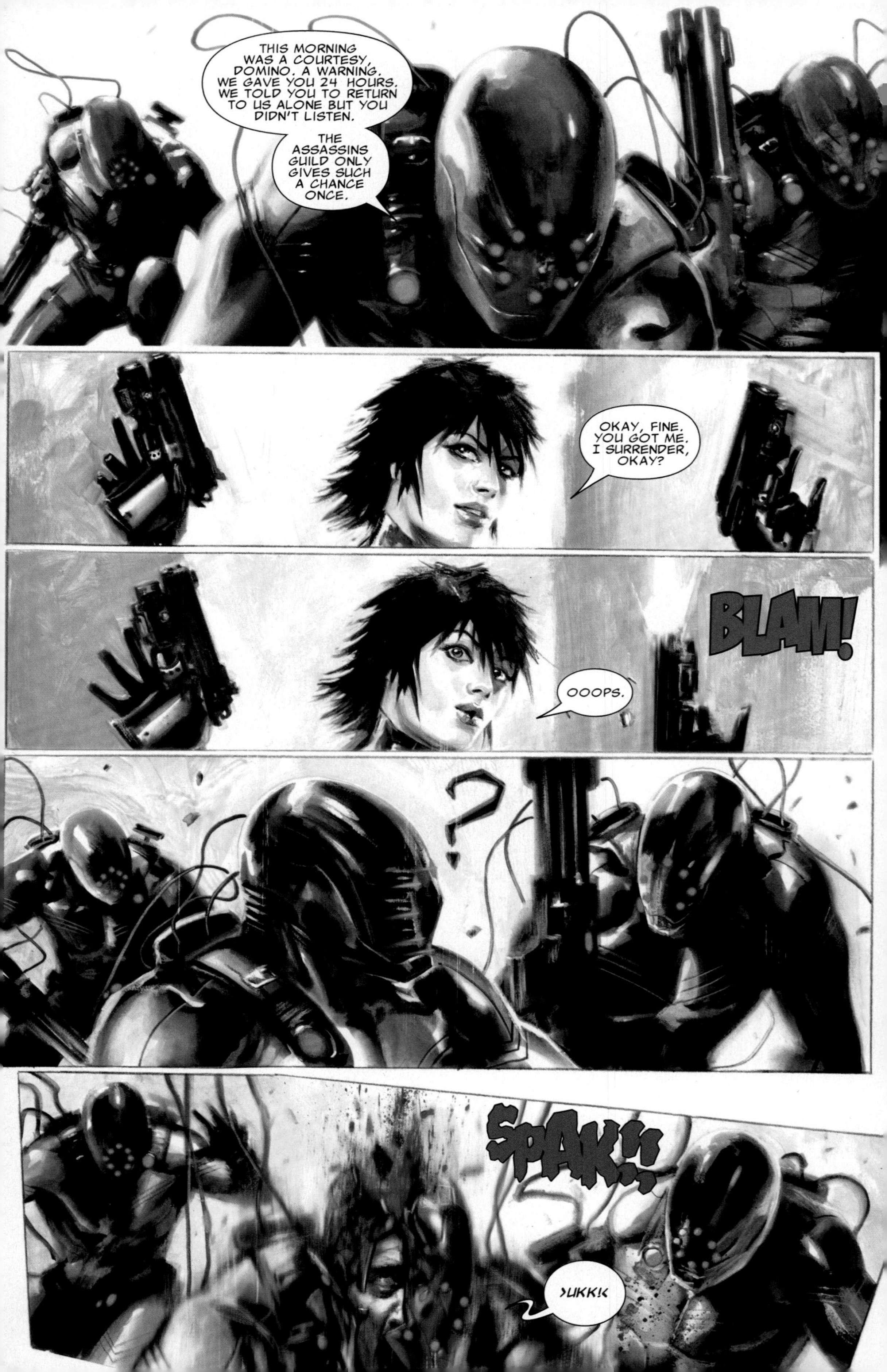
THIS MORNING WAS A COURTESY, DOMINO. A WARNING. WE GAVE YOU 24 HOURS. WE TOLD YOU TO RETURN TO US ALONE BUT YOU DIDN'T LISTEN.
THE ASSASSINS GUILD ONLY GIVES SUCH A CHANCE ONCE.
OKAY, FINE. YOU GOT ME. I SURRENDER, OKAY?
BLAM!
OOOPS.
?
SPAK!!
>UKK!<

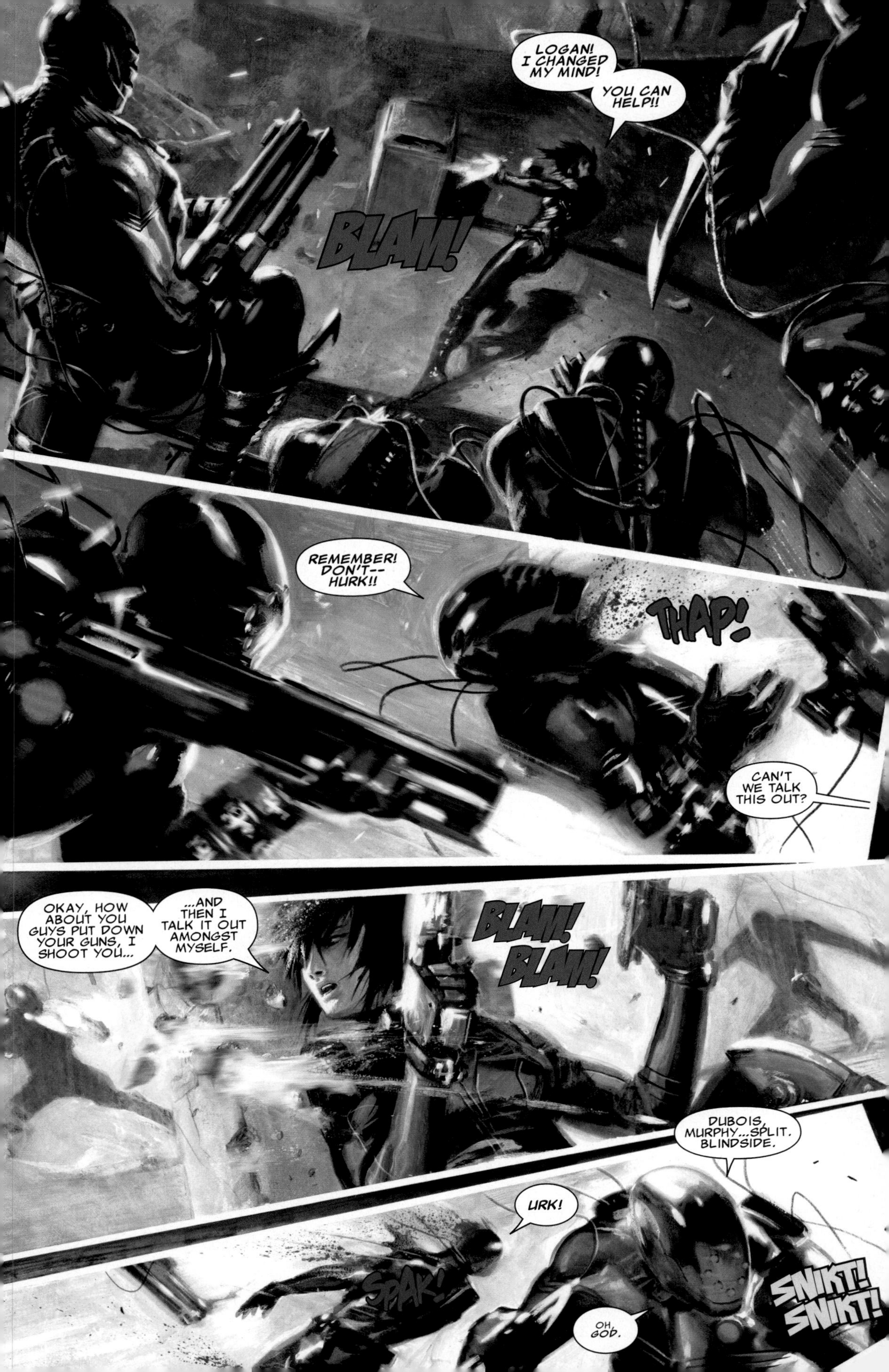
LOGAN! I CHANGED MY MIND!
YOU CAN HELP!!
BLAM!
REMEMBER! DON'T-- HURK!!
THAP!
CAN'T WE TALK THIS OUT?
OKAY, HOW ABOUT YOU GUYS PUT DOWN YOUR GUNS, I SHOOT YOU...
...AND THEN I TALK IT OUT AMONGST MYSELF.
BLAM! BLAM!
DUBOIS, MURPHY...SPLIT. BLINDSIDE.
URK!
SPAK!
SNIKT! SNIKT!
OH, GOD.

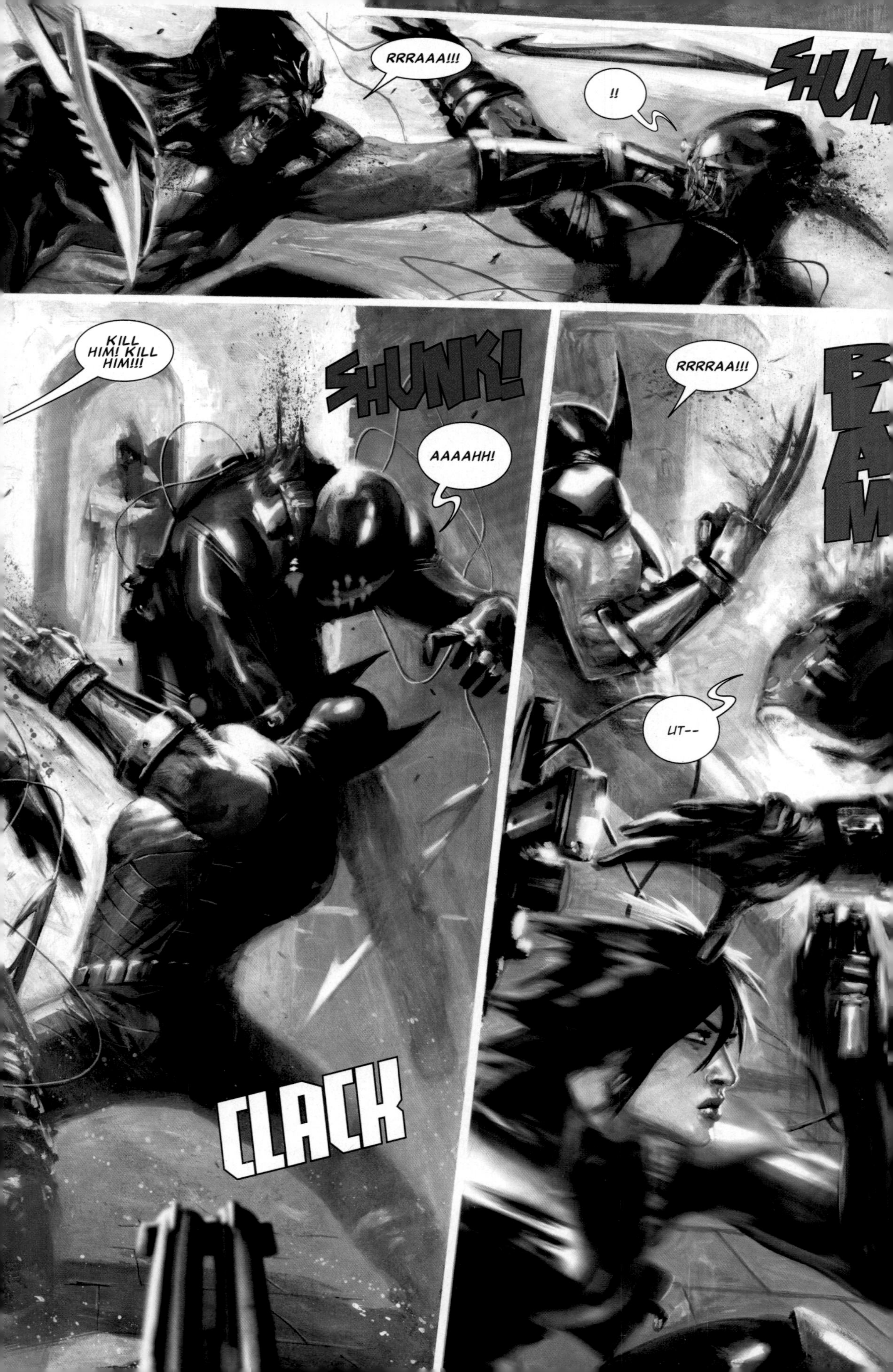
RRRAAA!!!
!!
SHUNK
KILL HIM! KILL HIM!!!
SHUNK!
AAAAHH!
CLACK
RRRRAA!!!
BLAM
UT--

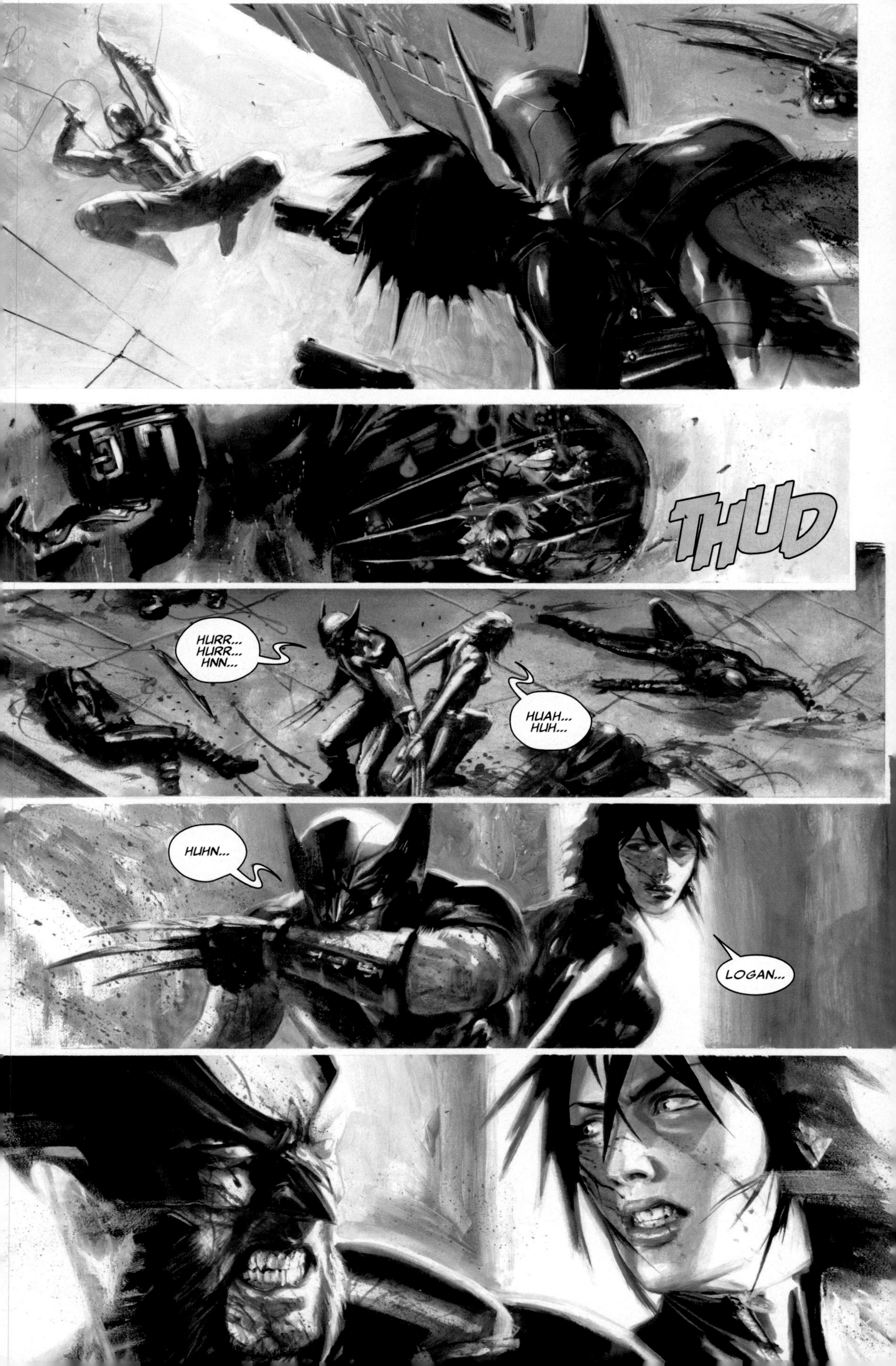
THUD
HURR... HURR... HNN...
HUAH... HUH...
HUHN...
LOGAN...

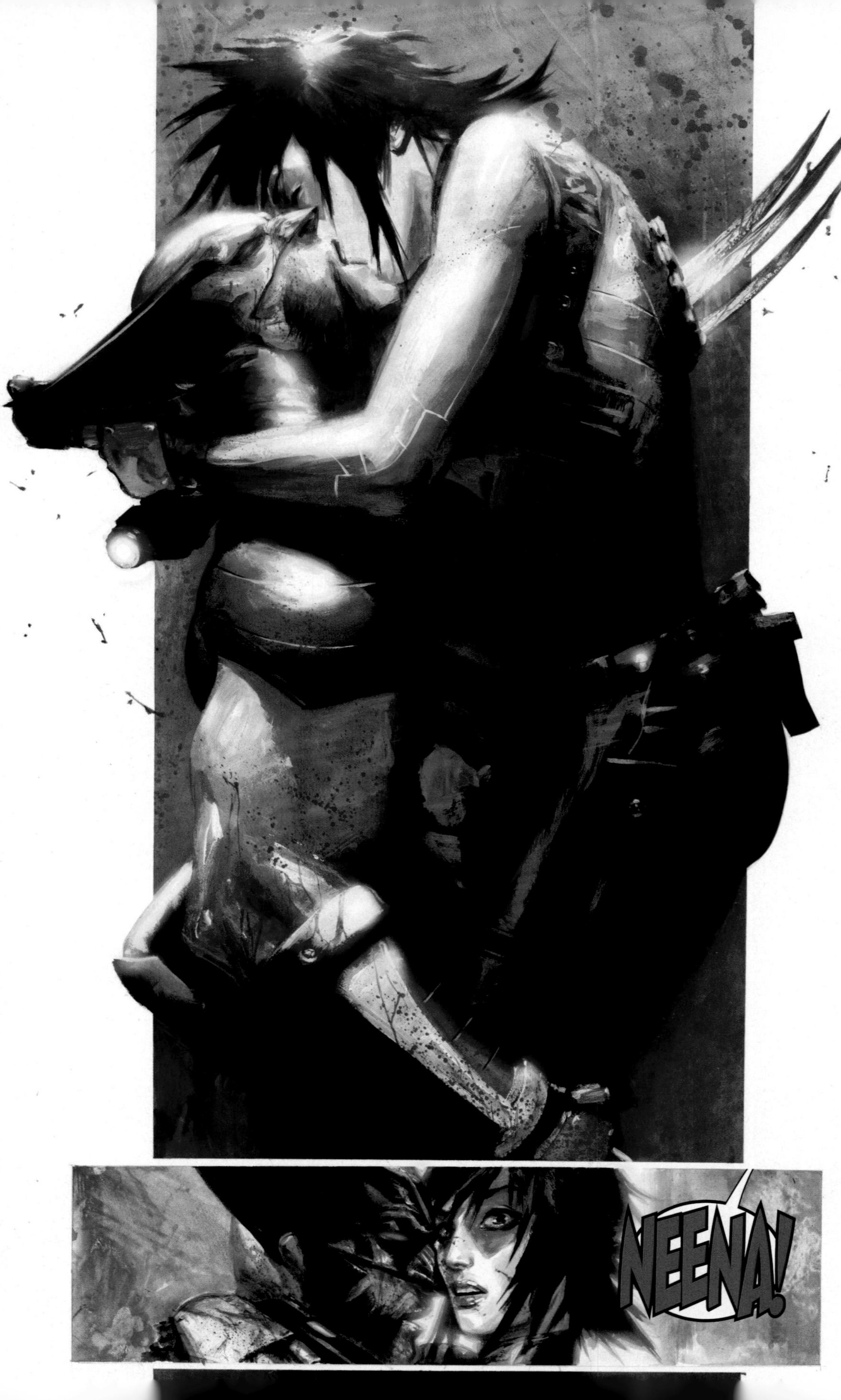
NEENA!

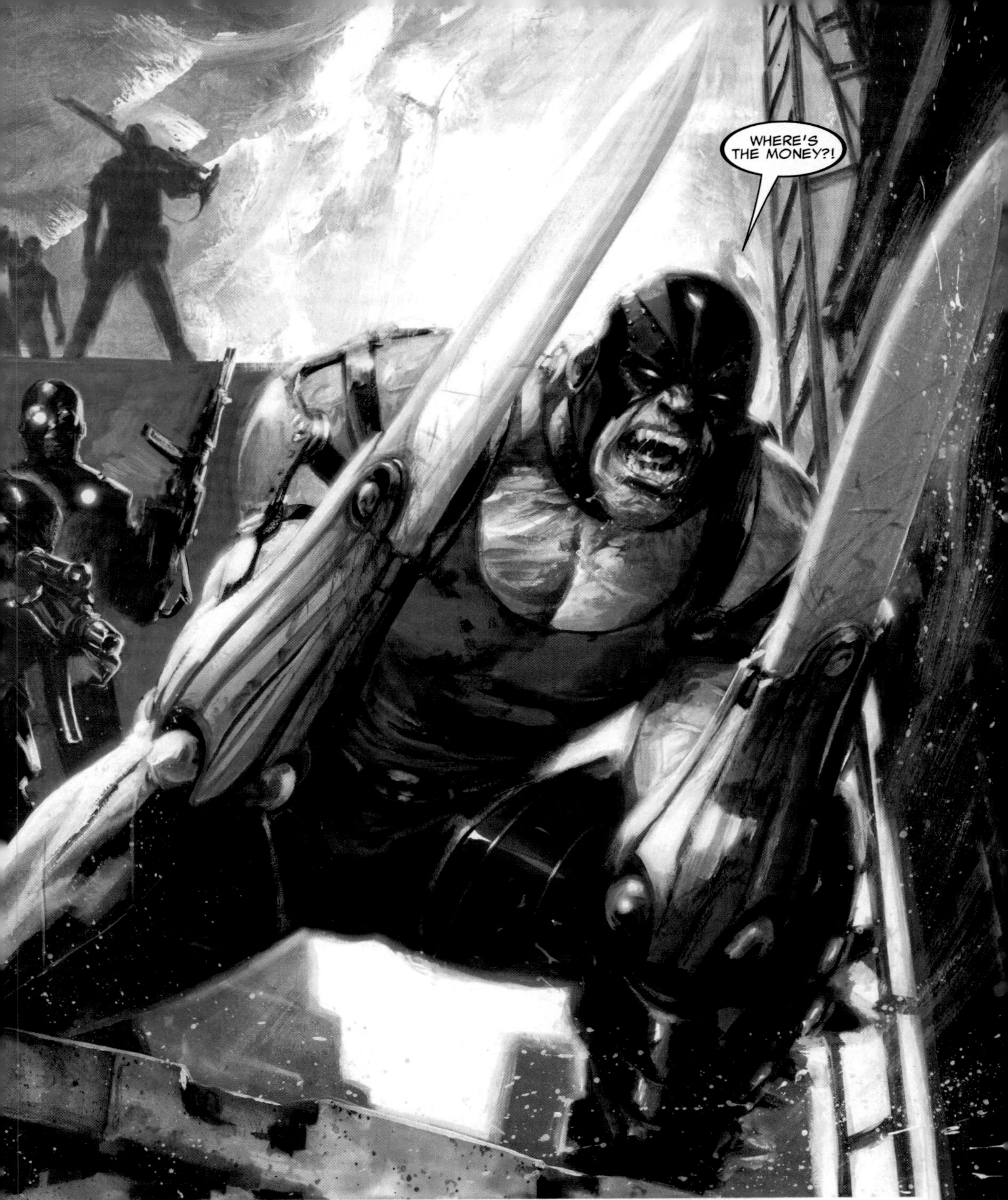
WHERE'S THE MONEY?!

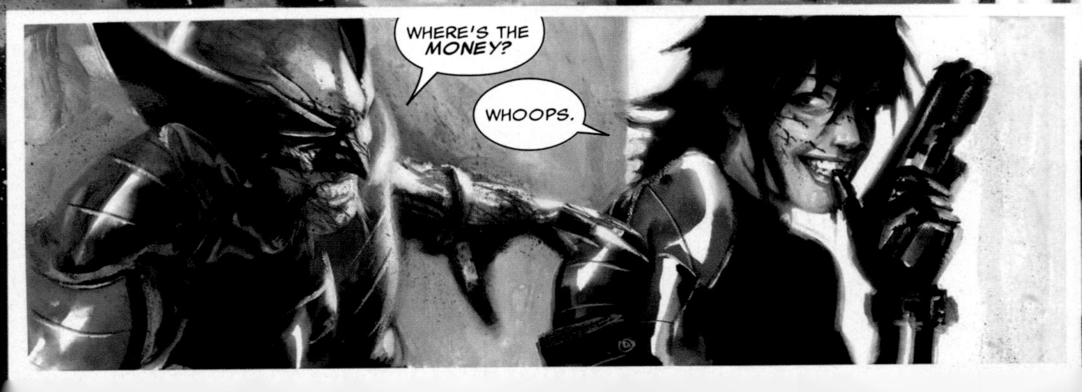
WHERE'S THE MONEY?
WHOOPS.

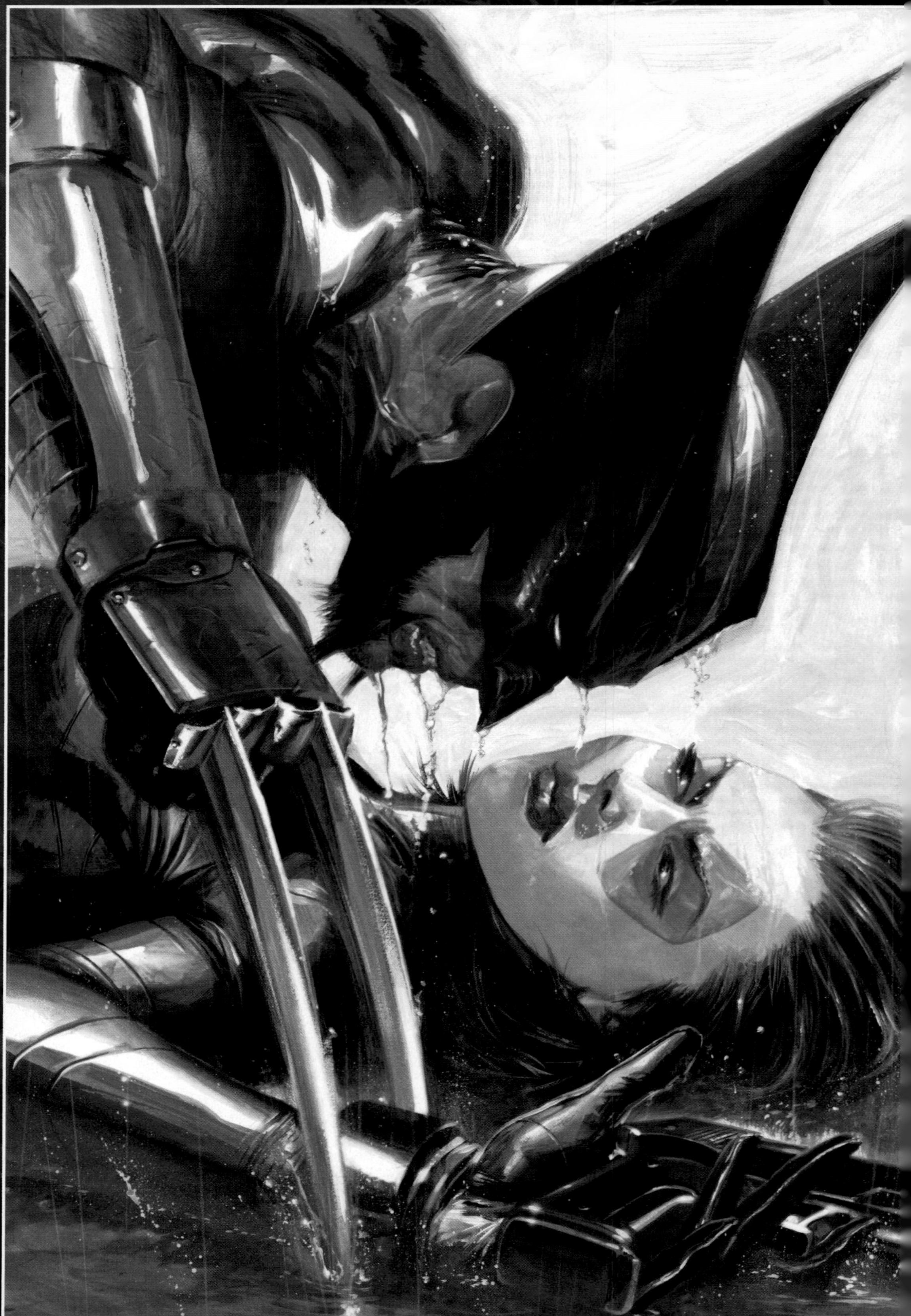

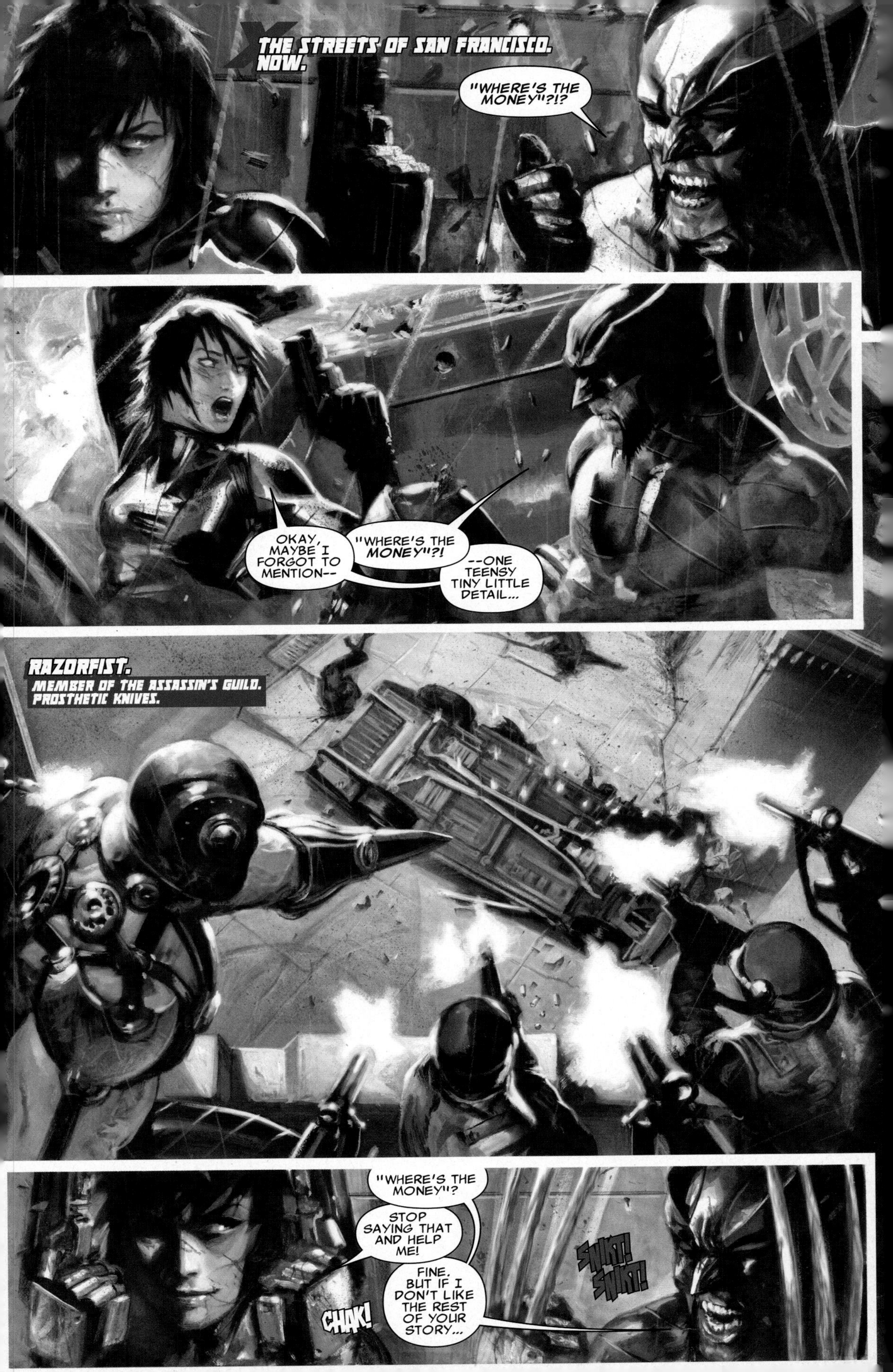
THE STREETS OF SAN FRANCISCO. NOW.
"WHERE'S THE MONEY"?!?
OKAY, MAYBE I FORGOT TO MENTION--
"WHERE'S THE MONEY"?!
--ONE TEENSY TINY LITTLE DETAIL...
RAZORFIST.
MEMBER OF THE ASSASSIN'S GUILD. PROSTHETIC KNIVES.
"WHERE'S THE MONEY"?
STOP SAYING THAT AND HELP ME!
FINE. BUT IF I DON'T LIKE THE REST OF YOUR STORY...
CHAK!
SNIKT! SNIKT!

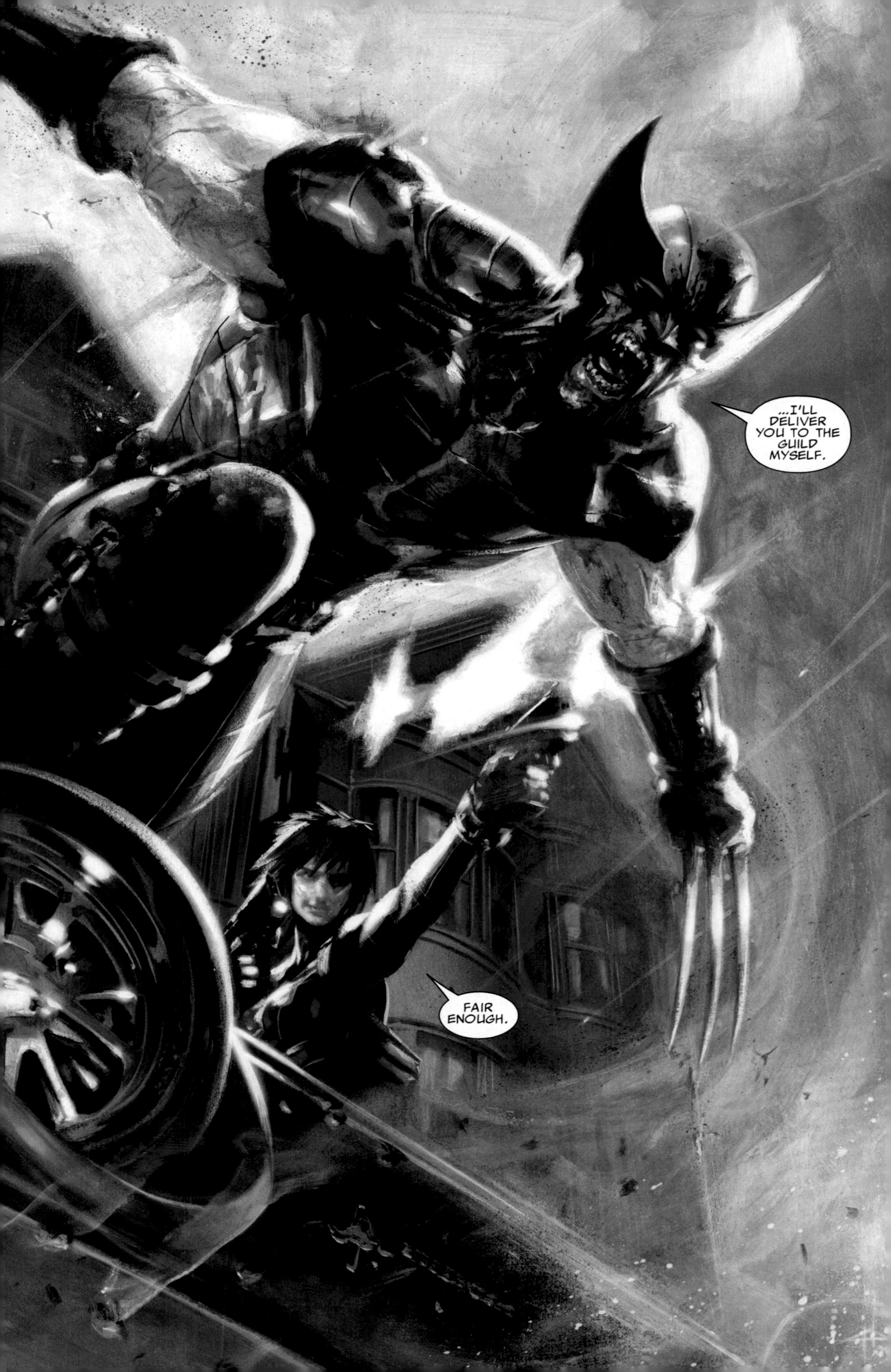
...I'LL DELIVER YOU TO THE GUILD MYSELF.
FAIR ENOUGH.

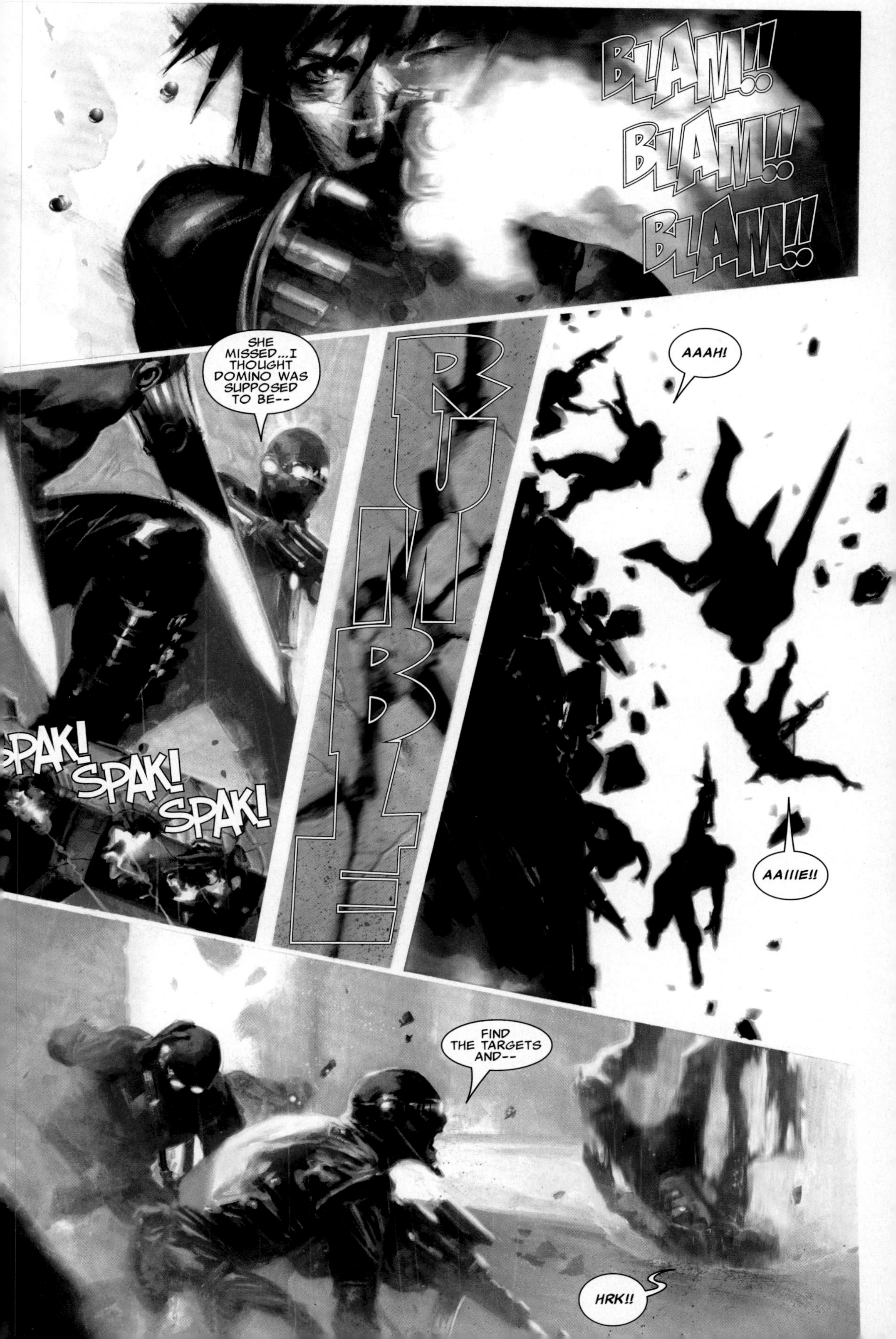
BLAM!! BLAM!! BLAM!!
SHE MISSED...I THOUGHT DOMINO WAS SUPPOSED TO BE--
SPAK! SPAK! SPAK!
RUMBLE
AAAH!
AAIIIE!!
FIND THE TARGETS AND--
HRK!!

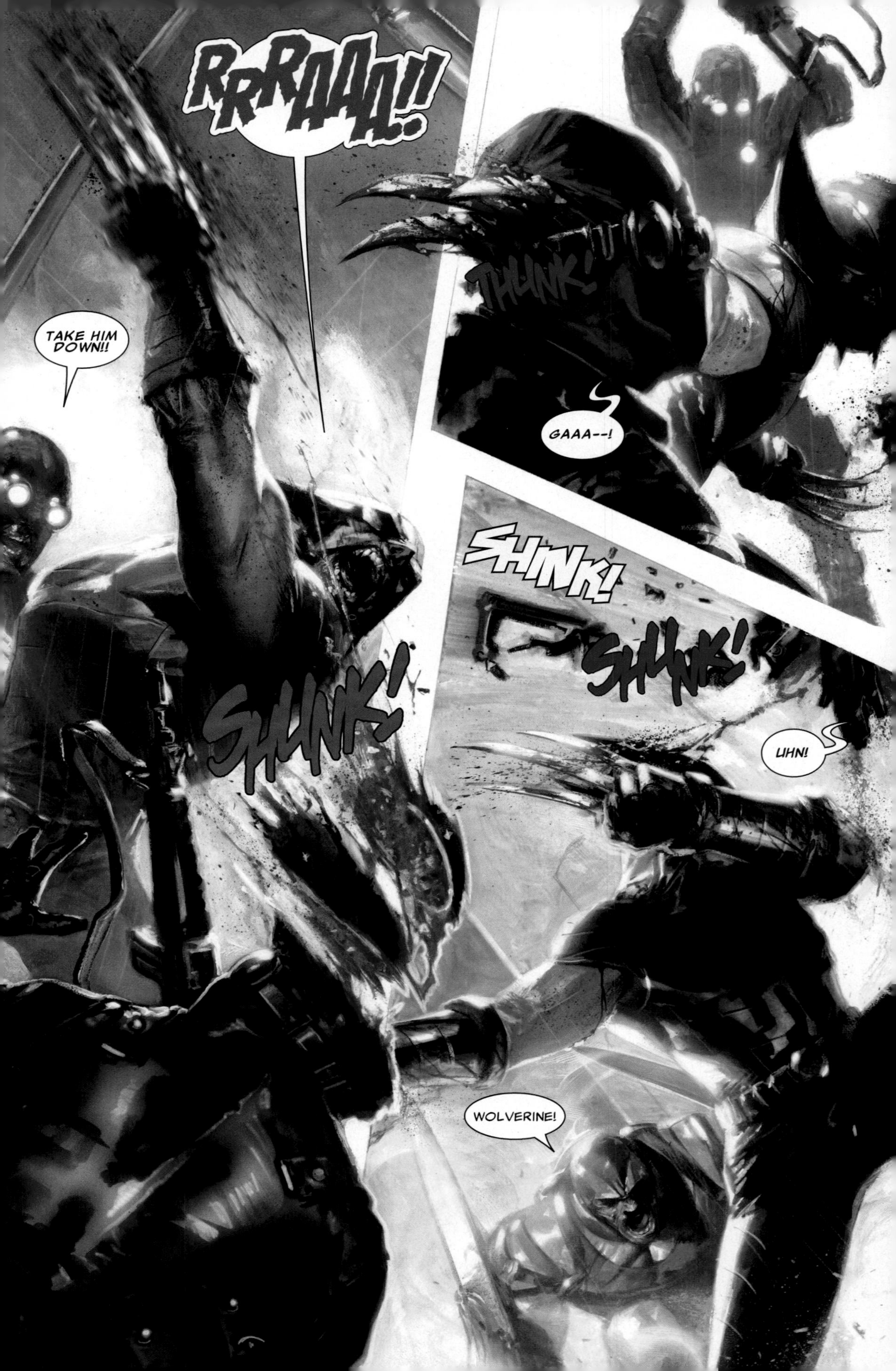
RRRAAA!!
TAKE HIM DOWN!!
THUNK!
GAAA--!
SHINK!
SHUNK!
SHUNK!
UHN!
WOLVERINE!

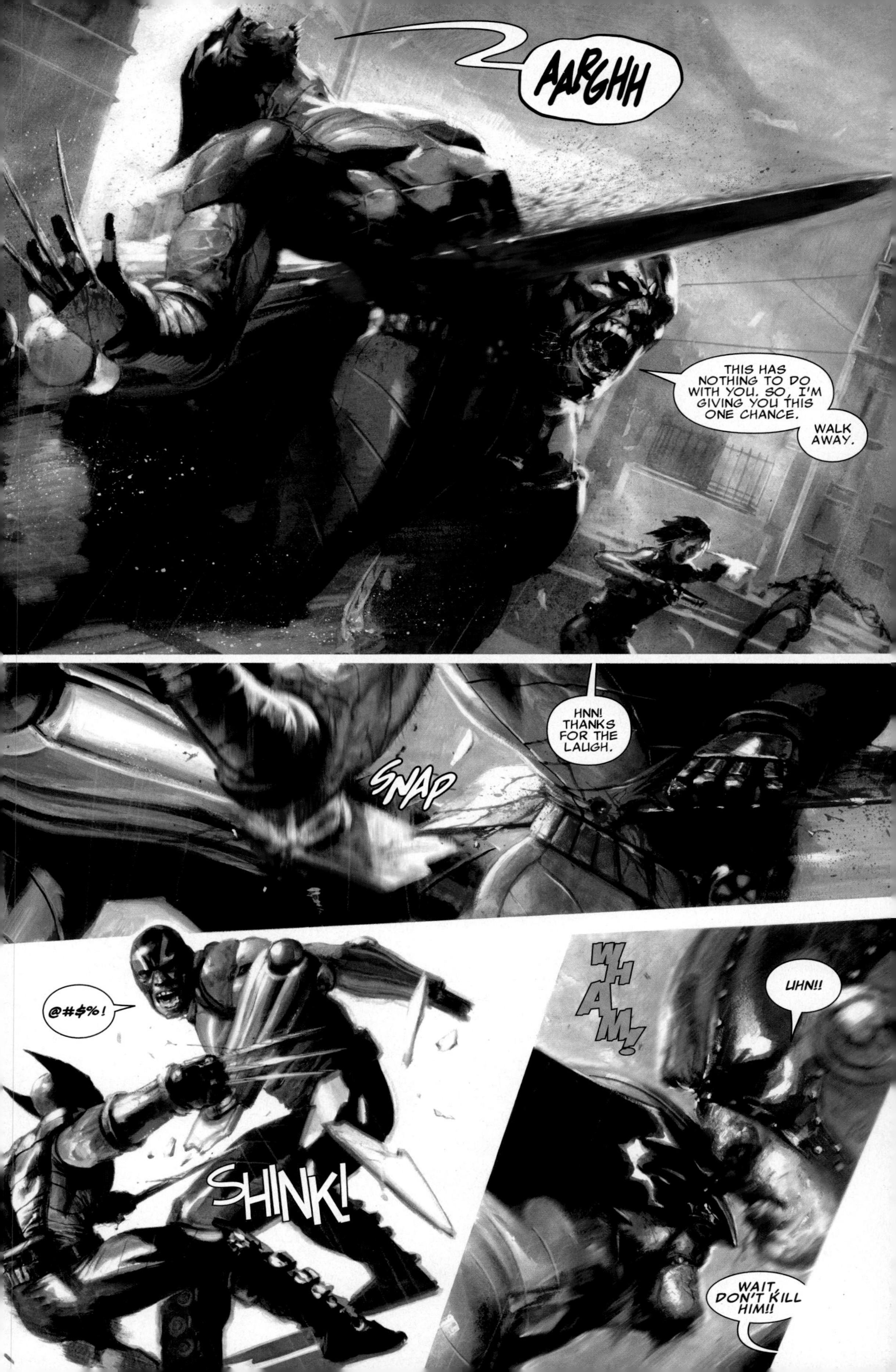
AARGHH
THIS HAS NOTHING TO DO WITH YOU. SO, I'M GIVING YOU THIS ONE CHANCE.
WALK AWAY.
HNN! THANKS FOR THE LAUGH.
SNAP
@#$%!
SHINK!
WHAM!
UHN!!
WAIT, DON'T KILL HIM!!

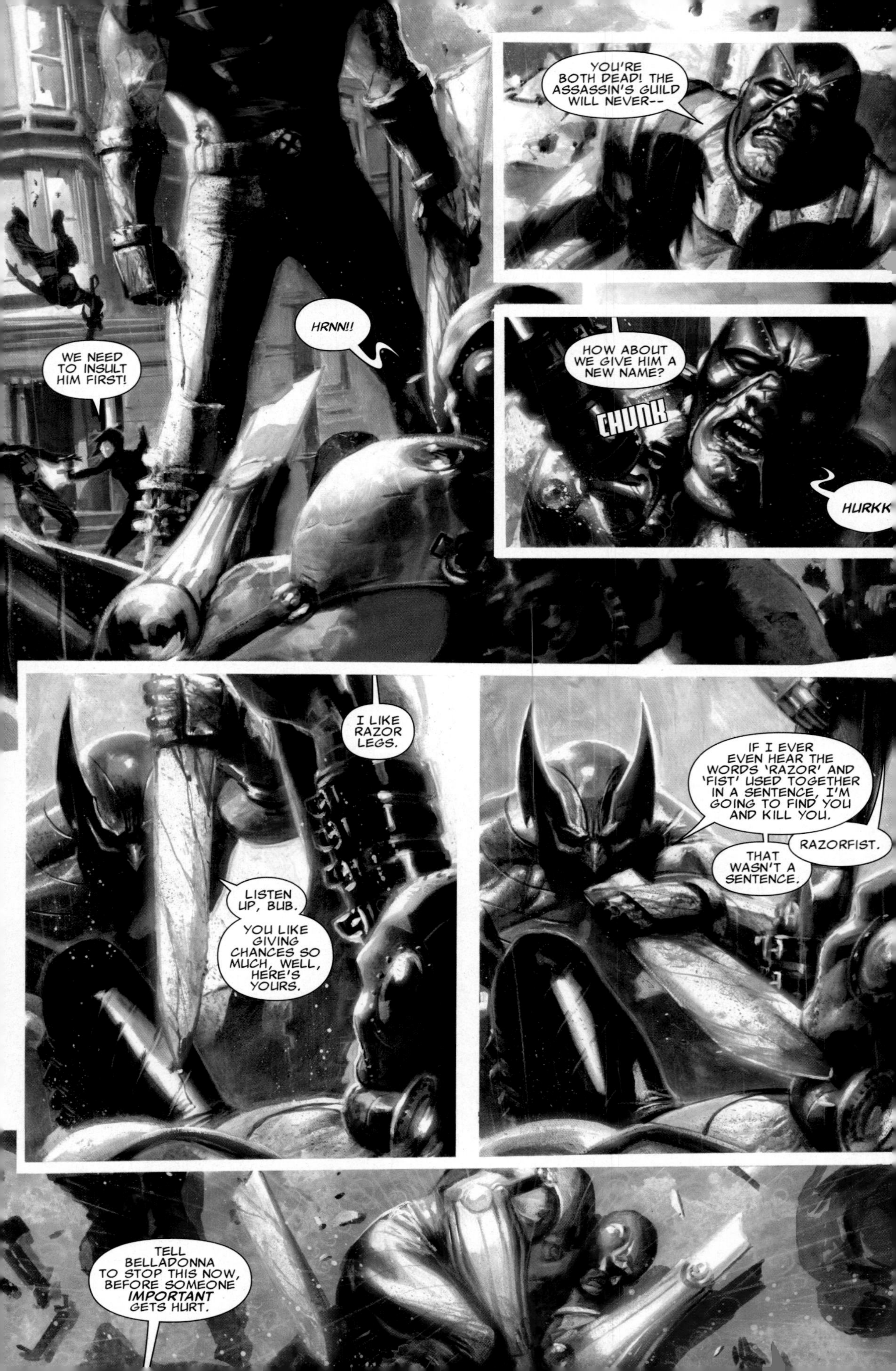
YOU'RE BOTH DEAD! THE ASSASSIN'S GUILD WILL NEVER--
WE NEED TO INSULT HIM FIRST!
HRNN!!
HOW ABOUT WE GIVE HIM A NEW NAME?
CHUNK
HURKK
I LIKE RAZOR LEGS.
LISTEN UP, BUB.
YOU LIKE GIVING CHANCES SO MUCH, WELL, HERE'S YOURS.
IF I EVER EVEN HEAR THE WORDS 'RAZOR' AND 'FIST' USED TOGETHER IN A SENTENCE, I'M GOING TO FIND YOU AND KILL YOU.
RAZORFIST.
THAT WASN'T A SENTENCE.
TELL BELLADONNA TO STOP THIS NOW, BEFORE SOMEONE IMPORTANT GETS HURT.

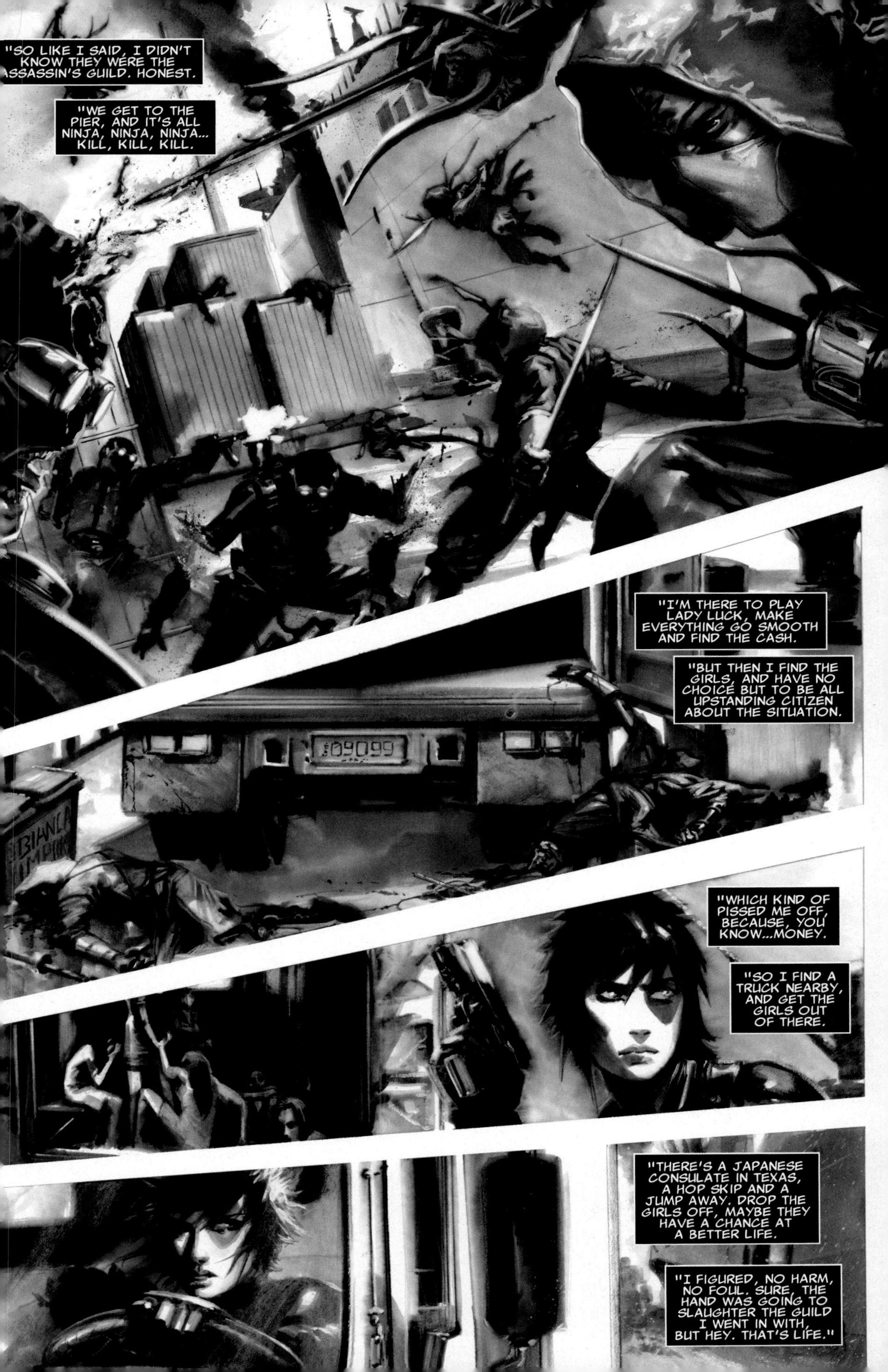
"SO LIKE I SAID, I DIDN'T KNOW THEY WERE THE ASSASSIN'S GUILD. HONEST.
"WE GET TO THE PIER, AND IT'S ALL NINJA, NINJA, NINJA... KILL, KILL, KILL.
"I'M THERE TO PLAY LADY LUCK, MAKE EVERYTHING GO SMOOTH AND FIND THE CASH.
"BUT THEN I FIND THE GIRLS, AND HAVE NO CHOICE BUT TO BE ALL UPSTANDING CITIZEN ABOUT THE SITUATION.
09099
"WHICH KIND OF PISSED ME OFF, BECAUSE, YOU KNOW...MONEY.
"SO I FIND A TRUCK NEARBY, AND GET THE GIRLS OUT OF THERE.
"THERE'S A JAPANESE CONSULATE IN TEXAS, A HOP SKIP AND A JUMP AWAY. DROP THE GIRLS OFF, MAYBE THEY HAVE A CHANCE AT A BETTER LIFE.
"I FIGURED, NO HARM, NO FOUL. SURE, THE HAND WAS GOING TO SLAUGHTER THE GUILD I WENT IN WITH, BUT HEY. THAT'S LIFE."

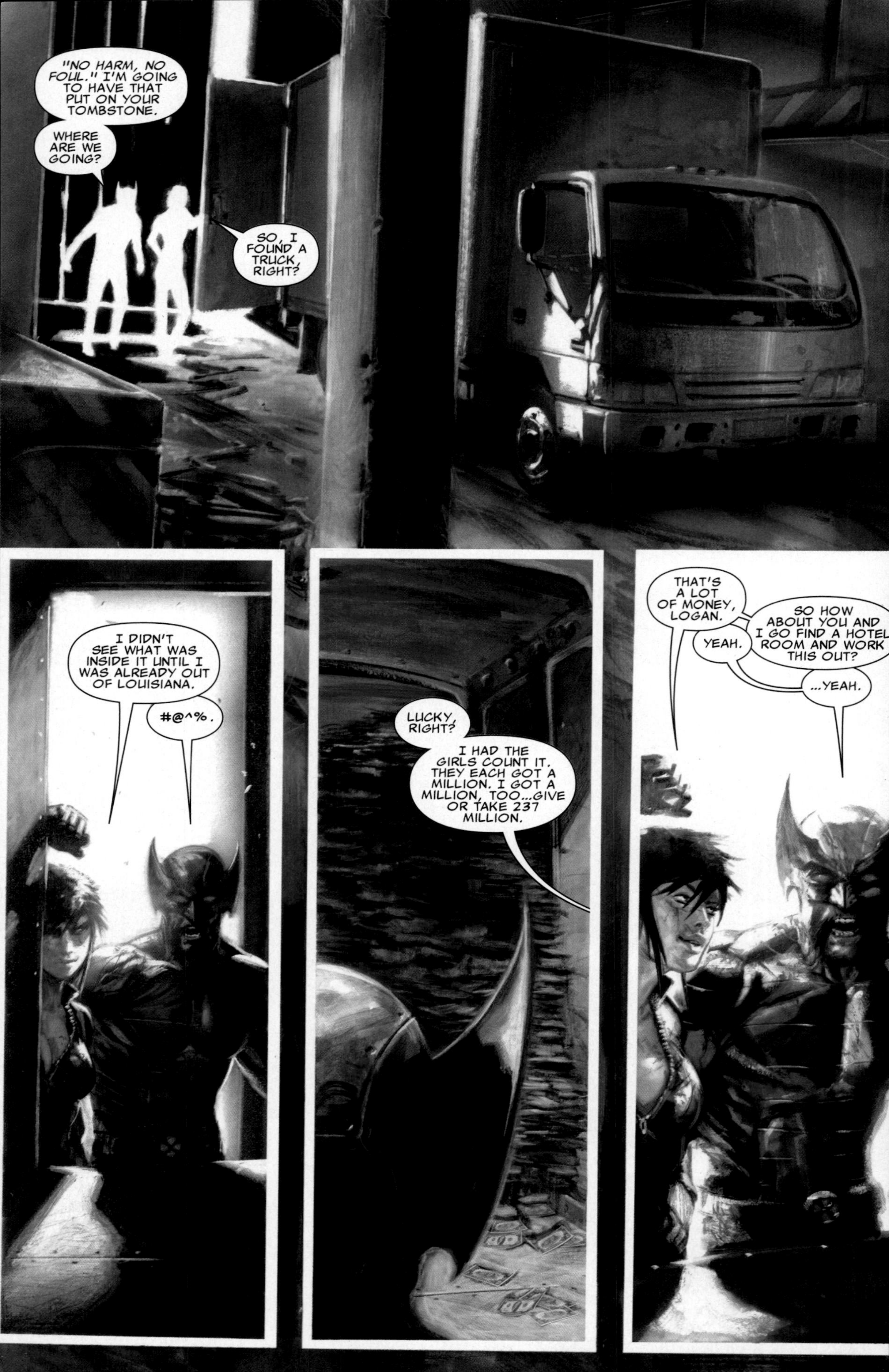
"NO HARM, NO FOUL." I'M GOING TO HAVE THAT PUT ON YOUR TOMBSTONE.
WHERE ARE WE GOING?
SO, I FOUND A TRUCK, RIGHT?
I DIDN'T SEE WHAT WAS INSIDE IT UNTIL I WAS ALREADY OUT OF LOUISIANA.
#@^%.
LUCKY, RIGHT?
I HAD THE GIRLS COUNT IT. THEY EACH GOT A MILLION. I GOT A MILLION, TOO...GIVE OR TAKE 237 MILLION.
THAT'S A LOT OF MONEY, LOGAN.
YEAH.
SO HOW ABOUT YOU AND I GO FIND A HOTEL ROOM AND WORK THIS OUT?
...YEAH.

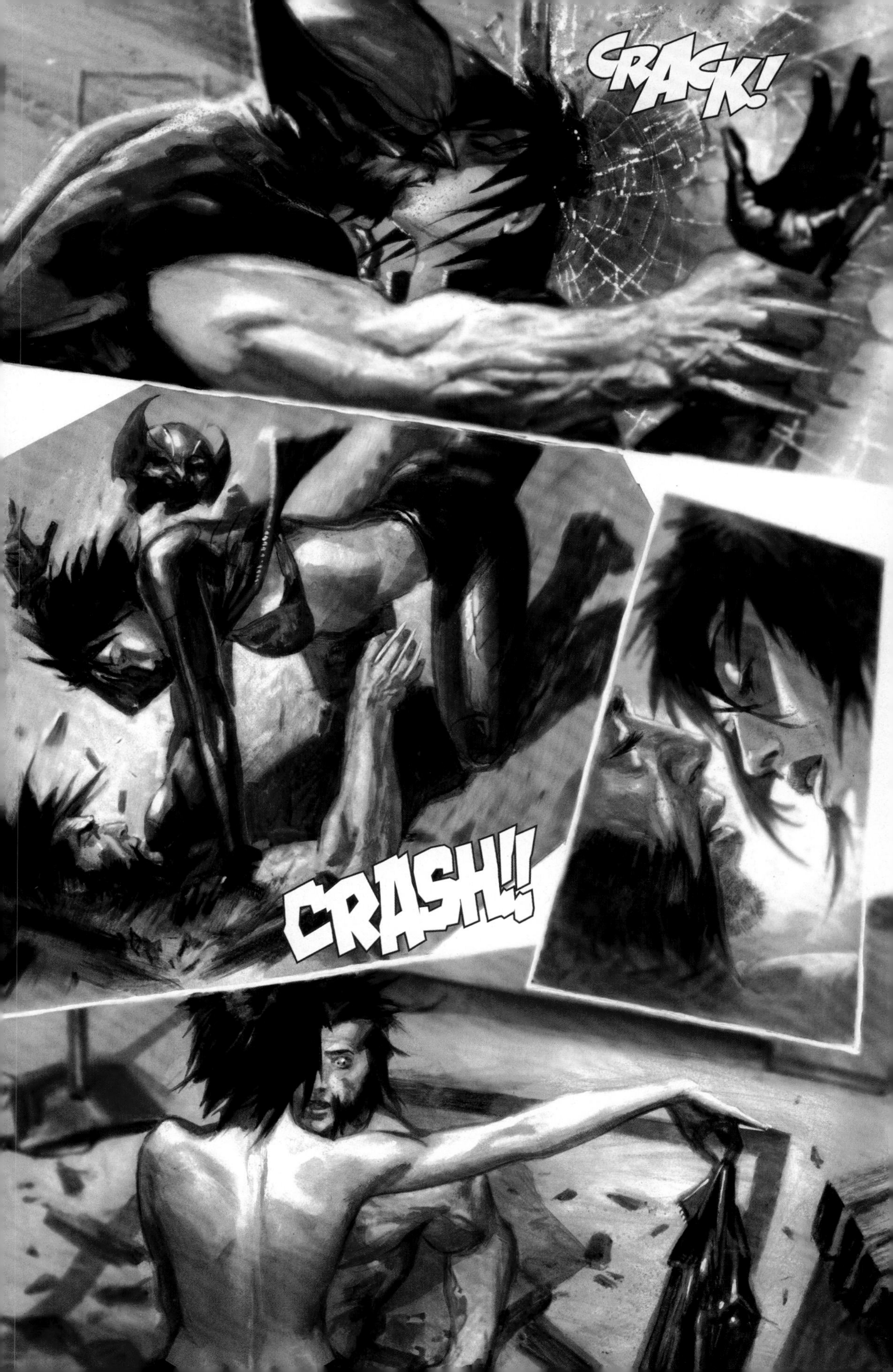
CRACK!
CRASH!!

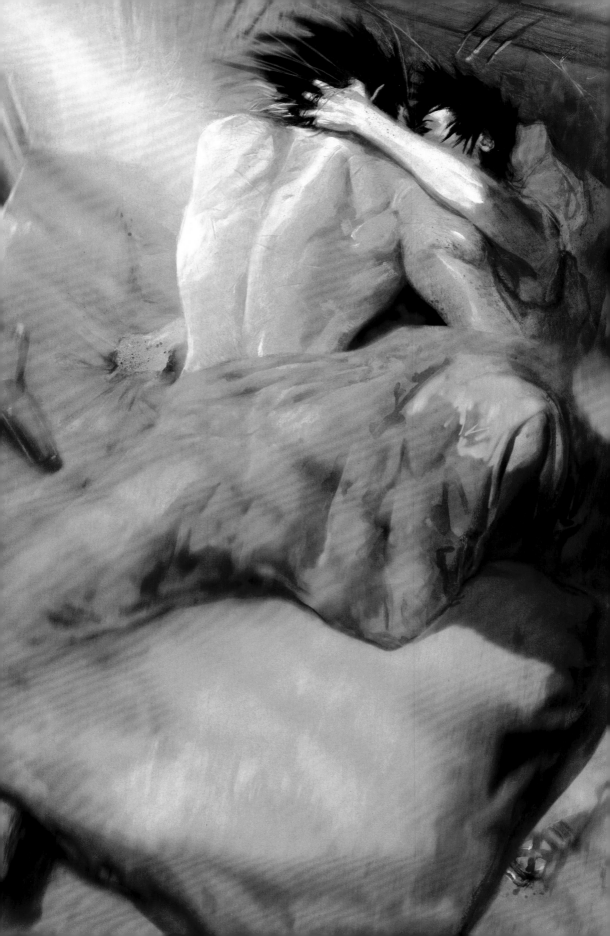

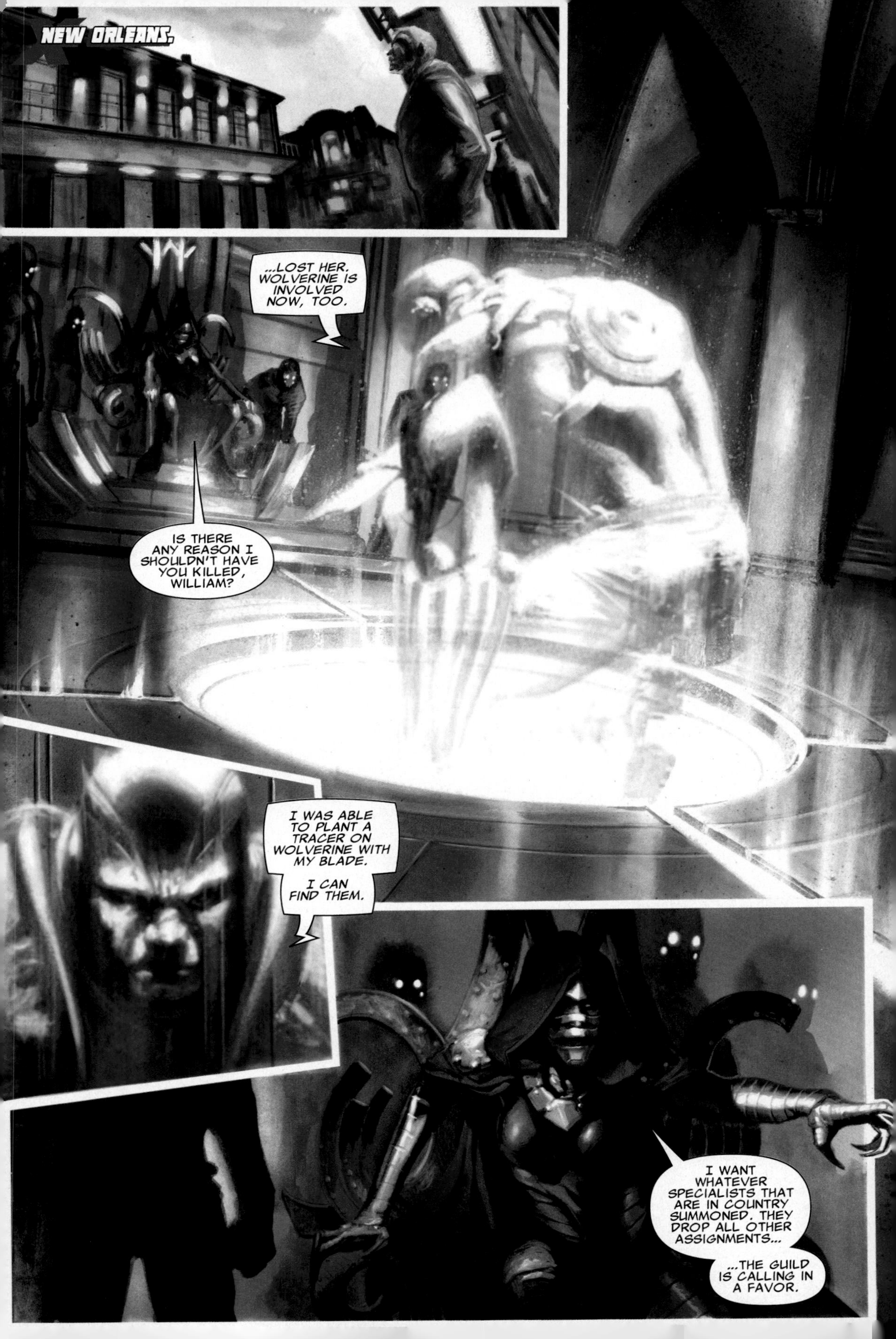
NEW ORLEANS.
...LOST HER. WOLVERINE IS INVOLVED NOW, TOO.
IS THERE ANY REASON I SHOULDN'T HAVE YOU KILLED, WILLIAM?
I WAS ABLE TO PLANT A TRACER ON WOLVERINE WITH MY BLADE.
I CAN FIND THEM.
I WANT WHATEVER SPECIALISTS THAT ARE IN COUNTRY SUMMONED. THEY DROP ALL OTHER ASSIGNMENTS...
...THE GUILD IS CALLING IN A FAVOR.

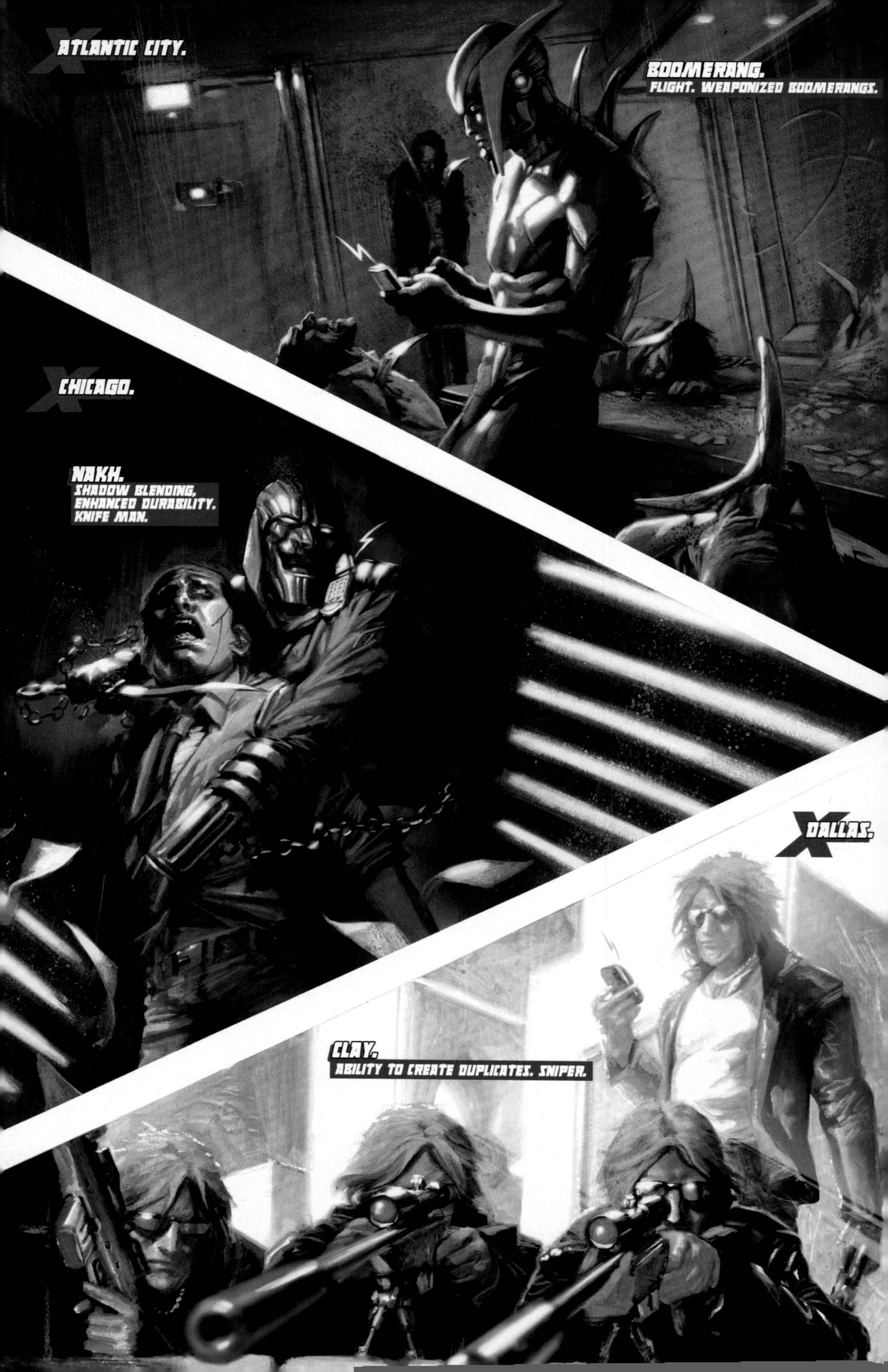
ATLANTIC CITY.
BOOMERANG.
FLIGHT. WEAPONIZED BOOMERANGS.
CHICAGO.
NAKH.
SHADOW BLENDING,
ENHANCED DURABILITY.
KNIFE MAN.
DALLAS.
CLAY.
ABILITY TO CREATE DUPLICATES. SNIPER.

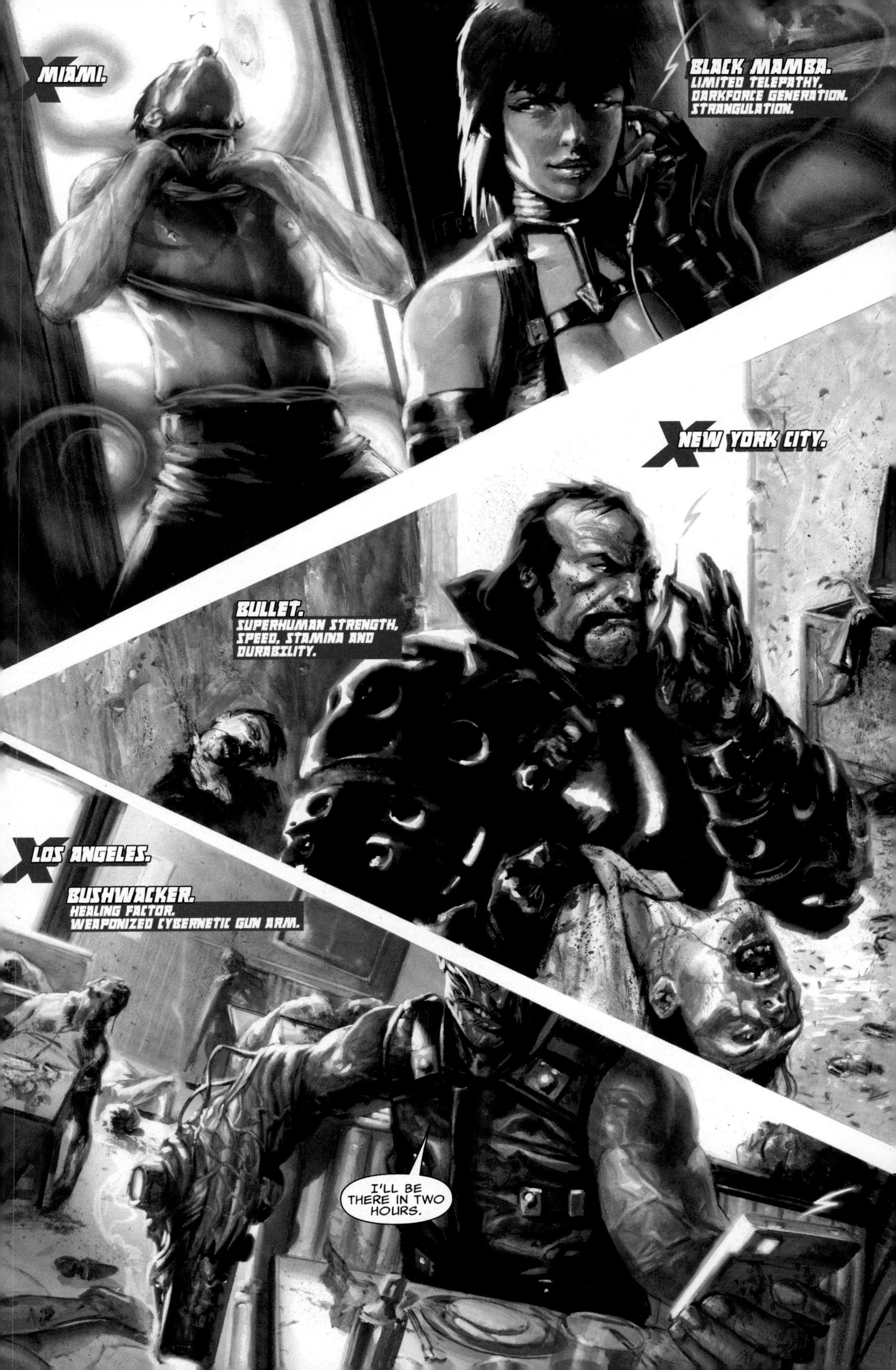
MIAMI.
BLACK MAMBA.
LIMITED TELEPATHY, DARKFORCE GENERATION. STRANGULATION.
NEW YORK CITY.
BULLET.
SUPERHUMAN STRENGTH, SPEED, STAMINA AND DURABILITY.
LOS ANGELES.
BUSHWACKER.
HEALING FACTOR. WEAPONIZED CYBERNETIC GUN ARM.
I'LL BE THERE IN TWO HOURS.

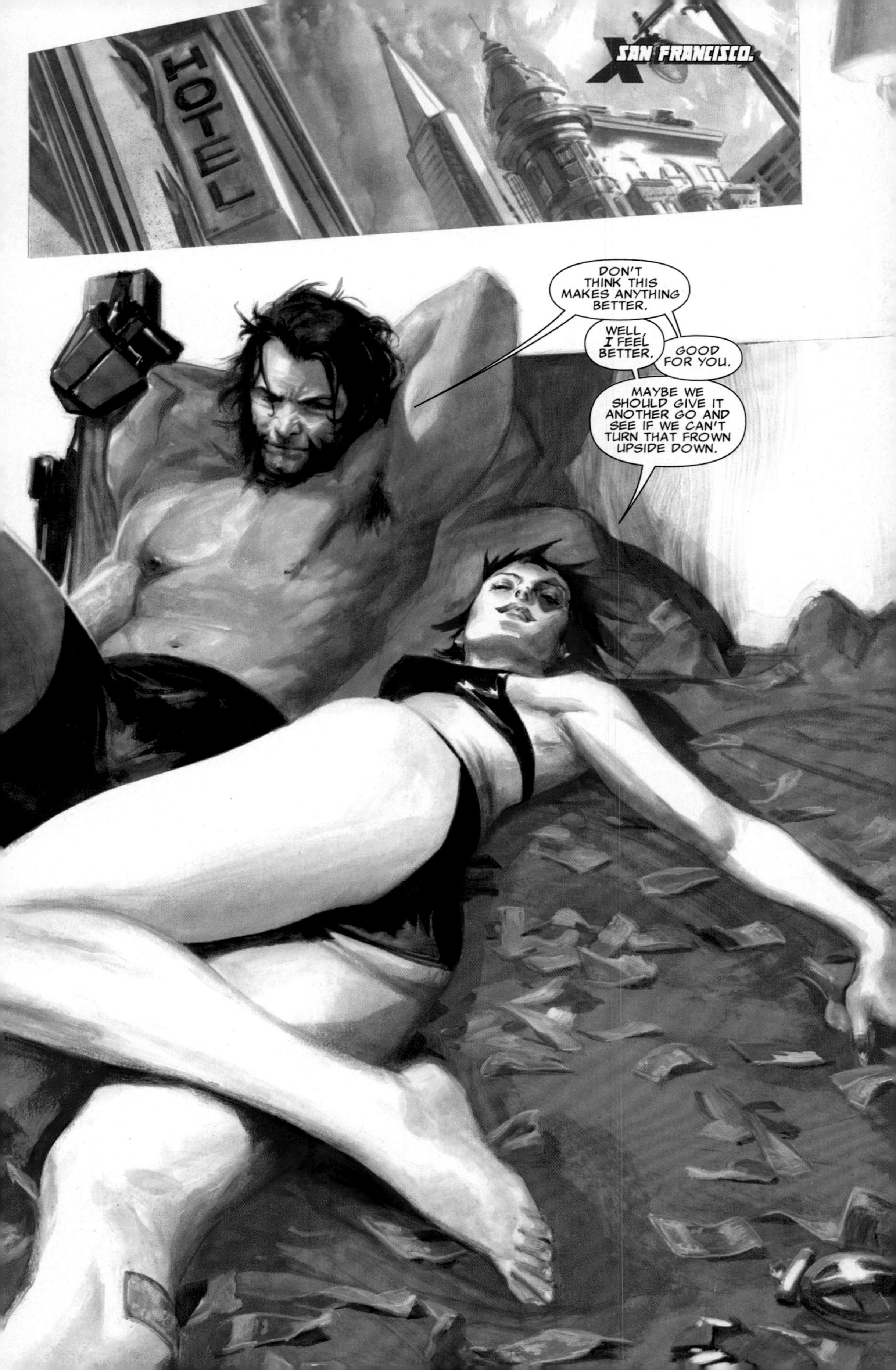
SAN FRANCISCO.
HOTEL
DON'T THINK THIS MAKES ANYTHING BETTER.
WELL, I FEEL BETTER.
GOOD FOR YOU.
MAYBE WE SHOULD GIVE IT ANOTHER GO AND SEE IF WE CAN'T TURN THAT FROWN UPSIDE DOWN.

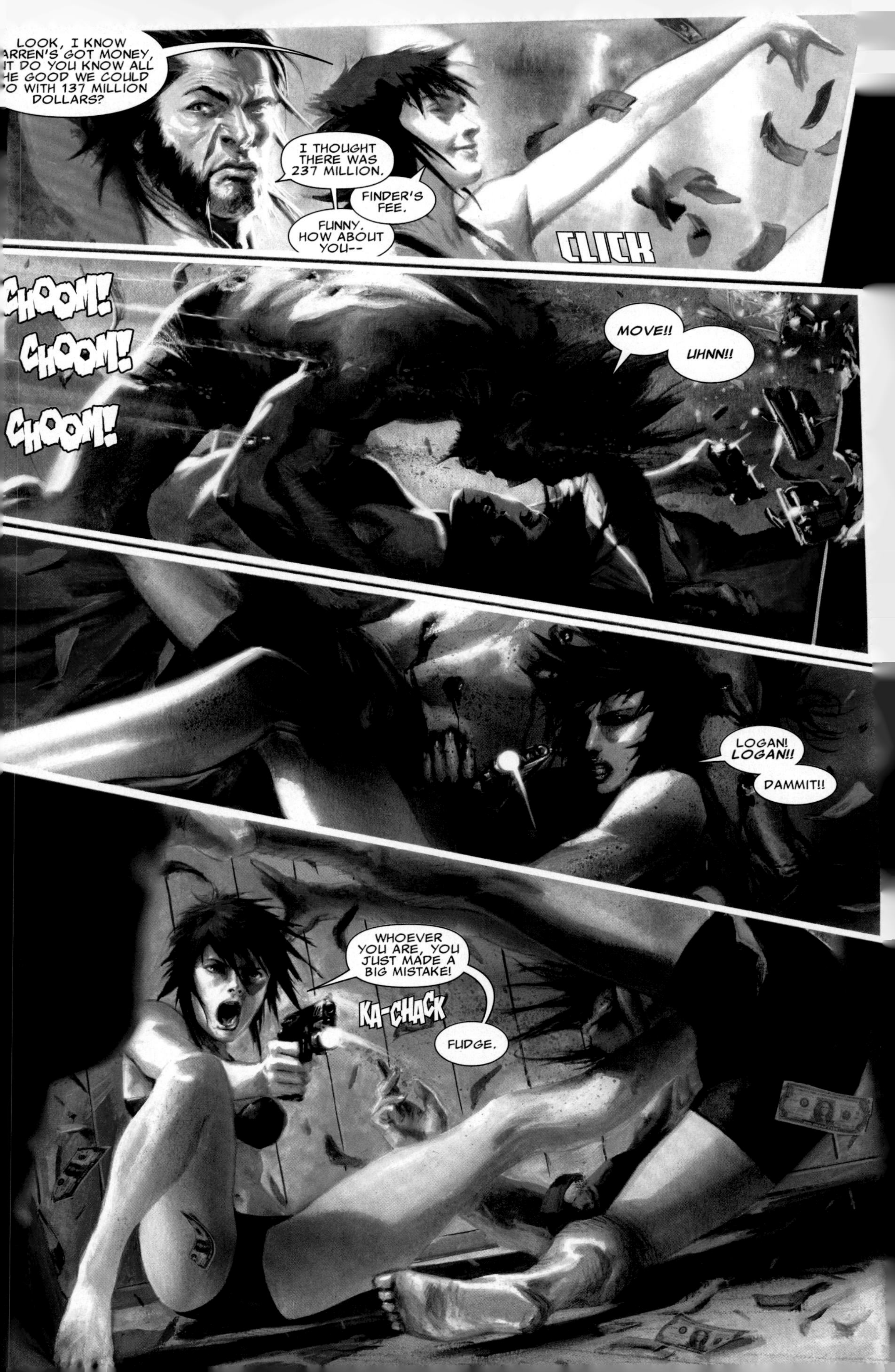
LOOK, I KNOW ARREN'S GOT MONEY, IT DO YOU KNOW ALL HE GOOD WE COULD O WITH 137 MILLION DOLLARS?
I THOUGHT THERE WAS 237 MILLION.
FINDER'S FEE.
FUNNY. HOW ABOUT YOU--
CLICK
CHOOM!
CHOOM!
CHOOM!
MOVE!!
UHNN!!
LOGAN! LOGAN!!
DAMMIT!!
WHOEVER YOU ARE, YOU JUST MADE A BIG MISTAKE!
KA-CHACK
FUDGE.

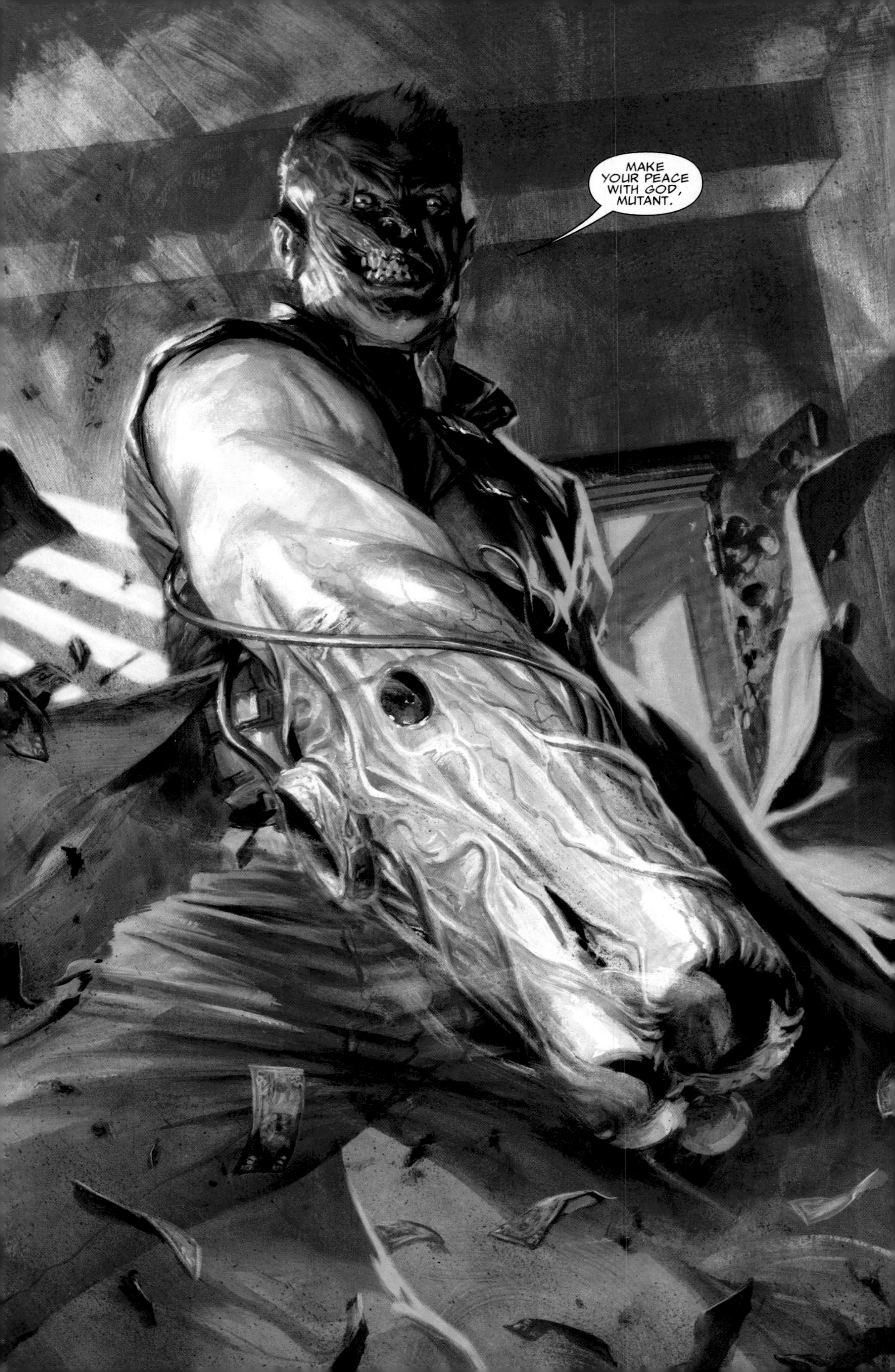
MAKE YOUR PEACE WITH GOD, MUTANT.

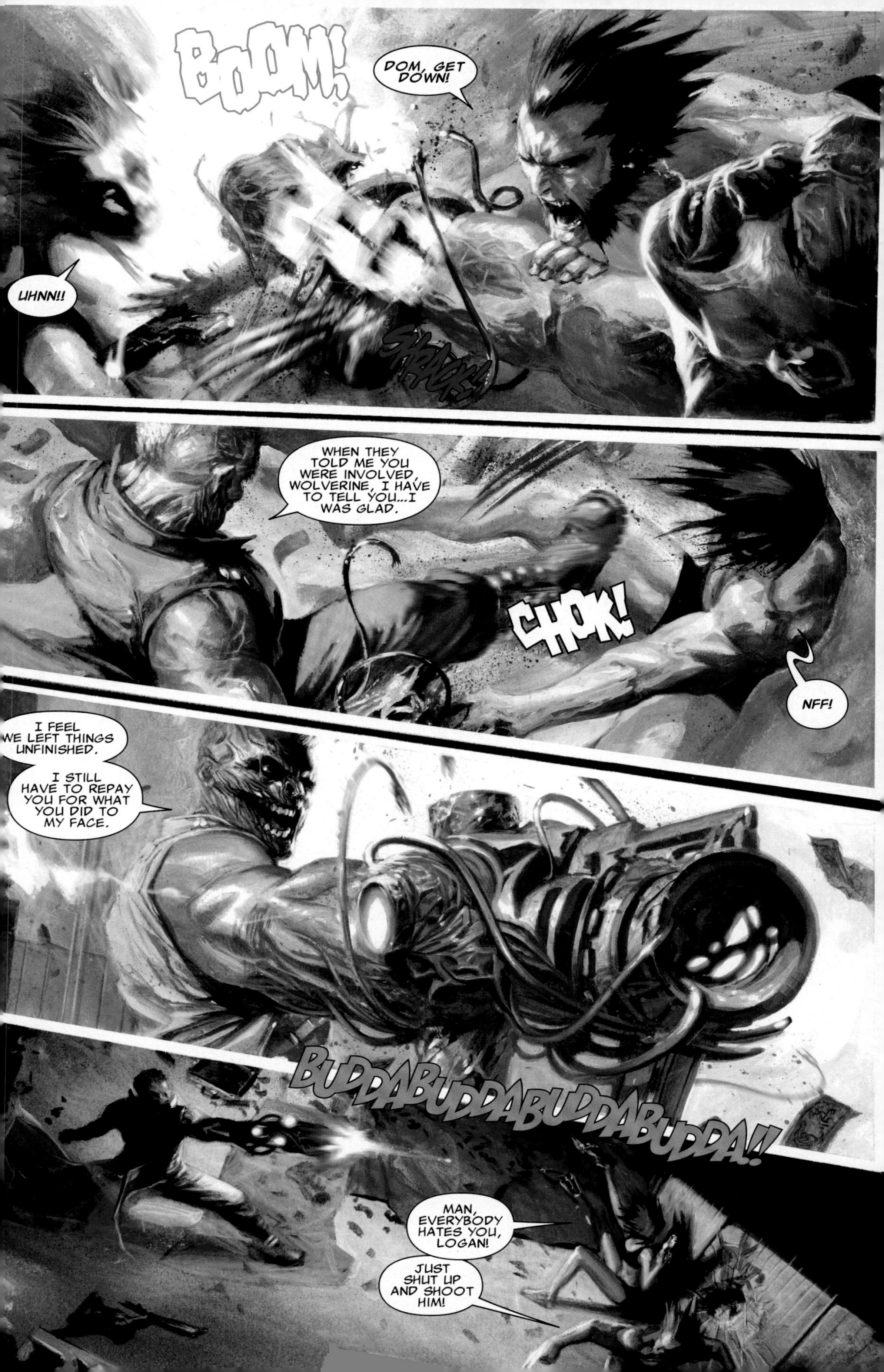
BOOM!
DOM, GET DOWN!
UHNN!!
SHRACK!
WHEN THEY TOLD ME YOU WERE INVOLVED, WOLVERINE, I HAVE TO TELL YOU...I WAS GLAD.
CHOK!
NFF!
I FEEL WE LEFT THINGS UNFINISHED.
I STILL HAVE TO REPAY YOU FOR WHAT YOU DID TO MY FACE.
BUDDABUDDABUDDABUDDA!!
MAN, EVERYBODY HATES YOU, LOGAN!
JUST SHUT UP AND SHOOT HIM!

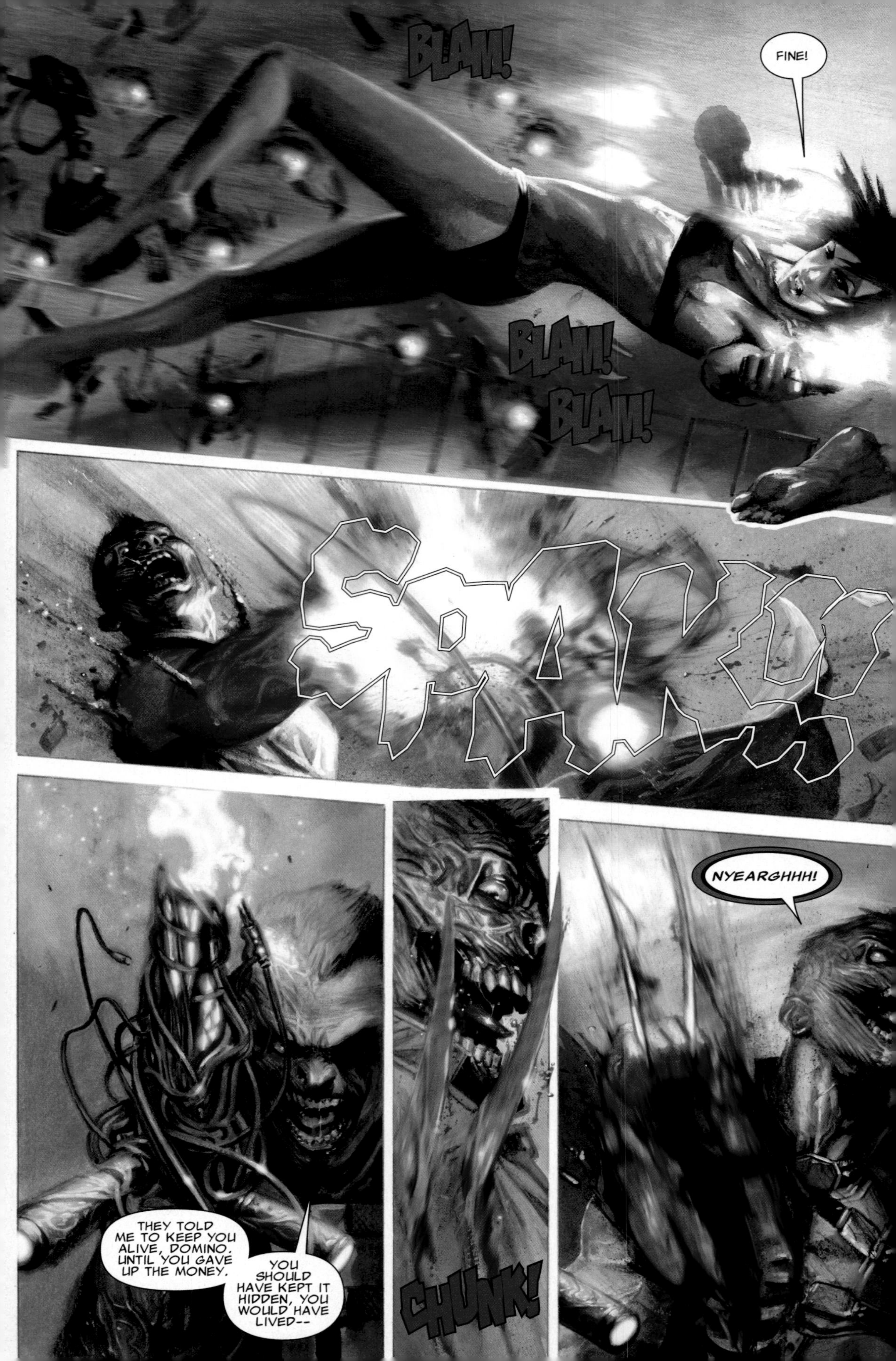
BLAM!
FINE!
BLAM!
BLAM!
THEY TOLD ME TO KEEP YOU ALIVE, DOMINO. UNTIL YOU GAVE UP THE MONEY.
YOU SHOULD HAVE KEPT IT HIDDEN, YOU WOULD HAVE LIVED--
CHUNK!
NYEARGHHH!

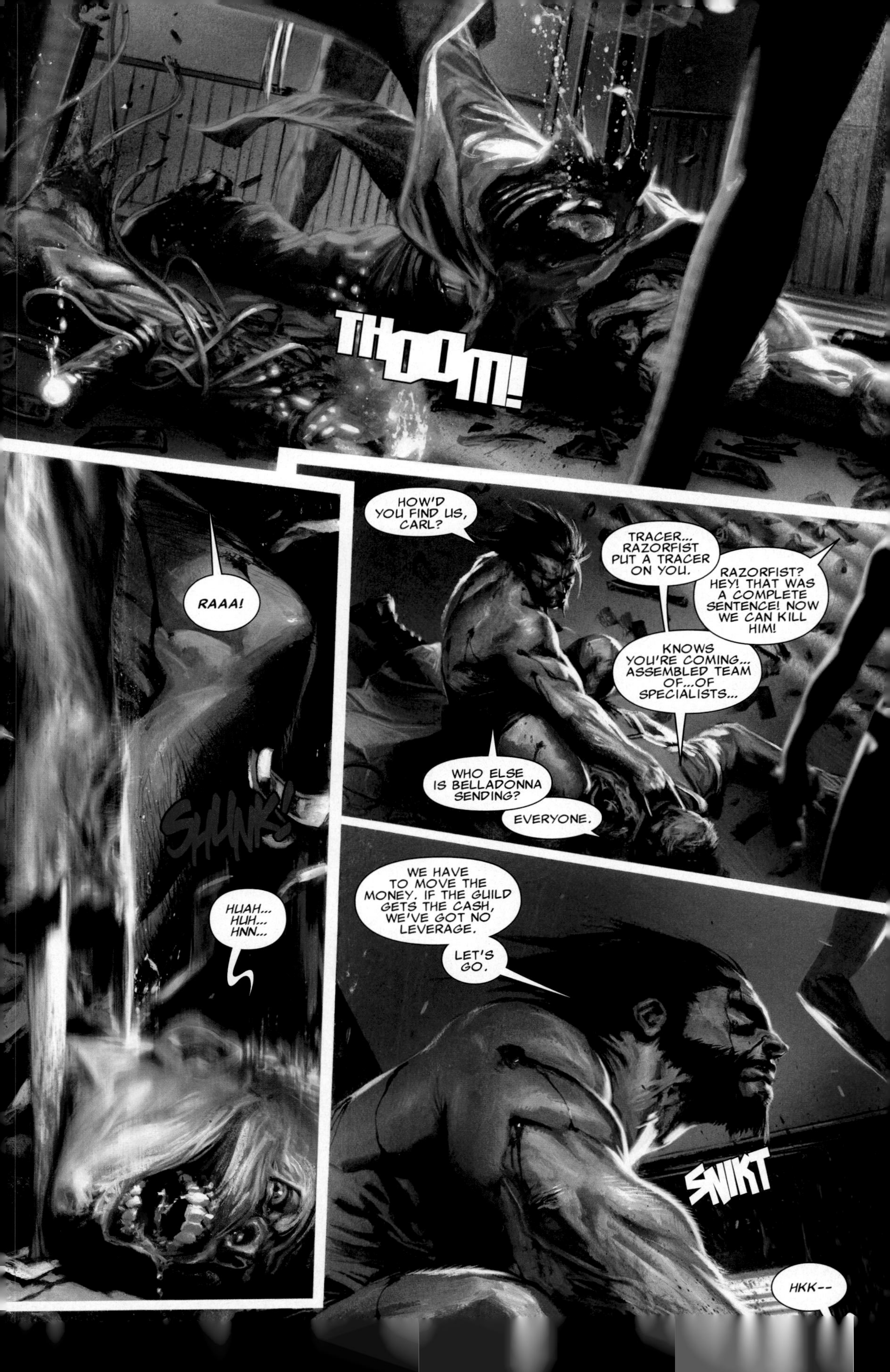
THOOM!
RAAA!
SHUNK!
HUAH... HUH... HNN...
HOW'D YOU FIND US, CARL?
TRACER... RAZORFIST PUT A TRACER ON YOU.
RAZORFIST? HEY! THAT WAS A COMPLETE SENTENCE! NOW WE CAN KILL HIM!
KNOWS YOU'RE COMING... ASSEMBLED TEAM OF...OF SPECIALISTS...
WHO ELSE IS BELLADONNA SENDING?
EVERYONE.
WE HAVE TO MOVE THE MONEY. IF THE GUILD GETS THE CASH, WE'VE GOT NO LEVERAGE.
LET'S GO.
SNIKT
HKK--

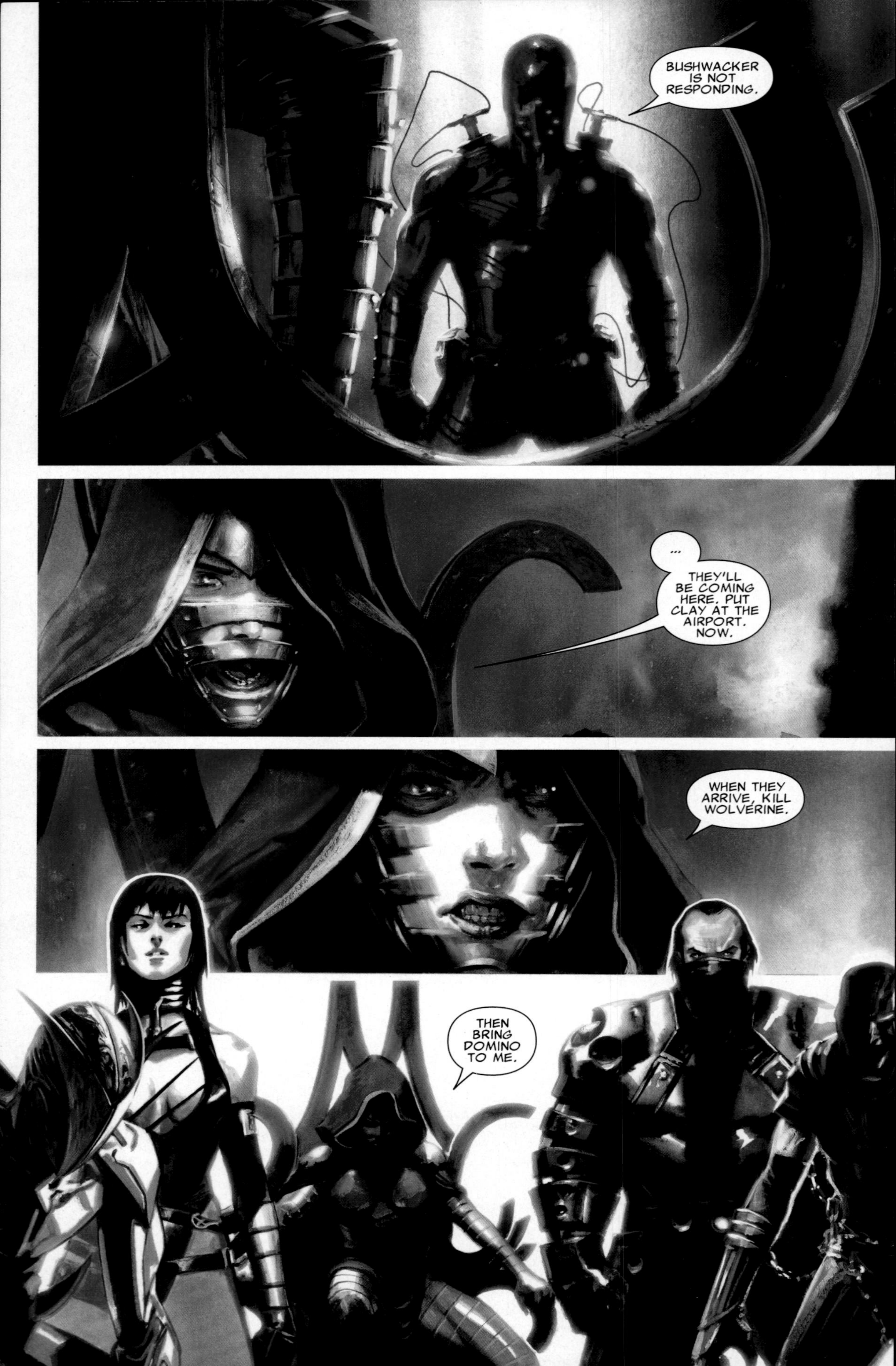

BUSHWACKER IS NOT RESPONDING.
...
THEY'LL BE COMING HERE. PUT CLAY AT THE AIRPORT. NOW.
WHEN THEY ARRIVE, KILL WOLVERINE.
THEN BRING DOMINO TO ME.

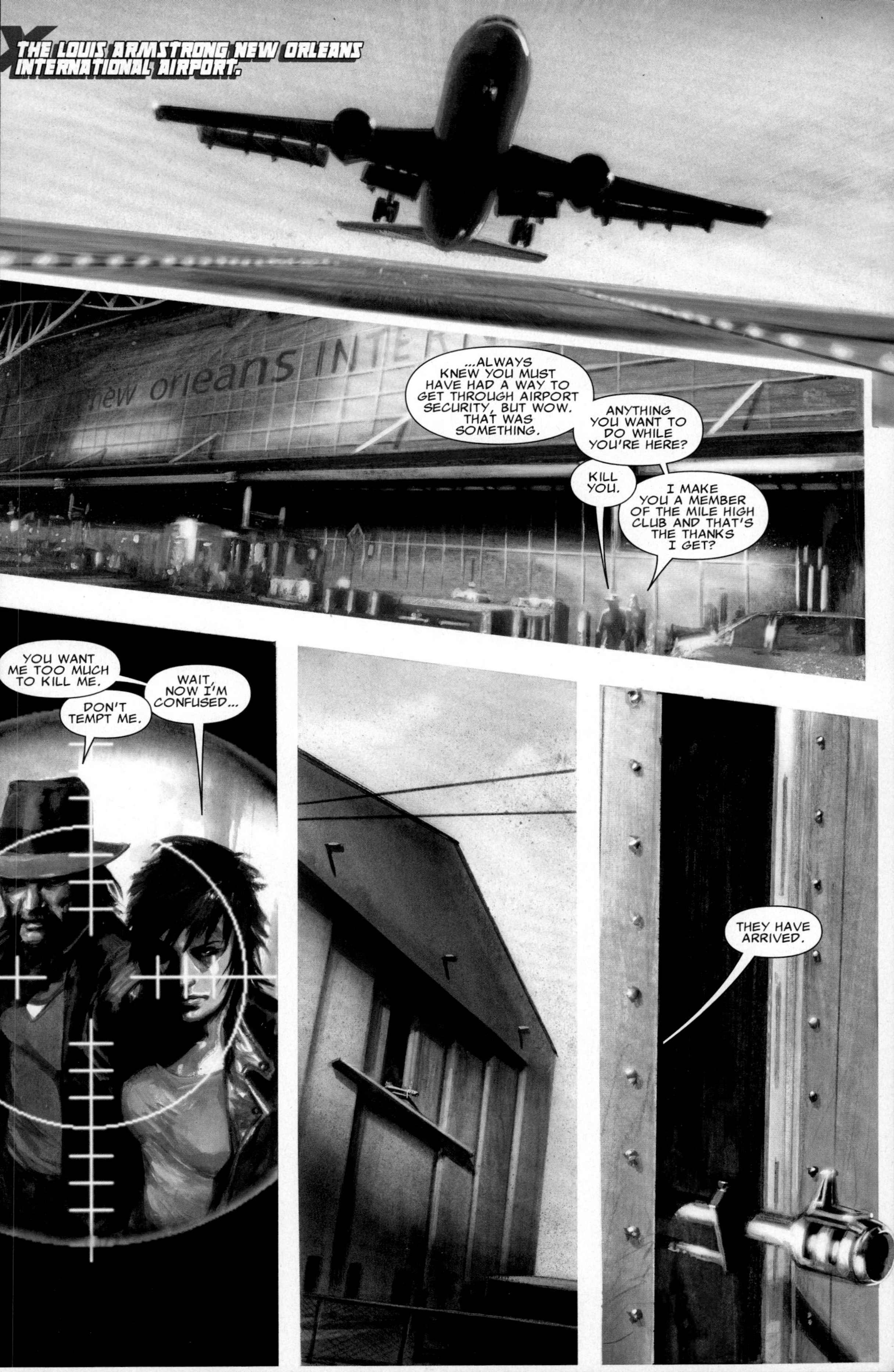
THE LOUIS ARMSTRONG NEW ORLEANS INTERNATIONAL AIRPORT.
...ALWAYS KNEW YOU MUST HAVE HAD A WAY TO GET THROUGH AIRPORT SECURITY, BUT WOW. THAT WAS SOMETHING.
ANYTHING YOU WANT TO DO WHILE YOU'RE HERE?
KILL YOU.
I MAKE YOU A MEMBER OF THE MILE HIGH CLUB AND THAT'S THE THANKS I GET?
YOU WANT ME TOO MUCH TO KILL ME.
DON'T TEMPT ME.
WAIT, NOW I'M CONFUSED...
THEY HAVE ARRIVED.

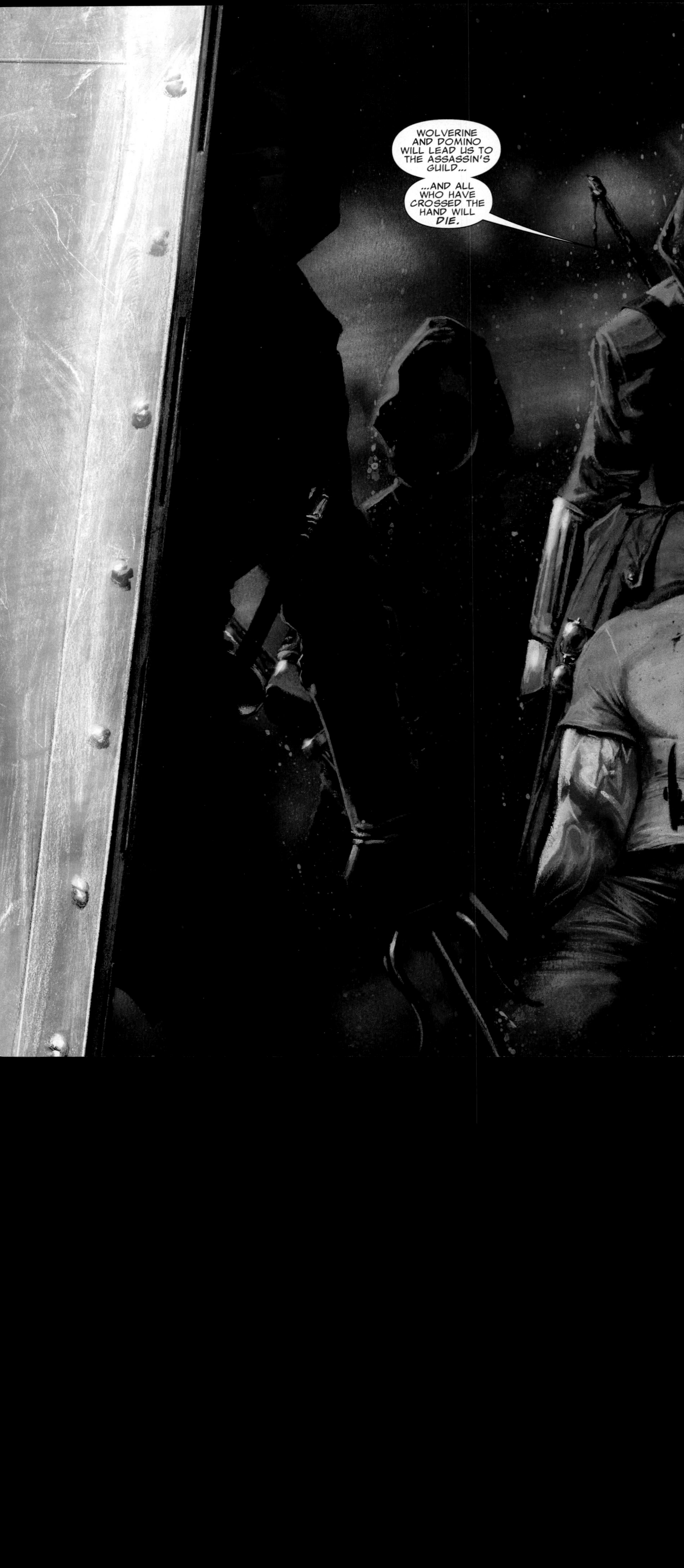
WOLVERINE AND DOMINO WILL LEAD US TO THE ASSASSIN'S GUILD...
...AND ALL WHO HAVE CROSSED THE HAND WILL DIE.

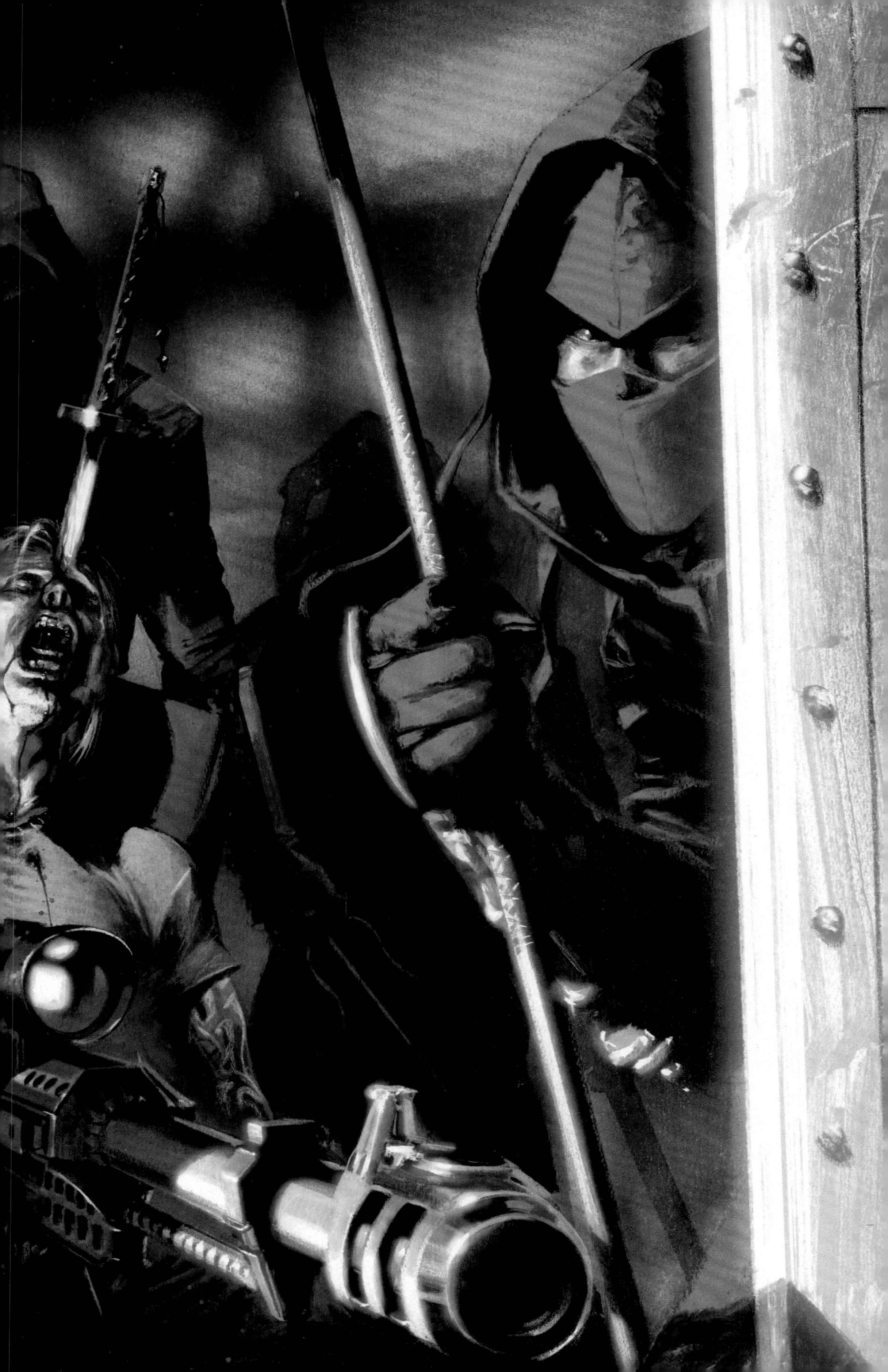

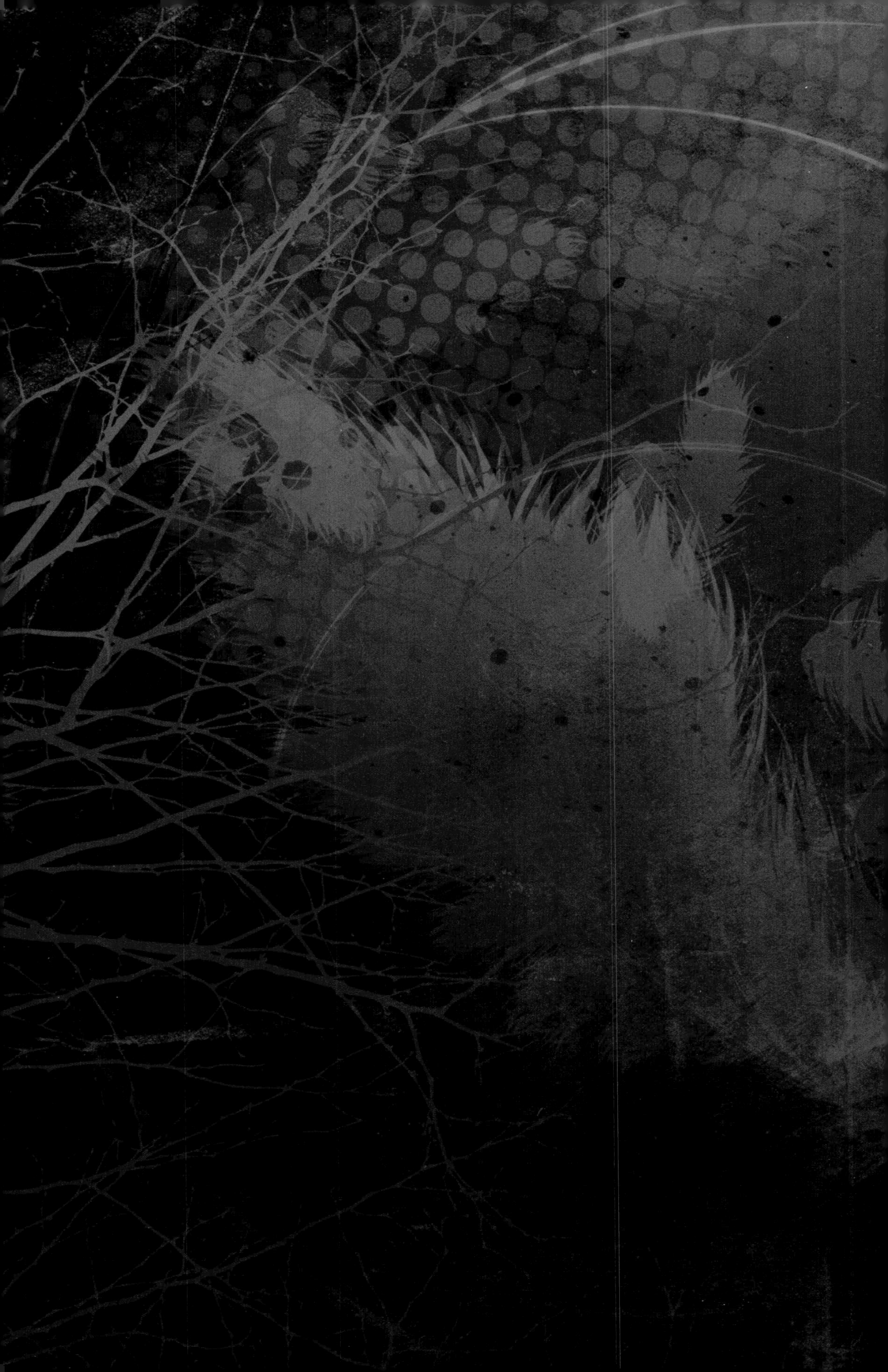

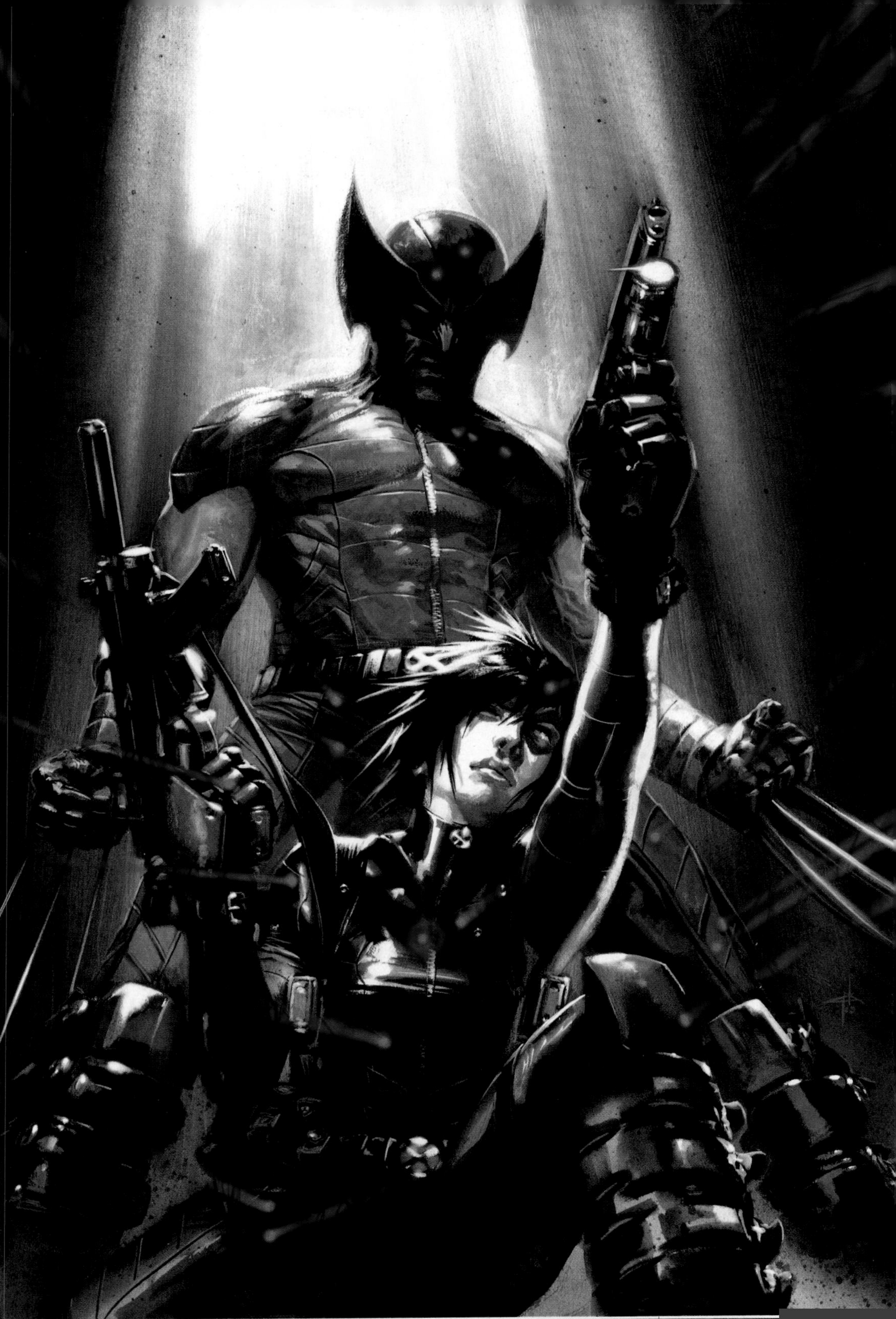

E #3

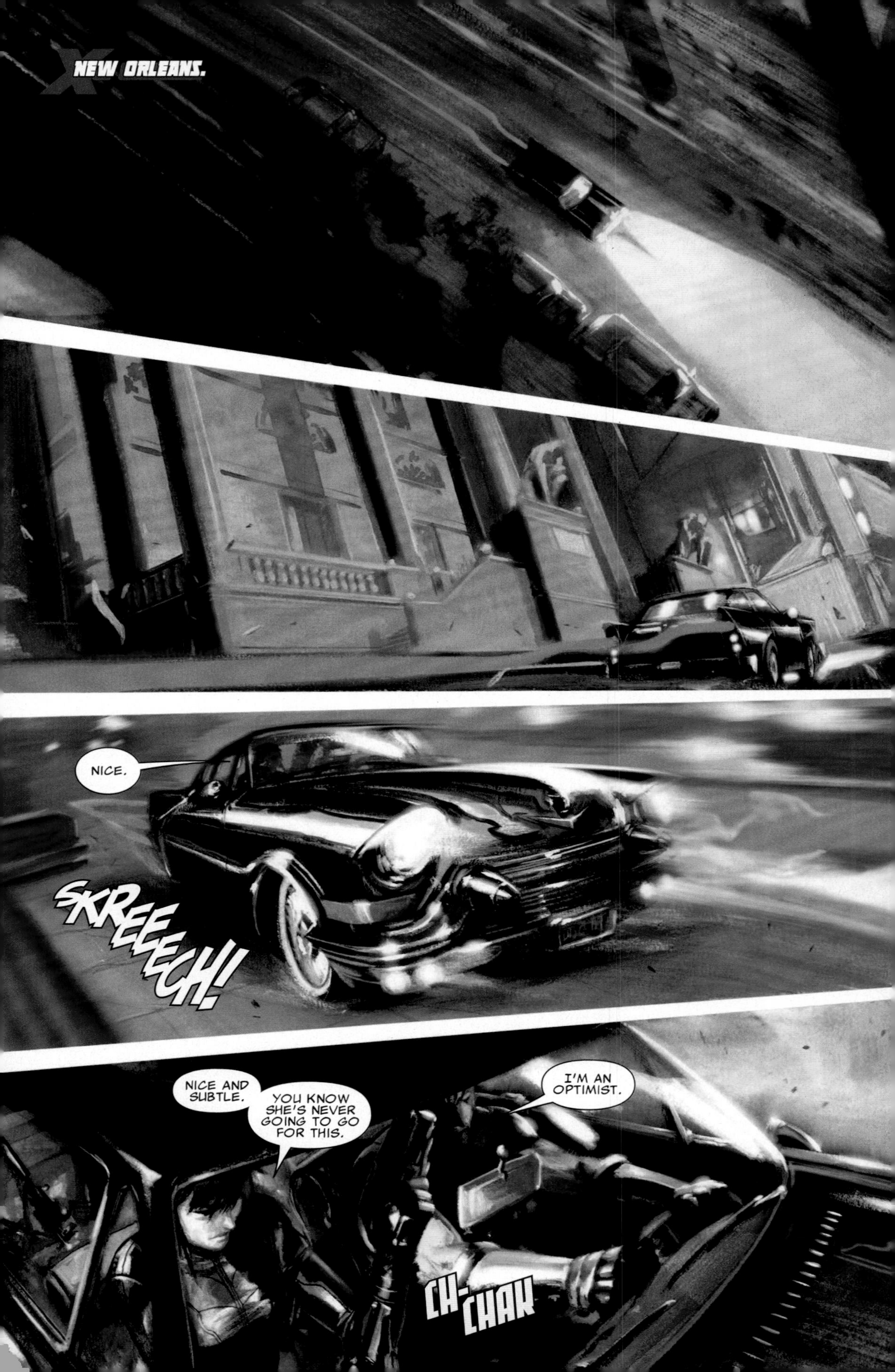
NEW ORLEANS.
NICE.
SKREEECH!
NICE AND SUBTLE.
YOU KNOW SHE'S NEVER GOING TO GO FOR THIS.
I'M AN OPTIMIST.
CH-CHAK

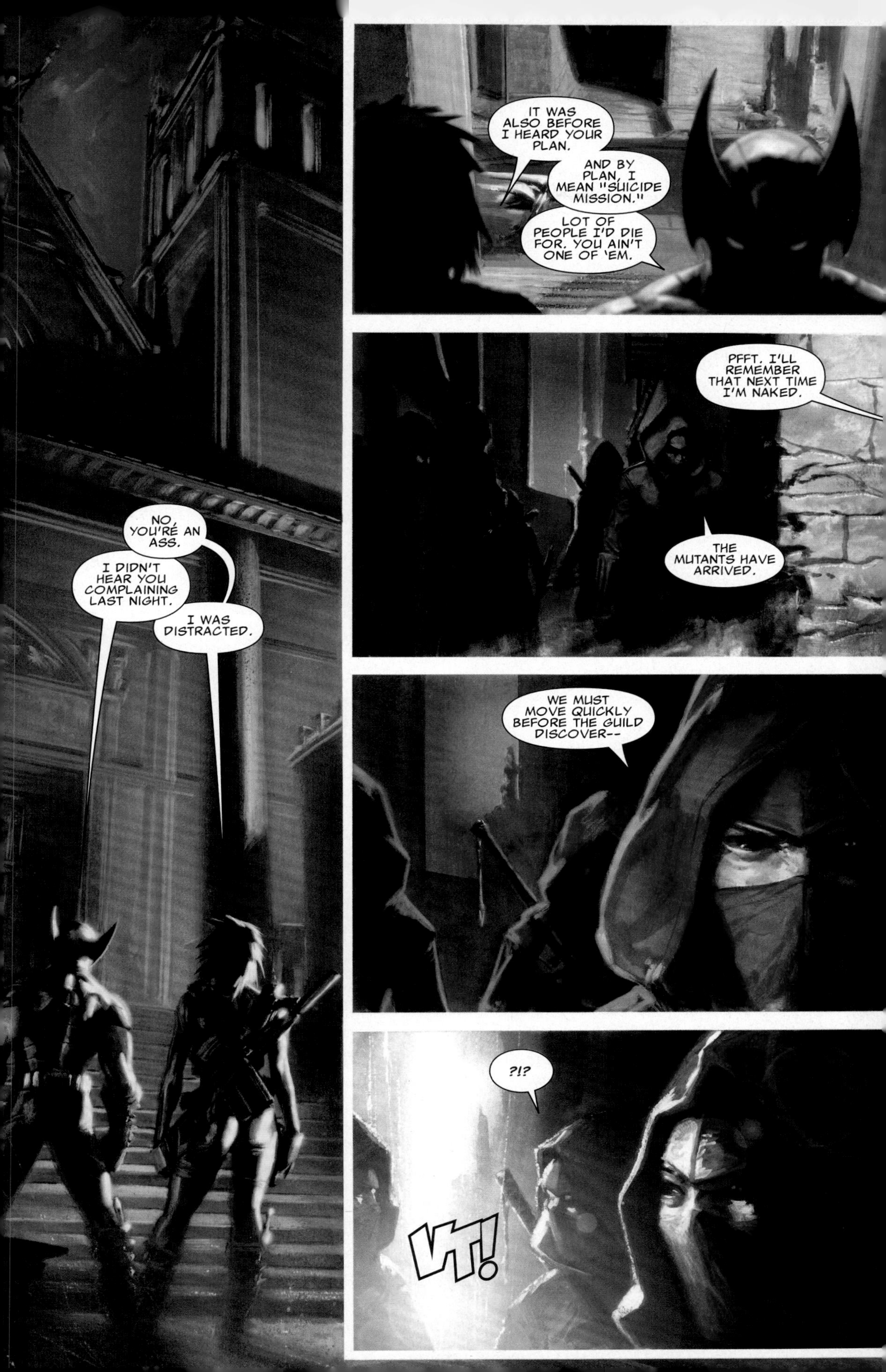
NO, YOU'RE AN ASS.
I DIDN'T HEAR YOU COMPLAINING LAST NIGHT.
I WAS DISTRACTED.
IT WAS ALSO BEFORE I HEARD YOUR PLAN.
AND BY PLAN, I MEAN "SUICIDE MISSION."
LOT OF PEOPLE I'D DIE FOR. YOU AIN'T ONE OF 'EM.
PFFT. I'LL REMEMBER THAT NEXT TIME I'M NAKED.
THE MUTANTS HAVE ARRIVED.
WE MUST MOVE QUICKLY BEFORE THE GUILD DISCOVER--
?!?
VT!

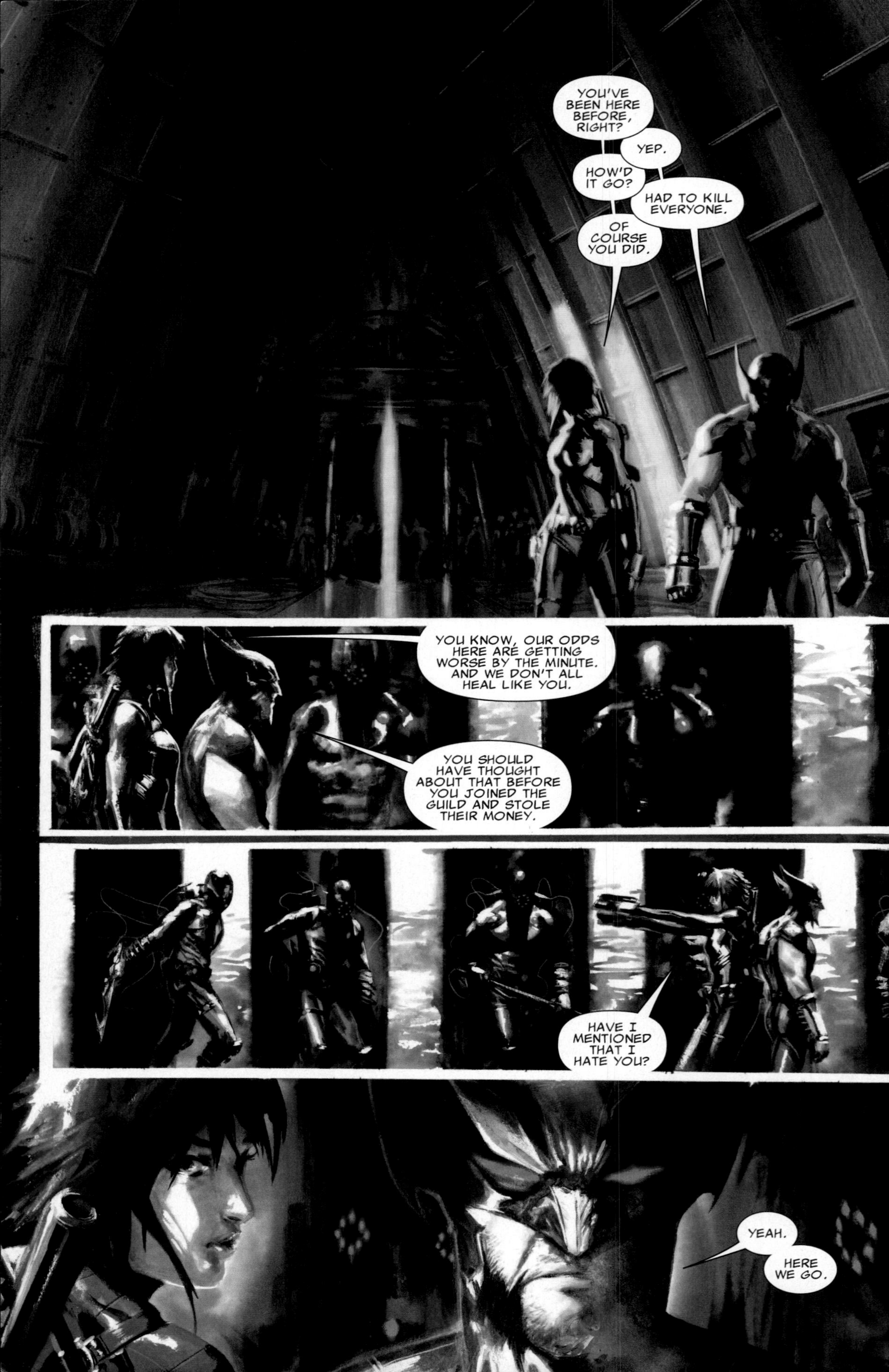
YOU'VE BEEN HERE BEFORE, RIGHT?
YEP.
HOW'D IT GO?
HAD TO KILL EVERYONE.
OF COURSE YOU DID.
YOU KNOW, OUR ODDS HERE ARE GETTING WORSE BY THE MINUTE. AND WE DON'T ALL HEAL LIKE YOU.
YOU SHOULD HAVE THOUGHT ABOUT THAT BEFORE YOU JOINED THE GUILD AND STOLE THEIR MONEY.
HAVE I MENTIONED THAT I HATE YOU?
YEAH.
HERE WE GO.

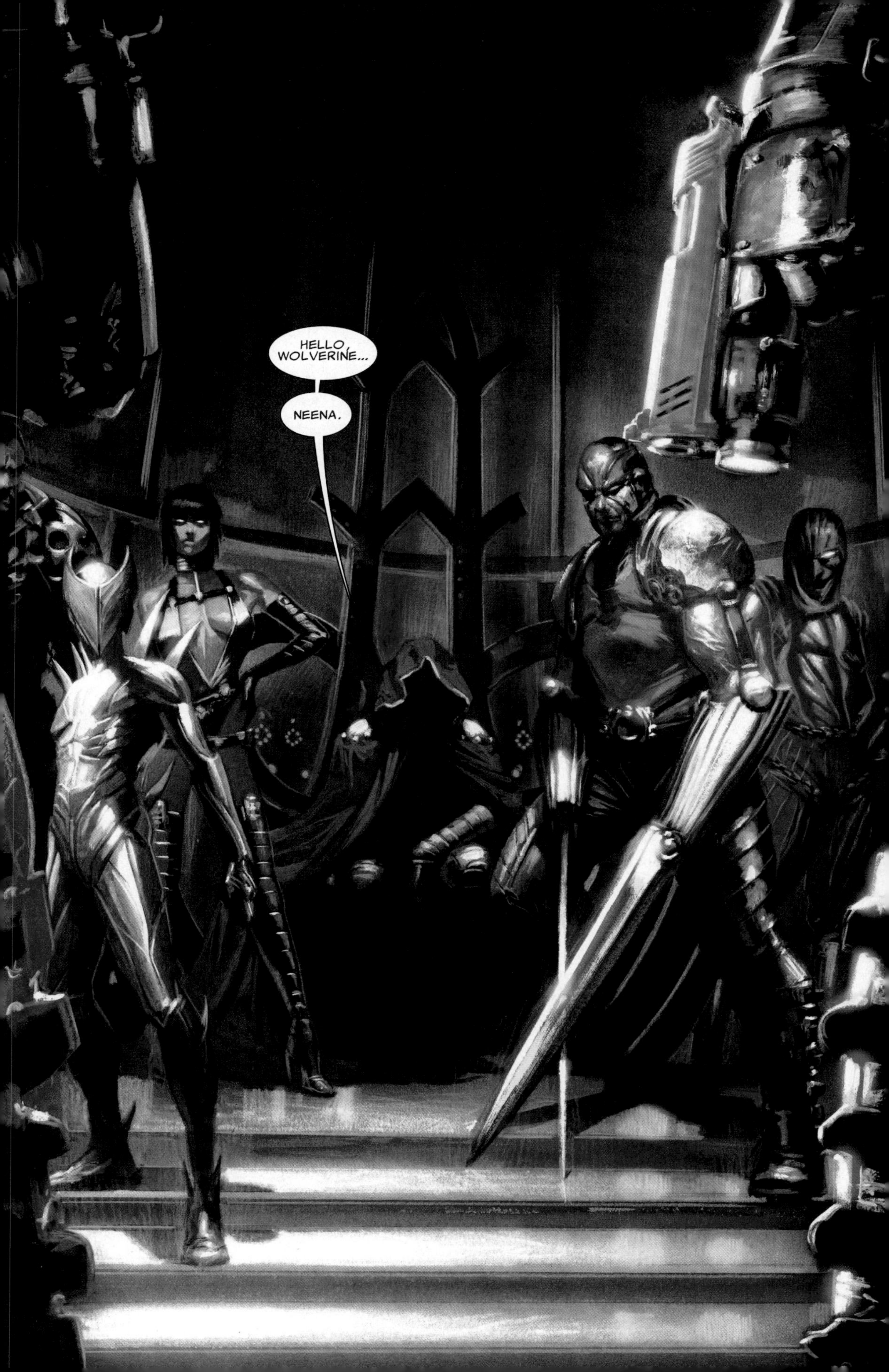
HELLO, WOLVERINE...
NEENA.

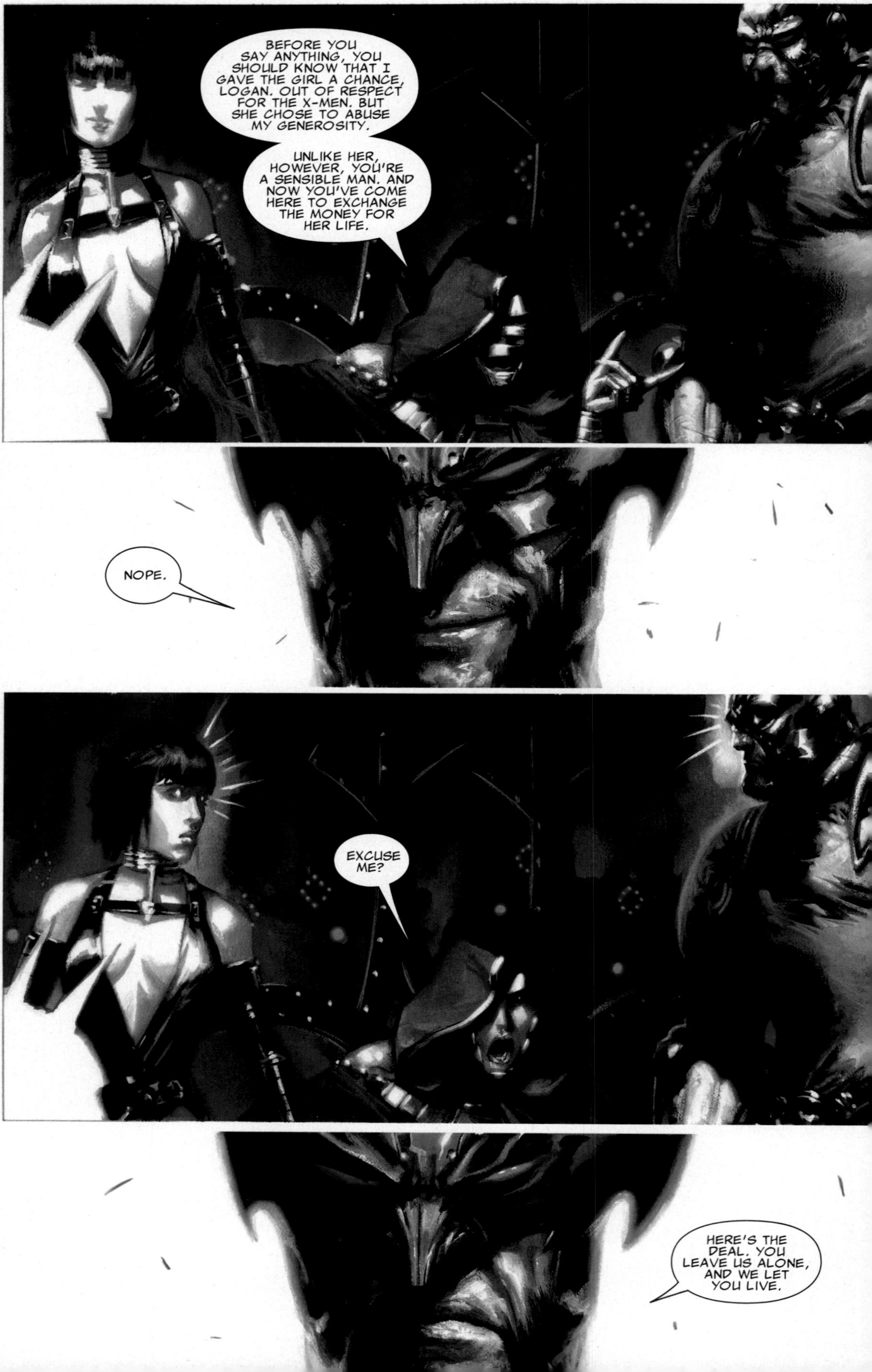
BEFORE YOU SAY ANYTHING, YOU SHOULD KNOW THAT I GAVE THE GIRL A CHANCE, LOGAN. OUT OF RESPECT FOR THE X-MEN. BUT SHE CHOSE TO ABUSE MY GENEROSITY.
UNLIKE HER, HOWEVER, YOU'RE A SENSIBLE MAN. AND NOW YOU'VE COME HERE TO EXCHANGE THE MONEY FOR HER LIFE.
NOPE.
EXCUSE ME?
HERE'S THE DEAL. YOU LEAVE US ALONE, AND WE LET YOU LIVE.

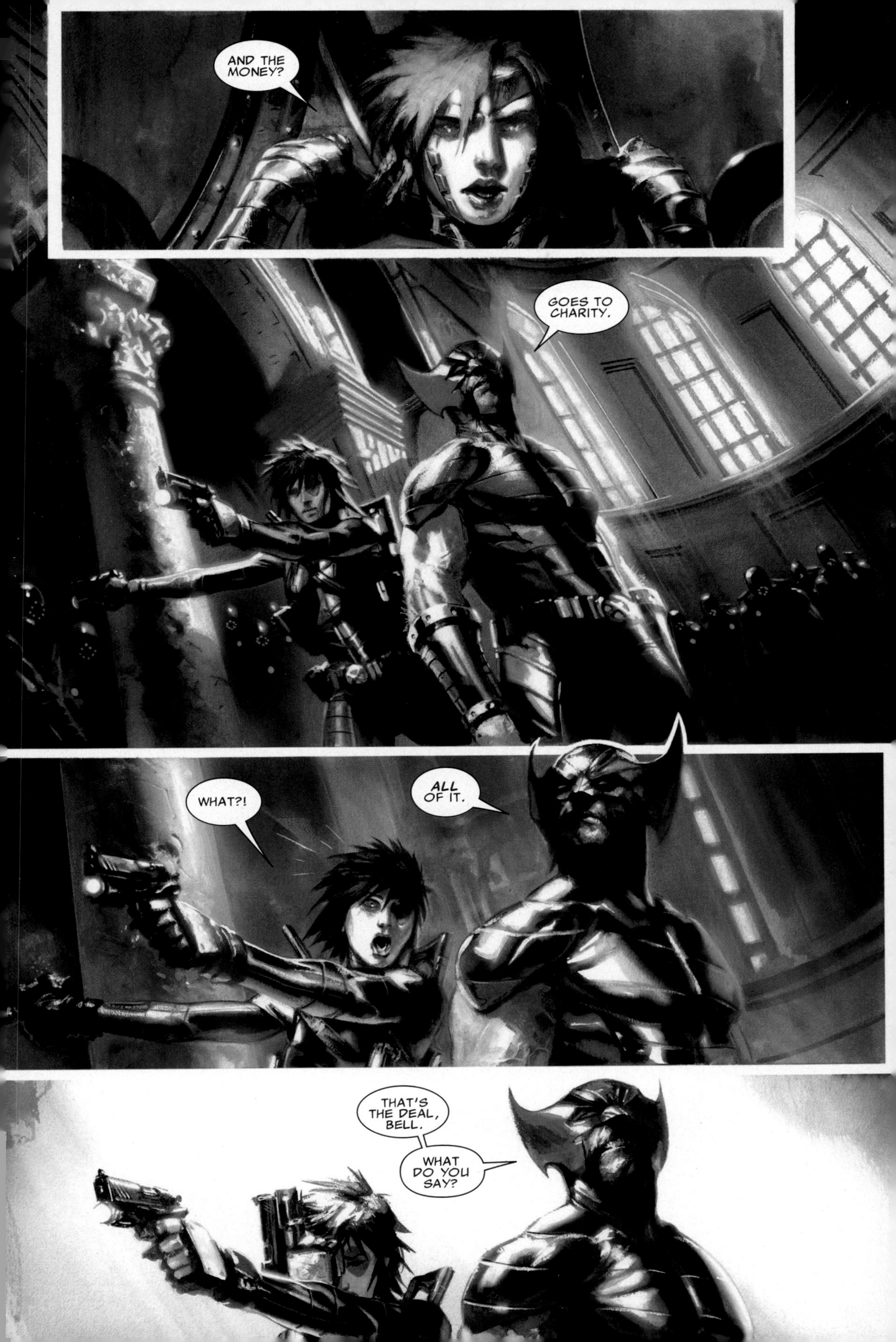
AND THE MONEY?
GOES TO CHARITY.
WHAT?!
ALL OF IT.
THAT'S THE DEAL, BELL.
WHAT DO YOU SAY?

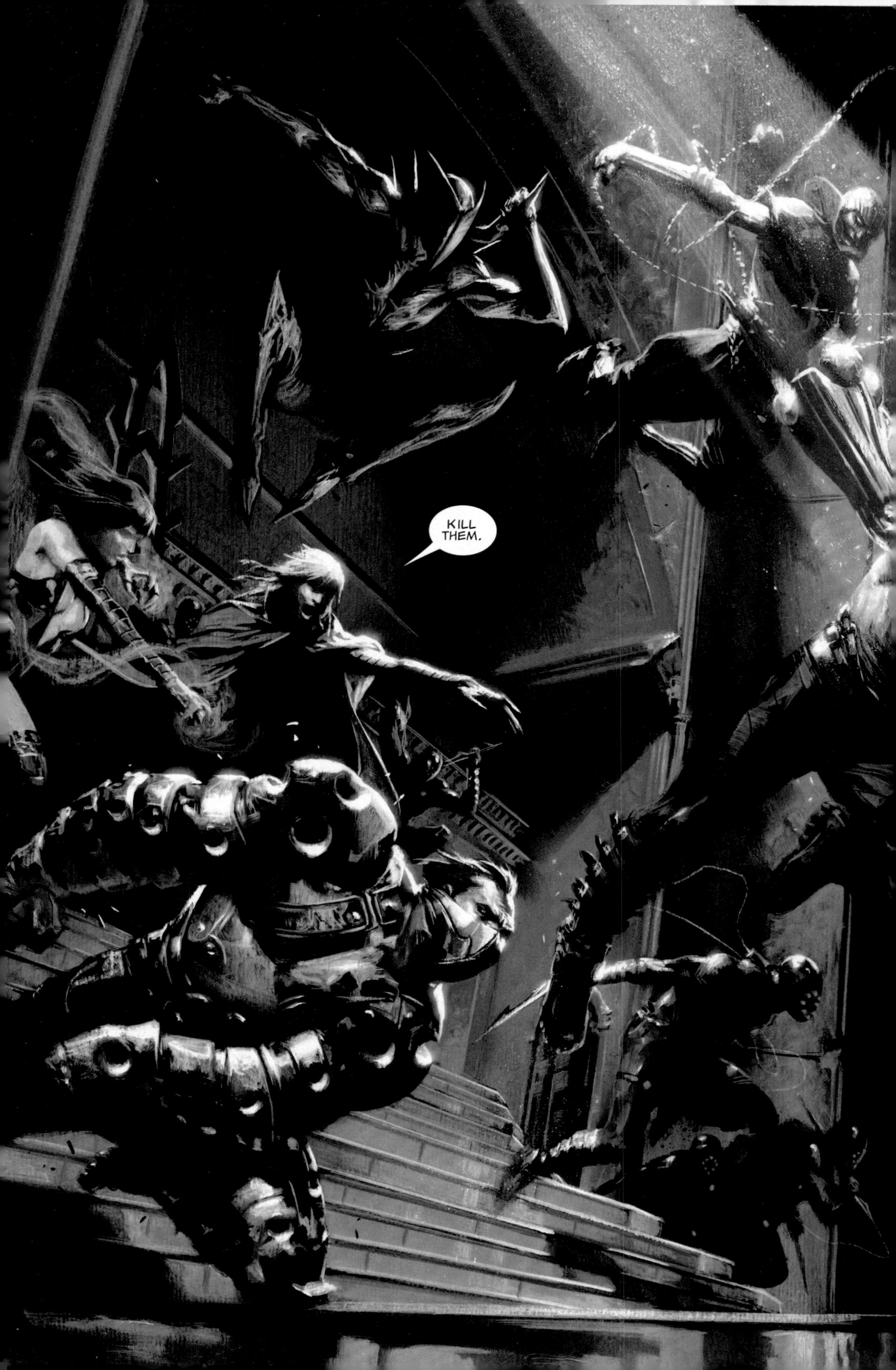
KILL THEM.

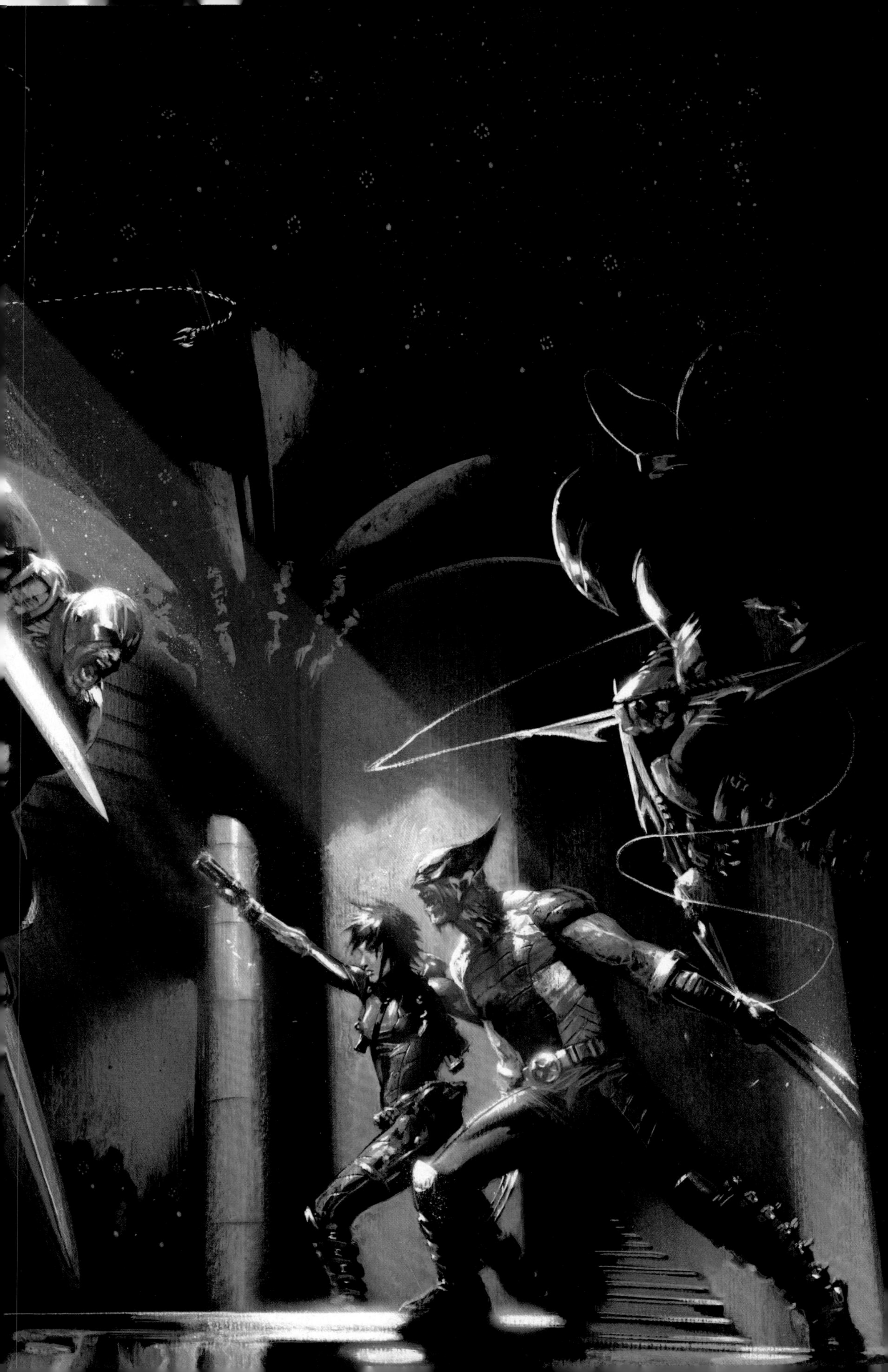

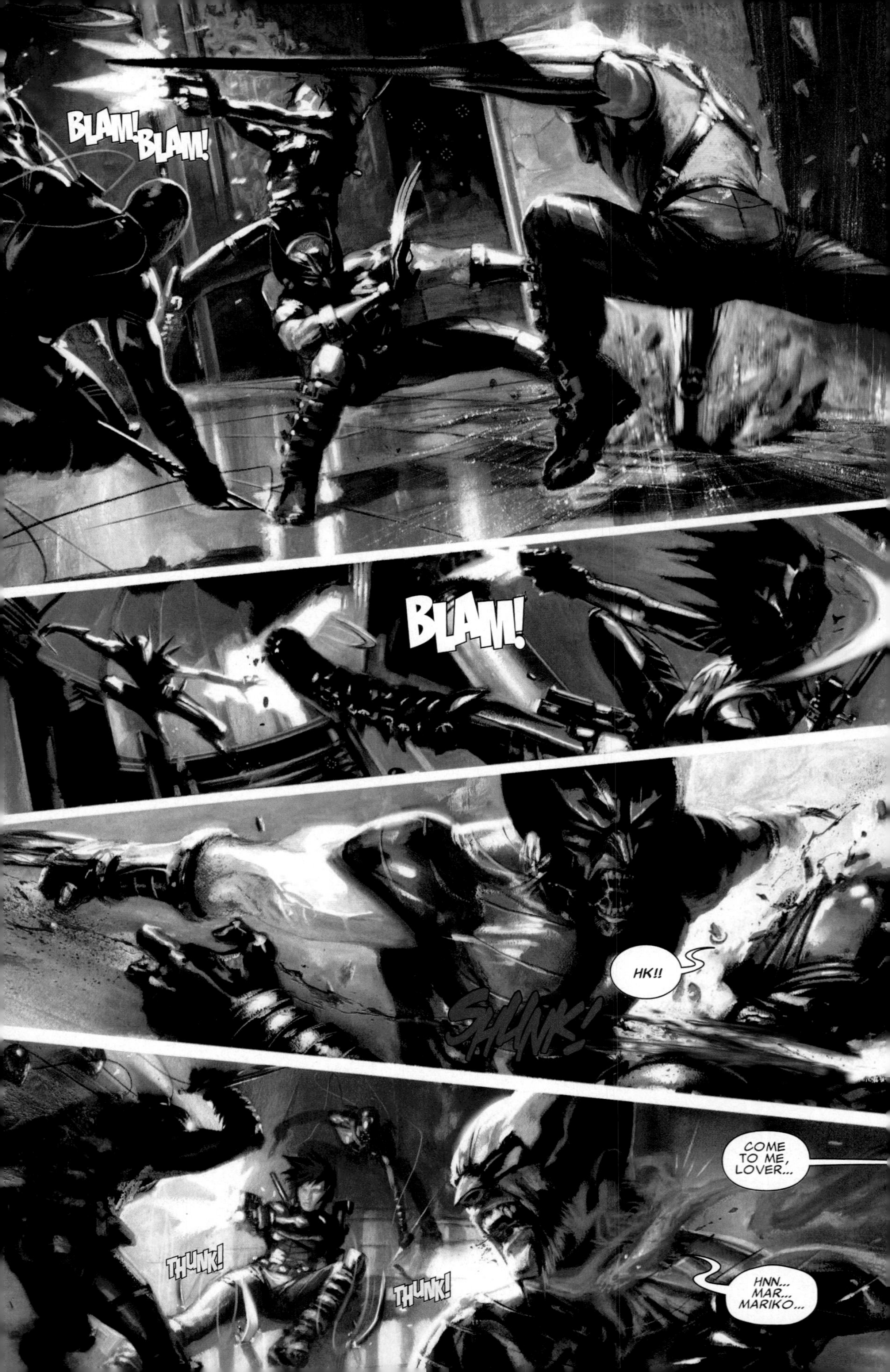
BLAM! BLAM!
BLAM!
HK!!
SHUNK!
COME TO ME, LOVER...
THUNK!
THUNK!
HNN... MAR... MARIKO...

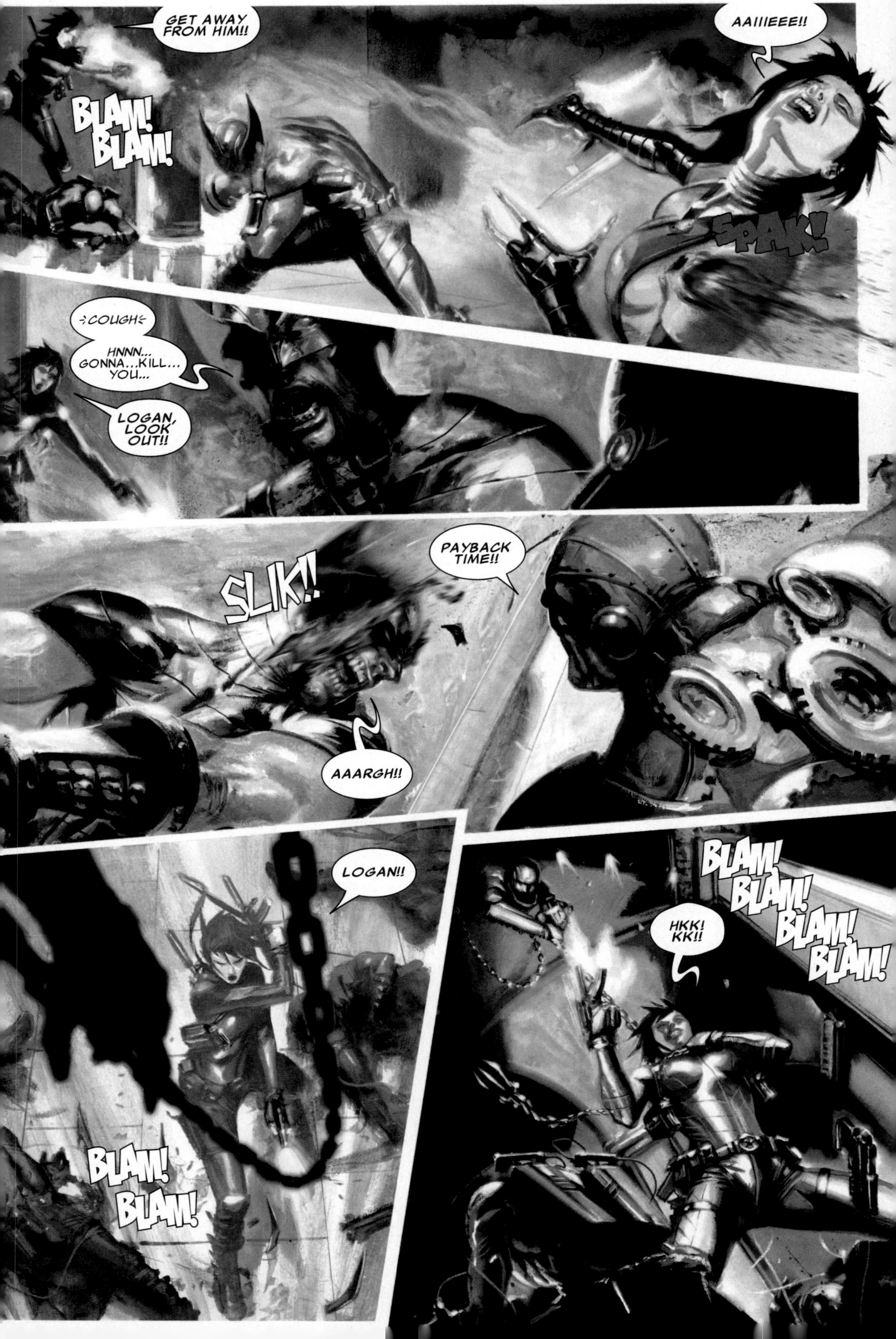
GET AWAY FROM HIM!!
BLAM! BLAM!
AAIIIEEE!!
SPAK!
COUGH
HNNN... GONNA...KILL... YOU...
LOGAN, LOOK OUT!!
SLIK!!
PAYBACK TIME!!
AAARGH!!
LOGAN!!
BLAM! BLAM!
BLAM! BLAM! BLAM! BLAM!
HKK! KK!!

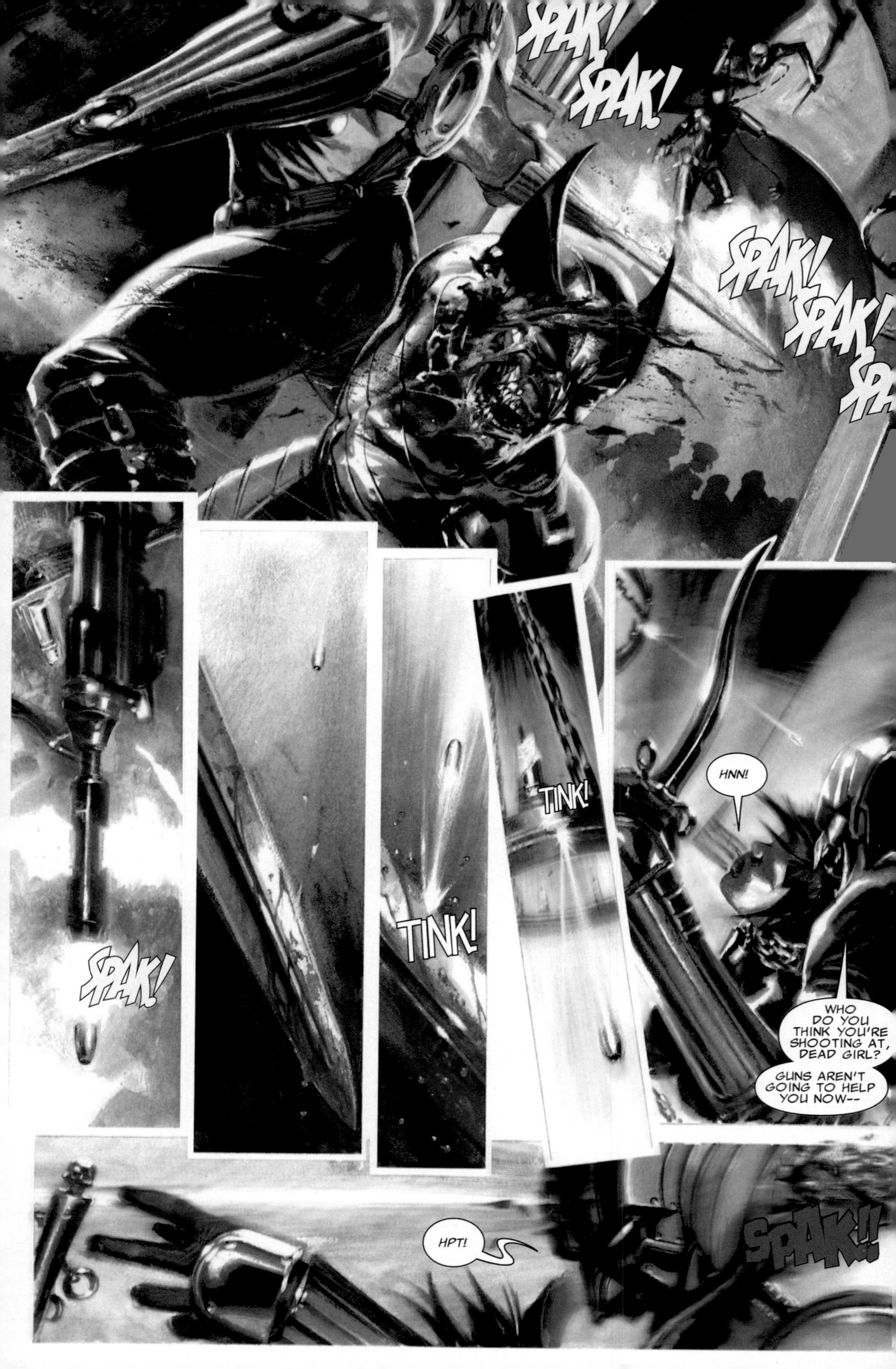
SPAK! SPAK!
SPAK! SPAK! SPA
SPAK!
TINK!
TINK!
HNN!
WHO DO YOU THINK YOU'RE SHOOTING AT, DEAD GIRL?
GUNS AREN'T GOING TO HELP YOU NOW--
HPT!
SPAK!!

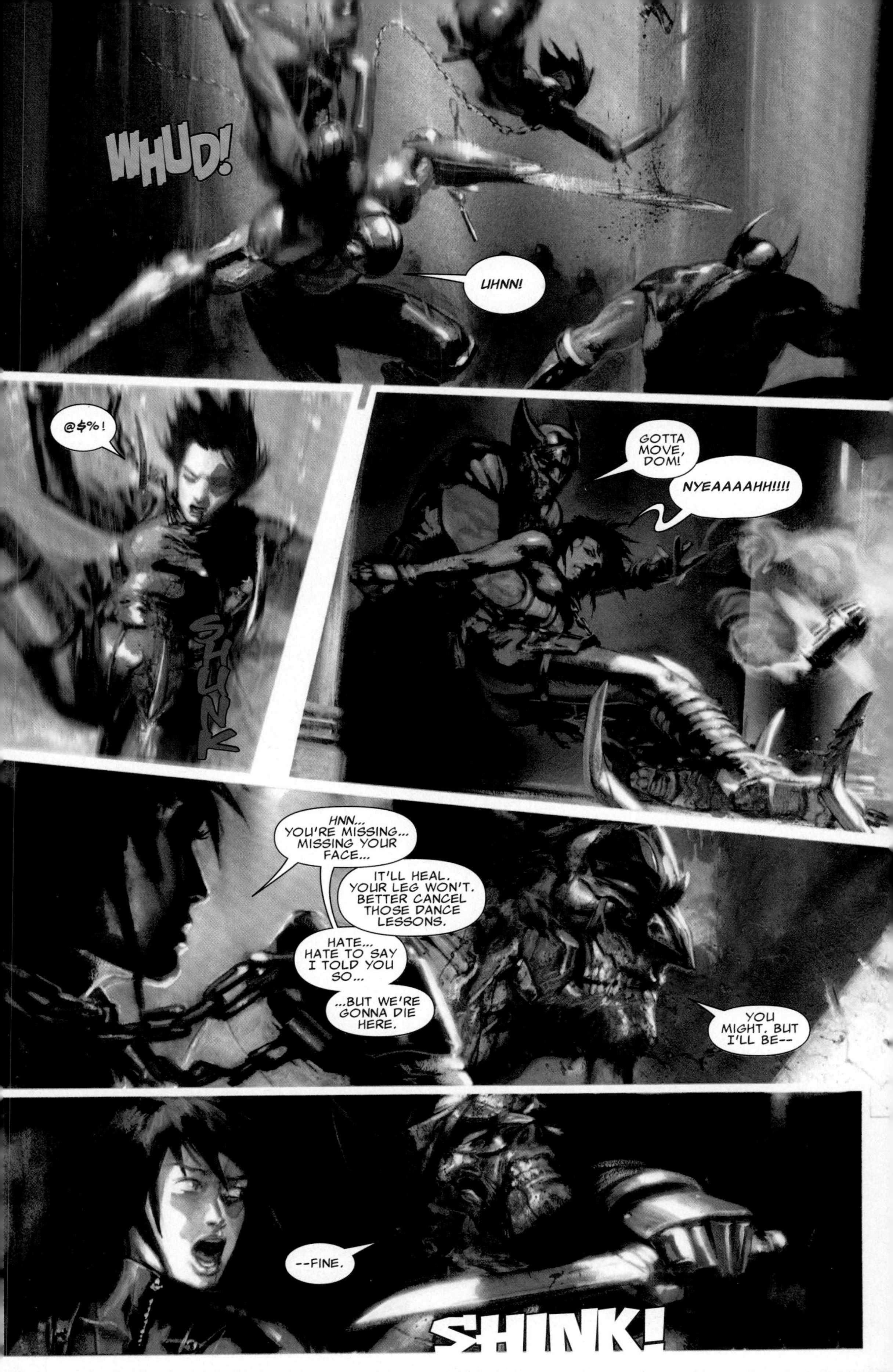
WHUD!
UHNN!
@$%!
SHUNK
GOTTA MOVE, DOM!
NYEAAAAHH!!!!
HNN... YOU'RE MISSING... MISSING YOUR FACE...
IT'LL HEAL. YOUR LEG WON'T. BETTER CANCEL THOSE DANCE LESSONS.
HATE... HATE TO SAY I TOLD YOU SO...
...BUT WE'RE GONNA DIE HERE.
YOU MIGHT. BUT I'LL BE--
--FINE.
SHINK!

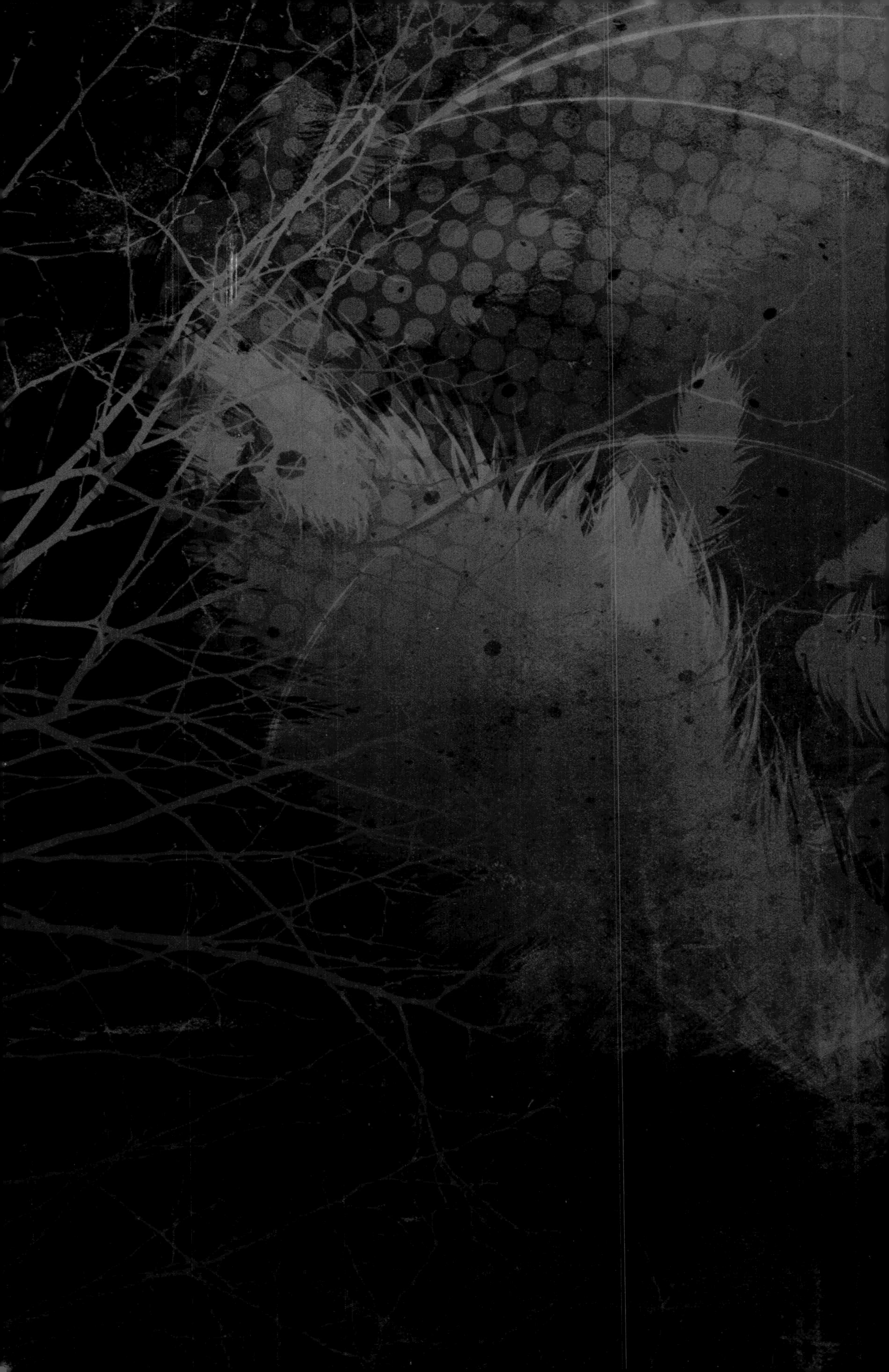

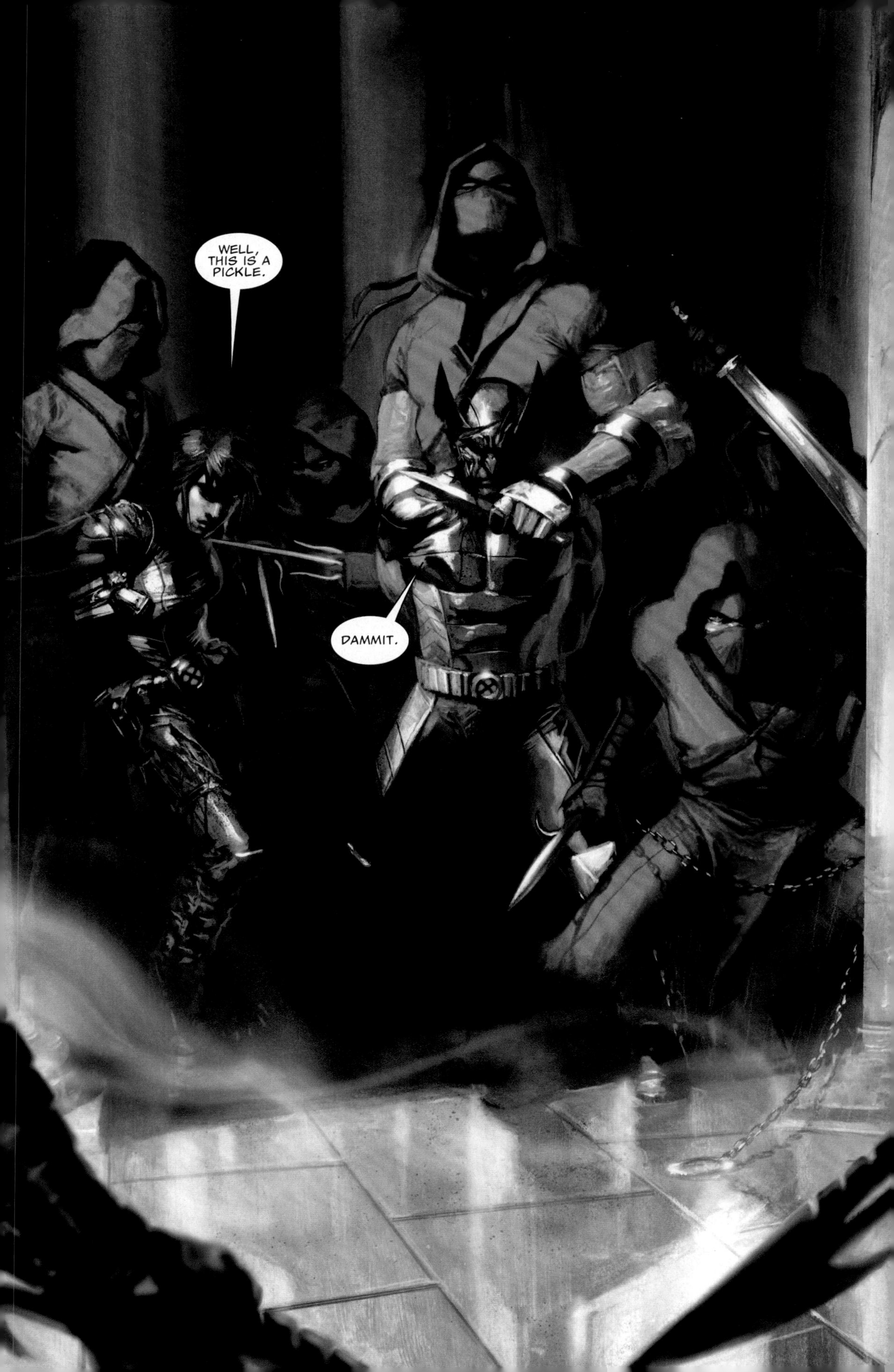
WELL, THIS IS A PICKLE.
DAMMIT.

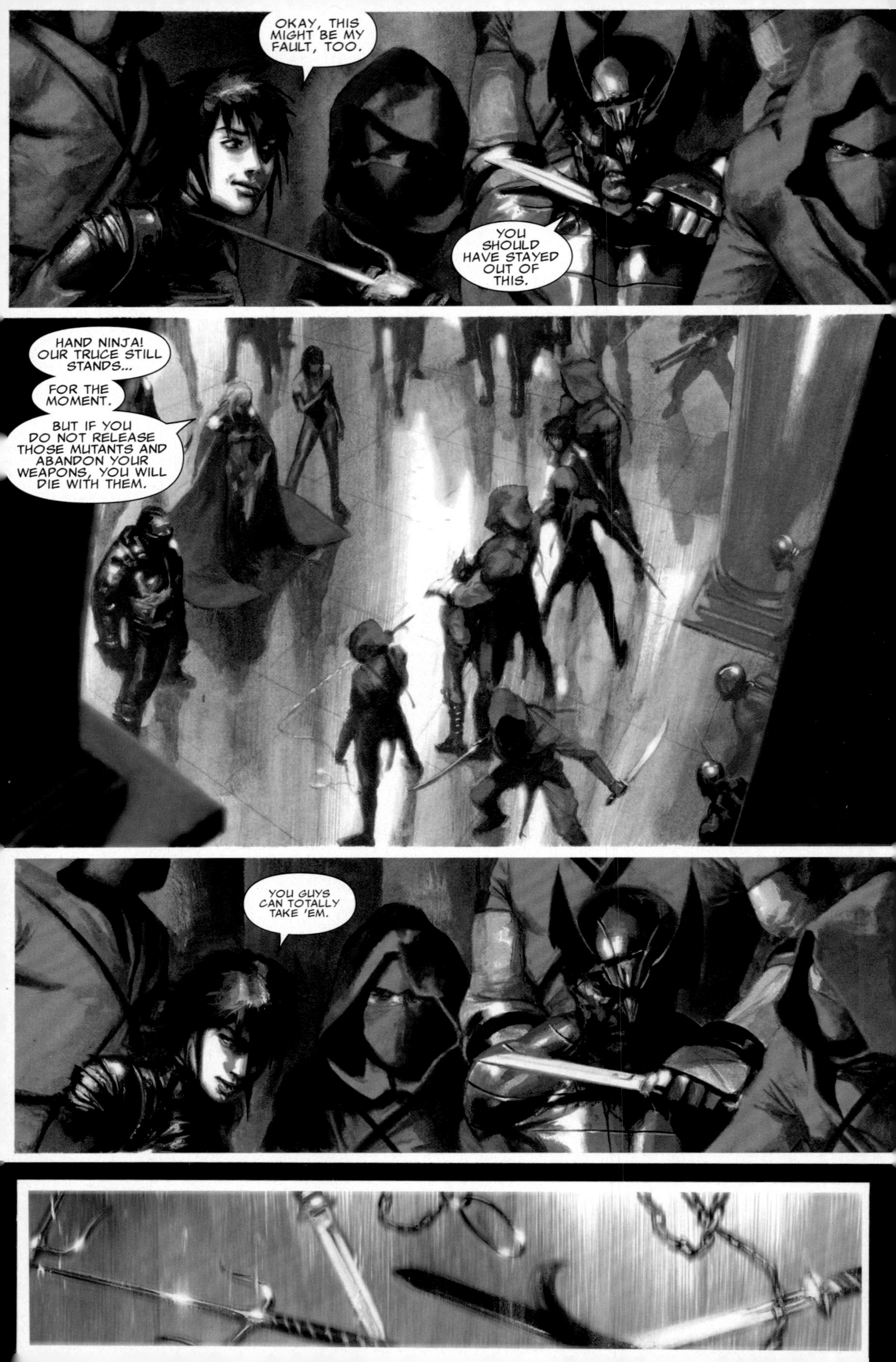

OKAY, THIS MIGHT BE MY FAULT, TOO.
YOU SHOULD HAVE STAYED OUT OF THIS.
HAND NINJA! OUR TRUCE STILL STANDS...
FOR THE MOMENT.
BUT IF YOU DO NOT RELEASE THOSE MUTANTS AND ABANDON YOUR WEAPONS, YOU WILL DIE WITH THEM.
YOU GUYS CAN TOTALLY TAKE 'EM.

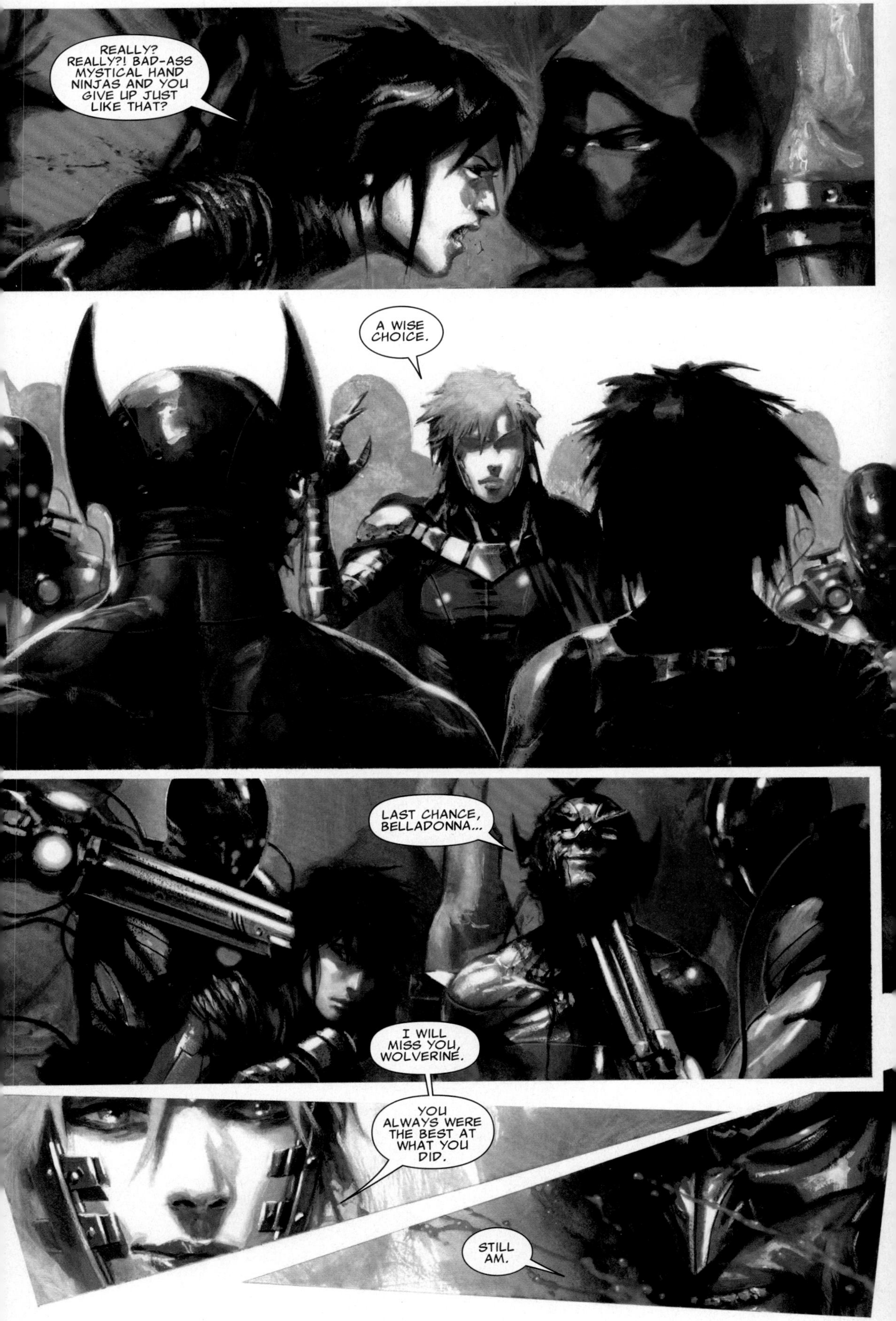
REALLY? REALLY?! BAD-ASS MYSTICAL HAND NINJAS AND YOU GIVE UP JUST LIKE THAT?
A WISE CHOICE.
LAST CHANCE, BELLADONNA...
I WILL MISS YOU, WOLVERINE.
YOU ALWAYS WERE THE BEST AT WHAT YOU DID.
STILL AM.

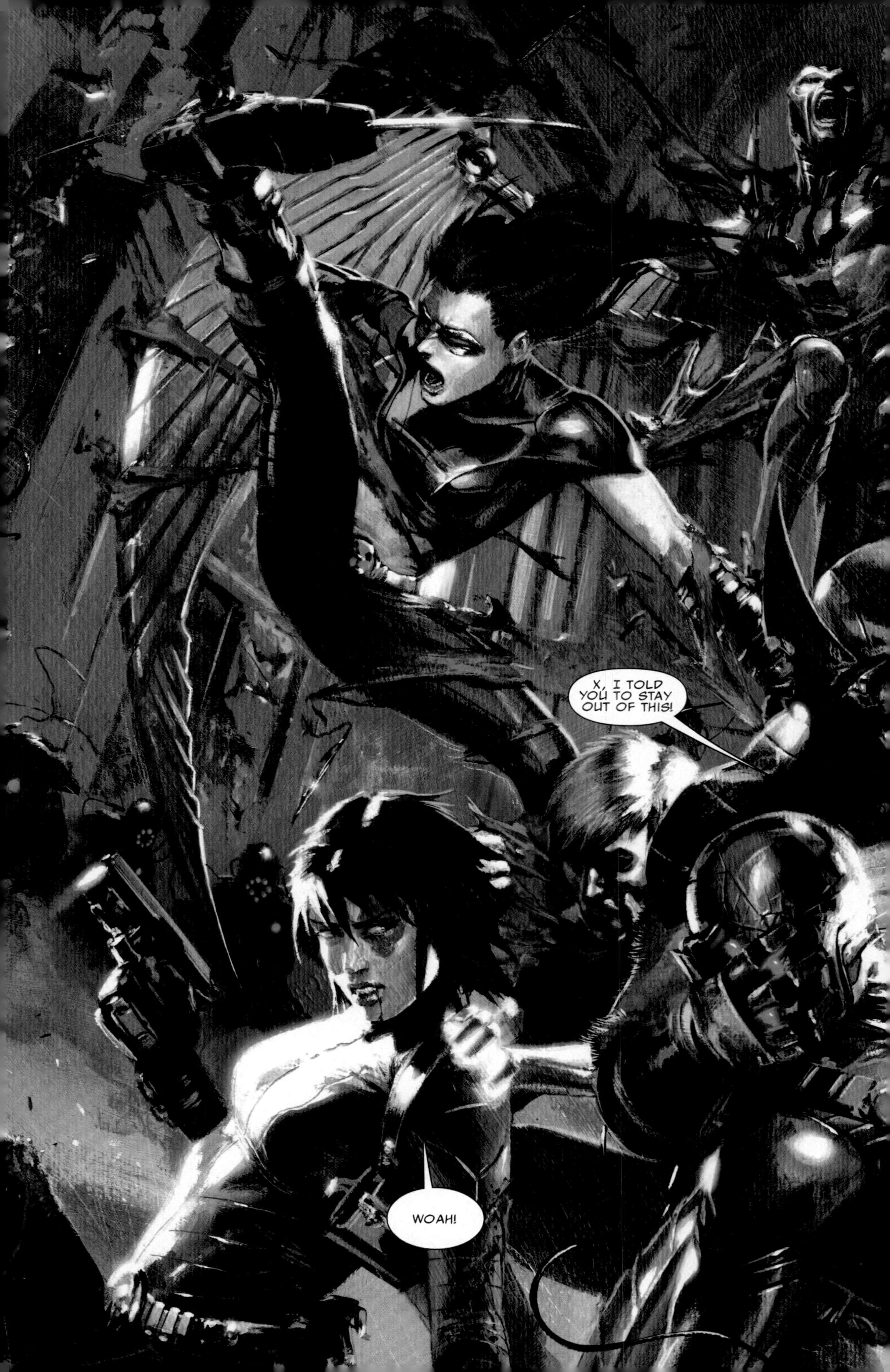
X, I TOLD YOU TO STAY OUT OF THIS!
WOAH!

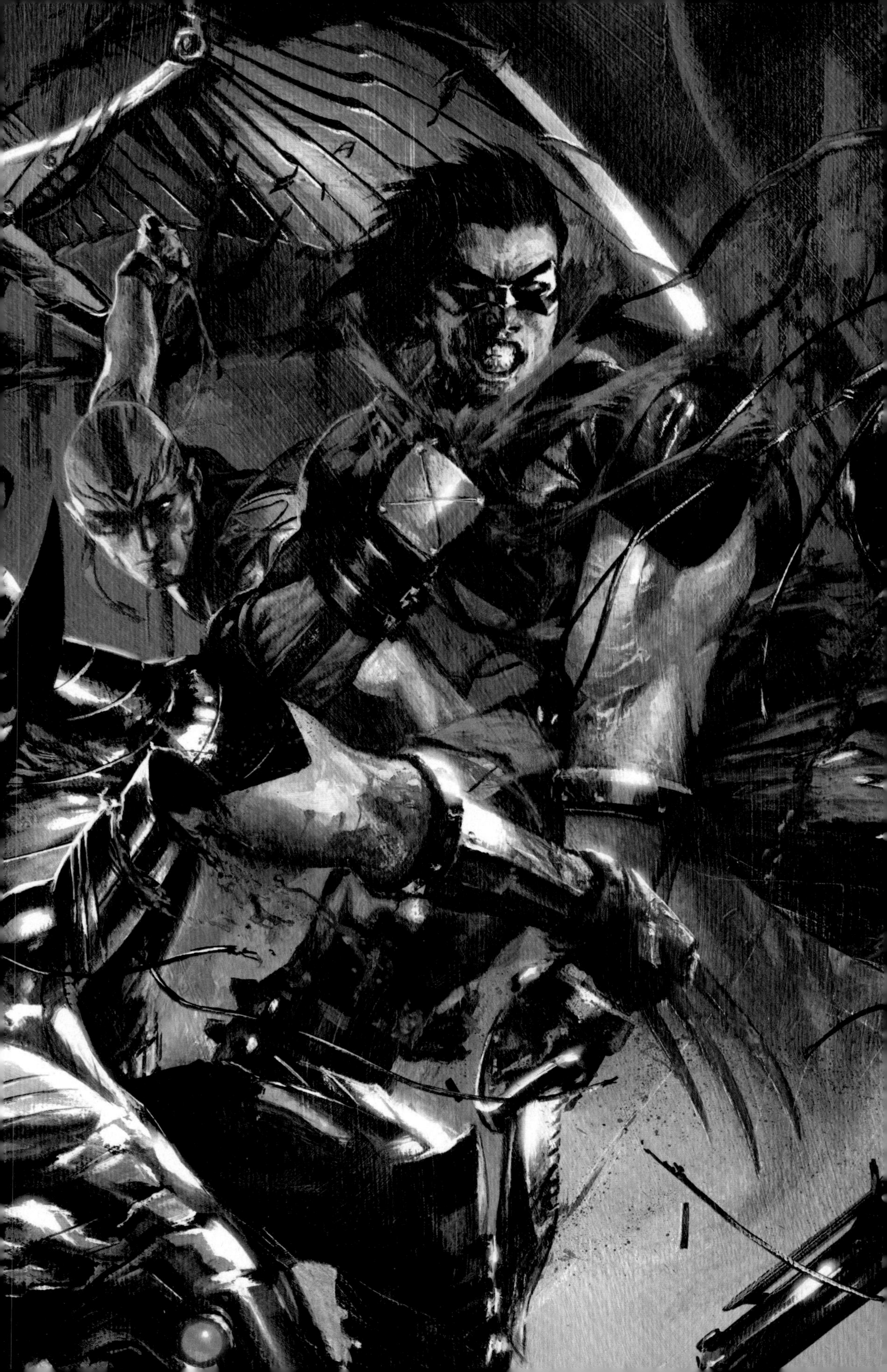

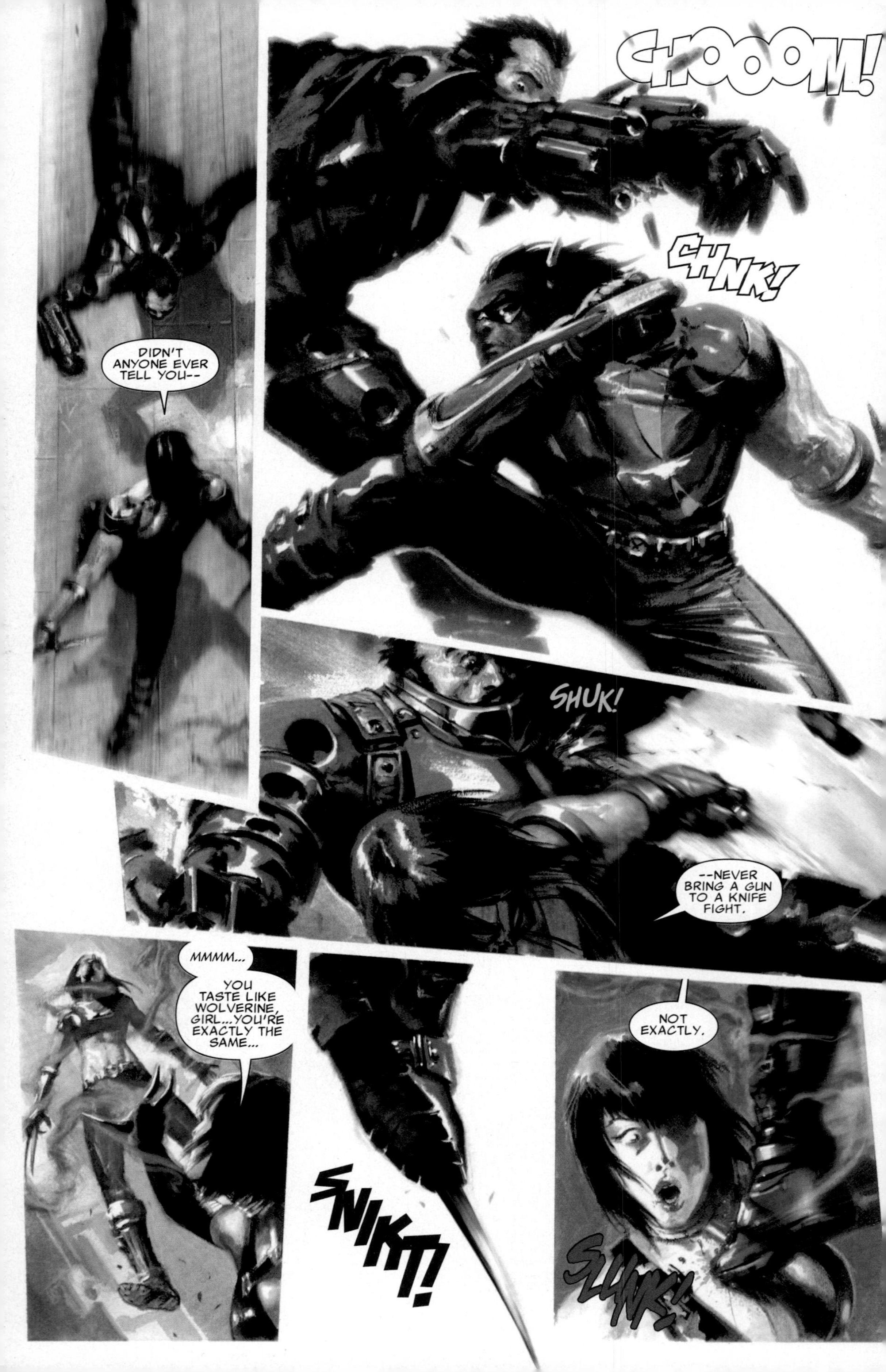

CHOOOM!
CHNK!
DIDN'T ANYONE EVER TELL YOU--
SHUK!
--NEVER BRING A GUN TO A KNIFE FIGHT.
MMMM...
YOU TASTE LIKE WOLVERINE, GIRL...YOU'RE EXACTLY THE SAME...
SNIKT!
NOT EXACTLY.
SLUNK!

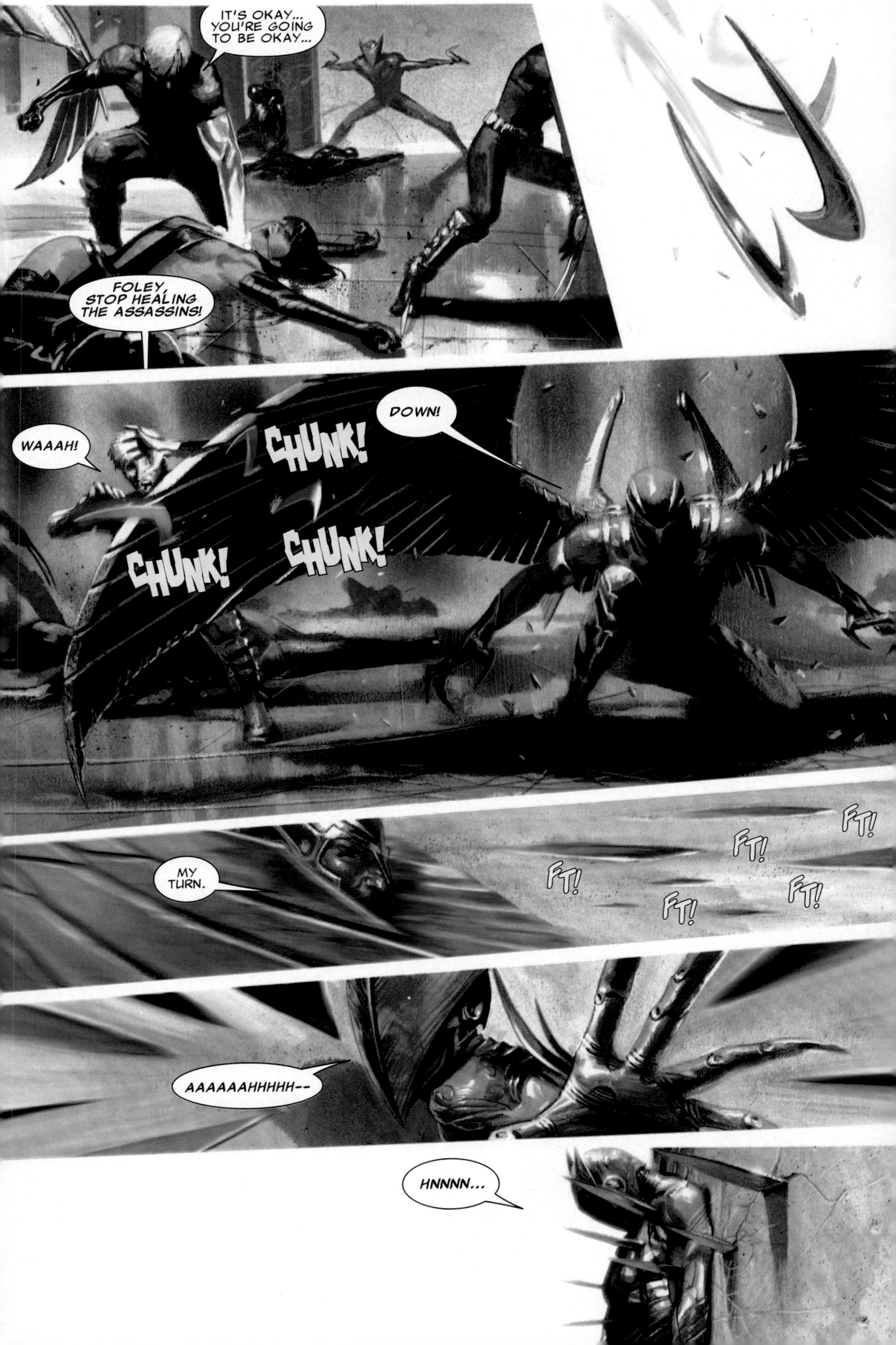
IT'S OKAY... YOU'RE GOING TO BE OKAY...
FOLEY, STOP HEALING THE ASSASSINS!
WAAAH!
CHUNK!
DOWN!
CHUNK!
CHUNK!
MY TURN.
FT!
FT!
FT!
FT!
FT!
AAAAAAHHHHH--
HNNNN...

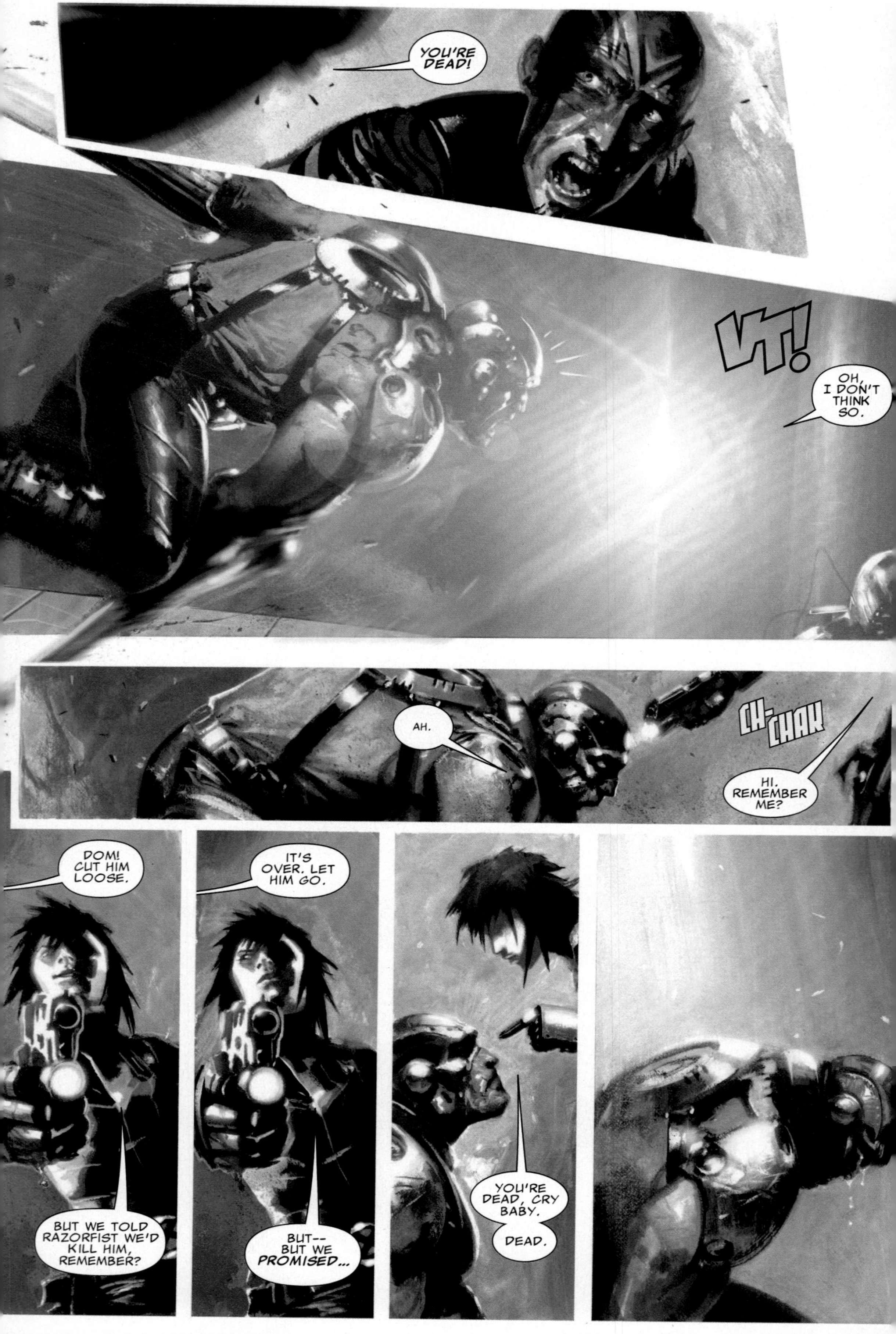
YOU'RE DEAD!
VT!
OH, I DON'T THINK SO.
AH.
CH-CHAK
HI. REMEMBER ME?
DOM! CUT HIM LOOSE.
BUT WE TOLD RAZORFIST WE'D KILL HIM, REMEMBER?
IT'S OVER. LET HIM GO.
BUT-- BUT WE PROMISED...
YOU'RE DEAD, CRY BABY.
DEAD.

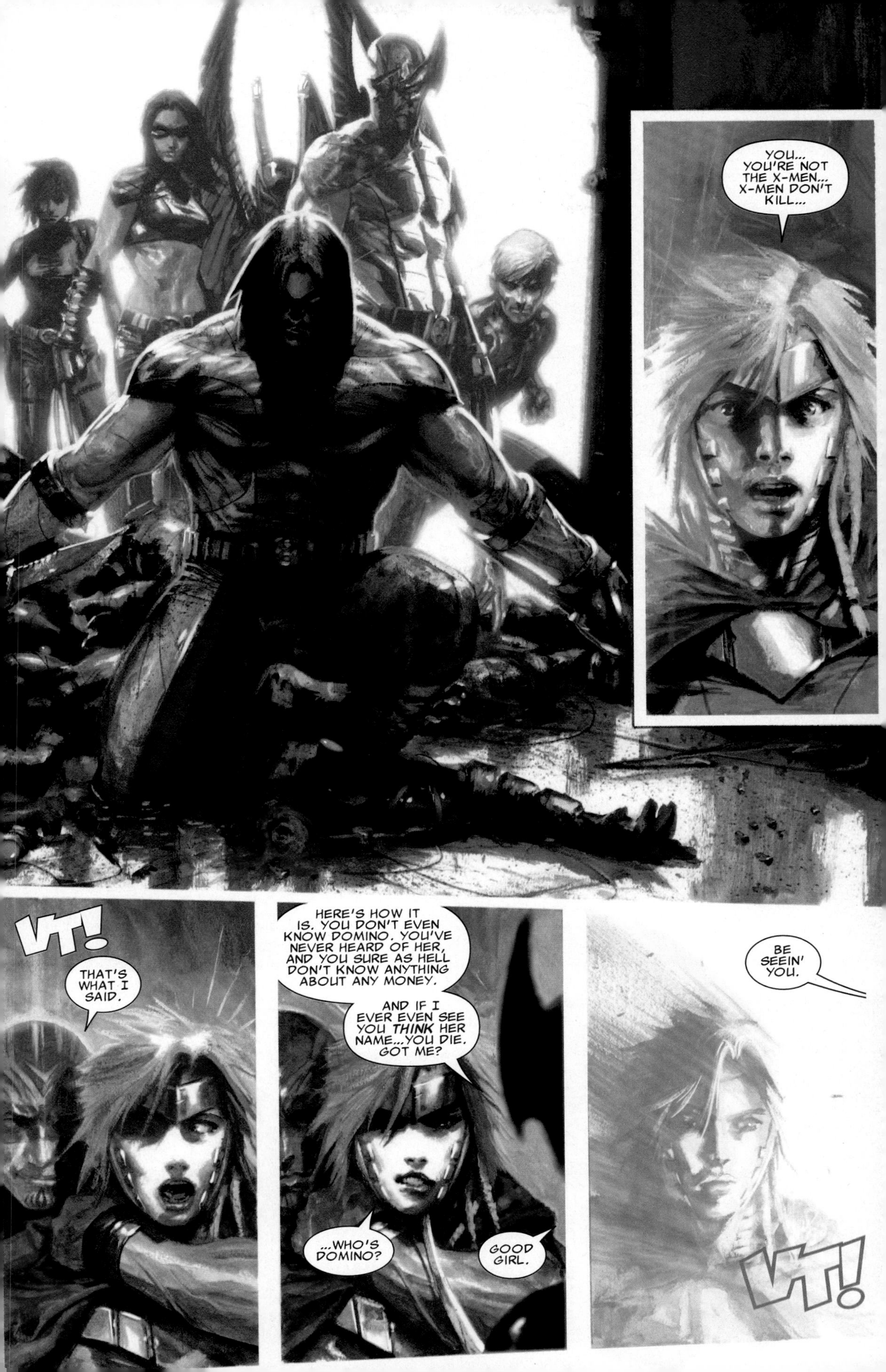
YOU... YOU'RE NOT THE X-MEN... X-MEN DON'T KILL...
VT!
THAT'S WHAT I SAID.
HERE'S HOW IT IS. YOU DON'T EVEN KNOW DOMINO. YOU'VE NEVER HEARD OF HER, AND YOU SURE AS HELL DON'T KNOW ANYTHING ABOUT ANY MONEY.
AND IF I EVER EVEN SEE YOU THINK HER NAME...YOU DIE. GOT ME?
...WHO'S DOMINO?
GOOD GIRL.
BE SEEIN' YOU.
VT!

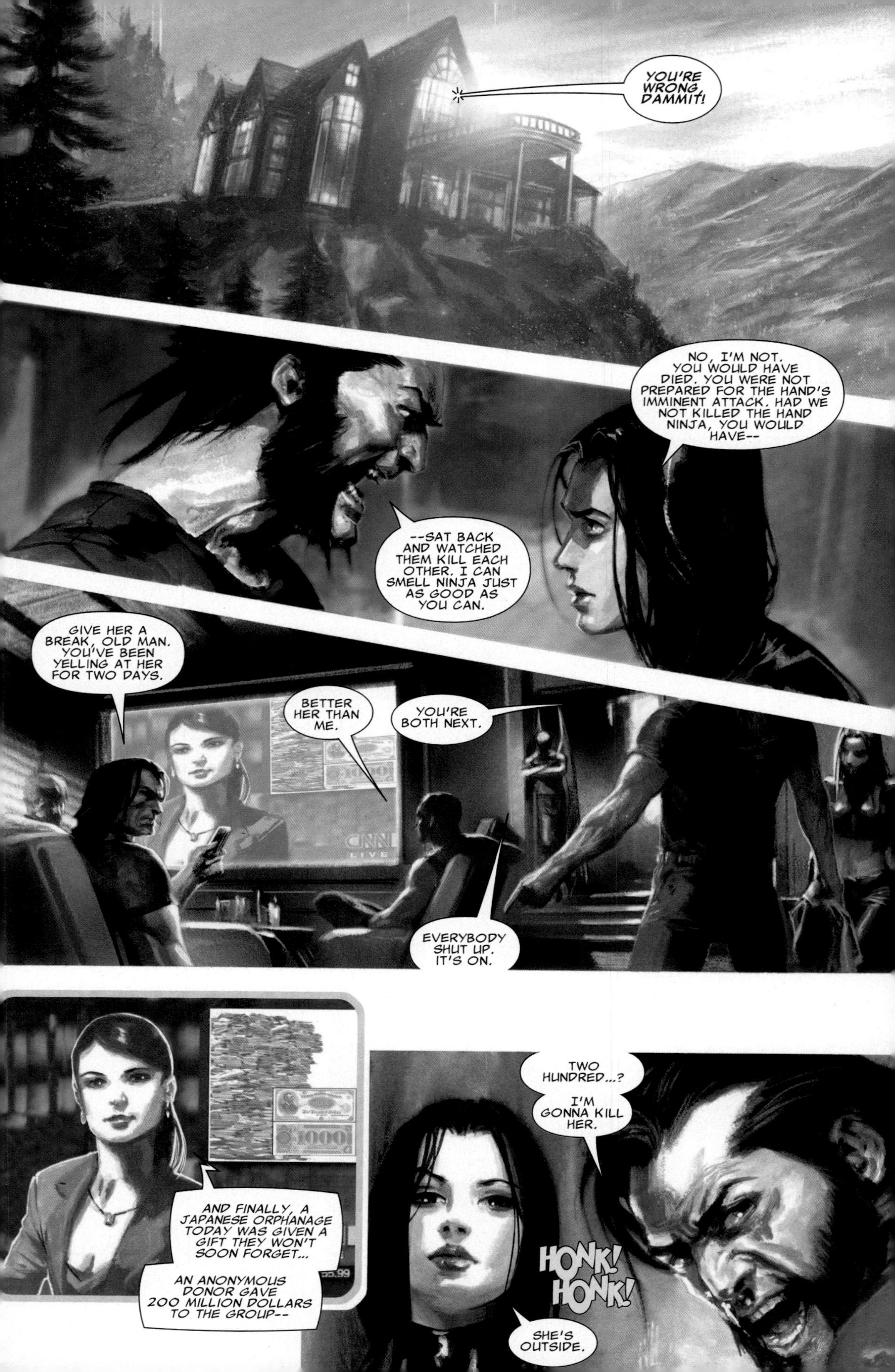
YOU'RE WRONG, DAMMIT!
NO, I'M NOT. YOU WOULD HAVE DIED. YOU WERE NOT PREPARED FOR THE HAND'S IMMINENT ATTACK. HAD WE NOT KILLED THE HAND NINJA, YOU WOULD HAVE--
--SAT BACK AND WATCHED THEM KILL EACH OTHER. I CAN SMELL NINJA JUST AS GOOD AS YOU CAN.
GIVE HER A BREAK, OLD MAN. YOU'VE BEEN YELLING AT HER FOR TWO DAYS.
BETTER HER THAN ME.
YOU'RE BOTH NEXT.
EVERYBODY SHUT UP. IT'S ON.
AND FINALLY, A JAPANESE ORPHANAGE TODAY WAS GIVEN A GIFT THEY WON'T SOON FORGET...
AN ANONYMOUS DONOR GAVE 200 MILLION DOLLARS TO THE GROUP--
TWO HUNDRED...?
I'M GONNA KILL HER.
HONK! HONK!
SHE'S OUTSIDE.

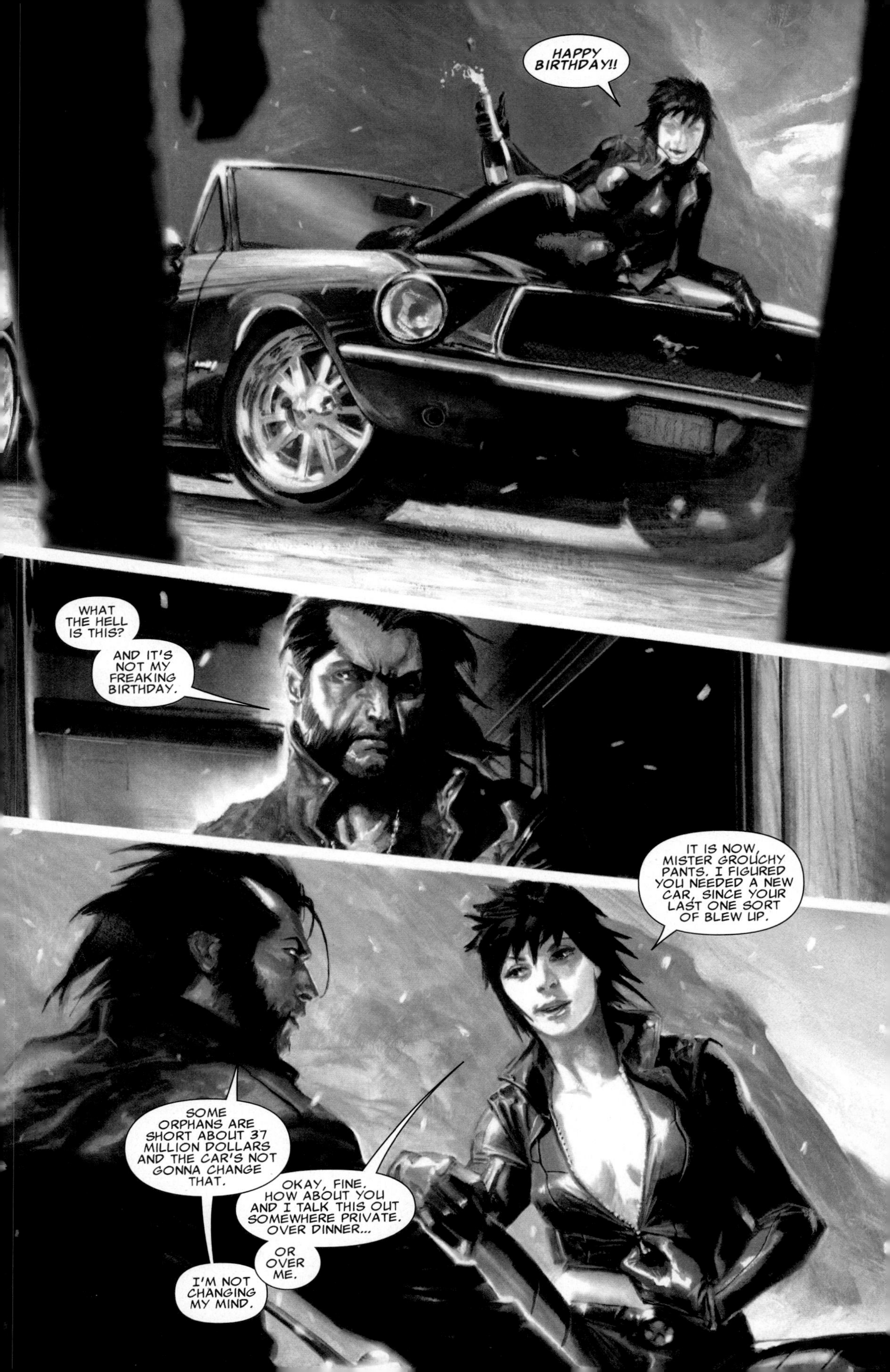
HAPPY BIRTHDAY!!
WHAT THE HELL IS THIS?
AND IT'S NOT MY FREAKING BIRTHDAY.
IT IS NOW, MISTER GROUCHY PANTS. I FIGURED YOU NEEDED A NEW CAR, SINCE YOUR LAST ONE SORT OF BLEW UP.
SOME ORPHANS ARE SHORT ABOUT 37 MILLION DOLLARS AND THE CAR'S NOT GONNA CHANGE THAT.
OKAY, FINE. HOW ABOUT YOU AND I TALK THIS OUT SOMEWHERE PRIVATE. OVER DINNER...
OR OVER ME.
I'M NOT CHANGING MY MIND.

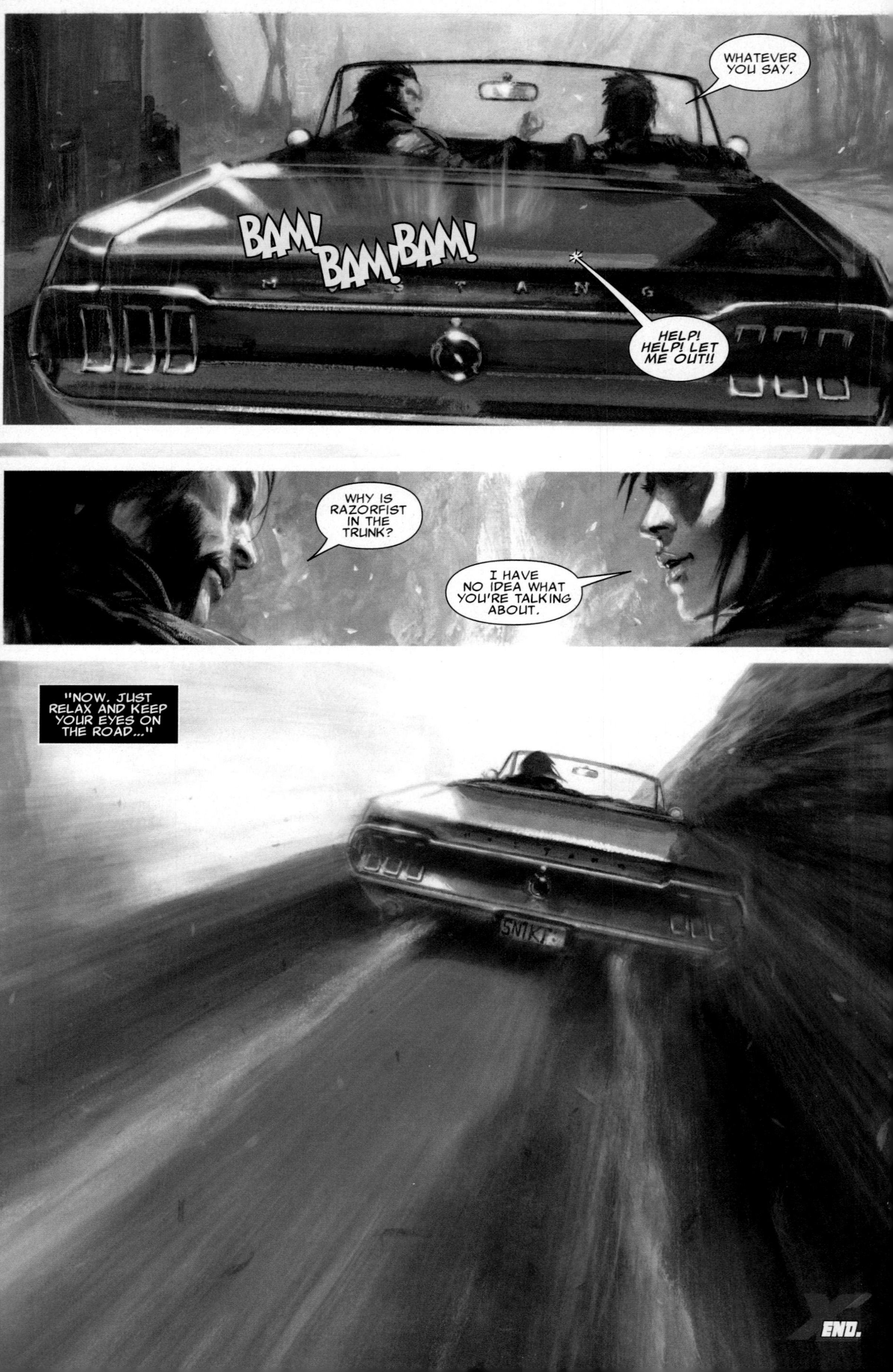
WHATEVER YOU SAY.
BAM! BAM! BAM!
HELP! HELP! LET ME OUT!!
WHY IS RAZORFIST IN THE TRUNK?
I HAVE NO IDEA WHAT YOU'RE TALKING ABOUT.
"NOW. JUST RELAX AND KEEP YOUR EYES ON THE ROAD..."
SNIKT
END.

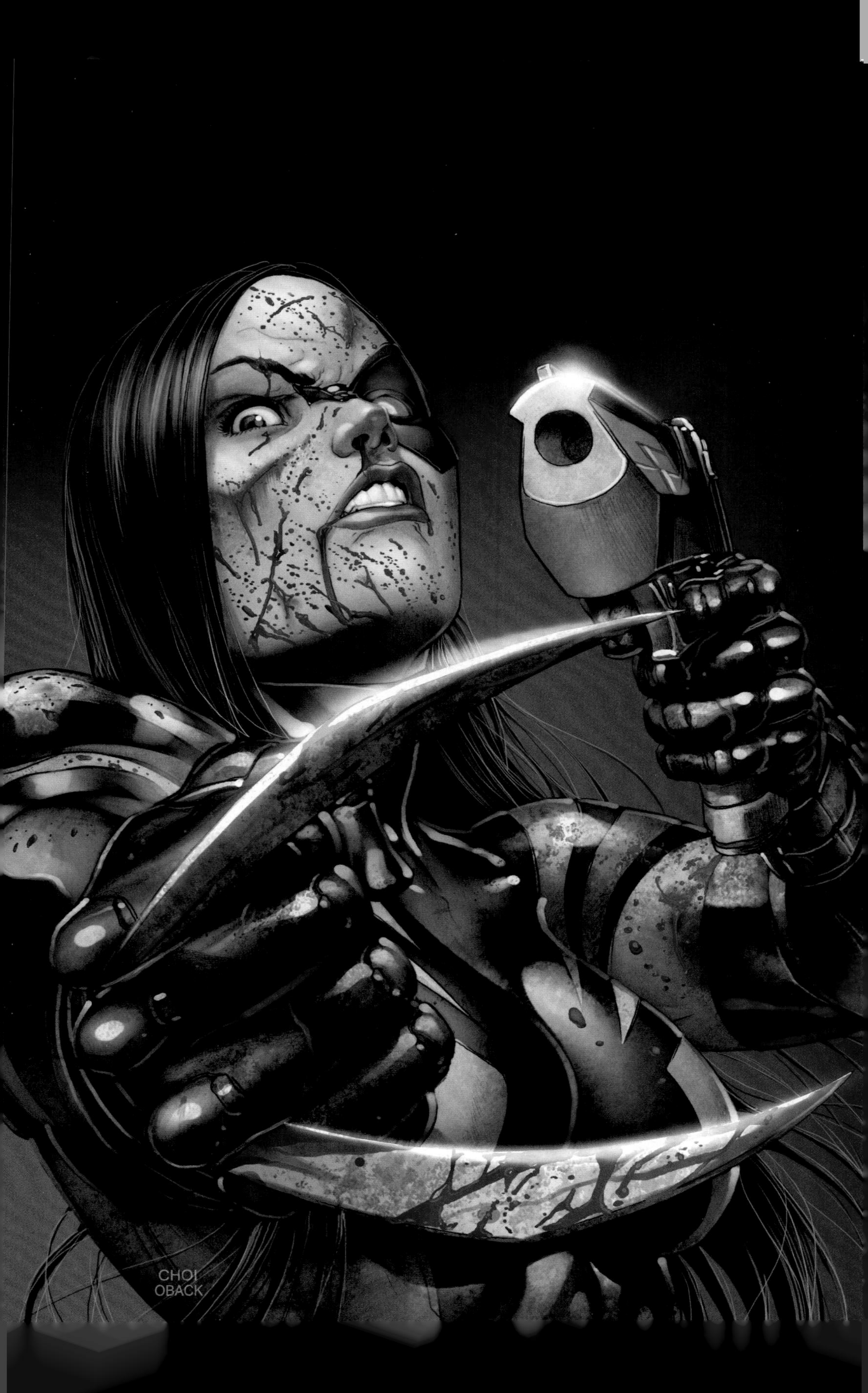
CHOI
OBACK

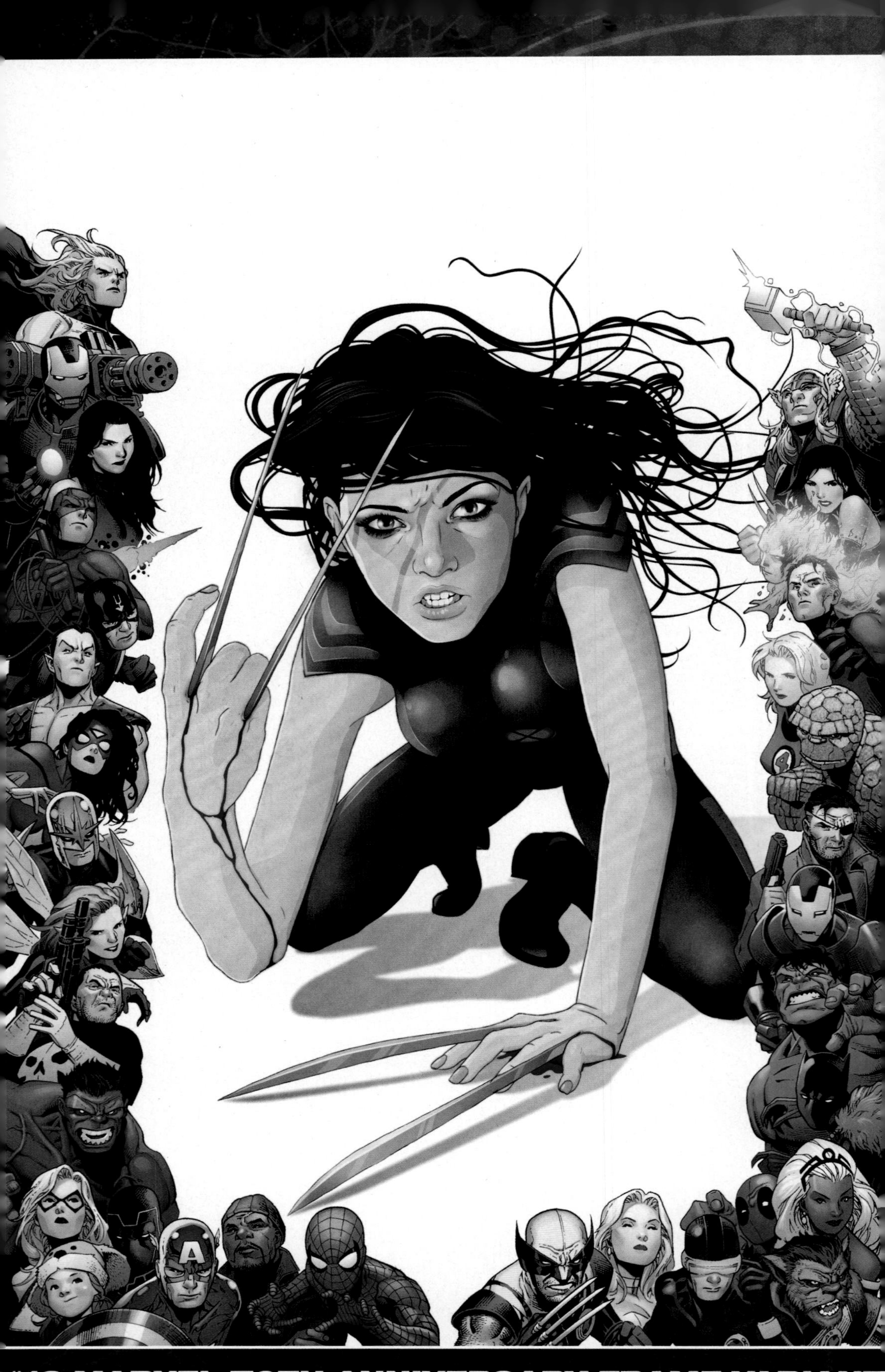

#18 MARVEL 70TH ANNIVERSARY FRAME VARIANT

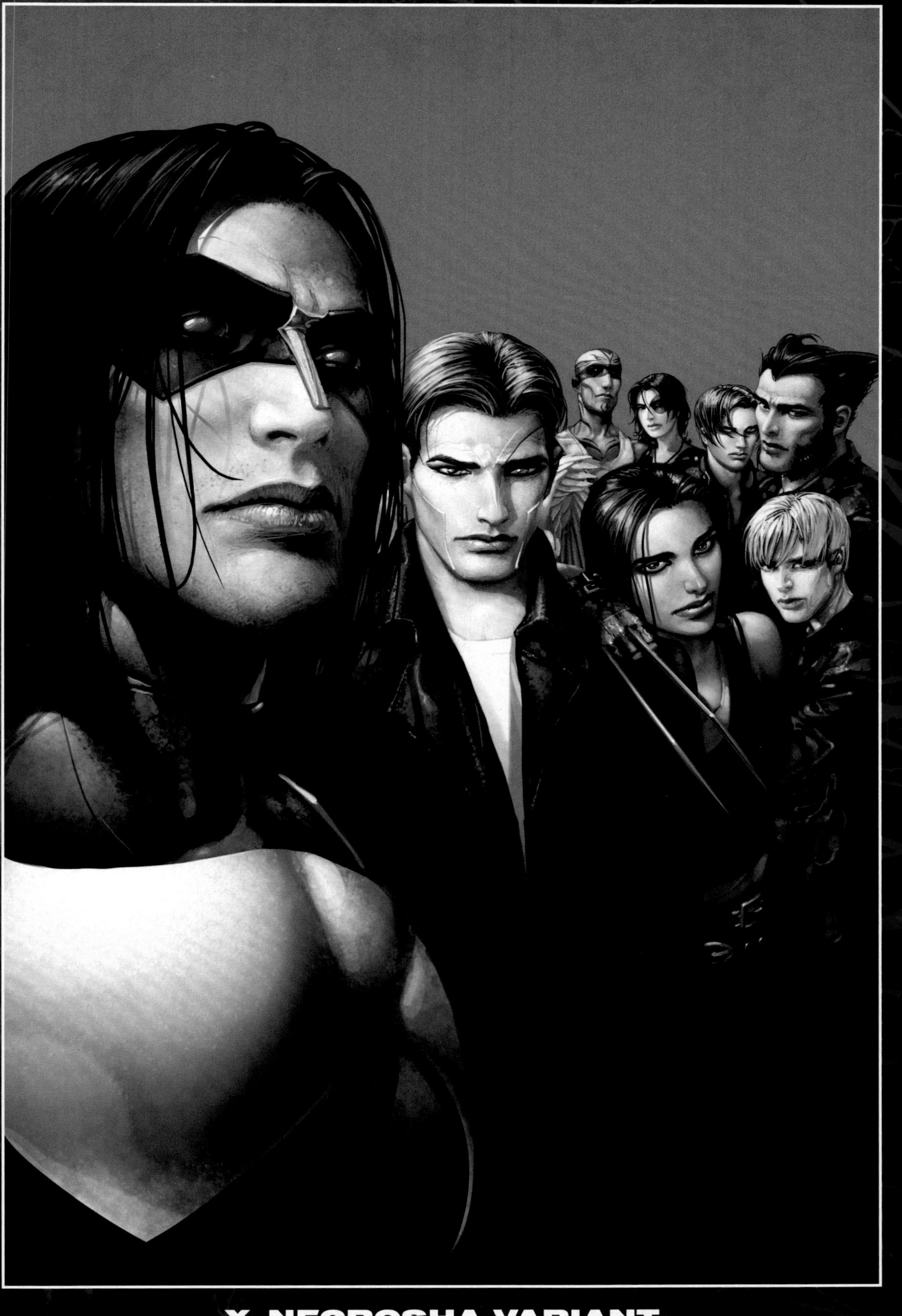

X-NECROSHA VARIANT

BY CLAYTON CRAIN

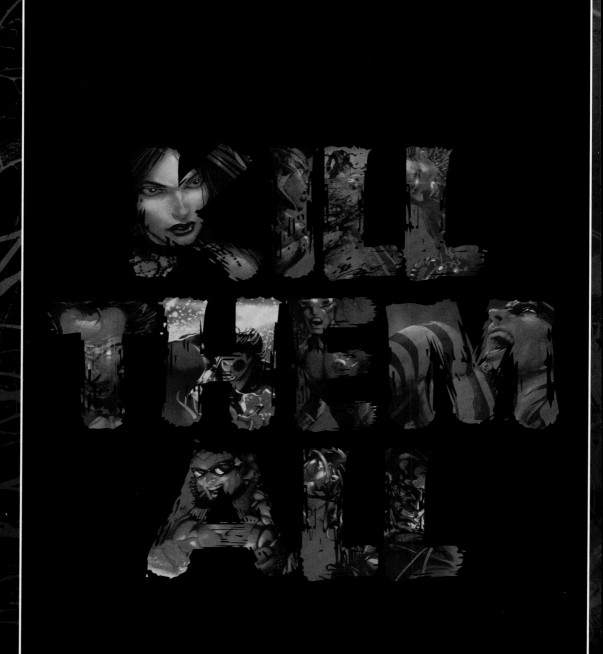

#21 2ND-PRINTING VARIANT
BY CLAYTON CRAIN

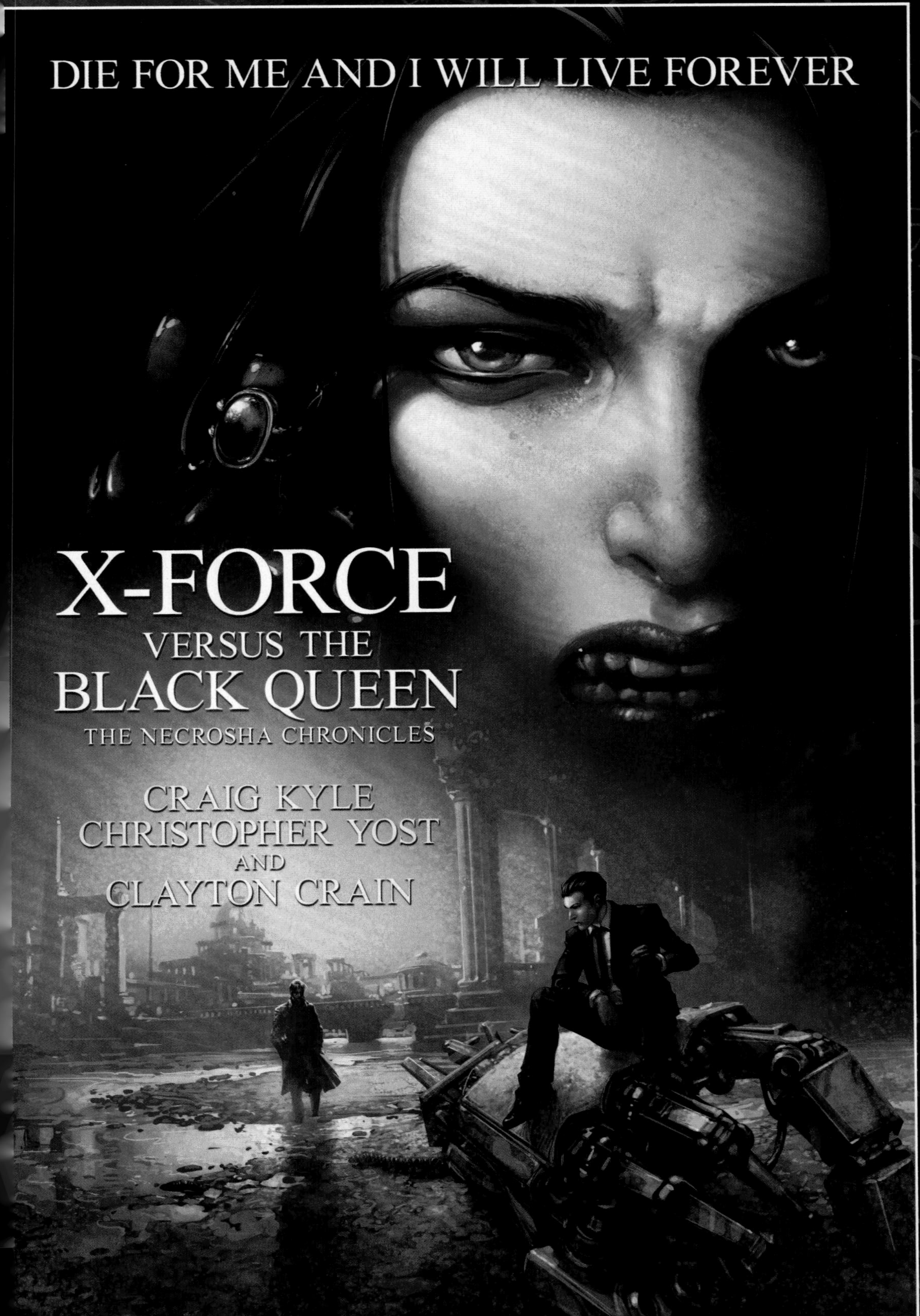
DIE FOR ME AND I WILL LIVE FOREVER
X-FORCE
VERSUS THE
BLACK QUEEN
THE NECROSHA CHRONICLES
CRAIG KYLE
CHRISTOPHER YOST
AND
CLAYTON CRAIN

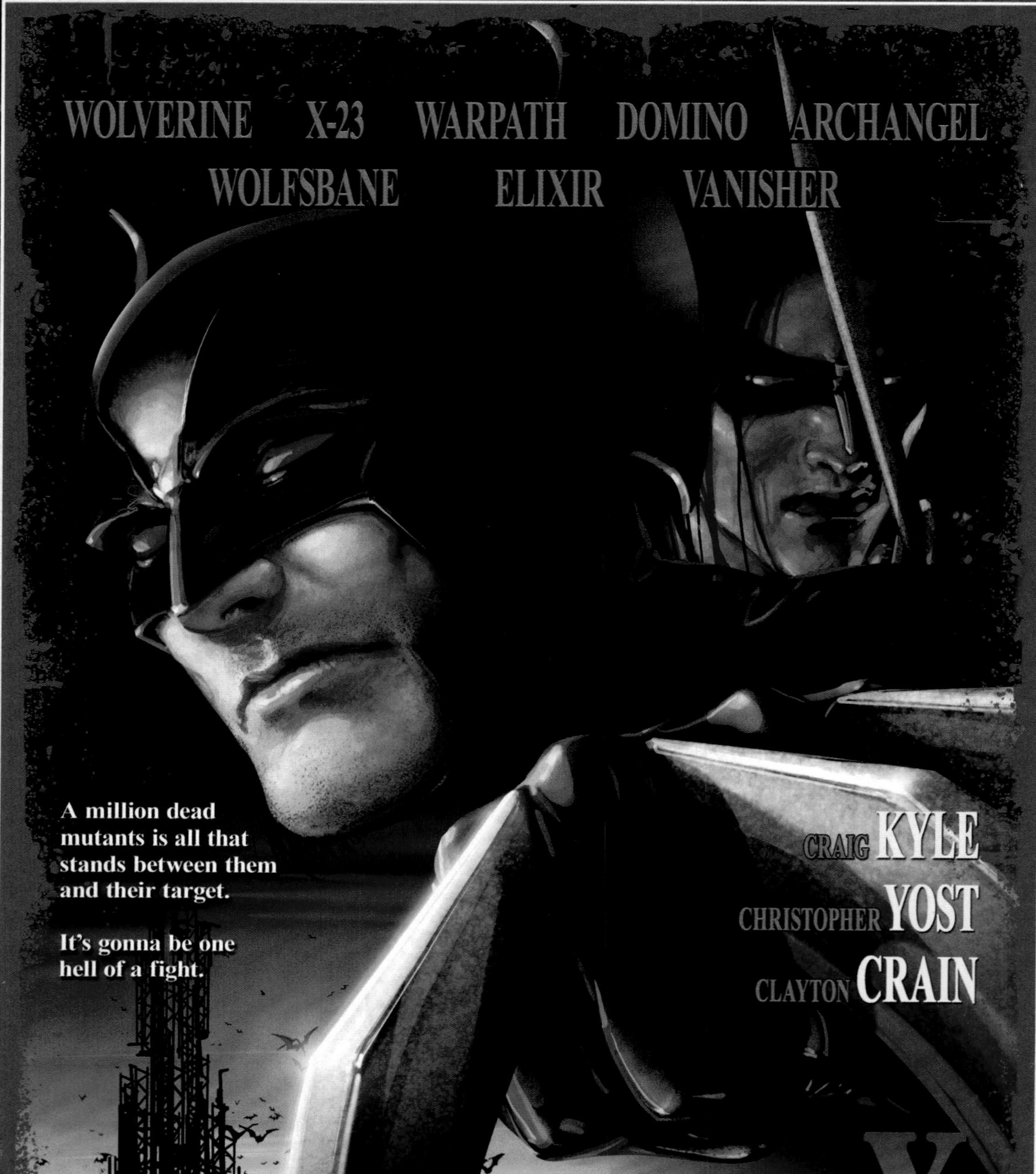

WOLVERINE X-23 WARPATH DOMINO ARCHANGEL
WOLFSBANE ELIXIR VANISHER
A million dead mutants is all that stands between them and their target.
It's gonna be one hell of a fight.
CRAIG KYLE
CHRISTOPHER YOST
CLAYTON CRAIN
X FORCE®

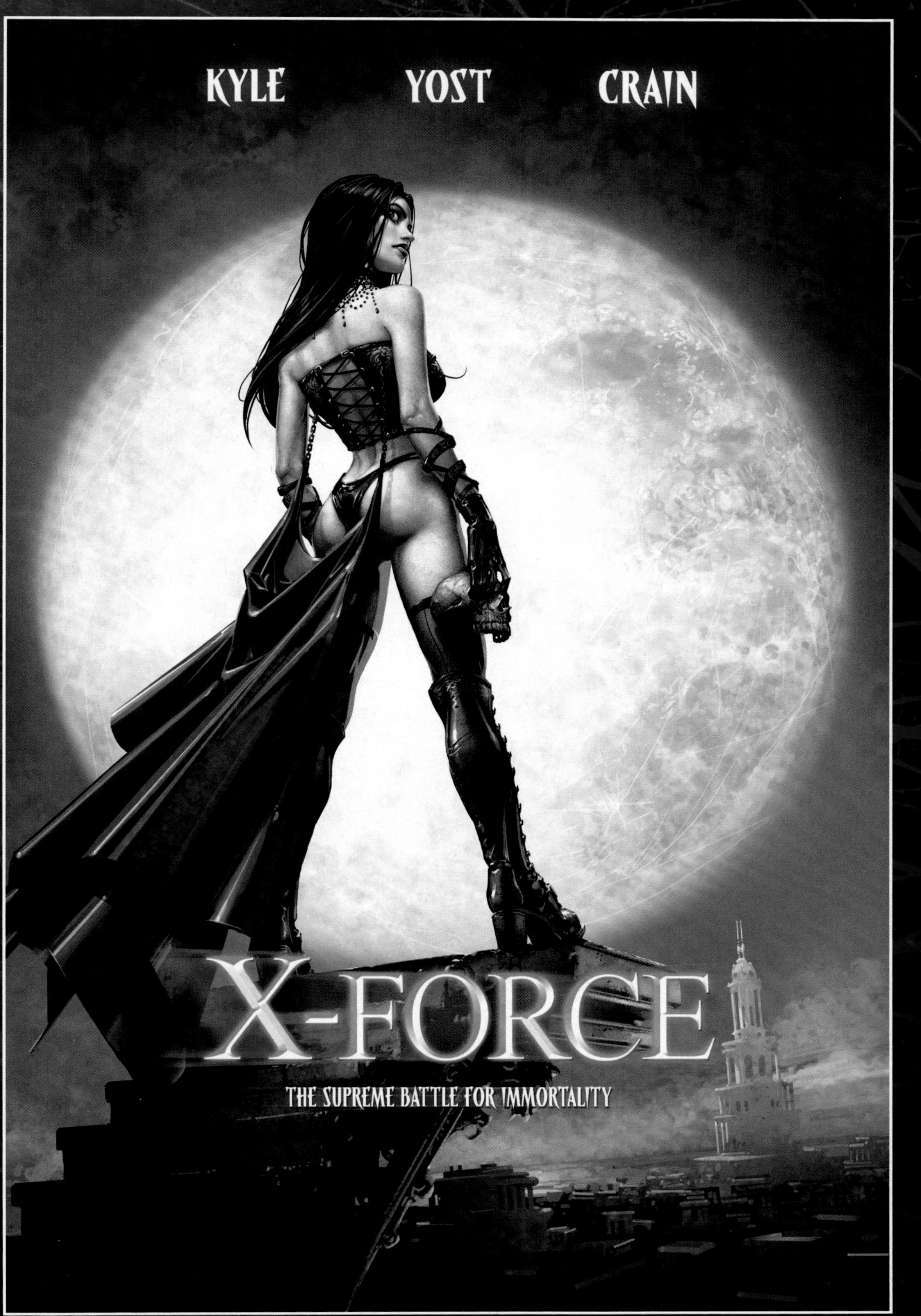
KYLE
YOST
CRAIN
X-FORCE
THE SUPREME BATTLE FOR IMMORTALITY

#23 VARIANT

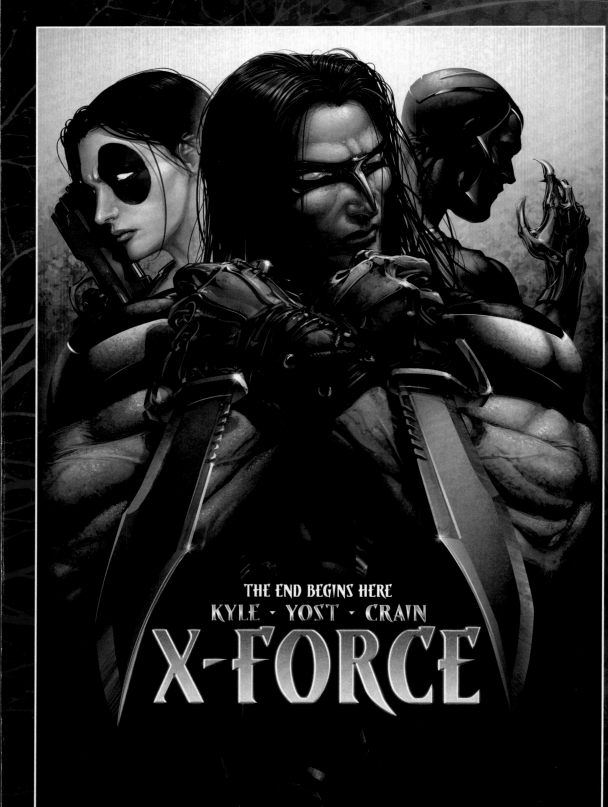

THE END BEGINS HERE
KYLE · YOST · CRAIN
X-FORCE

#24 VARIANT
BY CLAYTON CRAIN

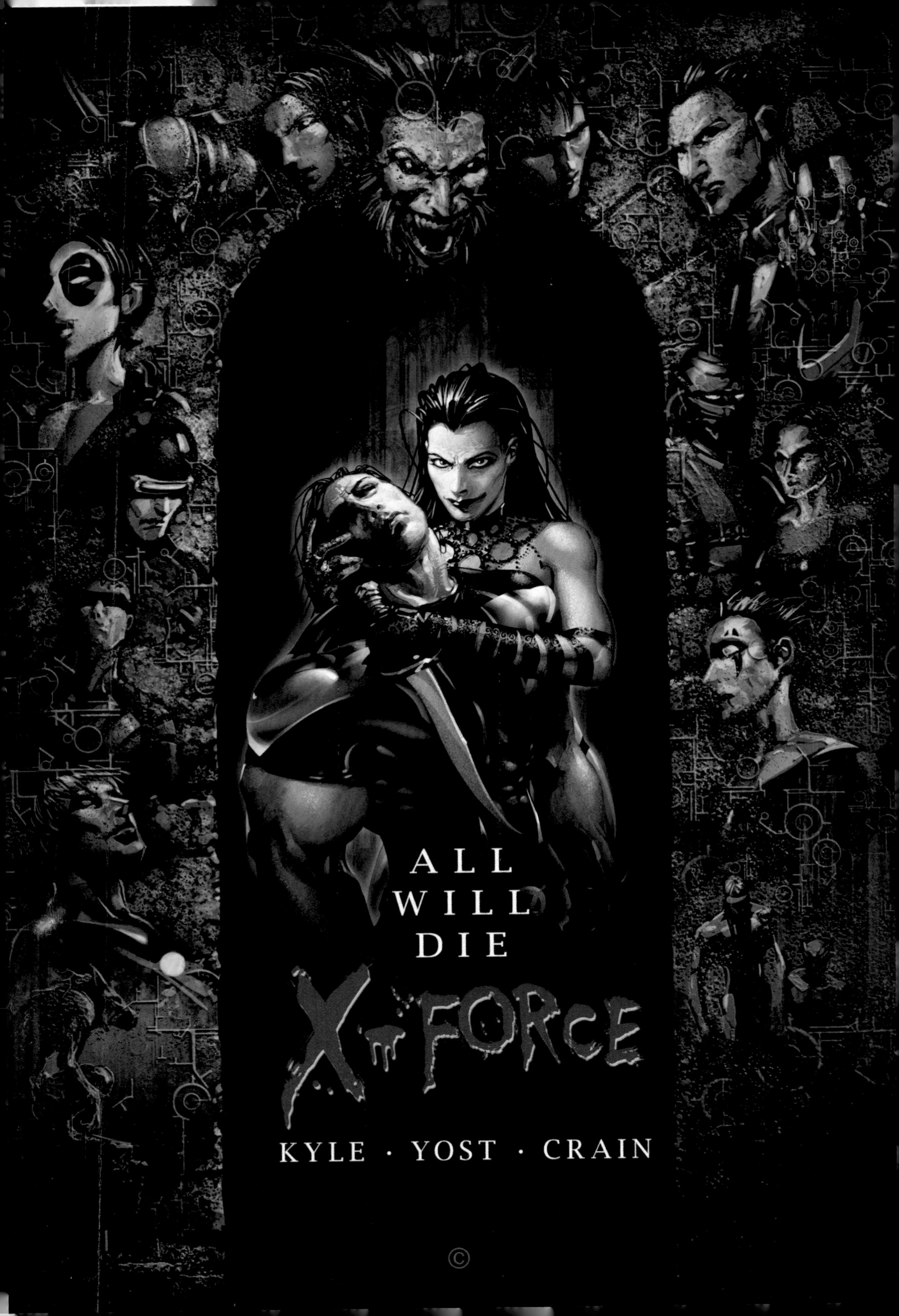
ALL
WILL
DIE
X-FORCE
KYLE · YOST · CRAIN
©

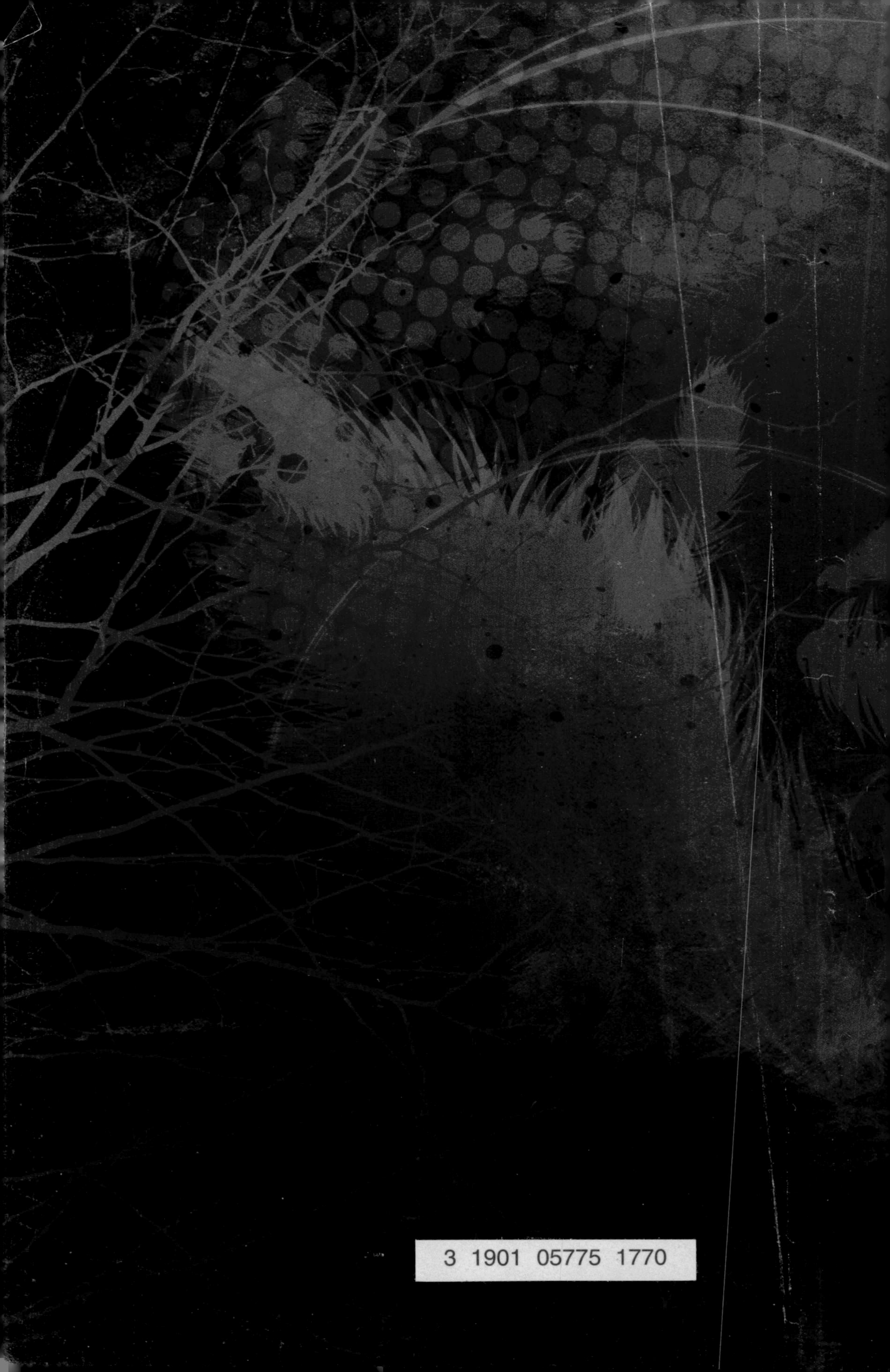